REVERSE ANGLE

ALSO BY JOHN SIMON

Acid Test
Private Screenings
Film 67/68 (co-editor)
Fourteen for Now (editor)
Movies into Film
Ingmar Bergman Directs
Uneasy Stages
Singularities
Paradigms Lost

John Simon

REVERSE ANGLE

A Decade of American Films

Clarkson N. Potter, Inc./Publishers, New York
Distributed by Crown Publishers, Inc.

We gratefully acknowledge the permission to reprint a number of articles which first appeared in: *American Film; Esquire; Horizon; National Review; The New Leader,* 1970–73, copyright © The American Labor Conference on International Affairs, Inc.; *New York,* copyright © 1975–77 by News Group Publications, Inc.; *The New York Times* © 1975 by The New York Times Company; *Unicorn,* © Unicorn Publishing Corp., 1978.

Inquiries should be addressed to Crown Publishers, Inc., One Park Avenue, New York, New York 10016

Printed in the United States of America

Published simultaneously in Canada by General Publishing Company Limited

Library of Congress Cataloging in Publication Data

Simon, John Ivan.
Reverse angle.

Includes index.
1. Moving-pictures—United States—Reviews. 2. Moving-picture plays—History and criticism—Addresses, essays, lectures. I. Title.
PN1995.S496 1981 791.43′75 81-15832
AACR2

ISBN: 0-517-54471-7 (cloth)
0-517-54697-7 (paper)

Design by Dennis J. Grastorf

10 9 8 7 6 5 4 3 2

To Ann Gordon
who deepened the meaning of friend *for me*
and goes on deepening it.

With thanks to the late Jane West
for her publisher's confidence, and to Nancy Novogrod
for her editorial prowess.

Contents

Preface

TITLES SHOULD NOT REQUIRE explanations. This one, however, may need a word or two. As some readers will know, a reverse-angle shot is one in which the camera, having focused on A, who, let's say, is talking to B, switches to an opposite vantage point and shows us B responding to A. Metaphorically speaking, all film criticism is a kind of reverse-angle shot to the film it is discussing. But, for better or worse—or, most likely, neither, only for different—my criticism seems to be at a reverse angle to much film criticism I have read. This may be most apparent in my reviews of American movies, of which this book is a representative selection.

Wherein does this difference, this reverse angle, lie? In the April 1981 issue of *American Film,* Stephen Farber addressed himself, in a rather too brief article, to the question "Why Do Critics Love Trashy Movies?" He adduced rave reviews from many prominent, and one or two good, critics for such movies as *Escape From Alcatraz, The Big Red One, Bronco Billy, Halloween, The Fury, Dressed to Kill, Scanners,* etc., which I too consider to be trash. Unfortunately, as I see it, the list Farber held up for guarded but genuine praise is, with the partial exception of *Norma Rae,* scarcely better: *Julia, Coming Home, Promises in the Dark, Brubaker,* and *Carrie.* More unfortunately yet, Farber's explanation—that contemporary film criticism is rebelling against respectably bourgeois, well-crafted, "classical humanist" films with "strong characters and strong stories" because it is ashamed of appearing old-fashioned—strikes me as inadequate.

The problem, to my mind, is that film reviewers, like anybody else, usually come to movies at an early age and that they tend to maintain certain puerile attitudes and associations, most of them under the rubric of escape from reality and responsibility, in their subsequent reviewing careers. By the time they have read serious books, looked at paintings, listened to classical music (if they have at all), these reviewers are older and less inflammable; moreover, such exposure probably occurred under some form of cultural or academic coercion. As a result, movies—and especially American ones, which have generally been aimed at adolescent or, at any rate, less speculative minds—have served as a psychic means of escape from adulthood, reality, truth. Note, for instance, the frequency and enthusiasm with which Pauline Kael, by way of supreme praise, applies the epithet "liberating" to a movie. America, as seen through the camera eye of Hollywood, became El Dorado for both American and European youngsters growing (or not growing) up into film reviewers.

My case—through no desert of mine, and in many ways to my detriment—is atypical. Living in Europe until the age of fifteen and a half, I too saw Hollywood's America as an Eden full of wonderful cowboys, gangsters, and happy endings. But, rudely transplanted to the real America at a still impressionable age, I began to see the European film—full of steamy sex, adultery, betrayal, failure, often unheroic destruction and waste—as the Lost Paradise of realism: of being honest, strong, and imbued with the tragic sense of life. In some strange way, these contradictory biases canceled each other out, leaving me to look at films with a different set of idiosyncrasies, predilections, fallibilities. Here they are.

INTRODUCTORY MATTERS: FOUR EASY PIECES

The Critical Condition

WHAT IS FILM CRITICISM all about? Praise for our product, says the industry. Recognition or, failing that, constructive suggestions, say the filmmakers. Reliable guidance, says the public. All of those things, say the reviewers, except, of course, praise only for good products. None of those things principally, say critics. Critics are after something harder and more elusive: pursuing their own reactions down to the rock bottom of their subjectivity and expressing them with the utmost artistry, so that what will always elude the test of objective truth will at least become a kind of art: the art of illumination, persuasion, and good thinking and writing. The industry is not to be indulged, any more than the filmmaker is to be told how he should make movies; the one would be dishonest, the other presumptuous. The public, to be sure, is to be guided, but not in the simplistic manner it hopes for.

It is not for the critic to do the reader's thinking for him; it is for the critic merely to do his own thinking for the reader's benefit. This may seem like a slight difference, but it is in fact tremendous. Artistic achievement cannot be measured by any foolproof method other than that of time. If the critic, instead of writing for a daily, weekly, or monthly, wrote for a decadely or, better yet, centurily publication, he could be very nearly infallible. But his life span would then have to be superhuman, just as his work, already done for him by time, would be supererogatory. So we can forget about objective truth in the evaluation of art; consumer-research criticism is equally hopeless: there is no way of guaranteeing the performance of a product for whose value there are no immediate yardsticks. There remains only thinking about the film.

But what kind of thinking? Either the kind that, without giving any compelling reasons, offers a bit of plot summary, a few quickie pronunciamentos, and a strong recommendation for or against the film—in other words, the kind that thinks *for* the reader, and is perfectly worthless. Or the other kind, in which the critic develops his thought processes, as it were, behind glass so that the reader can see how the critical mind engages the film and reaches conclusions. This is a sort of thinking aloud and in public, which the reader can fall in with, talk back at, agree or disagree with in part or in toto, on the basis of a motivation, a process, a methodology on full display. Although it brings a verdict, such criticism stresses its idiosyncrasy and particularity, and invites a dialogue with the reader; it is not a paternalistically pointing index finger, nor a tipster's inside dope, nor a brother-and-sister act: "We're all alike, and if I loved (hated) it, so will you." In truth, criticism at its best is an invitation to thinking.

Unfortunately, even with the best intentions, journalistic criticism cannot always function at top level. Sometimes there is not enough time, at other times not enough space, to develop views in sufficient depth and detail. But in an imperfect world the critic strives to do his imperfect best. And part of that is explaining to his audience what his values are, where he stands; for though the critic and his readers need not stand on the same ground, the readers must know where the critic is standing and then make the necessary adjustments. You can read any map once its scale is given you.

Here goes then. We often hear that film criticism is something very special, very different from other kinds of criticism, and particularly at odds with what is derisively referred to as a "literary" sensibility. Such arguments, I think, are always made by illiterates, even if they have advanced degrees in literature and are teaching in colleges, as more and more illiterates are. If a literary sensibility means anything, it is that the particular critic came to film from literature—but, then, so did the movies, which, from the very outset, tended to adapt works of fiction and theater. The fact that a screenplay still depends to a greater or lesser degree on good words, along with the fact that we still speak of "fiction films," proves that the umbilical cord has not been severed. And that some of the most film-as-film or movie-movie-oriented critics come from literary backgrounds shows that this particular term of obloquy is a fiction—and thus itself a literary product.

It may be, of course, that "literary" is being used as a synonym for "highbrow," and that the argument is that film is not a highbrow art, perhaps not an art at all, only a jolly good entertainment for all brows escaping in unison. Well, yes, films are of at least two different kinds: but so, too, are books. There are novels written for entertainment alone, with no pretensions (or only fake ones) to art; and others meant as art, whether or not they attain it. There were even, back in the Hellenistic age, novels that did not concern themselves with whether they were art, and still, in some cases, stumbled upon it. The same holds true in film: a Méliès, a Griffith, an early and better Chaplin may not have set out to make art, yet may have hit it anyhow; later on, like fiction, film went by one of two roads toward art or toward entertainment.

Books, costing less than movies to produce, can afford to be more exclusive in their appeal; a movie, to recoup its outlay, must sell more widely. Yet even this seemingly unalterable law is not really a law or unalterable. For the difference between art and entertainment is finally one not so much of direction as of degree: though all entertainment is not art, all art must include entertainment. "Entertaining" means interest-holding, and what bores and fails to involve has no real artistic value. Granted, art makes demands: it entertains those who are willing and able to feel, perceive, and think more deeply and arduously—more courageously, if you will—rather than those who *always* want to leave their thoughts behind, most likely because thought has abandoned them. I insist on the *always;* for *on occasion* everyone appreciates a well-made piece of fluff.

It is also true that a book reviewer can more easily afford to be a specialist. There are books enough coming out with high aspirations to allow him to ignore the Robbinses, Urises, and Micheners. In film, where the vast majority of the product is still escapist entertainment rather than artistic entertainment, the reviewer must accost all kinds of things or remain idle most of the time. So the film critic must be equipped with a sliding scale, and be able to assess both art and mere entertainment on their relative merits. What he must not do is to confuse or equate the two. But, then, art is nothing to be frightened of either; it is, in a sense, merely giving more than was expected: something not known, or known fully, or in that particular way, before.

This does not mean, of course, that because someone sees *The Passion of Anna,* or *L'Avventura,* or *The Rules of the Game,* he becomes a better person. It does mean, though, that if he can think and feel his way into the subtleties and implications of such films, he will become more aware of the complexities of life (and, coincidentally, art), and become a richer, more interesting person. But not necessarily wiser or better. You can think that *Bite the Bullet, The Day of the Locust,* or *Shampoo* is a wonderful film and still be a decent human being, but I seriously doubt that you then know anything about art. But a film that gives the large public exactly what it expects, i.e., sheer entertainment, is not to be ipso facto rejected (even if placed on a lower level)—as long as it does it well, like *Jaws,* rather than badly, like *Rollerball.*

Again, it must be stressed, a successful entertainment is preferable to a failed work of art. I don't mean a flawed work of art, like *Nashville,* which can be enjoyed and admired in part; I mean one that, except for its pretensions, totally misses the boat, like *The Passenger.* "Says who? Says *who?*" I hear someone impatiently remonstrating. Says this critic, says *only* this critic, thinking and speaking for himself—but in such a way, he hopes, that the reader can profit equally from disagreement as from agreement. That in fact is the test of valid criticism: that instead of merely eliciting rote consent or hysterical opposition, it stimulates thought. Thought, which is not the easiest thing in the world, which may require seeing the film even if—perhaps especially if—the critic disliked it; but thought which, in the long run, alone makes a human being human. Only not a thought divorced from feeling, but one that humanely collaborates with it.

August 18, 1975

What Is This Thing Called Love?

LET US NOW ACCOST THE ISSUE of film criticism, and what many people mistake for its opposite: love of movies. For it has come to that: in the untutored, or improperly tutored, mind, "to criticize" looms as the opposite of "to love." If you are the kind of critic who knocks a lot of them, you manifestly do not love the movies; whereas the reviewer who finds something good in most pictures—he, now, is the true lover of cinema.

This strikes me as a deplorable misconception. Two propositions I hold to be indisputable: (1) the person who really loves film will love fewer movies rather than more; and (2) what is popularly known as "loving movies" is no such thing; there is no loving of movies, only loving of good movies.

Whoever loves eating, loves to eat well. To eat well means to be a bit of an expert—gastronome, gourmet, person of taste; it does not mean stuffing yourself on frankfurters and hamburgers and feeling in heaven. To see movies well means not to like every other, third, or even fifth film. It means being demanding and discriminating, involved but not mesmerized, wishing to find what is good in movies but not attempting to justify, inadvertently or advertently, wasted time by proclaiming the trash that preempted it valuable or significant. There are people who like to gorge themselves on hot-dog movies sloshed with cheap mustard; I don't think they love movies—they merely dislike their lives.

There is nothing like film to elicit infatuation, obsession, addiction. For couples, it is the easiest and cheapest way of having an evening out (as prologue to a night in); for solitaries, there is always the comfort of being alone together with all those semi-obliterated masses of fellow moviegoers, of having one's private experience communally. There is nothing wrong with any of this until it starts to color one's judgment: the pleasures of moviegoing—atavistic or erotic, familial or convivial—having nothing to do with the intrinsic merit of a film.

Movies are potentially a great time-waster, being so easy to drift into (as opposed to picking up a book), and so hard to walk out on (as opposed to flinging aside an unfinished book). Quality, to masses of viewers and a good many reviewers, hardly matters. Even some of the feeblest flicks can be pronounced movie-movies, glorified trash, pure Americana, pop art, silly but harmless fun, or whatever term is thought to vindicate one's addiction best. I do not propose to review movies for addicts; to criticize them for addicts is a contradiction in terms.

Needless to say, I love good films. But how many of these are there in a week, a month, a year? There are others that have redeeming features or intermittent merit. This should be conveyed to people willing to settle for that, but *caveat emptor.* The movies are not to be turned into a substitute for living (they cannot be that good), nor should they be a lapse into blissful idiocy, like most television-watching (they need not be that bad). They can and should try to be art, or, failing that, damned good entertainment—though there are people who would say that they can't be an art, or, at best, only a popular one, like rock music. I say that they have demonstrated that they can be an art via Antonioni and Bergman, Buñuel and Bresson, Renoir and Fellini, Kurosawa and Ozu, Olmi and Troell, Welles and Wajda, Sucksdorff and Vigo and Truffaut *at their best;* and once a form has proved capable of greater things, why settle for lesser ones? To be sure, those lesser entertainments can be enjoyed; but should they be loved? This threatens to devaluate not only film, but also the very concept of love.

The problem—in America, in the world—is twofold: anti-intellectualism and rampaging pop culture, actually the two identical faces of a conman's coin that never comes up heads. This is not the moment for tracing the development of the anti-intellectual, anti-excellence, anti-high-art movement or cataclysm that has swept over us, but it may be the place for answering the obvious—too obvious—question: "But why *should* movies be art?"

It seems to me that whenever an art or quasi-art gets a close competitor, the former is driven to redefine itself, the latter to refine itself. When journalism became big and lively, fiction was pushed into art. When photography became more accomplished and popular, painting was forced into more cerebral and abstruse regions. When the movies became more effective and ubiquitous, the theater had to (or will have to) become more searching, experimental, and elitist. When television boomed into vulgar supremacy, the movies had to start rethinking themselves, and become more penetrating, special, artistic. I have often quoted Dürrenmatt's "It is inconceivable what would have to be played in today's theaters if the movies had not been invented, and screenwriters wrote plays." But that was said twenty years ago, and the problem has shifted ground: it is now fortunate that TV boxes, like so many litter baskets, line the avenues of film; those who want to produce instant trash are urged to drop it into those baskets or boxes. Not all television writers are that neat, alas; some of them do drop their litter all over film.

Certainly film, at its base, can and must continue to be an entertainment. In social and economic terms, it is only out of entertainments that works of art can arise. So—I cannot stress it enough—solid entertainments are to be hailed and enjoyed as the salt of the earth. But art—on screen or elsewhere—is the bread of the spirit. And now it behooves me to name the real enemy, who is not the mass that grooves on *Billy Jack,* ghastly as it is, and certainly not the crowd that wants a John Ford in its past, present, and future. The enemy is the jaded, frustrated, or factitious intellectual, often in the academy, sophistic enough to elevate his low cravings (perfectly all right until they are so elevated) by intellectualizing them. Take two examples.

First, a truly absurd essay on Bette Midler by Richard Poirier (professor of English at Rutgers) in the August 2 and 9 *New Republic.* This is a piece of perverse and sickening adulation of trash, in which Midler, "a pop artist whose whole tendency is classical," is repeatedly mentioned in the same breath with Joyce, Eliot, Pound, and Pynchon. Of course, our jesuitical juggler hedges his bets: ". . . Midler's particular way of expressing nostalgia needs to be taken as seriously, as studiously as some of the other literary manifestations I've mentioned, though this does *not* mean that we need think of it as equivalently good or satisfying." (We need not but, presumably, *may* think of them as equivalent.) And again: "It's easy to be misunderstood in these matters by high cultural illiterates, so let it be said carefully . . . structurally (not in quality, not in so-called contributions to Western culture, not in what it does to the traditions of art) but structurally, there is no difference between the juxtapositions of style in sections of 'The Waste Land' and juxtapositions that occur in sections of *Clams on the Half Shell.*"

After you strip this prose of its casuistic caveats, distinctions, and reservations, there still remains the "needs to be taken as seriously, as studiously"; there remains that "structural" identity that, at least for this high-culture illiterate, means flagrant gilding by association. It doesn't much matter that "structural identity" is meaningless—a toy airplane may have the same structure as a Boeing 747, but just try getting to Paris on it—or that certain differences are conceded in terms of "so-called contributions to Western culture" (why only "so-called," by the way? so that if Eliot and Pound are only so-called, Midler, eventually, can be so called too?); what matters is that if you mention high and low and non- and anti-art in the same breath often enough, they all end up becoming part of our staple polluted air.

For an example closer to home, consider a brand-new book by Michael Wood (professor of comparative literature at Columbia), *America in the Movies,* where you may read: "I do want to suggest that Hollywood movies, from the end of the 1930s to the beginning of the 1960s, from *Gone With the Wind,* say to *Cleopatra* (1963), were a *world* in the sense that the novels of Balzac were a world." This remark, as expected, does not come unhedged, either; elsewhere we read that this Hollywood cinema "is not life . . . and it is not realism, not even fantasy. It is *the movies* . . . a licensed zone of unreality, affectionately patronized by us all. . . ." Once again, in my high-culture illiteracy, I fail to understand why "a licensed zone of unreality" (which commissioner licensed it, by the bye?) is not tantamount to "fantasy," but no matter: I may not see the trees, but I see the Wood.

And so I say: we need a film criticism *not* based on adolescent bad taste. Most of the people in their forties and fifties who are today's leading film critics came to their calling by way of the trash they lapped up along with the popcorn in Palaces, Orpheums, and Bijous from Los Angeles to London, from Omaha to New York. They have become (some of them) literate and sophisticated, and they can make up wonderful-sounding arguments in defense of what Agee called intelligent trash. (Many of them even in defense of unintelligent trash.) It is for this reason that the Fords and Hawkses and Hitchcocks, even the Walshes, Vidors, and Sirks, all the way down to the Fullers, Ulmers, and Boettichers, become great filmmakers, subjects for study and admiration—artists. Now, some of these men were good, honest craftsmen; some clever hacks; some absolute nonentities. But our film "critics," remembering how they played hooky from school, how delicious those popcorn-scented Saturday double or triple bills tasted, what initiation into sex was dispensed by Veda Ann Borg and Patricia Medina, are slaves to their slobbering nostalgia, their onanistic mooning over their lost youth. And not only they, but even a younger generation of film critics, who graduated from film courses and art houses, but who inherit the sentimentality and the bad taste from their precursors, write pretentious articles and books full of auteurism, ontology, semiology, and whatnot to justify their arrested cinematic development. If that is love of the movies, no thanks!

August 25, 1975

"List, List, O List!" —*Hamlet,* I, v

If you are looking for a ten-best and ten-worst list of the year's films, don't look here. I have always considered picking the ten best or ten worst films the equivalent of determining how many angels can dance on the head of a pin.

One was a game for scholastics, the other is a game for cocktail-party chatterers. On the few occasions when I allowed myself to be talked into compiling a ten-best list (though never a ten-worst one!) I was writing film criticism in a relatively obscure publication and hoped, by getting my list into a more conspicuous one, to attract some readers to my regular film column. I am relieved not to have to resort to such stratagems any longer.

There is something antithetical to the very notion of criticism in the concept of a ten-best list: it is almost as deplorable as reviewing a movie by meting out to it one to four stars. The one critical absolute I know is that there are no shortcuts to criticism. In order for something to be criticism, it cannot be brief. An opinion can be minuscule: one star on a page, one minute of badinage on television, one paragraph or two in a magazine. This may have a minimal value: if you have complete trust in a reviewer (a risky business), you may find a snappy snap judgment sufficient. If a film is such an unimportant atrocity that a couple of epigrams is all a reviewer wishes to accord it, that is all right; it is humor rather than criticism, but not everything deserves to be reviewed, and humor can be a godsend anywhere, not least in critical writings.

Criticism at best, of course, is only a set of subjective opinions. But it is opinions expounded at some length: explained, illustrated with examples and quotations, supported with comparisons and contrasts to other works, related to certain standards of aesthetics and even ethics, and viewed in a larger context of human life. A novel by Pynchon or Barthelme, for example, may be a grand or cunning construct, but if it does not give expression to something greater than recondite gamesmanship, as a work by Beckett or Borges does, it will not pass muster. But criticism often enshrines such a construct by a kind of pseudo-explanation that must particularly be guarded against, as when three long overlapping strips of gray or pink felt by Robert Morris that spill off the wall onto the floor, the better to trip you up, are extolled by John Russell of the *Times* as "the kind of august plain statement for which we look to the architecture of the Lion Gate in Mycenae." This is a typical example of the critical shortcut, of the wordmonger undertaking to justify the artmonger by means of not merely false but downright meretricious analogies.

No amount of critical space could suffice to redeem, I would say, 99 percent of what passes for art nowadays; but often one could make out a far better case for or against a work—cinematic, let us say—if one had more, much more, space. To abrogate this critical *sine qua non* in order to declare films A, B, and C the best of the year, and films X, Y, and Z the worst, is not just to put the cart before the horse—it is to put the cart there before you have even acquired a horse. It could be argued, though, that these films have previously been reviewed by the list maker, and that all that is needed now is this final comparative assessment and reminder. But if the initial review had genuine merit, it told the readers what they needed to know, mercifully without pronunciamentos about the bests and worsts.

For how can one determine what was best or worst in a given year, or decade, or century? Yet even before I get to the concepts of "best" and "worst," I must protest against the absurd notion of "ten." The decimal system may be most efficient in mathematics and measurement, but what has it to do with art? The archetype here may, of course, be the Ten Commandments, or the top ten tunes of the Hit Parade; but the art of cinema, despite our neoscholastic buffs, is not a religion; and despite the raucous fans, not a mere pop entertainment. A college friend of mine used to amuse us by pretending to compile the five best Commandments; I was reminded of that in the years when I tried to compile lists of the ten best films and seldom got beyond seven or eight. There is something absurdly Procrustean about the notion of "ten best" or "ten worst"—the one usually meaning desperate stretching, the other preposterous elimination (worsts could, at best, be dealt with in hundreds).

But now, what in God's name is a "best" film? The question is particularly, though not exclusively, relevant to those compilers who presume even further by listing the ten in the order of supposed excellence. When something is in the "best" category, it must either stand alone and apart, or share the summit with a few equals. No sense at all, however, in trying to pick the *one* best. How, for instance, would one have chosen in 1953 between *I Vitelloni* and *The Naked Night?* Or, in 1961, between *Il Posto* and *Jules and Jim?* Was the Fellini *more best* than the Bergman, the Olmi *bester* than the Truffaut? Even if "best" means only "preferred by me"—which is, generally, what it means—how can one honestly choose between different but equal masterworks?

Let us, however, suppose that we are not limited to *one* best, and let us examine the problem in this year's terms. Can one put on the same list both worthy major efforts, however flawed, like *Nashville,* and very minor ones, like *Hearts of the West,* however consistently delightful? Can one have on the same list as fiction films a nonfiction film such as *Hearts and Minds,* to which entirely different criteria apply? Could one include a marvelous picture like Claude Goretta's *Pas si méchant que ça (The Wonderful Crook),* even if it was shown only at the New York Film Festival? If the list of films with artistic value turns out to be very, very short, should one include mere consistently funny trivia, such as *Young Frankenstein,* and perhaps even clever pieces of commercial entertainment, such as *Jaws?* In the end, would not the list become rather like a race among three-legged horses, and who really cares which is the fastest among *them?*

Yet the "best" and "worst" lists may have some perfectly acceptable nonprofessional applications. If a group of people after a good Christmas dinner should decide to draw up lists of favorites and pet peeves among the year's films and so end up engaging in a healthy discussion of movies, that is all to the good. Only let professionals keep out of it—at least in print. There is another game, however, that professionals may indulge in, though not without some peril. I refer to critical groups' picking the year's best film, director, performers, etc. This results in awards, and awards, though they go more often than not to the wrong effort, have at least occasionally been known to bring a worthy achievement back to our screens whence it vanished too soon.

December 22, 1975

Obiter Dicta

Lately I've been asked by a number of people (three, to be exact) why, if I resigned in protest from the National Society of Film Critics, I calmly joined the New York Film Critics' Circle.

The writer's profession, according to the immortal Sam Goldwyn, is a lonely one; but that of the film critic may, for two reasons, be even lonelier. First, the critic is primarily concerned with how much lasting, artistic value there is in a film; the paying customer is principally interested in having a good time. Now, art is a stern taskmistress: few pass the test of excellence that is the prerequisite of permanence, and the serious critic, who aims to preview the judgment of posterity, cannot help being severely selective in his criticism, which is meant to anticipate, however imperfectly, the strict eliminations of time. But the paying customer, who wants his investment of money and time to repay him in fun, and who wants to protect his good relations with whomever he took to the movie, may well condition himself to like most films. Existence requires affirmation, and where moviegoing is part of existing, it may inherit, often undeservedly, some of that existential affirmation. Here may lie the fundamental difference between viewing an art and getting on with life.

So the critic's apparent negativism sets him off from the happy-go-lucky (or, better, eager-to-be-happy) crowd, and makes him look intolerant, mean, and deserving of isolation. But—and this is the second reason for critical "loneliness"—when your fiction- or screenwriter departs from the taste of his consumers, he may bore, annoy, even infuriate them, but he does not threaten them. Let a critic, however, say that a movie the reader loved is worthless (which, of course, never means more than "worthless to the critic," but somehow always gets misconstrued), and the reader feels insulted and threatened: "This man considers me an idiot." And then, either insultedly, "I am not an idiot!" or intimidatedly, "My God! *Am* I an idiot?" So the tough critic ends up being rejected, not merely with indignation or scorn, but actually with hate and fear, which condemn him to greater aloneness. No help for this.

Now, if criticism is such conscious courting of isolation, it is apt to isolate the critic even more from his colleagues, who have every right to feel equally expert and tolerate disagreement even less well—and mind you, this works in the opposite direction, too: "He liked *that?* Am I, who disliked it, supposed to be blind?" Then what justifications are there for critical confraternities? Well, among others that need not concern us here—such as discussion, joint action to uphold certain standards, etc.—the giving of awards for "best achievement." Both the New York Film Critics' Circle and the National Society of Film Critics annually vote on a number of "bests."

The Society was founded by several magazine reviewers who, in those days, were not admitted to the Circle, which was reserved for newspaper reviewers, of whom there were then more than enough. The magazine reviewers felt that they were as good as the newspaper crowd, in which they were probably right, and deserved an equally audible collective voice. Some of them, no doubt, felt that they were also, as a group, superior to the newspaper people, and here they were on shakier ground. What is true, however, is that partly through the power and prestige of the *Times,* partly through his longevity as its film critic, Bosley Crowther was then a dominant force and influence in the Circle. Since there were certain kinds of films—usually foreign and small, and sometimes also profound—for which he had no use and whose chances he could scuttle, a counterbalance seemed indicated.

It appeared to me at the time that there was—over and above the occasionally interesting debates among members—an actual value in the Society's awards, if only because they were different, and made for (to use a somewhat grandiose image) bicameral legislation. Moreover, there was some vestigial notion of merit connected with membership: not every magazine critic was voted in, whereas every working newspaper film reviewer was ex officio admitted to the Circle. But merit, though an all-important consideration, is hard to assess. In areas where values have had more time to crystallize, the problem may be slightly less formidable: poetry and fiction criticism, say, having been around many centuries longer than film criticism, have standards that may be more readily recognizable.

Anyhow, the Society always voted on whom to admit to membership, and these elections were often hotly debated. Frequently they made no sense at all. Someone might be kept out year after year simply because most members disapproved of his sexual preference. Someone else might be voted in just because his publication had "clout," which struck me as equally nonsensical. A well-known novelist then writing film criticism that seemed to me quite amateurish was admitted because, as one member put it, "he would be an ornament to the Society." ("In that case," I said, "let's hang him from the chandelier.") A member I genuinely esteemed explained to me why he kept voting for people I thought he could have no use for; looking around our table, he said, he saw so many incompetents that he could find no grounds on which to exclude others no worse than they. My answer was that a plurality of nonentities seemed to me preferable to a majority of them.

Among the proposed members I recall voting for with conviction were Susan Sontag and Manny Farber: Sontag, with whom I often disagreed, because of my fundamental respect for her intelligence; Farber, with whom I almost always disagreed—and whom, on top of that, I considered unfathomable by any rational means—because so much selfless dedication to film deserved some kind of recognition. As it happens, Miss Sontag proved ineligible because she reviewed only very sporadically. Farber was elected, but left after a single meeting; according to some, because, when he had harangued us with rising fury for an hour about something that even his warmest supporters found totally irrelevant, and the chairman finally proposed that we move on to the election of new members, I suggested that we first add one further prerequisite: a sanity test.

In any case, in those days the Society's awards differed from those of the Circle, and one could say, at the very least, *"Vive la différence!"* But as newspapers began to bite the dust all around, the Circle—to be anything more than an arc and, as it were, make ends meet—started to admit Society members, provided they wrote for mass-circulation magazines. To be sure, there were some funny goings-on. For example, when one eminent magazine critic was considered for membership, the Circle's chairman inquired about the number of copies his publication printed. "One hundred fifteen thousand," someone said. "In that case," decreed the chairman, "let's make one hundred sixteen thousand the cutoff line." A couple of Society members turned down the Circle, one of them declaring he had nothing in common with most of "those people." But many accepted this dual citizenship, one of them shamefacedly muttering something about "power." In the end, there was precious little difference between the groups, and the overlapping membership inevitably spelled little difference between their respective awards.

A year came when ten new names were proposed for membership in the Society. Since I did not believe that there were ten people in the entire country—in and out of the Society—who lived up to the rigorous demands of film criticism, the very quantity seemed ludicrous. I remember Hollis Alpert arguing in behalf of Charles Champlin of the *Los Angeles Times* that, though he lived right there in L.A., Champlin, admirably, was not "bought by the industry." "Of course not," I said. "Why should they pay for something they can have for free?" Champlin was elected, and I resigned—which I would have done over other candidates as well, but Champlin preceded them alphabetically.

To belong to the Circle, however, is a different proposition. I think that a critical aggregation can exist on two defensible bases. One is that you try, however humanly and fallibly, to maintain standards of merit; the other, that you admit, ipso facto, the regular critics of every reputable publication. You do not then draw the line according to the number of copies published, but according to whether or not the publication is in some obvious way sectarian, and whether the critic writes about movies at sufficient length with sufficient regularity. To write only capsule criticism may discourage true critical thinking; to write less often than monthly may induce one to become negligent about keeping up with the medium. So, for example, it strikes me as ridiculous that the Circle should not include Stanley Kauffmann—either because *The New Republic* does not have a so-called mass circulation, or because its offices happen to be in Washington, D.C. Kauffmann himself, at any rate, is in New York, reviews films when they open in New York, and is read, I wager, much more in New York than in Washington.

Still, the Circle is ecumenical by some definition, and does not lie to itself and the world about admitting members on a basis of merit. Thus it becomes a cross section—or, rather, a representative average—of how the film-critical profession evaluates. Its choices may be preposterous, in which case the public can, at the very least, laugh at them. More important, since junky movies can generally make it on their own demerit, but good ones often need critical support, and since nobody—or, rather, no body or group—can be consistently wrong, even the Circle must do some good. In a world in which certain organizations do no good at all, and much harm, whereas others have no power to do harm but can occasionally do good, it seems all right to espouse, ex officio, the latter, as long as they do not harbor any delusions of serious merit.

January 19, 1976

FILMS

Marriage and Worse Coalitions

Diary of a Mad Housewife is the updated version of the "woman's picture," in which the trials and tribulations of a misunderstood wife who turns into a misunderstood mistress no longer soak the female audience's handkerchiefs as they did in the days when Joan Crawford and Joan Fontaine were being misunderstood. As Carrie Snodgress is misjudged and mistreated by her pompous, social-climbing lawyer-husband and clever but destructive novelist-lover, the matter is one for sophisticated nods, knowing snickers, and condescending chuckles. But, either way, the sensitive little woman at the apex is a cliché—once a heroic-pathetic cliché, now a wryly patronizing one—and the men at the vertices are oversimplifications of *machismo* or muttonheadedness, of one kind of immaturity or another, above whom our heroine has risen, melodramatically or comically, to self-realization.

Why is this such a formula? Isn't achievement of self-awareness a valid topic for art; isn't transcendence of the fickle lover by the noble beloved one of the great themes in literature? Think of Rilke's mighty Beloveds, *"die gewaltigen Liebenden,"* who "while they called out to him, jutted over the lover; who shot up above his head when he did not come back to them." But in the "woman's picture," old or new style, the woman is always seen complacently as basically superior to the men—by some female scriptwriter; or, patronizingly, as the helpless victim of her passions—by some male scenarist or director. There is no contest between different but equal partners, and the greatness of the little woman has to be taken on faith—the movies' bad faith.

I have not read, or wished to read, the Sue Kaufman novel on which this film, written by Eleanor Perry and directed by her husband, Frank, is based. But, I learn, the autobiographically tinged housewife of the book's title was really mad: angry, exasperated, in psychotherapy throughout. In the movie, Tina Balser is a perfectly normal little upper-bourgeois housewife who has the bad luck of being married to a fatuous young man, a lawyer intent on climbing all scales—social, financial, intellectual—and who finds that, try as she may, she cannot please him, being too direct, unassuming, and authentic. This housewife is not only not mad, she is, indeed, a paragon of sanity, functioning despite her husband's nagging, needling, bullying, and humiliating her; despite his tyrannical demands on her time, attention, energy; despite his being the kind of domineering yet also whining ass from whom any judge would grant her a divorce on sight. But she puts up, shuts up, waits on him hand and foot. Sanity? Hell, it's sanctity.

Or is the point that she is a masochist? No, because she is clearly shown not enjoying playing Psyche to her oafish Cupid, even being mildly horrified by it. Carrie Snodgress is good at pained reactions: at expressions half-reproachful, half-disbelieving that anyone could be as beastly as her spouse. Yet even that does not make sense: she has been married to him long enough (their daughters are aged, roughly, eight and six) to have long since left him, murdered him, or acquiesced.

If, as in the book, we were given the first-person narrative of a heroine in psychiatric treatment, the film might make sense as Tina's distorted view of the situation. But early in the film we have evidence to the contrary. In the elevator, Jonathan Balser is telling his wife what to pack for him for a short business trip: the plaid suit from Sills; two voile oxford and two Sea Island cotton shirts; the robe from Turnbull & Asser; the shoes—not the new ones—from Peal; socks—provenance unspecified; all into the oxblood suitcase from T. Anthony. As they leave, the elevator operator stares after them in dismay.

Incredulity is our reaction, too, from the very first scene. There is Jonathan upbraiding his wife, who is not really awake yet, for everything: for not being awake yet, for smoking, for not having enough vitality, for not shaping up, for being too skinny, for having straight hair, for—I can't remember what else. And she endures and endures, virtually without protest. It is preposterous. Meanwhile Jonathan is full of self-praise, and Tina doesn't demur at that either. Doubly preposterous. And as Richard Benjamin acts the part—and as Frank Perry directs it, and Eleanor Perry wrote it—it exudes exaggeration through every pore. Yet everything is played for laughs, so that Tina's suffering loses all dignity: the tenor is both more pseudosophisticated and more genuinely callous than when Olivia de Havilland or Bette Davis had to suffer for the three-handkerchief trade.

Of course, Tina's little girls are obvious changelings, imps of the perverse; she has every kind of servant and household trouble; Jonathan gets beastlier; and then—then!—she meets this famous writer, George Prager. Now in the novel, I gather, he is a tough sort of writer in his early middle age, a Mailer or Styron, all bumptious sexuality and hypermasculine aggressiveness. But Perry casts in this part Frank Langella, an actor of not inconsiderable talent but inconsiderable virility, with a rosebud mouth that Betty Boop might have envied. He woos Tina with "Tell me, does screwing appeal to you?" and similar well-turned phrases, not to mention an erection that, right in the middle of a party, he rubs against her groin. He finally gets her, partly out of fascination with his unvarnished caddishness, but mostly out of pique against her husband, to come to his fabulous apartment overlooking the East River from her fabulous apartment overlooking Central Park.

Here the churlish wooing continues, e.g., "Please don't start that la-di-da stuff with me, it makes me want to puke." Swept off her feet by this love talk, Tina falls into George's bed. After the act, George resumes the courtship: "Baby, you are a terrific piece of arse; are you always that good?" "No." "Well, so much for the compliments, but now what do we do?" "What do you mean?" "I thought you were good for a couple of screws, but this may get out of hand." And he explains: "The thing it all hangs on is: can you have a straight sex thing or not?" (The way Langella enacts him, one doubts that *George* could.) Well, such words are irresistible and Tina falls in love with George, and spends her afternoons with him whenever he deigns to have her. So now she is getting it both from an egomaniacal, exploitative husband and an egomaniacal, sadistic lover, with whom she has—again in his brilliantly writerly words—"pure and incredible sex," a line Langella delivers like a slightly overripe mango.

 Rather than go on summarizing this glamorized soap opera for illiterate sophisticates, let us get to the point. Mrs. Perry's writing (and, most likely, Sue Kaufman's) simply will not do. It is obvious and heavy-handed enough when she deals with children *(David and Lisa, Ladybug Ladybug, Last Summer),* but when she undertakes adults who are meant to be devious or pompous or crude, she hits us over the head. A mediocre writer's attempt at satire may well be the least digestible kind of writing there is. I have already cited the absurd catalogue of items Tina was to pack for her husband: absurdist humor (which was not intended, anyway) zooms around more fancifully; but even heightened realism cannot walk on such fallen arches. It is ineptly derived from Mary McCarthy's *The Group,* although there at least the boring brand names were an attempt at reconstructing a bygone era.

When Tina, angry at last, yells at George, "Save that for your bloody awful books!" the casual amorist runs after her enraged, suddenly hurt where he is most sensitive. He shakes her furiously and shouts, "Hey, wait a minute! Take that back!" That, you see, is the best a distinguished writer can come up with when wounded to the quick. And Tina obliges: "You're good. So good it doesn't bear thinking about." Now what is this? *The Sun Also Rises* filtered through *The Wind in the Willows?* One has the feeling that Mrs. Perry wants to switch here to a moment of seriousness, but her seriousness is indistinguishable from her satire, and both are kitsch. (If the dialogue is Miss Kaufman's, ditto for her.)

Now comes the obligatory intellectual-superiority bit. We've had other kinds of superiority before: dinner at Elaine's, an opening at the Feigen Gallery (always with the real names duly dropped) of a pop sculpture show by Allen Jones, about whose quality Mrs. Perry is careful not to commit herself. When Tina compares her innate gift for pleasing a man in bed to the gift Proust ascribes to Albertine, George bursts into a fit of immoderate laughter and informs his "poor baby" that Proust was a homosexual and Albertine really a boy. This comes as news to the poor baby, who was not taught it at Smith, though everyone in the audience who is going to get the point at all is presumably familiar with what the late Stanley Edgar Hyman called the Albertine Strategy. So it is oneupmanship for the half-baked, or halfupmanship. Then Perry cuts to the next scene (big laugh!): Tina in her conjugal bed trying to get to the bottom of this by reading *The Past Recaptured.* Since Albertine no longer appears in the final volume of Proust's work, we may assume that the Perrys' literary development stopped somewhere along *Swann's Way.*

Finally, after George has tormented Tina in much the same manner Jonathan has ("You have a pimple on your arse. You're getting too damned skinny . . .") and been unfaithful to boot, she erupts, "You're sick, sick! You've got to put on this big virile act because you're really a fag!" Incensed, George pushes her around a bit—rather gently for the sadist he is supposed to be—and turns her out for good. She goes back to her husband, who confesses that he has lost all their money in a socially prestigious but financially ruinous investment, that he is in trouble with his bosses at the law firm, and that he has been having an affair with a girl named Margo. Tina, guilty herself, takes it all in her stride, whereupon Jonathan exclaims gratefully and platitudinously (once again, we do not know whether this is satire or just bad writing): "Oh, Tina, you're wonderful. You're a fine human being, Tina. Do you think we can pick up the pieces and maybe have a better marriage than we ever had?" I guess it's both: satire and bad writing.

The last scene shows Tina in group therapy, being upheld by a couple of fellow patients and savaged by several others. How dare she complain, one of them shrills at her, when she has a husband, a lover, and an eight-room apartment? The audience laughs heartily at this, and the dishonest film ends with a predictable cop-out as Tina's eyes stare at us in mysterious closeup. Is she going to change, or is she just going to pieces?

And how has husband Frank directed *Diary of a Mad Housewife?* Modishly enough, with nervous camera movements in confined spaces, ironically commenting cuts ("Why don't you go to bed?" says Jonathan to Tina, and, pronto, we see her in bed with George), gratuitously nasty details that don't shed light on anything (a department-store Santa Claus picking his nose, followed promptly by two women wrangling over a taxi, only to have an insolent man steal it in front of their noses), a fair amount of arty lovemaking (e.g., underneath blue bed covers, with arms and moans protruding), and many exposures of Miss Snodgress's prepubescent breasts—quantity over quality, the perennial Perry formula for everything. Again the cinematographer is Gerald Hirschfeld, and, as in *The Swimmer,* he gives us his typically savvy but uninspired fashion-magazine color photography.

But where the director truly errs—over and above the casting of Langella as Prager, which makes the supposedly shocking revelation about him come as the slowest anticlimax this side of the New Haven Railroad—is in the consistent overstressing of what needs to be merely shown, omission of what might be of interest, and attempts at making something out of nothing. One example of each: a disappointing omelet is eaten by guests at a party with insulting contempt spelled out and underlined on every face; Jonathan's mistress, Margo, though not unimportant to the plot and listed in the credits, cannot be detected among the walk-ons by the most aquiline eye; and frequent training of the camera on a large Franz Kline painting on George's wall, though apparently meant to tell us something, remains as uncommunicative as Kline's work itself.

And there are the performances, also in part the work of the director. Richard Benjamin is allowed to turn Jonathan's priggishness into piggishness, and give one of the least restrained performances even in a Perry film. Carrie Snodgress has charmingly bewildered or ironic gazes at her command, and a voice that harbors not just one frog but a whole family of batrachians to delicious effect, though it is a little weak when fortissimos are called for. She has a nice ephebic figure and extraordinary eyes, but decision on her acting must await further exposure. The little daughters are several cuts below the Katzenjammer Kids, and minor characters like a Bronx baby-sitter and a bitchy, aging actress are overdone to a turn of the stomach.

September 7, 1970

A Mixed-Up Bag

FIVE EASY PIECES is an attempt at making an American film adult and artistic as well as commercial. As a program, this is admirable; as a finished film, rather less so. The opening reveals an oil rigger, Bobby Dupea, living with a waitress, Rayette, in a southern California oil town. Everything seems ordinary enough: the displeasure with one's work; restlessness in one's rented mobile-home quarters; resentment of one's pregnant and nagging girl friend with her dreams of becoming a pop singer; drinking and wenching forays with one's married buddy. But this series of typicalities is impinged on by another series of sprouting signs pointing toward Bobby's being really a displaced person, a refugee from upper-middle-class musical circles, and himself a not unskilled pianist.

When he learns that his father, paralyzed and struck mute, is close to death, Bobby decides to drive up to the family house in the woods of northern Washington. Rayette emotionally blackmails him into taking her along, and the journey is full of colorful little incidents—a pair of lesbian hitchhikers fleeing pollution and headed for Alaska; a roadside café waitress as domineering as she is obtuse—until they reach a motel near the Dupea house. There Bobby dumps his girl while, as he says, he investigates the situation at home. He meets again his patronizing concert-artist brother, Carl; Carl's newly acquired student concert-artist fiancée, Catherine; his dowdy, scatterbrained, kindly concert-artist sister, Tita; the mute, motionless father, a former concert artist and teacher; and an almost equally mute, uniformed male nurse. Promptly he starts seducing the ethereal yet sexy Catherine, and for her sake even sits down at the piano again, to serenade her with a little Chopin. When she praises his playing, he pooh-poohs her paean.

For Bobby, whose full name is Robert Eroica Dupea (Tita is really Partita, Carl is Carl Fidelio), seems never to be satisfied. And in the end he rejects, or is rejected by, both his worlds, only to run off north (Alaska, alas!) to escape the pollution that seems to be as much inside as around him. Yet Bobby's two worlds are seen only superficially, in images approaching and often achieving caricature, and his apostasy from his cultivated background is neither shown nor sufficiently explained. We do not even get to appreciate his human potential with whose waste we would have to commiserate if the film were to have serious merit.

Though Bobby says and does things that indicate his rootlessness and discontent, there is no real getting inside him; we never know whether we are watching a soul in torment or a set of jangling nerves. Bob Rafelson, the director and coscenarist with Adrien Joyce, tends to do things by doubles or by halves. Thus there are two traffic-jam scenes, two overlong sequences with a psychotic lesbian hitchhiker (played unsubtly albeit to great critical acclaim by Helena Kallianiotes), but almost nothing about what drew Bobby to Rayette in the first place, or how he discovers that things, as he puts it, have a way of going bad on him. Why does his brother's fiancée tumble into bed with him so readily? Why should this rather mannered, affected creature even begin to seem the *summum bonum* to him?

Other flaws include obvious transitions, like that from a couple about to have intercourse to a ball in a bowling alley racing toward an orgasmic scattering of pins; and grandiosely flashy shots such as those of the inactive machinery of the oil field looking, at nightfall, like a combination petrified forest and Calvary. Or take the scene that is supposed to explain Bobby's flight from home. At a gathering in the Dupea home, an arrogant neighbor woman is spouting intellectual slogans and, at the same time, being offensively condescending to Rayette. The scene is vulgarly written and grossly overdirected and overacted (by Irene Dailey). When Bobby gives it to her, we are clearly meant to side with him against these smug, superior, upper-crust eggheads. Bobby's friend at the oil field, though apparently an escaped robber, presents the lower-class concept of the good life in similarly oversimplified terms, and though Bobby rejects it, we are asked to feel a basic sympathy for his buddy's position.

Along with oversimplification, we get pretentiousness. The very title, *Five Easy Pieces,* strikes me as a bit of attitudinizing. It refers primarily to the five pieces of piano music performed at various times in the film (two Chopins, two Mozarts, one Bach), although I cannot affirm that they are really easy pieces. A parallel is presumably intended with the five women with whom we see Bobby making out: Rayette, two small-town hookers, one pickup in Los Angeles, and Catherine. Yet what is this analogy saying? Something about a parallel between music and sex, art and life? Something about everything in life being, or seeming, too easy for the disaffected person? Bobby himself does not play more than two of those piano pieces, however, and Tita finds one of the others anything but easy going. We are meant to feel some grand assertion or irony lurking in the title, if we could only seize it; but here as elsewhere the film fails to deliver.

Pretentious, too, is the color cinematography by Laszlo Kovacs, frame after frame looking like something destined for the covers of the photography annuals. Take Bobby leaving the oil field at sunset: a low-angle shot with an elaborate cloud formation (cumulo-stratus, if I remember correctly), filters for greater color contrast, and the solitary hardhatted figure jutting into the sky. Surely this is meant to be Tired, Suffering Man Against the August, Uncaring Heavens, a noble capitalizable commonplace.

What, more than anything, saves *Five Easy Pieces* from triviality is the acting. Almost all the performances are good; a few, excellent. I particularly liked Lois Smith as the well-meaning but fuzzy Tita, Karen Black as the banal but pitiable Rayette, and Billy "Bush" Green as the hero's buddy; all of them resisted the script's and director's nudging toward obviousness. Jack Nicholson, as Bobby, has some searing moments, but though I can believe him as a tough worker, he (or at least his voice and accent) cannot convince me as belonging to an intellectual and artistic milieu. I certainly can't see him playing any pieces less easy than "Chopsticks." Susan Anspach, an actress I have found thoroughly irritating on stage, is well used here in the role of the elusive Catherine; perhaps Rafelson does know how to handle some actors. The film certainly keeps our senses occupied as we watch and listen. I only wish it could also make a deeper kind of sense.

November 16, 1970

Hammering It In

LITTLE BIG MAN is the sort of movie that makes you wish you had read the novel. It is very good in spots, heavy-handed and obvious in others, tries too hard in places, yet occasionally darts with elegant ease to a perfect bull's-eye. It does not come off as a whole because it is too episodic, which works better in a book where there is more room to expand in, and because it is unsure of its style, which may not be the case with Thomas Berger's novel. But in Calder Willingham's screenplay, under Arthur Penn's direction, the film goes from realism to absurdism, from satire to sentimentality, without finding a consistent tone. This is as unnerving as having your fellow conversationalist's voice constantly shuttle between a resonant bass and a castrato's treble.

The film is the autobiographical narrative of a 120-year-old man, the sole white survivor of Custer's Last Stand, who tells the story of the West, the Indians, and Custer as it really was. He tells it in his hospital ward to a historian with a tape recorder. Unfortunately, we leave our hero, Jack Crabb, whom we followed from his capture by Indians at the age of ten, at a point where he seems to be in his mid-thirties, and the missing years strike me as an almost unbearable lacuna.

Another serious trouble is that Jack, for all that he is the only fully rounded character of the tale, does not develop into anything noteworthy or even discernible in the end. He may have learned the truth about red men and white, and some other colors as well, but we are not made aware of what the truth has done to him. In the latter part of the film, he becomes a dipsomaniac, but this seems to be only a phase, otherwise he would not have reached his phenomenal age. Or, if the point is that overindulgence leads to longevity, nothing is made of it.

Nevertheless, if you look at the film as a series of cavalierly tacked-together vignettes, a good many of these work, either in part or even in toto. Here the fact that some rather fantastic material is handled in a low-key, offhand way distinctly helps, and Penn has elicited several tasty performances. By far the most impressive is that of Chief Dan George as the venerable sachem, Old Lodge Skins; we are in the presence of a great Manitou-given acting talent.

Very pleasant, too, is Dustin Hoffman in the lead, always endearing with that sour-grapefruit face and voice of his, both of which, paradoxically, ooze the juice of human kindness. There is also a succulent piece of acting by Faye Dunaway as a lusty slut whose heart, like her hand, wants gold. In a good supporting cast—only Cal Bellini as a contrary Indian is unconvincing—I particularly liked Robert Little Star as a faggoty brave, and Amy Eccles as an enchanting (and too-good-and-pretty-to-be-true) squaw.

There are moments of vivid, almost scarring, visual loveliness, usually at times when the idyllic life of an Indian camp is about to be raped and destroyed by the U.S. Cavalry. Thus it is a somewhat tendentious loveliness, but no matter. Particularly handsome are the views of such a camp from across a river; the framing effect of the water and the general composition of the shots are admirable. In one remarkable sequence the cavalry is first heard but not seen, and then, ever so slowly, eerily, chillingly, beautifully emerges from the mists. At other times, Harry Stradling, Jr.'s color cinematography is merely ordinary, especially in the indoor scenes. The music, assembled or composed by John Hammond, though organic in its folksy, country-western way, is less than outstanding. Most of the scenes involving Custer strain too hard to be swingingly antimilitaristic, and end up being sweatily unfunny. Still, in a poor field of contenders, *Little Big Man* is several arrowheads ahead.

Husbands is John Cassavetes's latest quasi-documentary of boring middle-class lives. This roughly 140-minute film scrutinizes in exhaustive detail a four-day escapade of three close friends. Young-middle-aged husbands and fathers, the three attend the funeral of yet another friend, dead prematurely of a coronary. Frightened by the combined shadows of death, growing old, and ever more predictably monotonous existences, they go on a bender that begins with a group beer-drinking marathon in a bar, continues with an almost equally interminable vomiting and quarreling session in the men's room, and climaxes in an impromptu flight to London—for more drinking, gambling, and some wenching. They take three girls to their hotel rooms: the one husband who makes out best (and had the biggest falling out with his wife) elects to remain in London: the other two go back, unconvinced, to Long Island and their families.

As in Cassavetes's previous films, notably *Faces,* the actors improvise around the semblance of a plot for all they're worth. These improvisations, to be sure, seem to be first taken down on paper, then memorized and filmed, yet improvisations, group efforts, they remain, and thus the opposite of art. There is a terrible irony in all this, for Cassavetes desperately yearns to create art, but thinks that this is achieved by the ad hoc piling of dreary, footling detail on detail, and hoping for an immense, shattering truth—which is rather like heaping grains of sand on top of one another and expecting the result to be Mount Everest.

Or, better perhaps, it is as if the filmmaker shot the human face only in extreme closeup (actually what Cassavetes tends to do), concentrating on nothing but pores and pimples—every last one of them—on the assumption that the result will automatically be a searching analysis of the face and its owner. In fact, *Husbands* tells us very little about its three principals, and much of that is commonplace, even cliché.

Certainly, these are commonplace lives, but here, again, the penetrating and ordering imagination of an artist would be needed to reach beyond what we already know—and, above all, to curb the endless complacency and self-importance with which this film dawdles and maunders, like some senile imbecile traipsing about in his own excrement. The performances, however, are consistently good, as they are likely to be when actors are indulged at the expense of everything and everyone else. Cassavetes, Ben Gazzara, and Peter Falk give such impeccable embodiments to mediocrity as to make *Husbands* boring almost as much by its perfect naturalism as by its imperfect grasp of art.

December 28, 1970

Two for the Road and One for the Money

It is hard to decide whether films like *Groupies* and *Gimme Shelter* should be deplored or guardedly applauded. For these are cinéma-vérité films (once upon a time called documentaries) on interesting topics that are now dead for other filmmakers, who might have done better by them. On the other hand, other filmmakers might not have touched them, or been given the chance to do so, and perhaps we should be grateful for what we have. *Groupies* strikes me as the more cogent of the two because, however perfunctorily, it does try to get at the backgrounds and motivations of its people, if only by letting them chatter on. *Gimme Shelter* presents Mick Jagger and the Stones respectfully and superficially, in the manner of an official hagiography—which, in its way, the film was meant to be. It was commissioned from the Maysles brothers by the Rolling Stones, and its sins, accordingly, are not of commission but of omission: it leaves every Stone unturned.

Groupies, of course, are the camp followers of the rock musicians, but they differ from earlier and most contemporary fans and stage-door hangers-on. These girls (and, in some particularly maudlin cases, boys) are not stopped by the stage door or anything else. They tend to be ridiculously, pitifully young, and will often sleep with all the members of a rock group in rapid succession—including even their managers and entourage—afterward boasting to and comparing notes with fellow groupies. They frequently work in teams, from a brace of roommates upward to a dim constellation. The majority are outlandishly bedizened freaks, but quite a few could look very presentable, and some are beautiful and have genuine style. These become supergroupies and are famous; one of them married Paul McCartney. The typical groupie sports a characteristically garish look—that of a life-size rag doll made of cloths of shrilly clashing colors, and with hair out of imbricated polychrome Brillo pads.

Ron Dorfman and Peter Nevard's film tries to show groupies of every stripe against diverse but typical backgrounds: in rock emporiums, at home in weird pads, in dressing rooms, at disorderly parties. They talk about their pasts to some extent, about their presents in full and obscene detail, about their futures with hopes of getting out of groupiedom or proudly persisting in it. Many of them see their life as a vocation, an end in itself, the escape from conformity and mediocrity—as if nonconformity couldn't be just as mediocre. Some of them are not even aware of life-styles other than their own. And a few have defected from what they now consider a sick existence—though how they get along in more conventional circles is not examined in *Groupies.* The filmmakers boiled down eighty hours of footage to the present modest length, and claim, probably with veracity, that nothing was staged for the camera. Why should it have been? These are staged lives to begin with, however random the scenes and aleatory the sounds that emerge.

The trouble, apparently, was that some of the most celebrated groupies were unavailable to the filmmakers, or their footage was too dull, or, in some instances, too sensational. Thus the Plaster Casters (a pair of girls who orally arouse the organs of famous rock and movie personalities, then proceed to make plaster casts of them) were caught in action, but it was considered wiser to show them merely talking about their upstanding enterprise. Also, the very competent 16-mm photography comes out rather grainy in 35-mm enlargement; and though it was relevant to show some of the rock groups at work, we may have been given too much of that and not enough audience reaction and idolization. Otherwise, the film is effective and grimly instructive.

Audience reaction and star-worship of a dubious sort are the mainstays of the Maysles brothers' *Gimme Shelter,* which concentrates on the free concert at Altamont that ended the Rolling Stones' triumphal American tour. It was here that the Stones engaged the Hell's Angels as their bodyguards, and that one of these knifed a pistol-wielding Negro youth to death. Using the Altamont concert as a frame, the film shows scenes of a previous concert in Madison Square Garden, of the difficulties in obtaining a site for the free concert and the concomitant ruckus, of the preparations for that concert, of Mick Jagger and other Stones watching what happened on a Moviola, and of Mick and his sidekicks flitting about.

Unfortunately, the fact that a real-life murder accidentally got itself recorded on film tends to overshadow everything else in *Gimme Shelter;* one's eyes are continually scouring the screen for the killer Angel and his less than angelic victim. Still, what comes across clearly and unavoidably is the unruliness, the incipient and sometimes manifest savagery of the crowd, and, above all, the madness. Not a momentary crazed condition, but fundamental and sustained dementia. This surfaces in a variety of specific symptoms, such as a youth's stripping himself to the buff and getting the crowd to use him as a volleyball.

Even more disturbing is the behavior of the front rank of the mob, those within whose reach performers literally are. They stare at the Stones with an expression that could be described as stoned, zonked, glazed, but also hungry and somehow vicious—like a rabble that has just smashed the store windows and is getting ready to loot. Greedy polyplike arms stretch out toward Jagger and the rest; when repulsed, they tenaciously, tentacularly return to the task. You feel that this crowd is a Moloch that would as soon devour its idols as listen to them.

Yet where the Maysleses and Charlotte Zwerin, their editor now elevated to equal filmmaker status, err is with the Stones themselves. To be sure,

Jagger and his henchmen come across as archetypal creeps to me (just as to the young they appear to be archetypal demigods), but the nature and background of their quiddity is not even cursorily examined. Jagger, in his appalling way, is something to behold (not to hear, for the music is worthless, and so, doubtless, would be the words if one could make them out) whether he is performing or just existing, two conditions that resemble each other like allotropes.

The particular horror for me is his lascivious public enjoyment of his perfect androgyny: as if his male self were having continuous, ostentatiously lip-smacking intercourse with his female self, thus piling narcissism and exhibitionism on hermaphroditism and topping it off with pelf—for all of this is designed also for conversion into an unending stream of cash. Mick Jagger becomes a one-person Zeus and Danaë act. The Maysleses, though, catch this less well than does even such a dreadful quasi-narrative movie as *Performance.*

There are incidental epiphanies in the film. Among them I include the enshrinement of Melvin Belli as a legal superstar; he is a nonpareil of greasy self-display handling the negotiations for a stadium to accommodate the Stones. His office looks like the bar of a cruise ship; his press conference is a "radical-chic" party given by socialites for militants; his own person is an oily amalgam of a Lindy's habitué, Hollywood agent, and Mafia overlord. Not uninteresting, either, are the clothes worn by the Stones and especially Jagger, which clearly set the styles for the well-bedecked groupie. But most fascinating is one single look in the movie, given by a Hell's Angel to Jagger in mid-performance: a blend of amazement and contempt that intensifies into disbelief and disgust.

I cannot judge the photography, having seen it only on a small screen, where it seemed more than adequate. In fact, it becomes quite lovely during a night-and-dawn sequence when the Altamont race track is being converted into an outdoor concert hall and, again, when zooming in on Mick Jagger's particolored shoes. The murder itself is a bit of an anticlimax because, even in slow-motion replay and with stopshots, it unfurls hastily and skimpily—as these things do in reality without the services of scriptwriters and directors. But the Maysleses do not even probe the Stones' reactions to the killing beyond showing them watching the replay, and this has a staged look to it. If some notable comments were grunted out on this occasion, they certainly escaped me.

From these films, and a few others we have seen lately, we get a curious insight into our youth culture. It clearly apes adult culture without realizing it. It has its aristocracy, the college students; its middle class, the dropouts who take on various more or less flimsy jobs; its proletariat, the street people who hang around college towns to scrounge off students and their facilities; its warrior caste, the blacks and other militants; its artists and philosophers, the rock musicians and self-styled gurus; its whores and courtesans, the groupies and supergroupies; and its madness, however differently manifested.

Back now to the good old days, if such they were, in a film that purports to take place today, but capitalizes on old-fashioned sentimentality. I refer to

Love Story by Erich Segal, the young Yale classics professor who has written on and translated Plautus, but whose heart belongs to show biz. He has a few Broadway and off-Broadway credits, worked on the script of *Yellow Submarine,* and wrote the screenplays of *The Games,* which I haven't seen, and *R.P.M.,* which, alas, I have. Although *Love Story* began as a screenplay, Segal, before the film was ready, turned it into a novella by the same title. This tearjerker by our swinging classics prof has established a sales record, and been a best-seller for more weeks than you can shake a caduceus at.

I have looked at the book (all I could manage), and I have now read the film. I say "read" because this is clearly the *ur*-text, of whose writing Segal is said to be more proud than of his novelization, and because watching it is less a filmic experience than an exercise in mind reading, where one follows every twist of Segal's conning the customers into programmed exhilaration, heart-break, and catharsis. I suppose the plot is by now as well known as that of *War and Peace,* but in case some of you have forgotten both, I will sum up at least one of them.

Oliver Barrett IV, a Harvard jock and scion of a rich and social New England family, loses his heart to sassy, talented, but poor Jenny Cavilleri, Radcliffe music student and daughter of a Catholic baker from Cranston, R.I. Though the Barrett estate is bigger than the Cavilleri girl's state, the kids marry, only to have Oliver III cut off Oliver IV without a cent. Jenny teaches grade school to put her husband through Harvard Law School, and he does brilliantly. Upon graduation he lands a munificent job handling civil-rights cases with a venerable old New York law firm, and this permits the formerly struggling young couple to live in lavish style. Alas, Jenny develops some unnamed blood disease (presumably leukemia, but we do not go into any embarrassing details—Oliver doesn't even ask the doctor for a specific diagnosis). She dies beautifully, and in last speeches patterned after those of the heroine of *A Farewell to Arms,* urges Oliver IV to be a merry widower and to lie on top of her once more before she departs. Oliver III arrives to declare that all is forgiven, and the final shot repeats the film's first: Oliver IV hunched up and grieving in front of the snowed-in Central Park skating rink. His words, as near as I can bring myself to remember, are: "What do you say about a girl who was brilliant and beautiful and loved you and died at the age of twenty-five?" I think you say, "Very lucrative."

The film is so bad that for all its taking me back to some of the most enchanted locales of my youth—I, too, stood tremulously waiting for my date in the lobby of Briggs Hall, etc., etc.—and for all that I, too, loved a girl who died prematurely and tragically, it never once moved me. In fact, the one thing that did move me was Ray Milland's appearance: an actor whom I saw only yesterday, it seems, as a handsome matinee idol was so diminished of hairline and augmented of chinline as to be barely recognizable. That was sad.

The success of *Love Story,* as book or film, was as predictable as it is despicable. You take a boy who is rich and aristocratic and you make him an ace hockey player and have him fall out over a poor girl with his stuffy father (whom, in this day and age, he addresses as "Sir"—Segal, thou shouldst have lived in another hour!), thereby endearing him to those who resent wealth and social status. Then you make him into a brilliant lawyer who works on civil-rights cases. Perfect: not the ivory tower, but not a base or humdrum or useless occupation either.

Next, you bring in a Catholic girl. Very good: a minority group, but the oldest and most respectable of all—furthermore, she is a lapsed Catholic, so we have it all three ways. Her father is a baker. Splendid: working-class yet clean. Oh, the smell of good, fresh-baked bread—and in Rhode Island, not Alabama or the Bronx! Besides, the wench is dead right about the Köchel number of any Mozart composition and plays the piano charmingly. And in an age of casual sexuality these kids go in for puppy love and monogamy; they can count on the silent majority to shed rapturously inarticulate tears over them.

This exquisite Jenny could have studied in Paris with Nadia Boulanger, we learn. Any film with Köchel numbers and Nadia Boulanger is Culture—especially for people who don't know a Köchel from a streetcar number and who think that Nadia Boulanger is a French school of *cordon-bleu* bakery. Arthur Hiller has directed the film with a certain cleverness: young lovers gambol in the snow rather than in flowery meadows, and a disastrous family dinner is cunningly intercut with its aftermath, when Oliver and Jenny comment on it while driving back to school. Ray Milland does nicely by the stock part of the boy's posh father, but John Marley, as the girl's Catholic father, comes across rather like Segal's—a Brooklyn rabbi.

Ryan O'Neal seems absolutely right in every way as Oliver, but Ali MacGraw looks too old for her role and has to work overhard at being Jenny and very young. Moreover, she looks considerably less good than in *Goodbye, Columbus,* or is photographed considerably less well. In fact, Dick Kratina's work is unusual in this day of almost invariably competent color cinematography. His hues manage to be predominantly sickly: the Harvard Yard, for instance, comes out an unwholesome purplish shade, as though it, too, were dying of leukemia. Francis Lai's score is suitably syrupy.

I am told that Segal's book on Plautus is fine; I shall want to read *that* one of these days. I think it is very nice to make millions from one's work. But unless Segal is a Jackie Susann in academic drag, and a hopeless case, I issue this Horatian warning to him: *"Dignum laude virum Musa vetat mori. / Caelo Musa beat."* Let us not betray the Muse merely to amuse.

January 11, 1971

Ontological Thrillers

THE CREATORS OF THE DEPLORABLE *Bob & Carol & Ted & Alice* have done it again; in fact, Paul Mazursky and Larry Tucker have outdone themselves with *Alex in Wonderland,* for whose hero they have a perfect smart aleck in Donald Sutherland. Having been successful with their first movie (or second, if you count their script for *I Love You, Alice B. Toklas),* they have the nerve to see themselves in the position of Fellini after seven and a half important films, two or three of them masterpieces. In other words, they felt entitled to make an unstructured, improvisatory, self-aggrandizing film about a successful Hollywood director looking for his second film subject.

Though this is partly an *hommage* to Fellini, it is an even greater homage to themselves, or perhaps to their lack of ideas, which they parade across the screen in complacent detail. Alex, the young hotshot whose first film is not even released yet, already has problems not only with his next film and its potential producer, but also with buying a house, placating his wife, mother, and children, dodging his friends' good advice, and, most of all, with his teeming brain, which won't stop spewing forth sophomoric reveries about future films.

The whole thing is, once again, reduced to cabaret skits sloppily tacked together, but unlike *B&C&T&A, Alex in Wonderland* is not even vulgarly, not even intermittently funny. The reasons are obvious. Esalen, marital double standards and infidelities, orgies among friendly couples are topics that are very much in the air and provide both filmmakers and audiences with something palpable and close to home. But the thrashings of an allegedly sensitive soul in the spider web of Hollywood success is a rather tenuous subject if indeed it is plausible at all.

The only glimmerings of wit occur when Alex and his producer-to-be have lunch and dreams of glory together in the latter's office. But, unfortunately, the culturemongering grandioseness of Hollywood producers is a vein that has scant ore left in it to mine. Most of the other scenes are bits of waffling and woolgathering, much of it seemingly improvised in the hope of stumbling across some relevant truths but resulting only in aimless stumbling about.

Particularly embarrassing are the numerous allusions to and pastiches of *8½* and *Juliet of the Spirits,* which Mazursky and Tucker clearly admire, though their clownish adulation would drag down much better films. Fellini's own brief appearance in *Alex* is neither good nor bad, but Jeanne Moreau—looking rather sadly ravaged—is foolishly and demeaningly dragged into two scenes that are tasteless and depressing. So, too, is the social relevance that is roped in to give the film seriousness and class: a Negro uprising with bloody street fighting (ineptly staged) in which Alex imagines himself grieving over the body of his daughter.

Dreary, too, is a whole new shipload of manure about middle-class sex and drugs, not to mention a number of older and even drearier stereotyped Jewish jokes. And Donald Sutherland plays Alex again with that combination of sneering and sniveling for which the portmanteau word sneerveling may have to be invented. In the part of his wife, however, Ellen Burstyn performs humanly and credibly, and Mazursky himself is not unfunny as the producer. But his daughter, Meg, is horrid as Alex's elder child. Members of the Mazursky family had best avoid sympathetic roles.

The key line in the film is, "He's happy and sad like everybody—now why can't that be a movie?" Both the thought and the diction of that sentence epitomize the worst kind of triviality, the one that takes itself seriously and brandishes a moldering platitude as though it were a momentous insight. And that, I am afraid, is the essence of Mazursky and Tucker's "art."

Not much better is the new film by Robert Altman, whose *M*A*S*H* was a true albeit alloyed delight. *Brewster McCloud* is a pretentious, disorganized, modishly iconoclastic movie which, in the manner of its Icarus-like hero, aspires to fly high and merely drops dead. The screenplay by Doran William Cannon concerns an innocent boy who lives hidden in the bowels of Houston's Astrodome, where he is perfecting his body along with a pair of artificial wings for flying off into a better world. Right there the clumsiness of the filmmakers overwhelms us. The Astrodome may be a fine symbol for our denatured world, but only if you are faithful to your symbol and play out the whole film inside this dome, and refrain from transferring the action to the outer world, as the film does most of the time.

Brewster is helped by Louise, a mysterious blond guardian-angelish creature with wing marks on her shoulder blades and given to making nude appearances for the sole purpose of giving the film a Now look. Her pet crow liberates captive birds and, together with them, defecates on evil people who are subsequently found slain. The killings are apparently performed by Hope, a girl who works in a supermarket whence she steals food for Brewster, and who has orgasms all by herself while watching the boy do his body- or wing-building exercises. She has these orgasms under a blanket and seems to be simultaneously practicing her garrotting. As a character, or even as a symbol, she makes fully as little sense as Louise. The third female in Brewster's life is Suzanne, a heavily made-up teenybopper guide at the Astrodome, with whom the youth has his sexual initiation despite Louise's warnings to stay away from women and sex. Suzanne coaxes Brewster's secret out of him and becomes the instrument of his undoing. The character might make sense, but remains unexplored.

Do not for a moment think that the film is even as neat as this partial outline suggests. It is full of undisciplined, unintegrated, unfunny incidents and running gags, including the supposedly comic murders of wicked people, the humiliation of a cool supersleuth from the SFPD, the exposure of the pseudorighteous political bigwig, the incompetence of policemen and ultramodern methods of detection, a car chase that is so cute and interminable as to be more of a drag than a drag race, and, worst of all, a running gag involving René Auberjonois in one of his most outlandish performances. He plays a professor of ornithology who, in the process of lecturing on the habits of birds, himself slowly turns into various birds.

The lecture serves as a frame for the film and illustrates its muddle-headedness. Birds are, apparently, the symbol of naturalness, decency, and freedom, hence Brewster wants to become one of them. Yet the lecture, deliberately or inadvertently, makes birds sound absurd and ludicrously human. And the lecturer, who is the most avian of men, is both ridiculous and creepy. The birds, moreover, put the Indian sign on those about to be executed by crapping on them, and birdshit, visually and verbally wallowed in, becomes the film's favorite dirty joke—more infantile and unhygienic, alas, than daring.

In fact, what the movie lacks as much as a sense of direction is a sense of style, going as it does from the good old Alec Guinness comedy routines to the mod pseudosatire of the Michael Winner swinging-London films, from the Three Stooges to the trendiest black humor. It is also sloppily directed and badly cast, with Brewster played by Bud Cort, possibly the most spineless and gutless juvenile around. Sally Kellerman, as Louise, is beginning to repeat herself dangerously. As Suzanne, Shelley Duvall is the worst and homeliest thing to hit the movies since Liza Minnelli. As Hope, Jennifer Salt is equally deficient in looks, personality, and talent, and can boast only a famous actor boy friend and a successful screenwriter father. In a take-off on Steve McQueen's Bullitt, Michael Murphy vainly hopes to make his expressionlessness work comic wonders for him. Only William Windom comes across neatly as the Agnewish politico, but the part is easy and obvious, and I rather think that Windom has been playing it all his life.

The ending is a spurious variation on the standard Fellinian cop-out, in which everything turns into a dance or parade or procession—as in *8½*, *B&C&T&A,* etc. Here all the characters, including the dead ones, reappear as clowns and other circus figures, and only the fallen Icarus remains dead. This business of having it both ways proves more disorienting than devastating. The lesson of *Brewster McCloud* seems to be: stay away from sex with flesh-and-blood girls and stick to platonic but titillating nude bathing sequences with supernatural female beings. There is, needless to say, the obligatory rock score, complete with lyrics that desperately pretend to be saying something.

January 25, 1971

Women of Today, Men of Tomorrow

ELAINE MAY MAKES her film-directorial debut in *A New Leaf.* Miss May is suing Paramount for cutting and reediting her film and thus, allegedly, distorting and destroying it. From what I have been able to gather, her version developed the characters more fully, had rather more serious overtones, and was less of a concatenation of blackout sketches. I cannot pronounce on this issue, but her apparent persistence in her suit despite the rave reviews the released version, and she herself with it, received, suggests a person with character and artistic integrity that I cannot but applaud.

What, after this apparent defoliation by the studio, remains of *Leaf?* I should state that I saw the film at the Radio City Music Hall, which must be the worst place in the world to see anything, but particularly a comedy. For if audiences at the movies generally talk and bellow with uncontrolled laughter, in the world's biggest and most touristy movie theater the laughter is more excessive and delayed (the customers catching on to the first joke just in time to obliterate the second), the talk more persistent and unhushable than anywhere else. So I am likely to have lost a fair number of funny lines; on the other hand, I may be crediting lost dialogue with wit it does not possess. What I was left with was a mildly amusing, sometimes rather obvious, pleasantly inconsequential film, but far from being a work of comedic art.

Walter Matthau plays Henry Graham, a rich wastrel who finds himself suddenly bankrupt. His greedy uncle extends him a loan with a Draconian time limit; but before that term expires, and he is deprived even of his clothes, Henry hopes to realize his butler's suggestion and marry an heiress. Several possible heiresses having proved, on closer inspection, impossible, Henry settles on Henrietta Lowell (Miss May), a gawky, homely, utterly clumsy botanist: very rich, very unworldly, and presumably easy to murder—for that is Henry's plan.

But, clearly, a Henry and a Henrietta are mated in heaven. Although Henrietta's crooked lawyer tries everything to stop the marriage, it comes off. Henrietta's servants, in cahoots with the lawyer, are robbing her blind; Henry fires them. Now he can start to plot his own widowing. But Henrietta is every bit as generous and loving as she is wealthy and klutzy. Her life's ambition is to discover a new leaf or fern to which she can bequeath her name and thus acquire immortality as a footnote in the botany books. When she does discover a new genus of ferns, she names it after her beloved husband instead.

On an excursion to the Adirondacks, Henry gets his chance. Their canoe capsizes in the rapids, and Henry swims ashore while Henrietta is about to drown. But among the luxuriant riparian vegetation, a fine specimen of the fern that has given him eternal life catches Henry's eye. He rescues Henrietta and even accedes to her dearest wish: despite his detestation of work, he agrees to teach history at her school, so that every day in the school cafeteria they'll be lunching in midday marital bliss.

The film is palpably pieced together out of comic bits, Nichols-and-May numbers that have turned into Matthau-and-May, or whatever two characters happen to be on screen. This is not in itself a bad thing, except that in its present form there is something a trifle random and flaccid about the film: sometimes the events lack a chain; at other times, the chain lacks events. One episode is genuinely amusing. It involves a Grecian-style nightgown that Henrietta wants to be seductive in on her wedding night, without, however, knowing which part of herself goes through which aperture in the garment. She gets Gordianly entangled, and Henry, trying to help, only loses himself as well in that labyrinthine nightie. All this to the accompaniment of dialogue that, though I could not hear it from the roaring of the Radio City plebs, somehow *looked* funny.

It is unfortunate that *A New Leaf* was saddled with an inferior cinematographer, Gayne Rescher, who contributed so unhandsomely to *Rachel, Rachel.* Here, again, his colors tend to have a washed-out quality, rather like bad reproductions of paintings in a cheap art book. The cast is good, on the whole, though Jack Weston's conniving lawyer strikes me as too obvious; the actor simply lacks comic resources. George Rose and James Coco, as the butler and uncle, respectively, are better, even if not up to their very considerable best. But William Redfield contributes a delightful bit as Henry's lawyer, and Matthau and May do a very neat job of humanizing their highly exaggerated material. Miss May's direction is hard to judge without seeing her version of the film; here there are scenes that do not build properly, notably the last, which desperately lacks suspense and hardly makes us care about the outcome.

Science fiction reaches us with two extremely different films, *THX 1138* and *The Andromeda Strain.* The former is an expanded version of a prize-winning student short that called attention to its maker, George Lucas. It came out roughly simultaneously with *2001,* and many were the people who felt that Lucas had achieved more captivating effects on a shoestring than Kubrick with all his mammoth production values. I was not particularly impressed by either film, but the new, full-length *THX 1138* is rather different from its precursor. Now there is a plot that, while simple, manages to be both obscure and pretentious; but there are also visuals that I found almost always absorbing, indeed exhilarating.

We are in an evil, totally computerized utopia, where people have clean-shaven heads, are sedated out of all desire to make love (which is a crime), and bear not names but serial numbers, like THX 1138, the film's protagonist. THX, if I may refer to him thus familiarly, is rooming with a shaven-headed lass whose number I forget, and who de-sedates him sufficiently for them to have sex. Apprehended, he is tried and jailed with two other misfits, one of whom is a Negro but also an inadvertently materialized television image (whatever that means, and whatever it implies about the future of television), and the other Donald Pleasence of the already hairless head, and thus seemingly type-cast. It is a strange prison without walls, out of which our trio walks rather than breaks. They are pursued by various policeman-robots, making for some mildly lively moments. Our hero learns of his girl's death, flees with renewed zeal, and when the pursuit reaches a cost greater than the individual's worth to the state, is allowed to get away. He emerges on the earth's surface—we now realize that all this took place in its bowels—and faces an uncertain destiny.

The story, then, is trivial and confusing, and did not keep me from dozing off periodically. And, as almost always in sci-fi, the dialogue is devoid of interest. Even the various futuristic gimmicks are only moderately diverting. There remains the color photography of Dave Meyers and Albert Kihn which, combining with the ingenious set design, is not only visually thrilling but even, as it were, challenging to the intellect. The chief device here is to present a world of white on white: mainly white-garbed people against predominantly white backgrounds. It is as if snow had covered all these indoors, all these lives; only the faces, like great flesh-colored flowers, are vainly thrusting up through this chilling blanket toward a spring that will not come. It is a visual metaphor that is co-extensive with the entire film, and whose fascination never palls.

The Andromeda Strain, Robert Wise's film from Michael Crichton's bestseller about a satellite bringing back a dread germ from outer space, is another case of bipartite division. On the one hand, technology and science—everything from computers to microbiology; on the other, people and politics. Even though I enjoyed the film's jaundiced views of government, politicians, and the military, all that is routine stuff, slickly but unoriginally handled: the whole nonlaboratory part of the film is written and directed on the level of middling journalism. The technological part is arresting: the difficult, wearying, and often dangerous tests to establish the nature of the lethal substance and the race against time to find a way to neutralize it. Here the idea and treatment capture the mind, and one finds oneself puzzling along with the desperate scientists.

I suppose that where human beings are shown as merely minds behind procedures and issues, no matter how grave, their humanity always ends up foreshortened, indeed shortchanged. But Wise and his scenarist, Nelson Gidding, have not only come up with the usual clichés, they even stumble on stereotyped ways of trying to avoid stereotypes. Still, there is a certain beauty as well as horror in all that supergadgetry at work, giving the film some aesthetics as well as melodramatics. The grand finale is a rather too obvious *coup de cinéma* but, because James Olson and Arthur Hill are intelligent actors, it comes out a little less hoked-up than it might be.

Richard H. Kline's color cinematography is decent, the special effects are efficient, the music is appropriate. *The Andromeda Strain* is a tidy film, yet it completely fades from memory after its 130 minutes are over. Whether our entire planet will survive engages us very little in the cinema unless there is even one character in the movie about whose individual survival we can care. Not a one in this script.

April 5, 1971

Forman Against Man

It is hard to write about *Taking Off* without losing control. I cannot think offhand of any other movie as gracelessly, smugly, and stupidly antihuman, as self-servingly and gloatingly superior to all humanity. It leaves us with the impression that only the filmmaker is a knowing, sensitive spirit, who has every right to jeer at a humankind unfit to tie his shoelaces. And the fact that much of the audience and most reviewers have loudly endorsed this film almost proves him right. Almost, but not quite.

Taking Off is the first American picture of Miloš Forman, the refugee Czech filmmaker, whom I have always rated a highly overrated commodity. But some of his Czech films, though overvalued, were not without redeeming features, owing, no doubt, to such gifted collaborators as Ivan Passer. Forman's first film was a short called *Audition,* a cinéma-vérité item about girl singers auditioning for a Prague band. At least twenty minutes of *Taking Off* are devoted to girl singers auditioning before an unlikely panel for an unspecified job. This is rank self-plagiarism: but what in *Audition* was real and slightly touching (for example, Czech kids trying to cope with American songs), is in the present film pretentious, ugly, and evil. Next came another short, then *Black Peter,* Forman's best film to date, dealing with the conflicts of errant children and pompous parents, a theme taken up again, much more pompously and arrantly, in *Taking Off.*

Loves of a Blonde, Forman's biggest international success, was an unbalanced little comedy with moments that were meaningful and affecting, and others that were obvious and crude. It began with a precredit sequence in which a teen-aged girl in a cowboy outfit played the guitar and sang some silly pop song in dead earnest. *Taking Off* begins with a precredit shot of teen-aged girls dressed in costumes based on the American flag, singing a pop song in dread earnest. There was also a long closing sequence in *Blonde* involving the teen-aged heroine's bringing her pop-musician seducer home to meet her folks. *Mutatis mutandis,* it recurs here.

There followed *Firemen's Ball,* a ponderous blackish humoresque about a bunch of firemen as dumb as any Keystone Kops, who, among other things, conduct a beauty contest wherein some painfully plain girls are scrutinized in merciless detail. The song contestants in *Taking Off* are also, for the most part, ugly and even freakish, and are similarly lovingly—i.e., hatefully—anatomized. And the Society of Parents of Fugitive Children, which takes up a good part of this film (originally titled *S.P.F.C.),* not only carries on in much the same bumbling fashion as those firemen, but is, let me add, just as unfunny.

Taking Off concerns fifteen-and-a-half-year-old Jeannie Tyne, who runs away from her parents' affluently and militantly middle-class home and wanders into an East Village singing-talent audition that seems to be a nonstop affair. At least longer or shorter scenes from it pop up throughout the film, and the music and singing from it is sometimes heard in voice-over during the so-called plot scenes. Jeannie keeps coming home after brief disappearances, only to discover her parents drunk and disorderly and to flee again. The parents, Lynn and Larry, are seen either searching for Jeannie, often in the company of equally inept friends; or discussing sex absurdly and grossly; or having fights; or getting involved in various burlesque predicaments. There is a big S.P.F.C. banquet with speechifying, and a smaller S.P.F.C. meeting in an elegant upper-class apartment where the parents have their "first indulgence" (typical of their stilted language) in marijuana to find out what their children are up to. Finally, there is the dinner at the Tynes's to which Jeannie brings her hippie boy friend. But it is all much more horrible than it sounds.

The adults are crude, baffled fools. They screw too little, or too frenetically, and have to resort to risible devices to arouse one another. They smoke too much, and make asses of themselves trying to break the habit. They drink excessively, and cannot hold their liquor. And they know nothing, but nothing, about their kids. These adults are almost always caricatured; thus, for example, Lynn Tyne's friend, Margot, played by the chinless, fish-eyed Georgia Engel as a gaping or giggling imbecile; or the two men who try to pick up Lynn at a roadside nightclub and drop hideous jokes and their trousers with equally improbable alacrity. Adults shown in groups are even more disgusting. The S.P.F.C. members being taught how to turn on by a pothead version of Mortimer Snerd display collective cretinism to the point of asking questions like how fast are they supposed to count to ten before exhaling.

Don't go thinking, however, that youth comes off any better. The girls at the audition are, with a couple of exceptions, some of the unsavoriest specimens ever assembled: from acne to obesity, from toilet-brush hair to sick-sheep expressions, every form of unsightliness is caught by the lighting, photography, and editing in the most unflattering detail. A dreary song is sung over and over again by aspirant after aspirant, each given a bar or two and continuing from where the last one left off, so that brevity of appearance and giddiness of montage combine to make these unfortunates even more pitiful than they are. Forman actually steals a device from Camus's *Caligula,* whereby the main auditioner cuts off the applicants at an ever quickening rate, so that some poor no-talents have barely opened their mouths before the monosyllable "Next!" consigns them to oblivion.

But Forman does not stop at this. He throws in other phenomena of the pop-music scene, often without any rationale other than sensationalism. So he suddenly shows us an adipose nude girl playing the cello, Charlotte Moorman–fashion; or he gets Tom Eyen to write a particularly noxious song in his well-known "dirty" manner for some funny-looking kid gravely to perform. The song is entitled "Ode to a Screw," and consists of a catalogue of screwables such as "You can fuck the Russians/And the English too;/You can fuck the Germans/And every pushy Jew." Of course, it does not even have the courage of its moronic convictions, and ends with a cop-out: "But first of all fuck me!" (By the way, I first saw *Taking Off* at an invitational preview at the Museum of Modern Art, with an audience littered with show-biz personalities and sprinkled with reviewers; not only did they eat up the whole film, but they also carried on so orgiastically during this song that it seemed they were about to accord its precepts immediate application.)

The kids, I repeat, are made into idiots, too. Some of them gibber about the joys of drug-taking, some are cowardly, others are dolts, make-out artists and smartass operators, or Hell's Angels. Decency, like short hair, is out of fashion. The single character seemingly meant to be positive is young Jeannie, but to Forman this means only forcing her eyes wide open with wonderment or dismay at the world around her, and allowing her no more dialogue than four or five lines in the entire film. To equate mutism with virtue, though, is too easy. He cannot show us how she and her hippie musician make out, for it would be hard to turn the seduction of a barely nubile kid by a zonked zombie into a good thing. And I wonder whether Forman can be obtuse enough to regard the pretentious stuff some of these kids sing (or are made to sing) with anything but scorn: "I'm dying in a world that will die before death . . ."

The film is made out of total hate for man and beast alike. If a woman is seen leaning out of a tenement window, you may be sure that she is the *ne plus ultra* of fatness and repulsiveness; if two dogs are glimpsed, you may count on it that they are copulating. Now, of course, the great satirists—say, Juvenal, Swift, Voltaire—were also against most of what they saw around them. But they were also *for* something, whether it was the *pudor* they perceived beyond the *nefas,* or horses that were nobler than men, or gardens by whose cultivation one cultivates oneself.

The only truly positive value that Forman can offer us is himself. The Tynes drive on a wild-goose chase to somewhere three hundred miles upstate New York upon notification that their girl is being held there by the police for theft. "LYNN: What did she steal? LARRY: A Jap portable television set. LYNN (gulping with brand-name conscious awe): A SONY?" The girl turns out to be a friend who cravenly gave Jeannie's name as an alias; the police sergeant is an idiot; the parents are again made fools of. As they drive home through the night bickering and bemoaning their drab existence, the taillights and headlights of other cars on the highway whoosh past them, sportive red and white disks, like motorized Moholy-Nagy abstractions. This is a studio process shot, cheaper than actual night photography; but it is clearly meant to show the pictorial beauty that can be conjured up on screen for us in an otherwise crass, unlovely world.

Yet it is the people who made this film that are revealed as morally deficient and profoundly unlovely. It is not easy to say just who is responsible for what; the screenplay is credited to Forman, John Guare, John Klein, and Jean-Claude Carrière. Guare is the talented young playwright whose absurdist stage comedies are not devoid of human feeling; John Klein I know only as coscenarist of *The Collector,* an interesting and far from worthless film; Carrière is Buñuel's poorest scenarist, though I doubt that he had much to do with this film, having been on the project earlier, when Claude Berri was supposed to produce it. So Forman appears to be the chief perpetrator in every way.

And, surely, there is something richly distasteful about the way the main theme of the film is treated. The anxiety and despair of parents whose children are missing does not appear to be a fit subject for cheap comedy. For black comedy, perhaps, but the film lacks the stylization, the gift for hyperbole, black comedy involves; moreover, even such comedy, as written by the absurdist playwrights, has implicit moral values, however unconventional. Forman proves absolutely heartless here. Thus he shows a huge hotel ballroom during an S.P.F.C. banquet, complete with grandiloquently ludicrous chairwomen, orators, members who are thoroughly enjoying this social occasion. One mother of a fugitive daughter says to the father of another about her marriage, "Just looking for her has brought us together." As if that were not enough, she is saying it in the most flirtatious, provocatively coquettish way.

At the banquet, the parents all wear pictures of their missing offspring on their elegant lapels, or hanging amid expensive jewelry. They are asked to file past one particularly creepy girl who has just come back from a six months' underground escapade and might recognize some fellow fugitives and provide clues to their whereabouts. There ensues a passing parade of bedizened parents who have exercised their ingenuity to make the children's pictures blend in elegantly with their *haute toilette.* Some have made cute buttons out of the photos; others have even decorated these buttons with beads and flowers, to make them look like high-class *ex votos;* one father has suspended from his lapel a series of neatly tiered snapshots of his large missing brood. The scene ends with a characteristic gag: after repeatedly shaking her head, the girl finally says, "I've seen *her!*" at which the parent cries, "This is my son!"

I pass lightly over the arty and pretentious—as well as preposterous—sequence of the S.P.F.C. pot-smoking lesson in a fancy apartment where American primitives hang on the walls in prim black-and-white Colonial garb, and it looks at times as if the joints were being passed by austere New England patriarchs to their puritanically frowning helpmeets. The experiment is meant to elucidate the kids' behavior, but the parents, after displaying stodginess and naïveté beyond compare, promptly turn the occasion into fun and games, with stabs at adultery.

Even more unpalatable is the scene in which the Tynes and the other principal couple, the Lockstons, under the influence of grass, play a version of strip poker in the Tynes's apartment. This apartment, incidentally, is decorated with a bad taste that seems beyond the reach of even the grossest parvenus. There are, for instance, two separate kinds of dried ferns or flowers, whose names I unfortunately don't know, but both of which are, significantly, dead. There is also a picture representing a ship, a face, or a vase with flowers, depending on your angle of vision: "That's remarkable! That's what I mean by a work of art!" exclaims the dapper Mr. Lockston.

When the two couples play that card game, the director, typically, stacks the cards. While the Lockstons retain most of their clothing, the Tynes are reduced to nudity or almost. This is again a cop-out. Mrs. Lockston is played by an aging Doris Day type, whose exposed body would really be an act of cruelty of the sort Forman keeps sidling up to, a touch of the horror he wants us to feel. So here, when he has the chance to show his contempt for mankind, as it were, nakedly, fearless Forman chickens out.

Finally, there is that dinner scene. Trying to be broadminded and understanding, the Tynes have asked Jeannie to bring her Jamie to dinner. He turns out to be a cat so cool he is almost catatonic—it would be interesting to learn just what Jeannie sees in him, but the film does not deal in anything like insights or explications—and so out of sight that there is hardly a sound out of him. He is a rock musician, and when Larry, merely to make conversation, asks him, "Make any money at it?" Jamie answers quietly. "Last year I made two hundred ninety thousand." Larry, incredulous, asks, "What did you say?" and Jamie repeats the figure, adding modestly, "Before taxes." Larry, who has had to resort to hypnosis to break himself, painfully, of smoking, now grabs for the nearest cigarette. The film ends as the parents favor the kids with a rendition of "Stranger in Paradise." Lynn is at the piano, while Larry gestures, struts, and blares away ridiculously. Jeannie looks with quiet desperation at her parents' noisy one.

There are far more absurdities and vulgarities in *Taking Off* than I could begin to enumerate here. I haven't even had a chance to mention the grotesque casting and acting; for example, Lynn Carlin and Buck Henry do not look like a married couple by the wildest stretch of the uncomic imagination.

Moreover, Henry gives his customary soullessly exaggerated performance, and Miss Carlin merely repeats dimly what she did so lustrously in *Faces.* Linnea Heacock, as Jeannie, gives no evidence of acting ability, and the others, led by the already mentioned but utterly unmentionable Georgia Engel, are oafs.

As a critic, I am a moralist, though not, I trust, in a narrow, petty, moralizing sense. Whatever the case, I declare *Taking Off* an antihuman film: mean, arrogant, and thoroughly destructive. I consider Miloš Forman morally deficient to the utmost degree, and, as usually though not always follows, a worthless imitation of an artist. And I think that the army of his admirers, whether critics or audiences, are, at the very least, dupes and fools.

May 3, 1971

Youthful Indiscretions

NOTHING BUT YOUTH MOVIES this time round. Well, Woody Allen's *Bananas* is not exactly a youth movie—it is more of a retarded, or second-childhood movie. I tuned out on Allen after *What's New, Pussycat?,* and, tuning in again, I find that now as then nothing is new. Woody is still building card castles out of one-liners; no sooner has he piled up a few than the next one drops dead and the whole thing collapses.

Bananas concerns a little schnook who cannot make it for very long either with his odd job or his odd, revolutionary girl. He goes on a vacation to the Caribbean island for whose liberation the girl has been collecting signatures and marching. There he gets involved first with the Batista-ish president and then with the Castro-ish rebel leader, and . . . But why go on? None of it makes for sense or solidly developing humor, and much of it is in bad taste. Thus the opening scene, in which "Wide Wide World of Sports" televises the assassination of the island's president, complete with instant replay; and the last scene, in which Woody, having himself become El Presidente and returned to the United States, finally marries his activist girl, with the wedding night televised again by Howard Cosell in the manner and terminology of a sports event.

Somehow I do not much care for the figure of the little schnook as great statesman and lover in spite of himself. And I think it is the end of any so-called intellectual comedian, be it Mort Sahl or Woody Allen, when he really begins to believe all that stuff about his intellectuality. The fact is that intellectuals do not moonlight as stand-up comedians, and those who do have intellects that won't stand up. But a creeping pretentiousness spreads over their material, and pretty soon they are full of unfunny jokes about Kierkegaard and such, and instead of slipping on banana peels, they are making political satires about banana republics without knowing beans about their politics. The typical joke has Woody huffing amorously, "I love you," only to be passionately implored by the girl lying under him to say it in French. Hoarsely, he answers, "I don't know French. What about Hebrew?"

We come now to a brace of films about growing up in wartime: *Summer of '42*, about three boys lurching toward sexual initiation on a New England island; and *Red Sky at Morning,* about a boy's coming of age in the New Mexico of 1944. Both of these films depend heavily on nostalgia. But what, I ask, was so marvelous about the early forties that we should wax moony over them? There was an ugly war on, the fashions were unbecoming, the pop culture was all easy smugness based on the fact that God was on our side in the War.

Summer of '42 is the story, chiefly, of Hermie, who is emotionally ahead of his friends, although Oscy is bigger and more hard-boiled. In the process of playing the games of summer—stealing sex books from parental shelves, awkwardly buying prophylactics, fooling around with adolescent girls—Hermie meets an older woman of twenty, married to a soldier away at war. She lives in a distant beach house and Hermie carries her groceries for her. One evening he calls on her socially and finds her in a near-stupor: her husband has just been killed. A record is on the Victrola, and after silently, forlornly, clingingly dancing to it, they end up, with hardly a word spoken, in bed. The next day, the young widow is gone, having left a tender letter for Hermie. He never sees her again.

If this had been written by someone like Colette, acted by a young Gérard Philipe, say, and a Joanna Shimkus, and directed by someone with sensitivity and imagination, it might have been touching and beautiful. With Herman (formerly Hermie) Raucher's over- and underwritten script, Robert Mulligan's repetitious and floundering direction, the ordinariness of the supposedly sensitive Gary Grimes and the untalentedness of the pretty Jennifer O'Neill, what comes out is mostly drivel. But the world of 1942 is recaptured with deadly accuracy, for which dubious achievement Albert Brenner gets one of the top credits. Robert Surtees's cinematography, built around a watery, vaporous turquoise, is enervating in itself.

Red Sky at Morning is even less involving. A naval officer transplants his wife and son from Alabama to New Mexico, so they'll have a freer, healthier life while he goes back on active duty in 1944. The wife despises the Spanish-Americans, and slowly deteriorates between her mooching male cousin from Mobile and her decanter of sherry. The boy confronts a world where Anglo-Saxons are bottom dogs, and, with two chums (one a tomboy who does, however, end up in the hay with him), has more colorful coming-of-age adventures than I have the space or palette to evoke. The grandest ones involve a psychotic, knife-wielding Chicano, a madcap sculptor building a Mount Rushmore of his own, and the gun-toting, vengeful father of the two high-school whores.

Then the naval officer is lost at sea and the boy, whose maturing has progressed by leaps and bounds, now grows up at Keystone Kops tempo. He sets the paternal house in order and enlists in the navy. Mother becomes marvelously understanding, and the tomboy will wait for him. Everything about the film is thin and contrived, and James Goldstone's direction gives it ponderousness, not weight.

May 31, 1971

Crime Time

I HAVE NEVER BEEN PARTIAL to the criminal genre in any medium, though the nature of evil is an essential subject for artistic investigation. But the typical crime film, like most crime fiction, is not interested in that; it simply takes evil for granted and chronicles its exploits with unabashed relish, then slaps on a moralistic ending where justice triumphs—until the next time, that is, when another criminal marches forth toward glory. The appeal of the stuff to our most primitive needs is obvious enough; less obvious is that morality and righteousness, by popping up as a facile, contrived conclusion, become farce, made to look as bad as the company they keep.

Actually, the new tendency is to make morality, justice, the law look worse than the criminal and his crime. In one form or another, this motif appears in almost all contemporary crime films. About one, *The Anderson Tapes,* I would like to say something favorable, if only because leafing through the Twenty-fifth Anniversary Report of my Harvard class (1946), I found the picture and autobiographical sketch of Frank R. Pierson, the film's scenarist. In his sketch, rather better written than the screenplay (but, then, it wasn't based on a popular novel by Lawrence Sanders), Pierson tells us that out there in his "steel and glass and concrete box on the beach in Malibu" he is "fighting to maintain a lifelong anti-establishment position from the inside." There must be a moral here—either that it is hard to fight the Establishment from within, or that people who live in glass-and-concrete boxes should not throw bombs.

The Anderson Tapes concerns a heist plotted under the surveillance of a number of public and private agencies that for one reason or another keep hidden television cameras and tape recorders trained on those planning the robbery. The agencies do nothing to prevent it from happening, though—in fact, they erase the tapes after the crime is foiled, almost by accident, so that they will not become implicated. There is some sardonic criticism of our bugged society intended, but neither the scenarist nor the humorless and flat-footed director is able to get much mileage out of it. Worse yet, the framework keeps conflicting with the plot, the heist, which is further encroached on by a half-baked subplot: the quasi-love story between the master criminal and his calculating girl friend who, with leaden irony, leaves him for the more assured and respectable money of an oily businessman, thereby proving herself a true whore.

Sidney Lumet, surely the worst of the so-called better directors, has made the film choppy, diffuse, flabby, and wholly lacking in the good, unclean fun it wheezingly strives for. Sean Connery is dullish in the lead, with a muffled accent neither British nor American, and, thanks to the vagueness of the screenplay, unable to create a smidgen of character. As the whore with the heart dreaming of gold, Dyan Cannon gives a performance for which *amateurish* would be too kind a word. This is interesting only in view of the seeming excellence of her work in *Bob & Carol & Ted & Alice.* It is clear now that she was type-cast in the earlier film and equally clear that the movies can manipulate an inept performer into what looks like a highly accomplished performance.

Martin Balsam gives a heavy-handed portrayal of a lighter-than-air homosexual, and the film's running gag, whereby the unlikeliest people refer to him quite casually as a "fag," is neither funny nor in good taste. With the exception of Alan King, who does a surprisingly commanding impersonation of a high-class *mafioso,* the supporting cast is rather unsteady; such good stage actors as Christopher Walken, Janet Ward, and Anthony Holland do poorly. Arthur Ornitz's color photography is, at best, primitive; Quincy Jones's score fails both as music and as accompaniment to the action; and the plot, on top of its other shortcomings, is implausible. Most amazing is Ralph Meeker's police captain, only every fifth of whose words emerges intelligibly from the mush he keeps stored in his mouth.

June 28, 1971

There's Gold in Them Thar Hearts

PROSTITUTION PAST AND PRESENT is examined by two new Warner Brothers offerings. *Klute* takes us into the world of a New York call girl, and is very good while it sticks to simulated documentary filmmaking. It shows the heroine, Bree Daniel, at work and leisure: turning tricks, facing her analyst, trying to break into show business, neurotically resisting genuine feelings for a man. Writing, direction, acting, and cinematography combine to make this first half of the film convincing and full of quietly ominous fascination. But, alas, the movie then veers toward a rather conventional and contrived love-and-murder story, complete with a regeneration of the prostitute that would have made Alexander Kuprin wince and should make Erich Segal exult.

Nevertheless, for its atmospheric and incisive first half, *Klute* is to be commended and even, guardedly, recommended. Jane Fonda, as Bree, is as irresistible as a surfy beach in July: her performance washes over you like a tartly cooling, drolly buffeting liquid benediction, bringing wave after wave of unpredictable, exhilarating delight. There is a perfect blend here of shrewdness, acerbity, toughness, anxiety, and vulnerability. A quintessential feminity is caught in transition between a badly dented girlishness and a nascent womanliness as innocent of its past as a butterfly of its larva. Note the play of Miss Fonda's febrile hands when she is sweating it out with her therapist; the dartings and hesitancies of her voice, with its sudden leaps and falls of temperature; the faint seismic tremors of her facial play, indicating turbulences valiantly repressed. Truly this is one of our most valuable, loveliest young actresses—very possibly the most accomplished of them all.

But if Jane Fonda is Bree, Donald Sutherland, as the small-time investigator who uses, befriends, and finally loves her, should be Limburger, not Klute. What a malodorous actor Sutherland has rapidly become: when he is not insanely overacting, as in *Alex in Wonderland* or *Act of the Heart,* he is equally maniacally underacting. As John Klute, a provincial cop distinguished less for imaginativeness than doggedness, he emerges so simplistic, one-sided, stolid as to make me wonder whether Bree wasn't better off with some of her kinkiest lower-case johns, provided only that they belabored her with cloth rather than leather belts.

The supporting cast is uniformly evocative, as well chosen as the New York locales, tastefully photographed by Gordon Willis. Alan Pakula has directed more flexibly than in his one previous film, *The Sterile Cuckoo.* If only the initially able screenplay by Andy and Dave Lewis had eschewed the obvious, the film could have been thoroughly mature, and the boys could have rated billing as Andrew and David.

Prostitution, amiable skullduggery, and the viciousness of Church and Big Business are the subject of *McCabe and Mrs. Miller,* a film about the non-Spenglerian decline of the Old West. McCabe (Warren Beatty), a likable, penny-ante gambler, becomes the casino-*cum*-bordello operator of Presbyterian Church, a rising northwestern town. His enterprisingness is complemented by the shrewdness of his partner, Mrs. Miller (Julie Christie), as good a whoremistress as England ever exported. One of those shamefaced, grudging, antiverbal romances—naturally—springs up between them and all goes well (albeit unconscionably slowly and ramblingly) until big mining interests try to muscle in. McCabe resists them, and three varmints are dispatched to the town to dispatch him. The Brownian motion of the plot should now rise to the excitement of a showdown; under Robert Altman's direction it is a slowdown, a kind of low-comedy *High Noon* finish where—this is the twist—all are losers.

The movie is remarkably pretentious, its basic unit being neither a scene nor a shot, but a heavy hint or an arch symbol. Half the dialogue is delivered *sotto voce* out of the corners of people's mouths in a remote corner of the screen, or entirely off it; some of the sights are similarly relegated to the farthest crannies of the frame. The moviegoer now risks hurtling over the edge of his seat while straining to the utmost his eyes and ears (Julie Christie's accent is an additional burden on the latter)—rather as if he were a solitary sentinel on a foggy battlefield, with the enemy apt to strike anywhere, any moment. Unrewarding concentration, though, for there is not much to see in the film and even less to hear.

Vilmos Zsigmond's color photography is fine outdoors, though even here it must always be lowering, inclement weather; indoors, a special process meant to resemble daguerreotypy merely looks like badly blown-up 16-mm film. But by being forced to project one's sight and hearing as far as one can force them to go, one may get an impression of vasty spaces covered by *McCabe and Mrs.*

Miller. The film, moreover, is full of plot elements that are left dangling like a forgotten Pauline; but one imagines the filmmaker pontificating, "Such is life!"—as if art were supposed to be brute, undigested existence. Not that Altman's film is that either, crawling with audiovisual mannerisms as it is. The poor continuity is given conclusive disruption by the constantly recurring balladeering of Leonard Cohen, the Rod McKuen of the pseudoliterate.

July 12, 1971

Flailings of the Flesh

THERE ARE TWO KINDS of dishonesty: the kind that does not even care to pass for honesty, and the kind that implies or loudly proclaims it is telling God's truth. The old movies excelled at the former; the new breed, much more noxiously, tends to specialize in the latter. *Carnal Knowledge,* which garnered copious critical acclaim and is setting box-office records, is a fine example of a film that combines delusion of grandeur with delusion of honesty. Written by Jules Feiffer and directed by Mike Nichols, it carries the automatic cachet of the up-to-date, the with-it, the muckrakingly truthful.

Carnal Knowledge concerns two Amherst students, Jonathan (Jack Nicholson) and Sandy (Art Garfunkel), the one a juvenile Don Juan in the making, the other a naïvely idealistic, timid but lusting virgin. Sandy discovers Susan (Candice Bergen), a Smith girl, and falls for her. Soon both boys are sleeping with Susan (though Sandy does not know about Jonathan's doing so), and, eventually, she must choose between Sandy's ingenuous, one-sided puppy love and Jonathan's loveless but satisfying carnality. Uneasily, she opts for Sandy.

That was in the late forties; the fifties bring us a Sandy who is a doctor, a Jonathan who is a tax lawyer. Sandy is, more or less happily, married to Susan (whom we do not see any more); Jonathan is zestfully fornicating around town. They are comparing notes just above the Rockefeller Center skating rink, where a pretty blonde is pirouetting on the ice. Jonathan feels the pride of potentially possessing such a girl; Sandy begins to experience a hankering, and is only consoled by Jonathan's prompt castigation of all his conquests as castrators.

The next few vignettes take us to the sixties. Jonathan is involved with Bobbie (Ann-Margret), who has the immense breasts he has always craved; unfortunately for him, this aging good-time girl wants to get married and he is her choice. When they were merely living together, her slatternliness was a problem; now she is becoming a menace whom, as he says, he would even marry to get rid of. Meanwhile Sandy is having an affair with a sleek young career woman, Cindy (Cynthia O'Neal), as narcissistic a ballbreaker as you could not ask for. Jonathan tries to work out a swap, which drives Bobbie to attempted suicide and shames him into marrying her.

Finally, we are in the seventies: Jonathan has divorced Bobbie, whose alimony is bleeding him dry, though he is still living in high style; Sandy has gone hippie with a very young, frizzy-haired, and zonked flower child (Carol Kane) in tow. Jonathan shows them slides of all his past loves, with appropriately hateful comments about all. Leaving with his nonverbal girl, Sandy condescendingly lectures Jonathan about the true love- and life-style he is missing out on. Jonathan is finally seen being ministered to by a middle-aged whore (Rita Moreno), who must always go through the same ritual, word for word, extolling his virility while servilely abasing herself, so as to enable the now practically impotent lecher to achieve a precarious erection. Both men are losers, pitiful or laughable.

The film, too, is a loser, on any number of levels. First, the casting and acting. Jack Nicholson and Candice Bergen look like chaperones rather than freshmen at a mixer; Art Garfunkel looks youngish, inept, and ridiculous, but he accomplishes this through being the type, not by means of any noticeable acting. Yet it is not merely a question of ages: Miss Bergen cannot act any age even though, with every new film, she tries harder, which does make her a *rara avis* among no-talent actresses. Nicholson, who was marvelous in a character part in *Easy Rider,* is less than ideal for a leading man: his somewhat whiny, high-pitched voice lacks range, and he tries to compensate with rant; he has, moreover, a countrified, lower-class speech pattern that does not fit in here. He is also apt to overact.

It is Ann-Margret, as Bobbie, who is being hailed as the acting find of the movie. Type-cast hitherto as a sex kitten, and now grown too old for that part, she plays the familiar, heart-tugging role of the swinging bachelor girl who has become desperate for a husband and tries, with touching clumsiness and sloppiness, to keep house for her man. An utter failure at it, she retreats into longer and longer hours of sleep, and, like Cato on Carthage, keeps harping on marriage with her every pathetic peroration. This character, platitudinous or not, always wrings our hearts, and since Ann-Margret's career seems in some ways to parallel Bobbie's, the performance should truly drench a handkerchief or two. Actually, a Kleenex tissue can survive it.

True, there are those pitiful exposures of a famous body going to seed. We see the pushed-up breasts, framed by a low décolleté, the veins eerily prominent. Later, we see these breasts unveiled and jutting skyward even when their owner is supine: two uncollapsible, silly cones or globes, bespeaking man-made wonders. We get low-angle shots turning the naked buttocks into medicine balls, more suited to workouts than to amorous play. And we see the slightly sagging face, in relentless closeup, looking worried while trying to seduce. But something is lacking: a performance. Ann-Margret provides little more than the bulbous shell; missing are the quivering insides.

She is not helped by the screenplay. As has been remarked by others, Feiffer has given us a series of his cartoons; these, generally, represent two unchanging faces in a sequence of panels, with only the captions progressing. Similarly, the film is almost exclusively made up of colloquies between two less than mobile faces. Most often Nicholson and Garfunkel are framed in as tight a shot as can accommodate both heads in front of a fixed backdrop, such as the Rockefeller Center skating rink or a corner of P. J. Clarke's bar;

or they are gliding along at night, in a low-angle shot, against the summits of a row of lit-up skyscrapers along Park Avenue. When, very rarely, there are three characters in a scene, one of them is usually a silent observer, so that the Feiffer scheme is not unlike Greek drama before Sophocles introduced the third actor—but a far cry from Aeschylus, for all that.

The duologues gradually become repetitious, claustrophobic, and oppressive. To be sure, Nichols is sometimes able to infuse them with the old Nichols-May pizazz, but even that does not really work here. Those often very funny routines succeeded on stage partly because live performers gave us the illusion of improvisation, of spontaneity. More important, they were short and unrelated: a large number of anonymous prototypes were presented in rapid succession as outrageously and uproariously commonplace; sooner or later, one or another satirical shoe fitted everyone, from Cinderella to goat-foot satyr.

Once you start conflating these Feiffer cartoons or Nichols-May sketches, and try to derive sustained characterizations and narrative development from them, they simply do not jell. The dazzling clichés or cunning hyperboles piled on top of one another yield sagging superclichés—without the individuality, unpredictability, or aroma of the most mundane genuine character.

Furthermore, the Feiffer-Nichols approach is remarkably Procrustean. It takes the sexual quirks, skirmishes, and squirmings of Jonathan and Sandy (and, to a lesser degree, of their women) and cuts off everything else. There is no social fabric, no world of ideas, no history—except for the shallow oneupmanship of playing the right pop songs for the various periods, and getting the dresses and hair styles more or less correct. In short, there is no context. Nichols and Feiffer are probably proud of what they must consider their narrow, penetrant scanning of the sex lives of two typical American males, with no excess or irrelevancy of any kind. Yet whereas the sex life of certain insects having nothing except a sex life can be studied to the exclusion of all else about them, human sexuality is so inevitably and significantly tied in with other activities and concerns that this pinpointing reduces men to mayflies—mayflies not even free, but writhing at the end of a pin. The characters in the film are mere impaled specimens.

Carnal Knowledge could have been satirical. There is very little humor in it, however, and that is mostly concentrated in the college sequences. Nor is it informed by the love or hate that propels the jolly spoof or the biting satire. The dominant attitude is a sophomoric, smart-aleck, snidely superior smirk—and I use the nastily sibilant alliteration deliberately. It is very revealing, for example, that neither Susan nor Bobbie is shown again after the premarital episodes. This cannot be excused on the count that the story deals only with Sandy and Jonathan. There are times when the girls become central; besides, in our day, carnal knowledge is available and belongs to women as much as to men. But, of course, the film's aim is not carnal knowledge, but knowing carnage.

To reintroduce the women in later episodes would have required a subtlety of palette quite beyond either a Feiffer cartoon or a Nichols routine. For, from what we hear or can guess about them, the women have changed. While

Sandy and Jonathan remain the same under their changing surfaces, or change only in degree of ludicrousness or abjection, the women develop a duality. Susan must by now be both a stylishly glittering, efficiently coping wife and a disenchanted, wiser, skeptical or bitter woman. And Bobbie, as wife and divorcée, must be a strange mixture of bovine lethargy and spiteful defiance. For the sake of her alimony, she cannot have become the guilty party; yet she must have worn Jonathan down and driven him to divorce—though, at bottom, she must still be more pitiful than vicious.

To portray the more evolved Susan and Bobbie would require a measure of care, of probing awareness, of understanding if not affection—or, at the very least, of an antipathy that is analytical, not merely snotty. And of that, the basically little-boyish, clever but frozenly immature, talents of Nichols and Feiffer are incapable. This would-be drastic film is merely brattish.

The final difference, I suppose, between a cinematic confectioner and an artist is that the former simply manipulates his characters, whereas the latter is possessed, moved, manipulated by them. In *Carnal Knowledge,* no character is fleshy and thick enough to blot out the smirk on the faces of his makers that is always—depressingly rather than funnily—visible. Still, there is cleverness in the film, albeit secondhand cleverness. Thus Nichols, a steady Fellini admirer and emulator, has imported Giuseppe Rotunno, the cinematographer of *Fellini Satyricon* and the Fellini episode of *Spirits of the Dead.* Rotunno, in better films than those, has indeed proved himself an artist. Here he has done nicely by his director, especially in those closeups or two-shots where the texture of a wall or the fabric on a piece of furniture plays an important part—the sort of thing Nichols has, clearly, gathered from the films of Antonioni and Bergman.

Not that the latest aspect of Nichols's eclecticism (to call it by the politest possible name), his Bergmania, is wholly fortunate. When, for instance, he holds his camera on a face for a premeditatedly unendurable length of time—a risk you can take with a good script and the face of a Bibi Andersson or Liv Ullmann—he is stuck with a Candice Bergen or, at best, Jack Nicholson. The latter manages to make something out of a scene in which Bergen and Garfunkel are preparing for an outing and he, secret lover of the girl but excluded from the event, follows their movements with the hostilely oscillating pupils of a spectator at a tennis match between two equally detestable players. But when Miss Bergen is called upon to laugh and laugh and laugh right under the camera's nose, we are not allowed ingress into a soul, we merely keep bashing our heads against a façade.

August 9, 1971

Bogdanovich Rampant

Peter Bogdanovich is America's answer to the *Cahiers* phenomenon of film critic turned filmmaker; yet behind every answer there is a question. In this case, how good was he as a critic in the first place? The answer is that he was never a serious critic, only an auteurist hero-worshiper. And how is he as a filmmaker? His first film, *Targets,* handled a valid subject in a trashy way; his new one, *The Last Picture Show,* is a great hit with the reviewers, less so with the audiences, and strikes me as not bad by current standards. Inasmuch as Bogdanovich is in his very early thirties, this may augur well. But there is a "but" here, and quite a big, fat but it is, too.

The Last Picture Show takes place in the two-horse town of Anarene, Texas, in 1951, when the town's only picture show (i.e., movie theater) closed down before the onslaught of television, which brought the dream factory right into the living room. Sonny Crawford, co-captain of the high-school football team, is at the center of this one-year chronicle. We see him go from unsatisfactory pettings with his plain but busty girlfriend in the back of the picture show or in the front seat of his pickup truck, to an affair with Ruth Popper, the neglected middle-aged wife of the crude football coach; thence to an unconsummated affair and promptly annulled wedding with Jacy Farrow, a classmate who is the local pretty and spoiled rich bitch.

Meanwhile Sonny's best friend, Duane Jackson, the backfield captain, goes from being Jacy's platonic boyfriend to becoming, ever so fleetingly, her lover, thence to the army and the Korean War. Two lovable figures around town die: Sam the Lion—owner of the picture show, poolroom, and eatery, the three sole recreational centers of Anarene—a fine remnant of a more romantic West; and Billy, a little idiot boy whom Sam took care of and Sonny, often inadequately, protected.

Jacy goes from fooling around with Duane to getting herself deflowered by him merely to move in on the fast, smart set of Wichita Falls, where virginity would be held against her; thrown over by one of those megalopolitan rich boys, she returns to the local talent and takes on, first, Abilene, her mother's lover, then Sonny himself, only to cast him off. On the sidelines, there are two women watching and commenting: Genevieve, the hardy, good-natured café waitress; and Lois, Jacy's jaded mother, bored and exasperated by her loveless marriage to Anarene's oil millionaire.

All this is framed by an opening shot of the picture show still functioning, and a closing shot of it standing there on the town's main street, deserted. The former shows us a dry, windy, dusty, bleak day, and sets the climate of the film. The latter is a superimposition: Sonny, who has graduated and is already a forgotten outsider at the school football games, has sneaked back to see Ruth Popper, whom he so recklessly abandoned for Jacy. Ruth receives him nicely, gives him coffee, and then has her outburst: Why has she always been so self-effacing, waiting on everyone, Sonny included; why has she never asserted her rights? Sonny is remorseful, Ruth's moment of rebellion passes. Now they sit there, dejected, no longer lovers and not yet friends, holding hands unhopefully as their image dissolves into that of the abandoned movie theater of a godforsaken town.

Though schematic, this doesn't sound half bad. But look at the film more closely. The locale is captured accurately by Robert Surtees's black-and-white cinematography, and the time seems indeed to be 1951, as we are told it is. Told? Clobbered with it. Just about every hit song of the period manages to hit us from radios or jukeboxes; every major television program of the time seems to be watched by someone in the film at some point or other.

Yet this is fairly easy. The lay of the land has not changed much since Larry McMurtry wrote or lived the autobiographical novel on which he and Bogdanovich based this screenplay. I got my air-force basic training near Wichita Falls in 1944, and I can vouch for the area's being of the sort that a decade or two can barely make a dent in. The monochromatic photography is quite good, but in an era when almost everything is filmed in color, you can score easy points just by clinging to black-and-white—whether it is finally called honesty, nostalgia, or an *hommage* to your favorite directors of the period. And, certainly, the general outline of the film convinces: McMurtry lived it, wrote it almost without sentimentality or anger, and Bogdanovich approaches the material reverently—all too reverently, in fact.

McMurtry, who also wrote the novel on which *Hud* was based, considers himself a minor regional novelist, and engagingly mentioned at a symposium that, in working on the script of *The Last Picture Show,* he discovered how much better a novel could have been made from the material—and, by implication, how much better a film, had Bogdanovich not been so enamored of the published text. But as both Pauline Kael and Andrew Sarris (who have, unlike me, read the novel) pointed out, there were some minor yet not wholly insignificant changes made, adding up to a certain romanticizing of the matter. Thus the movies the kids see in the film are better than the ones in the novel (Bogdanovich even anachronistically drags in *Red River,* as a tribute to one of his auteur-heroes, Howard Hawks); Lois is not allowed, in the film, to have sex with Sonny, whom her daughter has just betrayed; Jacy's crude sexual bout with her mother's lover on a pool table, and the young bloods having intercourse with a blind heifer are also excised.

What is kept is not always particularly persuasive, either. I cannot believe the scene where all their classmates watch Jacy and Duane's sexual initiation from cars parked outside the motel; I do not see the need to make Lester, a two-bit operator (Randy Quaid), seem more idiotic than Billy, the real halfwit. I think it is a bad boiling down of the novel that introduces Sonny's father out of nowhere as an outcast, drops him immediately, and never tells us anything about Sonny's home life; the same goes for Duane and his family, with a mother making a belated, almost subliminal appearance. The character of Abilene, the town stud, is woefully underdeveloped; Sam the Lion is so idealized that we see him only in scenes where he can deploy generosity, righteous indignation, gracious forgiveness, or noble, homespun philosophizing. His basic, quotidian relationship to Genevieve and Billy is left completely unexamined.

The whole last part of the film proceeds by jerky, disparate lurches that do not blend into a balanced narrative, and the conclusion is so ambiguous (my interpretation, given above, is perforce quite arbitrary) as to be close to a mere effect. Worst of all, Sonny is unconvincing—whether in the writing, acting, or directing, or in all three, hardly matters. We are supposedly looking, for the most part, through his eyes, and he is meant to be a reasonable enough young fellow in the process of coming of age. Yet what has he really learned, or taught us, in the end? And how can we take him seriously if he is so stupid that when Genevieve observes the town is so small that no one can sneeze in it without all the other people holding out a handkerchief, he asks, "What do you mean?"

Indeed, almost all of these people are cloddish. The fact that Anarene is a cultural backwater may explain this, but does not necessarily reconcile us to spending two hours with its essentially dreary denizens. True artists, of course, can illumine the simplest people—in both senses of the verb—and can make plain words take on great resonance. Though McMurtry and Bogdanovich succeed once or twice, that is hardly enough to rouse one's sympathy from its sleep.

Potentially most gripping are those unfulfilled older women: Ruth, Genevieve, Lois Farrow. But none of them quite makes it. Ellen Burstyn is very competent as Lois, yet the part is too skimpy and burdened with drippy lines like "Nothing has really been right since Sam the Lion died." Eileen Brennan's Genevieve captures the essence of the likable tough broad of the old movies, but they, rather than life, seem to be the unfortunate source of the character. As Ruth, Cloris Leachman gives a poor performance: her weeping comes out comic, her shy love for a very young boy lacks genuine warmth and seems almost calculating, her face is usually a rather unattractive blank. She seems to be all nose and sharp bones; even a boy like Sonny might have found her no sexier than a Gillette razor blade.

Above all, Bogdanovich's direction is sheer derivativeness. To put it bluntly, it is cinémathèque direction. A John Ford shot is followed by a George Stevens one; a Welles shot by one out of Raoul Walsh. Even if every sequence is not so patently copied as the funeral is from *Shane,* the feeling is unmistakable that one is watching a film directed not by a young director in 1971, but by a conclave of the bigger Hollywood directors circa 1941. This may give the film visual authenticity, but of what kind? Imagine a present-day composer writing like Haydn, a painter working in the exact style of Vermeer. At best, such men are epigones; at worst, forgers. At its most successful, *The Last Picture Show* rises to the heights of pastiche.

There are also serious minor problems, the most bothersome of them being unsubtlety. When Sonny and Ruth make love for the first time, the springs of the bed do not just squeak, they ululate. If this were intended as deliberate heightening from a subjective point of view, it would have to occur throughout the film, which it doesn't. Sonny has a way of fondly turning around the baseball cap on Billy's head, so that the visor faces backward. He does this some half-dozen times in the film, and when *he* doesn't do it, Duane does. It becomes grating in its predictability. Or take Billy's death; the boy is run over by a truck. The scene is staged stiffly and ploddingly, and the gloom-inducing devices run amuck. Never, on those other windy days, has a shutter been banging in the poolroom; now there is one beating the Devil's tattoo. Never before has a single tumbleweed tumbled down the streets of Anarene; now there is a bunch of them doing enough tumbling for the main ring at Barnum & Bailey's.

At other times, instead of hitting us over the head, Bogdanovich does not make a point at all. When Sonny, after Billy's death, gets into his truck and drives off to leave this horrible town forever, we follow him along the empty road across scarcely less empty country until suddenly, for no visible reason, he makes a U-turn and capitulates. A reliable filmmaker would have taken us inside Sonny as the resolution to escape peters out; if nothing else, he would have found an objective correlative, the tiny external factor that undermines the boy's resolve. Instead, like so many things in the film, the change of mind has to be taken simply on faith.

The acting is far from consistently good. Aside from Cloris Leachman's and Randy Quaid's unpleasant work, there are Clu Gulager's Abilene, Timothy and Sam Bottoms's Sonny and Billy, and Cybill Shepherd's Jacy to leave one unmoved. Miss Shepherd is a model (though how, with that dubious figure, I can't imagine) whose face Bogdanovich found on a teen-age magazine cover. Although her face is absolutely right for Jacy, nothing else is. Ben Johnson does nicely by Sam the Lion, however, and Jeff Bridges is convincingly oxlike as Duane.

Another film of Bogdanovich's, *Directed by John Ford,* a rapturous auteurist tribute to a director enshrined in every auteur critic's Pantheon, is a feature-length documentary shuttling between various interviews and scenes from twenty-seven of Ford's close to two hundred films. These scenes lead up to a lengthy segment arranged chronologically, not by the dates of the films from which the excerpts come, but by the years of American history they are supposed to mirror. The implication, despite a limp disclaimer in the American Film Institute's program note to the film (produced by AFI), is that the director's enormous, heterogeneous, highly uneven output (about three or four Edsels to one Ford) constitutes a unified body of historical thought, and comprises a personal, historiographic as well as artistic, vision of the American past. This is auteurism on the rampage, and is amusingly deflated by Ford himself in the film.

In an almost grotesquely reverential scene, Bogdanovich interviews Ford in Monument Valley, known to film buffs as Ford Country. There, in his director's chair, sits the burly, purblind old man, as sharp and ornery as they come, with all the wonders of the West as his backdrop, or, perhaps more accurately, private backyard. In deferential tones, Bogdanovich inquires whether Ford's view of the West hasn't in fact progressively darkened between such films (I cite from memory) as *Fort Apache* or *Wagonmaster* and *The Horse Soldiers* and *Cheyenne Autumn.* Without hesitation, Ford emits the loudest, curtest "No!" ever heard in Monument Valley. When Bogdanovich tries to rephrase the question, Ford bellows, "Cut!"

Intercut with the sequences from Ford films (to which Orson Welles's by now insufferably fruity voice appends Bogdanovich's simple, if not simplistic, narration) are interviews with three major Ford stars: John Wayne, James Stewart, and Henry Fonda. All three talk of the master with a mixture of anecdotal jollity and sheer awe that I found quite touching, though perhaps a bit misplaced. For me, Ford remains one of the most skilled commercial directors Hollywood has produced, with a range extending from hack work to extremely solid entertainments, but as different from art as the Great Plains are from the Rockies. Sound commercialism is useful: it pays for the art of other filmmakers. But Ford is not to be venerated, or mistaken for an artist.

Whoever is inclined to doubt this should ponder Ford's answer to Bogdanovich's question about whether the director did not prefer silent films, whether he really approved of sound. "It's all right," Ford replies, "people expect it now." And he adds: "As long as the dialogue is crisp and cryptic, and there are no great soliloquies." This makes me wonder whether he knows the meaning of the word *cryptic,* never mind the meaning of art. He concludes: "Silent movies were hard work." Are we to gather that this new, highly evolved medium of combined image and sound is easy compared to something like *Straight Shooting,* a foolish 1917 silent that the AFI keeps publicly congratulating itself for having discovered in the Czech Film Archives, and restored to a Western world starving without it?

November 1, 1971

Laughing Violence

ALAS POOR KUBRICK! He is the American director for whom we had the highest hopes; who, alone among the younger crowd, promised achievements of lasting, international stature. Though I considered his beginning, *Fear and Desire,* far from auspicious, *The Killing* was a respectable small film and *Paths of Glory* worked effectively albeit blatantly up to its crashing cop-out. *Dr. Strangelove* was one of the very rare successful screen satires made in this country; before that, *Spartacus* and *Lolita,* both failures, had at least a few nice redeeming features. *2001* had some splendid gadgetry, even if not much else. Now comes the long-awaited *A Clockwork Orange,* based on Anthony Burgess's respected novel.

The novel was a poor choice for a film. It depends to a large extent on words, and particularly on certain curious, macaronic puns. *A Clockwork Orange* concerns Alex, a juvenile gang leader in some not very future England, who relates his first-person narrative in a teen-agers' slang consisting chiefly of Russian words given English spelling and a lower-class British pronunciation. For example, "good" or "well" becomes, from the Russian "harasho," the slangy "horrorshow"; since what Alex and his three "droogs" (pals) enjoy most are beatings, lootings, and rapes, that is what usually comes under the marvelously ambiguous heading of "horrorshow." Similarly, God becomes, from the Russian, "bog"—something to get bogged down in. Money is "deng," with unmistakable overtones of dung. A man is a "veck," an abridgement of "chelloveck"; a thing is a "veshch"—and can you disregard the sinister implications of the similarity between "veck" and "veshch"?

When the Russian words do not set up double entendres, their effect is nevertheless appalling in its suggestion of the communization of language, the world, the realms of the mind. Both English and Russian lose their dignity through this cross-sterilization that in itself becomes a metaphor for Burgess's overwhelming, but cheerfully expressed, pessimism.

It is quite wrong to read the novel, as some people do, as a plea for Christian free will (and, by the way, is free will necessarily Christian?). Alex is a jolly sadistic criminal until he falls into the hands of a quasi-enlightened socialist state that reclaims him via the Ludovico treatment: the enforced watching of filmed violence, murder, rape almost uninterruptedly for several weeks while strapped into a chair, his eyelids cruelly forced apart. Our teenaged hero is reduced to a meek monster of virtue whom violence, even in self-defense against walloping bullies, makes sick to his stomach. But a near-fatal fall restores the will-less milksop to the vicious punk he was: the "happy" ending has him daydreaming about once again cutting up the face of the world with his trusty switchblade.

Obviously Burgess does not like either alternative one bit—the proof is in the nomenclature. The nasty-minded Alex wallows in a kind of musical masturbation: listening to his hi-fi playing Bach, Mozart, and, above all, his favorite "Ludwig van's" Ninth Symphony (especially the last movement), he has onanistic fantasies of rapturous "ultra-violence." The new shock treatment that jellifies him is named after its fictitious inventor, Ludovico. An ironic parallel is intended. Hearing the highest and most ennobling music of Western civilization, and especially Beethoven's great "Ode to Joy," helps turn Alex into a ravening beast; the neo-Pavlovian conditioning—science at its most sinister—merely makes him into a perfect victim for others to vent their bestiality on. Thus Ludwig and Ludovico are equal banes: A plague on both their houses!

Stanley Kubrick, autodidact and self-styled intellectual, misses the three main points here. First, the relentless but laughing pessimism. Kubrick's Alex ends with the Beethoven blaring into his ears, his restored mind envisioning him gamboling in the snow in satyr's attire with a near-naked, serenely smiling blonde, while a bunch of beaming onlookers exude admiration. This, O my brothers (to use one of Alex's favorite locutions), is a huge cop-out, as big as the one in *Paths of Glory,* contrasted to Burgess's happy apocalypse with Alex "carving the whole litso of the creeching world with [his] cut-throat britva." When the chips are down—except, miraculously, in *Dr. Strangelove*—Kubrick's sensibility goes mushy.

The second great error is the mismanagement of the music on the soundtrack. Kubrick cannot lay off parading his musical "erudition." So we get, besides the Beethoven, a very mixed bag of minor music—Purcell, Rimsky-Korsakov, Elgar, and two popular Rossini overtures, as well as some electronic and pop music—loudly and constantly creeching at us. Now, during the Ludovico treatment, the violent film sequences are accidentally (?) scored with Beethoven, and Alex comes to abhor classical music as much as violence.

To have stuff like "The Thieving Magpie" and "William Tell"—not to mention the pop music—loudly smeared across the soundtrack both before and after Alex's conversion obfuscates the issue. Was Alex perhaps just as fond of second-rate and even trivial music? Is he, perhaps, just as capable of enjoying some or most music even after his treatment? In fact, he gives himself away to the man whom he crippled and whose wife he raped and, indirectly, killed by singing to himself "Singin' in the Rain," a song to which he once kicked the daylights out of the man. So we lose Burgess's grand ironic design: an Alex who relishes songs by Freed and Brown, and who can have erotic visions even to "Scheherazade," is no longer an object lesson in the failure of culture to civilize us.

The third great loss is the playing with language. Though some few of the Russian words are kept in the movie, they do not register on the ear as sardonically as on the eye—assuming that we can make them out at all under the Cockney accents. But lost, or impossible to catch in the film, is the tragicomic vandalism practiced on all language. "Two terrific and very enormous mountains" and "how to comport yourself publicwise" Burgess's Alex will say; or "Come and get one in the yarbles . . . you eunuch jelly, thou." These are blows to the very quick of language, spelling the doom of culture in letters (or crimes) more capital than knifings and rapings. But they are slurred over or omitted by Kubrick as unsuited to the medium of film.

Kubrick, indeed, drops almost all cultural references from his screenplay, although they are of the essence. Thus, in the novel, Alex and his gang knew "right away we were in Priestley Place as soon as we viddied the big bronze statue of some starry poet with an apey upper lip and a pipe stuck in a droopy old rot." How much these few words accomplish! J. B. Priestley, a mediocre novelist and playwright, but a socialist, is honored with a statue and a square by a socialist state, and it is all lost on the young for whom he is a "starry poet"—when poet is just what he wasn't, and starry still less, except that the word is really "stary": Russian for "old"! Similarly, "rot" is Russian for mouth—and English for what comes out of Priestley's.

Missing from the film, too, are the masks our punks put on for their criminal binges: "They were like faces of historical personalities (they gave you the name when you bought) and I had Disraeli, Pete had Elvis Presley, Georgie had Henry VIII and poor old Dim had a poet veck called Peebee Shelley. . . ." Kubrick reduces this to one big, ludicrous false nose. Gone is not only the subtle irony of "they gave you the name when you bought," but also the cruel jest that grinds culture and pseudoculture into common masks from behind which bestiality may strike, protected.

The problem is not only one of reducing the film to the level of illiterate masses—of all the Alexes among us. Even some unesoteric, perfectly filmable details of rich suggestive power are wantonly cut. To cite a single example: when the gang drives happily home in their stolen car after a night's brutality and destruction, they keep "running over odd squealing things." This hideous, low-level, casual heartlessness tends to be dropped in favor of splashier crimes, more artful sadism, and the basic "banality of evil" theme is forfeited. Worse, ingredients essential to understanding the work's meaning are jettisoned—as, for instance, the typescript of a novel, *A Clockwork Orange,* the gang's author-victim is working on, from which Alex contemptuously reads out a revealing paragraph.

The film's weaknesses, though, are often purely filmic. As frequently happens in movies dealing with some remote period whose full re-creation would be too costly, *Orange* has a fragmented look. Here a set, there a set, but very little of what connects them, so that each episode looks isolated, sealed off from the rest, making the film unduly episodic, and giving it an unpleasingly lurching and halting rhythm. The camera positions are amazingly predictable: for almost every entrance there is an establishing long shot with the new arrival entering from the back of the set. Accelerated and slow motion are used overabundantly. Field distortion by wide-angle lenses becomes wearying after a while; the lighting tends to be melodramatic and obvious. John Alcott's color cinematography is routine stuff, and John Barry's set design, though trying to be clever, is mostly derivative.

Malcolm McDowell is excellent as Alex; the rest of the casting is rather less felicitous. Why should the victimized writer, described as young and likable, be played by Patrick Magee, a very middle-aged, quirky actor specializing in being repellent? Could Kubrick be after something as trite as yet another generation-gap movie? He even overdirects the basically excessive Magee to the point where the actor's eyes erupt like missiles from a launching pad, and his face turns into every shade of a Technicolor sunset. The minor characters tend to be similarly overdone or travestied. There are, to be sure, a few lively moments in the film, including a well-handled scene or two, and some of the futuristic gadgets are fun; but no one ever questioned Kubrick's talent as a gadgeteer.

An almost perfect film of its kind is William Friedkin's *The French Connection;* still, both the "almost" and the "of its kind" present problems. The former is a matter of improbabilities and impossibilities; there is a goodly number of both in this story of large-scale dope smuggling from France into the U.S.A., based on fact though it be. But it must be conceded that as the story moves along swiftly and fascinatingly, we do not stop to ask questions, not even when a car, brutally and thoroughly torn apart by the police, is miraculously made whole again in a matter of hours.

The graver difficulty hinges on the phrase "of its kind," for *The French Connection* is typical of what might be called the New Brutality, a genre that serves up violence in loving detail: not just with a dab or two of ketchup, but also with a large amount of relish. Violent beatings and deaths are not only made extremely graphic, they are also treated with a nasty sense of fun. Thus a Marseilles murderer breaks off and munches on a bit of the *baguette* his dead victim has dropped, then tosses the rest jauntily back on the bloody corpse. And the blood-drenched victims of a fatal car crash are repeatedly scrutinized, almost anatomized, even though they are irrelevant to the main plot. Some connective material was cut out of the film here, leaving those mangled cadavers particularly gratuitous and shocking.

Yet when all this is said, the film, with a script by Ernest Tidyman, is tough, witty, exciting, paced judiciously a little too fast for full absorption of its foisoning details, but not so frantically as to make astonished involvement impossible. Even if its morality is suspect, it is full of good directorial touches that are not excessively arch, and it builds to several climaxes that are knowingly spaced and sensibly differentiated. The performances are all good, something that does not often happen in American films these days, least of all in thrillers. Most impressive is the bravura act of Gene Hackman as a fanatical, clever but outsmartable, rather repulsive but not unamusing detective, in whom stupid brutishness and inspired dedication are locked in continual, deadly alliance. Roy Scheider is effective as his partner, and Fernando Rey, Tony LoBianco, and Marcel Bozzuffi shine among the criminals.

Friedkin has used New York locations better than anyone else to date, and managed to keep the camera, appropriately, both fluid and choppy. There is one chase sequence that both scares the breath out of you and, at the same time, makes you smile at the wicked humor and sly comment it contains. Owen Roizman's color cinematography, grainy and grimy, is a brilliant rendering of urban blight. Roizman is particularly skillful at capturing a certain washed-out, bleary light of dawn among bridges and tenements, at recording a bluish equivalent of bone-chilling cold on winter evenings, and at rendering a spooky, greenish night illumination that may have some perfectly plausible optical explanation, but as surely symbolizes the viridescent phosphorescence of decomposing rottenness.

December 13, 1971–January 10, 1972

Unlikely Couples

Can there be such a thing as demotic satire? Hardly. Satire is a basically aristocratic genre in which one enlightened person speaks to another over the heads of the benighted; it is a word to the wise. It happens to be a witty word, and one that makes fun of human foibles, often including those of the writer and reader. A certain intellectual complicity is necessary, as well as a certain refinement, for satire operates through irony and indirection, through subtlety and deviousness. Anything less than that is not satire but a mere broadside, squib, lampoon, or pasquinade. The unsubtle or untutored mind does not get the point: "But, Dr. Swift, we do not eat babies!" Significantly, great satire flourished in aristocratic and cultivated eras, such as the Augustan and the neoclassical; whenever culture declines, satire, too, declines or vanishes.

Satire cannot be gross; if it is, it is vulgar sarcasm, the condescension of fools to even greater fools, ponderously witless spelling out of the obvious. And that, precisely, is the trouble with a film like *Made for Each Other.* The husband-and-wife team of Renée Taylor and Joseph Bologna were previously responsible for *Lovers and Other Strangers,* which I missed; here they have not only written the movie, they also have made it largely autobiographical and, accordingly, cast themselves in it. The fact that Robert B. Bean, the camera operator (not the cinematographer) is credited with the direction, suggests that the couple did not want a true, strong director, but someone whom they themselves could direct. They have turned out a film that, instead of being a sharp commentary on how today's marriages result from desperation—from the inability of parents to bring up healthy children, and the inability of these children, once grown up, to make healthy lovers and spouses—deteriorates into a series of obvious, noisy, heavily underlined and overacted cabaret turns. There is no controlled flow and progression.

Made for Each Other concerns Pandora (Panda) Gold and Giggi (Gig) Pinimba, a Jewish girl and Italian guy. She is a TV cue girl who has lost her job and yearns to be a stage and nightclub star; her doting, astrology-mongering mother overindulged her, while her philandering father neglected her. Her relations with men—married Chinamen, English satyrs, arty homosexuals—have always been hopeless. She has never had an orgasm. As for Gig, his father is a simple, warm Italian barber, his mother a simple, loving Catholic soul. But already as a seminarian he got expelled for womanizing with a maid in a broom closet; as a soldier, he was a total failure; now, in personnel work, he is getting women pregnant and suicidal. Panda and Gig meet in an emergency group-therapy session and spot each other as kindred misfits while they lie on the floor and, above them, the session gone berserk rages on.

The pair have sex on their first date in his cramped Peugeot 404. He is callous, but she persists. Soon he has given her her first orgasm and coped with the onslaughts of her mother. He witnesses her pitiful try at a nightclub act and tells her that it stinks; she blows up. They part, but he finds himself impotent with a far prettier girl. He ends up taking Panda, at her insistence, to a New Year's dinner with his family; ethnic and other resentments explode and the meal turns into pandemonium. Driving back, he gripes and chides, while she sits miserably silent. On the spot where they had their first intercourse, they erupt into a scene of tragicomic violence. But need wins out over neurosis, and they decide to get married.

Almost every one of these scenes could be a cabaret skit unto itself—indeed has been one before now, and better. If you removed the show-biz, psychoanalytic, Jewish and Italian (or Jewish vs. Italian) jokes of a vaudeville type, there would, in fact, be nothing left. But even those overused and unpromising topics could perhaps yield some satirical edge if properly treated. Taylor and Bologna, however, make their characters obvious to a degree equivalent to spelling cat "C-A-T."

The group-therapy session, for example, is as garishly caricatured as the encounter group in *Bob & Carol & Ted & Alice,* yet the authors have said on a talk show that they intended it sympathetically and respectfully. Are they liars or fools? I suspect the latter. Every member of the group, including the therapist and his wife, must promptly spell out his aberration and absurdity in a kind of telegraphic travesty that produces instant grotesquerie; only Gig and Panda are allowed to be lovably ridiculous, sweetly inept.

When Panda is to be revealed as an untalented performer—doing Sonja Henie on television, or Marlene Dietrich in a nightclub—her incompetence is made epically offensive, so that even the peasants can get the point, yet we are meant to feel involved and sorry for this oaf. If the Pinimba clan at the holiday dinner is shown as hostile to both of Panda's religions—Judaism and Freudianism—there is burlesque comedy but no point of view: you can be for or against any of the attitudes shown. "Subtlety never hurt anyone," Otis Ferguson carped about *Citizen Kane* (a film whose subtlety was monumental compared to this) "and those of us who aren't gaping yokels aren't alone." But *Made for Each Other* is a film made both for and by gaping yokels. Worse, it wants the gaping yokels to understand that it is S-A-T-I-R-E, and so it must not only crack its creaky jokes but also explain them as it goes along. When Gig and Panda have a row in the street, there must be a coolly self-possessed black leaning against a wall and observing their antics with mile-high *hauteur.*

If Gig's father gives Panda an improvised Christmas present of candy he got from someone else, he must say, "They're chocolate cherries; they make me sick." If Gig makes unfulfilling love to Panda in his tiny car, this must be stressed by the corny device of having her emerge minutes later from behind the front seat with her hat still on. If a character is to be identified as British, his every other word must be "bloody" or the like, yet he will be played by an actor who cannot even approximate a British accent, so tone-deaf are the filmmakers.

"That's why Giggi and I are so good for each other," Panda explains to her incredulous in-laws-to-be, "because we are two self-destructives confronting the Life Force." When Gig earlier called her "a textbook case," he was speaking truer than he or the authors knew. And when the couple fight their way from furious insults, shouting, and weeping into getting engaged, all in a few minutes, the transition is stunningly clumsy—if one compares it with the masterly handling of the same device in Chekhov's *The Marriage Proposal.* To clinch the humor of it, Gig must complain at the crucial point of how heavily his mother's dinner weighs on his stomach.

While explaining everything else, Taylor and Bologna never explain to us what brought Gig and Panda together. Or why, Casanova though he be, he should prove impotent with the gorgeous Ingrid (Connie Snow) once he has made love to the bovine Panda (Renée Taylor is unprepossessing beyond the call of satirical duty). Or what induces him to go so far as to propose marriage to her. The woods, after all, are full of self-destructives; why must it be these particular two who unite against the Life Force? What Taylor and Bologna have given us is not satire but made-to-order, mass-pandering nonsense: Taylor-made bologna.

Even less convincing is the couple served up to us in John Cassavetes's latest bit of improvisatory filmmaking, *Minnie and Moskowitz.* The conceit here is that a New York middle-class dropout, turned car-parker for a Los Angeles restaurant, can speedily woo and win a beautiful, tasteful art-gallery employee, whose bourgeois refinement and stylish living are continually assaulted by his vulgarity. Besides having this superior young woman marry this homely, brawling, monotonously wordmongering bluffer, the film ends with this unlikely couple joyously basking amid cherubic children and blissfully reconciled in-laws, to prove how possible the impossible really is.

No one, not even Cassavetes, could create people so staggeringly nonverbal for all their prattling. It has to be improvisation by actors singularly bereft of a way with words. Yet the sheer stupidity of it will spew up an occasional funny bit that forces us to laugh uneasily. Are people really as dumb, as crazy, as inefficacious, and as violent as Cassavetes would have them be (both Minnie and Moskowitz are human punching bags for nonstop pummeling)? If men and women are not really like that, the film is gross slander; if they are, the world is even worse off than I, in my pessimism, envisioned it, and there is no hope for any kind of survival, despite that mendaciously syrupy final cop-out. And the worst part of it is that Cassavetes seems to enjoy human incompetence, dote on it rather than ridicule or deplore it.

But parts of the film are very funny. The editing and color photography are much more accomplished than in previous Cassavetes films—occasionally, as in an all-lemon-yellow-except-for-a-bit-of-orange boudoir scene, downright arty. For the first time, too, Cassavetes has directed with a certain economy. Although several scenes (like the basically amusing one with Val Avery as an uncouth suitor) still go on too long, others are just right. The one where a lover (Cassavetes himself) emerges suddenly to beat up the innocent Minnie, or the one where the fellow later goes back to his wife and kids, are concise and pungent, and mark a distinct advance in the director's work. Most of the acting, too, is impressive, notably that of Gena Rowlands, the director's wife, and Katherine Cassavetes, his mother. A family-made picture can, unlike *Made for Each Other,* yield controlled performances. Only Seymour Cassel, who used up all his tricks in *Faces,* is repetitious as Moskowitz, and seems too crass both for his film mother and for his film wife.

January 24, 1972

Blue Shield Movies

BY A STRANGE DUPLICATION not infrequent in movie annals, we suddenly have two films making cruel fun of hospitals. American hospitals doubtless deserve every well-aimed kick they get, but both *The Hospital* and *Such Good Friends* weaken their cases either through ridiculous exaggeration or by dilution in sensationalism and irrelevancies. It may be that neither film's principal concern is the exposure and ridicule of our hospitals, yet considering how tawdry and spurious the other concerns are, I am left lamenting two missed opportunities.

The Hospital was written by Paddy Chayefsky and directed by Arthur Hiller, the team that gave us *The Americanization of Emily,* a ham-fisted satire of war heroes. Here we have a middle-aged chief of the medical staff of a big New York hospital, Dr. Bock, who finds his sexual potency gone, his marriage a failure, his son a dreary hippie and New Leftist phrasemonger whom he had to toss out on his ear, and his hospital a disaster area through which every kind of social, political, and medical chaos is rampaging. The most immediate calamity is a series of violent deaths befalling young doctors, interns, and nurses. The deaths do not arise credibly from some sort of basic disorder satirically magnified, but, in Chayefsky's lurid plotting, stem from a homicidal madman on the loose—a madman, by the way, displaying skills far beyond those of the average maniac in fact or fiction. Concurrently, the hospital staff is allowed to sink to the level of characters in absurdist comedy, out of keeping with the serious muckraking intentions the author seems to harbor.

I shall not even try to trace the convolutions of the plot. Suffice it to say that Dr. Bock, on the verge of suicide, is drawn back to life by the charms of a young braless hippie who has a thing for men in their fifties, and whom the doctor, after delivering an impassioned tirade in defense of impotence, throws to the floor and has sex with three times in a row. Swinger though she is, she nevertheless falls deeply in love with him, and starts luring him to New Mexico to minister to her needs as well as those of the Hope-eye Indians, as Diana Rigg pronounces it. But when wildly irrational extremist groups cause the resignation of the hospital's administrative director, Bock allows his sense of responsibility to prevail over the joys of rediscovered potency, and he stays on at the hospital.

It is all utter hokum, especially that hippie from Boston, played without a shred of credibility or aptitude by Miss Rigg. Pretentious and preposterous as the part is in the writing, she manages to make it even more ludicrous in the acting. She is, moreover, far too British, old, and smug for the role, and would seem much more competent to freeze vital fluids than to release them. Aside from some funny but crude gags and a number of good New York character actors contributing nice bits, the one thing that makes the film truly interesting is George C. Scott as the doctor.

Scott is somewhat of a mystery to me: he acts too "big" for the screen, with effects generally more suited to the stage, yet he manages to be effective and delightful on screen in a way that other "big" stage actors—say, James Earl Jones—are not. The reason may be a saving ironic flavor to his comedy, and the maniacally but quietly sustained demonism of his dramatics. When serious, Scott is a driven being; something from the outside takes possession of him. When outrageously farcical, as here, Scott gives his performance an ironic edge with a conspiratorial sardonic glitter in the eye and the barest tinge of mockery in his voice. I wish I could explain it better, but what it comes down to surely is something few actors can communicate: inspiration from above and intelligence from within. For Scott's performance alone *The Hospital* demands to be seen.

Otto Preminger's *Such Good Friends,* based on Lois Gould's semi-autobiographical novel (which I haven't read), is a movie that succeeds in being both brash and slick in such a way as to allow these potentially interesting vices to cancel each other out. Pushed a bit farther into brashness, it might have become genuinely chilling; with a shinier slickness, it might have been at least superficially funny. As it stands it has one good scene in it— that is all.

Julie Messinger is a young woman whose husband, Richard, is hospitalized for the routine removal of a mole; through a series of epic blunders, he goes from not so bad to worst. He is the art director of a big magazine and a minor writer; as his wife, the insecure, masochistic Julie is drawn into the semisocial, quasi-intellectual whirl of New York's marginal literati and lesser artists, where she is ill at ease. Searching for her husband's medical insurance, she stumbles on his little black book, which records impressive sexual bouts with all their female friends and acquaintances. While her husband is in a constant coma, Julie proceeds to have her revenge through dalliances with their male friends. Richard dies and Julie is (rather unconvincingly) liberated: as a predatory pack of friends and relatives jabber away in her apartment about what she should do now, she takes her two children and goes off into Central Park with them.

The plot is, in full, every bit as unrewarding as this brief summary. Its two main themes—the criminal bungling by supposedly expert modern medicine, and the repressed heroine's retaliatory and emancipatory adulteries—have nothing to do with each other; certainly Elaine May, who pseudonymously wrote the screenplay, fails to make them mesh. No less disheartening is the general superficiality of it all; thus the brief scenes of early maternal domination or desperate lesbian dabbling are both too skimpy and too cliché to explain anything, and the vignettes with calculating relatives and treacherous friends are both too obviously conceived and too ponderously executed.

There are three scenes in which Preminger's vulgarity equals that of Ken Russell at his worst, and that is no mean achievement. One shows us the aging and flabby Burgess Meredith, as Julie imagines him, dancing in the nude. Another has Ken Howard, as her husband's best friend, puffing and churning away on top of Julie in a temporary access of impotence (impotence, if I may wax paradoxical, seems to be "in" these days). The third has Julie performing fellatio on her fat and effete family doctor, James Coco, while he is kept on the phone by an irksome female patient. The first part of this jape has Coco trying to remove his girdle without letting Julie notice it; the second consists of incongruities and double entendres between what is happening verbally above and lingually below. The third part is worse yet: Preminger eliminated a shot of Julie getting up suddenly and colliding with Coco, but kept in his line "Did I hit you on the nose?" and that now takes on truly nauseating implications. Even when the film is not scraping bottom, it does not soar more than a few inches above it.

Dyan Cannon, as Julie, exudes a stupidity that strikes me uncomfortably as the actress's own contribution to the part; her one true talent is for bitchiness, a rather lowly gift. The rest of the cast have almost nothing to do, although that still proves too much for Jennifer O'Neill, whose lack of talent is stupendous. Most interesting is Nina Foch, as Julie's coldly distant mother; Miss Foch, who somehow never made it big as a leading actress, may yet do very well in character parts. Beyond that, there is that one good scene at lunch in the hospital cafeteria where the idiotic pseudowisdom of the specialists is funnily, frighteningly and, above all, convincingly lampooned. The scene points an accusing finger both at medicine and, alas, at the rest of the film.

February 7, 1972

Violence with a Difference

ONCE AGAIN THE SUBJECT is violence. Sam Peckinpah's *Straw Dogs* has aroused the anger of reviewers on both sides of the Atlantic, and there is no denying that this first Peckinpah nonwestern is, if anything, more brutal than his westerns. It might also be described as a western in eastern clothing, but that is unimportant here, except as it suggests that violence becomes more unnerving as it moves out of an exotic, mythical setting into something more like our own time and place. This, in turn, suggests the dizzying ambiguities and inconsistencies that surround the issue of "violence"—just as they used to, and still to some extent do, surround the issue of "sex."

The hue and cry about violence makes only a little more sense to me than the equally vociferous outrage about sex. In both cases, as reasonable persons have always argued, the questions are: To what end is the thing being used? How well is it managed? Is there some clandestine further motivation for it?

In no case does one advocate censorship, except perhaps for minors; still less does one want self-censorship, which made Cinerama submit *Straw Dogs* to the Motion Picture Association's psychological expert, who proceeded to snip some fifteen seconds of sodomy from the film, thereby reducing its rating from X (no minors allowed) to R (minors allowed only in the company of a guardian). I believe the violence and the sodomy in the film to be relevant to what Peckinpah and his coscenarist, David Z. Goodman, are trying to say, and I do not consider the violence to be in excess of what has often earned as ecumenical a rating as PG (parental guidance suggested). I may not particularly care for some of what the filmmakers are saying, but that is a different matter.

The worst thing about the current simple-minded violence-bemoaning is that it obfuscates the real problems. When a film like *A Clockwork Orange* pleases the majority of reviewers, the issue of violence either doesn't come up at all, or is dismissed with a simple, formulaic justification. Later, the same reviewers furiously pounce on *Straw Dogs* for its violence and see no contradiction. If, instead of using violence as a counter, it were subjected to serious scrutiny, that would be all to the good; what actually happens is that superficial arguments about quantity of violence deflect attention from the real issue: the nature and quality of the films.

The hero of *Straw Dogs* is David, a young American mathematics professor who has a grant and year's leave to work on the mathematical structure of matter on other planets. David has rented a Cornish farm from his English wife's father and hopes to work in peace there. How this retiring, cerebral

American academic could have met, let alone married Amy, a totally sensual, nonintellectual postnymphet from Cornwall, is almost inconceivable, but probability is not the film's strong suit, any more than it is that of, say, *The French Connection.*

The villagers are a rum lot and regard the American in their midst with ironic contempt if not downright hostility—not so much because he is a foreigner as because he is a remote intellectual, apparently helpless when it comes to practical matters, such as living. Even Amy, once again accosted by Charley Venner, a former swain of hers, is affected by the contempt of the villagers, particularly the gang of young men working on making the farm's garage habitable for David's sports car—as often as not, significantly, driven by Amy while David slumps back beside her.

By this stage, most of Peckinpah's main points have been introduced. David, the emblematic intellectual, prefers celestial mechanics to the mechanics of this world. Amy, Peckinpah's typical woman, is eager for sex and sexual domination, and ready to reject the man who cannot masterfully satisfy these cravings. The rustics are sanctioned to the extent that they are down-to-earth and rough-and-ready, but not for being treacherous and stupid. Peckinpah's vision is not so simplistic as some have assumed: Amy tries, to some extent, to penetrate her husband's world by studying up on chess and looking up what binary numbers are; David is not without his sensual side, and even if his desire is not overwhelming enough to prevent him from setting the alarm clock first, once he does get down to lovemaking, he goes to it heartily and very much on Amy's childlike level.

But the fact remains that David is imperceptive, weak-kneed, and absurdly conciliatory where the forces of evil are concerned, and here the casting of Dustin Hoffman in the part strikes me as ill-advised and damaging. I disagree on this point with Pauline Kael's in many ways cogent analysis of the film: I do not see Hoffman's hesitancies of speech, his throatbound voice that has to struggle up past a colony of frogs, his eyes that crouch nervously in their sockets as a proof of consequential ratiocination going on inside his head. I see it rather as an actor's bag of tricks, and not a very apposite one for this role. Hoffman is a "character" emanating a naïve or crotchety puniness; in this part, however, a more neutral figure, scholarly and aloof but not infantile or even doltish in appearance, would have been vastly preferable. Yet Peckinpah may have wanted his astral scientist to be so ingrained a graduate.

The petty nastinesses become more ominous. The unruly fellows hang Amy's cat by the light cord in the bedroom closet; still David cannot assert himself and fire them. Furious, Amy exposes herself half-naked to them at the window. David even accepts an invitation to go grouse-shooting with the boys; they abandon him at his post on the heath while two of them sneak back to the farm. Charley proceeds to rape Amy, who puts up some resistance, but then rather enjoys it, until the other chap, Norman, takes over and sodomizes her, and she submits only under extreme duress. This scene is considerably cut by the censor, and thus fudges the point that women will accept degradation as long as there is pleasure in it, are willing to become a thing while there is fun in it for them. It is an insulting view of women, but it is also consonant with Peckinpah's low estimate of humanity as eager for compromise, wallowing in reciprocal abasement, and balking at accommodation only when denied even its widow's mite.

Without fully understanding what has happened, David does finally dismiss his brutish workmen, but too late to assuage Amy's resentment of him. The town's magistrate brings the local clergyman and his wife for a visit. David's battle of wits with the Rev. Dr. Hood is perhaps the most curious episode in the film: Peckinpah, clearly unimpressed by either science or religion, enjoys the cleverness with which each scores off the other. We get a hint that when intellect becomes an aggressive weapon, Peckinpah can respect it.

There is a church fête attended by the entire town; though the minister performs second-rate conjuring tricks, he proves quite capable of putting down old Tom, the town's senior bully, when he starts heckling. Janice, Tom's daughter and the local teen-aged coquette, once again tries to captivate David, on whom she has a crush, but is rebuffed. Piqued, she turns to Henry Niles, the halfwit who has already committed some unspecified sexual offense, and lures him away. When their absence is noticed, Tom and the other toughs organize posses to track them down. Meanwhile, the church social where she has to mingle with her rapists has become too much for Amy; she asks David to drive her home.

The almost subliminal flashbacks in which Amy sees herself being raped and sodomized are sardonically juxtaposed with shots of the rapists dressed to the nines and acting as jolly good fellows and pillars of the village community. This is brilliantly horrifying and forcefully makes the picture's main point: under the veneer of civilized behavior and social order there exists a world of untamed and perhaps untamable violence that remains hidden from general view mostly because the general view closes its cowardly, hypocritical eye to it. Hardly a new idea, that, but one Peckinpah infuses with extraordinary new vitality. Here, for instance, it is the suddenness, speed, and utter unpredictability with which the horrible recollections pop up in Amy's mind that makes this montage as frightening as it is revealing.

On the drive home, in thick fog, David hits and slightly injures Henry Niles, who is escaping from the posse; hearing their approach, Niles panicked and accidentally strangled Janice. David takes him back to the house; Tom and his crew of rapists and other scum who worked for the mathematician find out where Niles is, surround the isolated farmhouse and demand the halfwit's extradition. David has had enough; at last he asserts himself. "This is where I live," he declares, and refuses to surrender the fellow. The magistrate arrives and tries to make order but, like many a peacemaker in Peckinpah's and our world, is accidentally shot dead for his pains. The five besiegers are now outlaws good and proper. Armed with a gun, some live rats, and vicious determination, they attack the house in earnest. David is also beleaguered from within: Amy, broken in spirit, wants Niles delivered to the posse, and Niles himself starts making trouble.

But David will fight, and such is Peckinpah's mastery that he has the audience, at first, in stitches at this absurd resolve; gradually, he wins them over to David's cause, until they end up cheering as each successive ruffian bites the dust. Peckinpah's rhythms are marvelous. The slow stages by which David, despite his reasonableness, cleverness, and mild charm, lost the audience's sympathy, are matched by his regaining (in the midst of utter mayhem) first our admiration, then that of his recalcitrant wife, and finally her and our love.

As Miss Kael observed, it is a partly acceptable view—that a man must defend his home and principles against bullies; and also partly unacceptable—that this kind of battling makes one a true man, justifies one's existence, and earns one a woman's respect and submission. According to her reading of the film, it is a brilliant, artistic defense of machismo, male supremacy through physical strength abetted by some brain power (David uses cunning devices to overcome his enemies), and female inferiority expressed in insubordination until the male conquers the woman by force. She accuses Peckinpah of fascism tinged with esteem for the intellect, but only when that intellect is at the service of masculine brawn and militancy.

Yet is there not something more to this? Is it not that Peckinpah sees the world as a hostile environment, a place where the individual must win respect for himself, and win it according to rules imposed on him from without? It emerges from Amy's taunting that David did not dare take a stand on some burning political issue at his university; he replies that he never pretended to be committed. By his own rules for living, in other words, he had not played wrong. But one does not call the rules of *this* game, a game so dirty that it can hardly be said to have rules. Still, since it is his scientific and logical resourcefulness that enables David to prevail over such great odds, a highly rational expertise is clearly seen as a prime factor in victorious commitment.

I disagree, then, with Miss Kael's calling the film a fascist work of art; it seems to me more misanthropic than fascistic, more a work of skillful entertainment than of true art. Though it deals with important matters, it does not examine them in sufficient depth and detail to qualify as art. But when it comes to artistry, which is the next-best thing, *Straw Dogs* abounds in it.

The movie is cleverly constructed as a two-ring circus: the main action is always happening simultaneously in two different places, from almost the first scene. David, in the pub, is awed by the tough nastiness of old Tom, and is also anxiously peering out at his car, where Charley Venner is flirting with Amy. At the farmhouse, we are always aware of two parallel but hostile worlds: that of David and Amy, trying to be civilized; and that of Charley, Norman, Causey the ratcatcher, and the others working on the garage, with their crude jokes and evil schemes.

With assured skill, Peckinpah and his three editors keep juxtaposing these two worlds, and letting the nasty one slowly infiltrate the other by a host of devices. There is, for example, effectively used foreshadowing throughout. When one of the fellows produces a pair of minuscule panties he stole from Amy's drawer, another says, "Bugger your trophy, I want what was in them," and the "bugger" spoken in jest points sinisterly to real things to come.

During the long, climactic siege, Peckinpah re-creates magisterially the tumult of fighting, the dislocation of place and time, of not knowing where and how it is all happening because the striking hand is quicker than the recording eye.

But just as the director can accelerate the tempo to good effect, so can he slow it down. A device Peckinpah used somewhat too floridly in *The Wild Bunch* is perfected here: as someone collapses into death, the film switches to slow motion. Since these collapses cannot last long, it is always only a snippet of slow motion rather than a sequence long enough to make us fully aware of what is being done. The retards come in the midst of fast, frenzied action, and, being virtually subliminal, take on a mystifying, hallucinatory quality.

Peckinpah is the master of countless effects. When David opens that closet and spots the hanged cat, he quickly slams the door shut; we thus see only dimly what happened and are projected into indistinct discomfiture, until the closet door is opened again and the full impact hits us, weakened as we are, all the harder. Later on, after the long fighting, the badly battered David bursts into a grin and mutters, "I've got them all," and we are relieved for and with David. Then, when he and we least expect it, one more thug comes at him—like the mathematician, we too have lost count, and the last, perhaps grimmest, ordeal rushes upon us. For the flash of righteous, defiant anger is spent, and all that is left is weariness—to say nothing of Amy's hesitance to help. This foe is hardest to overcome.

It is a corrupt world, as always in Peckinpah. David and Amy cannot even make love peacefully in their bedroom without young Janice and her likewise young brother spying on them out of the night. And the kids not only indulge in voyeurism but they also exhibit symptoms of incest. Yet this wicked world is also beautiful, especially as photographed by John Coquillon. Anyone can make strong colors look fine on screen; Coquillon wrests the thin, chary beauty from lean, almost niggardly colors. The visuals are cogently matched with Jerry Fielding's score, which imitates (perhaps actually quotes) the Stravinsky of the Concerto in D and the Dumbarton Oaks Concerto—spare, sinewy, nervous music.

The acting is flawless except for Hoffman's overbumbling—he even gets his own name wrong during a frantic phone call. Particularly compelling are David Warner's Niles, T. P. McKenna's magistrate, Colin Welland's Minister Hood, and Peter Vaughan's Tom. And as Amy, the toothsome Susan George is much more than frustrated nubility on the rampage; this already accomplished actress subtly communicates unformed responses through inchoate intonations and tiny changes of expression—visual quarter tones. And she makes bitchiness alluring.

While other films suffer from insufficient insight and point of view, a movie like Don Siegel's *Dirty Harry* has too much point of view, all bad. Written by two people with the inauspicious name of Fink, it is an argument in favor of Law and Order with enough holes it it to equip an oversize Swiss cheese. The only thing that need detain us about this film is the violence, which, though it has aroused some protest, has fared much better than that in *Straw Dogs.*

Now, *Dirty Harry* may be smeared with sadistically reveled-in gore, but it is also less credible, less real. And so we face once again the old paradox: violence, like sex, raises the more objections the better it is done.

This, clearly, is an unsatisfactory state of affairs. I am not saying, of course, that sex and violence must always be spelled out in realistic detail, rather than, for instance, be exaggerated into absurdity and presumable innocuousness. Neither do I consider naturalism the best or only acceptable style. Nor do I think—and this is my point—that realism should be penalized just for being realistic. The question is simply whether the realism is genuine and purposeful; whether the stylization, if that is what it is, is artistically and morally justified.

In *Dirty Harry* a raped and murdered body is a neat little sexual object, and orgies seen through windows are both reprehended and meant to turn you on. Violence is utterly brutal yet somehow fun. With the same dishonesty liberals are all shown as phonies or cowards, and their laws as affording protection to homicidal maniacs. The film's politics matches its aesthetics in doing violence to all—including to violence.

February 21–March 6, 1972

Scylla and Charybdis: Minnelli and Streisand

THE HIGHLY TOUTED movie version of *Cabaret* marks the fourth transformation of Christopher Isherwood's *The Berlin Stories.* It went from play to movie to stage musical to this movie musical; let us hope that it will finally be put to rest. Bob Fosse's film, handsomely photographed by Geoffrey Unsworth (the cinematographer of, among other films, *2001*), is much the best reincarnation of these stories, although still less good than they. Fosse has choreographed and shot the musical numbers as well as could be, and has done respectably by the rest of the material. The chief device is crosscutting—using the song-and-dance numbers at the Kit-Kat Klub as an ironic, or merely heightened, commentary on what happens in the story. Thanks to deft editing, much of this works impressively; only rarely is a point made too obvious through dawdling or repetitiousness.

But the trouble with the film is that it pretends to say more than it does. The basic connection between the decadence of a sleazy Berlin nightclub in the early thirties and the rise of Nazism, though continually hinted at, and sometimes leeringly rubbed in, is never truly demonstrated. The sets and costumes and German locations are marvelously authentic and inventive, the atmosphere is cogently derived from the paintings and graphics of the Expressionists. But we remain unenlightened about the connection: Is Nazism a product of the decadence, or is the decadence an attempt to escape from, and so a product of, Nazism? And was there no political-economic crisis that begat them both? It may be too much to ask a musical to be thoughtful and illuminating, but if it comports itself as if it were both of those things, we do ask questions.

Cabaret does not even do full justice to personal relations. The subsidiary love story falls quite flat, owing to the dull performances or personalities of Marisa Berenson and Fritz Wepper. But even the main threesome suffers from the casting. Helmut Griem has the looks and bearing needed for the bisexual Baron, and that is about all the part requires. Michael York does well enough by Brian, as the Isherwood figure is now called, though this essentially uninteresting actor is saved by the passivity of the role. But the film's irredeemable disaster is its Sally Bowles: changing her into an American was bad enough; into Liza Minnelli, catastrophe. Miss Minnelli cannot act any part without calling attention to how hard she is working at it and how far she is from having worked it out. She cannot even move right—in this case, like a sexy cabaret artiste and thriving nymphomaniac; instead, she rattles around gawkily and disjointedly, like someone who never got over being unfeminine and unattractive.

Plain, ludicrously rather than pathetically plain, is what Miss Minnelli is. That turnipy nose overhanging a forward-gaping mouth and hastily retreating chin, that bulbous cranium with eyes as big (and as inexpressive) as saucers; those are the appurtenances of a clown—a funny clown, not even a sad one. And given a matching figure—desperately uplifted breasts, waist indistinguishable from hips—you just cannot play Sally Bowles. Especially if you have no talent. In fact, Miss Minnelli has only two things going for her: a father and a mother who got her there in the first place, and tasteless reviewers and audiences who keep her there. She cannot even sing Kander and Ebb's admittedly inferior songs; if you want to hear real vocalism, listen to Greta Keller doing "Heimat" by way of intermittent background music. This was a mistake on the part of the filmmakers: the background sings the foreground right off the screen.

Still, Joel Grey is wonderfully sinister as the M.C., Jay Presson Allen's writing manages to get a fair amount of decadence into a script that had to earn a PG rating, and the crosscutting is sometimes brilliant, especially in that bravura scene that shuttles between Sally and Brian in bed, and Sally on stage singing about her bliss. But Liza Minnelli in bed?!

Peter Bogdanovich has followed up *The Last Picture Show* with another pastiche of past picture shows, this one evocatively called *What's Up, Doc?* It is an imitation "screwball comedy" in the manner of *Bringing Up Baby* or *His Girl Friday,* and, once again, it cashes in on Bogdanovich's aptitude for looking backward. With the help of three screenwriters, Bogdanovich has concocted a totally zany, but far from totally funny, farce about rival musicologists competing for a twenty-thousand-dollar grant; a man with purloined top-secret documents being chased by a secret service man; a rich dowager's jewels being stolen by a corrupt hotel clerk and house detective; and four identical suitcases in which these goodies or some rather less desirable articles are lodged. The valises keep changing hands, even as the shy hero keeps changing heads, depending on where he is with his bossy fiancée or with the (supposedly) charming kook who is out to get him.

I doubt whether this movie could have been a serious threat to Howard Hawks and the other expert screwballers even back then; today it merely seems a heavy-handed attempt at nostalgia. In his last film, Bogdanovich at least added some elements that its prototypes were not allowed to show or say; in this one, he sticks as close to the originals as he can, thus eliminating the slight *frisson* of introducing a drop of the new into the old wine in old bottles. The comic car chase is probably more lavish than it would have been in the old days—and here, indeed, the film scores most of its less than frequent comedic effects—but otherwise everything looks, sounds, feels and, if the word is permissible in this context, thinks 1937.

The movie is short on funny lines, even with the jazzy trio of David Newman, Robert Benton, and Buck Henry on script, although the audience at Radio City Music Hall laughed up a storm at the most pitiable inanities. It is shorter yet on performances. Ryan O'Neal, a personable and hard-working young man, is leagues below Cary Grant's league, and as for Barbra Streisand as that lovable kook, the sort of part that Hepburn, Lombard, and Jean Arthur made famous, she comes less close to the delights of Jean Arthur than to the debacle of Port Arthur.

In the present film, Miss Streisand looks like a cross between an aardvark and an albino rat surmounted by a platinum-coated horse bun. Though she has good eyes and a nice complexion, the rest of her is a veritable anthology of disaster areas. Her speaking voice seems to have graduated with top honors from the Brooklyn Conservatory of Yentaism, and her acting consists entirely of fishily thrusting out her lips, sounding like a cabbie bellyaching at breakneck speed, and throwing her weight around. Even her singing has become mannerism-infested, and a brief attempt at a Bogart impersonation may be the film's involuntary comic high spot. Miss Streisand is to our histrionic aesthetics what the Vietnam war is to our politics.

Among the others, only Madeline Kahn as the fiancée and Liam Dunn as a judge show true comic sparkle. The film's heavy, Hugh Simon (poorly played by Kenneth Mars), is said by Bogdanovich to be modeled on me. I am flattered, but since the character is both a Yugoslav and a plagiarist, I suspect that only deep-rooted modesty prevents Bogdanovich from admitting him to be a self-portrait.

March 20–April 3, 1972

Vonnegut 5, Puzo 1

JUST AS THERE EXISTS a genre called "the well-made play," there ought to be one called "the well-made film." This would mean a movie not quite deep, searching, or imaginative enough to be a work of art, but endowed with sufficient inventiveness, craftsmanship, and artistry to make it an authentic, enjoyable experience. It might even contain some food for thought—a thought sandwich, let's say, rather than a full-course meal. High among such movies I would rank *Slaughterhouse-Five,* a neat, amiable tragicomedy, cleverly and conscientiously crafted, and giving you the feeling of getting your time's, money's, and intelligence's worth.

From what I have been able to glean from a skimming of Kurt Vonnegut, Jr.'s novel, it is a little more convoluted, a little jumpier than Stephen Geller's screenplay. But the able scenarist may have come up with a script that is more satisfying than the book. It follows the real or imaginary (and no less real for that) adventures of Billy Pilgrim, who keeps slipping backward and forward in time. Captured by the Germans in World War II and a member of a work detail billeted in a Dresden slaughterhouse, he is one of the survivors of the terrible Allied firebombing that razed that beautiful open city.

Billy is, furthermore, an ineptly brought-up child, a passive husband and bemused father, the sole survivor of an air crash, a patient in a mental hospital. Eventually, he is killed by a psychotic former fellow G.I., who has sworn an insane vengeance against him. In between, however, he also inhabits the planet Tralfamadore, whither he has been mysteriously transported because its audible but invisible inhabitants want to study the mating habits of earthlings—for which purpose they supply him with the luscious starlet Montana Wildhack, barely audible but eminently visible and palpable.

"Unstuck in time," as Billy says, he travels perpetually among the phases of his extraordinary life, one that can befall only a true space-age Candide. And what ingenuity the film's director and editor exercise in making Billy's shifts from period to period, place to place, both surprising and persuasive! Matching shots tell us how one situation suggests another; crosscutting shows the similarities and differences between two vaguely related events. George Roy Hill, the canny director, and Dede Allen, his brilliant editor, have (along with the scenarist) deployed the most exhilarating skill in dovetailing the pieces of this jagged, jiggling jigsaw puzzle into a teasing, jolting, and ultimately compelling space-time continuum.

The matching shots are never obvious. For example, the delicate Dresden figurine of a dancer, which has just cost a good man's life, is whirling through the air, thrown away by the Nazi officers who ordered the execution. This leads into a shot of the toothsome Montana Wildhack pirouetting in front of the blissful Billy and his dog Spot, to show off the sexy nightgown the Tralfamadorians have fetched for her from Sears Roebuck. Consider how much is said with the juxtaposition of these two scenes and the way they are fitted together. Edgar Derby is the one wholly decent and committed, albeit not very bright, man Billy meets in his life's pilgrimage; but Derby is shot like a dog for "looting," when all he does is innocently pick up a figurine that is the exact duplicate of one he had loved. That first one was broken in a silly accident; this one has miraculously survived the firebombing of Dresden and seems to be a heaven-sent replacement destined for him.

This little dancer, however, leads Edgar straight into the dance of death: a life for a figurine that the very SS officers who order poor old Derby shot promptly throw away. What a cruel, unjust place this world is! But from the dancer tossed back into the rubble we cut to Montana doing her mating dance for Billy on Tralfamadore: another dancer, another good man, another world. Somewhere in the universe people do get their just recompense. But where is this enlightened planet? Vonnegut has cunningly constructed his novel so that everything Billy says about that wonderful place may be the quiet ravings of a gentle madman or gospel truth; a clinically explicable delusion or a mind-boggling miracle. There are signposts throughout rigorously pointing both ways. Why not? If you go south long enough, you get to the North Pole.

Slaughterhouse-Five is a film of finely wrought precisions: some crazy, some sane; some heartwarming, some heartbreaking. There is horror in it and laughter, and both, for better or worse, are double-bottomed. The mad drive of Billy's fat wife Valencia to the hospital where he may be dying is funny but results in her death—whereas he survives, a little madder perhaps, yet happier. Valencia, poor thing, is a bit of a monster, but such a well-meaning one. Everything is so desperately relative on this Earth where people actually believe in free will that one must escape to a realm of physical and metaphysical absolutes. If Tralfamadore didn't exist, it would have to be invented.

Sometimes the crosscutting is almost too studiedly dazzling for its own good. Derby's acceptance of the dubious honor of becoming the American POW's group leader is crosscut with Billy's accession to the presidency of the Ilium (i.e., Troy, N.Y.) Lions' Club. When Billy carries his faithful old dog up the stairs toward the privacy of a bedroom forever free of Valencia's gross presence, this is crosscut with the survivors' climbing from their dark shelter into the still blazing ruins of a sumptuous, historic city.

In the first instance, the point is ironic. Two very different elections (even the soundtrack turns antithetical: thunderous applause in Ilium, the sound of scarcely more than one hand clapping in the POW camp) are revealed to be equally meaningless. In the second case, one ascent leads to bliss and, ultimately, heaven on Tralfamadore; the other climb abuts on burning disaster, hell on earth. Still, heaven and hell—together they are this life. The point is brilliantly made, but the demonstration is a mite too ruthlessly geometrical.

George Roy Hill knows how to use the filmmaker's finest instrument: rhythm. Thus the deaths of various minor characters on the way to German imprisonment are treated with swift, cold casualness as befits the casualties of war: a quick shot of a body being marched past or trampled on, held just long enough for us to recognize the corpse. In contrast, the architectural riches of Dresden (photographed in Prague, a similarly baroque city) and the faces of people having to live under war are dwelt on lovingly, as if the camera wanted to stay with them as long as possible and protect them against death, destruction, oblivion. Particularly lingered over are the faces of young boys, American and German soldiers pressed into mutual murder—the visual equivalent of the novel's subtitle, *The Children's Crusade.*

To bring out the innocence and poignancy of these doomed young countenances and antique cityscapes, Miroslav Ondriček, the fine Czech cinematographer, virtually surpasses himself. Whether it is a populous bridge across the Elbe that looms slate-gray against an off-white winter sky; or whether the haze-wrapped steeples of Dresden file past the G.I.s arriving by train, the fine gauze around those baroque beauties prefiguring a shroud; or whether a wilderness of snow or a fiery inferno has to be evoked in monomaniacal white or red—Ondriček's camera is equal to all tasks. It manages to extract the visual, coloristic essences of things without calling undue attention to itself, and subdued expertise is mastery indeed.

Stephen Geller's adroit script sagely omits the dreary refrain that runs, or tap-dances, all through the book: "So it goes." The camera and Dede Allen's editing take care of that point. And the acting is—unusual for an American movie—flawless. A total newcomer, Michael Sacks, plays Billy with dazed kindliness, a halting decency that never becomes coy or cretinous. He is surrounded by an able band of actors, mostly New York–based and not yet overexposed. Ron Leibman is again excellent as one of those psychopaths he can make almost endearing, and Eugene Roche plays that lovable nonentity Derby with a gallant simplicity that is very touching. I would like to mention all, but can only single out one more talented novice, Valerie Perrine, who looks burstingly right as Montana, and can turn benightedness into an added sensual treat.

The question of the relativity of good and evil underlies, fuzzily and dishonestly, *The Godfather,* a violent film raved about by many of the same reviewers who criticized the violence of *Straw Dogs.* The difference is that *The Godfather*'s is old-fashioned violence: carefully prepared for, nicely spread across the entire film, and made to look palatable because all save one of the victims have been asking for it or aren't worth much to begin with. Besides, it is a genre film: it is, despite pretensions to newness and differentness, essentially an old gangster movie, skillfully manufactured except for one rather bad lacuna in the middle.

What does it say? That organized crime is not really such an ignoble way of life: immoral, yes, but exciting, heroic, and based (barring an occasional betrayal soon punished) on profound loyalties within the clan. It is, after all, merely a transitional phase poor immigrants traverse on the way to becoming respectable American capitalists. I cannot imagine why this film should have caused concern among Italo-American organizations or in the Mafia itself—even if all references to the Cosa Nostra had not been, upon some pressure, obligingly removed by the film's producers.

The basic dishonesty of the film lies in showing the Mafia mostly in extremes of heroic violence or sweet family life. Even the scenes of intimidation are grand and spectacular. Missing is the banality of evil: the cheap, ugly, petty racketeering that is the mainstay of organized crime and that neither the script of Mario Puzo nor the direction of Francis Ford Coppola could have made glamorous or so much as palatable.

The acting is predominantly good, with the exception of the highly touted and critically acclaimed performance of Marlon Brando in the title part. Brando has a weak, gray voice, a poor ear for accents, and an unrivaled capacity for hamming things up by sheer underacting—in particular by unconscionably drawn-out pauses. His make-up is good, to be sure, but only when the character is near death does Brando's halting, wheezing performance lumber into sense. The rest of the time he is outacted by Al Pacino, Richard Castellano, Robert Duvall, and so lowly a talent as James Caan's. *The Godfather* is raking it in at five New York theaters, while a film as great as *The Sorrow and the Pity* is struggling along in one.

May 1–15, 1972

Cats of a Differing Stripe

THERE ARE ESSENTIALLY two kinds of humor: for and against. For the easier acceptance of things as they are, which I shall call pro-humor; and against the status quo, which I shall call con-humor. These definitions are prompted by the simultaneous appearance of *Play It Again, Sam* and *Fritz the Cat.*

Pro-humor looks affectionately at the established order that, despite gentle ribbing, it would forever conserve. It may consider things slightly preposterous, and to that extent it wants to laugh them into harmlessness and acceptability; but basically it finds them foolishly likable, and would just as soon enshrine them in perpetuity. Such humor is to be found, for example, in *Life with Father,* Feydeau's *A Flea in Her Ear, A Comedy of Errors,* or, to descend a few thousand degrees, in *What's Up, Doc?* It is also, with differences more seeming than real, what operates in Woody Allen's *Play It Again, Sam.*

Con-humor, on the other hand, is humor on the warpath, humor that would change the world, if only it could be changed. To the extent that it believes the world susceptible of improvement, it may be satire of a socially or politically activist sort; if it has given up all hope for progress, it may be pure cynicism or black humor—partial vengeance on a world whose stupidity and uneducability deserve nothing better, and nothing less, than comic devastation. You find this sort of thing in Swift and, although disguised, in *The Importance of Being Earnest,* in *Dr. Strangelove* and *Endgame,* and again, in much more modest and erratic form, in Ralph Bakshi's X-rated cartoon feature, *Fritz the Cat.*

Play It Again, Sam, which Woody Allen adapted from his own stage play and stars in under Herbert Ross's direction, might appear on the surface a somewhat biting—let's call it snapping—comedy; actually it is very soft stuff, all right in its way, but not when it is also masochistic to the last degree, and thus unwholesome and distasteful. The only interesting thing about it, in fact, is that it is, despite its fundamental pro-humor quality, surprisingly unhealthy. It concerns Allan Felix, an apparently successful magazine movie critic (in San Francisco, in the film; in the play, more appositely, in New York) living in an affluence more compatible with ad-men. His ex-waitress wife, Nancy, has just left him; in despair, he turns to his only friends, Dick and Linda, a semihappily married couple.

Dick is a nonstop wheeler-dealer, one ear permanently buried in a telephone, instead of, as his wife would prefer, cut off as a Van Goghian love offering to her. Linda, a former model, is loved but neglected, and has become a confirmed tranquilizer-swallower, though in this department she is way behind the supreme hypochondriac, analysand, pill-popper, and hard-luck case, Allan. For our hero is a nebbish, a schnook and a schlemiel, and the fact that he is Jewish in the film (and, as Allen rather than Allan, in life too) is as significant as the fact that only Yiddish possesses sufficient *mots justes* for describing him.

There is, I firmly believe, such a thing as national humor. Or, more exactly, cultural humor. French, British, and Austrian humor, though subtly different under the microscope, are similar to the naked eye: the sophisticated wit of formerly mighty empires and monarchies fallen on lean years, still dressed in understated elegance despite a patched elbow or a slightly threadbare trouser-seat that is itself good for a cavalier joke or two. American humor, in contrast, is preeminently based on feeling superior to someone even more inept than oneself, or on making more or less harmless jokes about one's own blunders. So it was with almost all American stand-up comics, pre- and post-Lenny Bruce, whose reasonably or unreasonably natty jackets could not quite disguise the baggy pants.

From this indigenous American humor—itself based on feeling, rightly or wrongly, inferior to European culture—it is only a step to Jewish humor, the humor of unjustly hounded people who try to laugh at their miseries, or even exaggerate them for the benefit of their benevolent persecutors, the friendly anti-Semites, and who are thus imperceptibly drawn into self-caricature, self-hatred, self-abasement, masochism. In the end, the laugh that should take the sting off the hurt becomes a curse in its own right, and the cure may prove as deadly as the poison whose antidote it means to be. Allan Felix—that happy last name is itself an irony—is a nervous wreck. Significantly, we do not see him at his job, where he is an ostensible success; we observe him only in his all-consuming avocation, women, where he is not even a resounding failure. Sensing in advance that his dates will not end with a bang, he generally begins them with a whimper.

The film deals with Dick and Linda's efforts to set up Allan with various blind dates that all turn into blinding disasters. At last, the grass-widowed Librium-addict Linda falls into the arms of the abandoned Darvol-buff Allan, and, by way of a final cop-out, this pitiful one-night stand rejuvenates Linda's marriage and makes a man of Allan. But before we get to that absurd, mendacious finale, we see Allan continually beset by two imaginary presences: that of Humphrey Bogart, urging him on to ruthless conquests of women; and that of his absent wife, sneering at his sexual incompetence.

Typically, when Allan spots a girl for whom he is seized with instant lust, he'll either blurt out, "I love you! I want to have your baby!"—i.e., total reversal of roles, abdication of virility, masochism; or (my quotations are only approximations: I didn't have a pen with me) "She's gorgeous! For her, I'd sell my grandmother to the Arabs!"—i.e., making himself out to be a sissified grandma's boy who would still sell his beloved granny to the tribal enemy—in short, anti-Semitism.

Allan's schnookiness cries out from every frame of the film, and out of just about every gag. When Dick rightly suspects his wife of infidelity and tells Allan that words she spoke in her sleep betrayed her as dreaming of intercourse with another man, and the trembling Allan inquires whether she mentioned any names, Dick replies, "No—only yours." Allan, plainly, is beneath suspicion. And when, quasi-miraculously, Allan manages to make it with Linda—the Pepto-Bismol having, as she says, helped—he gushes with stud's pride: "I didn't have to get up once to consult the manual."

How horribly this sort of humor contrasts with that of, say, a Feydeau farce. Feydeau, too, concentrates on sex in general, and adultery in particular; yet the principal characters are funny because they are bigger than in real life, not smaller; and what they are in life is normal rather than sub- or abnormal. In Feydeau, a faithful but neglected wife toys with adultery, and is devastatingly funny in the brilliance of her toying as well as in her hairbreadth escapes. Thus both her intrigues and her ultimate chastity will be funny for being bigger, cleverer, and, finally, more chaste than life—not like Linda's and Allan's, more piddling, inept, and pitiable than reality.

And then, of course, comes the cop-out. The movie begins with the closing abdication scene from *Casablanca* reproduced *in toto,* and ends with a take-off on it: Linda and Allan simultaneously give each other up as she leaves for Cleveland with Dick, while Allan bids Bogey goodbye forever, having come of age sexually. But what has happened? Two whiny neurosis-breeding hypochondriacs have just barely brought off a night together, on the strength of which both are supposed to make out all right!

Tony Roberts is coarse and dreary as Dick; Diane Keaton is homely and untalented as Linda; Jerry Lacy's impersonation of Bogart is as amateurish as it was on stage; and Susan Anspach manages to be boring even in the short part of the wife. But Viva, Andy Warhol's ex-superstar, can make a two-minute bit histrionically and visually stomach-turning. She cannot even play herself on screen; yet so debased is our film criticism that she copped numerous plaudits.

Fritz the Cat is often sophomoric, and for every funny invention in it there must be two that are arty or *recherché.* Bakshi's drawing is sometimes quite artistic and imaginative in its three-dimensionality, subsuming of photographed sequences, surreal effects, and far-out transitions between episodes; at other times, these very effects become obstreperously self-conscious. Remotely based on some R. Crumb comic strips, the tale concerns Fritz, a tiger cat who drops out of NYU and burns his classrooms behind him, goes on a polymorphous orgy (e.g., a cat with an aardvark), is chased by the police (literally pigs) through a service in a synagogue all the way to Harlem, and there starts a black revolution that ends in catastrophe.

Fritz joins up with a swinging, liberated young woman (a bitch!) admirably named Winston Schwartz, and they start driving west together. Midway they prove incompatible, and he wanders off into the desert to get involved with a Hell's-Angels jack rabbit and his kinky horse girl friend. These two lead him to a viciously Weathermannish girl lizard, with whom he blows up a power plant, only to end in a hospital visited by three girls whom he balled at the orgy. Like a mummy returning to life, he sheds his bandages and the orgy resumes.

The film is sardonically insulting to everyone: blacks are depicted as ludicrous crows, Jews as bearded blitherers, police as porkers. Labor, youth, radicals, reactionaries—all emerge as screw-ups. Mankind is so many frantic animals whose only human parts are their insatiable genitalia. The only hope is in the survival of lechery and laughter—indeed, Fritz is an updated Mehitabel in tomcat's clothing. It's a ragged hope, but at least *Fritz the Cat* does not preach love for the schnooks.

May 29, 1972

Conflagration

The Trial of the Catonsville Nine is the film version of the documentary play Daniel Berrigan made of the trial of the seven men and two women who burned 378 draft records with homemade napalm at Catonsville, Maryland, in 1968. The play, first performed in Los Angeles, came to New York for a modest run—first in a church, then on Broadway—of 159 performances; or, roughly, one performance for every two-and-a-half records burned. I make this absurd calculation to dramatize the dearth of interest in this important play, written by one of the Catonsville Nine from his jail. True, people had read accounts of the case in newspapers and magazines; true, the play is only an edited version of the transcript with some minor explanatory additions. Yet over against this there was the fact that almost every New York drama critic had glowing praise for the play and production, and, above all, for the re-creation of a significant event and the sharing in a momentous experience.

To see the play was, in my opinion, to come into the presence of saints, and the film, though it throws a few obstacles in our way—some unavoidable, some not—still offers us this chance. For these nine human beings, as their testimony richly demonstrates, are or were (one of them has since died) saints. The fact that they were not burnt at the stake is irrelevant: giving up years of one's brief life to prison is no small sacrifice. And watching these people—or these actors who convincingly re-create the people—leaves me with little doubt whether the pyre or the gallows would have deterred them. Sainthood, like virginity, is not subdivisible; you have it, or you don't.

It might be objected that the Nine, expounding the events and complex reasons that led them to this act of civil disobedience, exhibit—along with their Christian and humanitarian concern—a certain smug or defiant self-righteousness, a measure of militant indignation. But why not? Or, rather, how not? A saint is, like other men, a little lower than the angels; and even angels, I suspect, come mainly in two varieties: militant or smug. Without some kind of satisfaction or righteous anger, no work can be done, not even a saint's; yet the occupational hazards of sainthood are nothing compared to those of ordinary solid citizenship: a self-righteousness and thick-headedness that beget war, racism, and social inequity.

What *The Trial of the Catonsville Nine* so clearly illustrates is that we have learned nothing from history and art: Joan of Arc was burned and canonized for nothing; Sophocles' *Antigone* taught us nothing. Why can't the Cauchons and Creons of today learn to revise, temper, or circumvent a law whose enforcement can only turn them into the same despised wretches? We will continue immuring or immolating saints, even though it is manifest that human law is in some cases inadequate.

The Catonsville judge seems to have been a decent, compassionate man and a good Catholic, like the defendants. He is reported to have shed tears for them. Why couldn't he have done the grand and glorious thing that one of them proposed to him: to address the jury differently and obtain acquittal for the Nine? Or, failing that, to let them off with some symbolically nugatory fine, like that farthing of damages Ruskin was made to pay Whistler? Oh, yes, the judge might have lost his job; but, in an unjust state, shouldn't he have? Which raises the question of what you or I would have done in his place.

Gordon Davidson, who directed the film as he did the play, and Saul Levitt and Father Berrigan, who collaborated on the screenplay, made one serious mistake. To show the draft-file burning and the Nine and their lawyer in informal discussions in the prison dining hall, and to intercut this with the trial, is a legitimate way of providing relief from the courtroom scenes; but the periodic cutting away to shots of the Vietnam war (including a recurrent image of bombs dropping in slow motion) and to antiwar protesters incurring police brutality, was, I think, a poor idea. All those burnt, dead babies are much too shocking an image for mere human beings arguing the inhumanity of war to compete with. The scenes, instead of stressing the urgency and nobility of the Nine's action, manage to minimize them. Protesters having their skulls cracked open have a way of making the calm, firm stand of nine defiant defendants look too quiet and self-defeating—almost too safe. Which, of course, it was not.

Even the rhythm of the film suffers from this device. And what on stage looked wonderfully filmic—having the testimony of one person flow into that of another as one actor stepped away from the witness stand in midsentence to make room for another—looks on film, paradoxically, rather stagy. Still, the camera movements and placements are often effective, and Haskell Wexler's color cinematography is, as always, highly expressive. Only a few shots from behind some sort of diaphanous curtain of glass struck me as unduly arty. The acting is good without being brilliant, and that, in a way, makes it all the more believable; but film, alas, does not give as strong a sense of being there as the stage was able to convey.

There is one subtly potent moment that the rest cannot quite match. Father Philip Berrigan explains that his position was reached in part by observing the injustices we inflict on Negroes: an act of solidarity with his black brothers. The government's prosecuting attorney happens to be a black, and is walking back to his seat as those words are spoken. The camera discreetly moves down from his face to catch merely a black hand as it momentarily freezes. But such cinematic gains do not make up for the sizable chunks of the play that have been omitted, possibly for no better reason than to accommodate that unneeded documentary footage. Nevertheless, like the play, the film proves that the letter of the law is immortal and invincible; only its spirit can be killed off or left unborn.

June 12, 1972

A Likely Candidate

A POLITICAL FILM out of Hollywood is a rare bird indeed (though all birds, alas, are getting to be that); a good political film is almost unheard of. Usually, we are given either pure hokum such as *Advise and Consent;* or impure hokum such as *The Best Man;* or else something exotic and remote from most of us such as *All the King's Men.* But now there is *The Candidate,* written by Jeremy Larner, directed by Michael Ritchie, and starring Robert Redford, so *Medium Cool* is no longer the only decent, serious political film made in America within recent years. Or should one say ever? Ritchie and Redford, who brought us the fine *Downhill Racer,* coproduced this venture, providing an impetus that would not have come from the customary uncreative sources.

The Candidate concerns the change that takes place in a fighting, progressive young California lawyer, Bill McKay, whom the Democratic Party runs as a dark-horse candidate for senator against the Republican incumbent, Crocker Jarmon, an entrenched, dyed-in-the-wool conservative smoothly and smarmily representing the forces of pious retrogression. Although Jarmon is depicted only in terms of his slick demagoguery and adroit manipulation of reactionary platitudes, he does not become a caricature—unless, that is, Nixon and his cabinet are caricatures too. McKay is a cogently conceived and executed figure: a clean, staunch young man, reasonably, not sacrosanctly idealistic, who discovers that there is no way of preserving one's purity while running for office.

This may not sound like a particularly novel statement for even a Hollywood film to make; but the subtlety, penetration, and wit with which it is made are certainly original and welcome. No melodramatic sell-out occurs: McKay is shown neither as perfect in the beginning nor as thorougly corroded in the end; he becomes merely somewhat shopworn and morally rumpled—still a good man, but one whose compromises have left him unsure of his footing and of himself, confused enough to be a likely candidate for further decline into genteel trimming. The film has something resembling a happy ending: the battling underdog ousts the smiling reactionary, but at the price of moral diminishment for himself, and watered-down representation for the people.

The Candidate is perforce a slightly less than profound analysis of the corruption, not of power but of the mere process of acquiring power, because it tries to cover so much: virtually all the funny, grim, grotesque, and saddening aspects of a victorious political campaign. What saves the film from superficiality is its ability to suggest a great deal more than it has time to show; its resolute avoidance of cliché by observing the most time-dishonored truths with a sharp, circumspect eye that sees everything as if for the first time; its judicious and witty selection of telling details without rubbing our eyes and ears in the obvious. There are two kinds of films: those that tell us what to think, and those that merely invite us to think; *The Candidate,* sensibly and sensitively, understates.

Bill McKay is a rather Kennedyish figure: glamorous, charismatic, quick-witted, essentially honest and well-meaning, with some fairly well-developed foibles, such as an appetite for attractive, available women. There is one such woman in the film (you'll have no difficulty identifying her prototype), seen first giving Bill a very special handshake, later whispering in his ear, still later hovering at a distance; but the only real hint we get before the comic denouement is a glimpse of a campaign poster where someone has scrawled "A toss in the hay with" just before the printed "Bill McKay." The camera never zeros in on the graffito; you either notice it in passing or you don't.

Similarly, right in the middle of McKay's first major political speech, you may just overhear a TV cameraman's callous, "We've got all we need." When McKay is outmaneuvered by Jarmon in an on-the-spot appearance at a Malibu brush fire, you may be able to read Bill's lips forming the words, "The son of a bitch!" or you may not. When Pat Harrington, Jr., patronizingly introduces Bill at a banquet, he compounds the offense with the malapropism "unequivocably," which may easily get past you. The political circus is there down to its puniest absurdities, but it is up to you to catch them on the wing.

Other things are less elusive. When Bill and his campaign manager, Marvin "Luke" Lucas—a rather mysterious figure who drops in out of nowhere to tempt, cajole, and provoke him into running for senator—are closeted for a conference in a water closet, the only place where they can escape the crowd, people bang impatiently on the door. Luke bangs back from inside and shouts, "Get your arse out of here!" But whose arse is really *in?* And where else does an arse really belong? Or is it politicians who truly belong in latrines, as E. E. Cummings suggested: "a politician is an arse upon/which everyone has sat except a man"?

Again, when McKay and his team are flying by helicopter to that brush fire, and Bill rehearses some of the points he will make to the assembled representatives of the media, his chief adviser tells him to drop some of those points: "Don't make this into an issues thing; it'll look like you're trying to make political capital out of it." What else, since he does not man the pumps, could he be doing in any case?

Ironies, big and small, jostle one another. But most of the people who surround McKay are themselves walking ironies. There is Lucas, who pretends to be helping Bill get his ideas before the people (the candidate is not actually expected to win), when he is merely using him for a fall guy in a race considered too hopeless for a reputable Democrat to essay. There is Klein, the TV image-maker who with his camera henchmen turns McKay from a genuine human being into a sexy commodity. When Luke wants a hollow McKay promise to fire the regents eliminated from one of the TV ads, Klein responds cynically that it "sounds good." Klein is Bill McKay's most evil demon, yet with every cheap, clever TV ad he puts out, up goes McKay's rating on the opinion polls by a couple of points.

Then there is Bill's wife, Nancy, looking very much like a Kennedy consort: cool, symmetrical, wrapped in a cellophane placenta. She is given to inimical banter and innuendos that imply less than meets the ear. Something is wrong between her and Bill, yet when their rapport is worst, their sex is best; though her ambition is much more naked and naïve than his, the two can be made to mesh. The family that preys together . . . And there is Bill's father, ex-Governor John J. McKay, who views his son as a hostile baby, calls him Bud, and would just as soon see him lose. But as soon as Bud begins to win over the public with an honesty that John mistakes for cunning, Dad is solidly behind him, even though his son merely wants him to keep out of it altogether. Help from this crass, wordly politician appalls his son the reformer.

And what of Bill McKay himself? He is, in the beginning, an embattled storefront lawyer, genuinely interested in social improvement and beloved by his youthful staff; but he is also interested in Luke's offer—half promise, half defiance. His ironic responses are a *via media* between idealistic intransigence and practical ambition. As he starts his campaign, he is disarmingly honest: when he has an answer to a question, it is as like as not an unpolitic one; when he has no answer, he admits it. The film records how his positions become coated over or thinned out by the men around him, and how their ideas seep back into his. The final question is at what point does the bearer of such compromised views become no better than anyone else—which is decidedly not good enough.

It is Bill's tragicomedy and ours, for we are in the picture too. Sometimes it is a skillful *reductio ad absurdum.* Crocker Jarmon is conducting a big rally under a huge picture of himself—an *hommage* to *Citizen Kane,* perhaps. Patriotic music is being segued in under his speech, which ends with grand clichés about keeping America beautiful. But who are these America Beautifulers in his audience? Cruelly but not unjustly, the camera picks them out one after the other. We notice especially a colossally fat woman who applauds frantically, stops long enough for a big, fat sneeze, then resumes her applauding undaunted. That perfervid, sneezing whale—is that what will keep America beautiful for us? Or is America to be kept beautiful for it? And what kind of beauty might that be?

The McKay followers are more couth or, at least, a little younger, for the most part; also, perhaps, more appealingly gotten up. But they, too, comprise garish hippies, beaming simpletons, silly matrons whose one thought is that Bill McKay is cute, swooning young girls who pin large McKay buttons on their panties just over the pudenda, movie stars who are as much concerned with getting themselves photographed with McKay as he is with getting photographed with them, and so on. Soon McKay drools over babies as repulsive as those Jarmon chucked under the chin, and the patriotic music at McKay rallies swells to climaxes every bit as rousing as the Jarmon crescendos.

Is there any difference? McKay does preserve a sense of humor and a simulacrum of independence, even if they can express themselves only in gratuitous acts. There is a ride in a limousine during which Bill makes up parodistic distortions of his campaign slogans, and a television program that he blows completely by uncontrollable fits of laughter, superficially without cause but with a deeper motivation: a sense of the absurdity of it all.

Michael Ritchie and Jeremy Larner have shrewdly allowed some *actes gratuits,* loose ends, red herrings to infiltrate their film—whether it be a religious fanatic walking the streets and heralding doomsday, or someone out of nowhere taking a swing at McKay, or a vending machine dyspeptically refusing to yield its Pepsi despite Bill's imprecations and kicks. These incidents, in context, acquire a certain left-handed relevance. Let it not be thought, though, that the film depends chiefly on such literary or ideological elements. It is also exultantly visual.

Ritchie will combine a crane shot with handheld-camera work to convey the sense of isolation and confusion McKay experiences when he first goes out to shake the hands of factory workers rushing homeward. The crane shot shows his smallness in that crowd that couldn't care less about shaking hands with obscure office seekers; the handheld camera echoes Bill's wavering, indeterminate movements. I don't know whether improvisation, too, was used here, but the scene is full of little awkwardnesses, contretemps, failures to connect that set the stage for bigger future mishaps.

Or consider the television debate between Jarmon and McKay. Throughout the film, TV screens and monitors have figured prominently: not only has the action moved from the big to the small screen, but also, at other times, it moved inversely, from the televised version to the event actually taking place. There is no longer a clear difference between the happening and its edited, broadcast version. As a result, both time and place become schizophrenic. The message thinks it is the medium, the medium thinks it is the message, and armies of stupefied viewers think nothing at all, except perhaps that McKay is cuter than Jarmon. That is why, as Bill's father boasts, he will not get his arse kicked.

But in the televised debate sequence, Ritchie has the multitude of monitors, glass partitions, control booths, and panels take over almost completely, while still allowing the human debaters their share of suspenseful, exacerbated humanity. By using frequent diagonal shots to create distortion, the film, often showing one face as really there and the other encapsulated on a TV monitor, suggests a world gone awry, where nothing is seen undistorted any more, and one cannot be sure where television ends and life begins. Equally brilliant is Ritchie's handling of the sound effects during a department-store harangue where the P.A. system goes haywire, or during an embarrassing address at a farmers' meeting hall that is almost empty, and where we mostly hear silences in which a chair abjectly scrapes against the floor or McKay despondently clears his throat.

No less adroit is the casting. The actors are either unknowns or near-unknowns who manage to look their parts with uncanny veracity; or else actual public figures, from politics and the media, doing what, alas, comes naturally to them. There are expert performances by a few known actors, too, like Peter Boyle's chillingly cynical, ominously subdued Luke, who nevertheless retains a minimum of vulnerability under his frozen eyes; and Melvyn Douglas's retired, hedonistic ex-governor, a figure of amiable repulsiveness. In a final scene, as he grins at Bill and cackles, "You're a politician, son!" the very grayish yellowness of his teeth (do I merely imagine food particles lodged among them?) contrasts sardonically with the whiteness of his son's, bared in a smile of frozen horror.

Thanks to both actors and director, expressions do much of the film's talking. So Redford carefully calibrates his degrees of bewilderment. It is modest when a girl pulls down the top of her dress and squeals: "Sign me, please, sign me!" It reaches proportions of dismay when a former coworker accompanies his handshake with "You and I both know that this is bullshit, but the point is: they are believing it!" Absolute alarm is attained at film's end, when the victorious McKay's call for help and Luke's laconic reply are drowned out by crowd noise; it is as if both anxiety and cynicism had reached some form of supreme purity beyond verbalization.

The film progresses by marvelous rhythms: chiefly hectic syncopation lapsing into moments of relaxation—either devil-may-care amusement, or doldrums of accidie. And when the McKay campaign winds to a close, Ritchie creates a splendid montage of ever shorter, ever more frenzied scenes that build pyramidally to an apex of terminal tension. Throughout, he is ably served by his scenarist, Jeremy Larner, who brings his experiences as a McCarthy speechwriter to bear on the script—yet Larner's work is not merely that of an alert political sideline observer; it is that of a skilled writer as well. *Drive, He Said* is forgiven and forgotten: Larner has now earned his premature acclaim, and possibly even a little something extra.

Robert Redford's McKay is right, down to his Teddy Kennedy looks: Redford is always believably complex, never settles for an easy or excessive effect, and communicates Bill's inner doubts without losing the enveloping grace of a winner, even if he is a winner who doesn't know what to do with his winnings.

There is only one other weakness in the film, besides the almost unavoidable quasi-superficiality. That is the utterly uninspired color cinematography of Victor J. Kemper. Kemper's colors lack definition and excitement; often it is impossible to tell whether they are washed-out on purpose or from ineptitude. Haskell Wexler's *Medium Cool,* besides being a more humane piece of political filmmaking, benefited from the acuity and inventiveness of Wexler's camera work. *The Candidate* could have used a Wexler. But, even so, it has my vote.

July 10, 1972

Failing to Deliver

THERE ARE TWO MYTHS that will probably keep cropping up as long as literature exists. One is the myth of lost childhood, of the personal, private Age of Gold that we once possessed and vainly try to recapture, returning to it only at the cost of losing our sanity or life itself. A good example of this is Alain-Fournier's *Le grand Meaulnes (The Wanderer)*. The other, in a sense its opposite, is the very masculine myth of rites of passage, the ordeal or ritual by means of which we become real men rather than boys. This usually centers on a test of severe physical, and sometimes also sexual, endurance that some pass while others fall by the wayside. Of this, James Dickey's novel *Deliverance* is a prime specimen. Both myths derive from a state of existential immaturity, no less seductive or eternal for being immature.

Deliverance, the novel, was a curious hybrid. It was seriously discussible and discussed in the better journals and had a literate following; but it also became a popular bestseller. The duality—as ancient and respectable as that of Greek drama—is manifest in the divergence of style and content, a divergence more real than apparent. The story is pure, violent adventure, almost completely devoid of "love interest," and all about a life-and-death struggle with hostile natural elements and fierce quasi-troglodytes, a struggle that tests and confirms one's manhood. The style, however, is vastly different, often very close to that of Dickey's excellent poetry; from its imagery and interior monologues—even from some of its intense descriptions—levels of meaning recede beyond the ken of the blissful bestseller reader. That the film caters to him exclusively is surely not to be blamed on the script, by Dickey himself, but on the avatars it underwent in the hands of John Boorman, the director.

The story concerns four middle-aged Atlanta businessmen who go on a weekend canoe trip down a faraway, little-explored, and essentially unnavigable river. They are spurred on by Lewis, a passionate sportsman and adventurer, who rather yearns for an atomic holocaust to bring about the kind of world in which he would become a leader. As a superman, he is more Nietzschean than Hitlerian, and he has genuine feeling for a wilderness soon to be dammed up into an artificial lake for the benefit of industry and tourism.

His principal disciple and admirer—almost worshiper—is Ed Gentry, the narrator. He is a successful yet restless advertising executive, whose life hovers at the junction of the bourgeois paterfamilias, the enthusiastic practitioner of archery, and the artistically tinged thinker and dreamer. The other two are Drew, a decent, hard-working company man, whose conventional nature is mitigated only by his proficiency on the guitar; and Bobby, a soft city slicker and a cynical "born salesman," who is at the lowest notch of Dickey's four-degree scale.

In the wilderness, strange things befall these men. The river proves a serious danger to life and limb; even worse are a couple of plug-ugly mountain men who capture Ed and Bobby and sodomize the latter. Before they can do further harm, Lewis shoots one of them dead with an arrow. The other escapes, intending to pick off the four canoers from the high banks of the river later on. Coming upon dangerous rapids, all four capsize and Drew dies, possibly gunned down by the surviving cracker. The remaining three adventurers are beached—Lewis incapacitated with a broken leg, and Bobby unnerved by the painful and humiliating assault. Ed has to take over as leader.

The typical *homme moyen sensuel,* who is also the author's chief alter ego, goes on to perform tasks of almost superhuman strength, skill, and intelligence. He triumphs over unclimbable cliffs, virtually untraversable rapids, the murderous mountain man (whom he kills) and, finally, suspicious lawmen; he brings his friends and himself back to civilization and safety. He succeeds in doing all this expertly, but at a psychic price: although the experience of the river will remain with him as a proud testimonial to his mastery, there will also be a lingering sense of guilt and anxiety. In the end, though, satisfaction prevails: we glimpse Ed in later life, clearly superior to the limping, chastened Lewis.

The three main subjects of the book, then, are the fear of stagnation and growing old that drives some men to seek unusual risks and challenges; the way men change under the destroying or annealing flame of danger, and how this connects with their previous and future existences; and the ultimate besting of the apparent superman by the seemingly more ordinary but actually more complex fellow. Dickey's book of diary jottings, *Sorties,* is full of these themes: "What is this fascination in me for attempting and spending a great deal of time on activities for which I have no natural ability?" "The only *raison d'être* for being middle-aged or old is the possession of an absolute mastery of *something.* . . . Without mastery, middle age is a joke and old age is hell itself." "It is the way the mind operates in . . . *extremis* that tells more about what we are than anything else possibly could."

Beyond that, the novel *Deliverance* is concerned, more cryptically and perhaps even partly unconsciously, with the nature of sexual relations, real or implied, between men and women, men and men, and men and idealized figments of their imagination, such as a girl espied in a quasi-sexual situation who remains a tantalizing chimera. Alas, the film manages to shave away most of the meaning and implications that made the novel interesting. By the mere fact of almost totally eliminating the prelude and postlude in the city (what little is left is more confusing than helpful), the deeper intentions were jettisoned. What we get is at best a triptych without the side panels; at worst, the long second act of a three-act play.

No less damaging than the cutting is the casting. Jon Voight, a young actor who looks even younger than his age, is far too handsome and existentially unthreatened for Ed Gentry. This dependable performer, moreover, gives one of his rare unconvincing performances, possibly because the truncated script does not offer him sufficient motivation and opportunity for emotional shading. As Lewis, Burt Reynolds is handsome and aggressively virile, but conveys no ideological or mystical superiority, and is a very shallow actor. Ronny Cox plays Drew decently enough, within the limitations of the script's not showing his city life; Ned Beatty, as Bobby, is good, though he overemphasizes the character's comic side. Dickey himself contributes a nice bit as the sheriff, and various back-country types are good and creepy.

The cinematography of Vilmos Zsigmond gets better, because less flamboyant, with his every new film. Here the glimmers on the river surface, the multiplicity of forest greens, the nocturnal climb up a steep rocky bank, the many tumultuous scenes of shooting the rapids are managed with a fine, unflashy fidelity. Sam Peckinpah having been unavailable, John Boorman was a logical second choice for director of this film combining the brutality of *Point Blank* with the nastiness and isolation of *Hell in the Pacific.* The violent sequences succeed well enough, as does even an occasional nonviolent one, such as the impromptu guitar and banjo duet and duel between Drew and a semicretinous mountain boy. But the larger and subtler implications are beyond Boorman's competence.

What is perhaps most acutely missing from the film is Dickey's poetry. The dialogue, probably the weakest part of the book, has been sensibly trimmed. But a voice-over interior monologue would have been appropriate to convey a little of the work's true texture. The novel is full of *trouvailles* such as "I lay awake all night in brilliant sleep," or this almost too clever evocation of Drew's widowed wife: " 'All right,' she said from far off, from the future, from all the years coming up, and from the first night alone in bed." Suppose one rejects the first of these images as unfilmable, the second could be rendered by panning to the conjugal bed soon to be half unused—assuming, of course, that the entire scene were not cut from the film, as it was. Yet how easily the camera could have conveyed, for example, Dickey's recurrent image of the hillbilly hinterland with its maimed rustics as "the country of the nine-fingered people."

Missing even is that vital passage where the book's title word makes its only appearance. While sodomizing his wife, Ed remembers the golden fleck he saw in a fashion model's iris, and muses "in the center of Martha's heaving and expertly working back, the gold eye shone, not with the practicality of sex, so necessary to its survival, but the promise of it that promised other things, another life, deliverance." Clearly, then, the title has much deeper meanings than just escaping from the river wilderness, meanings that add up to a quixotic search for deliverance from our transience, our mortality. And a scene like this conjugal buggery connects with the brutal sodomizing of Bobby, exemplifying the kind of near-parallel and disturbing echo on which the book thrives, and whose loss impoverishes the film.

Simpler things yet are gone, including the sense of unity between man and animals and nature—the profound underside of surface hostilities. Gone, too, is Ed's final, amoral victory; his ascent to true supermanhood for having been able to kill an inferior human being with impunity. The movie carefully avoids this ticklish central issue and substitutes a protagonist haunted by nightmares of retribution—the ultimate flattening compromise.

August 7, 1972

Drifting in Dreariness

THE CRITICALLY ACCLAIMED *Fat City* is supposed to mark the return of John Houston to his former mastery. Although I have some doubts about his former mastery, they are as nothing to my doubts about this film. I hear that Leonard Gardner's novel about a down-and-out prizefighter hitting the skids in Stockton, California, was quite good; I also hear that Columbia Pictures considered Gardner's screenplay and Houston's film too downbeat, and cut a lot of it out. To the film companies, cutting is what leeches were to medieval medicine: a cure for everything.

The film deals with some not very promising young ring hopefuls, and with some aging unhopefuls who nevertheless try to hang on: ex-fighters, fight managers, trainers, women of unclear vocation. Barflies and sporadic fruit-pickers, they are inhabitants of a prosperous burg whose affluence eludes them in real life, while, in their dreams, they inhabit Fat City. The film's hero believes in it until, in the end, he gives up altogether.

Tully, the fighter broken by a terrible defeat and his wife's desertion, is a likable and believable enough figure, but Gardner, at least in the movie, fails to make him interesting enough. Amiable braggart and fuzzy dreamer, he is always a decent, dull man who fails to command our concern. Ernie, the ambitious young fighter whom he takes under his wing, has a classic stupidity that is almost endearing, but his problems—such as being manipulated into marriage by a scheming little virgin whom he has dully deflowered—are finally too humdrum or too flatly presented. As for Oma, the sherry-guzzling drifter who forgets about her jailed black lover long enough to let Tully move in with her, she is your typical proud, alcoholic kook. She is defiant about being a lady, about the scorn heaped on "interracials," and about her morality: though she has had lovers of all colors, her creed is one race at a time, and she abhors "free love." She is altogether too cute.

There are others—those various marginal, atmospheric characters—and though they are credible, they do not capture the imagination the way a gravely ill Mexican fighter does, or a young black hopeful who delivers an outrageously inspirational tirade about why he will always win and proceeds to be knocked out forthwith. The trouble with this background part of the film is that the number of changes it can ring on petty failure is limited as well as limiting, so that the film itself seems to become a drifter confusedly wandering in search of significance.

And this is where the direction fails to come to the rescue. Although Houston, who himself was once involved in boxing, has staged and shot one long, obstinate, harrowing fight with great conviction, and has done well enough by the boxing atmosphere in general, the movie is not pulled together into a compelling whole. The many short, geographically scattered scenes do not coalesce, do not give us a sense of passing time, do not create a feeling for place. There is no feel of Stockton, of the relationships of different social strata and the way neighborhoods interlock, of the state of mind expressed through topography. Not only do individual scenes tend to lack that specific impact without which there is no cumulative one, but also there is no dovetailing of scenes into one another, no sovereign sense of where to begin one scene or end another. At least as released, the film is sadly disjointed.

Stacy Keach does not convince me that he is a lower-class semiderelict: he has a certain softness and gentility built into his appearance, manner, and speech that is too civilized for Tully. As for Susan Tyrrell, her Oma is no performance at all, merely a self-disembowelment with the performer spewing up her inner chaos, guts and all, untransformed by art or even self-control, for the delectation of idiotic viewers and reviewers who cannot tell the difference between creation of a character and embarrassing, unwholesome self-display. Only Jeff Bridges, as the stolidly well-meaning young Ernie, is just right.

Conrad Hall's camera work is, once again, tricky—as when it puts a gratuitous halo around Keach's head in the penultimate scene. Houston's direction goes to pieces in the last scene, where Tully watches some bums gambling behind a glass partition. He is in an all-night beanery where he has dragged Ernie for some talk; suddenly, the soundtrack goes mute and the camera comes in tight on Keach's face frozen with horror. We were not even shown very clearly what it was he saw behind the glass partition, and the enormous effect of it on him and the entire film is unearned—sheer rodomontade. To make things worse, Tully now waxes philosophical, and utters the supposedly clinching line: "Before you ever get rolling, your life makes a beeline for the drains."

That image simply does not work. The metaphor is nonvisual and slightly mixed, and the rhythm is off. We have to shift from a "you" that is rolling to a "life" that is making a beeline—as if you were traveling by car while your life rode on a bee's back—and, next thing, life is in the drains. But where is "you"? Compare with this the Arab's motto in Saroyan's *The Time of Your Life:* "No foundation. All the way down the line." That rolls off the tongue and sticks in the mind. But *Fat City* is like that awkward trope: unable to snap into place and incapable of reverberating in the memory.

September 4, 1972

Pinpricks in the Panacea

THE HOWARD SMITH–SARAH KERNOCHAN DOCUMENTARY, *Marjoe,* concerns the last months of Marjoe Gortner's ministry. The son of revivalist preachers in California, Marjoe (a portmanteau name derived from Mary and Joseph) received the call at the age of four and was preaching by the time he was five. He became a national sensation, causing rapture among the faithful and ruptures among elder fellow ministers. The film includes a good many clips from this period, and they are worthy of taking their place alongside the religious satires in the early novels of Evelyn Waugh.

Marjoe begins with the protagonist briefing the camera crew on how to behave while filming his revival meetings. Then we see him, alone or with other preachers, working on the faithful: arousing them to high pitches of hysteria, laying on hands, collecting pious handouts. Later, he is seen joyously counting the take while reminiscing about his childhood and upbringing and his break with his parents, who kept all the money he made. He is seen also at a Lucullan feast exchanging pieties with fellow ministers; making private pronouncements about the tricks of the trade and the phoniness of it all; preaching in tandem with his father, after an apparent partial reconciliation; and disporting himself with his black girl friend after the final break with religion.

The film documents human gullibility, fear, and hysteria, and how they are exploited. It shows that greatest of human weaknesses at work: the hunger for hope. But that weakness is not a bad habit, a psychological imbalance or a moral defect; it is, awesomely, the human condition in essence. Without hope, the human animal cannot go on; if the other animals can, how lucky for them. Marjoe and his fellow conmen, who bilk their pathetic white and black hordes even as they provide them with transcendent experiences, are not really cheating them at all. They may be selling a "Jesus" who does not exist, at least not in the form in which he is peddled. But what they are surely selling is hope, and it may be that those wretched widow's mites—crumpled twenty-dollar bills extracted from oldsters saving them for a rainy day—are not criminally extorted at all.

The chanting, shouting, swooning faithful whom we encounter here are caught in a downpour of miseries reflected in their faces and behavior. If their rainy days and nights are made more hopeful, their money may be wisely spent. Does it matter that their purchase has nothing to do with the truth? Are the other man-made saviors—hypnotists, psychiatrists, philosophers, theologians—necessarily more truthful? They are, of course, more sophisticated; but the grass-roots evangelists speak the medicine these humble wounds understand. A miracle can perhaps be judged best by the quality of hope it engenders; not by the honorableness of its method.

There are methods in miracles, and Marjoe the narrator betrays quite a few of these highly unprofessional professional secrets, yet even as one's indignation with the unscrupulous mulcters mounts, as one resents their oily self-righteousness, one cannot help shuddering at how much worse off their victims might be, left to their own devices. What good, then, is a film like *Marjoe,* which might rob the lowly of their seamy salvation? Well, it won't. It will not be shown in most of the places where evangelists thrive, and the most parched seekers after Jesus will give it a wide berth in any case. Should they somehow stray into a theater showing it, they would dismiss Marjoe as the one black sheep that turns up even among good shepherds.

The objections to *Marjoe* voiced by the more piously humanitarian reviewers is that it makes city slickers feel undeservedly and unpleasantly superior to the multitudes prostrating themselves before the Lamb of God. Why not? One of the very few compensations for enlightenment (feeble though it be) in this essentially enlightenment-hating land is the privilege of sneering at the culturally inferior. It would be cruel to deny the poor sinner the pleasure of giggling at the poor redeemed, which is *his* form of hope. Give the great unwashed the blood of the Lamb to wash in; give those unwashed in it the right to their smug but pleasurable laughter.

Nor will the objection made by Andrew Sarris hold: that if this film exposed the operations of popes and Billy Grahams, fine, but picking on small-time chiselers is cowardly and sterile. The chief value of the film, as I see it, is to those teetering on the brink of religious emancipation, who might liberate themselves through seeing it. For these people, if they are capable of logic, it will not matter whether the religious melodrama is big or small, splashy or austere, megalopolitan or rural. You can perceive the same "truth" in a drop of holy water as in all the fountains of Rome; the same "untruth" in a grain of dust thrown in your eyes in southern California or Madison Square Garden. For those of us who are free-thinkers, *Marjoe* is an amusing, appalling, and reasonably well-made documentary.

It is fascinating to watch the various techniques the evangelists employ to milk their flocks—some highly methodical, systematized, well-nigh rationalistic; others more emotional, improvisatory, belonging almost perfectly in the realm of the popular performing arts. Not for nothing does Marjoe Gortner now strive for a career in pop music or theater—at last report, he is being considered for the lead in a Broadway rock musical. His performances during revival meetings are every bit as good as what I have seen from leading rock musicians on film (and that is the only fair comparison); there is no artistic difference between Jagger selling sympathy and Gortner selling antipathy for the devil.

Then there are the faces, those primordially American faces that extend from Grant Wood to Thomas Hart Benton, from Norman Rockwell to Andrew Wyeth—*American Gothic* faces that seem lonelier and sadder than their equivalents from Asia and Europe. It may have something to do with innocence, with a certain naïve surprise that in a land of plenty one can feel so deprived. If there is anything nearly as pathetic as the look of defeated children, it is the look of defeated childish adults. At times, I am afraid, it also strikes one as ludicrous. *Marjoe* is a film one can weep or laugh at. Or both.

September 18, 1972

Sounder and Less Sound

MARTIN RITT's *Sounder* is a rare honest movie about people who work the soil under conditions of extreme rigor. *Sounder* is also a rare honest Hollywood movie about blacks, making it virtually unique. Based on a novel by William H. Armstrong, with a screenplay by Lonne Elder III, the film concerns a family of Louisiana sharecroppers in the thirties, exploited by their white boss. When hunger for meat becomes overwhelming, Nathan Lee Morgan, the father, steals a ham. For this, he is sentenced to a year of hard labor in a camp whose location is kept from his family. His wife, Rebecca, and older son, David Lee (ten or eleven), carry on without him—working the farm and raising the two tiny kids.

Later, David Lee goes off on a vain search for his father and is discovered along the way by a kindly black schoolteacher who promises to educate him. When the father, partially crippled, finally returns, David no longer wants to leave home. His courageous mother and farsighted father make him go, for the betterment of all their futures. So abridged, the story sounds banal, crude, and tearjerking. The film is none of these things. It is simple, forthright, and moving in its restraint. There are weaknesses, to be sure: Ritt is not a particularly imaginative director, and the screenplay (probably following the novel) does not explore character in depth.

But how could it? The characters are people who have not been permitted to explore the depths of their thoughts and feelings. Still, they manage to say a good deal with a look, a silence, an understatement, or a bit of indirection. In fact, the film's title is an indirection: Sounder is the name of the boy's beagle, which the sheriff shoots and almost kills. The dog disappears and does not return until its tongue and time have licked the wounds away. The Morgans and their fellows are in hiding, too, wounded but slowly licking themselves into health and strength.

Although Carmen Matthews is unconvincing as a decent white woman, the acting is generally good. Young Kevin Hooks is marvelously straightforward as David Lee. But the shattering performance is that of Cicely Tyson as Rebecca. Her strong emotions, deeply repressed, must register from behind layers and layers of imposed imperturbability. Miss Tyson does not indulge herself in a smidgen of histrionics—not even that kind of fake underplaying that Brando, for instance, capitalizes on in *The Godfather*—but her essential sentiments can be exhilaratingly glimpsed beneath the repressions, like bright pebbles at the bottom of a very limpid pond.

And now for the puerile grandiloquence division with *The King of Marvin Gardens.* What in Bob Rafelson's previous film, *Five Easy Pieces,* was pretentious vagueness of overstatement, here turns into pseudoprofound, hammy understatement. The entire film is an innuendo blared into your face, a children's game blown up to a tall tale. Locations and incidents are chosen for their supposed symbolic charge; everything reeks of atmosphere, fashionably emblematic defeat, and fragments of other men's movies drearily dragging about.

The plot is the old schlock classic: decent, obscure brother answers the call of glamorous, distant brother embroiled in the Great American Success Scheme. Mysterious Atlantic City, out of season and out of fashion: sumptuous, empty hotels, miles of deserted boardwalk, street names like Atlantic Avenue, Marvin Gardens, and all the childhood get-rich-quick dreams bred by playing Monopoly. Wheeler-dealer brother turns out to be only the lackey of successful black gangsters, and is nurturing a hotel-in-Hawaii fantasy like a castle in Spain. He plays around, meanwhile, with a woman of uncertain age and her simpering stepdaughter, and we get everything from troilism to lesbianism and the obligatory drug scene in chicly subliminal flashes. Innocent brother is partly sucked into all this, then jealous older woman shoots razzmatazz brother, and the other one returns to Philadelphia, a wiser and sadder man.

Apart from Jacob Brackman's modishly trashy script, in which incidents do not hang together and characters are only façades, there is the problem of Atlantic City refusing to take on mythic dimensions in the viewer's mind. Somehow being summoned from Philly to Atlantic City is not the equivalent of going from Europe to the heart of Congolese darkness, and the attempt to make that obsolete resort simultaneously the Valhalla of Monopoly players, a spooky ghost town, and a busy capital of crime, trips over its self-contradictions. Laszlo Kovacs's cinematography is too grandiose for its theme, and all performances except Bruce Dern's are either self-parodies or just bad. The direction is supposed to evoke Antonioni, but looks more like Patroni Griffi and his dreadful *Il Mare,* about Capri out of season. The name of the game is not Monopoly but monotony.

October 16–November 27, 1972

Unlived Lives

FRANK PERRY'S *Play It As It Lays* is a very bad movie made from the poor but prodigally overpraised novel by Joan Didion. Miss Didion's book was lauded especially for its extraordinary concision, its "unfeminine" toughness, and its evocative depiction of life and nonlife along the Hollywood-Vegas axis. As for the concision, a device meant to increase the power of suggestion, it is wasted on characters not interesting enough to make us want to pursue their reverberations into the "meadows of margin" surrounding Miss Didion's sparse text.

As for "feminine" writing, it is a meaningless term to which I am tempted to apply the uncouth neologism "sexist." What is wrong with a novel written by a woman from a female point of view—is it less human? Are *Middlemarch, Persuasion, Wuthering Heights* less good Victorian novels than those written by male contemporaries? And could one, without knowing their authors, be sure that they were written by women? They are neither frail nor gushy, characteristics often thought of as feminine but actually simply bad. If Miss Didion is "unfeminine" in any way, it is in the less than attractive sense of lacking sympathy for her characters, a defect I tend to think of (with inverse prejudice, perhaps) as more typically male.

We are thus at a loss about what to make of her heroine, Maria, a small-time movie actress caught in the Hollywood whirl, divorced by her upward-mobile director husband, tormented by her inability to reach (both literally and figuratively) an autistic daughter confined to a sanatorium, and finally driven over the brink, it seems, by an abortion her then husband, who did not beget the fetus, forced on her. When the novelist is inside Maria, recording her thoughts, the character seems moderately intelligent and sensitive, possibly Miss Didion herself. At these times, though, she is not different from whichever other figure the author slips into. Observed by the novelist from the outside, however, Maria becomes neurotic to the point of acute infantilism, if not imbecility, and behaves like a particularly amoral amoeba.

No good writer would permit such irreconcilable differences within a character, or such similarity between one character and all the others. That the society depicted is shallow and self-parodying is no excuse: the writer has to create more even when describing less. This undercuts Miss Didion's third alleged virtue, her power of evocation: she is all good eye and ear, but without the satirist's wit, the moralist's vision, or the poet's transcendent grace to put mind and soul behind those eyes and ears.

The film, with a script by Miss Didion and her husband, John Gregory Dunne, is at an immediate disadvantage vis-à-vis the novel. It has to anchor the elusive, vaguely suggestive effect of the laconic words in a specific, visually distracting place and an equally specific and limiting time, the duration of the film, which cannot, like printed paragraphs, be lingered over. When Maria, in the clutches of her neurosis, drives her sports car aimlessly and endlessly along the California freeways, our having to imagine this tentacular, pullulating inferno gives it a metaphysical dimension of sorts. Seeing the car, the traffic, the cloverleaves with all the lights and signs, photographed once more (even in a soft nocturnal focus that gives them a nonobjective Moholy-Nagy look as in, say, *Pierrot le Fou* and *Taking Off)* demystifies the nightmare.

Take a plainer example. Chapter 52 reads in its entirety: "Maria made a list of things she would never do. She would never: *walk through the Sands or Caesar's alone after midnight.* She would never: *ball at a party, do S-M unless she wanted to, borrow furs from Abe Lipsey, deal.* She would never: *carry a Yorkshire in Beverly Hills."* The effect, such as it is, depends on the expanse of white paper that surrounds this "chapter" and urges the reader to dwell on it in search of real or imaginary profundities.

In print, moreover, there is the sonorous fascination of proper names, the in-group cachet of knowing about the Sands and Lipsey's and that hip abbreviation for sadomasochism. There is, further, the provocative ambiguity of "unless she wanted to" and that curtly ominous "deal." And, of course, the titillating information about what distinguishes a superior swinger from a mere party girl: no easy pickups, orgies, kinky sex (except when the mood hits you), borrowed finery, drug traffic (as opposed to mere consumption), and, by way of poignant anticlimax, no public dandling of doll-like canines to assert one's regression into second girlhood. Well, one must at least concede some shrewdness to these observations, though I doubt if they deserve the italics lavished on them.

But on screen we see Maria and her husband's producer, BZ, a suffering, self-destructive married homosexual who is her best friend, strolling down a beach just before dawn. The catalogue of don'ts is delivered in stichomythic dialogue, with BZ smirkingly catechizing a pensively simpering Maria. S-M is explained, Abe Lipsey becomes "a store," and as the camera pans to the backs of our peripathetic philosophers, we see them walking into a resplendently breaking dawn. The verbal concentration is dissipated, the histrionic Technicolor and cutely colorful line readings rob the statement of even its spurious pathos.

The book can make use of such elliptic scenes in nonchronological order; at the speed of film it is all bewildering pieces of a jigsaw puzzle dumped pell-mell into your lap. You don't know what is happening, when or where or to whom, and what all the talk is about. As for motivations, you do not even presume to ask. Could an abortion really matter that much to a girl like Maria? And why would children, autistic or aborted, seem to her so important if she can calmly watch her only friend commit suicide before her eyes? Such contradictions are not necessarily beyond the reconciling powers of art, but they do enhance the blatancy of claptrap.

Frank Perry's direction strives sedulously for a chic, arty, complicated look and, unfortunately, succeeds in an endeavor where abstention would have been more honorable. From Jordan Cronenweth, his fashion-magazinish photographer, Perry gets the art-film aura he so hotly pursues, and from Sidney Katz's editing, the bedeviling dislocation of Father Daedalus' maze along with the vertiginous hurtling of Son Icarus' fall.

Tony Perkins does all right by BZ, though one suspects type-casting rather than acting; but type-casting, Tuesday Weld's only strength, is not enough for Maria. Miss Weld, a critics' darling, moves blandly, talks uninflectedly, and looks as blank as an unsigned check; she reveals, to be sure, a perfect inner emptiness, but that, alas, is not acting. Adam Roarke is as boring as the bits of his supposedly brilliant movies we are (unwisely) shown, and the others have scant chance of registering. At film's end, the institutionalized heroine smugly declares, "I know what 'nothing' means," a discovery *Play It As It Lays* is all too eager to share with the rest of us.

December 11, 1972

Adapted or Misadapted?

THANKS TO THE Christmas season, we are deluged with holiday movie fare, most of it, appropriately, tinsel. But there is also that occasional tastefully designed bauble, spreading charming, perishable joy. Such is *Sleuth,* directed by Joseph L. Mankiewicz and adapted by Anthony Shaffer from his own play. The fact that *Sleuth* is still running on the stages of New York and London—and, for all I know, Tulsa and Timbuktu—may be the biggest handicap the movie faces.

For by now almost everyone knows the plot of *Sleuth,* if only by hearsay, and a known ending is as embarrassing for a thriller as the mark of Cain for a fratricide. It is especially damaging for a plot whose basic device is reversals, and that progresses by putting one switcheroo in front of the other. Yet there is an even graver problem: both principals in *Sleuth* are improbably clever, witty, even brilliant, and outsmart each other with a zest and efficiency that are nothing short of prodigious. One of them, Andrew Wyke, a famous detective-story writer, might indeed be that fiendishly cunning; but what chance is there of a naïve hairdresser such as Milo Tindle (in the play, he was a travel agent; perhaps hairdressers are subtler) becoming, as the plot thickens, an ever rarer intellect?

The theater can get away with these things. Not, I think, because of any greater or lesser reality or stylization than the cinema's, or all those other customary explanations. It is, simply, that we are aware, however unconsciously, that in the movies it is the camera, the technology, that performs the tricks, and they had better be perfect. At the theater, we tacitly realize that these are human beings up there, naked but for a bit of make-up, costuming, and a trick or two of lighting: the faking is all up to the actor, without benefit of process photography, retakes, splicing together, stunt men, and what have you. In other words, though both media depend on stylized or simulated reality, we somehow keep in mind that the stage actor has so much less up his sleeves—has, virtually, no sleeves at all—and so fall in more lovingly and admiringly with whatever *trompe l'oeil* he can pull off.

What the movie *Sleuth* must chiefly depend on is the literacy of the screenplay, the proficiency of the direction, and the bravura of the acting. In all these categories it does well enough or better. Shaffer's respect for verbal finesse, savoring of ultracivilized repartee, ability to blend psychologically revealing dialogue with wittily pyrotechnical hyperbole survive in the film version, even though a mild form of self-censorship has been exercised. The extremes of Wyke's chauvinist xenophobia have been trimmed, and such presumably eyebrow-raising lines as the one about "a passing sheep rapist" are delivered *sotto voce* and in long shot. Yet the film remains what the play was: a battle of *wits* in the double sense of intelligences and epigrammatists.

Moreover, scenarist and director have wisely refrained from "opening up" the play—from introducing additional people and places beyond some bedrooms, a basement, and a garden. Even this much expansion may at times weaken the sense of two men pitted against each other in a space almost as confined as the boxing ring; but, on the whole, the intimacy of the contest is maintained. The direction is more like that of the old Mankiewicz, respectable if not great, than that of the recent Mankiewicz responsible for *Cleopatra, The Honey Pot,* and *There Was a Crooked Man.* It does have one mildly irritating aspect: overmuch hovering over automata, figurines, moving skeletons, pictures, and various bric-a-brac Wyke has collected. This is meant to make the atmosphere more ominous and to introduce, as it were, further characters, even if they are mere automata or effigies. It may help avoid facial monotony, yet it adds a whiff of glacial artiness.

But the drawback is more than compensated for by the acting and cinematography. Laurence Olivier makes the aging crime writer and *bon vivant*—a man who could commit murder to maintain the illusion of his cerebral and sexual supremacy—into a bright, magnetic though mean and ridiculous, and ultimately pathetic figure; he kneads more than usually diverging elements into a piece of credible human clay. There are times when Sir Laurence is a little too grand for the part—too much the great actor to be squeezed into such miniature shenanigans without slightly ripping them. And, though he handles accents quite well, they don't seem to come to him with ease. But he does bring to the part an almost bewildering variety of effects, a charm that may well be unrivaled in our theater and cinema, and a laudable restraint in never pulling out all the stops of his supremely powerful instrument.

Michael Caine has some difficulty with Milo. Caine is more personality than performer, has a limited emotional range, and is poor at accents—a particular minus in this part. And his prolonged breakdown scene as he faces imminent death (splendidly managed by Keith Baxter on stage) is not so sustained and convincing as it might be. Even playing Milo with a faintly lower-class accent—presumably the one Caine is most comfortable with—is a mistake. But Caine has a very real charm of his own: an impudent enjoyment of his masculinity, a canny proletarian refusal to be snowed by excessive refinements, and the self-confidence of the plebeian risen by sheer shrewdness.

This is good in itself, but even better when pitted against Olivier's consummate artistry. It gives the film an added—perhaps irrelevant, but irresistible—mythic fascination: the duel between the great stage actor and the lionized movie-star personality. The film's (and play's) underlying theme—the skills of experienced, crafty age versus the resourcefulness and vigor of youth—is thus couched in histrionic as well as human terms. Let me cite also two splendid finishing touches: the cinematography of Oswald Morris, whose sensitivity to color and shading makes dusky interiors as various and poignant as other cinematographers' sunny exteriors; and the score of John Addison, whose simple main theme sounds deceptively familiar at first, but, through clever orchestrations and barely perceptible departures, leads to unfamiliar, tantalizing entrancements.

An even more peculiar adaptation is *The Heartbreak Kid,* which Neil Simon wrote and Elaine May directed from Bruce Jay Friedman's very short story, "A Change of Plan." The usual bad adaptation is like a bad marriage; what we have here is a bad *ménage à trois.* Clashingly thrown together are Friedman's absurdism, Elaine May's protracted monologue or duologue technique, and Neil Simon's customary farce. Some attempt at an amalgam is discernible: Simon has gone relatively easy on the gags, May has slightly shortened her cabaret routines, and Friedman has been pretty much ignored. Still, the picture does not quite know what it is doing, where it is heading, or why it is there in the first place.

What Friedman has written in an absurdly rushing style and preposterous foreshortening—rather like a comic film sequence in accelerated motion—is the account of how a young Jewish man dumps his unprepossessing bride in the middle of a Miami honeymoon to dally with a blond Minnesota hoyden and, despite the opposition of the girl's staid middle-class family and all manner of complications, manages to woo and win the midwestern nymph—

only to begin, in the middle of his second wedding, to lust after his new bride's mother. The trick—and it is a pretty feeble one in this relatively unsuccessful story—is the speed and casualness with which these bizarre yet binding events scramble on and on.

The movie had several problems: how to fill out a story of less than ten pages; how to make its outrageous events a bit more believable to suit the more fleshed-out characters; and, finally, how to introduce a little morality into this amoral tale. One method is elaborate contrast: Jewish milieu versus WASP ambience, ridiculously downgrading the former into crassness and ridiculously upgrading the latter into snobbish prissiness. But ridiculous is not necessarily funny.

The other method is provocative ambivalence. So Lenny is both a bumbling Jewish comic and a determined, persistent, ungainsayable suitor—stretching ambivalence to the point of self-contradiction. So, too, the first wife, here called Lila, has to be a nagging grotesque who is then turned into a pitiful victim—giving her supposed depth at the cost of simple believability. Friedman's middle-class Minnesota girl, Sue Ellen Parker, becomes wealthy and spoiled Kelly Corcoran, wisecracking sophisticate but also obedient, corn-fed virgin. She goes from cool *demi-vierge* to Lenny's willing bedmate and back to Daddy's docile daughter at two fell swoops. And Daddy—despotic, rocklike, near-incestuously adoring his girl, and adamantly opposed to Lenny—must paradoxically crumble into acquiescence the moment Lenny refuses to be bought off.

Among the many muddled things, the ending is muddiest. Why is Lenny, who has gone over so well with the proper Minnesotans at the wedding, suddenly left haranguing two kids who, presently, also leave? What are we to make of Lenny, forlorn and dejected, alone on a sofa as the film ends? Is it that he has bored and lost this alien world? Or that he feels out of place among these goyim? Or just that when you finally possess your hard-won dream, you no longer want it? Here, I think, the filmmakers' third device, moralizing, takes over, and they have ineptly tacked on a *Room at the Top*–style comeuppance. Incongruity has become rampant.

Elaine May's direction is uncomfortably reminiscent of Mike Nichols's, but most of the actors (except for cute Cybill Shepherd) are good or excellent, and Owen Roizman's camera work is clean and elegant. As for Neil Simon's new seriousness—I never thought it would come to my wishing he'd put back the gags.

January 8, 1973

Kid Stuff

IT'S TIME AGAIN for my annual Barbra Streisand piece. The film this time is *Up the Sandbox,* based on a novel by Anne Richardson Roiphe: I have skimmed Mrs. Roiphe's novel and find it rather less enchanting than the reviewers did in 1970. My quarrel is not with the author's anti-women's-lib orientation, but with writing that is essentially a slightly higher-brow version of women's magazine fiction. To put it bluntly, no one who can write "Motherhood is always a greedy affair and eventually the suckling-off of the suckler"—whatever the meaning of that opaque maxim may be—has an ear for the cadences of English prose.

In the novel, Margaret Reynolds is married to Paul, a brilliant young professor of history at Columbia. She has a small daughter, a baby boy, and several elaborate reveries as she sits in the park watching the children in the playground. Her humdrum life is filled with drudgery and uncertainties about her marriage and identity; her daydreams make up for this with gallant, thrilling adventures. Having just once forgotten to insert her diaphragm before intercourse, she finds that she is pregnant again; amazingly, the marriage is revitalized by this, exactly as in reams of women's fiction and hours upon hours of soap opera. Yet it must be said for Mrs. Roiphe that her fantasies retain a certain amount of restraint and dignity, and that her descriptions of life among genteel but hectic, literate but bourgeois Upper-West-Siders are possessed of a decent enough fidelity to second-rate truths.

The screenplay by Paul Zindel and the direction of Irvin Kershner, however, turn the movie into quasi-Nichols-and-May cabaret-style skits loosely linked into a sappy plot line and often collapsing into cheap farce; sometimes, too, the aim is for social significance replete with arty camera lyricism that touches the surreal. The Vietnam fantasy of the book is omitted as being, perhaps, too controversial; a rather plausibly managed Amazon exploration in the novel becomes a crude African adventure, psychologically inappropriate and not even funny. Where Mrs. Roiphe has her confused heroine imagine her seduction by a Fidel Castro who is really a woman in disguise, the movie Margaret resists the female Fidel and keeps even her id spotlessly clean.

The sequences of daily living suffer even worse. Instead of the rather quiet events of the original—the wistful speculations of a young mother who finally resigns herself to most of the donkey work her husband is spared—the movie gives us coyly virulent in-fighting, outbursts of jealousy, garish family parties, and sophisticated cosmopolitan soirées. There is also a slew of lesser fantasies such as the one where Margaret's breasts, in competition with those of an admiring, bosomy female whom Paul flirts with at a party, suddenly puff up to cantaloupe dimensions; totally ignored by Paul, they deflate themselves back to their usual size. Or there is an imaginary scene in which Margaret is awed into accepting a female professor's ongoing affair with Paul when it is couched in high academic terms. Worst of all, there is a lurid fantasy about an abortion clinic that our heroine spectacularly escapes from to have her third baby, approved now by the very husband who previously inveighed against such irresponsible overpopulation.

The movie vulgarizes away with a vengeance. Thus the book's interior monologues—Margaret's ruminations expressing a vague discontent with her life that nevertheless end in acceptance of the wife and mother's traditional role—become in the movie gab sessions with a farcical assortment of other bench-sitting mothers, ranging from bristling liberationists to adoring slaves and, of course, the obligatory black. The heroine's oppressively middle-class mother and relatives, whom the book is content to leave in a New Jersey limbo, are brought on the scene in stereotypical comedy situations, and Margaret is allowed some supposedly hilarious *mots* and tirades against them.

As the movie presents her, Margaret is the exploited worm that finally turns and asserts herself; but then her readiness to settle for a weekly day off from the kids and imminent saddling with yet another baby is a sentimentalization and falsification of the whole problem. The film therefore becomes a piece of corrupt claptrap, ostensibly chronicling the rebellion of the existentially shortchanged housewife, only to make her capitulate in a Central Park pastoral in which dialogue, photography, and especially her brains grow soft and fuzzy—and all for that one day off. Just how the busy teacher, researcher and author will manage the children is no more explained than what the wife will do with her precious chunk of emancipation.

If Zindel's script and Kershner's direction provide a fair share of meretriciousness and vulgarity, it nevertheless remains for Barbra Streisand to drag the film down to the bottom of incredibility and coarseness. The mere fact that in a family milieu as militantly Jewish as that, say, of the Cantrows and Kolodnys of *The Heartbreak Kid,* Streisand should appear as a "Margaret Reynolds" already strikes a false note. Miss Streisand comes on as fundamentally Jewish as Woody Allen, only she represents the other side of a stereotype that, like a coin, has two sides. Whereas Allen is the beleaguered, repressed, self-depreciating little man, masochistically wallowing in his littleness, weakness, homeliness, Miss Streisand is the shrewd, aggressive shrew, domineering to the point of sadism, blithely unaware of her ugliness or bullying everyone into accepting it as beauty. I think it would be nice if at least Jewish filmmakers could stop caricaturing Jews in this fashion.

Quite aside from her persona, however, I find Miss Streisand's looks repellent. Perhaps this is my limitation, but I cannot accept a romantic heroine who is both knock-kneed and ankleless (maybe one of those things, but not both!), short-waisted and shapeless, scrag-toothed and with a horse face centering on a nose that looks like Brancusi's Rooster cast in liverwurst. I believe in beauty or in a performer's ability to make herself or himself attractive in one way or another even when lacking outstanding physical endowments. Think, for example, of those English leading ladies like Celia Johnson, Dorothy Tutin, Joan Plowright, Maggie Smith, Rita Tushingham, and a host of others—plain women who, through make-up, acting ability, or, most likely, a spiritual intensity that suffuses their faces, make themselves lovely. Streisand remains arrogantly, exultantly ugly.

And she is no actress. Her speaking voice consists either of a husky stage whisper (originated by Marilyn Monroe, another nonactress parlayed into an alleged comic talent by special pleading) or a terrible fishwife's screech. In big, emotional scenes, her accent goes Lower-East-Side and completely undermines the cultivatedness she is supposed to portray or the gentility she presumes to affect. In anger, her face assumes shapes and expressions that turn a movie into a horror film. Unlike a real comedienne—Jane Fonda, for instance—she lacks the variety, modulations, little inventive eccentricities, ability to underplay that add up to genuine humor. She does not embody a part, she defies it. But she is undoubtedly a great inspiration to the legions of unsightly women whose banner she has carried to the heights of stardom and critical adulation that extends from Pauline Kael all the way to Rex Reed.

The film is photographed in overpretty, almost deliquescent colors by Gordon Willis, and in the abortion-clinic fantasy the camera and opticals run Ken-Russellish riot. The very idea of representing such a hospital, in this day and age, as a den of iniquity where patients look abject or mentally unbalanced, and the head doctor is an ominous lesbian looking and acting like a stevedore in drag, strikes me as gross reactionary propaganda.

Though some of the minor parts are well played, David Selby, as Paul, is as stiff and stilted a performer as Miss Streisand is a garishly grotesque one. The height of the ridiculous is that the African scene was actually shot in Kenya; for what registers on screen, New Jersey would have done as well. But what can you say about a film that begins with a closeup of a baby's bottom and ends with a yellow—nay, golden—cab carrying Barbra right through the middle of Central Park? Is the implication that even the rosy resolution is just a pipe dream? If so, this is a particularly sneaky way of having your happy ending and eating your words too.

Sam Peckinpah's *The Getaway* is a sourly disappointing, ugly, and unbelievable film. I am not in a high moral dudgeon about the criminal couple's getting away with their ill-gotten loot to carefree safety in Mexico, but I am disgusted with the great lack of artistry the gifted maker of *The Wild Bunch* and *Straw Dogs* exhibits in this unimaginative, preposterous film. Bank robbers, after all, do get away with it on occasion, and sympathy for the outlaw is nothing unusual in the movies, especially those of Peckinpah. The man is half Indian, and the redskin whom the paleface turned into a homeless outlaw has every right to pay back the debt with moral anomie.

Yet, unfortunately, there is more to it. There is something truly repellent about the vicious, wounded gangster who gets a veterinarian to patch him up, then abducts the fellow and his kewpie-doll wife whom he has just seduced. We are treated to a subplot in which the punk and the little woman, traveling by car and staying at hotels, variously taunt and torture the unfortunate husband. At night, they tie him to a straight chair (perhaps the only straight thing in the movie) and force him to watch them having intercourse in a comfortable bed; after a couple of days of this, he hangs himself. The filmmaker relishes the sadism much too much, and his sympathies, very clearly, are not with the victim. Also, it is no longer possible to avoid the notion that Peckinpah thinks of women as generally inferior beings who always attach themselves to the stronger and more powerful man, no matter what loyalties are betrayed, what lives destroyed.

The plot of *The Getaway* is lurid trash; the characterizations are devoid of humanity. If we care about the principals, it is only because Steve McQueen and Ali MacGraw look much better than anyone else in the film. McQueen, who does not exactly act and is rather too genteel for his part, at least has a presence: an easygoing self-assurance that stops short of cheekiness. Miss MacGraw cannot act at all. At the screening I attended, people were laughing out loud at her delivery of dramatic lines—rather like a grade-school pupil asking to be excused to go to the bathroom. Miss MacGraw, we can tell now, was a fluke in *Goodbye, Columbus,* where she played herself and was convincingly pretty, spoiled, and insecure. Here—a little older, much more smug, and not type-cast—she flounders, forlorn and simpering, and is somehow always beside the point.

The film hasn't a shred of believability. Consider, for example, the episode where hero and heroine are sucked into a large garbage truck and have every kind of metallic and other waste hurled at and heaped roof-high over them. Miraculously, they are spewed out onto a dumping ground with only a small scratch on her and no mark on him. If Peckinpah keeps piling this kind of garbage on his talents, they, alas, will not emerge similarly unscathed.

It was a bad day when the western discovered its mythic significance and its allegorical potential. Primitive art is still a humble form of art, but premeditated primitivism is pure sham. The deliberately mythic-allegoric western is like a folk song contrived by a city slicker, a naïve painting by a highly trained academician, or a sober man's attempt to recapture his drunken ebullience—it all comes out arch, brittle, contrived. This is the problem of both *The Life and Times of Judge Roy Bean* and *Jeremiah Johnson,* both with screenplays wholly or partly by John Milius. On this unsavory character, see Pauline Kael's splendid exposé in *Reeling.*

John Huston's *Bean* starts out as a sort of absurdist western and quickly deteriorates into cutie-pie bloodthirstiness and bloodcurdling allegory. *Jeremiah Johnson,* on the other hand, is a kind of Zen western, full of comic yet supposedly profound quirkiness, and ending with one more apotheosis of the justly murderous white superman. *Bean,* despite a few amusing moments, becomes wearying with its relentless striving to be offbeat, and repugnant with its hypocritical celebration of the hanging judge as a moral hero. Paul Newman's efforts notwithstanding, it remains poor stuff, undeserving of further comment; but *Jeremiah Johnson,* artfully directed by Sydney Pollack (whose *They Shoot Horses, Don't They?* was an important film), does bear some looking into.

Robert Redford portrays a soldier disgusted with the Mexican War who goes west to become a mountain man, a trapper who can ignore the vile contentiousness of the plains. He learns his trade by chance meetings with a couple of bizarre, experienced loners, and sobering encounters with various Indians and their victims. He adopts a fatherless boy and accidentally wins an Indian maiden for a wife, and begins to settle into a facsimile of bourgeois family comfort in a nice log cabin amid God's plenty. Then the army calls upon him to help rescue a stranded wagon train and, in so doing, he is obliged to violate a sacred Crow burial ground, whereupon the Crows kill his family—why them rather than him, the soldiers, or the wagon party makes no more sense than anything else in this movie. He becomes a Crow-slaying avenger, surviving countless attacks on him and killing innumerable braves.

The Crow chieftain is forced to call a truce, and a weary, battered but unbowed Jeremiah has earned his right to being a great, white, unmolested hunter.

What makes the film so absurd is that while it strives for picturesque but ostensibly demythifying realism in showing its hero bumbling his way through to survival among genuinely harsh and even harrowing conditions, it nevertheless presents a white man who can ultimately outhear, outsmell, outwit, outkill, and outlive any old Indian. The hero is your trendy dropout from bellicose, greedy society, pretentiously and improbably addressed as "Pilgrim" who, by devious and sometimes ironic ways, becomes as great a destroyer of men and beasts as anyone in the despised plains. Yet he is glorified by *faux-naïf* ballads that infest the soundtrack, and his progress is a series of seriocomic incidents that are kept calculatedly oblique, oddball, sardonic, and, above all, random, so as to maintain an aura of cosmic irony.

The only thing that escapes reprehension and ridicule is Pollack's ability to make individual scenes have an authentic look and feel to them. But the moment you start analyzing anything at all, it falls apart. And, like *Judge Roy Bean,* the film promulgates in mythico-allegorical terms the notion that in today's violent, evil world only the tough, bloody, and amoral man can carve out a quiet niche for himself.

February 5, 1973

Burning Dim

SAVE THE TIGER was written by Steve Shagan and directed by John G. Avildsen, who made *Joe* and, regrettably, *Cry Uncle.* The movie covers a day in the life of a Los Angeles Jewish garment manufacturer, one part magnate, one part idealist, and two parts desperate man barely ahead of bankruptcy, compelled to rig his books and hire an arsonist to burn down one of his factories for the insurance money. His wife goes to New York and he is lonely; an important client whom he sets up with a favorite call girl has a heart attack in mid-sex before he could put in an order; there are troubles with various associates and employees; and an all-important fashion show produces a temporary nervous breakdown. He looks back upon his fighting at Anzio as the key event of his life, but the hippie girl with whom he spends a night has never heard of our being at war with Italy. And though he repeats old baseball scores to himself as if they were Holy Writ, a bunch of happy kids in the park exclude him from their ballgame.

It is a film with good, serious intentions, and thus a somewhat touching failure. *Save the Tiger* can abjure neither sentimentality nor glamour; it cannot make its hero's disappointments and predicament unshiny or, at the very least, unexotic. And in Los Angeles, where success has a way of looking like failure, it is hard to come up with a failure that does not resemble success. Jack Lemmon's acting is good most of the way, but cannot encompass the deeper moments; writing and direction are a bit slick and predictable. Why is it so damned hard to make a grown-up film in America?

Images shows us Robert Altman at his most trivial. The film is a psychological thriller about one of those rich young women who can apparently afford the most extraordinary hallucinations and outbursts of violence without being put away. In the present case, the heroine is haunted in her isolated hunting lodge—or perhaps hounded in her haunting lodge—by the ghost of a dead lover and the presences of a weak husband and an overbearing would-be lover. These figures get confused in her imagination, so that sometimes a real person is seen by her as an unreal one, sometimes an unreal one is real, and sometimes, for all her paranoia and schizophrenia, a real one is unpleasantly real. The writer-director's game is to keep the audience guessing which of the three possibilities obtains at any given moment, the sort of game I find just a little less absorbing than tag.

To be sure, Altman decks his film out with all sorts of fancy, indeed pretentious, auditory and visual trappings. One works: the color cinematography of the astute Vilmos Zsigmond is a romantic enough rendering of the Irish countryside for the camera to have been nurtured on early Yeats. The acting is good enough for this sort of charade, though I wish that Marcel Bozzuffi's English were more penetrable and that Susannah York had not picked a moment of fairly advanced pregnancy to show herself in the nude. There is, of course, a trick ending, but after all that trick beginning and middle, it hardly registers.

Much of this stuff has been done appreciably better in Roman Polanski's *Repulsion,* although I did not care for that film, either. When I asked Altman whether he had been influenced by *Repulsion,* he said he had not seen it when he made *Images.* This has become the stock answer of filmmakers to that type of question. I wonder, don't they see any movies, or are they just fibbing?

Just about scuttled by Warner Brothers back in 1971 when it failed to impress the New York critics, *Billy Jack* has since been sweeping the country, has become a youth-cult film, and is well on its way to turning into one of the all-time box-office hits. So now Warner is giving it a big, heavily advertised première engagement in its second run.

The film, by the husband-and-wife team of Tom Laughlin and Delores Taylor, stars both of them and was directed by Laughlin. The couple previously gave us a very successful motorcycle movie, *Born Losers,* but it is with *Billy Jack* that they have hit upon the kind of archetypal trash that will make you wealthy and famous. As they proudly proclaim in the published screenplay, *Billy Jack* has become "the greatest youth-culture picture of our times."

The plot is hardly worth dwelling on. It concerns Jean, the plucky mistress of an ultra-Montessorian school for dropouts on a southwestern Indian reservation, and the hatred her long-haired pupils who are acquiring a do-it-yourself education inspire in the silent-American population of the neighboring town. Whenever the townspeople become too vicious to the pacifist teacher and her gallant brood (many of whom are Indians, Chicanos, and blacks), Billy Jack, an indomitable halfbreed Indian, appears on the scene. As Jean puts it, "We just contact him Indian style. We just want him and somehow he shows up." This combination mystic and superman can beat up a whole town when required and so save the situation. Sometimes the telepathy gets short-circuited, though, and Jean gets raped and a nice Indian boy murdered. But, in the end, Billy Jack's staunchness and Jean's nonviolence combine into a true albeit modishly muted victory.

The writing, directing, and acting are as amateurish as they are tendentious, and obviousness and preposterousness are made to go happily hand in hand. Yet a number of critics, including Pauline Kael, have given this sorry mess their more or less guarded approval. The saving grace most often cited is the film's sincerity, its genuine belief in Shoshone and Paiute mystical lore. Thus Billy, in a solemn ceremony, becomes Brother to the Snake by allowing a rattler to bite him repeatedly. He survives thanks to boundless faith and an Indian antidote, and, under the influence of his brother's venomous bite—though not with his brother's forked tongue—proceeds to preach a mystical doctrine of universal brotherhood. The school is saved, and there is hope as it turns out, even for those with short hair.

Sincerity a virtue? Almost all successful trash is as paved with sincerity as the road to hell is with good intentions. Jacqueline Susann and her ilk succeed precisely because of their sincerely naïve belief in their message and genius. This gives them that vulgar charisma that reeks of sincerity, wherever on the scale between Miss Susann and Grandma Moses it pitches its tent. *Billy Jack* is mostly Grandma Moses but with a sufficiency of Susann; it has something in it for both sincere purists and sincere impurists, provided only that they do not think.

March 19–April 2, 1973

Escapism Old and New

WELL NOW, GOOD PEOPLE, what is your candidate for the worst picture of the last year or two? I limit the time range, for there is no point in overcomplicating what is already a tough question. (If only the Oscars had such a category, a little honesty could be infused into the proceedings.) I must ask you also to restrict yourselves to so-called A-pictures, since there is no need to swat obscure, almost invisible flies. This regrettably eliminates movies like *A Place Called Today,* the one film I know of that used the same man as cinematographer and composer. You might nominate *Portnoy's Complaint* or *Play It As It Lays, Fellini's Roma* or *Pope Joan, Alex in Wonderland* or *The Spider's Stratagem,* or any number of other excellent choices. But you will sweep them all away before a contender that must have arrived in garbage rather than film cans, Ross Hunter's musicalized *Lost Horizon.*

Hunter, I agree for once with Judith Crist, is perhaps the only man around who would remake a 1937 movie into a 1932 one. The picture clearly should be called *Shangri-la Melody* or *Lullaby of Shangri-la,* and when you consider that it cost six million dollars to produce and makes *The Sound of Music* look like *La Règle du jeu,* you will have to admit that never was tackiness purchased at a greater cost. The story itself—one of genteel escapism from a Hitler-threatened world—was appropriate trash for 1937; the correct equivalent for 1973 is not to turn James Hilton's Shangri-la into the Shangri-la Hilton, but to cough up something like *Godspell.* But let's not anticipate.

The solitary honest moment in *Lost Horizon* occurs when Peter Finch as Conway, the idealistic hero, remarks to his Shangri-la schoolmarm-sweetheart, Liv Ullmann, "I am certain there is a wish for Shangri-la in every man's heart," that all good people "secretly wish they were in a beautiful place like this." "Well, if they were," she replies, "it wouldn't be beautiful for long."

Even the average American might catch this fatal glimpse of truth: the earthly paradise is no longer paradise when the many invade it; wherever hordes come hurtling toward Shangri-la, Shangri-la is defiled, devaluated, and ceases to be. The basic absurdity of Hilton's novel is that if humanity outside the ring of magic mountains were to destroy itself, the blessed valley would surely not be large enough to contain all the righteous. Moreover, the children of the elect would have to leave the tiny paradise and, presumably, form another mutually destructive race in a less miraculous climate. Even utopian thinking nowadays realizes that it cannot lead people to an outside paradise; it must create paradise inside man, here and everywhere. The current escapism is inward rather than outward.

What this movie offers looks like a composite of various old, exotic Hollywood sets and a number of the more pretentious Bel-Air interiors. Since the one law that governs Shangri-la is "Be kind!" there is, clearly, no need for science, art, or good taste in the place. Its one library consists of books that are manifestly not read by anyone; there is an obvious class system but no technology; there are obliging women to carry water on their backs; and the clothes, like the furnishings, are stunningly garish. Women, by the way, exhibit no flesh, however warm it may get; men, however, are revealingly stripped for a scarf dance ludicrously choreographed by Hermes Pan. At least, they are described as "the men of Shangri-la," though they appear to have been hand-picked for purposes of population control.

Everything about this Shangri-la looks like a set; even the books in that library (designed, it seems, more for dancing than for reading) are all leather-bound sets—only authors of Collected or Complete Works are chosen by the lamasery (lamaserialized?). Ross Hunter has declared that all the flowers in the film were real; and so, perhaps, they were until the set decorator, director, and cinematographer got through with them, by which time they looked like perfect imitations. One of Hunter's earlier films, incidentally, was a remake of *Imitation of Life,* an imitation of an *Imitation.*

Not only Hunter's films are synthetic; so, too, are his name (really Martin Fuss), his hair, and, as far as I could glean from one conversation, his mind. His favorite boasts are that he does not allow sex, nudity, or four-letter words in his movies, and that he gives the public what it wants. That may indeed be so, but I am more convinced that he gives them what *he* wants, and honest-to-goodness sex and a little racy talk would be much too real for him. I hear that he collects glass and ceramic lemons; and, truly, the lemons he has been producing do not even have the juice of life.

Charles Jarrott, the director, has already given us two paltry historical spectaculars, *Anne of the Thousand Days* and *Mary, Queen of Scots;* he now proves equally gifted with the ahistoric spectacular. For, to be able to elicit a non-performance from an actress as good as Liv Ullmann—worse yet, to make her look totally unattractive—is a spectacular achievement all right. To be sure, everyone in the movie manages to look silly, although John Gielgud succeeds in making Chang, the Oxford-educated Assistant High Lama, amusing in a campy way, and Peter Finch knows how to look intelligent even while forced to sing (or to have someone's voice sing through his face) such stuff as "Will I find/There is really such a thing/As peace of mind?" and "Have I found Shangri-la/Or has it found me?" Burt Bacharach's tunes and orchestrations, I hasten to add, are every bit as vulgar as Hal David's lyrics. One feels surrounded by idiocy and the crassest fakery—transported, in fact, into the heart of Nixon's America.

The script sinks to the illiteracy of "When you lay down to sleep," and has poor Finch say "I am desperately trying to keep my emotional feelings and my spiritual needs from clobbering each other to death." This drivel—including the subliterate tautology of "emotional feelings"—was concocted by Larry Kramer, who wrote the screenplay for *Women in Love,* which might cause admirers of that movie to ask themselves some belated questions. The only question I ask is: Will *Lost Horizon* be a financial success? If so, there may be some hope for the American movie industry, but none whatever for American moviegoers. They will be clobbered to insensibility not only by emotional feelings and spiritual needs, but also by mental vacuity.

April 16, 1973

Fake Antique

WITH *Paper Moon,* Peter Bogdanovich continues his progress into the past. Not a real past that he knew or creatively imagined, but the past of trashy old movies that he religiously lapped up as a buff and now proudly regurgitates as a director. If *The Last Picture Show* was Bogdanovich's *King's Row,* and *What's Up, Doc?* his *Bringing Up Baby, Paper Moon* is, as Vincent Canby correctly diagnosed, his *Little Miss Marker.* That, of course, is oversimplification; our fan-turned-filmmaker has ingested enough Hollywood trivia to be able to cough up artful syntheses of scenes from scores of movies, some known to most of us, and some that only an Andrew Sarris could extract from his own comparable grab bag. But as long as Bogdanovich can remold the old genres he knows by heart (he is said to be planning a John Wayne western next—

clearly, there is a Ford in his future), he may prosper: the public's appetite for updated yet nostalgically backward-harking kitsch remains hearty.

Even so, he may get his comeuppance. Either he may run out of his borrowed tricks, or he may, puffed up with the arrogance he flaunts in interviews and on talk shows, attempt something on his own hook, for which there is no clear antecedent. Something like that, in fact, happened with his first, unremunerative film, *Targets.* In *Paper Moon,* however, he is playing it safe. There is, first of all, plenty of jolly nostalgia for the thirties—indeed, the credits list almost as many old radio performers and recording artists as they do names of present actors and technicians who worked on the film. Hardly a minute goes by without a display of some vintage Nehi poster, cigarette package, railway ticket, popular song or radio show—the latter two usually cut off after a while to give a sense of them as airy fragments wispily haunting our recollection.

But if you want nostalgia of a harsher sort, you are treated to images of slatternly, rural graveyards, with ramshackle tombstones looking like scattered corpses; or to views of *Grapes of Wrath*-like Okies struggling grimly along desolate, dusty roads; or to pious, impoverished widows on whose gullibility the film's hero preys. For Mose Pray is a fake Bible salesman (his favorite among many petty larcenies) extorting modest sums from the newly bereaved by a conman's trick. Seen against a stark yet comical Kansas background, Pray's prayerful preying is supposed to charm us: it is such small, naïve, almost bumbling conmanship and, in the Depression, a well-nigh acceptable form of survival of the fittest.

Almost accidentally, Mose finds himself stuck with nine-year-old Addie, an orphan whose illegitimate father he may have been. Addie bullies Mose into not sending her off to her relatives in Missouri, and soon exhibits a greater shrewdness than his, both for humbugging people and for keeping the ill-gotten gains prudently and parsimoniously stashed away in a cigar box—a real Bogdanovichian period piece of a cigar box, of course. More than merely Mose's accomplice, she becomes a strategist, bailer-out in tight spots, treasure of a treasurer, and moral influence as she jealously breaks up his dalliances with floozies. A reverse-parental relationship results, not unlike that between Chaplin's Tramp and the Kid, and there is hardly a parent or kid in the audience whose emotions are not preyed on by this claptrap.

For claptrap it is. The child is much too clever for her age, and the adult is rather too dumb for a man supposedly living by his wits. Thus Mose falls for an obvious trollop and carries on about her as if she were a real lady, although he is presented as a man who has casually consumed his share of tarts. But getting him deeply involved with Trixie Delight gives Bogdanovich and his scenarist, Alvin Sargent, a chance to show off Addie as a mini-machiavel, which is too good to miss even if it is too good to be true. Altogether, the movie is perfectly happy running from tearjerker to comic strip and back, and the devil take the hindmost.

The black-and-white cinematography by Laszlo Kovacs has its moments of truth, but also others that are patently showy—such as a picnic by a solitary, stunted tree; or a road that is, by some kind of trickery, seen winding into infinity and looks like that cartoon road along which the Roadrunner eludes his eternal antagonist, the Coyote. The acting is rather cartoonish on the whole, especially that of Madeline Kahn and Burton Gilliam; as for Ryan O'Neal, he simply depends on his youthful good looks. But his little daughter Tatum is quite an actress already; what merits the film does have are largely hers.

June 11, 1973

Games People Shouldn't Play

LET ME SAY AS LITTLE as possible about Sam Peckinpah's latest, *Pat Garrett and Billy the Kid.* It has obviously been cut and recut by Jim Aubrey (who deserves to be made an honorary or, rather, dishonorable member of the film editors' union), and no less than six names are credited with the film's editing. Ever since *Major Dundee,* Peckinpah has been denied the final cut for one reason or another. But things have reached a point where I no longer care: the present film could not have been that much better in any version, for what is left is unremittingly trashy, obvious, or pointless, defiantly irrational or doggedly repetitious. Some of it Peckinpah has done very much better before; the rest of it should not have been perpetrated once.

Though I pass over most of it in silence, I must mention the appalling dual presence of Bob Dylan: on film, as a puny and expressionless nonactor; on the soundtrack, as the fabricator of abysmal lyrics and tunes. He plays a supposedly mysterious character named Alias—a clumsy steal from Eugene Loring's ballet *Billy the Kid* to Copland's score. There Alias was the collective name for Billy's victims, the same dancer dying and rising again, to symbolize the nemesis that Billy, try as he may, cannot wipe out. Here the name and character of Alias are beyond comprehension.

I am forced to conclude that Peckinpah is a man lacking taste and perhaps intelligence, but gifted with a fine cinematic sensibility. When his scenarist is good, the results can be impressive; when, like Rudolph Wurlitzer in the present case, he is incompetent, the film will be a mess. Even a concurrent low-budget film on the youth of Billy, by two ad men, Charles Moss and Stan Dragoti (the latter of whom directed), is more effective; entitled *Dirty Little Billy,* it has a somewhat simplistic debunking purpose, rather trying at times, but not outright boring.

An extraordinarily distasteful film, *The Last of Sheila,* marks the joint screenwriting debut of Stephen Sondheim, the Broadway lyricist-composer, and Anthony Perkins, the movie star. Both scenarists are devotees of games and puzzles, and the entire film is a series of involved charades, double- and triple-bottomed conundrums, some of which may make sense but are impossible to keep up with, others of which can be followed but do not make the slightest sense. Several of these games are supposed to solve a mysterious death; several elicit further killings requiring more unscrambling. Sense, I repeat, is scarce; probability nonexistent; but nastiness of a peculiarly smug and condescending sort is absolutely omnipresent.

James Coburn is a sadistic producer whose mistress Sheila has been killed by a hit-and-run driver. He invites the suspects to his yacht off Cannes for a week of exacting games that are supposed to unearth the truth. At any rate, they are to reveal some ugly hidden facts about the players who, for inconceivable reasons, consent to play. They are Richard Benjamin, a hack screenwriter, and Joan Hackett, his rich wife; James Mason, a movie director on the skids, and Dyan Cannon, a maliciously wisecracking talent agent; Raquel Welch, a rising movie star, and Ian McShane, the gigolo whom she is keeping. Each, it seems, is modeled on a real-life person, and an additional unsavory game is for the audience to figure out on whom.

It is all attitudinizing—for we are to consider these characters horribly fascinating, whereas they are merely mildly clever bores; self-serving—because Sondheim and Perkins, show-business celebrities, are touting the glamour of showbiz celebs; pretentious—for we are to view maniacal game-players not as immature but as an intellectual elite; and hopelessly trivial—because not even a decent thriller comes of it. Yet there is worse: a genuine ugliness and unhealthiness. Every relationship shown is based on petty or sadistic mutual humiliation and cruelty, and the final good takes the form of blackmailing the murderer out of his millions, letting the creature dangle forever at the end of a string, and royally screwing the rest of the world. Thus the difference between moral acceptability and insufficiency is simply that between a successful and an unsuccessful criminal.

The direction by Herbert Ross and the acting by an all-second-rate-star cast (except for James Mason, who was once first-rate) ranges from slick to inept. Dyan Cannon is getting more repulsive with every appearance, James Coburn more stuck in a tooth-flashing rut, and Raquel Welch more unable to cope with the rudiments of acting. Ian McShane and Mason have a few better-than-average moments, and Richard Benjamin is surprisingly inoffensive. But the hollow ostentation and epicene bitchiness of *The Last of Sheila* more than make up for that.

July 9, 1973

Mortal Coyles

The Friends of Eddie Coyle is a rather accomplished gangster movie. Even the fact that it takes place in Boston may add a little class to it. Eddie Coyle (Robert Mitchum) is a smalltime crook who cannot afford the two years of prison he faces for transporting stolen whisky in his truck because his wife and children would have to go on welfare. He has had his hard times: every bone in his hand was once broken by some vengeful associates in crime, and he has served time before. Now he is over fifty and trying to live more or less straight—except for a little dealing in stolen guns, where, however, he is strictly a go-between—not even the middleman, but a sort of middleman's middleman. After all, man cannot live by trucking alone.

Peter Yates's film, based on a novel by George V. Higgins (said to be dry, tough, stark) and a script by Paul Monash, is effectively gray despite the color photography. Victor J. Kempner always struck me as a drab color cinematographer, and here his limitations become a virtue. The locales around Boston are well chosen: they have flavor but are not self-consciously atmospheric. The pacing is good, the continuity tidy, the dialogue convincingly puny yet also racy. The various criminal life-styles are deftly sketched in; there is a rising action and a haunting sense of injustice as the more likable crooks get it in the neck while the archvillains prosper. And police tactics are revealed in all their plodding shabbiness and fallibility. Why then is all this merely not boring instead of gripping?

The reason is the twofold undercutting of Eddie: first, the plot is allowed to stray too far from him, so that for long stretches we are more involved with a cool, swinging stolen-gun-seller (juicily underplayed by Steven Keats), or with the mechanics of bank robbery as performed by Scalise's gang, in which, again, Eddie is not directly involved. Second, Eddie is not—whether as played by Mitchum, or else as conceived by the novelist, scenarist, and director—an absorbing enough character.

There are three ways of making a gangster or hoodlum interesting. The chap may be a dazzling master criminal whose intellect fascinates us while we are also eager to learn what minor oversight, trick of chance, or unexpected bit of humanity will bring low that computerized mind. Or the fellow may be a creepily spellbinding psychotic (in the Richard Widmark–George Macready–Robert Hossein tradition) whose vicious doings we watch as the Hellenes watched their tragic heroes, for perhaps only in this kind of supreme, mad evil can pure individuality still assert itself today—hence the spell cast by a Charles Manson. Or the criminal may be shown as intensely human (ourselves but for the grace of God), good, chivalrous, responsible underneath his unfortunate deviation into crime. The grand master of this humane criminality was and is Jean Gabin—no supercrook, only an ordinary, passionate, suffering human being. But Mitchum is a little too ordinary, softpedaled, and victimized to compel identification with him. At best, he is pitiable; Gabin, at the right moment, would have been tragic.

Two other films are worth noting here for their curiously timely complementariness. In *Shaft in Africa* (written and directed by whites), the blacks are braver, finer, more civilized, and more beautiful than the whites, most of whom are fools, psychos, or swine. Shaft, the black private eye, makes mincemeat of the white villains, except when they are attractive women—in which case he beds them and lets some evil white make mincemeat of them. Shakespeare, he tells us, was a johnny-come-lately: Africans were grooving on poetry a thousand years before.

In the latest James Bond film, *Live and Let Die,* all the villains are black and 007 makes mincemeat of them, except when they are to be bedded down first—in which case some evil black makes mincemeat of them. It is interesting to see black and white trash run side by side and neck and neck, as it were, in brotherly competition. Guy Hamilton's Bond film is the better of the two, but it lacks such historic insights as when Shaft tells a French police inspector: "Listen, you motherfucker, my people were building churches when yours were still living in caves."

July 23, 1973

Yesterday's Gardenias

LOOKING BACKWARD IS ONE THING; looking backward while pretending you're looking straight ahead is quite another and worse matter. *A Touch of Class* is a mildly funny and fiercely dishonest little film that clearly thinks it is telling a timeless tale in strictly up-to-date terms. What it is really, though perhaps unconsciously, doing is reshuffling a hoary Hollywood formula to conform to so-called contemporary standards of medium-fast living, and not offend seriously even the most delicate, antiquated sensibilities.

Steve Blackburn is an American marine insurance adjustor working in a gorgeous London office overlooking the Thames. (What an American is doing there can be explained only by saying that George Segal couldn't have played the part as an Englishman.) During a jolly softball session in Hyde Park, he "meets cute" a divorced Englishwoman, Vicki Allessio, by knocking down her child. She is a divorcée and working in fashion design, for both of those reasons frankly in need of a man; he has a nice wife, two nice kids, one nice dog, but . . . Anyway, soon he is in Marbella for a week investigating an accident at sea and Vicki is with him. They are on their own sexual collision course with problems like a married couple, friends of Steve's, watching and butting in; a dislocated back that temporarily puts Steve out of amatory commission; and one of those nonstop mutual heckling contests that couples in thirties and forties movies were always engaged in.

For this film by Melvin Frank and Jack Rose, two old Hollywood hands (sometimes spelled "hacks"), is really a forties movie where adultery was taboo, and the screenwriters' entire ingenuity, such as it was, was taken up with devising ways to postpone—never mind interrupt—the coitus until ninety minutes of film could elapse and the would-be lovers could part as cute as they met. Or, alternatively, if the picture was "serious," they could part bittersweetly and tearfully. But the sanctity of marriage had to remain as inviolate as the realms of truth, whose very threshold these pictures were careful never to darken. In *A Touch of Class,* adultery—prudently, only on the man's side (boys will be boys!)—must finally be accosted, but it must happen late and soon turn elegiac.

When the couple set up a home away from home in Soho, things must proceed comically yet charmingly just long enough to establish that the two really love each other, that theirs was no casual tumbling into bed. Presently, however, things must deteriorate, until a definitive break becomes inevitable, even if, as shown, it makes no sense. For Steve seems not to care a rap about his wife and children, who are ciphers anyway, whereas he and Vicki appear to be perfect for each other. But we must not stretch middle America's new-found elasticity too far: Steve must go back to his family, the culprits must cleanse their souls with condign freshets of tears, and Vicki must, in a new encounter, refuse another married man.

To make it all contemporary and sophisticated, the film must be crowded with marginal sexuality and sexual innuendo; but for the sake of universal endorsement—and also because Glenda Jackson, who plays Vicki, is so homely all over—as little bare flesh and sex as possible must be shown. A homosexual character is presented in the typically bifurcated way of this movie: part of the time he is allowed the dignity of a witty personage at ease with his deviant sexuality; part of the time he is still a silly swish of the Franklin Pangborn vintage. Even if they dared to be of our day, these screen-writers wouldn't know how.

At a crucial point in the film, Steve and Vicki weepily watch *Brief Encounter* on television. This is not merely an *hommage;* it is the filmmakers' (Melvin Frank also directed) attempt to forestall charges of flagrant derivativeness: their hope that by admitting it, they can get people to call it a variation on a theme. They might have gone farther and shown us the lovers, on another night, watching *Private Lives,* for this, too, has heavily influenced the movie. There is, in fact, nothing original about *A Touch of Class;* even the jokes are recognizable variants of old gags. It may be that all jokes are, but in a new context they can at least acquire a fresh sparkle; here we laugh guiltily like men caught in a brothel hoping that those who caught us will themselves feel too ashamed to snitch. A typical gag has Vicki, trying to cook supper, knock on the door of the hooker upstairs; "Do you have oregano?" "I hope not," comes the reply, "I just had a checkup last week."

A cheap film, then, but slickly made, its tired jests about complicated gearshifts (are gearshifts ever that complicated?) and fights over who'll sleep on which side of the bed (do people really fight over such things?) given a bit of new life by the very able acting of Glenda Jackson and George Segal, and a good supporting cast, in which Paul Sorvino, playing a slightly updated Jack Carson part, is outstanding. Miss Jackson is a bit on the crude side, as is her wont, yet she is masterly with both comic and pathetic exasperation. George Segal is always George Segal, but he is getting to be very good at that.

In fact, this summer marks, I believe, the definitive emergence of Segal as a star; he is equally winning in Paul Mazursky's odious film, *Blume in Love.* What makes the actor so likable despite his lack of versatility (he cannot even get rid of a slight Jewish inflection) and his rather undistinguished looks (his head, for instance, is much too big for his body) is that he falls exactly midway between Robert Redford and Woody Allen, between virile hand-someness and amusingly hangdog schnookiness. If you blink as you look at him, he is dashing enough for women to crave and men to envy him; at a closer look, men can feel comfortable and women motherly. Segal wins both coming and going. But he is also a decent enough, hard-working actor whose face can sustain tricky grimaces for a long time, and is good at rapid or slow dissolves into quite antithetical expressions.

August 6, 1973

The Lamentations of Jeremy

SMALL FILMS, inexpensively and independently made, have great appeal: one looks to them as a promising alternative to mass-produced mammoths from the big studios, especially when they do not come from the trendy, narcissistic, obscurantist underground cinema. *Jeremy* ought to fill the bill: it was made locally by the writer-director Arthur Barron, who teaches film at Columbia and created quite a stir with his TV documentary on birth and death. The fact that Joseph Brooks, who wrote one of the film's songs, claims to be a co-author, need not detain us here.

Jeremy is a New York high-school sophomore, artistically and intellectually inclined, who falls in love with a new girl at school: a junior and a transfer student from Detroit. He is shy and bungling about getting to know this older girl, but his talent as a cellist and her interest in becoming a ballet dancer bring them together. They become friends, then happy lovers; but Susan's father gets another job and takes his daughter back home with him. Heartbreak, and end of film.

As you can guess, the movie deals with the basic problems and relationships of adolescence, one of the oldest topics going, and thus requiring a maximum of honesty, perspicacity, and freshness of outlook. Otherwise, even if it manages to avoid the more obvious traps of the cliché, the sentimental, and the maudlin, it is apt to collapse under the weight of all that competition from previous literature, drama, and film. One good thing can be said for Barron right away: he does not make it easy for himself by inventing a blood feud between the families or giving one of the youngsters an incurable disease. A father who left a Detroit ad agency under a cloud is exonerated and recalled from his temporary job in New York to an even better one in Detroit—that is all. It may smack a little of a plot device, but does not strain our credulity unduly.

Still, what is *Jeremy* really about? Is it about being a teen-aged boy and girl together in an era when high-school kids quite naturally have sexual intercourse? Or is it about the unsettledness of contemporary existence, whereby two adolescents who love each other sensitively and deeply, and might even grow into spouses, are suddenly and irrevocably torn asunder? These are two major and separate problems, and demand, each of them, pretty nearly full-scale attention. Either we should have seen how the kids live with and fight for their precocious, city-buffeted love, or the shock of parting should not have been delayed till nearly the end of the picture, so that its effects and aftereffects cannot be adequately explored.

A great artist—can it be often enough repeated?—makes his own rules, and gets away with murder, or incurable diseases, or the most extraordinary coincidences. Such a one could have carried off *Jeremy*'s asymmetrically bipartite construction. Barron, though, leaves us feeling slightly cheated. For example, when Susan's father is amazed at her taking their return home so badly, and remarks that she has hardly known this Jeremy, the girl, without a moment's hesitation, blurts out the exact number of weeks and days she has been seeing him. Perfect. When Jeremy's more "experienced" classmate Ralphie (a bit of a stock character altogether) thinks there is nothing to asking the "older" girl out for a date, Jeremy remonstrates: "She probably expects me to be interesting," which rings wonderfully true and is nicely ironic to boot, Jeremy being so unusual.

But now take this exchange: "SUSAN: Someday I'll find out who I am. Do you know who you are?—JEREMY: Sometimes." I do not believe this. It may well be what the kids are thinking or, more precisely, feeling; yet it is expressed much too abstractly, too theoretically. On the whole, the growing love between the kids is very well handled, but their relationship to the world and sense of themselves is rather less surely grasped. The parents, in particular, seem unduly petty and plodding; their lack of communication with their children would be much more gripping if it occurred inevitably, in spite of genuine sympathy rather than as here, because of narrow-mindedness or self-absorption.

Especially unconvincing is the kindly, aging music teacher who gives Jeremy cello lessons. The casting of Leonardo Cimino, a second-generation Italian-American and third-rate actor, is typical of a certain carelessness that informs this movie, for the bookshelves in the musician's apartment display Peter Altenberg, Rilke's *Rodin* in German, Burnshaw's *The Hebrew Poem Itself,* and other items denoting a first-generation Austrian or German Jew, a type of displaced Central European intellectual whom the rather mafioso-like Cimino doesn't begin to suggest. And such feeble lines of his as "The music expresses life. Play it that way!" do not help—unless intended as parody, which, clearly, they are not.

What it comes down to is that when you are dealing with such simple, elemental, prototypical subjects, you have to be absolutely, nail-on-the-head right, and Barron (or whoever—even the boy who plays Jeremy claims to have contributed two key scenes) misses too often. Moreover, the cinematography by Paul Goldsmith, who almost certainly had to shoot this in 16 mm, emerges as unimpressive; in view of all that straining after urban pastoral effects, this becomes quite a drawback. The two songs are abominations ("Jeremy, your love for me/Awakened the woman asleep in myself;/Now she is lost to you, to me . . ."), and there is altogether too much manipulativeness in the script. Thus Jeremy invariably picks the winners in horse races but never actually bets (why, since he is infallible?); he loves and plays classical music soulfully, but listens to rock while doing his homework; he is scared witless of making a date with Susan, yet a couple of weeks later makes flawless love to her; he studies hard and gets top grades, but is also a hell of a basketball player, and so on.

Nevertheless, the film has its charming or moving scenes, not the least because the principals, Robby Benson and a newcomer, Glynnis O'Connor, are so natural, persuasive, and winning. And, as Roger Greenspun correctly noted, the film is ultimately saved from the slickness it flirts with by the roughness and amateurishness it cannot quite escape. In the end, you do feel that categorical severance as strongly as, before, you felt the fumbling grace. You are moved, though not, as in true art, illuminated and transfigured. But certainly moved.

September 3, 1973

Faith, Hope, and Charity

BY NOW, I suppose, everyone has encountered *Jesus Christ Superstar* as a best-selling record album, a lavishly tasteless Broadway musical, or one of those sundry traveling companies that performed this self-styled "rock opera" in concert style. Norman Jewison, who scored a hefty hit with his overblown movie version of *Fiddler on the Roof,* must have been casting about for an even bigger Jewish musical—with ecumenical values, of course—and what better property to acquire for actual filming in the Holy Land? Since *Jesus Christ Superstar* is a youth show, it would bring in the young; since it takes place in Israel, it would draw the Jewish audience; since it deals with Christ somewhat radically—at least enough so to have earned picketing by and protests from various religious groups—it may be counted on to lure the more inquisitive Christians; and since the record sold millions of copies, providing many a household with wall-to-wall trumpeting, it ought to bring in all those who, according to the immortal P. T. Barnum, are born one every minute.

As a body who considered the rock opera mostly throwaway din, and the Broadway show a throwback to the megatherium, I would say that the movie version is—although in many ways odious and in all ways absurd—better than either of those. The reason has to do with those sprawling yet also towering sandstone formations that look like the discarded works of Le Corbusier, the melancholy ruined columns that sprout from the desert like a lost patrol of the Roman legions, and the surreally bizarre under-sand caverns and oubliettes that either nature or the clever production designer, Richard MacDonald, has come up with. These are among the principal backgrounds for the film, nourishing at least the eye while the mind is starved and the ear force-fed to bursting.

It is not in the name of religion that the film should be faulted. If this Christ has among his followers nothing but cavorting Jesus freaks, making him a kind of Pied Piper of Hamelin and the entry into Jerusalem a children's crusade, this is not, in itself, an impious variation on the theme. Pier Paolo Pasolini, in his vastly superior movie, *The Gospel According to St. Matthew,* made Christ into a furibund Marxist revolutionary, yet the Pope was, by all accounts, pleased as Punch: not only was there no ban by the Vatican, the film actually copped a number of Catholic awards. Besides, Jewison and his coscenarist, Melvyn Bragg, covered themselves by presenting the cast of characters first as a busload of itinerant players coming to perform the story of the Seven Last Days on native ground. Though this humble framing device reappears at the end, things in between become pretty cosmic, with some virtually metaphysical Todd-AO 35 sunsets and sunrises—to say nothing of the Israeli Tank Corps and Air Force—contributing their eschatological services.

Cautiously, too, the movie departs from Tom O'Horgan's more controversial stage version in that it makes the relationship between Christ and Mary Magdalene no longer carnal but, if I may mix my Hebraism and Hellenism, platonic; and though Herod's entourage still boasts some campy, epicene figures, it is no longer a hotbed of mincing transvestism. In fact, the entire story is presented without any original point of view, the only slightly significant departure being Christ's virtually provoking and coercing Judas into betraying him so as to fulfill the grand design. But I doubt if, at this late date, that is likely to give rise to a new heresy or serious schism.

No, the offense is of a different order. It is, first, in the text, which is faithfully that of Tim Rice for the "rock opera," and translates the sublime prose of the gospels into witless doggerel. "Listen, Jesus, I don't like what I see/ All I ask is that you listen to me," Judas expostulates with his master; whereas Mary Magdalene pleads with the weary Jesus: "Close your eyes, close your eyes and relax/ Think of nothing tonight." Caiaphas concedes: "One thing I'll say for him:/ Jesus is cool!" while his fellow priests complain of "A man who is bigger than John was/ When he did his baptism thing." The apostles chant, somewhat anacoluthically, "Always hoped that I'd be an apostle,/ Knew that I would make it if I tried;/ Then when we retire, we can write the gospels,/ So they'll still talk about us when we've died." Jesus himself gives out with things like "Then I was inspired,/ Now I'm sad and tired" and "My time is almost through,/ Little left to do. . . ." As Judas puts it to Jesus, "But every word you say today/ Gets twisted round some other way," which will also serve as a fair description of Tim Rice's lyric-writing.

But if the words are all bad—sounding like the unholy writ of Edgar Guest in collaboration with Norman Vincent Peale—the music by Andrew Lloyd Webber is not *all* deafening commonplaces. Though it is not exactly the kind of rock you can build a church on—sometimes, in fact, it sounds like recycled Massenet—it does have its tuneful or rousing moments. These, unfortunately, tend to succumb to Rob Iscove's choreography, which fluctuates between show-biz ethnic and discothèque disheveled, either because the choreographer cannot think bigger or because the likable performing amateurs could not do better. Yet the supreme failure is the director's own for trying to fill in the vacuity of the material with desperate stratagems of montage and camera trickery, and by feverishly latching on to bits of contemporary relevance that no other cat would have dragged in.

So during the endless procession of song-and-dance numbers the camera incessantly vomits up its entire repertoire of jump cuts, zoomings in and out, telephoto lensing, freeze shots, superimpositions, crane and helicopter shots, lap dissolves, slow motion (in which, for instance, Jesus is scourged, thus simultaneously flogging the Savior and a dead horse) and other such paraphernalia calculated to detract our attention from all that isn't there as well as the little that is. Once or twice the montage actually works, as when Jewison cuts from frantic followers' hands jigging toward Christ to Christ's face in closeup, thence to a flock of vultures wheeling in an etiolated sky, and, again, to a covey of black-robed priests buzzing all over a scaffolding like a colony of hypertrophic rooks. Or, again, later, when Douglas Slocombe's camera swoops across those highly sculptural mesas while a lone trumpet ululates on the sound track.

But even such rare felicities are soon devaluated by iteration. Then other kinds of trickery are summoned to the fore. The Temple is now no longer infested merely with moneylenders: all sorts of modern products, from postcards to machine guns, are being marketed here. Instead of lashing out at people, Jesus takes an ax to these consumer goods, an edulcoration meant to placate people-loving but possession-lacking flower children. At one point, Judas is chased through the desert by five tanks with ithyphallic turret guns (shades of a marvelous scene from *Ballad of a Soldier,* from which this is probably cribbed); later he is very nearly mowed down by low-flying jet fighters, a sequence so incongruous as to be explicable only as an inducement for us to sell more planes to Israel as long as they are going to be put to such peaceable, histrionic uses. Another time, Jewison introduces out of nowhere a fast montage of famous pictorial representations of Christ through the ages, a sequence that might well be used as a rapid identification test in a survey course in fine arts, but is jarringly pretentious here.

The ear, however, gets assaulted worse than the eye. Overamplification, which seems to be not so much the occupational hazard of rock musicals as their very *raison d'être,* exacts a heavy toll. Whether it is Carl Anderson, the otherwise rather personable Judas, shrilling away in a falsetto to drive dogs rabid; or Ted Neeley, the otherwise handsome and dignified young Christ, leading the Jesus freaks with his high-treble Jesus squeaks; or whether it is merely André Previn conducting the orchestra in Webber's own arrangements (which have a way of sounding like an aural salad doused with three different kinds of dressing), the ear is put through such a wringer that, on the rare, brief occasions when the sound track shuts up, the silence seems not just golden, but positively platinum.

There is, needless to say, no such thing as acting in a film like this, but much depends on the performer's ability to look and sound right, and to strike the proper attitude. In this respect, the already mentioned Neeley and Anderson are fine; Barry Dennen's Pilate, Bob Bingham's Caiaphas, and Kurt Yaghjian's Annas, perfect; but Yvonne Elliman's Magdalene, though she sounds lovely, looks like someone who could do much better business as a saint than as a whore. The acting fiasco of the film, though, is Josh Mostel's Herod, who allows the work's best number, the campy Charleston with which the Jewish king taunts the King of the Jews, to fall as flat as the stylish marina on which the number is performed. Young Mr. Mostel, who manages the difficult feat of reaching the grotesque while totally bypassing the funny, has not inherited any of the Mostel from his father, only the Zero.

Jesus Christ Superstar ends with a faintly stylized cross silhouetted against a gorgeous Palestinian sunset even as the bus with the Passion players regretfully leaves the Holy Land—as if to remind us that this venture, so far from being any kind of spiritual exploration, is just a giant FitzGerald Travelogue. Some six decades ago, the distinguished German aesthetician Konrad Lange accused the then nascent world film production of being in the hands of "semieducated, aesthetically feelingless, ethically indifferent, in short, spiritually inferior people," and as one watches this movie, it would be hard to disagree. It is extremely doubtful even whether one can forgive them because, as the King James version had it, they know not what they do, or, as the present text prosaicizes it, they don't know what they're doing.

George Lucas, who made *American Graffiti,* previously showed high promise with the two versions of *THX 1138,* a science-fiction film the young director first made in short form while he was still a graduate student and film instructor at U.S.C. In this his second feature, he re-creates his final high-school days when many a graduating Heracles found himself at the crossroads between college somewhere far away and slipping into a more or less plausible job right there in the Bay Area. It is 1962, still the period of ducktail and flattop hairstyles, ponytails and pleated skirts, sock hops and nighttime cruising about in chrome-smothered cars; of groups like The Beach Boys, The Platters, Flash Cadillac and The Continental Kids; of no political commitment, and action in Vietnam as unheard of as the Punic Wars.

Before you dismiss the film automatically as nostalgia (assuming, that is, that there are still people left who dismiss nostalgia rather than lapping it up), let me hasten to say that it does not do what your standard nostalgia vehicle does: it implies neither that things were ever so much rosier in those wonderful days, nor that they were so sidesplittingly idiotic that we must love them for their campy, absurd charm like Gibson Girl calendars or tap-dancing Pullman-porter dolls. Lucas and his coscriptwriters, Gloria Katz and Willard Huyck, merely ask us to look at this period with judicious amusement, affectionately yet critically aware that though its follies were different, they were neither bigger nor smaller than ours are today.

The movie concerns four boys on their last Friday night together in a small northern California town. Steve, a Jack Armstrong figure, good-looking in a Norman Rockwellish way, was the president of his graduating class; he is all set for his departure tomorrow for an Eastern college. Curt is the nice, somewhat dopey-looking class intellectual; having won a fellowship from the local Elks, he too is off to the same Eastern college, but rather unsure about whether he'll catch that plane. Big John is the town's drag-racing champion and drives "a '32 custom Ford deuce coupe" as the official synopsis puts it (I wouldn't know—to me it's just a fancy hot rod); he is a ladies' man, the "grown-up" of the group who disdains such perpetuations of puerility as going away to college. Terry is a year younger and homely, and hero-worships the others, for which Steve gives him the use of his grand Impala while he is away. During the night, the four boys cruise around separately, some with old girl friends they are about to leave behind, some with potential new ones they chase after or are chased by. They get into a variety of scrapes, such as uneasy involvement with members of a youth gang, challengers to drag races, or car thieves. In the morning, there are some fairly predictable surprises about who does go off to college and who yields to a steady girl friend's desire to keep him at home.

It is a film in which little things keep happening thick and fast, but which, somehow, seems plotless all the same. For even though these events in some cases determine the futures of the boys and their girls, they are, in themselves, insignificant enough. The movie ingeniously manages to keep them in dual perspective: trivial and ludicrous, as they seem to us; and also exciting, frustrating, and momentous, as they are to the kids. The continuous circling around the main drag in various more or less prestigious vehicles; the flirtations, provocations, and downright insults hurled from car to parallel-running car; the periodic reencountering of the same faces and places in the course of this endless-seeming ballet on wheels give the film an exhilarating rhythm, but also the hallucinatory character of a gay, silly dream that nevertheless threatens to spill over into nightmare. The motorized ballet is well choreographed: it has a visual refrain—Mel's Burger City, the drive-in hangout from which the boys depart and into which they keep dropping back as the night progresses; and an auditory refrain—Wolfman Jack, the real-life disc jockey playing himself, to whose patter and platters the kids keep listening on their car radios, and who becomes, in the end, an important plot element. What orchestrates these modestly aspiring or defiantly abdicating lives is the popular songs: the unending flux of mundane music and paltry verbiage pouring from the radios, disbursed equally to all, insinuating itself into and absorbing the lives it carries along on its shallow yet sedulous stream.

Almost every nation has, in one way or another, made this film. The French version was called here *The Girl Chasers;* the Italian, *La Notte Brava;* the British, *The Girl Getters.* The American variant is, characteristically, by far the sweetest and most innocent. Nowhere here, as in the French film, does a character cry out, "I have already resigned myself to not possessing all the women in the world, but at least I must sleep with as many as I possibly can." Nowhere here, as in the British version, is there a heartless seducer (even granted that he reforms in the end); nowhere, as in the Italian model, does violence burst out full blast. True, these kids are a little younger, but so is, or was in 1962, the country. In a way, *American Graffiti* is a significant document: it explains the innocence, the almost guilty innocence that led to our stumbling into Vietnam, the Pentagon Papers, and Watergate—stumbling into them and remaining stuck there. It could especially happen here.

I shall not try to list the excellent but little-known actors who pour themselves into these existences, scribbled like living graffiti on the walls of the night. Almost all of them are already experienced performers, yet we tend to be unable to place them, which gives them the combined advantages of professionals and amateurs. George Lucas has directed with a remarkably firm but unostentatious hand, two virtues equally rare in a young filmmaker. He has, moreover, avoided the pitfall into which another successful young director, Peter Bogdanovich, keeps hurtling—indeed, hurling himself: that of deliberately imitating the films and directors of the period or genre in question. Lucas's film, though it re-creates an epoch most faithfully, does not espouse the style or conventions of anyone or anything, and resolutely creates its own quasi-formless form.

The script, too, even while immersing itself in the mores and lingo of the era, exudes humor and humanity that transcend the boundaries of time and place. Let me cite one example. When the class cheerleader pleads with her steady beau, the class president, not to go off to college, the following front-seat colloquy takes place: "It doesn't make sense," Laurie marshals her argument laboriously, "to leave home to find a new home, to leave friends to find new friends, to give up your old life for a new life." Steve stares at her uncomprehendingly and blurts out, "Could you say that again?" The meaning means nothing to him; only the sheer, long-winded eloquence astounds and impresses him. But, of course, such hard-won rhetorical triumphs are unrepeatable; Laurie merely glares at him, exasperated. A small film, but with a rich ore of truth in it.

Another second feature by a young director—albeit one with considerable experience in the theater—is John Hancock's *Bang the Drum Slowly.* I have seen little of Hancock's theater work; his first feature film, *Let's Scare Jessica to Death,* was a mess; his preceding short, *Sticky My Fingers, Fleet My Feet,* based on a cute *New Yorker* story about a middle-aged man playing touch football in Central Park, was too sticky by half. But in this film, based on a novel and screenplay by Mark Harris, Hancock comes, not yet into his own, but into the ranks of those younger directors who aim for more than mere commercial successes.

This is technically a baseball story, but—take it from one who knows nothing about baseball—it works handily on various other levels, including the best of all, that of basic human relationships. Henry Wiggen is the star pitcher of the New York Mammoths: he has the raucous approval of the fans, the love of a pretty young wife, and useful supplements to his income from being a successful author and insurance salesman. But he also has an albatross round his neck: Bruce Pearson, a drab, benighted, unappetizing Georgia farmboy who is not even a very good catcher and, on top of that, is slowly dying of Hodgkin's disease.

Gradually but irresistibly, something compassionate in Henry's rather flip nature draws him into a tightening friendship with Bruce, who becomes his roommate and for whom he sticks up in the most gallant and arduous ways without truly liking him. He tries hard to keep Bruce's ghastly secret from the team, but it does leak out. From tough manager to barely English-speaking Puerto Rican rookie, from boisterous coach to a cool cat of a black player, everyone reluctantly slips into humanity. Bruce is coddled and bullied into becoming a happy man and efficient catcher until the illness reaches its final phase and he has to be sent home. Then everyone forgets him; only Henry goes to Georgia, when the time comes, to be his pallbearer.

This synopsis omits all the spunky, wry, droll, hilarious, and tragic details in which *Bang the Drum Slowly* abounds. There are some mouth-wateringly flavorous conversations, trenchantly observed characters, and perkily etched incidents enlivening this movie. It accosts its essentially grim theme with admirable, never callous cheerfulness, and exemplarily eschews the maudlin. Hancock and Harris are to be congratulated, for example, on their handling of the roommates' final leave-taking at the airport: avoided alike are false heroics and mawkish pathos. Similarly, Henry never becomes too unselfishly good; he mostly gets a kick out of being the dumb kid's big brother. And Bruce—here is the wonder—remains throughout a likable oaf, whose oafishness never quite dispels his likableness, any more than his likableness lets you forget that he is an oaf.

In this, the film profits immeasurably from the performance of Robert De Niro, a Northerner who completely transformed himself into the Georgia cracker with the fatal crack running through him. De Niro accomplished this partly through patient research, and partly through sheer inspired acting. The way Pearson wraps his knowledge that he must die in forgetfulness, so that life can go on while it can; how amid all those spurious kindnesses, he is saved not by his insight but by his obtuseness; these things are beautifully conveyed by a certain slowness, tentativeness, or excessive alacrity—a rhythm that is always a bit off. And there is the half-comprehending gaze that remains a little clouded, but amiably so, like an overcast day about which one notices less the lack of sunshine than the merciful absence of rain.

A bravura performance is given also by Vincent Gardenia, an impeccable character actor, as Dutch Schnell, the epitome of the tough but lovable manager. "Tough but lovable" is no longer a cliché after Gardenia gets through with it. He shows it up for what it really is: not some glorious American amalgam of virility and kindliness but shrewd stubbornness laced with wisecracking indifference to all but one's narrow, immediate concerns. Gardenia's Dutch, a purposively snorting bull, is magnificently funny without stooping to caricature; if impersonators of baseball greats get their own Hall of Fame, this performance can be sure of its shrine. Michael Moriarty has a bit of a struggle with Henry's smart-aleck phlegm and mush-mouthed diction: one sees the actor working at lowering himself into the character with canny but conscious effort. Still, it is an honorable piece of work, and many of the lesser parts are executed with dazzling precision. Note, for instance, the team owner's imperturbably domineering wife, stunningly created by Barbara Babcock down to the imperious way she clamps her bare foot on the couch on which she squats.

Hancock deserves praise, too, for such good work with his actors, though elsewhere he does slip up. He cannot resist recurring slow-motion shots of baseball plays which, initially effective, soon become as illegitimate and painful as beanballs. Or he will let a fine scene, in which the modest achievement of a mammoth dance ensemble is serenely wrecked by Bruce's elephantine footwork, go on well past the making of the comic-pathetic point. And he lets his cinematographer, Richard Shore, get away with mediocrity. Yet this is a humane, unsentimental film, truly diverting despite the smell of mortality it bravely does not wipe away. Moviegoers who reject films they can call "depressing" must face the fact that it is not that at all—merely, at times, sad.

October 1973

Put It in Escrow

Two solidly established genres of film as well as fiction, the-most-unforgettable-character-I-ever-met story and the glory-and-agony-of-schooldays, tale, are welded together into *The Paper Chase.* The movie is based on a novel by John Jay Osborn, Jr., a kind of second-best-seller Osborn wrote as a student at Harvard Law School. It deals with the love-hate that Hart, a first-year student, feels for Kingsfield, his haughty, sardonic, mean but brilliant contract-law professor. Kingsfield, who either ignores his students or sarcastically browbeats them, is one of the stars of the Law School faculty who teaches by the Socratic method and rules his students with a Socratic rod of irony. Hart, a bright, unassertive midwesterner, so fears, idolizes, and resents Kingsfield that it becomes his ruling passion to impress, astound, or even confound him—indeed, to turn into him.

The other part of the plot, as noted, concerns the glory and agony of being a student. The glory consists of Hart's getting picked up by a pretty young woman in the nocturnal streets of Cambridge when she needs protection from someone who has been following her, a meeting cute scene that quickly—and through rapid cutting even more quickly—develops into an affair. Susan, the temperamental young woman, turns out to be Kingsfield's daughter, which gives coincidence roughly the role Fate used to play in Greek tragedy, and nicely thickens the plot. For the agony, we get the immense hardship involved in making it through the first year of school: the study group formed by Hart, Ford, and four ill-assorted fellows who manage to irritate more than help one another; the near-suicide of one of the group who cannot keep up; the frantic cramming for examinations; the breakup with Susan when work forces Hart to neglect her. Of course, there is a happy ending on both the academic and the romantic fronts.

It might have made a very decent film if any of the main intentions had been realized by James Bridges, either in his script or in his direction. John Houseman, the celebrated producer and director who here makes his belated starring debut, is a fine Kingsfield: he exudes the proper amount of icy intelligence and fastidious prissiness, and subtly suggests even the underlying emotional alienation. But such a figure would impose itself through keenness of mind, dazzling epigrammatic sallies, and here the writing lets Kingsfield down. About the best he gets is an opening remark to his students: "You come in here with a skullful of mush and you leave thinking like a lawyer," and a bit of insult humor when, during a class, he offers Hart a dime with which to call his mother and tell her he'll never make a lawyer. Of legal brilliance, he is never allowed one example—perhaps because we in the audience, coming in with our skullfuls of mush, might leave feeling inferior and disgruntled.

Hart's obsession is not made palpable either. Timothy Bottoms gives his best performance to date in the role, but he is, finally, one of those actors who prevail (if they do) through looking likable and not doing anything really wrong rather than through the flexibility and taking of risks that truly are acting. Still, it is more likely the script's fault if most of his inner life is amputated. Back in 1926, Virginia Woolf wrote that at the movies, "as smoke pours from Vesuvius, we should be able to see thought in its wildness, in its beauty, in its oddity. . . ." *The Paper Chase* fails to make thought visible.

The best scene is that of the first nocturnal breaking into Langdell Hall by Hart and Ford. Bridges shoots their feet through the frosted-glass floors illuminated by the boys' flashlights: moving patches of light through which glide blotches of darkness, the intruders' shoes. There is mystery in that shot, a sense of adventure and awe, of student pranks that are more than bravado: rites of passage into the realms of the Law. On another night, the boys break into the Law Library to peruse Kingsfield's notes, and the notebooks of bygone notables, bound in red buckram, emit a weird, orangy glow by flashlight; it is like George Meredith's Lucifer beholding in the stars "the army of unalterable law." Hart exclaims: "This is the unbroken chain! This is the ageless passing on of wisdom!" and some inner life begins to stir in the film, only to vanish after a couple of fitful flickers.

The study group is drolly portrayed by a handful of little-known New York actors, but the affair with Susan is, except for the absence of a lethal illness, worthy of *Love Story*. Bridges, whose one previous film was the insufferable *The Baby Maker,* has no feeling for the *genius loci.* Take a sequence like the one at Kingsfield's cocktail party, where the strained texture of such an academic gathering is flatly missed: the director cannot find the tiny telling details that fasten the whole thing to reality. But in the Susan of Lindsay Wagner, he has hit upon the very essence of a Radcliffe girl's looks, sound, and demeanor. Miss Wagner is so true that she almost hurts—at least those of us who have spent some of our best years in love with Radcliffe girls.

December 1973

Gulling the Audience

No, I HAVE NOT READ *Jonathan Livingston Seagull,* but, O my God, did I ever see the movie! Seagulls, as the film stresses, subsist on garbage, and, I guess, you are what you eat. Judging from the screenplay, Richard Bach's flyaway best seller must read like Kahlil Gibran with feathers. (True, Bach legally contested some of the dialogue in the movie he wrote with Hall Bartlett, the director, but I am told that it is still no more unfaithful to the original than a hooker to her pimp.) The film, at any rate, closely resembles every other predigested, semiliterate, mistily mystagogic piece of hopemongering with which seekers after Great Life-giving Truths in small packages have been traditionally gulled.

This is the story (if a little bird hasn't already told you) of a seagull that flies higher and dives deeper than others, and seeks to reform the seagull diet from garbage to fruit of the sea. But an evil Elder stirs up the seagull multitudes against Jonathan, who, banished, circles the globe, dies (apparently), and is reborn in a seagull Shangri-la whose sachem is actually called Chang, where he has a platonic love affair with Maureen Seagull. But he must return to his flock. With the pious platitudes learned from Chang, he turns the crippled Fletcher Seagull into a supergull, who, however, kills himself in a display of aerobatic skills. Jonathan resuscitates Fletcher, all the while denying that he is the Son of the Great Gull, and departs to do good among other flocks, leaving this one to Fletcher's ministrations.

As if this were not nauseating enough in itself, Neil Diamond composed and sings an ear-splitting and stomach-turning background score, its platitudes and decibels running abreast and amuck. Jack Couffer's color cinematography looks like a morganatic marriage between the *National Geographic* and *Vogue*, but the aerial tracking shots of Jonathan soaring over exotic landscapes have, just before they turn soupy, moments of breathtaking visual bravura. The special effects by L. B. Abbott, before they, too, turn corny, are likewise impressive. The dialogue—for the birds—is supplied by uncredited voices that speak in tones usually reserved for biblical epics and heartwarming B-movies about boys and their pet hamsters.

Most provocative, though, are not the sequences of a lone gull in flight across the vastness of rear projection or the rousing crowd scenes of the flock swarming, revving up, and taking loudly to the air like gallant RAF squadrons in World War II movies. True pathos is achieved only briefly in scenes where Jonathan, so glorious in the air, is shown pitifully sidling athwart a sandy or snowy waste, leaving behind his daintily diagonal footprints looking like a doomed attempt to hemstitch a glacier or desert. Here one is movingly reminded of Baudelaire's symbolist sonnet about the albatross, that winged voyager who, on the ground, is clumsy and laggard, his giant wings impeding his walk. Alas, even at such moments, one was tempted to say that what Jonathan, sinking into the snow, needed was a good pair of galoshes.

A couple of years ago there appeared a very brief short, *The End of One.* It took place on a litter-strewn beach overrun by seagulls. From among those teeming, sleek birds, a brownish, bedraggled one wearily dragged itself into some concavity in the garbage. While the others, resplendent in their white bibs, heedlessly fluttered about, this old bird slowly, agonizingly sank into itself and into death, as the camera, in extreme close-up, concentrated on the glazing over of an avian eye. This short should be programmed with every screening of *Jonathan Livingston Seagull* as a prophylactic against all that saccharine uplift.

The Way We Were purports to be a candid look at the mixed and mixed-up marriage of Jewish Katie and WASP Hubbell, whose seeds were sown in college in the late thirties. During the war, Katie, who has a modest job in radio, runs into Hubbell, an officer in the Navy, and spirits him away from his rich Christian girl friend by means of her charming bohemian poverty, leftist politics and right attitude in the sack, good Jewish cooking, and, above all, indomitable chutzpah. They marry, and Hubbell, a budding novelist, moves to Hollywood with Katie; here they get involved with the big movie director filming Hubbell's first book, and with an assortment of prototypical movieland oddballs. Comes the era of blacklisting and witch-hunts, and loyalties are severely strained. Marriages begin to creak and crack. Katie divorces Hubbell and returns with her daughter to New York, more leftist (or is it merely liberal?) politics, and another, this time unmixed, marriage. Demonstrating against the Bomb in front of the Plaza, she runs into Hubbell with his new, unkosher lady. There is a moment of bittersweet rapprochement as Katie tells him about their daughter (whom, for purely tearjerking reasons, he is not allowed to see), then the two go their separate ways.

The script, by Arthur Laurents from his own novel, is sheer, piddling hokum, most so when it huffs and churns toward high seriousness. The college scenes strive for bubbly lightness, but the humor is vestigial when not ponderously cute. The scenes in New York City, where Katie woos and wins Hubbell, are on the level of average Hollywood gag writing (as, for instance, in *A Touch of Class),* but marred by Laurents's sweaty straining for significance. This is particularly gauche coming from someone who can't decide even whether he wants to extol or patronize Katie's leftist activities. Still, Laurents does capture to an extent the way in which World War II confused certain political issues, and gets something of the laissez-faire politeness of the wealthy, too graciously lax to respond even to Katie's insults with commensurate indignation. But he cannot begin to show us what makes his heroine so allegedly irresistible, despite her all-too-strident humor, lack of self-criticism, and brand of loving-kindness that uncomfortably verges on tyranny.

Here, to be sure, matters are not helped by Barbra Streisand's performance. Sydney Pollack, the director, has tried to tone down her brashness and shrillness, but has hardly made a dent in that basic pugnacious charmlessness that is beyond redemption. The difficulty is that even when Miss Streisand labors to appear sensitive and vulnerable, she cannot conquer our impression that, were she to collide with a Mack truck, it is the truck that would drop dead. And, as always, I am repelled by her looks; by the receding brow and the overcompensatory nose, which, unlike Cleopatra's in Pascal's famous dictum, would not, even if it were shorter, change the face of the earth—merely blot out a smaller part of it. Only very plain women, in their wish-fulfillment fantasies, could accept without flinching the dashing Robert Redford's passion for, and bedroom scenes with, Barbra Streisand.

Yet it is not until the action shifts to Hollywood that things get thoroughly out of control. Laurents's fatcat director is a paper-thin cliché, and the rest of the colorful characters come in hues no subtler than those of a hand-painted necktie. The proto-McCarthyist persecution and mob scenes are tritely conceived and listlessly executed by Pollack, which is surprising from a director who so skillfully conveyed social unrest in *They Shoot Horses, Don't They?* And what the embattled spouses hurl at each other is not so much searing truths as grating commonplaces.

The dialogue lacks authentic period flavor; anachronistically, Katie calls someone a fink or tells a gathering of students, "You are beautiful!" an ugly misuse of the word that we were spared until quite recently. What hurts more, though, is the cuteness. When Hubbell asks the studious young Katie, "What are you always carrying your books for?" she answers, "That's to help me get across the street." Whereupon he promptly gives as reason for his drinking, "to celebrate your getting across the street." And here is the same pair, now young-middle-aged ex-spouses, just as drippingly cute: "You never give up, do you?—But I'm a very good loser.—Better than I am.—Well, I've had . . . more experience." Some things, I suppose, never change, like that tie Redford wears in two scenes that take place many years apart.

Redford is a racy, unmannered, often incisive actor, but here he does little to convince us that he is a novelist. The supporting players, with the happy exception of James Woods, either walk through their parts, like Patrick O'Neal, or ham them up, like Viveca Lindfors. The color cinematography by Harry Stradling, Jr., is insipid, and the music of Marvin Hamlisch cannot even manage the unabashed schmaltziness we got from Max Steiner, Franz Waxman, and other glossy old-timers. And something else: the entire picture reeks of prophetic hindsight, whereby the cleverer characters so splendidly predict the future, thanks to the author's writing them years after the fact.

Robert Altman's *The Long Goodbye* was briefly released some months ago, when public disapproval caused it to be withdrawn. Audiences allegedly thought that this private-eye movie, based on one of Raymond Chandler's Philip Marlowe novels, was to be taken straight, as if Bogart were still playing Marlowe, with Howard Hawks directing. Whereas, it seems, Altman and his star, Elliott Gould, were giving us a send-up of the genre, and so, for the current release, the publicity campaign is alerting us to this fact. It is a sorry state of affairs when a joke has to be labeled "JOKE" and I am not sure to what extent the new interpretation is not merely the counsel of despair.

Elliott Gould has none of the characteristics of the tough, canny sleuth: his face and expressions, slack and self-indulgent, do not betray any signs of quick and sharp thinking—or, for that matter, of any other kind. Casting him as Marlowe would, indeed, seem to be an intentional jest of a satirical sort; otherwise, though, Leigh Brackett's screenplay hardly departs from what has become paradigmatic for the genre: a tone of wisecracking ruthlessness and a plot in which unsavory characters savor outsmarting and doing in one another. There may be one or two more farcical elements here than is customary, but for a real send-up you would have needed Woody Allen rather than Gould who is all wooden.

Without knowing the book, I still assume that in this late work Chandler perceived his detective hero as even more dogged and less heroic than usual, for this Marlowe makes his discoveries by snooping through windows, and shoots only once, and then at an adversary both unarmed and unsuspecting. The screenplay, in any case, has less complexity than could be found in previous Marlowe films—although it still has one quite incomprehensible twist in the plot—and the whole thing lacks the fascination of even such a minor piece of Marloviana as Robert Montgomery's *The Lady in the Lake.* But it may also be a question of the acting: Gould's cutesy mumbling is no way to deliver Marlowe's mighty lines; Nina van Pallandt's casting can be explained only in terms of her highly publicized association with Clifford Irving, and her acting is certainly a fake; Sterling Hayden's attempt at portraying a Hemingwayish novelist whose unwritten books are drowning in booze is much too simplistic for my taste. Writers need not be particularly writerlike in real life; in art, though, something more is required, and I could no more believe in Hayden's novels than in Redford's.

Two other bits of offbeat casting—Jim Bouton as a suspected wife killer, and Henry Gibson as a sinister psychiatrist—come off equally unpersuasively, but Mark Rydell is good and juicy as a drolly mean Jewish gangster, and Jo Ann Brody does well as his devoted girl friend who is rewarded with a Coke bottle smashed in her face. Altman's work, however, does not seem to concentrate on performances so much as on effects. With his steady cinematographer, Vilmos Zsigmond, Altman has evolved some stunning ones, and others which, as in the two men's previous collaborations, call excessive attention to themselves. Thus a private conversation between van Pallandt and Hayden takes place just behind the picture window of their Malibu house while Gould, as instructed by them, walks about on the beach. The camera shoots right into the plate glass and blends the agitated talkers behind it with the man moseying around the beach in one overrich image, a sort of single-shot double exposure, a metaphysical fusion of worlds within and without: an ocean ominously projected into a house while people, seemingly safely anchored in their living room, are adrift on a sea of reflections.

It is spectacular, but it is too much. There is, however, a sequence immediately following whose mixture of awesomeness and concise efficacy could hardly be surpassed. Hayden has walked out into the ocean to drown himself; it has grown dark, and the breakers are unusually vehement. Gould and van Pallandt, dressed as they are, rush into the water to save him. The nocturnal beach is all blacks and whites, but on color film (perhaps by means of filters or a special mode of processing) these blacks and whites assume disturbingly lurid tinges. The waves come rampaging in—one thinks of Turner and Hokusai—and figures loom against the white crests or vanish into the dark interior of the billows. The family dog races in to the rescue, but dares not do more than cavort in the shallows. As Hayden disappears into the deep, and a drenched and exhausted Gould barely manages to drag van Pallandt back to safety, the dog arrives with his master's cane between his jaws. Those colorless colors in the hallucinatory light, that dog proudly retrieving the now useless cane, make this a vision of bone-chilling horror for whose brief duration the film pulls itself up into art.

Soon, unfortunately, Gould is trying to act again: he has a drunk scene in which he is scarcely different from his sober self. But for Robert Altman, whose films since *M*A*S*H* have been generally disappointing, *The Long Goodbye* is at least a step back up again from its predecessor, *Images.* Altman, though he can go terribly wrong, is misled by ideas rather than by incompetence. In his next film, or the one after, they may once again pay off.

What may well prove the year's most overrated film is Martin Scorsese's *Mean Streets.* The young American-Italian director returns here to his early haunts, New York's Little Italy, which provided the setting also for his first feature, the equally clumsy but less pretentious *Who's That Knocking at My Door?* The enthusiastic reception of *Mean Streets* may be due in part to its being largely child's play—and rather sloppily written, improvised, acted, photographed, and edited child's play at that. But in a period when moviemaking has reached a high plateau of soulless slickness and glitter, when any number of directors can put together neat little scenes into a triumph of the art of assemblage—the only trouble being that the entire thing is hollow and pointless—a movie oozing amateurishness from every hole in the plot and every crevice in the continuity may come across as endearingly genuine, unassuming, and direct.

In a way, it all goes back to early Godard, where supposedly serious events were first rendered—I think only half consciously—in terms of grown-up children playing with guns, cars, sex, and other potentially dangerous toys. It could be called the Bang-Bang-You're-Dead school of filmmaking, and *Mean Streets* is a fairly good example of it.

The movie centers on Charlie, a young man of average niceness, lust, and greed. He is the nephew of Giovanni, a Mafia boss, and hopes to obtain a restaurant when his uncle eliminates its present owner for nonpayment of debts. He is a friend of Tony, who runs the bar where everyone hangs out; of Michael, who lends money to people; and, above all, of Johnny Boy, an all-round goof-off heavily in debt to Michael and unconcerned about paying him back. Charlie has an affair with Teresa, Johnny Boy's epileptic cousin, and another with God, in whose church he periodically mopes about sin and damnation.

The film proceeds through a series of loosely connected episodes in the course of which Tony gets a tiger, Teresa an epileptic fit, Johnny Boy a bullet that kills him, and Charlie nothing. (The gunman who shoots Johnny Boy is, surely not accidentally, played by Scorsese himself.) In between there are assorted con jobs, barroom brawls, an incomprehensible and preposterously staged gangland murder in a men's room, various abortive flirtations with girls, several portentous but unpenetrating encounters between Charlie and Uncle Giovanni, and repetitious attempts by Charlie to straighten out Johnny Boy. None of this is quite convincing enough: con jobs are managed too easily, fights look unreal and leave no wounds, Giovanni's influence is inadequately conveyed, and the affair with Teresa is seen in conventional, surface terms. We don't find out why Charlie is so devoted to Johnny Boy, or why the latter is so crazy. Even individual sequences don't come off: we don't believe in Tony's tiger or the nice Teresa's nastiness to Negro hotel maids (though such things occur), or in the facile way Johnny Boy gets gunned down. Worst of all, the talk in this screenplay by Scorsese and Mardik Martin sounds all too frequently improvised by actors with no gift for extemporization.

The result is a film without structure, whose episodes might as easily be fewer or more numerous, begin or end anywhere, or not exist at all. And it is very hard to evince even superficial sympathy for these characters. Charlie is as average as a pebble on a beach, rounded and polished by waves of happenstance into perfect ordinariness. His one unusual feature is his solicitude for Johnny Boy, the supposedly amiable nut who, alas, despite Robert De Niro's bravura performance, remains more nutty than amiable, and so cuts out the ground under Charlie's one claim to our affection. As for Johnny Boy, he is beyond pity and beneath terror. Comparisons to Fellini's masterpiece, *I Vitelloni,* glibly enunciated by certain critics, are otiose: not only do Fellini's characters exude a comic-pathetic humanity that Scorsese's never achieve, but also there is organization in Fellini's film, so that events build toward climaxes and resolutions, however wan they may be—whereas *Mean Streets* merely slaps an arbitrary and unenlightening ending on ramblings that could go on forever, and indeed seem to do so.

Ken Wakeford's cinematography captures the griminess of the milieu, but only with the artless, accidental *trouvailles* of primitive paintings; the background score is an accumulation of jukebox flotsam that functions efficiently enough; and the performances are passable, with Cesare Danova (Giovanni) and Amy Robinson (Teresa) better than that, and De Niro sustainedly fulgurant but lacking in nuances. All in all, an amateurish film; and amateurishness, in itself, is not an asset.

The two truly indigenous forms of Hollywood filmmaking are, of course, the western and the gangster movie. Both genres have undergone decades of refining, and *Charley Varrick* is one of the more accomplished specimens of the latter. It falls, to be sure, into the comic subcategory, which defenders of the genre's purity may downgrade, but it does provide more than adequate, simple-minded entertainment of the kind movies had better manage if they are to survive at all. The idealization of the clever, affable, independent criminal who outsmarts both the Mafia and the police, and makes off with the loot, is morally queasy; but it is not worth expending moral outrage on in this cardboard context. In his last film, *Dirty Harry,* Don Siegel exalted the fascist cop; in this one, he exalts the anarchic criminal. The two aberrancies cancel each other out—to worry about them would mean questioning the validity of all popular nonculture, and wasting one's time.

The script by Howard Rodman and Dean Riesner, from a novel by John Reese, is full of improbabilities but fast-paced and amusing, and there are good performances galore. Walter Matthau plays a thinking man's crook with his customary gruff suavity and split-second timing, and among the supporting players I enjoyed most William Schallert's sheriff—the quintessence of decent, bumbling bravado. But what gives the film its modest but genuine interest is chiefly Siegel's direction.

The auteur critics are, of course, fools to have made Siegel and most of their other favorites auteurs, i.e., directors whose alleged artistry triumphs over Hollywood's commercialism by imbuing every frame of a formulaic film with a marvelously personal style. It is very much like cigarettes: blindfold the champion of a given brand and he's most unlikely to recognize it by its taste. Remove the credits from a film, and your most obstreperous auteurist won't know a Budd Boetticher from a Don Siegel, a Vincente Minnelli from a Stanley Donen, an Edgar G. Ulmer from a Joseph M. Newman. What makes a *Charley Varrick* fun to watch, though, is that Siegel makes use of the accumulated wisdom of Hollywood through the years, all the jointly elaborated, shrewdly tactical tricks of the trade. A piece of coral is not the worse for being just one piece off a great, anonymous reef. But not the better, either.

January 1974

Black Friday

For the ultimate low I commend to you *Ash Wednesday,* directed by Larry Peerce, who has my vote for the most offensive young director in Hollywood today. Since his initial *One Potato, Two Potato,* Peerce has been turning out moldy potatoes in ever larger sizes and numbers; and even if *Goodbye, Columbus* was not a complete stinker, items like *The Sporting Club* and *A Separate Peace* made up for it by being stinkers-and-a-half. The current opus is a preposterous concoction about a rich woman aged fifty plus who has a total face-and-body-lift at a chic little French clinic, then goes on to a luxury hotel in Cortina d'Ampezzo, where her unfaithful husband, a Detroit lawyer, is to join her for a second honeymoon. To lure him back, the woman (Elizabeth Taylor) has secretly undergone that grueling operation; now she looks to be a creepy thirty-five and is the cynosure of Cortina—so gorgeous that her grown daughter doesn't recognize her for the longest time, and that the ski resort's prettiest and most eligible gigolo (Helmut Berger) has his heart doing telemarks over her. But when hubby (Henry Fonda) finally joins her, neither the wonders of surgery nor the magic of a mountain Mardi Gras, nor even Liz's passionate or angry clawing, can win him back. He returns to his new and younger girl, offering Liz divorce and eternal friendship. Her rage yields to an embryo smile: with a thirtyish body and face, and with Ash Wednesday here, can spring, or, at any rate, Resurrection, be far behind?

This ghastly claptrap, complete with dialogue in desperate need of surgical rejuvenation or euthanasia, was written by one Jean-Claude Tramont, who was born a Belgian, which explains a great deal, and began as Milton Berle's cue-card boy, which may explain the rest. "Isn't it simply that we all refuse to accept reality?" someone pontificates; or Liz explains, "I was the last of the sex-in-the-dark generation," as the script oscillates between fake cleverness and genuine banality. But it is Peerce who is the master of the phony effect. No matter how full a cable car may be before Liz gets into it, it empties out immediately upon her entry, the better to mirror her melancholia. If she steps into a jewelry store, we must follow the reflection of her face as it floats hauntedly, hauntingly from one gem-filled glass cabinet to another. If a girl in a fancy, sophisticated restaurant slaps her escort's face and leaves, the entire clientele stares in mortifying silence at the victim until, at the snap of the headwaiter's fingers, the orchestra and life resume their courses. At the clinic, Peerce shamelessly cuts back and forth between plot scenes, nauseating in their lack of authenticity, and documentary shots of plastic surgery, nauseating in their authenticity.

The movie's main premise, voiced by Fonda, "We've both changed: we don't satisfy each other's needs any more," is never demonstrated or examined, and all the characters act to suit the whims of the plotting. Thus the divorced daughter first refuses to hop over from Paris to Cortina to see her mother—cruel callousness; then, inexplicably, arrives at the Venice airport and tries to make Mummy face the facts of Daddy's disaffection—cruelty only to be kind; then promptly returns to Paris, lest she call the attention of Cortina's swains to her mother's real age—exquisite tact. And Peerce's direction plods from closeup to closeup indoors, as outdoors it turns every frame into a genuine two-lira postcard. The cinematographer is the same Ennio Guarnieri who was responsible for that mushy camerawork in the wishy-washy *Garden of the Finzi-Continis,* and I particularly relished one panoramic shot of Cortina zooming in on a painted backdrop. But even when photographing the real Cortina, Guarnieri's camera performs a kind of cosmetic surgery, with soft-focus shooting through gentle snowfalls, as if the very Dolomites had sutures behind their ears.

It makes one wonder at which producer's son's bar mitzvah Larry Peerce's father, Jan, might have sung for free, to get his own son into the movies. *Ash Wednesday* is so bad that even Liz Taylor's performance becomes almost inconspicuous in it. Fonda and Keith Baxter do act a bit, but only just, and Helmut Berger doesn't even try, which seems to come naturally to him. Complete with syrupy score by the once-talented Maurice Jarre, this is the sort of film that used to be called a woman's picture. Today, with more and more women becoming liberated, they will need their hankies not to wipe away gentle tears, but to bite into during fits of justified fury. *Ash Wednesday* is not so much about plastic surgery as about plastic.

February 1974

Cops, Crooks, and Cryogenics

ONE INTERESTING THING about movies is that they can always surprise you—sometimes even pleasantly. No sooner had I declared in these pages that Sidney Lumet was a pretty hopeless director, than he proved me wrong: his *Serpico* is as enjoyable and engrossing as a film can be without being a work of art. The film is the story of Frank Serpico, an honest New York policeman who joined the force out of idealism and cannot abide the various forms of dishonesty he encounters there. These range from the brutalizing of suspects, indifference to public safety, and petty bribe-taking, to large-scale graft and totally corrupt cynicism in high places.

At first Serpico tries to ignore the ugliness around him; he merely abstains from joining in, at the cost of being considered at best a dolt, at worst a dangerous troublemaker, by his colleagues and superiors. He is continually transferred, never promoted, and his highly original modes of detection are generally scoffed at. When he sends out urgent messages to his superiors for aid and, above all, justice, he is rebuffed or strung along. Finally, with the help of a few decent fellows in various positions, he starts the mechanism that leads to the Knapp Commission and the shake-up of the entire police department, but he has to pay a bitter price for an only temporary victory.

In fact, Serpico pays all along. His work does not permit him to marry (or so he feels), and he loses one girl, a ballet dancer; another, a nurse and a more serious type, is driven away by Frank's taking his professional grievances out on her, and by the danger he keeps exposing himself to—not so much from criminals as from fellow policemen. He becomes a loner, a scholar, an artist, almost a saint. A scholar because he studies Spanish to get closer to his constituents, and even ballet to come nearer to his girl friend's world. An artist because he comes up with ever more fanciful disguises in which to infiltrate the underworld, and indeed, when the ballerina introduces him to her bohemian friends, these proto-artists, cool at first to a cop, gradually warm up to him. A sort of a saint or hermit, who talks to his pet cockatoo as Saint Francis did to the birds, and is followed by his sheep dog as Saint Jerome was by his lion.

Yet here, good as it is, the film begins to desert our needs. It cannot, qua film, have the scope of a long book. If it addresses itself to something as big as police corruption—in fact, human corruptibility in general—it must make certain choices. It can turn into a documentary, or staged quasi-documentary, and bring out all the facts. Although it is a true story, *Serpico* refuses this option, because naming names might lead to litigation and other unpleasantnesses. Or it can become a large, fictional fresco, telling of the whole, vast operation in slightly disguised form. This is partly what *Serpico* does, but it prefers the third possibility: concentrating on one man's role in the events. Only in that case we want to have more analytical detail than we are given.

We would like to know what made Frank Serpico into a holy fool, an intransigent idealist—and we get almost nothing about his personal background. We would like to know something beyond his professional and sexual involvements, which are all we are let in on, and on the latter only superficially at that. We would like to know Serpico from the inside, whereas the film contents itself with a very workmanlike but outside view: enough for us to feel for him, but not enough to understand him.

Still, the script by Waldo Salt *(Midnight Cowboy)* and Norman Wexler *(Joe),* based on the biography by Peter Maas, is intelligent and adroit. It does not pretend to explain what it doesn't know; it has a good sense of rhythm, meaning that it knows not only where to accelerate but also where to slow down; it is not afraid of making Mayor Lindsay and some of his bright young men look like knights in very rusty armor; and it does not even remotely imply that because corruption has been dealt a body blow, it has been toppled forever. As for Lumet, he is a thorough product of New York, and brings to the film a love-hate for the city that makes it so real that you shudder with affectionate loathing as the screen conveys the megalopolitan odors and grime directly to the respective centers in your brain.

Serpico is a street movie, like *The French Connection,* like certain films by Elia Kazan and Jules Dassin, because to these directors, as to Lumet, a back alley and a boulevard are as real as their bedrooms and bathrooms; because they seem more at home with wall-to-wall asphalt than with wall-to-wall carpeting. In such films the cameraman is extremely important, and *Serpico*'s Arthur J. Ornitz has the requisite ultrahigh sensitivity to light and shadow locked in Manichaean combat over the city, to the way faces flatten out into vapidity in overilluminated offices, or become prematurely eclipsed in sunless metropolitan chasms.

No less helpful is the excellent casting. None of these actors' faces is a household commodity, except perhaps Tony Roberts's, but Roberts is cast against the grain. The players are recruited mostly from the New York stage; or else, like John Randolph and Biff McGuire, they have the kinds of faces that dissolve into the parts they are playing. And, as the protagonist, Al Pacino is spectacular. He began on the stage, specializing in vicious psychopaths, and a soupçon of menace still tends to cling to his gentlest moments. But he has now learned how to convert this fierceness into a look of intense moral commitment or zanily lovable passion, and so turn the fuzzy implications of the script into disturbing realities. Pacino has the happy gift of suggesting a mind ceaselessly mobile under a fixed façade, some beast within perpetually coiled for action but as likely to spring into the form of a gamboling lapdog as into that of a lethal panther. He conveys, moreover, an ever ready wit, crouching in the corners of the eyes and flickering in the pupils; and always he suggests funds of untapped energy.

The film does not do full justice to Sergeant David Durk's role in support of Serpico; called Bob Blair in the movie, and played ably by Tony Roberts, the character remains, nevertheless, rather sketchy. But myth demands a single giant-slayer: two Davids, even if they reach only up to Goliath's knees, are a team; but there is nothing that our team-spirited democracy hungers for more than the image of the solitary, stubborn little man singlehandedly disposing of tentacular, corporate ogres. A more serious flaw, however, is the film's score, by Mikis Theodorakis, a hero and martyr of various Greek socialist resistance movements, but a perfectly dreadful composer. In *Zorba the Greek* and *Z,* where his ineptitude was mitigated by Hellenic folk authenticity, all right; but in non-Greek films like *State of Siege* and *Serpico,* his thematic vulgarity and battering-ram method of driving in musical points become offensive. I am all for giving Mr. Theodorakis his political freedom of speech; only his composing voice ought to be silenced.

Finally, *Serpico* benefits greatly from Dede Allen's editing. Miss Allen has an almost uncanny knack for sensing the right moment at which to cut off a shot. It is not that her editing is always fast; it is only that she makes a scene end before it has overexplained itself. She lets it speak to us, as it were, subliminally, and the eruption of joy with which we realize that we have worked out its meaning is the very energy that carries us forward to the next scene.

An action film, more funny than grave, deserves our fullest attention. The comedy-thriller, *The Sting,* works endearingly without a hitch. George Roy Hill's film concerns conmanship in Chicago in the thirties, and the exploits of a few independent confidence men banding together against a big gang boss and his henchmen. This is one of those precarious movies in which murder must look absurd or funny—except in one case, where it has been taken seriously—and it is to Hill's and his scenarist's, David S. Ward's, credit that they just about carry off this colossally queasy task. It must be said right away that certain plot elements in these cinematic rodomontades are bound to be unbelievable; the question is merely to what extent the filmmakers, con artists in their own right, can carry off the caper without allowing us time to unsuspend our disbelief. The main tools at their disposal are surprise, wit, credibility in trappings and details, fast pacing, and good performances. *The Sting* possesses them all.

Sets, costumes, and locations could not look more authentic—Chicago hasn't changed that much since 1936, and neither has Edith Head, the costumer—and the supporting cast, again actors either unfamiliar or used in an offbeat way, adds believability. The plot has more twists to it than a boa constrictor taking its constitutional, and even if you guess something correctly, you are made to abandon your hypothesis only to have it prove right after all, and so have been had, anyhow. There are funny lines and situations throughout, and no pretensions whatsoever. Well integrated subplots fill in the gaps of the main plot, and Hill has a good sense of camera placement for getting bustle or moodiness into a shot.

Robert Surtees is a better cinematographer in black-and-white than, as here, in color; but if his colors are conventional, at least they aren't jarring. The background score by Marvin Hamlisch, having been adapted from Scott Joplin rags, is better than his usual work. The three principals—Robert Redford, Paul Newman, and Robert Shaw—are exhilarating in a very nice balance between acting and star quality, and they get fine support from everyone around. My one small quarrel is with the inapposite unattractiveness of the women the glamorous Redford is made to shack up with, but I suppose, once the dangerous precedent of his romancing Barbra Streisand in his last film was established, only embracing someone like Dimitra Arliss can top that unappetizing act.

Woody Allen's latest, *Sleeper,* is his best film to date. An amiable little New Yorker, a dealer in health foods and wisecracks, goes into a hospital for minor surgery and ends up the victim of an experiment in cryogenics. He wakes up in the totalitarian America of 2173, becomes the subject of historical curiosity among doctors not yet brainwashed like the rest of society, an escapee from the state police, and the unwilling agent of the revolutionary underground—

but why go on? Suffice it to say that in this movie Allen makes less of his sexual fears and social ineptitudes: the Jewish self-pitier is largely supplanted by a new persona, a near-regulation Gulliver amid Brobdingnagian technology and Lilliputian spirits; also, the visual elements are more carefully worked out than in Allen's slapdash yesteryears.

Woody is slowly getting away from a comedy based chiefly on one-liners and throwaway gags, and tending toward a more structured and disciplined dramatic whole. At the same time, he stresses visual comedy more than before, with mixed results. Nevertheless, the script by Allen and Marshall Brickman manages to be more often funny than not, and funny more often uproariously than mildly. Allen also composed and plays some of the jolly jazz score, and acts and directs with greater poise than ever. Above all, he adds to our cinematic repertoire political and cultural satire, almost as sorely needed as a change in our politics and culture themselves.

March 1974

The World, the Fish, and the Devil

PROVIDENCE NEVER SENT A COPY of *The Exorcist* my way, knowing perhaps what I would have done with it. But a review copy of William Peter Blatty's next book, *I'll Tell Them I Remember You,* unaccountably ended up on my desk. I am always interested in what hacks who have made one great killing do for an encore, so I perused this little volume that deals chiefly with the adventures of Mr. Blatty's mother, before and after her death. Before death, she was a poor, tough Lebanese immigrant whose husband abandoned her with five children, but who indomitably peddled, scrounged, chiseled, lied, and bulldozed away to bring up her darlings, four of whom didn't come to much, but the fifth of whom lived to write *The Exorcist.*

One fatal day, when his mother lay dying in a West Coast hospital, Blatty, an already thriving screenwriter, did not attend her bedside, but stayed home reading the papers and waiting for a phone call from his estranged wife. That evening, Mrs. Blatty, Sr., died, leaving her adoring, idolizing son disconsolate and unable to forgive himself. Then, as the remainder of the book tells us, Mamma proceeded to haunt Blatty in various ways, even appearing to his daughter as a visible ghost. For him, however, the hauntings culminated when mechanical birds that had not been wound up sang—on three separate occasions—while he was thinking of Mamma. That proved to him that "she had done it. She had beaten death."

Well, this may strike you as proof either of the infinitude of the human soul or of the finitude of the human brain, depending on your beliefs or lack of them. The real surprise, though, comes on the book's penultimate page in the form of this palinode: "The birds did sing. That you can rely on. Yet we do not need paranormal events to find proof of our God or of our life everlasting. The phenomenon of love is proof enough. A love like my mother's is miracle enough. Whatever existed in the primal gas could never evolve, even given an eternity, to one fragment of a heart like my mother's. No amoeba could learn how to love like that. . . ." Perhaps not; but almost any amoeba could learn to write like this, or better. Now, I ask you: if love, which we have all experienced, is enough, why do we need such paranormal garbage as Mr. Blatty's *The Exorcist,* book or movie, to prove what we already know?

The answer is that most people love scabrousness, goose pimples, and facile uplift beyond anything else. Scabrousness, because their daily lives are boringly proper; goose pimples, because nothing exciting ever happens to them; and facile uplift, because they are depressed by the insignificance and monotony of their existence. So if a trashy book comes along that gives them all three in one gloriously noxious package, it is almost doomed to become a bestseller, be translated into umpteen languages, and be turned into a ten-million-dollar movie that will increase the birthrate of suckers from one to a hundred per minute.

In *The Exorcist,* Regan MacNeil, a twelve-year-old girl, has accompanied her movie-star mother, Chris, to Georgetown, where the latter is making a movie. Regan becomes possessed by the devil, urinates in public, obscenely defaces the statue of the Virgin, masturbates with a crucifix until her vagina is bloody and then rubs her mother's nose in it, howls out disgusting remarks in a ghastly bass voice, begins to look like Mickey Rooney in drag, and vomits into people's faces in pistachio green, chrome yellow, and probably other decorator colors. Science can do nothing for her, but the desperate Chris chances upon Father Karras, a Jesuit psychiatrist who has been losing his faith from exacerbated guilt feelings ever since he let his mother die in an unfashionable hospital.

The priest calls in a famous exorcist, Father Merrin, and together they undertake the exorcizing of the devil from little Regan. It is high time. She has already caused the demise of her mother's movie-director friend, found dead at the foot of a street of stairs, with his head turned around a hundred and eighty degrees—a trick that Regan herself, like others diabolically possessed, performs with hideous glee. Why the director, who was merely pushed out of the window by Regan, should also be doing that trick in death, remains, like much else, unclear. The devil puts up one hell of a fight against exorcism: Regan's bed rattles around like Magic Fingers gone berserk, furniture is tossed about the room as if all seven Santini Brothers were in the process of moving the MacNeil household, Regan's body levitates high enough above her bed to turn the Guru Maharaj Ji green with envy, and the little girl fights with the strength of four grown men or two Jesuits.

Father Merrin dies movingly on the job, and the younger Jesuit carries on alone. Meanwhile, a nice Jewish detective has also been snooping around, but getting nowhere, except for finding at the foot of the death stairs the same demonic figurine that Father Merrin dug up archaeologizing in Iraq during the first reel of the film, which has nothing to do with the subsequent reels, except that it sets the source of the deviltry in Assyria, obviously meant to symbolize Lebanon, the cradle of the Blattys and their ancestral curse. As for the statuette's ending up in Georgetown, scholars of the paranormal will doubtless explain it by the fact that W. P. Blatty, a good Catholic, attended Georgetown University, and there learned about the 1949 case of a boy in nearby Maryland who was possessed by the devil until his priest, after two months of strenuous exorcizing, succeeded in expelling the fiend. Father Karras succeeds likewise, but only at the cost of inviting the demon to take possession of him instead, which he, yearning like other poor devils for upward mobility, eagerly accepts. Whereupon Father Karras, spreading out his arms to look like the Crucified, or merely the better to emulate an airplane, flies out of the window and lands smashed at the foot of the aforementioned fatal stairs. Here a conveniently passing fellow Jesuit gives him extreme unction, thus foiling the devil, as proved by the fact that Father Karras faces forward even in death, it taking more than a mere devil to turn a good Jesuit's head.

This would all be only risible, were it not for certain factors that make it repugnant. There is, first, Blatty's mixture of sanctimoniousness and arrogance: the tone of *The Exorcist* (as well as its author's pronouncements) leaves no doubt that Blatty believes he has created a work of great moral, religious, and artistic import. There is, second, the expensive, near-DeMillean grandioseness with which the film was made by William Friedkin, who brings to it the same blend of meticulousness and sensationalism with which he endued *The French Connection.* The director, for example, was dissatisfied with the looks of the Georgetown house that had been built as the principal set and on which protracted shooting had already taken place; so, at enormous cost, the house had to be rebuilt and the scenes reshot. Such perfectionism at the service of trash takes on a lurid, almost indecent, character. Still, Friedkin has a crass expertise with which he can keep the average moviegoer from laughing at these absurd goings-on, and he certainly gets great performances, not from his actors—who, with the exception of Jason Miller and Lee J. Cobb, are defeated by the material—but from his special-effects and make-up men, who carry the film. And Friedkin showed strength in being able to keep Blatty, who was both producer and scenarist, out of the cutting room during a long, fussy period of editing.

Disturbing, too, is the MPAA's R rating for a film that would have surely been X-rated had it not cost a major Hollywood studio a fortune; Valenti, Stern & Co. have a way of becoming most accommodating when survival of the industry whose hirelings they are is at stake. And then there is the Society of Jesus giving its blessing to this fetid venture, with three of its members acting as technical advisers and two of them as performers in it, showing that the good fathers' thespian ambitions are second only to their theological fervor. *Inter faeces et urinas nascimur,* the Church Fathers observed; no doubt the worthy Jesuits felt that the birth of renewed faith, too, must take place between the urine of Regan and the excrement of William Peter Blatty. New York audiences, sure enough, have been forming three-block-long queues in freezing temperatures outside the theater where *The Exorcist* is playing, but whether out of incipient piety or coprophagous prurience remains to be seen.

For Blatty, in the meantime, I have found in a letter of Béla Bartók's a nice old Hungarian folk curse: "May your towels pour out flames, and the water you wash in turn to blood."

The offensive thing is, I repeat, not so much that Blatty, despite pans from the more civilized reviewers, is laughing all the way to the bank, like so many hacks before and after him. The horror lies elsewhere. If you read Blatty's mother-book carefully, you find in it many people and incidents the author transposed or translated into *The Exorcist,* and none of them more clearly than himself into Karras. Thus he himself is the guilty, suffering, and ultimately magnificent savior of mankind. I can only marvel at a pious public that accepts this moral megalomania from the man who previously served up *What Did You Do in the War, Daddy?; John Goldfarb, Please Come Home,* and other such less than pious Blattitudes. As for the impious thrill-seekers and obscenity hounds, have they no pride? *The Devil in Miss Jones* is one thing, but the devil in Little Nell is quite another—devious, craven, hypocritical—way of coming by one's smut. Is there no honor left among thieves?

Things are not much better with the other long-awaited blockbuster, *The Day of the Dolphin.* I am told that Robert Merle's novel, on which Mike Nichols's film is based, has merit. But, as I am further told, Buck Henry's screenplay departs considerably from the book, a piece of French Marxist, naïve but ideologically explicit, anti-Americanism. In order to make the movie salable here, Nichols and Henry had to make the attack both more circumscribed and more vague, a mutually contradictory narrowing and expansion that proved, predictably, deleterious.

The story concerns Dr. Jake Terrell, a scientist who, under the auspices of the Franklin Foundation, is trying to teach dolphins human speech. A true idealist, he proceeds from love of knowledge and of his fellow creatures, but the foundation's motives appear to be murky. Terrell, his young and pretty wife, Dr. Margaret (Maggie) Terrell, and a team of somewhat unlikely young men and women are working in absolute secrecy on an island off the Florida coast; yet Harold DeMilo, the foundation executive in charge of the operation and a clandestine homosexual, allows a shady self-styled journalist, Mahoney, to blackmail him into persuading the Terrells to let him come to the island. There Mahoney is prevented from seeing the work and play of a pair of amorous dolphins, Alpha and Beta—Fa and Be to their intimates—whose passion for each other is almost equaled by their love for Jake Terrell, whom Fa actually views as a father substitute. In fact, Jake and Fa have learned to talk to each other, in pidgin, or dolphin, English. Mahoney leaves, ominously intimating that Terrell will soon need his services.

Now a group of bigwigs is brought to the island by the venal DeMilo. They are senators and congressmen of a particularly reactionary sort. DeMilo extorts from Terrell an exhibition of Fa's skills (Be, a comparative neophyte, is less advanced), and the muckamucks then retire to their yacht anchored off the island. Next, the Terrells are lured on a pretext to the foundation's mainland office, and detained there while a traitor among their assistants fishnaps the dolphins and kills Mahoney's sidekick. The Terrells return to the island, as does Mahoney, who belongs to some unspecified, but apparently more benevolent, government agency watching the sinister bigwigs; he reveals the traitor to be in their service and indicates that the dolphins will be put to some unknown nefarious use. Why he couldn't warn the Terrells earlier is, like many another thing, left unexplained.

The evil panjandrums, in cahoots with DeMilo and, apparently, the entire Franklin Foundation, trick the dolphins into believing they are friends of the Terrells and teach them to carry underwater bombs to attach to the president's yacht—miles away, but no problem for a talking dolphin to ferret out. Fa smells a plot, and, under the abductors' gunfire, escapes back to the island, once again delighting his overjoyed protoparents, the Terrells, with such conversational tidbits as "Fa loves Pa" and "Fa loves Ma." Mahoney, his brain perhaps even subtler than a dolphin's, figures out the nature of the plot, but it may be too late: a marine Eve more seducible than her Adam, Be has already been dispatched on her diabolic living-submarine mission. Pa explains matters to Fa, succinctly and with no blah, and forthwith the purposeful porpoise darts off to save the Great White Da. He catches up with his lady friend in the nick of time, and they promptly hotfin it back to the other yacht and hoist the villains with their own petard.

But this is an adult fish story, and there is no happy ending. The unnamed evil powers whom the villains represent are now gathering their forces, to the tune of one rather measly helicopter, to strike against the Terrells, and all a disgruntled Jake can do is to send the dolphins back to the deep, enjoining them to forget all about vile and treacherous man, and so be safe and happy. Fa, confused and hurt, leaves with Be, hurling falsetto imprecations at his retreating father figure, even as the heartbroken scientists seek refuge among the island's sparse vegetation, where even a mangy helicopter should nose them out easily.

Nichols has once again attempted to direct in the grand manner: fancy underwater photography for the aquatic ballets of the dolphins; satirical skits in which Jake bests various wise guys, snoops, and nasty senators; a supposedly suspenseful aura of mystery hanging over the entire plot (which has trouble taking off in all that fog); and a grand, final dolphin chase to equal, *mutatis mutandis,* corresponding chases in terrestrial thrillers. But the various elements, on top of their intrinsic dubiousness, pull in different directions. Since George C. Scott wanted to costar with his new wife, Trish Van Devere, the middle-aged Jake is given a youthful spouse, a scientist herself, setting up a vestigial rivalry or jealousy motif, perhaps even a love triangle: Maggie, Jake, and Fa. But, of course, nothing much can come of such a small red herring among all those great silvery dolphins. Similarly, the cabaret skits (Nichols cannot quite live down his origins) in which Jake tangles with nosy questioners at a women's-club lecture, a bitchy executive secretary, or a scurvy senator, are of a tone not easily floatable on that dolphin-torn, that bomb-tormented sea.

Worst of all is the suspense plot, simplistic enough to be rather more laughable than the high-pitched, anile voice in which the bottle-nosed dolphin *(Tursiops truncatus)* shrills his truncated banalities. On the other hand, the dolphins, while performing unanthropomorphically in their aqueous element, are marvelous to watch—unfortunately dwarfing their human fellow-actors even beyond the trivialities inherent in Buck Henry's script. But then the dolphins, too, are dragged down by their small talk, and also by being unphotogenic in closeups, in which they look like sharks wearing hardhats. A sawtoothed, brachycephalic hardhat, even gamboling in the water, is hard to warm up to.

Yet I was moved to briny tears by the final scene in which Jake must deny his affection, and hearts, both human and cetacean, are breaking. And Peter Moss has trained the dolphins as magisterially as William A. Fraker has photographed them above water, and Lamar Boren under. But all this cannot make up for an inept screenplay, leaving the actors as stranded as dolphins out of water, and for Nichols's choppy, episodic direction. A special word of dispraise must go to Georges Delerue, the once delightful composer, whose recent scores have all been boring or, as in the present case, bombastic.

April 1974

The Lower Shallows

It is a curious fact about American movies in general, and recent ones in particular, that they do not (cannot? dare not?) cope with serious, contemporary, middle-class, adult problems. If the film is to be a drama, it can deal with the western frontier, the historical past, some war or other; with the criminal classes, occasionally spies, possibly even law-enforcers; more rarely with the lives of famous people (rarer nowadays, when the common man is more in than ever), and now and then lovable prostitutes, impoverished blacks, or exploited Indians. What is virtually nonexistent is serious filmmaking about the urban bourgeoisie and its ordinary problems of existence and co-existence—not something about beautiful young women dying of mysterious diseases, to say nothing of demonically possessed teen-agers.

Yet most of us are urban bourgeois, and the sort of discoveries we made about ourselves in the films of Antonioni, Bergman, Fellini, Buñuel, Ozu, Olmi, Truffaut, Louis Malle, Carol Reed, the early David Lean, and a few others, we are very seldom afforded by American moviemakers. Virtually every notable American film is a genre film, a frothy little comedy, or a specialty number, and, with the best of intentions, I cannot sensitize myself by viewing *Psycho* or *Rio Bravo, My Darling Clementine* or *The Maltese Falcon, 2001* or *Catch-22.* It is so rare that an American movie about middle-class living proves anything but ludicrous or pathetic or both, that it is arguable that, in this direction, the American cinema might as well give up trying. Rather than such abominations as *Blume in Love* or *Summer Wishes, Winter Dreams,* I'll take the twentieth version of *Billy the Kid,* or the fiftieth movie about a bunch of cozy burglars bungling their way to riches.

Robert Altman's latest film *Thieves Like Us*, which has been garnering solid raves, is, characteristically, a new filmization of Edward Anderson's 1937 novel on which Nicholas Ray's 1947 *They Live By Night* was based. More important, it is almost servilely derived from Arthur Penn's *Bonnie and Clyde.* Still more important, the people in the film are barely on the fringes of the middle class, the period is the already-remote thirties, and the characters are criminals and their womenfolk. And this is how close we have come to a serious adult film thus far in 1974.

Thieves Like Us is the story of three escapees from the Mississippi penitentiary and the smalltime bank robberies they pull off, becoming more reckless as they go along. One of the men is a "sensitive" young murderer, Bowie; another is the brutish quarter-Indian, Chicamaw; the third, jolly, aging T-Dub, is the leader of the trio. They are not particularly ingenious criminals, but they are up against banks and police forces that are even less clever than they are. What finally does them in is their women: T-Dub is so enamored of his silly young beautician bride that he signs his real name to their marriage license, which results in his doom; Bowie wants Keechie, his child bride, to have the comforts of the family motel, which was T-Dub's legacy to Mattie, his sister-in-law. But Mattie, whose husband is in the pen, doesn't want Bowie around, and in exchange for leniency for her spouse, ends up by betraying Bowie to the police. Keechie, who never had another man and genuinely loved Bowie, nevertheless disowns him and her past as she goes off to bear his posthumous child.

It is true that the screenplay by Calder Willingham, Joan Tewkesbury, and Altman does not explicitly blame the Depression and society for the trio's way of life. But it does have T-Dub casually refer to the bankers as "thieves like us," and Bowie wonder whether a stray dog he picks up is a "thief like me." So the feeble philosophical framework is established: rich man, poor man, dog—everyone lives by scrounging, stealing, surviving. Beyond that, the film is only interested in establishing what good family men these robbers are—except for the uncouth Chicamaw, whose meanness is implicitly blamed on being ugly and unloved—and how it is through their virtues, not their vices, that the gods destroy them.

The characters seem real enough, but authenticity without some appeal isn't worth very much. It is worth even less without some fresh insight into social and psychological problems. The supposedly superior Bowie is distinguished from his comrades only by a certain finickiness about shedding blood, but even this is not gone into. He genuinely loves Keechie, but perhaps only because he is sexually almost as inexperienced as she is. Keechie, in turn, loves three things: Bowie, making love, and guzzling Cokes, though in what order the film never makes clear. Typical of the prevailing pseudosophistication is that when Keechie, while nursing the wounded Bowie, first yields to him, the radio is playing some sort of serialization of *Romeo and Juliet,* enacted by simpering voices, and periodically interrupted by a fruitily orotund announcer's voice declaring: "Thus did Romeo and Juliet consummate their first interview by falling madly in love with each other." We hear this inane comment not once, which would be funny, but three times, which is not.

What are we to conclude from that? Altman's film makes even more persistent use of period radio programs than Bogdanovich's *Paper Moon* did. Such heavy leaning on a device, even if it is consistent with contemporary mores, calls undue attention to itself after a while. So Altman tries to justify it by extracting irony from it—by, for instance, having Bowie listen to "Gangbusters" while waiting at the wheel of the getaway car for his pals: the simplistic triumphs of fictional law enforcement are belied by reality. So, in the love scene, the clumsy, Coke-swilling sex of Bowie and Keechie is meant to appear truer, I think, than the fanciful literary love-troth, further denatured by broadcasting. Yet aside from the fact that irony goes stale in triplicate, there remains the question of why we are to consider these lovers superior, or even just equal, to Shakespeare's? The level of awareness, to say nothing of the level of expression, of Altman's pair is infinitely crude, and resembles less Shakespeare's than the radio announcer's sensibility. But if *that* is the point, why waste such attention and affection on them?

Even as irony, the radio leitmotivs fail. By the time these radios have spewed up everything from Rudy Vallee to F.D.R., from The Shadow to Seabiscuit, dubious irony deteriorates into indubitable nostalgia, exactly as in *Paper Moon.* In the end, Keechie's addiction to Coca-Cola (which is advertised even on the sign of the state penitentiary) must be meant to elicit wistful recognition of her as a child of her time. There is even something touching, not to say sweet, about the way she bowdlerizes the memory of the dead Bowie, although this is an obvious borrowing from the brilliant, tough ending of Faulkner's *Sanctuary,* without, alas, the toughness.

But when it comes to borrowing, the all too manifest source is *Bonnie and Clyde,* another film for which I had little use. Almost everything has been lifted: the rattling around in vintage cars through lush landscapes that become a playground for larking crime sprees until the game suddenly turns horribly earnest, the sentimentalization of criminals' love affairs and family ties, the use of slow motion at tragic climaxes, the obliteration of the protagonist by a barrage of bullets whose depersonalized mass production of mortality deprives death of its dignity, the betrayal by a basically well-meaning wife who becomes a police tool. Penn, Benton, and Newman almost deserve screen credit for *Thieves Like Us*—for better or worse.

Even the sappiness of *Bonnie and Clyde* is faithfully echoed by an image such as Bowie's mangled body being roughly carried out wrapped in the patchwork quilt Keechie inherited from her grandmother, the quilt Bowie and Keechie had loved so much. From the quilt, the body is brutally dumped into a mud puddle in the mercilessly pouring rain. But what the film has especially in common with *Bonnie and Clyde* is the sympathy for the criminal based on the wholly unproved proposition that he is nowise different from the rest of us. In a novella such as *Michael Kohlhaas,* the great artist Kleist was able to make the outlaw thoroughly sympathetic by methods Altman might profitably have studied, instead of resorting to facile appeal to trendily anarchic sentiments. The film, in fact, is so sloppy that it never begins to explain

Bowie's unlikely acquisition of a sheriff's credentials with which to spring Chicamaw from prison.

The most interesting thing about the movie is the photography by the superb French cinematographer Jean Boffety, here making his American debut. Boffety's cinematography was more overwhelmingly penetrant in films like *Zita* and *The Things of Life,* among others, but here the colors have an extraordinary way of looking as if painted on glass, with the milky tones so achieved. Whether this was deliberately intended to suggest the look of naïve painting I cannot say, but it is insidiously effective. The acting, too, is commendable, with Keith Carradine a believable Bowie, his charm properly undercut by a certain callowness; and Shelley Duvall a most persuasive Keechie: a *jolie laide* whose clumsinesses, though they may be personality rather than performance, fit in perfectly with the character's hesitant, awkward burgeoning. And, as usual in an Altman film, the supporting cast, besides acting competently, has a usefully unfamiliar look. In fact, Altman has most of the qualifications for a major director except the supreme one of having something significant to say.

A not dissimilar atmosphere pervades the other attention-getting quasi-meaningful film of the winter season, *The Last Detail.* It was directed by Hal Ashby, whose unenviable record includes *The Landlord* and *Harold and Maude,* and based on a novel by Darryl Ponicsan, who earlier adapted another one of his novels into the sentimental, pseudotough drivel of *Cinderella Liberty. The Last Detail* has at least the slight advantage of another scriptwriter, Robert Towne, although no one could make a silk purse out of Ponicsan's sow's ear. I use the phrase advisedly, for Ponicsan, obviously drawing on his own navy experiences, revels in his swinish ear for old-salty dialogue, in which obscenities invade every part of speech, with the possible exception of prepositions. It was quite depressing, by the way, to see the movie with a youthful audience that greeted every four-letter word with five-bell-alarm peals of laughter.

Two career sailors, Sergeants "Badass" Buddusky and "Mule" Mulhall of the Shore Patrol, are detailed to conduct a sad sack of an eighteen-year-old sailor, Meadows, from Norfolk, where he unsuccessfully tried to pilfer forty dollars from the polio collection box, to Portsmouth, New Hampshire, and eight years in the marine brig plus a dishonorable discharge. The tough, self-styled "lifers" are willing to take on this detail because with seven days' time and allowance for a two-to-three-day job, it becomes a bit of a paid vacation. What they did not bargain for is a growing sympathy for the pimply, kleptomaniacal, underprivileged and overpenalized youth, which makes them slow down their journey and devote themselves to his sentimental education. They work on instilling in him self-respect and self-assertion, then, less successfully, indignation against the navy (eight years because polio happens to be the Old Man's old lady's favorite charity!), and, finally, enjoyment of the better things of life: food, drink, and wenching. In solid intake, Meadows progresses from cheeseburgers to hero sandwiches; in liquid ingestion, from sodas to Heineken ("the finest beer in the world—President Kennedy used to drink it"); in sexual output, from zero to two cracks at a little whore whom his doting guardians purchase for him in a Boston brothel.

When Meadows reaches self-realization, he can prove his manhood only by a foolishly ineffectual attempted escape, forcing his escorts to maul him and hand him over bloodied to the untender ministrations of the "grunts." The sergeants leave Portsmouth deeply demoralized: Meadows will now find prison more unbearable, while to them the long years to come in the navy also begin to seem like imprisonment. Even if the concept of these soft-core toughies is old hat, there is a film in all this; Ashby and his cronies, however, have not found it. Their movie is too schematic in its rote ups and downs, too predictable in its calculated alternation of drama and farce, and too whorish in its playing to the gallery.

Thus, for instance, Buddusky insists that they take a detour for Meadows to visit his mother (his father has long since left), only to discover, on the Lord's day, the mother gone God knows where, and the house a shambles littered with empty bottles. No wonder poor Meadows turned out bad! Then there is Meadows's saintly unwillingness to blame the navy, which drives the enraged Buddusky into smashing his fist through a door, without so much as scratching that mighty hand. Scarcely more likely is the inexperienced Meadows's blissful first experience with sex, particularly when the whore is played by Carol Kane, scrawny and scraggly, with her eyes dementedly staring from the bottoms of two large, dark pits. Mule is black, which prompts the filmmakers to turn him meretriciously into a figure of stoic self-control and serene sagacity, a sort of Marcus Aurelius in bell-bottoms.

What lurks under the crust of obscenities is perhaps less a soft heart than a soft brain. The dialogue, even in its most self-possessed moments, never rises above the level of "Welcome to the wonderful world of pussy, kid!" or "Marines are really assholes. It takes a kind of sadistic temperament to be a marine." Ashby's direction is plodding, always settling for the obvious shot, and betraying not a hint of a personal vision. Worse yet is the cinematography of Michael Chapman, which, even if the film had been shot in 16 mm and then enlarged, would still look inexcusably coarse-grained and washed-out. Chapman also makes a brief appearance as a cab driver, on which evidence his future appears no brighter in acting than in cinematography. And then there is the blatant and banal score by Johnny Mandel.

As Buddusky, Jack Nicholson gives what many consider a superlative performance, and what strikes me as yet another example of his customary turn, which consists of delaying the reaction time to most stimuli in order to accelerate it on one or two others, and letting the emotion either seep or hurtle to the surface toward a slightly exaggerated, distorted climax—sometimes even an overstated indifference, a hammy silence. Most of this derives from Brando, and often misfires even for him. And one cannot get around the feeling that the basic pigment of all Nicholson performances is an impasto of smugness. As Mule, Otis Young is as good as the imposed idealization permits. Best of all is the Meadows of Randy Quaid. He has a way of acting in half- or quarter tones, making apparent the promise of a feeling rather than the feeling itself, and, when called for, allowing a basically benighted, opaque look to turn gradually diaphanous and radiant, the way an old iron stove becomes glowing and translucent with the fire within.

No mention of *Blazing Saddles* can be brief enough. Mel Brooks's film, like his previous *The Producers* and *The Twelve Chairs,* is a model of how not to make a comedy. It is like playing tennis not only without a net but also without a court, and with twenty balls simultaneously. All kinds of gags—chiefly anachronisms, irrelevancies, reverse ethnic jokes, and out-and-out vulgarities—are thrown together pell-mell, batted about insanely in all directions, and usually beaten into the ground.

With several gag writers huffing away full blast, it is no wonder that a few one-liners come off; what I found more amazing is that, in one of our better theaters, a civilized-looking audience laughed loudest and longest at a scene in which a bunch of cowboys sit around a campfire eating beans. One after another, they raise their backsides a bit and break wind, each a bit louder than his predecessor, the turn, in a continuous crescendo, coming back to each three times. If that is what makes audiences happiest, all hope for the future of the cinema is gone with the wind.

May 1974

Lovers on the Lam

CURIOUS, the way things come in clusters. After some delay, we are finally getting *Badlands,* the first film by a young Texan, Terrence Malick, former Harvard man, Rhodes scholar, and MIT philosophy lecturer turned filmmaker with remarkable perception and quiet bravura. *Badlands* bears a superficial resemblance to *The Sugarland Express* and *Thieves Like Us,* but is immeasurably finer than both those films rolled, or unrolled, into one. It is, in fact, the next-to-last word about the virulent alienation youth has been going through, a subject on which the last word can probably never be spoken. Wisely, Malick refrains from even trying.

The film is based on the Starkweather-Fugate case, but sensibly permits itself the freedoms of fiction. The time is 1960, the place a South Dakota town, where Kit Carruthers, a feckless twenty-five-year-old garbage collector falls for Holly Sargis, a bored fifteen-year-old high-school student, whose widowed sign-painter father rules her with a brush of iron. Kit loses his job, and may also lose Holly, whose father forbids her to see him and, by way of punishment, even shoots her dog. When the father tries to stop Kit from running off with Holly, the boy shoots him and burns down the house. For a while, the kids live idyllically in a tree house in a cottonwood grove, subsisting on what they can pluck or scrounge, and thriving on fantasies. Holly, an avid reader of movie magazines and dime fiction, when not doing the housework, reads aloud to Kit or looks at stereopticon slides. Kit is Robinson

Crusoe and Great White Hunter combined, and instructs Holly in gunmanship, handy should she have to carry on alone. The pastoral is soon passed: they are discovered, and Kit shoots the bounty hunters.

The couple seeks refuge with Kit's fellow garbage man, Cato, whom Kit ends up shooting when he seemingly attempts to turn them in. The kids become famous: alarms and posses are out from Texas to Montana. After a period of nerve-racking concealment in a rich man's house, they make off in the man's Cadillac, driving not along roads, but across the bumpy, desolate badlands. Rough riding and deprivation soon pall on Holly; even Kit is not always sure they'll make Canada, where he hopes to become a Mountie. Kit talks and acts strangely now, even by the bloody escapade's unusual standards.

When a helicopter cop sights the pair, Holly announces she won't go any farther. Enraged, Kit lets her surrender and escapes alone, but not until making an improbable date with her in the distant future. Discovered by a passing sheriff as he tries to buy gasoline, Kit leads him a merry chase, then deliberately gives up. He endures captivity with perfect bonhomie, chatting amiably and courteously with policemen and reporters, and alternating between preposterous hopes for a future and grand gestures of life-contemning resignation. During his last meeting with Holly, he is talkative and not unhopeful; she, distant and taciturn. Holly's voice, which narrates much of the film, now informs us that she got off with a suspended sentence, married her lawyer's son, and settled down to respectability. Kit, on the other hand, was asleep in the courtroom when the death sentence was pronounced. This we hear; what we see at film's end is Kit gazing out of the plane carrying him to judgment across banks of stratocumuli eerily reddened by the setting sun, but already turning to ashen gray.

The film is admirable visually, verbally, psychologically. It took guts for a neophyte filmmaker still in his twenties to fire two cinematographers before a third gave him what he wanted; yet the result is seamlessly impeccable. In the early sequences, there is a visual dialogue between bucolic lushness and sardonic undercutting—as if Grant Wood were being superimposed on Norman Rockwell. Thus Holly's father paints a grotesque sign in the middle of a lyrical landscape; so, shortly before the shooting of Cato, Kit's face, even in tight closeup, is ironically framed with intensely innocent greenery.

But when the escaping lovers drive into the badlands, nature and human beings merge in a unison bizarre yet beautiful. Instead of ironic contrasts, an all-embracing hallucination prevails. Strange little animals disport themselves by the roadside during the day; at night, towns glitter spectrally in the distance. There are dizzying light changes in the sky, as if some divine madman were improvising on a color organ. Often a whole scene is told through images, as in that excruciatingly sad and lovely episode when, in the heart of the nocturnal wasteland, the car radio picks up Nat "King" Cole singing "A Blossom Fell." (Until then, there were no period songs on the radio; *this* film shuns gratuitously nostalgic atmospherics.) The couple get out of the car to dance in a narrow streak of brightness cast by the headlights. The camera indulges in its own dreamy dance around them; what remains fixed is that slender runner of light thrown across pitch-blackness, on which two precarious lightrope walkers seem to be sleepwalking toward the abyss. In long shot, this is an abstractionist painting, subtly implying the ineluctable, fatal geometry underlying gallant little human whimsies. Both the song and the glowing headlights linger on in a slow dissolve, as dawn obtrudes slowly, soberingly.

Verbally, the film shows equal control. Thus Holly's voice-over narration, commenting from a vantage point beyond these turbulent events, stands in significant contrast to the actual dialogue. The girl's sensibility is formed, or deformed, by her shoddy reading. "Each lived for the precious hours when he or she could be with the other, away from the cares of the world," Holly's voice muses early on—and note the devastating irony of that assiduously grammatical "he or she" drowning in sentimental drivel. Again, in the treehouse sequence, the voice ruminates: "We had our bad moments, like any couple; mostly, though, we got along fine and stayed in love." This from a fifteen-year-old accomplice who eloped with her father's slayer, to describe a sylvan interlude that lasted a couple of weeks!

But what are the conversations like? After Holly's sexual initiation, the kids emerge from the bushes; the girl, still shoeless in her bobby socks, inquires: "Did it go the way it's supposed to?" "Yeah," answers Kit, buttoning his trousers. "Is that all there is to it?" "Yeah." "Gosh, what was everybody talking about?" "Don't ask me!" Never was deflation presented less inflatedly on film. (But we should recall Stendhal's *Lamiel:* "—There's nothing else? said Lamiel.—Nothing at all, Jean replied. . . . So this vaunted love, that's all it amounts to!") Then the dully monosyllabic Kit swings over into his opposite self. He picks up a heavy rock from the spot where they made love and offers to crunch their hands with it in memory of the experience. When she objects that it would hurt, he reprimands her: "That's the point, stupid!" Implicit in all this is an inchoate disillusionment with the incommensurateness and transitoriness of feeling: even Kit himself, deciding to keep the rock as a souvenir, drops it in favor of a lighter one.

This scene finds its echo much later, when Kit, tired of running, lets himself be captured, but spends his last free moments erecting a little cairn to mark the place of *his* surrender. From the transience of love, we have moved to the more fundamental transience of life itself. In the Montana wilderness, emblematic of the bewilderment in which he lived, Kit needs to put up a monument to his outlaw's career, some sign of his earthly trajectory. Yet the meanness and impermanence of the memorial presages total oblivion. Even Holly forgets apace.

In proposing to illustrate Malick's verbal control, I have wandered into his psychological penetrancy. But the two are closely related. There are three main ways in which dialogue functions. It can record faithfully how people talk, and so convey a cultural climate. In the middle of nowhere, Kit asks Holly what she knows about Montana. "The state bird is the meadowlark," she responds, like any spotty schoolgirl. Later, fed up with the adventure,

Holly complains that there is "no place to get anything good to eat," the exact naïve phraseology of the sulky adolescent.

Language can also, through imaginative intensification, elicit deeper sympathy for the speaker. As Holly sits listlessly by the driving Kit, her hair dutifully up in curlers, she plays a touching little game: "I sat in the car and read my maps and spelled out entire sentences with my tongue on the roof of my mouth, where nobody could read them." Under the romantic kitsch, under the basic prosaism even, the girl has a flash of genuine poetic invention; by endowing her with it, Malick makes her more three-dimensional as well as more engaging.

Lastly, language can portray character: reveal the speaker's innermost psychic mechanisms. When a cop asks Kit whether he likes people, the reply is, "They're okay." "Then why did you do it?" "I don't know. I always wanted to be a criminal, I guess; just not this big a one." There is the essential dichotomy: Kit is too rebellious to accept the doldrums of rural America, but not demonic enough to be at ease with his rebellion, a well-adjusted supercriminal. Throughout, he is shown as an orderly and mannerly fellow who dislikes litter and makes Holly take her textbooks along on their flight, so she won't "fall behind." He ought to have made a model garbage man instead of ending up himself in a disposal unit.

Kit and Holly's relationship is rich in complexities. He clings to her tenaciously, but who knows whether as to a lover or merely as to an audience; when he is gunned down at last, he says, he doesn't want to die without a girl there to shriek for him. Most eloquent is the moment when Holly reads from a fan magazine to the driving Kit: "Rumor: Frank Sinatra and Rita Hayworth are in love. Fact: True, but not with each other." From behind a spreading, ineffable smile, Kit murmurs, "Yeah." Has he perceived a parallel? As for Holly, at the very height of their idyl she wonders what the man she'll marry will look like; later, she narrates, she made up her mind "to never again hang out with a hell-bent type, no matter how much I was in love with him." Uncannily right: the split infinitive, the dime-novel phrase "hell-bent type," and the immature assumption that this was a great love.

Badlands sees alienation as it is: the incapacity or unwillingness to recognize the humanity of others; a huge blind spot of affectlessness amid otherwise standard attitudes. When Kit kills her father, Holly feels mild surprise, inability to believe what she is seeing. But no grief, no sense of the act's enormity. Kit has the same problem writ larger. Holly asks him about Cato: "How's he doing?" He answers: "I got him in the stomach." "Is he upset?" "He didn't say anything about it." Holly then has a little chat with the bleeding Cato about his pet spider, and is oblivious to the fact that he is dying from her lover's bullet.

The clear-eyed unawareness and casual sociability with which the pair accost their terrified victims—usually with a friendly "Hi!" which, in context, is devastating—constitute the crux of the movie. Laudably, Malick does not explain this, as it were, geological fault in the hero's and heroine's psyches. True, Holly lost a mother in infancy, was uprooted, fell under the thumb of an embittered, tyrannical father. And Kit seems to have no family at all.

There is also a hint of the stagnancy of Middle America: if the Communists must drop the bomb, they might as well do it right in the middle of Rapid City, Kit declares. But Malick does not offer these as sufficient explanations, nor will he blame society—a refusal that radical youth may easily hold against him.

Yet there is nobility in this abstention. Unlike, say, *Easy Rider,* which portrayed confusion confusedly, and summed it up with the gnomic phrase, "We blew it," *Badlands* depicts a state of confusion with meticulous clarity and insight, but refuses facile didacticism. Whether these kids were taught footling rules without having the grand design revealed to them ("Disobedience is bad!" but not, "Life is sacred!"); whether Kit is simply a psychopath; whether Holly is a mere innocent victim (as Malick seems to believe) or, in her spiritual abulia, more tainted even than Kit (as I am inclined to think); to what degree these atypical youngsters might be mere exaggerations of what lurks in all of us—these and similar questions are not answered, although quite enough is presented for each viewer to work out his own conclusions.

Let us not overlook the film's poetry, either, the quality that confers on it its ultimate distinction. It lies in the perception of beauty even in horror—not in a glib espousal of juvenile destructiveness, but in admitting the exhilaration in the spectacle of, say, a stuffy, dreary, old frame house going up in flames. This is not latent pyromania, only delight even in the illicit conversion of ancient, entrenched ugliness into a brief, cleansing bit of fireworks. Here, as elsewhere in the film, the musical score is brilliantly suggestive. It was inventive to alternate pop music with Satie and Orff, letting the musical duality reflect the characters' inner sundering.

Poetic, too, is the presence of mystery, of little things in the film that are neither realistic details, gratuitous excrescences, nor symbols exactly, yet things that are felt to belong without definable reason. Such an element is Kit's crazy walk after disposing of Cato's body, a kind of jerky, twitchy pacing back and forth, rather like the mating dance of some exotic bird. Or take an action Kit performs even as Holly narrates it: "Before we left, he shot a football that he considered excess baggage." Is this just a mad whim, or a symbolic farewell to normal young manhood, or the killing of someone in effigy? Who knows? Malick himself may not, but it feels subrationally right. As right as this dazzling film, which is not even autobiographical, the sort of thing beginning filmmakers can sometimes pull off, without being able to manage other subjects afterward. Malick chose to start with something much more demanding, and his success is doubly impressive.

If we compare *Badlands* with *The Sugarland Express,* the difference between the artist and the mere smartass becomes overwhelmingly manifest. Steven Spielberg's film about a kooky couple on the lam, escorted by what seems to be the entire Texas police force (unable to stop them because of a cop they hold as hostage), has a certain cinematic knack, but is all effect and no real humanity, all manipulation and splash, and no attempt at honest insight. When Spielberg wants laughs, which is most of the time, his couple is zany and cute with a vengeance; when he wants tragedy, a good cop turns arbitrarily into a bastard, the dumb principals become even dumber, and the cinematography goes as arty as only Vilmos Zsigmond can make it.

The film lurches from one sophomorically bright idea to the next: one time, when the police motorcade must suddenly renew its pursuit, a goodly bunch of policemen is bedewing the urinals and then shown comically changing courses in midstream; another time, when the pursuit starts up again, some idiotic cop won't stop repairing his captain's headlights, so the boss drives the car right out from between the tinkerer's hands. And not only is characterization walked all over by gags and thrills, the principals are also too stupid for us to care about them.

Even the acting is mostly caricature. True, William Atherton cannot give a bad performance, but the usually able Michael Sacks overdoes the policeman hostage's naïveté, and Goldie Hawn plays the screwy young mother with a rising pitch of exaggeration that ends in sheer self-indulgence. Contrast this with the immaculate performances Malick gets from Martin Sheen, a splendid actor who here reaches new heights of understated suggestiveness, and Sissy Spacek, who was touching in *Prime Cut,* yet is even finer here by not playing on our sentiments. While Sheen changes mercurially from emotion to intricate emotion, she maintains a wistful abstractedness across which flicker hesitant ambiguities.

Francis Ford Coppola's *The Conversation* starts out auspiciously enough as a quasi-documentary about wiretappers at work, a chilling display showing the expertise with which the privacy of even shrewd and suspicious people can be invaded. But the icy fascination soon succumbs to two forms of excess. One is Coppola's growing infatuation with the technical aspects of his subject, which drenches us with ever splashier aural effects, closely combined with scarcely less frantic visual hocus-pocus. The other is a mystery story that thickens into ever greater contrivance, improbability, and opacity, at the same time obliging the protagonist, a master wiretapper with an awakening conscience, to become progressively, not more human, as intended, but weirder and less believable.

Gene Hackman heftily overplays both the character's quirkiness and his emotional paralysis, and though the rest of the cast is effective, Cindy Williams (so good in *American Graffiti)* is woefully unconvincing as a *femme fatale.* And there is something profoundly irritating about a movie that presents its hero as a celebrated mastermind, and then proceeds to have him fall for a row of transparent stratagems. Bill Butler's cinematography is uninspired, and the film disintegrates into the very thing it purports to attack: an invasion of the spectator's privacy with glaring visual jolts and aural jabs.

June 1974

Gatsby De-greated

When will the movies learn not to adapt great, or even good, novels to the screen? This is not the place to debate into which of those categories *The Great Gatsby* falls; either way, it is a work of art because of its style, and there is no way in which a written style can be turned into a cinematic one. Partly out of exploitativeness, but partly also out of stupidity, producers ignore a fact that the very schoolchildren of today have mastered: the form is the content. The shape of the novel on the page, its paragraph and sentence structure, the imagery and cadences of the prose, and all the things that are left to the imagination, these, as much as plot and character, are what the novel is about, and these, in good and great novels, cannot be transposed on screen—do not even yield cinematic equivalents. To a short, sleek novel like *Gatsby,* where the slight action moves forward like a capricious swimmer (now at a leisurely breaststroke, then at a furious crawl, then again with a dainty backstroke or a splashily showy butterfly, but always cool and elegant) nothing could be more destructive than slow pace, top-heavy lavishness, and overexplicitness. Under these impositions, the film version sinks to the bottom.

Yet even if the film were paced better—and it is about to receive some postmortem cutting—it would be no use. Much, if not most, of the book's life is in the descriptions and animadversions of Nick Carraway, the naïve yet thoughtful narrator, whose gradually waning starry-eyedness and nascent sobriety provide the basic flavor and progression. But even though Francis Ford Coppola's screenplay incorporates some of this as Nick's voice-over narration, indeed smuggles some of it into the dialogue, a great deal of it inevitably gets dropped. The unfortunate attempt has been made, however, to translate almost every missing textual element into a compensatory silence, a lingering over something, a marking of time, and it is often as if the screen were invaded by visible lacunae and hiatuses slouching and dragging themselves about among the performers.

There are no fewer errors of sheer incomprehension. Take, for example, the case of a single line: In the book, Nick says of Daisy, "She's got an indiscreet voice," and breaks off hesitantly after, "It's full of—" to which Gatsby responds *suddenly* (as Fitzgerald states) with, "Her voice is full of money." Jack Clayton, the director, allows Robert Redford's Gatsby to be Method-actorishly introverted and speculative: "It's full of . . . full of . . . the voice is full of money." How deeply wrong those pauses are! Gatsby is not an analytical, philosophical soul; if he were, he wouldn't be Gatsby. His rare insights, and this is one of them, are slapdash and almost fortuitous, which is what makes them so touching and even tragic: they are truths from the mouths of babes who should long since have grown up; and, like other such truths, they go by ignored, first and foremost by the babes themselves.

Or take a short scene. Gatsby, followed by Nick, is showing Daisy his house and riches for the first time. As Fitzgerald puts it, "He took out a pile of shirts and began throwing them, one by one, before us, shirts of sheer linen and thick silk and fine flannel, which lost their folds as they fell and covered the table in many-colored disarray." The "soft rich heap [mounts] higher" and Daisy bends into it and cries "stormily," explaining between sobs: "It makes me sad because I've never seen such—such beautiful shirts before." Now Clayton and Coppola, presumably to make the scene more dramatic, have Gatsby toss out shirts ever more frantically, not really on the table before Daisy, but all around on the floor. The meaning is thrown away with the shirts: what is intended as an awkward, foolish love tribute, a wooing of Daisy with these absurd yet to her not at all irrelevant trappings, becomes in the film an act of display for its own sake, a pointless frenzy of excess. And when the inept Mia Farrow then starts sniffling and simpering, instead of crying stormily, we do not get that sense of heart-rending preposterousness, of too much not soon enough, of lives wrecked for the want of a hundred silken shirts. The audience, both times I saw the movie, merely laughed. They should have laughed and wept.

Clayton's and Coppola's directorial and scenaristic faults, despite, and even because of, superficial striving for fidelity, are legion. It is a big mistake to introduce many of the same characters during *both* big-party scenes at Gatsby's house and so convey a certain consistency and stability where all should be flux and transience. It is an error to belabor the T. J. Eckleburg sign more than Fitzgerald did, clobbering us with what should be a symbol only for the pathetic Wilson, and certainly not appear to be some God-oriented moral message of the entire work. It is a dreadful idea to have the bereaved Wilson consoled by an elderly, almost slow-witted comforter (unsubtly played by Elliot Sullivan), when Fitzgerald deliberately made the character young and not semidoddering—to show that not even the young and strong can help one another in a world grown senile around them.

There are many such lapses, most of them on the side of simplification or obviousness. Others, though, derive merely from the pitfalls inherent in the change of genres. Personally, I would be happier if neither novel nor film contained that supererogatory, quasi-poetic ending about America having loomed as the last great promise to its discoverers, but that Gatsby and his likes failed to realize that the dream was already behind them. Yet under no circumstances should part of this commentary be distributed as dialogue between Nick and Gatsby: it is bad enough for the author to be overexplanatory, but unforgivable for a character to know what he cannot know. After such knowledge, what forgiveness?

Then there is the wretched cinematography of Douglas Slocombe. His colors are often those of primitive twenties postcards, faces in a sunset, for instance, doused with a flat orange yellow light coming from the wrong direction! Everything in the picture gleams and glistens, or else dreamily blurs; but when, in closeups, human eyeballs begin to sparkle like Christmas-tree ornaments, we suffocate in all that pomp and zirconstance.

The acting and casting also deserve castigation. Redford cuts too elegant, civilized, almost overeducated a figure to convey the fishily and insecurely risen Gatsby; conversely, Bruce Dern is too crude and oafish to be a born and Yale-bred millionaire: he, not Gatsby, emerges as the outsider. Mia Farrow, whose voice is all crooning and squawking, embodies Daisy's superficiality, but not her charm and attraction. Ironically, her skull-like face looks much too unhealthy to suggest carefreeness careering into carelessness. Karen Black is miles away from Fitzgerald's Myrtle; no simple, totally sensual older woman, she is merely a grosser version of Farrow's insipid sex kitten. Miss Black's histrionic range is not just limited—it seems actually to shrink with every new picture. Scott Wilson's Wilson is too weak and hysterical from the outset, but Lois Chiles makes an acceptable Jordan Baker, and Roberts Blossom a believable Gatz Sr.

Sam Waterston, who specializes in good-natured dopiness whether or not his part calls for it, is perfectly cast as Nick and comes off much the best. But to turn *The Great Gatsby,* nervous and rapid, into a slow, uninvolving "The Good Carraway," is seedy business indeed. I doubt if the novel ever bored anyone; at the end of the film's one big preopening screening there was only dull, exhausted silence. Not even the freeloaders and sycophants could work up the energy to applaud.

July 1974

Jacobin—Not Jacobite

PETER BOGDANOVICH'S *Daisy Miller* shows what happens to an eclectic director when he has no clear prototypes to emulate. Bogdanovich was at loose ends, looking for a subject that might suit his girl friend, Cybill Shepherd, when he hit on *Daisy Miller.* He decided that Henry James had written the novella with Cybill in mind, and that the least he could do to oblige Miss Shepherd and Mr. James was to make this film, even if there were no analogues and precedents, as for his previous movies. It is hard to determine to whom he has done the greater disservice: to his author, by assuming he could bring him to the screen, or to his inamorata, by assuming he could get her to act.

James's Daisy is a charming but uneducated girl, an American innocent abroad, who founders not so much on the ancient and sophisticated wiles of Europe as on the narrowness of Europeanized Americans, whose conventional proprieties she carelessly flouts. Daisy's characterization is a tour de force: James manages to make her both superior in her naturalness and irritating in her flirtatiousness; delightful in her native taste and wit, but also rather trying in her uneducatedness and capriciousness. By observing her intermittently and somewhat uneasily, through the fascinated but fearful eyes of his narrator, Winterbourne, James maintains a slightly ambiguous haze around his heroine: Bogdanovich and his coscenarist, Frederic Raphael, have labored to make the ambiguity obvious.

Daisy is now ignorant and crass enough to start applauding her admirer's aria before he has anywhere near finished, and she is assigned such utterly trivial (not to mention anachronistic) badinage as: "You're fun!" "Am I?" "Uh-huh." She rattles on soullessly, yet we are meant to share Winterbourne's tragic bereavement at her death. Barry Brown, who plays Winterbourne, said of him that "he'll always be haunted by what happened," which is clearly implied in the camera's final receding into the distance, leaving the figure of Winterbourne, alone in the cemetery, becoming smaller and more forlorn, until the image turns sickly yellow and fades out completely. Not so in James, where the man returns to Geneva, for what may be further studies, or a dalliance with "a very clever foreign lady." The movie Winterbourne is a would-be Othello spying on Daisy from behind church columns, more intensely and ridiculously jealous than the story Winterbourne, and more crushed and lost in the end. The tragicomedy of social and sexual misapprehension becomes a sentimental tale of loss.

Works of true literary art never translate well to the screen, but a novella in particular runs the danger of inadequate additions—and I am not even concerned here with such anachronisms of dialogue as "I like just hanging around," or having the Roman ruins illuminated at night by what seems to be indirect lighting some forty years before it was heard of. What does concern me is making Daisy's little brother, Randolph, into an even less tolerable brat by the accretion of nasty new exploits; having Daisy's mother prattle insufferably even when Daisy is dying, at which point James gives her some dignity; turning Eugenio, an ordinary liveried courier, into a black-clad, evil-eyed figure of menace; foisting on Giovanelli faulty, pseudocomic English, whereas James stressed his command of it; and so on. Some things are fulsomely overexplained ("malaria: that's what the Roman fever is," and, at the Colosseum, you can even hear the buzz of the anopheles) so that the most ignorant can get them; others are cravenly omitted or toned down (Randolph is no longer called an infant Hannibal, and a "Comanche savage" becomes, redundantly, a "Comanche Indian"), lest anyone take offense.

Superficially, Bogdanovich's direction is competent enough. He once joked that critics would call this his "homage to George Cukor," but even Cukor would have managed things better. For example, when Daisy and Winterbourne drive away from Chillon, there is a lingering long shot of the castle prettily framed in the carriage's rear window. But this nostalgic shot is not from Daisy's point of view, for she does not give a hoot for castles, history, and culture; nor can it be from that of her swain, who has eyes only for Daisy. The direction, in short, is pictorial rather than psychological, preferring effect to truthfulness. When Winterbourne, drawn by the sight of an unwonted hansom waiting outside the nocturnal Colosseum, approaches the ruin, we get a fancy wide-angle shot of the edifice from Winterbourne's seemingly overawed point of view, though he is merely a midnight stroller whose curiosity has been piqued.

The director has an eye for the bizarre, as in a scene in which he evokes the curious way in which one took the waters circa 1878, but he lacks psychological sensitivity. Thus he allows little Randolph to become an actual thief, or permits the sound track to tinkle out *"La donna è mobile"* via some unseen player piano as a hotel clerk informs Winterbourne of Daisy's death—an irony that is not just heavy-handed but downright inept. Still more obviously, Bogdanovich cuts from Randolph aiming his alpenstock at the hero and going "Bang!" to a matching shot of the departing promenade boat blowing its siren as its stack discharges smoke—a self-conscious cuteness that establishes neither a useful similitude nor a significant contrast. Particularly unfortunate is a scene with Daisy and Giovanelli at the piano, singing songs at Winterbourne, designed chiefly to exhibit Miss Shepherd's modest vocal endowments, and derived more likely from Harry than from Henry James.

And what acting! Cybill Shepherd's Daisy looks right and is dressed right by the British designer John Furness, with the exquisite taste James attributed to American young ladies; but there the similarity ends. Miss Shepherd's conception of the part—whether her own, or Svengalized into her by her director-lover—consists of reading all her lines prestissimo, with equal lack of emphasis, and then, when the subject suddenly becomes personal, staring intently at Winterbourne and letting the ensuing embarrassed pause do her acting for her. Consider: a chatterbox is not necessarily a robot; a charming chatterbox in particular is not a windup toy, but puts a certain variety and playful styling into her chitchat. But the very few times Miss Shepherd does not sound like a recorded message played at accelerated speed, she sounds like a ponderous coquette belaboring her gentlemen with a cleaver—a verbal Lizzie Borden.

Fully as bad is the Winterbourne of Barry Brown. Picked for the part because he looked to Bogdanovich like the rare actor who has actually read a book, he manages to look and sound like someone who has indeed read one book—*Little Women,* say, or *Uncle Tom's Cabin.* His expressions are two: a would-be debonair but actually wan and fumbling smile, and a look he reserves for Daisy—the gaze of a lovesick calf. This look, to do him justice, he is able to heighten: it progresses to lovesick wallaby and lovesick potto, until, at Daisy's graveside, it culminates in lovesick onager.

In the supporting cast, young James McMurtry looks a perfect Randolph, but recites his lines by vacuous rote; the vastly overrated Cloris Leachman makes Daisy's mother even more of a gibbering nitwit than Daisy, which is carrying family resemblance, whether deliberately or not, to disastrous lengths. The sometimes effective Mildred Natwick hams up Mrs. Costello, and the generally gifted Eileen Brennan lacks upper-class hauteur as Mrs. Walker. George Morfogen merely scowls as Eugenio, and Duilio Del Prete's Giovanelli is a caricature. But caricature is what Bogdanovich thrives on—what his three successful films wallowed in; thus here, when a Swiss guide shows disapproval of Daisy and Winterbourne's conduct, he makes not one but three disparaging gestures. Bogdanovich once said in an interview (in which, as usual, he dismissed the European art film and extolled the commercial movies of Hawks, Hitchcock, Ford, and their ilk): "My best days as a filmgoer were around the time I was ten. My taste was purest then." On the evidence of *Daisy Miller,* this was self-depreciation: Bogdanovich's taste has lost none of its ten-year-old's purity.

August 1974

Jaundice of the Soul

WITH *Chinatown,* Roman Polanski makes a comeback. True, in some ways a throwback to all those private-eye movies, often based on novels by Dashiell Hammett or Raymond Chandler, that supplied the cinema of our formative (or merely impressionable) years with one of its juiciest genres. But *Chinatown* is not just another *Maltese Falcon* or *Big Sleep,* to be dismissed as a contemporary painting that apes, however skillfully, an Old Master. It is, rather, a subtly updated version: an equivalent with significant albeit subcutaneous differences that puts Polanski, after the monstrous fiasco of *What?,* back into the running.

The plot could hardly be more archetypal. The capable private investigator, J. J. Gittes, slightly soiled but basically honorable, is employed by a beautiful woman with a husband problem, a woman who may, in fact, be criminal herself. Gittes has the properly ambivalent relationship with the police lieutenant who is working parallelly, or obliquely, on the same case: once they were partners in uniform, now they nudge each other with a mixture of respect and mistrust. Gittes is sucked into a world of intrigue in which, typically, he gets about as many beatings as he delivers. Finally, though he solves the case, success turns bitter in his mouth. Life is a cracked bowl of mostly rotten cherries.

So what else is new about *Chinatown?* Quite a bit, actually. The hero, even though the time and place is Los Angeles in the thirties (which is to this genre what Paris 1890 was to bedroom farce), is played by Jack Nicholson as an emblematic man of today. Unlike the Bogartian hero, he is not coolly sure of himself all the way down the line. His wisecracks are more brittle, he is occasionally gauche, his aplomb is muted by a sense of moral ambiguity. He can break up at other people's jokes as retold by himself, a childlike trait as remote from Bogey as the somewhat high-pitched voice and thinning hair, both of which render Nicholson's Gittes more fragile, as does his slightly ridiculous name: can you imagine Hammett calling a Spade a Gittes?

The lovely but shopworn heroine, Evelyn Mulwray (Faye Dunaway), is also faintly off-center. Under the beautiful, battered exterior there lurks neither the untouched innocent who can settle down snugly into a happy ending, nor a fascinating wrongdoer for whom the electric chair is the fitting final seat. Even the chief villain is not your typical racketeer, sadist, or madman; his evil has sociopolitical coloration and even a certain pathos; too bad that John Huston, a living *hommage* to *The Maltese Falcon,* gives an essentially lazy, unresonant performance opting for easy charm. The others are mostly genre types, but the police lieutenant (Perry Lopez) is a Chicano, whose position is ipso facto precarious, which brings us back to social implications.

What primarily distinguishes the film from its models is the new sensibility of the director and scenarist, and the new technology, wide-screen and color, which interestingly distort the old simplicities. Thus the "Chinatown" in which the final reckoning unfurls is not so much a place as a concept, a symbol. Gittes, when still on the force, was stationed in Chinatown, where the wary police motto was, "Do as little as possible." In this Chinatown, he loved a woman and tried to keep her from being hurt, but "ended up making sure that she *was* hurt." Throughout the film there are quietly ominous references to this Chinatown where "you can't always tell what's going on," but where your very life is changed even as you endeavor to do as little as possible.

Gradually, then, we become aware of a Chinatown of the mind, to which, the film says, all roads lead. Unlike Rome, it is not a place to which we want to be led, for in it *we* do not have a Chinaman's chance. Because the film works honestly and contemporaneously with real locations (instead of, say, the fancy opium-den setting, smelling more of studio than of opium, where the Martha Vickers character is shown in *The Big Sleep),* it must use the available Chinatown of Los Angeles, which is not quite the place of sinister mystery we might demand from an objective correlative. This is somewhat disappointing visually, but has the virtue of forcing us toward the symbolic rather than realistic values of the concept. What is more troubling is that the references to Chinatown seem at times to be dragged arbitrarily into the conversation, and that the various Chinese servants, who also serve as visual reminders, no longer exude the disquieting "Oriental inscrutability" they gave off when private-eyehood was in flower.

Yet it is not just some philosophic overview that differentiates this film from its predecessors. Nor do I mean the greater sexual freedom in language and incident. So, for instance, the film begins with a series of black-and-white stills, mostly of copulation, accompanied by grunting on the sound track. By degrees we realize that we are looking at telephoto snapshots of infidelity being examined by a Gittes client, and that the groans are not the lecher's but the cuckold's. In an old folks' home, we are allowed to glimpse an elderly inmate grabbing a nurse's buttocks. The brief affair between Gittes and Mrs. Mulwray, for all its tactful understatement, is still more suggestive than was once possible: "I didn't see anyone for very long," says Evelyn about her psychosexual disarray. "It's difficult for me. . . ."

The main modernity of *Chinatown* is of a different order. Robert Towne's screenplay (so superior to that for *The Last Detail)* is at times much more speculative than the old genre films dared to be: "Politicians, ugly buildings, and whores all get respectable if they last long enough," the aged millionaire-villain will say. Things also get more Rabelaisian: when a policeman taunts J.J. with an unflattering interpretation of how he came by his nose injury, our hero replies, "No. Your wife got excited and crossed her legs a little too quick. . . ." But what really brings the film into the 1970s is the loss of innocence that permeates its world: the boundaries between right and wrong have become hazy even in the good—or better—people, and the two genuine innocents of the film are both, in one way or another, victimized. The entire world is headed for its Chinatown, and when, in the end, Gittes, faced with a dreadful recurrence of loss, mutters dazedly, "As little as possible," what may have once been shrewd strategy becomes a counsel of universal despair.

Entirely new is the approach to violence. There is less of it than in the Marlovian heyday, and much less than in the Spillanian decadence; what there is of it, however, is more discriminating, disturbing, and real. When Gittes is to be given a warning, an ugly little punk (played by Polanski himself) slices up his nose with a switchblade knife. It happens quickly, too quickly for immediate comprehension, with the full new awareness that speed, brevity, and opacity vastly increase the horror quotient. The sight is grisly, and the aftereffects are precisely observed: J.J.'s nose, for the rest of the film, is bandaged, and though the bandages decrease in size with clinical accuracy, even the big sex scene, with the bandages temporarily removed, has to be played with a nose from which the freshly torn sutures protrude like a carp's whiskers. A lesser villain, whom Gittes roughs up, sports a suitably bandaged head next time round. And the final bullet hole of the film has the true disfiguring ghastliness that could not have been shown formerly. Yet the film is at the other end of the scale from those movies where excess of violence is allowed to immunize the viewer with surfeit.

So, too, the sex is treated with a nice adultness, and the only place where the film becomes childishly preposterous is the very end, when a policeman pulls off the kind of fatal marksmanship that is as improbable as the fatuous nonmarksmanship in certain films by Godard and Truffaut. Otherwise, *Chinatown* is a cogently low-key thriller, in which action and even suspense must take a backseat to atmosphere: a sense of general corruption far more unsettling than the conventionally localized evil of the standard genre film, however explosive it may be.

Historically and visually, the ambience is laudably right. Anthea Sylbert's costumes, and her brother-in-law's, Richard Sylbert's, sets could not look more Los Angeles circa 1935, but without any ostentation. Granted that in few places has time stood so ponderously still as in the capital of film and sunny living unclouded by thought, there are still details here that are wonders of re-creative exactness, whether it is the goose-pimpled brown leatherette covering on binoculars, wooden-slatted Venetian blinds, or stacks of Pears soap in a bathroom cupboard. And never does one of Faye Dunaway's outfits call attention to itself as it would had it been designed, say, by Theadora van Runkle. Jerry Goldsmith's score avoids repetition of an obvious theme (it is, in the ordinary sense, almost tuneless) and can eerily subsume the sound of a leaky faucet in a murdered woman's apartment. Sam O'Steen's editing is happily uncommitted to modish hyperexcitation, and will linger appositely over the desolation of a dry riverbed.

Very fine, too, is the cinematography of John A. Alonzo. It makes use of the wide screen in various cunning ways, managing even to convey strong verticals, as when Gittes is spying on Mulwray from roof- or hilltops; but it can also be cleverly procrustean when it shows just enough of Miss Dunaway's breasts for erotic spice, but not too much to deflect attention from the dialogue. Yet it is not just a matter of framing shots (which, in any case, is more the director's doing), but also of using an ingeniously muted palette, with emphasis on tawny or burnished tones that somehow suggest a bygone era preserved in amber.

The final question is whether a mystery film, however concerned with moral climate and psychological overtones, can transcend its genre. The performances Polanski elicits are certainly unusual. Jack Nicholson has never trod with greater assurance the fine line between professional cynicism verging on sleaziness and a still untarnished self-respect and concern for at least the less demanding decencies of life; he looks wonderfully in period with his hair almost in a center part, and he manages emotional shadings miles above his self-indulgences in *The Last Detail.* Faye Dunaway, too, carries off a neat balancing act as a woman whose sophistication cannot gloss over her woundedness, and whose neuroses and sound instincts are at war beneath a translucent coat of not-quite-chip-proof polish. These people are much more vulnerable than their genre antecedents, which is what ultimately makes for *Chinatown's* originality and distinction. Still, the hold of the genre is so strong that, even with sensational plot twists kept at a minimum, there simply isn't room enough for full character development—for the richer humanity required by art.

October 1974

No Dice

OF TWO NEW FILMS about gambling neither hits the jackpot; both *California Split* and *The Gambler* merely hit us over the head with their points or pointlessness. The subject of gambling does not interest me very much, but it is the duty and prerogative of art to create concern where none was previously. I have become deeply involved with black sharecroppers, Italian shoeshine boys, and Swedish Lutheran pastors to whom, before seeing certain films, I consecrated nary a thought; the trouble with *The Gambler* and *California Split* is that even if gambling preoccupied me, I wouldn't give a damn about them.

Gambling, surely, must be seen not as an end in itself but as a symptom. The figure of the gambler becomes interesting in terms of what his gambling is an escape from or excuse for. The two great classics of gambling, Pushkin's *The Queen of Spades* and Dostoevsky's *The Gambler,* both intimately involve their heroes with women: behind each gambler there is a woman being used as a tool or pretext. So, too, the great womanizers in history—Casanova, for example—tended to be gamblers as well, wenching and gambling going traditionally hand in hand (e.g., *The Rake's Progress*). Indeed, in Renaissance English "to game" meant both to wench and to gamble. To separate gambling from virtually everything else, as Robert Altman does in *California Split,* is not to see it more sharply, only to see too little.

To gamble is to pursue luck—personified, not for nothing, as Lady Luck, which brings us back to women. The gambler, like Don Juan, is always in transition toward a new and greater conquest, either to recoup past losses or to win at still higher, more prestigious stakes, against still greater odds. Like Juan, he sets up an artificial, parallel world—the game of love or roulette—which becomes a model of the real world, but smaller, more controllable, and, when controlled, conferring money, power, and love upon one. Which is to say, all the emoluments of the real world, as the simpleton sees it. Gambling means competing in an easier, more tractable game; it is presumed to be simpler to win at cards or seduction than at serious work. The game, then, is a model of life, which, like model trains, becomes the real thing. And, like the seducer, the gambler must go on, to evade the difficulties of staying put, of maintaining a relation to life.

California Split has Elliott Gould and George Segal as two smalltime gamblers gambling away at, and with, everything. The difference is that Gould is your straight comic gambler who turns all things into a joke, most often infantile; whereas Segal is your seriocomic gambler whose agonizing teeters on the ledge between the ridiculous and the pitiful. One night, after they win at poker, they are rolled by the losers, and the team that is preyed on together, plays on together. They win a little at various games, lose a lot, and finally make a killing, only for Segal to discover that victory is meaningless, a taste of ashes in his mouth. That is a puny and wizened revelation for a monomaniacal two-hour film to be huffing, puffing, and churning its way up—or down—to. Consider, by way of contrast, Casanova: "So I spent the two hours playing . . . winning, losing . . . in complete freedom of body and soul . . . enjoying the present and snapping my fingers at the future and at all those who are pleased to exercise their reason in the dreary task of foreseeing it." Gambling as the disenfranchisement of reason, then, and the embracing of an absurd universe.

Now take Dostoevsky in *The Gambler,* a semi-autobiographical novel: "No, it wasn't the money that I wanted so much. . . . I wanted that . . . all these [burghers], all these headwaiters, all these elegant Baden ladies . . . should be talking about me, that they should all be telling my story, that they should all wonder at me, admire me, and worship my . . . success." That seems to me to get at the essence—coming from a great writer who was also a great, abject gambler: gambling as a conquerable microcosm that can eventually absorb the real world.

This is the sort of insight that I would want *California Split* to dramatize for me; but neither Robert Altman nor his scenarist, the actor Joseph Walsh, is concerned with, or capable of, such an undertaking. True, they do show the winners basking in brief bouts of celebrity and adulation, but this would make a point only if the other side of the coin were visible, too: what is it that Gould, the petty gamester living or partly living with two call girls, and Segal, the middling magazine writer separated from his wife, are escaping from and failing to grapple with? And when Segal, a disillusioned winner, mutters in the end, "I'm going home," what kind of an actual or metaphorical home has he in mind? The film, enamored of mere atmosphere and cunningly inconsequential incidents, couldn't care less.

But even on its own level, the movie suffers from Altman's apparently ever more unshakable idiosyncrasies. Foremost among these is the notion that life is a series of tragicomic whimsies—that it is, somehow, sadly cute. All right, if only Altman could convince me that the wistful joke is truly the building block with which life and movies are constructed. It may be that these paltry gamblers are in fact funny-pathetic; but are the two call girls who put up

 Gould regularly and Segal sporadically also funny-pathetic? And the aging, obese singer-pianist at a Reno casino who croaks out unlistened-to songs from under her bleached hair? And the obstreperous young woman whom Gould talks out of betting on a winning horse, and who ends up pelting him with her luncheon oranges? Funny-pathetic, of course! And how does Gould beat up the gambler who rolled him? And how do Gould and Segal rout a middle-aged transvestite client who threatens to preempt their girls? You guessed it: funny-pathetically. Which is also how the piddling bookie who underwrites Segal sees himself. And how does Segal's attempt to make out with the younger prostitute end when the older one comes in to retrieve a copy of *TV Guide* mislaid somewhere between the girl's sheets? Funny-pathetically, yessir.

And how does Altman apprehend his questionable reality? Structurally, by tiny, more or less repetitious incidents, vaguely cute and inconclusive, rather like a bunch of O. Henry stories with their punch lines removed. Technically, with an eight-track recorder and up to eleven microphones. His idée fixe is that reality strikes us as the world does William James's paradigmatic baby: as a big, blooming, buzzing Babel of sounds and voices, from which the significant dialogue emerges only after you've hacked your way through layers of irrelevance. The lesser problem with this is that by the time your machete cuts through to what you were meant to hear, it proves too measly a reward for such Herculean labors. The bigger problem, though, is that certain ways of representing reality can become more real than the thing itself, and fatally overshoot the mark. In life, even in the most crowded and clamorous places, we can easily segregate what we wish to listen to from what we don't, or we'd go mad with frustration. In Altman's 111 minutes we haven't the time to go mad, only to be thoroughly exasperated.

Performances in an Altman movie also tend to pile up frail, idiosyncratic trifling into parlously overweening card castles; Gould, for example, is encouraged to carry on his cutesy nonstop monologues (the world perceived in a bubble of gum) at outlandish lengths, and even Segal is made to rely on his boyish charm more heavily than that slender crutch will bear. There are, however, some good supporting performances, notably from Ann Prentiss and Gwen Welles as the whores—the lesbian undercurrent of their relationship is, in fact, the film's most subtle and penetrating touch—and from the late Barbara Ruick as a barmaid. Other roles, however, are grossly exaggerated, especially those of Jeff Goldblum and Barbara Colby as Segal's boss and receptionist.

Paul Lohmann's cinematography is, as they say, moody and evocative, but, again, the graininess and haziness rather overextend themselves. In general terms, there is nothing wrong with concentrating on atmosphere, if only it doesn't devour everything else, or become too self-conscious, or rub its excogitated casualness in our faces, all of which we get here. But I may be harder on Altman than I would be on someone else precisely because I detect a mind at work in his movies, so that his floundering strikes me as more wasteful than that of the typically mindless Hollywood director, old or new.

A much more annoying movie is Karel Reisz's *The Gambler,* from a script by James Toback. I have been rooting for Reisz to make a good film after such interesting, or at least provocative, failures as *Saturday Night and Sunday Morning, Morgan!,* and the front-office-mangled *Loves of Isadora;* alas, *The Gambler* isn't it. There had been advance reports that Toback was deriving his script, at a remove, from Dostoevsky's short novel (which had previously served as the basis for Robert Siodmak's *The Great Sinner,* a pygmy peccadillo), but there are only two distant tributes to the Russian master: naming the hero Axel, after the novel's Alexei; and a brief but embarrassing classroom discussion of *Notes from the Underground* led by Axel, who, like Alexei, is a teacher, albeit not a private tutor but a professor of English at a New York university.

What we get is a shabbily conventional story about an otherwise nice young man's addiction to gambling—a story that does make wobbly obeisances to integrating the gambling mania with certain social, psychic, and sexual phenomena, but makes them so superficially, self-consciously, and self-contradictorily as to be worse than worthless—pretentious. Axel approaches gambling in a sometimes frenzied, sometimes blasé manner, which is neither new nor interesting. And here I begin to wonder whether gambling isn't a subject unsuited to film. Womanizing, for example, involves relationships with other human beings who act, react, interact. But the gambler at roulette, say, interacts only with objects like a revolving disk and a small metal ball, and with a croupier scarcely more animate than they. Other gamblers sit around, but are all likewise locked into their unvoiced perceptions. A kind of gambling that involves visible skill, such as pool, may be more photogenic, and a kind that involves the give-and-take of bluffing, such as poker, more dramatic; but it is all, essentially, internalized, solipsistic, and far better dealt with by fiction or autobiography.

Axel has a curious relationship with his mother, who gives him all her savings to cover his gambling debts, but this is not gone into very much: "Have I been such a failure that I raised a son to have the morals of a snake?" she wonders, less than searchingly. Axel also has a curious relationship with his grandfather, a poor Jewish immigrant who acquired enormous wealth, but will not pay Axel's debt and berates him for getting involved with the Syndicate. When Axel reproaches the oldster with his own shady past, the overworked reptilians crawl out again: "I dealt with those vipers because I had to, not because I wanted to," an arresting piece of casuistry that remains unscrutinized. When Axel and his rather benighted girl, Billie, are aroused in the middle of the night by an irate bookie demanding to be paid off, Billie inquires: "Do you like people breaking in on you like this when you're asleep? 'Cause I sure don't." No reptiles here, but not much soaring language of insight either.

One looks for a pattern in these relationships that might shed light on Axel's predicament, but there isn't one. And as an English professor, Axel feeds his students blatant banalities, whether about Dostoevsky or William Carlos Williams's *In the American Grain* (a curious curriculum, too, come to think of it). The students, in turn, are shown as deserving no better, either giggling like junior-high cheerleaders or driveling densely or arrogantly. Have we reached this sorry level thanks to open admissions? And if so, where: at the universities or at the film studios? The prize for pretentiousness goes to a scene where, after a considerable killing, Axel and Billie relax in their Vegas hotel room. Billie recalls a former lover who brought her here, and whom she watched being horribly mutilated by the Syndicate. "Buffalo Bill's defunct," Axel murmurs. "What's that?" asks Billie. "The first line of a poem." "What does it mean?" "What it says." Now that dialogue has everything: Hemingwayish toughness, cocktail-party literacy, sophomoric depth, and total irrelevance.

Nevertheless, the film does try, feebly, to explain gambling with limp statements such as, "I like the threat of it—the uncertainty of it. . . . That I could lose, but I won't. . . . And I love winning, even though it never lasts." And this inadequate verbalizing doesn't even reap the benefit of competent visual support. Reisz, who has written the definitive book about film editing, does not even establish a compelling tempo, except in the opening scenes, nor does he exhibit much visual sensitivity. His Las Vegas gambling emporium is skimpily and stagily faked in (here Altman has it all over Reisz); the sinister hoodlums are either more humdrum or more absurd than in less pretentious movies, and even such a scene as the grandfather's birthday party hardly captures the idiosyncrasies of nouveau-riche refugee life, which Karel Reisz, a Czech living in England, might be presumed to have a special eye for.

There is one beautifully framed shot, though, where the noisy background movement of some hoods contrasts effectively with the immobility of Axel's anguished face shown in closeup in the lower right corner of the frame. Axel has fixed a student basketball game, and is petrified with guilt while the contented mobsters, in soft focus, move diagonally out of the frame to the left. Axel's face, unnervingly off center, remains surrounded by the cold empty greens of the deserted gymnasium. Here, as in some other shots, the usually undistinguished Victor J. Kemper's cinematography is striking, for which Reisz must surely get some of the credit.

But the director has done less well with his actors. James Caan, who has been getting better and better, here slides back almost to his very inauspicious beginnings, and does not begin to convey the drivenness of the protagonist. We feel neither Axel's ghastly compulsion nor his intermittent exultation—granted that he gets very little help from the script. From the Billie of Lauren Hutton one would not, God knows, expect much acting, but here even her facial radiance becomes strangely etiolated. And the generally excellent Paul Sorvino is only one of several supporting players who fail to score through no fault of theirs.

Apropos score, Jerry Fielding's adaptation of Mahler's First Symphony is in the worst possible taste, both because of its meddling with Mahler, and because of its dragging him into this in the first place. Yet at least the recurring cuckoo motif is apt in view of the cuckoo eggs Fielding and Toback sneaked into the nests of Mahler and Dostoevsky to be hatched. The plot, finally, goes quite berserk when, in a fit of ultimate masochism, Axel infiltrates Harlem and provokes a black pimp to kill him, but manages only to get a whore to slash his face to ribbons. We are, I dare say, supposed to see a parallel between Axel and that other quasi-defunct Buffalo Bill of gambling, perhaps even perceive the addiction as a giant death wish and, heaven forfend, maybe an allegory of the current state of America. I would rather venture into the worst gambling den of Macao than enter into this game of symbols and profundities.

A few other corkers demand cursory chronicling. Sam Peckinpah's *Bring Me the Head of Alfredo Garcia* is an all-out preposterous horror, except for a fine performance by Isela Vega and the clever way in which the protagonist is sneaked into our consciousness. As one who touted and defended *The Wild Bunch* and *Straw Dogs,* I am particularly disheartened: Peckinpah clearly doesn't lack talent; what he lacks is brains. Every one of his dubious old chestnuts resurfaces here (civilization is just corruption of instinctual nobility, simple Mexican peasants are the salt of the earth, even the best women crave rape by beasts, a man with a mission can mow down dozens without, etc.), and there is nothing sadder than watching so much technique at the service of ideas that, for all their rehashing, remain half-baked.

That insufferably cute and crass filmmaker Paul Mazursky is back with *Harry and Tonto,* in which a much abused New York senior citizen packs up his beloved cat and heads west. All kinds of arch, sticky, and achingly recherché adventures befall them, and the whole thing is rife with Mazursky's maniacal striving to fuse the offbeat and the slick into the indigestible. Art Carney's performance is inexpressive and dull enough to earn him an Oscar, Josh Mostel and Melanie Mayron are there to make the younger generation keep up in unappealingness with the older, and some worthier actors flit by in cameo roles. The cat acts best, and with condign condescension.

November 1974

Mainliners

MURDER ON THE ORIENT EXPRESS is that unusual thing: an inflated trifle that actually works. The director, Sidney Lumet, is hardly known for his light touch, but with a competent screenplay by Paul Dehn based on a pleasantly frivolous Agatha Christie mystery, unaffectedly craftsmanlike color cinematography by Geoffrey Unsworth (of *2001* and *Cabaret* fame), an agreeably slumming score by the serious composer Richard Rodney Bennett, tastefully opulent production design and period costumes by Tony Walton, and the presence of enough stars for a minor galaxy, how could the thing go wrong? Well, it still could have, and if, for the most part, it doesn't, thanks be also to Lumet.

Those stars really sparkle in their self-assurance! Who but an actor's actor, like John Gielgud, could so perfectly play a gentleman's gentleman? What poise Richard Widmark brings to, not an ugly, merely an odious American! With impeccable smoothness, Jean-Pierre Cassel impersonates a polyglot and multifaceted sleeping-car steward. No less masterly is Ingrid Bergman's portrayal of a stolid yet batty Swede, the very thing she isn't—stolid yet batty, I mean. Lauren Bacall does tidily by a rich, upper-crust busybody; Wendy Hiller dithers and fulminates with equal ease as a faintly unhinged Russian aristo- and autocrat; and Rachel Roberts as a German lady's companion is ablaze with *furor Teutonicus.* I expected less from Martin Balsam, Michael York, and Sean Connery, and, alas, got it; Anthony Perkins's part was a bit too juicy for him to be able to restrain himself, and Vanessa Redgrave's a mite too empty for anyone to enliven. But there is no accounting for the usually dependable and always charming Jacqueline Bisset's malfunctioning, unless she was aware of how bad a thirties hairdo looks on her. But, on the credit side again, there is a whole nebula of lesser stars to do wonders in smaller roles: George Coulouris, Denis Quilley, Jeremy Lloyd, and Colin Blakely, among others.

That leaves Albert Finney in the principal part of Hercule Poirot, the Belgian master detective. Finney's gusto and self-confidence triumph over a questionable French (or Belgian) accent; linguist-cartographers could have fun tracing the more or less incomplete trajectory of his phonemes from Lancashire to the land of the Walloons. In fact, he does not so much produce a genuine accent as send up trial Walloons. Otherwise, though, a very jolly performance, studded with neat little tics and quirks yet not unpleasantly mannered, and good down to his make-up and general bearing. Finney manages to look as squat and pale as a leek (in French, *poireau,* a homonym for Poirot), and nicely shuttles between jaded languor and voluble enthusiasm in his work, thus providing an entertaining film with a fine, comic capstone.

The gifted director Bob Fosse comes to grief with *Lenny.* I am no Bruce expert or enthusiast, though I enjoyed him the one time I saw him perform, and considered him by far the most unusual and valuable of stand-up comics. But I cannot condone the current attempts to canonize him as scapegoat, martyr, prophet, and universal sage; which does not, however, mean that he is unworthy of a screen biography, either straight or fictionalized. But that is just it: the film, with a script by Julian Barry from his own quite different but equally unsatisfactory stage play, is a mess—precisely because it is neither fact nor imaginative fiction. Fosse and Barry never figured out for themselves how this nothingy little comic grew into a heroic figure and, rightly or wrongly, a legend; they further becloud the issue with "arty" fragmentation and time shifts, so that past (the unknown, two-bit comedian), present (the phenomenally risen and fallen, one and only Lenny Bruce), and future (his mother, wife, and agent spinning out his myth in posthumous interviews with a heard but unseen journalist) are utterly scrambled, and we cannot even superficially follow the transitions, evolutionary and deteriorative, that marked the man's story.

The filmmakers were clearly hampered by the need to appease Bruce's widow and mother. But with a marvelous mother like the one on screen, no boy could have grown up troubled; and with a basically so loving husband-wife relationship, whence came the divorce, and all those marital and postmarital agonies? Would his work and milieu have permitted the young Lenny such childlike innocence? Could the older Bruce have remained so pure amid his drug addiction, litigiousness, and despair? The film's dishonesty is epitomized by the scene in which Bruce gets his wife, Honey, to have sex with a lesbian as he watches and, eventually, joins in. The idea is to evoke moral deterioration, have a daring and salacious scene, and still not offend any moviegoers. So the event is shown as the simple consequence of living among West Coast show-biz freaks, and entered into by both Lenny and Honey with a joylessness darkening into tragic despondency. In bed with the other woman, Honey either shoots desperate glances at Lenny, implying, "I only did this to please you, now please, please, get me out of it!" or mingles with her partner in cheerless submissiveness.

Lenny, meanwhile, surveys the scene with saturnine impassivity that barely masks pain and revulsion; when he introduces himself between the two gloomy women, he looks like the most luckless of Lucky Pierres. Now one can have such a mini-orgy because one is stoned out of one's head, goes in for genuinely kinky sex, or is in the grip of overaroused curiosity. In none of these cases, though, would one carry on like a painfully dying gladiator, any more than *Deep Throat* could be played as if it were *Oedipus Rex.* But who could resent such profusely suffering sinners? And who deny Fosse and Barry their "candid, fearless, adult" film that could, as an added bonus, turn on a few susceptible souls?

The fragmented structure, furthermore, prevents us from seeing the Bruce routines whole; the best ones, indeed, are absent altogether, perhaps because Dustin Hoffman couldn't manage them. Hoffman, in fact, manages very little. As young Lenny in love, he is the bumblingly coltish Graduate again, quite out of tune with the sleazy nightclub atmosphere, which Fosse goes to excessive lengths to establish. (Likewise, we get the points about sexual, social, and legal hypocrisy with much greater speed than Fosse credits us with.) As the adult Bruce, Hoffman is still too nice, cool, and lucid, with little of the madness and meanness that were mixed in with the messianism. And, as usual, idealization spells dehumanization, spells diminishment. Bruce Surtees's unexciting cinematography is, at least, in appropriate black-and-white; Valerie Perrine and Jan Miner do the best they can with the unreal wife and mother, though the agent figure, who (presumably because his identity could be disguised) is allowed a dose of villainy, may be a mite overdone by Stanley Beck. Most painful about this lackluster film are the bits of barbershop Freudianism in the posthumous interviews: "He had to prove it to himself."—"Insecurity?"—"Insecurity."

February 1975

(The) Brotherhood Is Always Beautiful

THE GODFATHER seemed to me one of the sleazier films to achieve overwhelming public, and considerable critical, success. Yet there is logic in this. For as all-time top-grossing picture it is followed by *The Sound of Music* at a distance of no more millions than can be explained by lower rates of admission back in 1965. And these two films are surely the two sides of one soiled and worn-smooth coin: family pictures in the same sickening sense, though in different form. At a casual glance, the family that stays together by praying and yodeling together may seem vastly different from the one that stays together by preying and O-sole-mioing together. But in both cases we are dealing with fierce clannish loyalties and faiths that move mountains: one putting the Alps and Nazis behind it, the other shoving aside the twin peaks of Business-and-Finance and Law-and-Order. And both families, Corleones and Trapps, are glued together with strong Catholic faith, and lots of music and singing. If the Corleones also kill, that is a relatively minor difference: murderers are famous for their sentimental sides; sentimentalists have throughout history waged—in the name of country, religion, or race—ferocious wars and bloody persecutions.

The sequel to *The Godfather* (which, for reasons I'll soon make apparent, could not, alas, be called *Son of Godfather)* is entitled *The Godfather, Part II,* and strikes me as better than its predecessor, though this is lukewarm praise at best. The new movie is, I gather, made out of leftovers from Mario Puzo's original novel as well as from additions by Puzo and his coscenarist Francis Ford Coppola, who directed both films. The rationalizations and mass appeal are the same. We are told that the Mafia is not really different from other big business; whether you rub out an enemy or merely ruin a competitor comes to the same thing in a materialistic society. But whereas big business is even internecinely cutthroat, the Mafia is The Family, reveres its womenfolk, rewards its loyal males, accepts and remunerates even outsiders, provided they are faithful and obedient. They don't even have to be Italian; the Corleones' trusted legal counsel is an Irishman.

If these things endear the Mafia (at least on film) to men, women respond to the wonderful family feeling: the emotional shelteredness, absolute respect, creature comforts, and multiple offspring accorded to wives and mothers make your upper-echelon *mafioso* as good a matrimonial prospect as pining females from Paris to Peoria could ask for. And there are other attractions for all. First, that an illiterate Italian immigrant can rise through the Mafia to the pinnacle of power and wealth must appeal to all the aspiring underprivileged. Then, the way *Godfather* I and II are set up, those whom the Corleones kill are always a little, and often a lot, more reprehensible than their slayers, so these films become the surrogates for the now ethnically taboo cowboy-and-Indian movies. Lastly, there is an exoticism, a Catholic-meridional colorfulness about these people, fatally fascinating to the pallid inheritors of the Protestant ethic.

What makes Part II slightly more attractive than Part I is, first of all, the absence of Marlon Brando. For Brando gave an unpardonably cheap performance (though perhaps no worse than the rest of his depressing latter-day work), the kind that consists entirely of some phony accent, a fixedly vacant stare, and eternities of portentous pauses. In the sequel, which shuttles between the prehistory of Part I and its posthistory, Robert De Niro plays the Brando part, Vito Corleone, as a young man, while Al Pacino again does his son Michele, now Michael, who has taken over as Don from his dead father. Though the binary structure, the shuttling between the stories of two almost co-equal heroes, might damage a better film, here it makes for relief. When we tire of the icy, secretly smoldering Michael, grandly operating all over Nevada, Miami, Cuba, we get a respite by switching to the story of easygoing young Vito, first as a Mafia-persecuted child in Sicily, then as a nice husband, father, and nascent mafioso in New York's Little Italy. And when the small and simple crimes of yesteryear begin to pall on us, we are whisked forward in time to big national and international intrigues: the near takeover of Cuba by the Syndicate, the Kefauver Committee and its hoodwinking, and other such weighty matters. And if Pacino's acting magic begins to wear thin, there is De Niro's in full bloom.

We get, furthermore, a newly political horizon. Before, the Corleones tangled merely with crooked policemen (more rarely honest ones), Hollywood producers, Las Vegas hotel proprietors, and rival branches of the Mafia; now they take on corrupt Nevada senators, a flavorous Jewish supergangster (modeled on Meyer Lansky), Batista's Cuba, the FBI, and a whole congressional investigation. Granted, this makes for pretentiousness when unsteadily supported by dialogue like, "Michael, we are bigger than U.S. Steel" and "If anything in this life is certain—if history teaches us anything—it's that you can kill anyone." Worse yet, it makes for a tendentious political nihilism, trendily cashing in, on the one hand, on current political alienation, and, on the other, facilely abetting such disaffection and cynicism: better an honest gangster than a crooked politician, the film is saying, as if those were the only possible choices.

Repellent as these stances are, they at least occupy the mind that tries to oppose them. There was nothing to think about in *The Godfather* except when, of what sort, and how big the next bloodletting would be. Here there is less bloodshed, more scheming and counterscheming, which is more interesting. True, Puzo and Coppola turn even this to dishonest advantage when they have Michael say (ungrammatically but magnanimously): "I don't have to wipe everybody out that are my enemies"; we are to sympathize with today's Mafia even because it turns out a widow's mite's worth fewer widows! Still, the new emphasis on political intrigue, petty and sometimes droll chicanery in the De Niro episodes, even an occasional bit of kinky sexuality (ever so guarded—mustn't lose that R rating!) do add spice to the previously almost unrelieved holocausts.

Part I had some solid performances, but no bravura ones, not even from Pacino. Here, besides De Niro's extraordinary work, there are stunning bits from Italian actors, realistically permitted to speak in subtitled Italian—especially from Leopoldo Trieste as a slum landlord, and Gastone Moschin as Fanucci, a Mafia district boss. And there is a bull's-eye performance from Lee Strasberg—yes, Strasberg, the grayest eminence among teachers and directors in the American theater—here making a movie-acting debut comparable to last year's triumph by John Houseman, and no doubt likewise slated for an Oscar (if anyone still cares about such foolish trivia). On the debit side, the supremely untalented Diane Keaton, as Kay, is worse yet in Part II, but one of her big scenes has been mercifully cut from the released version, and the other is so bad as to be deliciously giggle-provoking.

However, the final argument in favor of Part II is that it is better made, of sounder workmanship. Coppola is getting to be a more competent director: a scene here is allowed more leisure and breathing space, is less like a guided missile trained with dumb, mechanical determinism to explode on a specific target. Thus the characterizations of Hyman Roth, the Jewish gangster (Lee Strasberg), and Pentangeli, an aging Mafia *capo* losing his grip (Michael V. Gazzo, in another juicy performance), create a dense, credible atmosphere rather than just advance the plot. Granted, Coppola still goes in for repeating his fancy effects: there is far too much backlighting to reveal altogether too many stark silhouettes, and much too much interior underlighting to make rich *mafiosi* look like troglodytes in hiding.

There are other forms of cheating, too; so Michael seems happy only when playing with his children. All the rest of the time he must embody the tragic grandeur of the Mafia boss; as his errant but reformed sister Connie puts it, "You were just being strong for all of us, the way Papa was, and I forgive you"—absolution for such trifles as the killing of her husband and, by prolepsis, the impending murder of their weak, and thus dangerously untrustworthy, brother. Yet there is considerable skill in the way Coppola juggles the Pacino and De Niro episodes, knowing exactly when to switch from one to the other; when to use a slow dissolve, and when a fadeout. True, he does fall back on the tricks of Part I: beginning with a gay festivity with troubling undertones, and ending with a rapid pileup of major murders and suicides followed by Michael's dark, lonely supremacy. But, somehow, the hand is steadier here, the sensationalism kept at bay, except for a couple of smirkingly suggestive scenes of perversion, which parents may find hard to explain to their puzzled children.

Gordon Willis's color cinematography is better than in Part I, because the obsession with graininess (not so much for a documentary look, I suspect, as from nostalgia for old-time movies and film stock) is just about gone, although the dominant colors are still reddish brown and burnished yellow, as in old paintings turning sere under excessive coats of varnish. Nino Rota's music, though hardly his best, has its moments, and the film moves along for its 200 minutes without actually boring us. The moral defects are undeniable and repugnant—no amount of canting comparisons of the Mafia to the Roman Empire or tributes from Michael Corleone to Fidel Castro's revolution can alter that—but the movie is well put together and steadily watchable. One could ask for more, but nowadays one is likely to get much less.

March 1975

Down in Mabel's Dumps

I WOULD JUST AS GLADLY have passed over the dreadful *A Woman Under the Influence* in condign silence, but the success it begins to garner calls for a cry of protest. The history of art is rich in examples of genuine artists who were not particularly bright human beings: one can write exquisite lyrics without burdening one's head with anything so prosaic as a brain, and many an able painter's eye was backed up by nothing deeper than an optic nerve. Cerebration, though, is a downright impediment to the nonartist, a label that fits John Cassavetes as perfectly as a stretch sock. In film after film he has put actors or nonactors in front of a camera, encouraging them to improvise their guts out on some sketched-in topic, confident that great existential truths will thus be apprehended. He might as well have gone about catching them by sprinkling salt on their tails.

Granted, Cassavetes claims that his films are thoroughly scripted by himself (he used to say, as I recall, 93 or 95 percent; now, with inflation upon us, he has gone up to 100), but I prefer to think that he is fibbing. Indeed, the blackest lie would be preferable to the authorship of stuff like *Husbands, Minnie and Moskowitz,* and now *A Woman Under the Influence.* This last is the story of a blue-collar worker's wife who, though her husband insists that she is not crazy, acts more and more like a madwoman, crazed partly, perhaps, by her husband's long working hours away from home. She begins by picking up a man in a bar (such is the film's incompetence that we cannot even be sure whether she has met him before); pretty soon she is accosting strangers in the street with absurd outpourings, or forcing her bewildered guests to dance ballets with her. Finally, at the family doctor's urging, her husband has her committed. When she is released after six months, hubby invites a whole crowd for a welcome-home party, even though there is neither food nor drink in the house. She might be frightened by all those people, and so he is finally persuaded to send away all but the immediate family. In the end, the spouses are loving and fighting again, and the cycle seems ready to recommence.

The film's incidents, however they were arrived at, look and sound like improvisations in which a dreary little situation is stretched, worried, reiterated until any spectator with a sense of the value of his time must turn as blue in the face as the hero's collar. There is no external authenticity even: we never quite figure out what Nick Longhetti's exact job is, what it is that drives Mabel Longhetti out of her mind, or what the couple's long separations are all about, since no union would permit the endless hours Nick seems to be putting in. In a typical scene, Nick brings his buddies home for lunch and Mabel spouts endless drivel or shy-making questions at them, to which they respond with dull, inarticulate answers. People are also egged on by her to sing, and, worse luck, they do. There was a similarly tiresome singing scene in *Husbands:* when in doubt, have a songfest.

The film staggers and stammers on for two hours and thirty-five minutes. At the end of its New York Film Festival screening, I asked Cassavetes during the customary press conference whether the main characters of this long movie changed in any way, and, if so, how? Or, if they didn't change, why not? Visibly taken aback by what seemed to him a most unexpected query, he said that this was a very difficult question, and passed the buck to his wife, Gena Rowlands, who plays Mabel. (If you haven't got the answers to such fundamental questions, it seems to me you have no business making the film.)

While ostensibly agreeing, director and star managed to contradict both each other and themselves. Mabel could not change, but did; was quite crazy, but was unjustly committed by her husband—who, however, truly loved her, or, perhaps, didn't love her enough all along. *He* did, however, change, because he sent all those guests away. (Big deal—when Mabel and the whole family demanded it, and there was nothing for them to eat or drink!)

The very attitude of the film toward its "little people" is contradictory: it worshipfully hangs on their every action and word, yet it patronizingly lets them go from ludicrousness to boringly uneventful repetitions of minutiae. As Mabel, Gena Rowlands lets it all hang out ubiquitously and continually; if feelings were laundry, she'd be the city of Naples. As Nick, Peter Falk acts devoted beyond the call of duty, expansive beyond the call of nature, and dogged beyond the call of the wild. Why did Cassavetes, who could act pretty decently, want to become a filmmaker? Upward mobility is a dangerous thing in an actor. Whereas a bank teller might logically become president of his bank, or a waiter understandably work himself up to restaurant owner, an actor does not normally progress into a director, though to a bored or ambitious performer this might seem the natural step up. Yet the mimetic and receptive talents of the actor are the opposite of the cerebral and aggressive ones of the filmmaker. On the American movie scene, besides Cassavetes, only George C. Scott seems to have maneuvered himself into this untenable position. Both men have demonstrated great determination and energy, but these misplaced qualities yield only misdirected films.

April 1975

Soft Soap

ANY MORE WRITTEN AS one word has always struck me as a barbarism, though it may be the least barbarous thing about *Alice Doesn't Live Here Anymore,* Martin Scorsese's first nonshoestring movie. Although it looks more professional than *Mean Streets,* and offers us, instead of boys growing up absurd in Little Italy, a young woman finding her identity in the great southwest, it suffers from much the same defects: trying too hard and delivering too little. Atmosphere is poured on thick, the characters are meant to be so real that you are to think you can blow your nose into their handkerchiefs, and the women's liberationists are supposed to be thrilled by this meaty part for a mature actress to sink her teeth into—not to mention the wonderful manner in which Alice in the end gets both her way and her man. Yet the whole thing is as labored, superficial, and old hat beneath the trendy veneer as anything Hollywood has been grinding out in its pre-Enlightenment decades.

A prologue—all in red, like a demented valentine—shows us Alice Hyatt as a foulmouthed eight-year-old in Monterey, California, piteously squeaking out "You'll Never Know" and defiantly vowing to become a singer. Twenty-seven years later, we find her living in Socorro, New Mexico, married to the crudest, most unsympathetic truck driver you have ever seen; the mother of twelve-year-old Tommy, a monstrously precocious, bespectacled brat; and running a hideously prototypical southwestern house without help from anyone. Donald, the husband, reads magazines before dinner, makes no conversation at table, watches television in bed, and when Alice bursts into tears, gives her a little sex as a pacifier. And Tommy is up to every conceivable mischief; when Alice, between sewing and cooking, laments: "I don't know, I'm an okay sort of person—how did I get such a smartass kid?" he replies in his best smartass tone, "You got pregnant," and does not budge to help out. No wonder Alice beats her fists against her shabby-genteel curtained French doors and shouts, "Socorro sucks!"

We are not so much in the heartland of America as at the heart of soap opera, only soap opera whose mouth has *not* been washed with soap, as befits that mature medium, the New Cinema. This New Cinema, which purports to deal with adult matters, labors under two handicaps. First, for all its adulthood, it is meant to be comprehended by the most immature minds in Socorro, or any other sucking town; and, second, it is made by filmmakers whose minds are mature only by the standards of fifteen-year-olds. In fact, most of *Alice* could have been written by Tommy Hyatt. We wonder right off: If Alice is such a good wife, understanding mother, pretty and witty woman, what on earth made her marry that Coca-Cola-truck-driving brute? Paws that refresh, apparently. When Tommy questions her on that score, she answers, "Because he was a great kisser." "That's why you married him?" Tommy exclaims with justifiable incredulity; "How great can you kiss?" Alice retorts, "Ask me again in a couple of years, and I'll tell you."

That brings us to the second question: How are we to believe this great comedy act, this mother-and-son repartee marathon that rattles across the southwest after Donald is killed in a collision, and Alice and Tommy start their drive to Monterey, where she hopes to make it as a singer? In the car, in soulless motels, through vacant landscapes and hollow towns, the comedy turns never flag. If, for example, Tommy is restless in the car, Alice enjoins him: "Relax and enjoy life!" "Life is short!" he snaps back. "So are you!" comes the clincher. Now this sort of thing might just barely go on between a mother and son in a sophisticated megalopolitan setting, though even there it would quickly become odious. In Socorro and parts west, among these simple folk, it is both odious and incredible. Also tasteless: when Tommy mumbles "What?" several times in rapid succession (his mind obviously preoccupied with thinking up their next comic routine), Alice erupts, "What do you mean, 'what?' Who are you—Helen Keller?"

Now comes the third puzzler. When after innumerable cutenesses as well as quite a few minor heartbreaks (Alice cries nine or ten times in the picture, fights back tears four or five times, and hovers twice between laughter and weeping), the mother finally lands a job as a singer-pianist in a cheesy but respectable Phoenix saloon, why must she, with all kinds of men making passes at her, pick Ben Eberhart to have an affair with? He is impudently, obnoxiously persistent; dumb—"Hya, Hyatt!" is his opening witticism, and it's all downhill from there; eight years younger than Alice, and God knows how many years younger than Tommy; unsavorily employed—he packs gunpowder into bullets; and is a leering, swaggering lout. But that's not enough; he must also turn out to be a wife-beating, knife-wielding maniac; presumably, however, he, too, is a great kisser. Twice burned, once shy, Alice escapes with Tommy to Tucson.

Here, alas, the only job she can get is as a waitress in a hash house, and though her and Tommy's scintillating exchanges continue unabated, other things do change: mother and son make new friends. Tommy meets Audrey (as young Doris likes to call herself), a fellow music student who thinks all Tucson is "weird," though she, a cocotte's daughter of Tommy's age who shoplifts, takes drugs, and talks in a contralto voice much more brazenly than Tommy, is the weirdest of all; in fact, she does not come across as a little girl but as a juvenile transvestite. Alice, at Mel and Ruby's Café, meets her two fellow waitresses: Flo, who can out-foulmouth her or anyone without batting a brash false eyelash, but who wears on her capacious bosom a large cross she herself has made, held together, as she says, by safety pins—just like herself; and Vera, always rushing around in a dither, fouling up, and continually in tears—yet, after work, donning a motorcycle helmet, and driven home by her swinging old man, Daddy Duke, on his powerful bike. Surprises, surprises! Best of all, there is David, the big, tough, decent, quietly smiling rancher, whose beard Alice eventually cannot resist touching, finding it soft—like his heart, no doubt, and perhaps even his brain. He first wins over Tommy, then Alice, and when he shows her around his hard-earned ranch nestling under mountains as rugged as he, instructs her in the mental prowess of various livestock, and points with sovereign calm to a patch of land as he explains casually, "That's alfalfa, or will be in two months," he has conquered Alice from alfalfa to—oh, omega. By a lucky coincidence, he, too, seems to be a great kisser.

Notice how simplistic it all is. For Tommy, a little girl friend tougher than he, and David who takes him riding, fishing, and helps him with his guitar lessons. For Alice, two contrasting waitresses neatly epitomizing the extremes of her own nature, but with little surprises tucked away inside them, like the messages in fortune cookies. And, above all, a strong, silent man, with all the virtues her previous men lacked, plus the one they had. Everything could end now in the most conventional way, as behooves this basically conventional film, but that would militate against its maturity. So Scorsese and his scenarist, Robert Getchell, trump up the most spurious fight between David and Alice, based on David's giving Tommy a mild spanking after he had been carrying on even more insufferably than usual, whereupon Alice flares up, and it emerges that David doesn't take her ambition to become a singer in Monterey entirely seriously, which really arouses her new-found protofeminist sense of self, and a rupture ensues.

After a few more peripheral peripeteias and turnings on of the waterworks, Alice and David are reconciled in a nauseatingly cute scene worthy of the coy happy endings of the thirties and forties. It is one of those having-it-out sequences ending in a passionate clinch that begins as Alice is waiting hectically on the lunchtime crowd and David remonstrates with her from the café door. After he capitulates on every point, Alice flings herself around his neck as Vera, in the nick of time, rescues the B.L.T.'s about to hurtle off Alice's tray, and the enraptured customers applaud lustily. Later, by way of a beau geste, Alice gives up Monterey, though not her singing, and Tommy looks forward to school in Tucson, and all ends with a telephoto shot of the two of them blending happily with Tucson's downtown traffic.

But what of the film's technical achievements? Well, Scorsese has learned the syntax of moviemaking and uses it demonstratively. Give him a car about to leave with Alice and Tommy, or a sewing machine or piano with Alice seated at it, and he will track around semicircularly from right to left, then from left to right, sometimes even full circle, but intercutting this with close-ups of the heroine, and making sure that, if Alice is performing at the center of a circular bar, there should be plenty of blurry customers' backs temporarily blocking the camera's vision. He also knows how to pull back his camera from Alice at her home piano, dolly out through the window and across a hedge, then change to a lateral motion and track along with Tommy slinking away and administering a naturalistically brattish kick or two to the sand. Beyond that, when he is trying to convey the farcical chaos of the café or the lyricism of an Arizona ranch, he is as stereotypical and bathetic as all our good old Hollywood hacks.

Yet those hacks at least employed cinematographers better than Kent L. Wakeford, to whom, and to that boring actor Harvey Keitel, Scorsese is absurdly faithful. True, Keitel fits the role of Ben Eberhart well enough—but how dreadful he was in *Mean Streets;* and Wakeford does make the southwest look washed-out and sleazy, which may be his intention. But I somehow cannot trust a cameraman who, for no good reason, will make an entire tree come out blue. Like Keitel, he seems merely to have a crudity that sometimes fits the setting. Some of the other performances, notably Diana Ladd's as Flo, are very able in their straightforward ways, but Alfred Lutter's Tommy may be even more slap-provoking than required, making us feel, inappropriately, as hostile toward Alice as toward a tympanist pathologically unable to hit his kettledrum.

Ellen Burstyn (who, one hears, had an uncredited hand in the script) plays Alice impeccably, lifting both the wisecracking and the tear-shedding out of the Roz Russell and Jean Arthur movies that begot them into something very like contemporary reality. What she deserves is an equally meaty role, but one whose meat has been kept under proper refrigeration. As David, Kris Kristofferson seems unable to cope with all that placid serenity, and comes to life only in his one angry scene. There is also, typically for Scorsese, a soundtrack bursting with the pop songs of yesterday and today as if there were no tomorrow; but the garishness of Toby Rafelson's production design is faultlessly on target. Altogether, though, the film has a heart conceivably bigger than a bread box, but a brain surely smaller than a bread crumb.

An even more misguided operation is *Shampoo,* cowritten by its star, Warren Beatty, and Robert Towne, scenarist of *Chinatown* and *The Last Detail,* and directed by the latter's director, Hal Ashby. The movie concerns forty-eight hours in the life of George, a Hollywood celebrity hairdresser and superstud, to whom his grateful women clients give both heads and head, not to mention their hearts, but who heeds only his pleasure and his ambition to acquire his own hair salon. In the former pursuit, he is foiled half the time—the film shows or implies four instances of coitus interruptus, and four of fulfillment; in the latter, he is frustrated completely, neither his bank nor his potential Maecenas staking him to the needed capital. The bank turns him down because doing Barbara Rush's head seems insufficient collateral; the millionaire businessman, Lester, because he discovers that George is making it with his wife (annoying!), teen-aged daughter (amazing!), and mistress (too much!). You may safely conclude that one of the film's themes is the sexual corruption of Hollywood at the time of the action: Election Day, 1968.

Here the other, more portentous, theme rears—to invoke an appropriate metaphor—its ugly head. Thus at a fancy dinner party at Le Bistro, given for a Republican senator and other choice guests, people are watching the election returns on television. Bits of speeches by Nixon and his henchmen are seen and overheard—all about an open administration and greater integrity—and the screen is awash with facile irony. There is supposed to be a connection between these acquisitive rich people and the Nixon debacle, as if the poor had not voted for Nixon, and as if most campaign promises did not ring hollow and ludicrous seven years later. Still, the idea of responsibility for what may have been our worst president ever is worth developing and examining; but nothing is achieved by just tossing it out and letting it lie there. Next we go to a party where they are not watching the election on TV, but where successful hippies are tripping amid booze, pot, strobe lights, naked bathing, merry copulation; yet the film never stops to ask whether these orgiasts are more, less, or equally to blame for the Nixon years to come.

Everything about *Shampoo* is vague, attitudinizing, and lacking in true insight. Not one of its characters is worthy of sympathy, and George's final heartbreak leaves us doubly cold because we cannot believe in it and do not give a damn about George. Even his supposedly fabulous heads look no better than the preposterous hairdos worn by stars on Oscar night, and should this be intentional, it still wouldn't make George any more endearing. When he tells us that he cannot envision a future with his current main girl friend—a dumb, budding actress dumbly but not very buddingly played by Goldie Hawn—yet insists that he could spend his life happily with a former girl friend who is now Lester's kept woman—rather too lackadaisically played by Julie Christie—we cannot see much difference between these equally two-dimensional creatures, or why, if the latter is so superior, George let her go in the first place.

Let me give examples of two characteristic, recurrent flaws. One: obviousness. At the hippie party, the camera catches in the background a young mother boozing at the bar while nursing her baby—a nice piece of observation if kept subtly at the fringes. But no, here it is shown immediately in closeup, so that every idiot gets the point. Two: sloppy inaccuracy in details. At Lester's party, the senator makes a political speech that consists largely of his doing an Indian chant at inordinate length. This quickly ceases to be funny or believable even as a hyperbole. The senator then switches to singing *"Tamo daleko,"* a Dalmatian folk song, which deprives him of any ethnic credibility: a Dalmatian Indian, what's that supposed to be?

There are some better jokes here and there, but nothing incisive and biting enough to make *Shampoo* a genuine satire; having neither satirical trenchancy nor some kind of sympathetic immersion in its characters, the film has no raison d'être. Well, yes; George confesses to his finally wised-up girl to relations with his clients: "Let's face it, I fucked them all. That's why I went to beauty school. It makes me feel I'm going to live forever." It just might be that the beauty schools of America subsidized this pretentious movie that manages to be simultaneously slick and inept, and that enrollment, especially by heterosexuals, in our beauty schools will climb to a record high.

Actually, the relationship of that rather rare bird, a heterosexual hairdresser, to his glamorous but shallow Beverly Hills clients might have made an interesting movie, but not the way Beatty & Co. merely skimmed along its surface. Of course, from the moment in the opening nearly pitch-black sequence (in which two bodies can be dimly discerned fornicating) when the first loudly uttered word is a monosyllabic obscenity, our enlightened audience is in stitches, which may yet make *Shampoo* a huge success. I just wonder whether that makes the audience responsible for the Ford Administration?

May 1975

Better Vietnam Than Barbra

THE STEPFORD WIVES is a sleazy rather than slick thriller (by Bryan Forbes, who can do better) about a suburban men's association that replaces its members' wives with nearly identical but more curvaceous, sexually submissive, and mindless robots. Its one interesting feature is its being peddled in some quarters as a feminist picture because one of the wives is *almost* smart enough to avert her doom! This film will do very little for women of any sort, but another item from Columbia Pictures, *Funny Lady,* may do a great deal for women of a nonfeminist persuasion. It stars Barbra Streisand, who is not a mindless but a shrewdly singleminded robot, which may mean getting the worst of both possible worlds.

If Miss Streisand did not exist, she would have to be invented, as, I believe, she was. There may be uglier women in the world than she is, but surely none that wears her ugliness—enhanced by monumental arrogance—with more bravura (Italian), panache (French), and chutzpah (Yiddish). She was a singer once, but, as the mannerisms with which she has almost completely overlaid her voice attest, that was not the point. She may even have been a potential actress, as I recall from her Broadway debut, but that certainly wasn't the point. The point is that all the masses of people—female, male or other—who feel, justly or unjustly, unloved, undesirable, untouchable, or simply gross (or who are some or all of these things without realizing it) have finally got someone who is all of these things and then some to identify themselves with. A Jane Fonda, a Julie Christie, a Jacqueline Bisset, a Joanna Shimkus, a Geneviève Bujold have both looks and talent, which make them suitable alter egos for *some;* but how much better a Streisand, about whom *all*—even the most utterly graceless—can feel, without need for mental sleight of hand, "There, but for the absentmindedness of God, go I."

I missed the first screen installment of the Fanny Brice story, *Funny Girl* (I saw it on the stage, and deemed that enough), and can make no comparisons, but the even solecistically titled sequel, *Funny Lady,* for all the cleverness of the people who worked on, if not in, it, ranges from mildly to vastly distasteful and, on top of that, has an open ending, implying that we are yet to be blessed with *Funny Grandma.*

Funny Lady purports to be the story of Fanny Brice's collaboration with, marriage to, and divorce from Billy Rose, and when you consider that the real-life Rose, a greasy, unprepossessing pygmy, is portrayed here by a tall, handsome, and well-scrubbed James Caan as a long-stemmed Rose, you can promptly divest yourself of any misguided notion that the film has anything to do with reality or honesty. To be sure, it might convey to some viewers the sordidness of how two showbiz figures, gifted with the low, dog-eat-dog cunning the ghetto breeds into one, and desperate to make it in the cutthroat jungle of Broadway, proceed to bully, insult, adulate, and exploit each other right into marriage. "This is a shrewd kid," says singing Fanny of songwriting Billy, "I think I'll marry him—I hate paying for his material." Later, proffering an engagement ring, Rose the hustler announces: "I paid retail!" Was ever woman in this humor wooed? Was ever showman in this humor won? Such viewers may feel that these two horrors amply deserve each other, but do we deserve their 140-minute story? To the archetypal Streisand fan, however, the film happily demonstrates that beside Sharif, Segal, Montand, O'Neal, Sarrazin, and Redford, Barbra can also get James Caan—that there is no end to the conquering potential of militant repulsiveness.

The movie is very skillfully directed by Herbert Ross, whose directorial coming-of-age it marks (even if the influence of Bob Fosse is, especially in the show-within-a-film numbers, a bit too noticeable), magnificently photographed by one of Hollywood's grandest veterans, James Wong Howe, designed and costumed with appropriate brashness yielding occasionally to genuine beauty; equipped with good old Billy Rose and passable new Kander-and-Ebb songs, dazzlingly orchestrated by Peter Matz, stuffed by the scriptwriters Jay Presson Allen and Arnold Schulman with bright remarks ("Childbirth easy? It was like pushing a piano through a transom!") and bitchy jabs (wife to stunned aquastar caught in hubby's bed: "So don't just lay there, honey—swim something!") that to unfastidious palates may taste like epigrams, and the whole thing is opulent and polished-looking from start to finish. But in the place where its soul ought to be there is, at best, a perfect void. The old musicals may have been tamer and even dumber, but they at least seemed to believe their own make-believe, and were selling romances rather than selling selling. "I'm a STAR!!! I don't need *you!*" is the most memorable line Streisand spews out, epitomizing both Brice and herself in the full glory of their show-biz stardom: status carved from chopped chicken livers and mounted on a jangling cash register for pedestal.

The leading men are less than distinguished but suitably sexy. Omar Sharif reappears briefly as Fanny's first husband, the gambler Nicky Arnstein (another likely bit of casting!), and makes me glad I missed *Funny Girl* where he had the male lead. His lips quiver with fake sensitivity while his voice drips genuine molasses, and his calorific regard could still, as in *Zhivago,* melt all the snows of Russia. As an actor, he is of no earthly use; perhaps the navy could use him as an icebreaker. James Caan is better than that, though I preferred him before he was infected with thespian delusions; here he shuttles between Brando doing the Godfather and Tom Pedi doing Tom Pedi.

There is nothing unbearably wrong with show business until it starts publicly kissing its own feet, as it does here. Take the final scene where, ten years after their divorce, a redivorced Billy shows up to offer the ploddingly successful Baby Snooks of radio another crack at Broadway. He starts playing one of his old songs, "Me and My Shadow," on the piano, and asks: "Remember that?" Comes the reply in the most reverentially outraged tone: "Are you kidding? One of your *best!"* And soon he is promising Fanny a fabulous musical comeback at the Ziegfeld Theater, which he has just bought, featuring nothing but the finest: sets by Salvador Dali, Stokowski in the pit, songs by Rodgers and Hart, book by Kaufman and Hart (obviously a show with plenty of Hart). One wonders: Do the filmmakers intend this as satire or do they, as I suspect, really consider *that* art with a capital H?

Similarly, there is nothing wrong with Jewishness, but when all the worst features ascribed to it by the most sedulous anti-Semites are first smeared across the huge expanse of this overlong film and then, as it were, bathed in a heavenly radiance and sanctimoniously held up as wonderful human qualities, you have yourself a movie that, if by some unconscionable error it were to be shown in downtown Cairo, would cause instant resumption of the Mideast war.

Even so, *Funny Lady* is ineffably superior to Peter Bogdanovich's resounding dud, *At Long Last Love,* which may be the worst movie musical of this—or any—decade. Bogdanovich, whose entire filmmaking prowess is not much more than a mnemonic feat, has here accosted a genre where the gift of total recall and studious emulation is no match for the utter lack of genuine sophistication. For, of course, Bogdanovich opts for the sophisticated, high-society musical (as opposed to such more modest subgenres as the college, armed-services, show-biz, or fairy-tale musical), and makes the further mistake of hiring himself as scriptwriter. His notion of urbane wit is having unskilled actors rattle off sophomoric drivel at a breakneck pace, but with a condescending sneer built into every other slurred syllable. Sitting through this movie is like having someone at a fancy Parisian restaurant who neither speaks nor reads French read out stentoriously the entire long menu in his best Arkansas accent, and occasionally interrupt himself to chortle at his cleverness.

This is one of those films too dumb to spoof its targets, themselves almost too dumb to bear spoofing, yet it proceeds to do so, groaning under the double burden of Bogdanovich the director's heavy hand, and Bogdanovich the scenarist's immoderate borrowings. Why, already the credit sequence is the most brazen aping of some of Bergman's and Jean Renoir's credit sequences. The genuinely disturbing thing, though, is that the sixteen Cole Porter songs around which the film is—not built—just pinned together are made to sound as witless and formulaic as the rest of the goings-on: mostly lists of one kind or another, e.g., "You're the something in my something," or "Like a whosits without a whatsit," and so on, endlessly. If Bogdanovich achieves anything at all with his film, it is to ruin Porter for us.

And what performances! Cybill Shepherd, Mr. B.'s inamorata, plays a poor little snotty rich girl with a notion of sophistication that is underpassed only by her acting ability. (I will not even sully my pen by making it describe her singing and dancing.) If it weren't for an asinine superciliousness radiating from her, Miss Shepherd would actually be pitiable, rather like a kid from an orphanage trying to play Noël Coward. In fact, she comes across like one of those inanimate objects, say, a cupboard or a grandfather clock, which is made in certain humorous shorts to act, through trick photography, like people. Well, Bogdanovich is truly in love with Miss Shepherd, so one cannot call his slapping her into the lead of almost every one of his films the casting-couch approach; yet even those crude old-time producers who did have the crassness to use that method at least had the good sense to cast the girl, not the couch.

As for Burt Reynolds as a jaded millionaire playboy . . . there is in *Funny Lady* a buffalo named Charles, whom Billy Rose insists on displaying in a musical, where, on opening night, he creates havoc by improvising a one-buffalo stampede. Well, put a dinner jacket on Charles, and you've got Reynolds in *At Long Last Love,* except that he never musters enough animation for a stampede. And, just as in the old musicals, there had to be a secondary couple here for the primary couple to get its emotional wires crossed with. So we have Madeline Kahn as a second-rate musical comedienne, a part that should have suited her only too well, but the film cheats her of the chance of making it even to second-rate. Opposite her, as a merry Italian Lothario, we get Duilio Del Prete, an Italian nonactor whom Bogdanovich has also used disastrously in *Daisy Miller,* and whom he is clearly adding to his repertory company. Mr. Del Prete might conceivably play a street arab, but in a sophisticated role, with his thick accent and thin talent, he has as much charm as a broomstick with a smile painted on it, and turns every Porter lyric into a verbal jigsaw puzzle we are supposed to piece together on the wing. The supporting cast is made up of rather more talented performers, but the script and direction reduce them to the level of the stars.

The one paltry idea of the film is to make its art-deco scenery and costumes mostly black, white, and gray, and then shoot in color for the oddball effect. Used sparingly, this device can be impressive—indeed, has proved so for a variety of directors. (No one should make the rash assumption that any idea, however minuscule, is Bogdanovich's own.) But used as relentlessly as here, it succeeds only in making Laszlo Kovacs's cinematography, which has often looked unpleasantly flashy but not incompetent, look washed-out and—incompetent. This may well be the first color film ever to have come out almost completely black-and-white.

Certainly the most significant and probably best of all recent films is Peter Davis's documentary about our involvement in Vietnam, *Hearts and Minds*. It is always much harder for a critic to deal with a political documentary than with a fiction film, because criticism can treat compellingly only aesthetic matters, whereas in even the most impartial political documentary, aesthetics is secondary to ideology. On an issue like the Vietnam war, no one can be without opinion except a moral and intellectual imbecile, which, unlike certain other filmmakers I can think of, Peter Davis surely isn't. So when you see his film—and people of all political persuasions would benefit from seeing it—do not be surprised that Davis is against our role in Vietnam as much as he is against war in general. What should be surprising is the evenhandedness with which he sought out all kinds of views on the war from all sorts of people involved with it in influential or representative ways, and gave everybody a fair chance to hang or redeem himself. He was, unfortunately, not granted entry into North Vietnam, but made excellent use of North Vietnamese footage he got from other sources, and I must confess that I would have never guessed that the able production team did not set foot in North Vietnam.

It is virtually impossible to resist reporting scenes and statements from the film, but resist it I must. First, because of the faces, intonations, backgrounds of *Hearts and Minds*—even its small gestures and sometimes very long pauses speak as eloquently as its words, yet cannot be reproduced here. Second, because despite everything we have heard and read about the subject, so very much of this film seems novel and unique, inviting insights that each of us should make without prompting from anyone, filmmaker or critic. I would hate to deprive my readers of the sense of discovery they must have during and after the viewing of the film. There is one example I will, however, give—that of an anonymous South Vietnamese who walks by while Davis and his crew are filming. "First they bomb us," he mutters disgustedly, "then they come and photograph it all." An impromptu bit like this (and the film is full of them) makes two revelations: beyond its more obvious horrors, war also means divisive misunderstanding among people who feel the same way (the Vietnamese man and the sympathetic filmmaker, for example) and ghastly invasion of privacy.

Note two of the film's less immediately apparent yet ultimately well-conveyed points. One is the lack of communication between Americans and the people they are fighting with or against; the only levels on which they have contact are the black market, prostitution, and patronization, e.g., the condescension with which an American officer speaks of a Vietnamese, one he professes to admire, yet whose actions he can see only through a mist of clichés. The other point is what people—from those who masterminded the war, led our armies, or participated in various ways in the fighting, to those who lost a son in it, or were themselves harassed, tortured, or ruined, or actually profited financially—learned or failed to learn from it. There is a revealing sense of before and after, which, unfortunately, are not always so different as even the wisest and best participants, looking into themselves, would have them be.

One thing the film should make patent to all is the fallacy of arguing that things could have been worse without our intervention. For it suggests that (a) whatever we sought to avert, at disastrous costs, is inevitably yet to come; and (b) what did happen *was,* in many ways, the worst. The film is saliently and salutarily (though not consciously and slavishly) influenced by Marcel Ophüls's seminal *The Sorrow and the Pity,* only, dealing with more recent matters, less detached. Such paternity and filiation should be equally gratifying to begetter, begotten, and beholder.

June 1975

Our Movie Comedies Are No Laughing Matter

Is THERE SOMETHING new and wonderful happening in American film comedy? Great claims have been made for the year 1975, ushered in with Mel Brooks's *Young Frankenstein,* and now celebrating its summer solstice with Woody Allen's *Love and Death.* In between, the enthusiasts point a sanguine finger at Blake Edwards's *The Return of the Pink Panther* and Mike Nichols's *The Fortune.* One swallow, we know, does not make a summer; do four films constitute a bumper year of American comedy?

The first thing to strike me about this quartet is that none of the films is truly a comedy. *Love and Death* is a curious olio of night-club patter, revue sketches, and one-liners, most of them quite funny but uneasily stitched together. What comes out resembles a movie only as something midway between a crazy quilt and a potato sack resembles a suit of clothes. Now, there is nothing intrinsically wrong with that: like anything else, film can accommodate a great many forms or lacks of form of a madcap, one-shot, *sui generis* kind. But there is a grave problem with *Love and Death,* hilarious as much of it may be. This sort of film wears thin too easily; laughter that is largely pointless becomes in the end exhausting. This does not necessarily happen within a single Woody Allen film, which, kept wisely short, can generally squeeze by without our realizing until later that we have been exercising our jaws in a vacuum—that we could have gotten roughly the same effect from laughing gas, sneezing powder, or a mutual tickling session with a friendly prankster. As a result, we approach the next Allen film with increased trepidation.

But for the more discriminating viewer a certain, as it were, postcoital depression sets in even earlier: say, midway through the film. It is in the nature of gags not to be all as funny as the best of the lot: a set of perfectly matched jokes is infinitely harder to come by than a necklace of perfectly matched pearls. To avoid inevitable letdowns, the jokes, however, have a remedy unavailable to pearls. They can be helped by what they are strung on: plot, character, existential implications. These strings, in comedy, should be visible; unlike in necklaces, they have their impact to make. What put *Sleeper* above Allen's other films so far is that it really was about something besides gags—about what was wrong with present-day society revealed in terms of a grimly caricatured but all too plausible future.

In *Love and Death,* however, the joke is everything; if it misfires, we promptly begin to wonder what it is that we have been laughing at, anyway. The film starts out as vague satire on Russian novels (do we need that?), but soon scatters toward all kinds of targets, from anti-Semitism to Jewish sexuality (or lack of it), from pretentious pseudophilosophical chitchat to village idiots, from take-offs on Ingmar Bergman to attempted plots against Napoleon Bonaparte's life. Overworked and unsupported, the gag begins to sag. *Love and Death,* says the title, and we think that the film may work its way up to some comic insights into these two big subjects, better yet, about how they interrelate. Yet while it boasts gags galore about both, it has nothing much to say about either, let alone about the two of them together.

This is particularly saddening because Woody Allen is more than merely funny: at his best, he exhibits a penetrating intelligence—indeed, intellect—well beyond the mental means of our run-of-the-mill farceurs. Such intelligence can uncover, ridicule, and perhaps help laugh out of existence genuine evils, and a little, a very little, of this elixir survives even in the anomic laugh-fest of *Love and Death.* But the movie stoops far too often to such things as a facile sight gag about a convention of village idiots that, when you come right down to it, yields laughter that leaves you with a bad taste in the soul.

The other three items in our great comic revival are not really comedies but farces. Now, a farce operates through a total exaggeration, which is all right as long as we know what is being exaggerated and why, and as long as we can feel some sense of recognition or relevance at the core of our laughter. In this fundamental respect *Young Frankenstein,* modest as its aims are, works best of the three. It is principally a funny send-up of the horror-film genre, first by spelling out absurdities to which most of us have at one time or other paid emotional tribute; and, second, by bringing to the surface things latent in the genre that have not dared to become conscious: the intense sexuality masquerading as horror, and the secret double identity of the only superficially monstrous monster as object of our lust as well as of our repressed empathy. Under the surface, of course, the genre always exploited the public's repressed sexual nightmares and longings, but not till *Young Frankenstein* did we get an ithyphallic monster that turns frigidly prissy women into raving sex maniacs. I am not saying that a person who laughs loud at the film's jokes must be fully aware of these implications, but I do think that, consciously or unconsciously, the unifying undercurrent of hidden meanings made all but manifest helps make the laughter steadier and happier.

I don't know exactly why *Young Frankenstein* is so much superior to Mel Brooks's earlier features. It may be that Gene Wilder, the film's star, who had the original idea and collaborated with Brooks on the screenplay, has more discipline, more self-control than Brooks. Then, again, the horror film, which *Young Frankenstein* successfully spoofs, is a limited, formulaic genre, whose solid, satirizable clichés enclose the scenarists and prevent them from wandering off. Moreover, the horror film is absurd by definition, in contrast to the show-biz film *(The Producers),* the comic chase film *(The Twelve Chairs),* and the western *(Blazing Saddles);* it can absorb any number of excesses and still not be desecrated.

Unlike most horror films that are low-budget affairs with, at the utmost, two or three real actors in them, here there are several good performances even in minor parts; and the tiniest of cameo roles, that of a blind monk, is played delightfully by none other than Gene Hackman. And the movie has a real histrionic find in Marty Feldman, a bug-eyed British television comic, whose Igor (pronounced eye-gore) is a source of galloping merriment, rather like Igor's hump, which shuttles between his right side and left side with inscrutable aplomb.

With *The Return of the Pink Panther* and *The Fortune,* we come to the most typical abuses of farce: ways of turning the principal characters into bigger idiots than any audience can conceivably contain. Such movies offer their spectators the edifying experience of feeling superior to the sheer imbecility of the screen personages, and so lets them feel justifiably entrenched in any crassness of their own, which must now look, by comparison, like divine wisdom. In *Panther* there is also a desperate attempt to make all kinds of put-out-to-pasture jokes race again, or to make short-distance jokes run many miles on a soggy track, or simply to make jack-in-the-box gags leap at you out of every nook, cranny, or closet until you become totally slap-unhappy.

Granted, there are tried old formulas that work even here, particularly since Peter Sellers is still a grand jester—as when, sitting at the edge of a swimming pool, he leans backward to follow the form (physical, not technical) of a pretty diver until he himself ends up immersed; or, again, when dapperly crossing a dance floor, he runs into the flying hand of a cavorting young woman, and promptly lands on his back.

But how sorry the more extended, less split-second gags tend to be! I am not even going into the patently poor construction of the movie, which has two half-baked plots that never mesh into a whole: one concerning Christopher Plummer as a master jewel thief trying to get at the bottom of the one theft he did not commit, and another concerning Sellers as the bumbling Inspector Clouseau not really tracking down the stolen diamond but dodging his police chief, sparring with his Chinese butler, or trying to seduce Plummer's glamorous wife.

I *am* talking about the sheer old-hat idiocy of it all. Take the following sequence of shots. Sellers-Clouseau arrives at the Swiss resort where Catherine Schell has lured him. He jumps into a taxi and commands the driver to "Follow that car!" The driver promptly leaps out and starts running after Schell's car. The sense of déjà vu worsens as Sellers asks a passerby whether he knows the way to the Palace Hotel: "Yes," says the man, and walks on. As Sellers arrives at the Palace, he is crossed by the cabbie still chasing after that now emptily returning car—a panting rather than running gag, if ever there was one. Stepping into the Palace lobby, after another superannuated gag with a revolving door, Sellers is accosted by a smooth-talking, suitably accented fellow who asks him successively whether he may have his coat, hat, gloves. Sellers suavely obliges, taking him for a hotel employee, only to have the man—a thief—disappear with the surrendered garments.

This is not merely ancient; it also depends, like most of the film's comedy, on stupidity and incompetence. Indeed, the overwhelming majority of the gags and routines in the film depends on Clouseau's or someone else's abject stupidity and incompetence. Yet this is even more disturbing in the case of Mike Nichols's profoundly unsatisfactory and unlikable *The Fortune.* Here a petty married crook (Warren Beatty) needs an even pettier but unmarried crook (Jack Nicholson) to marry an heiress (Stockard Channing) for him. The time is the twenties, and Beatty must get her off to California, away from her powerful father, but the Mann Act makes transportation of women across state lines for immoral purposes a dangerous business—hence the marriage of convenience. A rather farfetched premise, this—by Adrien Joyce (scenarist also of the vastly overrated *Five Easy Pieces* and the impossible-to-underrate *Puzzle of a Downfall Child),* but let that pass.

Having arrived in Los Angeles, both men vie more or less successfully for the heroine's favors until she discovers that they mostly want her money, which she then vows to donate to charity. The men decide that the only solution is to kill her and split the fortune between them. The main part of the film concerns their fumbling and comically foiled efforts to do away with the heiress. Now, funny movies about the queasy subject of unmurderable victims do exist—they go back at least as far as *The Ladykillers.* Here, however, the jokes are all based on the phenomenal dumbness and clumsiness of the three principals, and are not, by and large, funny enough. That is fatal. What gets killed is not the heiress but our sympathy for the characters: if they are that stupid, we begin to feel, they don't deserve to live, and, forthwith, the film has made misanthropists out of its viewers.

Do not make the mistake of assuming that all farce capitalizes on human stupidity. Think back on the great theatrical and cinematic farces, and you will recall that their humor lies in making fun of stupidity only coincidentally, and concentrating on such more amiable human foibles as lechery, eccentricity, mendacity, absentmindedness, snobbery, laziness, and the like, and that the characters amuse us by the outrageous ways in which they outsmart one another. In *The Fortune,* all they can do is outstupid one another. Thus the would-be killers are birdbrained enough to think the heiress can drown in a birdbath; she, in turn, clambering out of a closed trunk accidentally washed ashore by the ocean, refuses to believe the police when they later tell her that her husband and lover tried to kill her.

Murderous or suicidal idiocy is not an apt subject for laughter (as outwitted murderous cleverness can be), and Nichols makes his film even sleazier when he allows a nocturnal shot of Beatty and Nicholson slinking away from the beach where Miss Channing may have been drowned by them to take on (in John A. Alonzo's excellent photography) an unearthly loveliness. This sort of dissociation of sensibility is a further demonstration of callousness, of moral tone-deafness. Whether one laughs at these characters out of smug superiority or deadly contempt, the laughter is equally unwholesome and, I repeat, turns against the laugher.

Go and see *The Return of the Pink Panther* and *The Fortune* if you must, go ahead and laugh at them if you can, but do not tell me that they make for an *annus mirabilis* of cinematic comedy.

June 29, 1975

Nightmare of the Locust

IT IS A CALAMITOUS IDEA to transfer a great or even very good novel to the screen. The reason is obvious to all except the unfortunates who undertake the project, whose numbers, somehow, never decrease. Nathanael West's last novel may be only very good, not great, but it is far too formalized and idiomatic a piece of writing to allow itself to be dragged with impunity into another medium. *The Day of the Locust* derives its particular strength from two sources: the cool, clear control with which it apprehends matters of extreme turbidity, vehemence, and tawdriness, and the intense concentration with which it encapsulates sprawling, turbulent subjects riddled with implications. It is a novel so condensed as to be made up less of plot and dialogue, or sentences and paragraphs, than of metaphors. The emblematic character of a passing comment, the paradigmatic aspect of a piece of observation strikes the reader like an electric discharge that fills the atmosphere with ozone, exhilarating to breathe in, yet also a potential poison.

For example, when West describes the silly California house that Homer Simpson, the émigré from Iowa, purchases, we read about the enormous hinges on the front door: "Although made by machine, the hinges had been carefully stamped to appear hand forged." On one of the bedroom walls of this pseudo–New England house "was a colored etching of a snowbound Connecticut farmhouse, complete with wolf." Even if the film tried to reproduce this house and this etching, which it doesn't, how would it convey the impact of that bitingly concise and suggestive "complete with wolf"? Yet of such verbal dazzlement is West's novel composed.

John Schlesinger's film, like the book, concerns Tod Hackett, a young painter just out of Yale, trying to make it in a Hollywood studio's art department. He lives at the sleazy San Bernardino Arms, where he falls for a neighbor, seventeen-year-old Faye Greener, a very pretty, very ordinary, very dedicated would-be star working as an extra. She becomes the object also of the inchoate aspirations of Homer Simpson, a repressed accountant from Wayneville, Iowa, one of those many nonentities who come to southern California to die. Faye gets involved with both men in an intricate but platonic relationship with unwholesomely teasing overtones. Around these three revolve several minor figures, mostly ciphers or grotesques, and there is also an outer circle of barely glimpsed human flotsam. The book ends with a riot at a Hollywood première, which is characteristic of West's sensibility: though Homer gets killed by the crowd and Tod is fairly badly injured, it is still a very insignificant riot; things do not go up in flames, what holocaust there is remains in Tod's imagination. Unlike in the movie, the little people around the crowd's perimeter have their not-quite-innocent fun: the edge of violence consists of stupid social and sexual banter among gabbing gapers. In the pettiness, which carries in it the perpetual seeds of violence, lies the true horror.

Even things that could have been managed on film are not, thanks to the incompetence of Schlesinger and his screenwriter, Waldo Salt, who, in contradistinction to the Great Waldo Pepper, will have to be known as the little Waldo Salt. Take almost any scene in which the film tries to follow the book—such as the one where Homer sits in his shabby garden, killing time and being killed by it. "By moving his chair in a quarter circle," West writes, "he could have seen a large part of the canyon twisting down to the city below. He never thought of making this shift." Although Schlesinger begins with a panoramic shot, he does not make clear this almost perverse obtuseness, does not show beauty behind Homer's back. Moveover, the oranges dropping from the tree are not allowed to thud hollowly in a lonely silence; instead, the sound track is polluted with John Barry's mushy music. And the lizard Homer is watching does not become the ultimate in insignificance; seen only in extreme closeup, it takes on the aspect of a giant Komodo dragon, or some legendary basilisk, and so makes the footling fabulous.

Or let us take a bigger example of the film's inflationary methodology: the collapse of the studio set on which the battle of Waterloo is being filmed. In the movie, this becomes a grandiose disaster prefiguring the final Armageddon, and is followed by what Andrew Sarris has called a mini-Watergate: studio executives covering up a gross malpractice. In West's prose, it is all merely a grim joke: "The French killed General Picton with a ball through the head and he returned to his dressing room. . . . The Scotch Greys were destroyed and went to change into another uniform. Ponsonby's heavy dragoons were also cut to ribbons. Mr. Grotenstein [the producer—in the film, the fellow has been prudently de-Semitized into Grote, and a very non-Jewish Helverston placed above him] would have a large bill to pay at the Western Costume Company." When the movie cuirassiers charge up Mont St. Jean, "It was the classic mistake, Tod realized, the same one Napoleon had made. Then it had been wrong for a different reason." Here, "In Wellington's absence, one of the assistant directors, a Mr. Crane, was in command of the allies," a man in a checked cap who is later "sent to the doghouse by Mr. Grotenstein just as Napoleon was sent to St. Helena." In the book, all is satire: "The armies of England and her allies were too deep in scenery to flee." In the film, we get dramatic spectacle, complete with Tod, the separated lover, searching anxiously for the possibly wounded or killed Faye Greener, like Tolstoy's Natasha for Prince Andrei.

The point is that what makes the book distinguished is, as Edmund Wilson correctly noted, "its peculiar combination of amenity of surface and felicity of form and style with ugly subject matter and somber feeling," whereas the film always operates on one simplistic level: obvious grandioseness, obvious sleaziness, or obvious obviousness. Take, for example, the pivotal character of Faye. Karen Black is a poor actress—unsubtle, repetitious, unable to add any personal richness to a part; though, at thirty-three, she is only sixteen years older than Faye, she conveys someone already quite corrupted by the system, a full-fledged little floozy. Yet the very script seems to call for a sexual tease—Harry, Faye's father, is made to spell it out in the crudest terms—in whom innocence and sincerity, even in tarnished form, are never glimpsed. One gets, at best, stupidity, which is not quite the same thing.

Now, West tells us explicitly yet poetically, "her beauty was structural like a tree's" and "she was as shiny as a new spoon," her expression "a subtle half-smile uncontaminated by thought." Karen Black, however, is overmade-up, artificial in look and demeanor, generally scheming and contaminated by unworthy calculation. This contributes to the film's extreme misogyny, its often quite inappropriately homosexual sensibility. So, for example, the distinctly unhandsome hero of the novel is hardly the well-acted but much too pretty, adorable Tod of William Atherton; the book's transvestite entertainer is far less dashing than the movie's; Maybelle Loomis, mother of the film brat Adore, is much less evil in the book; and in the novel Adore himself is not an epicene creature rather resembling Faye, so that when Homer stomps him to death amid much orgasmic panting, it is not the obvious sexual vengeance it becomes in the film. And so on. But to return to West's Faye, we read about her that "she was not hard-boiled"; whereas Karen Black, gum-chewing, eyelash-batting, lip-wetting with a come-hither flick of the tongue, is as hard-boiled as a chalcedony decorator's egg.

The filmmakers are, deliberately or otherwise, unmindful of how different visual images are from the words they purport to be literally illustrating. So when Harry, Faye's pathetic salesman/clown father, dies unbeknown to the girl who is tracking down a pimple on her face in a nearby mirror, West makes this a mere absurd, painful fact of life. In the film, it is spelled out in an ugly, insistent shot suggestive of callous female narcissism. Suffering from vulgar gigantism, the film must always inflate things that West scrupulously left as small as life.

How fundamentally the filmmakers misunderstand the book! They turn it, first and last, into an attack on Hollywood, with suggestions in between of the rise of Nazism and the coming world war. So they introduce all kinds of irrelevant Hollywoodiana while, at the same time, never missing a chance to drag in Hitler via headlines, newsreels, and radio newscasts popping up with studied casualness. Indeed, Homer is made to look rather like Hitler, and Adore even taunts him with, "Nazi spy!" But West's attack is never confined to such specific targets; his attitude, under the surface compassion, is one of universal condemnation: the little people are everywhere, and the day of their settling on the world like a plague of locusts is ever at hand. With partial (in both senses of the word) exception of the quasi-autobiographical Tod, all the characters in the book are deficient in humanity, potential locusts.

I wonder whether it is out of trickiness, dishonesty, or mere slipshodness that Schlesinger never explains (as West does) that Tod is making sketches for a huge painting of *The Burning of Los Angeles.* It is certainly trickiness to show cars passing in front of a street bench and, after each car, as after an objectified wipe, reveal one more desolately staring person sitting on that bench. It is similarly tricky that when, wounded in the riot, Tod begins to hallucinate, the drawings he has made should come to life as actors in ghastly masks mingling with ordinary people. These living masks out of Goya and (as Pauline Kael suggested) out of Ensor and Francis Bacon—but mostly out of putty—are too obvious, too vulgar contraptions on screen: they carry no greater mystery than that of the studio make-up department. The nightmare is too literally contrived to be scary, suggestive, or symbolic.

Literal-mindedness is yet another of Schlesinger's failings. Where West has a few lines about the preposterous religious cults of southern California, Schlesinger and Salt invent an extraneous and tiresome sequence about an Aimee Semple MacPhersonish revivalist, complete with facile and unoriginal jokes derived from the crosscutting of fervent believers' faces with the greedy hands of Big Sister's assistants raking in and totting up the take. It was all done much better in *Marjoe.*

Then there are the depoeticization and deintellectualization practiced by the film. Thus the al fresco dinner scene where three men bestially lust for Faye is poeticized by West with such a bittersweet evocation of a quail's call answered by the call of another quail, this one "a trapped bird, but the sound it made had no anxiety in it, only sadness, impersonal and without hope." In the movie, the scene is all incipient lechery and attempted rape. Again, Audrey Jenning, the madam, is in the novel conscientious, solicitous of her girls, and "really cultured." When her clients "wanted to talk about certain lively matters of universal interest . . . she insisted on discussing Gertrude Stein and Juan Gris." (Note how the irony cuts both ways.) In the film, she is played creepily by Natalie Schafer, and is deintellectualized, like everything else, to the level of the book's archetypal ignoramus, "the barber in Purdue," who wants from his movies merely "amour and glamour."

But the picture's worst sin is all the stuff Salt has written into it. Because the book is lean in incident and rich only in detail, it was thought necessary to invent all manner of episodes and add considerable dialogue, all trivial, downright sacrilegious. Let me cite just the added prologue and epilogue. In the former, Tod arrives at the San Bernardino Arms to find in his apartment-to-be a huge crack in a wall, left over from "the big earthquake." He impishly sticks into it a paper rose, which can be seen jutting out in various shots, sometimes seeming to bleed. Later he refers to the décor of his place as "early earthquake," which the filmmakers proudly, chortlingly reiterate, even though it patently harks back to Gloria Grahame's comment on Glenn Ford's apartment in *The Big Heat,* "early nothing." In the epilogue, a chastened and apparently repentant Faye returns to Tod's apartment, now finally needing him. But he is gone; only the paper rose hurls its reproach at Faye. Is this a conventional comeuppance or more homophile antifeminism? In any case, West ended on no such note.

None of the major performances quite works; Donald Sutherland in particular plays *into* the foolishness and obtuseness of Homer Simpson, not against it, thus making him imbecile rather than ridiculous and pathetic. Burgess Meredith and Billy Barty come off best, but these are small assets in a film in which everything hurtles toward that final, fruity cataclysm, trying to make West's subtly ambivalent novel into the definitive disaster movie. *The Day of the Locust* certainly is a disaster of a movie.

Where moral, aesthetic, and several other kinds of indignation might, however, be put to better use is in *Supervixen,* by that abject no-talent Russ Meyer. Meyer is a filmmaker arrested technically somewhere between home movies and television commercials; emotionally, in the hollow between two hypertrophic female breasts (with very little interest shown in other parts of the body); and, intellectually, somewhere between the ages of seven and eight. Well, not quite; he seems to have learned from one of our callowest movie reviewers, Roger Ebert (with whom he collaborated on *Beyond the Valley of the Dolls),* what sophomoric humor is, and he tries to use it here to defuse his extraordinary nastiness. So we get cheap jokes as an overlay for the most nauseating brutality—like the slow, sadistic murder of a woman shown in the goriest, most gleeful detail—but the putative defense, "Have you no sense of humor?" ostensibly ready to hand. It was instructive to hear a male voice pipe up in the screening room after that murder: "That's what they all deserve!" Maybe that, too, was a joke. But the real joke is on us, on a world in which allegedly serious critics such as Richard Schickel and Raymond Durgnat write lengthy articles on or analyses of Russ Meyer in respectable journals, and where the Yale Law School Forum honors this Neanderthal hack with a retrospective of his soft-core pornography.

And now we have a remake of *Murder, My Sweet* (1945) under its true Chandlerian title, *Farewell, My Lovely;* by either name, the film smells unsweet. In Edward Dmytryk's version, Dick Powell earned James Agee's plaudits as being better than Bogart; what I recall mostly is the scariness of Mike Mazurki and the convincing whorishness of Claire Trevor. In the current version (with a script by David Zelag Goodman that, most likely, does not improve on John Paxton's), the plot remains hard to follow and less than persuasive, and Dick Richards's direction seems to fall short even of Dmytryk's. There is, however, ingenious color cinematography by John A. Alonzo, who here, even more than in *Chinatown* or *The Fortune,* conveys period atmosphere through his very palette, and seediness or menace through superb lighting. No less satisfying is the production design of Dean Tavoularis, and those wishing to feel nostalgia for 1941 can get it here.

Then there is Robert Mitchum, looking more than ever like a bloodhound that has seen too many horrible truths to stir so much as a jowl, and reading lines with his customary incertitude whenever they come in bunches bigger than five or contain words with more syllables than two. But he certainly looks and growls his part, and may equal Dick Powell's thespian gifts. Charlotte Rampling, a poor actress who mistakes creepiness for sensuality, is no match for Claire Trevor, and in the supporting cast only Harry Dean Stanton and John O'Leary are outstanding. And Jack O'Halloran is either a much less frightening monster than Mazurki or else we have become more used to living with the monstrous.

August 1975

The Amazing Shrunken *Nashville*

PARAMOUNT PICTURES HAS, I suspect, done Robert Altman a grave disservice in not releasing his *Nashville* in some longer version. Not since the Roman sibyl, to punish the skepticism of Tarquin the Proud, kept burning successive thirds of her prophetic books have we been tormented by stories of such woeful progressive diminution. From an eight-hour version to a six-hour one to be released in two parts, from a three-and-a-half- to its present two-and-a-half-hour version, the film kept shrinking with nothing reaching us except rumors of its decrease. Not even Pauline Kael's gallant stand on behalf of a somewhat longer *Nashville,* which she reviewed before the final version was assembled, was able to halt the march of the scissors, and merely earned her the gibes of fellow critics envious of her advance look at the film. What has finally been vouchsafed us strikes me as highly interesting but ultimately insufficient. The film is unorthodox enough in more radical respects; why boggle at a mere matter of length?

Length, after all, is organic and appropriate in a movie that dispenses with conventional plot for the sake of a thickly woven texture and its sedulous scrutiny. There are—or were—twenty-four main characters in this account of five days in the life of Nashville, the country-music center of America, and the film was (and truncatedly still is) a chronicle of how these two dozen existences parallel or intersect one another, interact or fail to do so, in that slice of time and space. In a sense, the film resembles Joyce's *Ulysses:* more or less interconnected, self-important but essentially humdrum lives strutting in a brief time span against the more important backdrop of an exceptionally raucous but second-rate city, and the whole thing functioning on two levels. But there are two sizable differences: the nonliteral level in the book is mythic, not merely allegorical; and the novel is a work of genius, the film only of talent.

Still, this is an absorbing film, Altman's best so far, and look what the drastic cutting has done to it. We encounter, for instance, a mismated married couple: an elderly farmer husband (Bert Remsen) and his flighty young wife (Barbara Harris) who keeps eluding him to take stabs at becoming a country-and-western singer. We see so little of their relationship—almost nothing of Remsen—that the surprise climax, in which Harris against all probability gets a sensational start on the road to stardom, lacks the petty beginnings against which to resonate. Such fragmentation diminishes most of the characters and relationships in the released *Nashville,* which now comes across rather like a huge novel turned into a telegram. It whets the appetite and then lets it down so many times as to make this a veritable feast of Tantalus.

We are left with questions upon questions. Why would Tom (Keith Carradine), a Casanova of a rock musician briefly in Nashville for a recording session (with Bill and Mary, fellow members of his trio) and currently enjoying the favors of three more available and plausible women, so crave a fling with Linnea, played by the horse-faced Lily Tomlin? True, she is the white lead singer of a black gospel chorus, the middle-class wife of a male-chauvinist lawyer, and the mother of two deaf children—all of which might make her a somewhat exotic morsel for Tom's jaded palate. Still, we want to know the details of why this self-absorbed, indolent fellow makes such assiduous efforts to seduce her; and though we have been told by more than one middle-aged female movie critic that this is the one affair Tom will find hard to forget, on present evidence that is only a middle-aged female fantasy. In a fuller version, it might be the gospel, or country-and-western, truth.

We should like to know more about the significance, symbolic or otherwise, of the "tricycle man," a fellow who pops up everywhere doing paltry magic tricks or merely riding his outlandish bike with its far-flung, delicate front wheels and squat, bulky rear wheels, which make it the mechanical equivalent of a crossbred giraffe and hippopotamus. We want to know more about the Pfc. on furlough and the escaping mother's boy who are, respectively, the good and evil angels of Barbara Jean (Ronee Blakley), Nashville's reigning C. & W. queen. And why, we wonder, is the very countrified and Protestant Barbara Jean's husband and manager the extremely urban and Jewish Barnett (Allen Garfield)? And what is the nature and cause of Barbara Jean's psychic disorder that has her forever hovering on the verge of a nervous breakdown? We can make up answers to these and similar questions, and a work of art may certainly raise more queries than it answers; still, we are entitled to ask of the film, here and there, a little answering of its own.

The biggest problem, however, despite the flavorousness, humor, and even excitement of the literal level, is the uneasy symbolism. We are led to the symbolic level adroitly enough, to be sure. Running through the film is the invisible presence of Hal Walker, a third-party presidential candidate. The movie, in fact, begins with Nashville waking to campaign speeches blaring from Walker's cruising sound truck, which proceeds to weave its way through much of the film. We also see high-school drum majorettes and other youthful campaign workers for Walker impinging on or overlapping with the C. & W. world. A major character is John Triplette (Michael Murphy), Walker's suave but unsavory advance man, busy arranging a stellar C. & W. telecast on behalf of Walker's campaign, to be broadcast from that curious replica of the Parthenon that gave Nashville its spurious honorific, "the Athens of the South." Country music, television, Parthenon (culture), and Walker (politics)—we see which way things are pointing. Walker's speeches, with their blend of horse sense, half sense, and nonsense, nicely parallel the inane yet somehow pawky lyrics to the C. & W. songs that celebrate the very values of Walker's Replacement party, with its quirky populism and fanatical free enterprise.

There are parallels, too, in the barely disguised political aspirations of Haven Hamilton (Henry Gibson), the reigning male C. & W. star; in the tearful and smoldering reminiscences of his consort, Lady Pearl (Barbara Baxley), about the assassinated Kennedy brothers she worshiped and worked for; the quasi-political rivalry between Barbara Jean and the number-two female star, Connie White (Karen Black, here wisely cast in a role sufficiently vulgar for her), who is Barbara Jean's occasional replacement (note the parallel with the Replacement party). All these point to the film's climax: the insane, protopolitical assassination of Barbara Jean during the televised Parthenon concert, causing the Walker motorcade that arrived with sinister aggressiveness to beat a hasty and humbled retreat. Clearly, metaphorical significance is intended—but what exactly is being signified?

In one brief interview with the *New York Times,* Altman managed to contradict himself about this twice. "*Nashville* is a metaphor for my personal view of our society," he stated, and promptly added that Nashville "is the new Hollywood, where people are tuned in by instant stars, instant music, and instant politicians." And a little later: "It's the Hollywood of forty years ago. Recording studios, singers, musicians are everywhere. You get off the bus carrying a guitar and, with luck, in two years you have a guitar-shaped swimming pool." Well, which is it: the old Hollywood, the new Hollywood, or Our Society? I am all for Nashville (or *Nashville)* being different things to different people, but I am less happy about its being three different things to the same person, especially if he happens to be the filmmaker.

An even blurrier picture emerges from another interview with Altman in the Sunday *Times.* Here he says: "It's my view—my distorted view—of the culture. But I don't have any philosophies. I don't have anything to say. I don't believe in propaganda. In *Nashville* there's certainly not a definitive study of a culture. . . . It's not even supposed to be accurate. It's just an impression." Much worse than merely confusing the old and new Hollywoods and our society is not distinguishing among philosophies, propaganda, and having something to say. It is to Altman's credit that his film is better than his interviews, but something of the same confusion pervades all. What point is there in devising an elaborate metaphor for something as trivial and passé as the old Hollywood? Or as trivial and well-nigh passé as the new Hollywood? For a film about something as small and specialized as that, no need to resort to symbolism or allegory, modes reserved for vast topics, often metaphysical ones, which require such more devious, roundabout strategies to encompass them.

Our society—now, that is something else. But in that case, how does the symbology work? Easy fame, easy money, easy sex, uneasy competitiveness, all stemming from a dubious commodity, C. & W. music—meaning presumably that our materialistic, appetitive, and competitive society produces unwholesome social climates and political ideologies. Yet does the fanatical production of musical claptrap really parallel the political, let alone the cultural situation? Does one become a politician the way one becomes a C. & W. musician? And isn't our culture to a large extent, alas, precisely C. & W. and rock music—in which case, how can the thing symbolized do double duty as the symbol? And what is the point of symbolizing unless new light is shed on the thing symbolized, yet I cannot find anything new about America in the movie, however much it may hold my interest. But maybe a fuller version would have yielded something more.

I doubt, though, whether any version could make the climactic shooting of Barbara Jean by Kenny (David Hayward), a mother's boy fleeing Mom's authority, believable, granted that the singer had just praised Dad and Mom in her song. Clearly, if the film is to represent our society, such a seemingly meaningless assassination belongs in it. But whereas this makes a kind of sick sense in the political arena, where a powerless nonentity may imagine he is appropriating a great leader's power by killing him, what power can Kenny absorb from poor, daffy Barbara Jean, teetering on the edge of collapse? She has musical fame, but the film does not make clear that Kenny is after that; and, in any case, is fame without tangible power enough to trigger off assassins? If so, I would like to recommend a few movie stars to their attention; but the facts would not bear me out. Any resemblance to the Sharon Tate case, by the way, is purely coincidental.

So the film's grand design, which would crumble without the murder, crumbles even worse with it. It is likewise foolhardy and self-destructive for a film that so trades in metaphors to hold up to our unmitigated ridicule the one character in it who likewise spouts them. This is Opal (Geraldine Chaplin), the BBC television journalist, the film's most repellent and least convincing personage. No one that unprofessional, foolishly garrulous, and ineptly pushy would work for the sedately respectable BBC (whatever other incompetent and importunate interviewers Altman may here be paying back). More important, this steady nuisance and intermittent fool is allowed some valid insights among overwhelming imbecilities, some pregnant metaphors among others that are totally barren. This confusion may derive from the fact that Altman and his scenarist, Joan Tewkesbury, wanted to give even the backwoods filmgoers, who would identify themselves like crazy with all the other characters, at least one preposterous foreigner to feel superior to; or it may be simply that as all the actors were encouraged to improvise, so was Miss Chaplin, and she merely proved worse at it. Either way, Opal is a crude device.

There remains, finally, the nature of the vehicle picked for the main metaphor, the country music with which the film is awash. Most of these countless songs were written and composed by the very actors who perform them and strike me as no different from bona fide C. & W. hits. But if any rank amateur can do as well at something as the established professionals (and that includes delivering the songs), there can't be much to that thing. And, indeed, I found most of what was sung close to excruciating, except for one number ("200 Years") that has some satirical value, and two others, both by

Keith Carradine, that actually bear listening to. Why couldn't Altman use the classical music field for his metaphor? I guess not even he could envision Beverly Sills getting shot.

But it is time to advert to the virtues of *Nashville,* which also are numerous and real. Take, first, the acting. Following the lead of such master directors as Kurosawa and Bergman, Altman has sagely been assembling a repertory company. Yet whether gleaned from its ranks or a total newcomer, almost everyone here is cast against character or previous experience, with generally stunning results. Aside from Miss Chaplin, only Shelley Duvall misfires, being rather in excess of even the excessive groupie she is playing. All the rest, however, are, or are directed into becoming, good or indeed outstanding. Even performers with rather too grand a manner, like Barbara Baxley and Keenan Wynn, are orchestrated into a harmonious ensemble.

Then there are all those bravura scenes. Take the harrowing striptease at a political smoker, as flawlessly acted by Gwen Welles as it is written and directed. Sueleen Gay (the name is, like all the others, apt), a countergirl without a shred of musical talent but hell-bent on becoming a C. & W. star, has been conned into stripping for a group of affluent Walker backers. The scene is cleverly poised between comedy and pathos. Sueleen is not a delicate, virginal victim; the ogling men are not preternaturally brutish; the girl will later get a real chance in exchange for her present complaisance; and although she comically bungles the removal of some garments, at other times she manages to mimic the real thing almost too convincingly. Her singing, moreover, though plainly insufficient for a singer, might just do for a novelty stripping act. So by avoiding romantic pathos and concentrating on routine, minor-key humiliation, the scene achieves the genuine chill of a matter-of-fact, almost jocular degradation. And Altman's camera is always in the right places, as when, at the end, the naked girl forlornly trudges away, all attempts at sexiness abandoned, and the camera does not follow her closely but lets her vanish behind a distant door—a small, used-up figure to be instantly forgotten.

Or take the scene in which the rising rock star, Tom, performs his latest song in a local night spot; the number is called "I'm Easy," and he dedicates it to a special woman in the audience. Three women listening have recently shared Tom's bed: the outrageous groupie, Opal, and Mary who, with her husband Bill, is part of Tom's trio. Each woman thinks the song is for her, but with what different feelings! Opal, who has just a while ago announced her having bedded down with Tom, is ridiculously exultant; Mary, who bristled at Opal's announcement, is torn by contrary emotions; the groupie just beams idiotically. Yet the song is actually for the befuddled housewife Linnea, who has accepted Tom's suggestion that she come to the joint almost against her wishes, and who now sits there in flattered, shy amazement. She is beginning to yield—why, the very lyric, "I'm easy," is a thinly veiled proclamation of Tom's sexual prowess. The way Altman intercuts among the four women with their variously affected, even agitated, expressions, and Tom, smugly imperturbable in his professional assurance as performer and seducer, makes for one of those scenes where the staccato editing, the nervous rhythm successively catching widely differing facial expressions, creates a riotous sense of life collaring us from the screen.

Other fine scenes, briefly noted. Barbara Jean's mental wanderings during a performance, causing some of her more fickle fans to turn hideously against her as she babbles on about her childhood—the ghastly psychic equivalent of Sueleen's physical stripping. Or, in a similar vein, Albuquerque (Barbara Harris) getting at last a chance to sing at a stock-car rally whose roar turns her performance into a laughable dumb show for those few who pay her any heed. Or the fascinating set of sequences in which the very different Sunday church services all the characters dutifully attend or even perform in are shown, some of our people fitting predictably into their particular church setting, others revealed in a surprising new light. We are delighted by Altman and Tewkesbury's skill in such scenes even if the Draconian cutting of the film sometimes leaves us shortchanged and puzzled.

Paul Lohmann, only for the second time cinematographer on an Altman film, captures suggestive color tonalities; the expert set and costume design always gets the right look and feel of things. Even Altman's previously irritatingly distracting multiple sound track works here: where there is no plot-advancing dialogue to follow, we don't care what we miss by tuning in on one conversation to the exclusion of another. All conversations are equally important, but it is their cumulative, discordant unimportance that gives this self-important bustle its comic punch.

In *Nashville,* the sum of the parts is, unfortunately, greater than the whole, but, bit by bit, they are mostly well worth attending to. Even if they do not signify much that is new to us about our society, they do represent a significant advance in Altman's filmmaking. There is something more mature and subtle here that confirms Altman, for all his faults, as Hollywood's most rewarding director. May his faults grow fewer as his rewards keep growing.

September 1975

One Dog Day or Three Condor Ones?

HERE IS *Three Days of the Condor,* loosely based on James Grady's *Six Days of the Condor,* whose title apparently had not been Sanforized. We have here a spy thriller in which the villain is the CIA—or, rather, a seditious faction within it (we mustn't make our anti-Americanism too sweepingly irreversible)—and the hero a lowly, bookish operative whose job is reading spy books for the CIA. He stumbles onto an embarrassing secret and has to be eliminated by his employer—or a cabal within the organization.

The film's trendy climate is early post-Watergate, a long gloomward step beyond its most closely related predecessor, *Scorpio* (1972). What is significant about the movie version of *Condor* is the way the book has been rewritten by the screenwriters, Lorenzo Semple, Jr., and David Rayfiel. That the action has been relocated from sleepy Washington to furious New York City, that almost all the names have been changed, that the plot has been vastly overcomplicated, is of lesser interest than that a potentially straight genre film has been overloaded into an elegy of private, political, and, finally, cosmic pessimism, a kind of national, if not indeed metaphysical, guilt film to enchant the disenchanted. Over against the somewhat desiccated leanness of the book, the movie is positively baroque.

Consider merely the changes in the boy-girl relation. In the book, the hero is Ron Malcolm, who, like the girl, Wendy, owns the record album of the score for *Black Orpheus.* In the film, the hero is Joseph Turner—a nice, painterly sort of name—who holds forth at lunch counters about Mozart and van Gogh. Wendy works for a law firm; is relatively easily convinced by Malcolm, who abducts her at gunpoint in order to hide out in her digs, that he works for the CIA; and comes quite eagerly to his bed. Kathy, her movie counterpart, is infinitely more suspicious and uncooperative and complex, has a lover waiting for her up north for a cross-country trip, and is much harder to bed. But the real difference is that she is a photographer who takes strange, moody pictures of lonely, unyielding landscapes which, when Turner sees them on her walls, make him exclaim: "Not autumn, not winter, but in between; I like them." Later, when she is drawn to Turner, it emerges that she has taken even stranger pictures that she herself cannot recognize as an extension of herself. Someday, she says, she will be close enough to Turner to show them to him, but she never does. She takes her portentous secret—and deep aloneness—off camera with her.

The Kathy-Joseph affair evolves along grandly neo-Hemingwayesque lines. Take this, spoken in a tone as flat as Nebraska: "I don't remember yesterday. Today it rained." Or Turner's declaration of love: "You've got good eyes. Not kind, but they don't look away, and don't miss anything. I could use eyes like that." When he asks Kathy to bed, he blurts out that he doesn't want love, only a few hours' oblivion, surcease, rest. And when they do make love—in an oddly fiftul, spasmodic, yet also childlike way—the director, Sydney Pollack, keeps cuting away to Kathy's photographs: black-and-white shots in the midst of color film, loneliness at the core of sex, and, in sudden closeup, a Nikon camera with its rubescent lens cover for a symbol: the camera eye inflamed like an aroused penis, the photographic and the phallic eye both searching for something hidden or lost in an unpeopled November landscape. And when, after Kathy has performed some far-fetched sleuthing services for Turner ("You can always depend on the old spy-fucker," she tells him), the two part forever in a railway station—he going toward possible death, she to her eagerly waiting lover—this is their last colloquy: "Is he a tough guy?"—"Pretty tough."—"What will he do?"—"Understand."—"That *is* tough."

Now, ladies and gentlemen, you may consider this fine writing, and filmmaking, or you may consider it kitsch, or even an artful blend of both, but it does wreak havoc on your genre film. Imagine yourself nonchalantly inspecting some pleasant genre paintings, by, say, Gerrit Dou or Pieter de Hooch, and suddenly having a troubled Rembrandt self-portrait stare at you from among them, transfixing you with its implicating gaze. Once Robert Redford and Faye Dunaway start their uneasy jockeying, their exacerbated love-or-power play ("Have I raped you? Are you surprised I haven't?"—"The night is still young"), what spurious interest the CIA or CIA-within-a-CIA plot might generate plummets into oblivion.

It is not that Pollack, Semple, and Rayfiel haven't tried hard. They have developed characters from the book and added new ones, have made the plot intricate enough to cease having truck with mere sense, have written in oodles of bright or at least brightish dialogue, and have sent the nervous camera scurrying and prying around locations all over New York and environs. Not for nothing, the cinematographic services of Owen Roizman, who did so well by the original *French Connection,* were enlisted, and here is the city in all its tawdry splendor and coloristic chaos, caught in all kinds of light and weather to exhilarating effect. You don't even have to be a foreigner, watching the film in Bratislava or Benares, to want to live in New York. But silliness prevails.

Joseph Turner does not make sense even foisted on the capable shoulders of Redford. So incompetent in the beginning as to have to say on the phone "At fourteen-thirty? All right, that will be two-thirty?" he speedily evolves into a modest mixture of Sherlock Holmes and 007, who can, even during a deadly fight, find time to turn on a photographer's floodlight to blind his assailant. And I cannot endorse the old shell game of making everyone look highly suspicious throughout contrary to any logic, and then, in the end, shoving almost all guilt onto one arbitrary person and letting us even feel a grudging admiration for Jaubert, the hired killer who likes children and has a sporting sense—though he, too, shuttles between superhuman cunning and dumb mistakes.

Over all this hovers, as mentioned, the vague but all-inclusive malaise of Watergate, yet with an equivocal ray of light allowed to pierce the gloom. Most curious is Turner's final staking of his life—if not, in fact, America's future—on his belief in the wisdom and power of the *New York Times,* the kind of act of faith one might have thought went out with Bernadette of Lourdes. But rare is the downbeat film coming out of Hollywood (or New York) that doesn't try to have it both ways.

Sydney Pollack is a puzzling director. A man of ability and finesse, he can make a film as good as *They Shoot Horses, Don't They?,* and pull off some very well-turned scenes in the otherwise unconvincing *Jeremiah Johnson,* then go on to such amateurish nonsense as *The Way We Were* and *The Yakuza.* Here he does offer some nice atmospheric sequences against crowded or deserted cityscapes, but does little for the more private moments. As a starring twosome, Redford and Dunaway fail to ignite. Have his sideburns grown too shaggy, or has her coloring become too drab? Or is it that, although both perform at their still more than acceptable second-best, the script and direction make inappropriate demands on them? Redford is always at his peak when his charming competence, easy intelligence, and mild indifference join in a cool, low-gear efficacy; as a desperate man up against overwhelming odds, he is not exactly unbelievable, but not compelling either. And obliged to underplay her sleek sexiness, Dunaway emerges as only respectable, both as character and as performer. Max von Sydow does well as the hired assassin, a part for which a lesser actor would have been quite sufficient; Cliff Robertson is sensibly type-cast; but John Houseman, who looked so impressive in his first major screen role, is already repetitious the third time around. The lesson I derive from the film is that we must, after all, be grateful to the CIA: it does what our schools no longer do—engage some people to read books.

Dog Day Afternoon is based on a true story that took place in Brooklyn, and Sidney Lumet shot his film there. It concerns a bank robbery by two oddballs: Sonny, ex–bank clerk and Vietnam veteran, intelligent and likable, but not cut out for criminal work; and Sal, his somewhat slow-witted, slightly mad ex-buddy, also likable under his creepy veneer. Everything goes wrong from the start—an accomplice crumps out in mid-holdup, there is hardly any money in the vault, etc.—and our two robbers find themselves confined with nine hostages to a tiny bank lacking creature comforts, while, outside, half of New York's finest spiked with a few feds are laying siege to them.

The film proceeds along several levels, not all of them sufficiently developed, and most of them getting into one another's way. Much of it is comedy about a somewhat less than brilliant policeman and an FBI type (rivals, as is customary in such films) trying to negotiate with Sonny, who is keenly alive to the fact that this is his moment of power and glory, but who has troubles with Sal, the hostages, his parents, television reporters, his fat wife, Angela, their two children, and his other "wife," Leon, a disturbed young homosexual hospitalized at some place like Bellevue, whose change-of-sex operation (in some place like Sweden) the robbery was meant to finance. Most of this is treated as comedy or farce, but it is social comedy, sexual comedy, domestic comedy (intolerant father, overprotective mother, hysterical Angela, near-catatonic Leon), religious comedy (Sonny and Sal are good Catholics), and even absurdist comedy confusingly cheek by jowl. Outside the bank there are young liberals who see Sonny and Sal as victims of another Attica, and gay libbers who are making Sonny, after his public announcement of his homosexual marriage, into a hero-martyr. In the course of all this we learn a fair amount about Sonny, but nowhere near enough about Sal.

Yet the real problem is those jarring, warring types of comedy that suddenly veer into seriousness, and the blurry values of Lumet and his scenarist, Frank Pierson. It is always hard to mix comedy and drama, and particularly so when there is no clear moral attitude at work. It is impossible to tell whether these underprivileged and maladjusted veterans are ultimately treated with compassion or ridicule; whether homosexual marriage is accepted or made fun of; whether the law enforcers are viewed as put-upon, befuddled creatures attempting to do their best, or brutish villains; whether the hostages are little people doing their utmost in trying circumstances or a variety of buffoons and poltroons either lighting up indecently in the spotlight or just turning yellow.

Ambiguity is, of course, a perfectly valid artistic device, but I felt here more in the presence of commercially calculated ambivalence ("We neither know for certain nor care, but will make sure to provide something for everyone") than in that of genuine philosophical and artistic ambiguity. Still, there are good scenes in this fairly long, or long-seeming, film; and there is some commendable striving for psychological and sociological accuracy—note, for example, the mixed reactions of various policemen to Leon's eventual outpourings. This homosexual "wife," by the way, is superbly played by Chris Sarandon, who must tread the delicate line between the maudlin and the grotesque, as heterosexual viewers might see it, and who with consummate histrionic restraint and human dignity, neither over- nor underacts, where a lesser actor would have done both.

As Sonny, Al Pacino is back in fine fettle after what seemed like marking time in *Godfather II,* and several supporting players contribute handsome bits. But other supporting parts are less happily handled: John Cazale cannot bring much dimension to Sal, and Carol Kane once again proves one of our screen's more untalented and graceless presences. Sidney Lumet's direction is middling—the crowd scenes, for instance, are routinely handled—and Victor J. Kemper's cinematography may be unduly grubby. But Dede Allen edits with her usual razor-sharp eye, and there are scattered moments of wry humor, sudden pathos, and correct observation throughout.

September 29, 1975

How the West Was Winning

THE TEMPTATION TO OVERPRAISE a movie like *Hearts of the West* is considerable. It is rather like a scruffy, affectionate mutt that follows you in the street and demands adoption, even though you already have a whole menagerie of impeccable pets and can ill afford this additional piece of shaggy, flea-infested affection. Yet, after it has trailed and nuzzled you for a while—or, to revert to film idiom, somewhere in the second reel—resistance becomes useless. *Hearts of the West* is a commercial film, dopey and wiseacreish by turns, but merry, endearing, and—is it possible in this day and age?—genuinely innocent. Its director, Howard Zieff, has somewhere—more in the eye, perhaps, than in a deeper part, but somewhere—a true touch of the artist about him.

Remember Zieff's one previous feature, *Slither?* A very, very uneven movie, yet with aspects of (to borrow a phrase so shopworn it will never have to be returned) inspired lunacy about it. There, too, people were driven toward good or bad or some quaint mixture of the two by forces that were nothing short of demonic, even though these forces chose to inhabit persons seemingly more suited to being plaster dwarfs than stirrers-up of tempests. Our protagonist now is Lewis Tater from Iowa in the thirties (when it was even more Iowan than today), who wants to be a writer of "western prose" and is lured to a dump in Nevada by two petty crooks who promptly dump on him. Outsmarting, or possibly outdumbing them, he escapes into the deadly desert with their ill-gotten gains, and is miraculously saved by a film crew making rotten westerns on location. They take him back to Hollywood, and thenceforth it is a combination old-time-movie-industry and innocent-pursued-by-bumbling-villains story, the two elements wonderfully cross-fertilizing each other, and the whole thing adding up to farce, romance, suspense, local color, and nostalgia in artfully balanced and blended dosage. Unless you want deep seriousness or high comedy (which this is not), you couldn't ask for more.

Based on a script by Rob Thompson, which is a young man's work in the nicest sense—cinematically knowledgeable, uncynical, willing to take chances—the film moves along in leisurely, uninsistent fashion, content to sacrifice the chase after big laughs for the sake of consistent joviality. Soon you are surprisingly involved with this young hayseed whose delusions of seedy grandeur bifurcate toward the twin goals of western writer and cowboy star, Zane Grey and Tom Mix. It is a most engaging, downright modest, kind of gimcrack megalomania, made of pure crazy enthusiasm and not a shred of arrogance. The people Tater encounters along his dubious climb are types, to be sure, but types with gusts of individual life puffed into them by Thompson, Zieff, and a cluster of equally vigorous leading and supporting actors among whom only Donald Pleasence seems more blatantly freakish than necessary.

Throughout, Zieff's good eye and good sense are joyously displayed. That Kessler, the two-bit blowhard movie director, remains a role underemphasized in length and importance is in itself a masterstroke: give Alan Arkin too long and prominent a part, and it'll be at best an interesting but uneven performance; give him a medium-sized role and restrain his mannerisms, and you get highly textured and suggestive comic craftsmanship. Pick for your heroine neither an empty sexpot nor one of those currently preconized so-called New York actresses (more or less pathetic weirdos like Carol Kane, Susan Tyrrell, Marcia Jean Kurtz, and their ilk), but the not especially beautiful yet wholesome, canny, and talented Blythe Danner, and you fill your screen with something like essential humanity. In lesser ways, Zieff gets the same thing from Andy Griffith and a lot of other, often quite unknown, players, e.g., an atypical but arresting minor heavy (light-heavy, since he is rather cadaverous) from Anthony James.

And then, as Tater, there is Jeff Bridges, clearly the most—or should I say only?—gifted member of the acting Bridges clan, and getting better all the time. His specialty is a very likable one: making average looks, intelligence, and skill assume a basic dignity, even stature, through honesty, gallantry, rough-and-tumble charm, or some kind of dogged, reckless self-reliance. He has, in fact, the quality that has made American movie actors universally beloved: a boyishness so perdurable, so monumental, that it surpasses mere manhood. It is what established Gary Cooper and James Stewart, for example: a kind of hopeful, naïve vulnerability that, when sufficiently provoked, will sweetly, innocently mow down its antagonists.

Even more than with his casting and handling of actors, Zieff impresses us with his fine sense of visual detail and the ability to toss off nonchalantly powerful pictorial effects, the way certain actors can score with throwaway lines. Thus when a caravan of film-crew vehicles departs through the cold desert night, the one white thing in all that darkness is a horse swathed like a granny in protective canvas wrapping—a rather mangy-looking creature jutting forlornly from the back of a receding truck, yet also the most impressive item in that caravan, and fittingly so, since it is the ultimate, irreducible star of the horse operas being produced. Or consider how Zieff treats the various episodes in which Tater the extra, stuntman, aspiring actor, comes to comic grief: never an obvious pratfall photographed head on, but, rather, a subtly choreographed bit of absurdity whose impact slowly, sneakily overpowers our awareness.

Some effects misfire. Whether or not intended as an *hommage,* it is wrong for Tater to wear his hat while soaking in the bathtub; not only is this old hat by now, it is also out of character. And there is that bitter confrontation scene on a private beach during a fancy Hollywood brunch, a scene that, in writing and direction, takes itself too seriously, strives too sweatily for pathos. The actors are lined up in a row in a medium shot in front of the relentlessly rolling-in breakers—the shot is heavy with color contrast, framed and held equally relentlessly, followed by another in which the pages of a manuscript are angrily scattered to the winds. The whole thing is reminiscent of the excesses of films like *Alex in Wonderland* and *The Long Goodbye.* But such failings are few and brief. Mario Tosi's pastel cinematography also occasionally overdoes certain tricks like soft focus, but it is generally pleasing, and the predominantly eclectic and nostalgic score by Ken Lauber and four able assistants is exemplary: old music well chosen, cleverly orchestrated, and used with just the right amount of humorous or sentimental nudging, but without undue ostentation. *Hearts of the West* manages to reinvent its old jokes, reimagine its conventional story line with such unabashedly amiable cheekiness as to insinuate itself into the most hidebound, most eastern, hearts.

Hester Street is about Lower-East-Side Jewish immigrants at the turn of the century; it is the first film of Joan Micklin Silver, and, if it is any indication of her talent, may well be the last. It is in sleazy black-and-white, amateurishly photographed by Kenneth Van Sickle, with a platitudinous script by Mrs. Silver from a story by Abraham Cahan (whom I never knew as an author, and I now see why), and is played by some actors who are dependably bad and others who have been known to be good until working with this director. Even the music by the not untalented William Bolcom is, like the rest of the film, pallid and derivative. Only Mel Howard, who is not a professional actor but shows restraint and dignity, emerges unscathed.

Much of the film is in Yiddish, although the actors seem to have had only the most superficial coaching in it; the rest is in Jewish-accented English, often equally unconvincing; both fall unpleasantly on the ear. But the aural chaos is as nothing to the banality of the plot and dialogue and the filmically illiterate handling of the camera and performers; I have seen work by second-year film students that delivered more than this. Nevertheless, the film may appeal to some—those who share its Jewish-immigrant background, or those who are ardent enough feminists to hail the work of a woman director, however untalented, and who are perhaps also impressed by the genuine gutsiness of the independent distribution methods devised by Raphael Silver, the producer, distributor, and director's husband.

Still, you have to be more than Jewish and a feminist to enjoy *Hester Street:* you have to be cinematically, literarily, artistically unsophisticated. And you have to have a stomach for ugliness to endure the face of Carol Kane—to say nothing of the zombielike expressions she mistakes for acting—for the inordinate amount of screen time it gets. It is not life in the ghetto but nonlife among stereotypes that the film conveys; its publishing equivalent would be one of those volumes of spiritual-uplift poetry that come in a steady trickle and treacle from the vanity presses.

October 13–20, 1975

A Miss Is as Good as Her Smile

IT IS EASY TO MISTAKE *Smile* for immoderate satire, as I did when I first saw it some months ago. Having seen the film again, I have come to the conclusion that *Smile* isn't any of the things for which some critics have so virulently attacked it—neither a gratuitous potshot at a sitting duck, nor smug condescension to Middle America, and hardly satirical exaggeration. I find myself in the position of Alfred Jarry, asked by a shocked woman visitor whether the enormous stone phallus on his mantelpiece was an enlargement. "No, madam," Jarry replied, "a reduction."

Smile concerns the California finals of the Young American Miss competition, a fictitious event closely modeled on several others that egregiously exist. On one level, the film is a quasi-journalistic retelling of what happens during the several days of preliminaries and the final selection in the goodly town of Santa Rosa, where the Jaycees are sponsoring the event, and the Bears and other organizations, not to mention the entire enthusiastic citizenry, all join in the good, clean, dirty fun. Clean, because it is "inner beauty" that is supposed to count; dirty, because both younger and older townfolk have themselves an orgy of covert nymphet-ogling; and good, because the exalted purpose is to spread a tidal wave of hypocritical cheer.

"There are only two things to remember: just be yourself, and keep smiling," the girls are told early on by Brenda, a contest official, former winner, and unfulfilled wife of Andy DiCarlo, a frustrated sports-trophy dealer who is now in cups of a different sort. But to be themselves is precisely what these girls are not allowed to be; they are coaxed, goaded, bullied into posing as the embodiments of the sweetness, joy, and hope that faded out of the lives of their elders. As for the compulsory all-purpose smile they affix to their faces as a bank robber does his mask, it either conceals ruthlessly competitive egotism, or else it is the near-imbecile reflection of ingrained hebetude. This eponymous, endemic smile is, in short, either phony or meaningless. Yet there are a few genuine, nonidiotic innocents among the girls, notably Robin; even they, however, are severely threatened by the corruption of fake, dime-store concepts of contentment through service that the contest, the community, the country are stuffing down their smiling faces.

Does Brenda, that walking baked Alaska, dedicate herself to the pageant with such relentless jollity because Andy drinks? Or does Andy drink because Brenda is frigid? And what about Big Bob Freelander, the mobile-home supersalesman and chief judge of the pageant? He sells like a demon, spouts platitudes that give more uplift than a lifetime supply of Maidenform, and could make the gargoyles of Notre Dame say "cheese." Pressed, he concedes: "Yeah, I got my applecart upset sometimes. I just learned a long time ago to expect a little less from life." He learned it particularly from having once spent a lot of money and expectation on a blind date with Liz Taylor, who stood him up and eloped with the son of "that hotel guy." "Now," Big Bob concludes in a tone less gibbous than usual, "I'm married to Roberta and I'm happy about it, even though she's a little less than Liz Taylor."

Using the farcically deflationary, hilarious but mildly gruesome incidents culled from actual beauty contests as the outer layer, and the two DiCarlos and one Freelander (Mrs. F. is, like many others, only sketched in briefly but suggestively) as the core, the film conveys lives of noisy desperation in which it is just as bad to believe as not to. It evokes a world that the hideously believable M.C. of the competition (about which everybody always insists that it is not *really* a competition) sums up when he addresses the winner, the losers, and the audience of lifetime losers with the oily rhetorical questions: "Isn't she lovely? Aren't they all lovely? Isn't everyone lovely?" Michael Ritchie and his scenarist, Jerry Belson, have captured on screen a society that makes do across the board with something that is a lot less than Liz Taylor—except that, in this case, more would still be less.

The picture says mean truths about mean lives, but it is not mean-spirited. It plays fair with people who beg to be ridiculed by giving all, or almost all, of them moments of generosity, of near-insight even. Whereit goes wrong, I think, is in running out before being able to follow through on what happens to its three main adult characters, one of whom opts out in favor of we know not what, one of whom readjusts her blinders yet more tightly, and one of whom backs away from the brink of recognition through a process of resignation that the filmmakers unfortunately skip over. Even so, this film is about something important. And I sympathize neither with those reviewers who scorned it for shooting sitting ducks—some ducks have to be shot down, alas, whatever their position—nor with those who dismissed a teen-age beauty pageant in a small California town as too insignificant or uncharacteristic a target—since when can't the social commentator, like the poet, see the world in a grain of sand?

But I am least in sympathy with those critics who rail at the film for allegedly condescending to its subject. They simply want to believe that grass-roots America is full of wonderfully adjusted or naturally sane and happy people—otherwise who will make this country survive, and, more important yet, appreciate their writing, take their advice on movies, be their grateful audience? But watch even once the full-grown Miss America Pageant on television and try, if you have a shred of perception and honesty, to accuse *Smile* of falsifying or patronizing.

Granted, it has some minor flaws. It starts out too much *in medias res* dumping us instantly into its world of blissful vapidity and sanctimonious hypocrisy rather than letting us discover it gradually. The Jaycee executive, especially as played by Geoffrey Lewis, is too obviously smarmy. The wryly sympathetic boozy maintenance man (played by the always unsubtle Tito Vandis) emerges as more of a cliché than, as intended, a benevolently comic chorus. Big Bob's relapse, as already mentioned, is not duly motivated. Young Robin's wising-up and reunion with her mother are too pat a happy ending, particularly as seen through the suddenly tearful eyes of tough Miss Anaheim, whose former opportunism and whorishness seem now facilely justified by lack of maternal love.

Apart from a few such errors—not so much of omission or commission as of reaching for shortcuts—the film is funny, sobering, and strong. In Big Bob, Brenda, and Tommy French, the cynical but not inhumane has-been choreographer who stages the pageant (and is the one genuine, life-giving breath of foul air in an atmosphere reeking of moral detergents and deodorants), it has created three rounded, ungainsayable characters. As Big Bob, Bruce Dern is frighteningly as well as deliciously perfect, and Barbara Feldon's Brenda and Michael Kidd's Tommy are not far behind. Nor are Eric Shea, as Little Bob Freelander, a Huck Finn in Norman Rockwell clothing; Joan Prather, as a Robin both impressionable and perspicacious; Annette O'Toole, as the Machiavellian Miss Anaheim; and Nicholas Pryor, whose Andy DiCarlo at thirty-five nicely portrays the transition from boyishness to incipient sodden obesity. Many others also shine.

The theme that runs through Ritchie's movies is that of lost innocence: in *Downhill Racer,* our own Olympic skiers going unclean; in *Prime Cut,* the formerly less spoiled heartland proving more evil than the city; in *The Candidate,* a Lochinvarish liberal politician getting co-opted and morally rumpled; and in *Smile,* fresh high-school girls being turned into pious dissemblers. It is muckraking cinema, not always deep enough, yet often able to say much through quick, throwaway scenes or even, in *Smile*, the furnishings of a house. It would be a serious loss if such a tidy job of holding up the mirror to denaturedness were ignored for the sake of a few tactical errors.

November 3, 1975

The Night of the Rooster

ROOSTER COGBURN is a sentimental journey into nausea. I have nothing against senescence or even senility on screen if the subject is treated with honesty. It is then, in fact, one of the enduring subjects of art, and can be approached from any direction, tragic or comic. But as an excuse for mendacious sentimentality, old age has always struck me as particularly infelicitous and tasteless. It is not great swashbuckling fun to be old; it is not sexy and romantic. When you are pushing seventy like John Wayne and Katharine Hepburn, you are not playing Wyatt Earp and Calamity Jane any longer, and the attempt to turn a frozen back and floating belly, a caved-in face and quavering voice into a Beatrice-and-Benedick act is even less persuasive than trying to get us to melt at the spectacle of a sensitive adolescent being initiated into manhood by a kindly hooker—a physiological as well as a psychological lie.

The movie is a spin-off from *True Grit,* which was a decent picture, though it, too, somewhat softened the novel it was based on. There was something believable and even touching about a girl on the verge of adulthood and a man on the far edge of his prowess joining hands in an unlikely adventure on which only an idealistic adolescent and an aging (but not yet old) codger aiming to go out with a bang could have gambled. But Wayne and Hepburn today, acting coy and doing a platonic mating ritual when not defying or destroying a horde of desperadoes, are about as convincing as Virgil Thomson and Betty Friedan would be in those parts.

We are introduced to Hepburn as a fearless New England schoolmarm helping her preacher father to care for the Indians at some godforsaken outpost in the Arkansas Territory. We know that Miss Hepburn is from New England because of the peculiarly digestive way in which she says *eyah* every five minutes, even as we know that the man is her father because he has white hair and looks a good two years older, and as we know that we are in Arkansas because the scenery is so unmistakably Oregon.

As for Wayne, in his second go at the roistering Rooster Cogburn, we meet him again being stripped of his deputy marshal's badge for having, singlehandedly and in self-defense, shot down a bunch of murderous varmints who just killed his sidekick. How comforting it is to see a cross between Felix Frankfurter and Judge Hardy meting out from his bench in Fort Smith, circa 1880, such enlightened post-My Lai justice, even as we guess that he will soon be eating crow as he sends out Rooster to catch the Hawk and his homicidal gang of robbers without so much as a single man to assist him. Actually, as an animated cartoon, a rooster versus a hawk might be good avian fun, but too many crusty old birds turn the movie into an inanimate cartoon. Rooster agrees to redeem himself under the skeptical gaze of his beer-swilling cat and Chinese cook from central casting.

This should more or less suffice about a film whose witless dialogue by Martin Julien, plodding direction by Stuart Millar, and penny-postcard cinematography by Harry Stradling, Jr., compete for the palm of predictability. Movie buffs can savor the dubious pleasure of sorting out clichés from *hommages,* and determine whether such and such a ludicrous plot device is a rip-off of *Deliverance* or a tribute to *The African Queen.* For sheer horror, however, I must cite the scene in which Richard Jordan, as a remarkably uncharismatic outlaw leader, directs a cylinderful of intimidating bullets all within inches of various parts of Miss Hepburn, while she, undauntable and assuming her best Hepburn-impersonator's vowels, hurls hortatory Bible verses at him.

And, again, the final scene, in which Wayne, looking like the ghost of John Ford, and Miss Hepburn as carefully swathed and prepared as a mummy of the Middle Kingdom, bid adieu in the saddle till the day when they are reunited—not, as you might expect, in the great beyond, but in the Indian settlement her father started, where Hepburn and Wayne, their missionary work and derring-do completed, will settle down to romance and sex at the age of, one surmises, eighty or ninety.

The stars are carefully surrounded by actors who cannot, or were forbidden to, act, and out of special deference to Miss Hepburn, by not a single noticeable actress. Their performances consist of the most outrageous self-caricature (which always seems to be the last talent to leave a performer), and they are pitched, particularly by Miss Hepburn, directly at the audience, which, on the evening I attended, rewarded her first appearance with lusty applause. As one of our more trenchant TV reviewers observed about this yoking of venerables, "perfect chemistry between two great legends." The trouble with legends is that, however good they may be at chemistry, they are even better at self-parody.

The Sunshine Boys is even less funny on film than on stage. Neil Simon writes comic turns whose excess needs living but distanced presences, and that suffer both by losing one dimension to the screen and by having the other two vastly enlarged. Accordingly, Walter Matthau, who plays one of the two now warring former vaudeville partners as if he were regurgitating a lifetime's worth of chewed-up scenery, becomes quickly insufferable; whereas George Burns, who meticulously restrains himself as the more silent partner, is a pleasure to see and hear. Richard Benjamin contributes one of his customary greasy performances, while Herbert Ross's direction remains painfully dry.

Simon's stuff is doggedly theatrical—all geared to actors. Thus on stage, where Jack Albertson's Clark was better than Sam Levene's Lewis, Clark emerged as the hero; now, thanks to the superior Burns, it is Lewis we feel for. On stage, the flesh-and-blood performer can almost make a show; on screen, rather more is needed.

November 10–17, 1975

Unholy Writ

One Flew Over the Cuckoo's Nest is a sacred writ of the counterculture; in that sense it is as much beyond the reach of critical dissuasion as a *Billy Jack* or *Walking Tall* film with built-in audience appeal wholly irrespective of quality. I have not read Ken Kesey's novel, but I have sat through two separate stage adaptations of it by Dale Wasserman, and have had a sufficiency of people relate its finer points to me. It would, therefore, seem to me that this script by Lawrence Hauben and Bo Goldman, as directed by Miloš

Forman, is faithful to the general outline and adequate to the trappings of Kesey's work, but misses its essence.

As I understand it, the basic conflict between Big Nurse Ratched and Randle McMurphy is not merely one between the Establishment and the counterculture, but also one between two sexual antagonists: one who enforces sterile, orderly chastity and *embourgeoisement* in all their castrating antilife aspects, and one who makes of his jovially randy, unremitting masculinity a priapic force meant to have a liberating, life-enhancing effect. The locale—a state insane asylum—is intended not only as a metaphor for our overbureaucratized, regimented world, but also as a battleground where healthy but repressed instincts, chiefly sexual, struggle against the forces of repression. Consequently, McMurphy must defeat Nurse Ratched, who is trying not only to break but also to unsex him, in two ways; defeat her as a restrictive authority figure and also as a sexual inhibitor. She, in turn, must perceive him not only as an anarchic figure to be tamed, but also as a man of unbridled lusts whose subduing becomes her surrogate sexual victory.

Unfortunately, the film flubs the complexity of this basic conflict. This has to do as much with casting as with script and direction. The excellent Jack Nicholson disappoints as McMurphy; he isn't intrinsically suitable, as Kirk Douglas was in the original stage production. Somehow Nicholson radiates a wise-guy quality, the ability to outsmart through clever trickery, and not (as Douglas did) through being fundamentally right, and strong in that rightness. There is too much of the trickster-comedian about Nicholson; you do not see him as representing some greater salutary principle, only as an operator outwitting others who could as easily embody dumb honesty as cunning oppression. Nicholson does a lot of things very well, and has much charm, but he just isn't elemental enough.

As for Louise Fletcher, the Mattie of *Thieves Like Us,* she is a fine, expressive actress, but wrong for Big Nurse. She emanates kindly, womanly understanding—sometimes troubled intelligence; and, of course, she tries hard to be ominous and smoothly sinister. But I don't believe her; some deep-seated decency and common sense are always too much in evidence. This is the sort of part for which, but for accent and size, Glenda Jackson would be only too right. For there is also the question of size: Miss Fletcher's Ratched is not, as in the book, big and ample-bosomed, exuding an overabundance of the very thing she is trying to suppress. So the conflict between her and McMurphy becomes desexualized and ceases to be central in importance. What remains of it is purely about power; so much so that when McMurphy makes his final attack on her, he does not, in the movie, go for her huge breasts—which she has, as it were, denied—but for her throat, trying to throttle the very life out of her. As a result, his subsequent lobotomy does not seem so cruel and unusual a punishment. Moreover, the film suppresses the nurse's vengeful role in that lobotomy, and her cold triumph in it.

The idea, presumably, was to "civilize" Kesey's book; but this is quite wrong. Even though McMurphy himself is not meant to be mad, only a man who resorts to simulated insanity to beat a mad system, the others in the story, except for the Indian, have been driven mad by the world, and McMurphy is meant to be their all-but-successful savior. To make him less heroic, and the contest less mythical, is to deny the work its primitive strength—essentially bogus, but strength nevertheless. Kesey is, probably unconsciously, a Laingian, and however much the filmmakers (and I) may reprehend his position, the film's effectiveness depends on respect for it.

This is, all the same, Forman's best film since his first Czech effort, *Black Peter,* and vastly preferable to his American debut, *Taking Off,* which I found reeking with Formanian antihumanism: contempt for people expressed with snickering condescension. Defending Forman against my attack, the exiled Czech critic, Antonín J. Liehm, writes in a forthcoming book: "Forman doesn't pass judgment, and he doesn't shout. All he does is point his finger and smile knowingly." But that is what makes it so ugly: the insistently pointing finger and the superior, self-serving snigger. There is little if any of that in the new movie, which is a sound commercial piece of filmmaking with appropriate pacing, a good eye, and fine cinematography, even though artistic disagreements necessitated the employment of three cameramen. The entire supporting cast does well, my favorites being Brad Dourif as Billy Bibbit, and Will Sampson, who is quite the best of the three Chief Bromdens I have seen. But if the center does not hold, the best periphery cannot save a film.

And there is finally something distasteful about a film (and, I take it, book) in which Big Nurse prods a disturbed young man into suicide. It is one thing to say the Establishment is blind, stupid, and uncaring; another, and irresponsible, to say it is deliberately murderous. But that sort of thing, as Lionel Trilling sadly noted, is "the measure of how desperate is the impulse to impugn and transcend the limitations of rational mind."

December 1, 1975

Coming to No Good End

When I saw Gerard Damiano's *The Story of Joanna,* it struck me as a cheap steal from the novel *Story of O.* After seeing the movie version of the latter, *The Story of O,* I find this film of Just Jaeckin's more of a ripoff than Damiano's. Finally, though, both films fail, as pornography on screen almost invariably does. *The Story of Joanna* is worth discussing only in the framework of contemporary cinepornography, and that, when even the Sunday *Times* devotes an article to it, can no longer go uncommented on here.

It is typical of our sorrier reviewers that, with reference to such Damiano offerings as *Deep Throat, The Devil in Miss Jones, Memories Within Miss Aggie,* and now *The Story of Joanna,* they should pontificate about how the gap between the porn movie and the art film is rapidly closing, so good have Damiano's blue, or true-blue, movies become. Now, it is undeniable that thanks to what some call enlightenment and others permissiveness the serious filmmaker can show much more explicit sexuality than he previously could, and that in the hands of a genuine artist this can be both arousing and significant. In the hands of a moderately clever pseudo-artist, like Bertolucci, it can still be somewhat arousing (like the first sexual encounter in *Last Tango in Paris),* but not very significant. In the hands of pornographers, hard- or soft-core, it is neither very arousing nor artistically relevant.

A film, I believe, becomes pornographic not when it tries or manages to arouse us; it becomes pornographic when it is a bad film—when it engages us only as curiosity-seekers and mutterers of wisecracks in the dark. There is nothing wrong with the celebration of sex on film when you consider that erotic poetry, fiction, and painting also celebrate sex and have, despite some former attempts to censor them, long since become accepted. It would be a ludicrous piece of hypocrisy to deny the screen what paper and canvas are permitted to do. Actually, as a method of arousal, film, which is generally seen in public, is less efficacious than a book or (reproduction of a) painting, which is enjoyed in private and allows instant leaping to sexual action. One exception, to be sure, is the practitioner of the sub rosa, or sub Aquascutum, system of self-indulgence; another is described by Brendan Gill in his article "Blue Notes" *(Film Comment,* January-February, 1973): "Often there will be found standing at the back of the [homosexual porn] theatre two or three young men, any of whom, for a fee, will accompany one to seats well down front and there practice upon one the same arts that are being practiced upon others on screen." Which gives the old moviegoer's exclamation, "Down in front," quite a new meaning.

The reasons for the failure of *The Story of Joanna* are symptomatic. They occur, first, at the so-called creative end. No serious artist, with the possible exception of Alain Robbe-Grillet (assuming that he is one), has, to my knowledge, attempted an outright pornographic or, to use a less loaded term, totally erotic movie. This is only partly owing to the fact that most real artists aren't that one-sided, that erotomaniacally circumscribed. Some might be secretly, and, with some nudging, even publicly. I am sure that if anyone had commissioned a straight sex film from Buñuel—not now, but during his middle period, when he was less prolix, furtively oblique, and unfunnily jocular—he might have made a far more interesting pornographic picture than his last five quasi-metaphysical and pseudosocial ones rolled into one. But the fact remains that it is very, very hard to arouse those who are not highly susceptible by means of cinema.

Even if Damiano, for instance, had all the directorial requisites, he'd still be stuck with his actors. His current leads, who play Joanna and her seducer-(tor)mentor Jason, are not going to turn out to be great turners-on. Though they go by such WASP names or *noms de guerre* as Terri Hall and Jamie Gillis, they look like two nice Jewish kids who have nothing of the lovely maiden in distress and the *homme fatal* about them. You can look at Miss Hall's body, but raising your gaze higher will not lift up your heart; as for Mr. Gillis, he is not suave and commanding, only callow and faintly oily. And, of course, they cannot act. If they could, they would be in bigger, better, and better-paying productions. The exception in recent years was Marilyn Chambers, who, but for her uncommonly common-looking hands, was wholesome and attractive in *Behind the Green Door,* and was fine until her second film, where she had some dialogue, alas. A chap like the punnily pseudonymous Harry Reems, who appears in a great many porno films, has neither talent nor looks; what he does, apparently, have is dependable erections.

So that is one part of the problem: that although porno performers desperately depend on their looks, the overwhelming majority haven't got them, and haven't got the acting ability either with which to create an illusion of seductiveness. Yet to be effective, pornography must engage the fantasy of the viewer, which even a lot of comely performers would not necessarily do. Which is why the inspired pornographer sticks to literature and leaves his characters relatively undescribed, so that the reader can graft onto them faces and bodies of his own choosing. But what if the cinepornographic leads were stars, with whom most of the viewers are a priori in love? The way things are going, might this not happen soon? One of the early porn kings, David F. Friedman, is quoted by Turan and Zito in their book, *Sinema:* "If they make a [porn] picture with Ali MacGraw and Steve McQueen . . . it's gonna really be sucking and fucking with kid gloves on and ain't nobody gonna go see Linda Lovelace if they can see Ali MacGraw." But it isn't that simple: suppose that the naked Ali isn't up to the clothed one? It would ruin not only the film but also the career of Miss MacGraw. Or has she already managed that even with her clothes on? Jeanne Moreau and Jane Fonda proved that they could have been great porno stars; both, however, could do more and better elsewhere.

Another part of the problem is that comedy is a detumescent agent. In a "serious" work of pornography there is no laughter, or only of a hellish kind. But in most pornographic films there is either ineptitude, which is funny, or deliberate humor to cover up the technical inadequacies—and out goes the eroticism. Damiano's dialogue is risible, especially when it aspires to sophistication and lapidariness; so, too, is his notion of elegance—or is it ominousness—as when the camera tracks for the umpteenth time along the ceilings of Jason's mansion, while the sound track bursts into Albinoni's *Adagio.* This, to be sure, is right out of *Last Year at Marienbad;* but things get funnier yet when the music is that of Edward Earle, whoever he may be, and switches to pop songs with lyrics by Damiano.

There is also another difficulty, inherent in the medium itself. Sexual activity is not all that photogenic and dramatic. To quote Gill again: "Simply as theater, cunnilingus isn't a patch on fellatio. . . ." And, after a while, straight sex isn't a patch even on kung fu. This is why the variations, or what is rightly or wrongly called perversions, soon make their entrances. Because sadomasochism, with its bondage, whips, etc., is visually the most spectacular, and psychologically the most dramatic (with the exception of incest, but that is extremely hard to convey on film—with poor porno actors, downright impossible), it gets the most play. But there may be a deeper reason for this. If George Orwell is right, and the typical pornographic work is ultimately about "the pursuit of power" and, by implication, its complement, the pursuit of being overpowered, sadism and masochism are what all pornography tends toward.

The problems of visualization are responsible for many of the anomalies of pornocinematography. Thus, in order to prove that the male performer is actually experiencing orgasm, it becomes imperative to withdraw the penis at the crucial point, which leaves the viewer with an unpleasant sense of coitus quasi-interruptus. Again, certain forms of aberrant behavior are aphrodisiac only to a minority of viewers; so the scene in *Sensations* in which a woman urinates on a man has to be conveyed aurally rather than actually shown. Suggesting rather than showing would be fine if the director knew how to utilize fully the power of suggestion. But if he did, he would be an artist, and would most likely be making other kinds of films. In fact, it can be posited as a general rule that suggestion is more stimulating than demonstration, but also more difficult, more demanding of artistry, which is precisely and fatally what the pornographer tends to lack. And now that most screen sex is actually performed rather than simulated in pornographic movies, the act automatically precludes acting: during orgasm, Duse is no better than Streisand.

Yet the most self-defeating aspect of pornography may be the teleological. For the end is not what an unknown (to me) bone-deep thinker, Robert Bone, is quoted as saying in William Rotsler's *Contemporary Erotic Cinema:* "God invented the orgasm so we would know when to stop." Aside from the fact that God seems to have invented nothing to tell us where to *begin,* which makes pornography vastly extensible in the other direction, there is also the simple observable fact that most pornography does not stop with the orgasm. Thus Susan Sontag, in her challenging essay, "The Pornographic Imagination" (in *Styles of Radical Will),* asserts that the pornographic entelechy is nothing short of death: "Tamed as it may be, sexuality remains one of the demonic forces in human consciousness—pushing us at intervals close to taboo and dangerous desires, which range from the impulse to commit sudden arbitrary violence upon another person to the voluptuous yearning for the extinction of one's consciousness, for death itself." Though Miss Sontag doesn't quite follow through on this, the death can, presumably, be that of either partner: murder or self-annihilation. If this is so, the thorough, which is to say truly artistic, porn film would take us to realms into which the average customer is not prepared to follow, and so becomes uncommercial and, like its protagonist, suicidal.

Violence and killing, spiced with sex, are, granted, very much to the public's taste. But however many of his or her favorite playmates bite the dust, the protagonist with whom the audience identifies itself *must* survive. True, Jason has an incurable disease and finally gets Joanna to shoot him; still, after a brief, full life, he dies in beauty, not as a victim. And Joanna, the real protagonist, inherits the mansion, the servants, the sexual equipment, and, presumably, Albinoni's *Adagio,* and carries on.

But why, you may ask impatiently, this whole piece on pornography? Well, go of a late afternoon to the Fine Arts theater, where *Exhibition,* the first hard-core film to be shown at the New York Film Festival, is playing, and watch, not the film, but the audience. It is packed with matrons with their Bloomingdale's shopping bags, with couples and individuals of all ages, classes, and sexes. Though there may be no clear evidence that the audience is enjoying itself, neither is there the slightest sign of shock. Yet less than ten years ago such a thing would have been held impossible by most decent bag-carrying Bloomingdalians. What has happened, and how do we account for it?

Is Miss Sontag right when she says: "Everyone has felt (at least in fantasy) the erotic glamour of physical cruelty and an erotic lure in things that are vile and repulsive"? *(Exhibition,* by the way, is not particularly repulsive; but viler things are, or will soon be, getting similarly ecumenical and contented audiences.) Or is it merely that people are inquisitive and sheeplike, and want to see what is there and what other people are seeing? There is not only safety in numbers but also respectability. I don't know what the answer is, and I am certainly not for suppressing anything. But I am for investigating what people feel they are getting out of it. The discoveries so to be made, while of little use to the artist, should prove invaluable to the psychologist.

December 15, 1975

Million-Dollar Blimps

ONCE WHILE CONVERSING with Tennyson, Thackeray was interrupted when his younger daughter, thitherto immersed in her reading, asked: "Papa, why do you not write books like *Nicholas Nickleby?*" Well may we ask the same after seeing Stanley Kubrick's movie version of Thackeray's *The Luck of Barry Lyndon.* And we might also ask Kubrick, not why he didn't make *Nicholas Nickleby*—Alberto Cavalcanti beat him to it by some thirty years—but why he can't make movies like those other filmmakers who care for the characters in their films. In the works of Kubrick, to quote a verse Matthew Arnold wrote in a different context, "Thin, thin the pleasant human noises grow."

Barry Lyndon is a curious choice for Kubrick, who has become more and more estranged from the taste and smell of human experience. Already *Lolita* was an exaggeration in the direction of the grotesque; *Dr. Strangelove,* which I consider his best film *(Paths of Glory* being marred by a final cop-out), was all caricature and could dispense with flesh-and-blood people; *2001* was about machines, and such men as were in it were (deliberately, I hope) much less human than the computer, HAL Burgess's novel *A Clockwork Orange* is, despite its linguistic and other eccentricities, a humane book, but as Kubrick filmed it, it became more bizarre, sensationalistic, effect-ridden, and vastly inferior. But why *Lyndon?* What interest it holds lies in the discrepancy between the rascally protagonist-narrator's assessment of himself and the rather different evaluation the reader (nudged by an occasional author's footnote) is allowed to form. Beyond that, there is the social canvas, where Thackeray lovingly re-creates his beloved eighteenth century; lastly, there is the style, unexciting but conscientious, full of tiny but well-observed details. The reader carries away with him a pervasive moral tone and a set of characters who, as David Cecil long ago noted, are exactly like people one has met.

A moral tone is hard to convey on film; the discrepancy between reality and the first-person narrator's self-estimate, impossible when there is no such narrator—Kubrick has voice-over narration, but from an omniscient, third-person point of view; and unspectacular, minor-key incidents don't fit well into movies of would-be epic stature. Kubrick has tried to compensate in three ways. He has invented, as writer-director, a number of more pointed episodes, such as Cousin Nora's ribbon having to be fetched out of her bodice by the timid hero, or the climactic duel between Barry and his hate-riddled stepson. He has taken existing episodes such as the worm's-eye view of the battle of Minden (in which Thackeray may have been influenced by Stendhal) and has turned it into something more absurd and satirical than Thackeray describes, making the British strategy, or lack of it, supremely stupid and wasteful of human lives. So, too, he has taken such a minor incident as Barry's refusal to oblige his bride and stop smoking during their first postnuptial carriage ride, and magnified it into something more emphatically nasty. Finally, he has omitted (often, but not always, for the sake of necessary abridgement) a great many episodes that make for density; the resultant impression is of a series of vignettes, a jumping from highlight to highlight. One is unhappily reminded of Dwight Macdonald's wise warning against making films out of "lots of Big Moments, but no small ones."

Indeed, watching the movie is like looking at illustrations for a work that—partly through Thackeray's, but more through Kubrick's, negligence—has not been supplied. Striking as some of these illustrations, often in long or extreme long shot, are, they do not encourage our getting involved with the characters in the story. This has something to do with the episodic nature of the film, but mostly with the fact that the director seems more concerned with landscapes, architecture, period interiors, costumes, etc., than with what happens to the people in them. The very casting bears this out. As Barry, Ryan O'Neal looks engaging (although the chubbiness that sits well on him when he is supposed to be fifteen never forsakes him), but his performance, except in one or two scenes, does not rise above the level of a nice try. An Irish accent, for instance, despite his name, remains outside his reach. Marisa Berenson, as Lady Lyndon, does even less. She appears first somewhere around the middle of the film, and has four or five lines of dialogue—surely a record for the female lead in a movie lasting over three hours. Any more lines might have been more than she could handle, but that only proves how little importance Kubrick attaches to acting.

The supporting cast, which comprises some good actors along with many indifferent ones, is given trifles to work with, although for the highly repetitious Murray Melvin as Chaplain Runt, and Patrick Magee as the Chevalier, that may be more than enough. Magee has a way of turning every syllable he utters into overripe Limburger cheese; he is one of the few actors I can think of to whom one listens with one's nose. Marie Kean, though restrained as Barry's mother, makes too little of what might have been a bravura part—did Kubrick hold her down? He certainly stacks the cards when he casts the physically repellent Leon Vitali as Lord Bullingdon, while little Bryan, as played by David Morley, is so bloody adorable that you know the angels will want to claim him for their own, and you merely wish it wouldn't take them quite so long.

The cinematography by John Alcott, whom I suspect of being totally Kubrick's creature, is exquisite, but there is a surfeit of soft focus. Indoors, this may be the result of that special, ultrafast Zeiss lens, which allowed for shooting by genuine eighteenth-century candlelight; but even in the sumptuous outdoor shots a delicate haze of dancing motes envelops the landscapes, a sort of subtle film-upon-the-film. The candlelight photography is only one of many aspects of Kubrick's mastery of technique and historical accuracy, to which his humanism, alas, cannot hold a candle. It is typical, for example, that a missing leg is made to look more convincing here, as the camera shows it from all angles, than I have ever seen it faked before; yet I prefer the kind of movie where I worry about what happens to the characters to the kind where I wonder how the deuce they managed that amputated leg. At that, Kubrick will turn inconsistently soft when it comes to aging Marisa Berenson; she remains virtually unaltered; only her wigs grow old, most gracefully. And never, as in Thackeray, does Lady Lyndon grow fat.

In reading the book, we may object to a certain inconsistency of tone. What is meant to be a toughly picaresque novel modeled on *Jonathan Wild* has a way of turning suddenly sentimental. But even clashing tones are, at least, tones; the film is almost entirely cool to the point of near-tonelessness, exuding, along with visual splendor, an aura of detachment, if not indifference, out of which the death of Bryan resonates with a doubly plangent, and so particularly inappropriate, note. And speaking of notes, even the score, which Leonard Rosenman has arranged from baroque or classical works, except for a Schubert trio, appropriate to the period (and one, by Frederick the Great, almost an in-joke), remains bland, unemotional—not even, as one might have supposed, witty.

Alas, poor Kubrick! He expects to beat all box-office records with this film. But how does one attract crowds with a humdrum story about unprepossessing characters played by mostly undistinguished actors? No stars, no sex, no violence, no rollicking *Tom Jones* humor. Are the masses to be brought in by their interest in neoclassical architecture?

The cost of *Barry Lyndon* hovers somewhere between eleven million dollars and fourteen million dollars; so too does that of *Lucky Lady,* which, however, does not even have such visual bounties to offer. Stanley Donen, its director, is a delightful man who, sweetly and innocently, enjoys elegance, opulence, romance on screen—which is why he was the wrong person for this script, assuming that anyone could have been right. Essentially, this is the story of how three two-bit liquor smugglers in the Gulf of Mexico circa 1930 buy a modest shipload of hooch, and manage against all odds—bigtime gangsters, the coast guard, their own bumbling—to cash in on it; they keep expanding their business and become improbably rich. They are a young wetback-runner's widow, played by Liza Minnelli, and her two lovers: the ebullient but frequently fumbling Burt Reynolds; and the mysterious, strong-and-silent, close to infallible Gene Hackman. They form a sassy *ménage à trois,* for the sake of which Liza eventually gives up a chance at a rich, respectable marriage. But the bigtime gangsters will not be bearded forever; into a rather obvious trap walk Gene and Burt and a nice kid who has been assisting them. The kid is brutally killed, and only a miracle (or the stupidity of the powerful gangsters) lets the severely wounded Gene and Burt get away alive.

Liza, who has developed a business genius she patently lacked in the earlier part of the movie, and the boys now assemble what we are to regard as *good* smugglers—small but expert independent operators, with all kinds of picturesque traits and getups worthy of a come-as-a-cute-crook fancy-dress party—who form a navy big enough to defy the considerable naval force of the *bad* smugglers, meanies who machine-gun clean-cut young kids. It all builds up to an "epic" and highly idiosyncratic naval engagement (directed by Ricou Browning, who performed similar chores for James Bond films), which ends in the triumph of the good baddies and comic annihilation of the bad baddies. There was an epilogue (just cut, I learned), taking place decades later, in which an ineptly aged Burt and Gene (they look like a couple of self-made-up actors in a high-school theatrical) and Liza, who looks scarcely different—age cannot wither, nor make-up stale, her infinite sameness—burrow in a merry gambol under the sheets of the biggest triple bed you've ever seen. But, of course, nothing is shown, here as elsewhere, that might upset the film's PG status.

The script by the young married couple Willard Huyck and Gloria Katz, who became big and expensive names on the strength of *American Graffiti,* was somewhat tougher before Donen took over. It is he—best known for musicals like *Singin' in the Rain* and polite thrillers like *Charade*—who kept asking for and getting more glitter and comedy as the shooting progressed, and who finally rejected the original ending he himself had filmed, in which Gene and Burt are shot by the coast guard, and Liza, married to the wealthy square, is seen years later wistfully recalling it all. Almost everyone involved with the film has made statements praising the original ending, but also justifying the new one in terms of the requirements of a public now, allegedly, more than ever in need of being comforted. What it means in plain language is that up to X million dollars a film may have artistic pretensions; beyond that, it will have a nice, escapist ending, and forget about "art." Lest, however, you start worrying that something fine and authentic has been betrayed by this *Road to Utopia* ending, let me assure you that the whole thing is mirthless trumpery, no more undercut than a Hallmark card by a closing rhyme of *love* and *dove.*

Seldom have I encountered so large a collection of old and unfunny jokes—like the martinet of a coast guard captain repeatedly falling on his face, or the waiter so overwhelmed by the sight of three in a bathtub as to continue pouring a drink after the glass is full. And seldom, too, have I seen anything that so clearly ought to be (if it must be at all) a story told in grisaille, shot in black-and-white and with a seedy look to it, so gussied up, so bursting with rockets in the air. Geoffrey Unsworth, who also shot *Cabaret* in this manner, gives us not only oodles of backlighting, but also visible light sources bursting into bloom like luminous sunflowers around the actors' heads. Donen has committed here in spades what the classicists reproached the romantics with:

mélange des genres. He has directed what, despite a couple of songs, is a straight film as if it were a supermusical, and introduced into it elements from other genres: the *Road* pictures with the Hope-Crosby-Lamour "fun threesome," the hard-boiled-lovers films with the likes of Bogart and Bacall, the merry-outlaws-brought-up-short-by-real-blood movies initiated by *Bonnie and Clyde,* and the macho-twosome flicks with Newman and Redford.

This is a heavy load for any film to bear; for this script and these actors, crushing. The thirtyish Huyck and Katz can recall the *American Graffiti* era perfectly well; for the Prohibition, however, they must depend on research, which they do not wear lightly. Hardly a line of dialogue is allowed to slip by without some piece of twenties or thirties slang pinned onto it like a donkey's tail. But in case you miss that, Ralph Burns works in some evocative Bessie Smith or Fats Waller song. If even that won't suffice, the art director gives you enough art deco to get visually drunk on. It all merely alerts us to the lack of more substantial things.

Neither Reynolds nor Hackman strikes sparks: the former's face looks like an armored car made, inexplicably, out of meat; the latter has a visage that looks so convincingly hoboish in the early sequences that it can't be debummed in the later ones. As for Miss Minnelli, she is herself a perfect *ménage à trois* in which lack of talent, lack of looks, and lack of a speaking voice cohabit blissfully. Donen sensibly concentrates on her best feature, her legs, but he unfortunately can't wrap them around her face. Her head always hangs into her fellow actors' faces like a sloppy waiter's thumb into the soup. Meant to convey a tough outcast clawing for a place in the sun, she suggests a wallflower flailing for an invitation to the junior prom.

Not even the big sea battle works, because it introduces yet another genre, the 007 film. There are good supporting players, but not enough good lines or actions to support *them.* Donen tells me that although only three get credit, seven editors worked on the film; with that many cutters, you could have started a small clothing business.

December 29, 1975

Over the Mountains, Beyond the Pale

THE MAN WHO WOULD BE KING is John Huston's best film in twenty-three years, or since *The African Queen.* It is an unpretentious adventure story based on Kipling's tale, and is, but for two aspects that most people will blissfully ignore, a happy piece of hokum, derring-do, and entertainment—just about the only film for the holiday season that can be viewed with round-the-family contentment. It is not a great work, but it is a solid bagatelle, like those new, creative toys for children that are made to be attractive, safe, and also a bit mind-stretching.

Well, the idea content of the film is somewhat marred, owing to Kipling's Queen and quirks. The main didactic impact—that ambition is, up to a point, a magnificent albeit amoral force—is acceptable enough. Daniel Dravot and Peachy Carnehan, two ex-soldiers of Her Majesty's Indian Army, whose conmanship has led them out of the military and just barely out of the clutches of the judiciary, disguise themselves as a mad dervish and his servant and, after numerous hardships and adventures, make it across the mountains into Kafiristan, where the white man has not been a burden since Alexander the Great. Here they become—through ingenuity, guts, dumb luck, and vestigial honor among thieves—the sacred king and commander of the armies, respectively. Dravot enjoys playing Alexander's heir more and more, while Peachy is just waiting for the right time for them to abscond with the temple treasures.

Then, alas, on top of his newly found passion for kingship, Daniel also picks a proud native beauty, Roxanne, to become his queen. He celebrates his wedding over Peachy's misgivings, over the priests' and populace's open hostility, and over, as it turns out, his dead body. All this would be in the best tradition of high adventure, but for one Victorian and one more specifically Kiplingian stricture. The Victorian drawback is, simply put, racism. There was no question in the British Imperial mind that the people of Kafiristan are "lesser breeds without the Law," and the fact that they play polo with their luckless enemies' heads is viewed with condescending amusement. At their noblest, they may sacrifice their lives to save their British overlords, strictly from Gunga. The more particularly Kiplingian blemish, however, derives from our author's misogyny, which, in turn, stems from his fear of sex. Perhaps the nastiest verse in all English poetry is Kipling's "And a woman is only a woman, but a good cigar is a Smoke." Accordingly, the trouble in *The Man Who Would Be King* starts when Dravot chooses to take a wife. Earlier, the two Englishmen helped each other resist the temptations of the flesh; now, even legal marriage to a native girl—the racist motif harmonizing with the antiwoman one—proves catastrophic.

Huston's direction is pleasantly ungimmicky, and that splendid veteran cameraman, Oswald Morris, delivers fine, unpretentious cinematography. Somewhat less can be said for the production design of one of the greats in the field, Alexander Trauner, whose re-creation of a forgotten Greek city from the days of his namesake, Alexander the Great, is adequate but less than stunning, though budgetary limitations may have played a role. The costumes, by the venerable Edith, are suitably raggle-taggle, but do come to a Head with a wedding gown that is strictly boutique-Grecian. Maurice Jarre continues his career as a dependably commercialized composer, which is rather saddening from someone whose early scores were well above average.

What really makes the film is racy acting combined with niftily dissembling location photography. That Morocco should be a good stand-in for India is perhaps less surprising than the excellent impersonation by the French Alps around Chamonix, which manage to look as Hindu Kush as all getout. Sean Connery, craggy in his own right, makes a good, blustering Dravot, and Michael Caine, after all too frequent miscastings as an upper-class intellectual, takes to playing a canny Cockney as a duck to water, or, better yet, a *canard* to *l'orange.* It is gutter gallantry at its juiciest. Christopher

Plummer, who plays the author as he portrayed himself at the start and close of his tale, is hardly a Kipling in his early twenties; but he is the very essence of Kiplingishness, for Plummer is one of the screen's most versatile actors, and one would almost have to go back to the late, sorely missed Pierre Fresnay for a performer so gloriously able to disappear into the role he is playing.

We need not concern ourselves much with the once powerful Sam Peckinpah whose latest, *The Killer Elite,* makes even his recent, beyond-the-pale films pale by comparison. This is one of those new anti-CIA films that are a priori doomed. For if they really knew the truth, they wouldn't be allowed to tell it; so they must rely on ominous clichés, nebulous hints, torrents of violence to obscure the lack of facts, and ultimate inscrutability. It all has to do with a CIA-sponsored organization either protecting or doing away with people who know too much, including some of their own. The audience, not knowing what the hell is going on, is luckily safe.

Peckinpah and his unsavory scenarists pile on every form of brutality and gore, worsened by the fact that the dishing out and enduring of pain become the measure of masculinity. Then, in the middle of all this, we get jesuitical sermons about human dignity and not allowing oneself to become a pawn in the murderous game played by the powers that be. I suspect that all this means is that we should be free to maul and mangle others for our *own* pleasure—otherwise why this charnelhouse of a film that exhibits such relish in all its mean details?

January 12, 1976

Pink Croutons in Blue Soup

PAUL MAZURSKY's *Next Stop, Greenwich Village* appears to aim at being, and very possibly is, truly recollected autobiography. But the truth has a better chance in a convex mirror than filtered through Mazursky's concave mind. I would be hard put to find another director who combines so much phony-pathetic slickness with so much mendacious cuteness without any of that dubious cleverness that could at least weld them into a semblance of reality. So this film, like Mazursky's others, shuttles flat-footedly between scenes that are meant to catch at your throat and scenes that are supposed to suffuse you with a warm glow as you murmur, "How true! How sweetly funny! How like me when I was young!" It takes very little to love a film like *Next Stop, Greenwich Village*—just very, very little brain, and no taste at all.

This is the story of how Larry Lapinsky (alias Paul Mazursky) leaves Brownsville, Brooklyn, in 1953 for Greenwich Village and an acting career. He leaves behind the Jewish mother to end all Jewish mothers, and a father compared to whom your average eunuch is a model of virility. In the Village, he has a pad, a complaisant girl friend named Sarah, and a bunch of cronies that include the older, comically suicidal Anita, the coldly egocentric yet somehow honest poet-playwright Robert, the campy black homosexual who cutely calls himself Bernstein, a roly-poly tomboy of a good girl, and several other lesser friends but no lesser clichés. What happens to them in two close-to-interminable hours is everything you always didn't want to know about coming of age in Greenwich Village but were always mercilessly told and told again. There are ludicrous acting classes with a gassily verbose but ever-so-real coach, days put in behind a lunch counter run by an obstreperous but drolly, golden-hearted Jew, lovers' quarrels and reconciliations, diaphragms and abortions, mad parties and suicides, parents repeatedly dropping in at the worst time, terrible scenes with one's hysterical mother, betrayal by one's true love and one's best friend, and—at long and much-delayed last—departure for a movie role and Sunset Boulevard, a rather truer apotheosis than merely walking into the sunset hand in hand.

To repeat, Mazursky has two modes: cloyingly cute and touchingly "real." To both he brings such a platitudinous sensibility, such an eye geared to cliché details, such an ear for stereotyped dialogue that the film is not so much like tossing coins for two hours and seeing which of Mazursky's two sides will come up (bad enough), but rather like tossing a trick coin that has tails on both sides (worse yet). After one of Anita's mock suicides, her gray cat is seen slinking among her accumulated bric-a-brac; after her final, real suicide, the gray cat is again slinking among the bric-a-brac. When Larry rehearses an Academy Award–winner's speech in an empty nocturnal subway station, a wry cop tells him his performance stinks and to forget about acting. (Sample dialogue: "I would also like to thank the author of this film, that great Jewish writer Eugene O'Neill—thank you, Gene!") In Larry's nightmares, he is rehearsing an Odets love scene, not with his acting partner but with his termagant mother—whom he, however, dearly loves. When he is leaving in triumph for Hollywood, the usual busybody of a neighbor leans out of her window to butt in in her usual way, kids are playing ball in the street, and an old man is playing the violin on the sidewalk. We get a long shot of the near-tenements that Larry is seeing for the last time.

Here is the wit: "SARAH: Maybe I should go to an analyst. LARRY: You'd be better off in Mexico. SARAH: Maybe I should go to a Mexican analyst." Again: "ACTING COACH: Nobody can be a Marlon Brando every week. LARRY: I'd settle for Laurence Olivier. GIRL STUDENT: I'd settle for ZaSu Pitts." In-jokes and topical references abound, as befits a nostalgia vehicle, thus: "WOULD-BE ACTOR: I studied with everybody. With Sandy, with Stella, with Lee, man. LARRY: I study with Herbert." ("Ah," exclaims the hip moviegoer, "how clever of me to know who all those people are!") When Sarah says she likes Larry's mother because "there's something strange about her," Larry explains, "She invented the Oedipus complex." And everybody is always, *always* doing imitations, impersonations, accents—usually quite badly—because that's what growing up in the Village in the fifties was all about!

When Mazursky could tell us something real, he doesn't. What is Sarah's home life like, and what does she do away from Larry? To know that might explain her leaving him for Robert, who doesn't love her, but that sort of thing requires insight and willingness to look beyond himself when young, so we don't get it from Mazursky. Nor does he know where to put his camera. When Mother, finally reconciled to her son's going to Hollywood, says tearfully, "Sweetheart Larry, if you will ever see Clark Gable, tell him that your mother saw his every picture, and that I loved him all my life," surely the camera should slowly come in on Pop, to show his pain and humiliation, but no such thing occurs. And in the sexual scenes, Mazursky is much more interested in the quaint undergarments women wore in those days than in what happens between Larry and Sarah.

As the inventor of the Oedipus complex, Shelley Winters manages to wrest new horrors from the cliché of the Jewish mother, but without shedding new light on it. Between her profound personal charmlessness and the thick overlay of Actors' Studio tricks, there is no room for the merest spark of genuine humanity. As Larry, Lenny Baker looks every bit as homely as young Paul must have looked, and struggles gamely with a role that is all commonplaces and impersonations of Brando, Olivier, Edward G. Robinson, and even Shelley Winters—but how can he compete with Shelley Winters's impersonations of Shelley Winters? Occasionally, he has an interestingly ambiguous expression, which the director forces him to hold much too long. Christopher Walken contributes his standard bit of frozen narcissism, and the others range from adequate to awful. But the real find is Ellen Greene as Sarah; Miss Greene, who started as a singer, is developing into an authentic actress. Her playing has a wonderful concentration that gets at the essence of things with a minimum of mannerisms. Arthur Ornitz's cinematography strives too hard for a fifties' Technicolor look in which blues predominated: the actors' faces float like pink croutons in blue soup.

February 9, 1976

Hack Work

WHAT MAKES SEEMINGLY QUIET Americans suddenly go berserk, loners turn into murderous psychopaths, has been the subject of several movies, from Peter Bogdanovich's dreary *Targets* to Terrence Malick's brilliant *Badlands,* but the problem continues to attract and deserve attention. Now Martin Scorsese's *Taxi Driver* offers us Travis Bickle—the name is well chosen—a strictly brought up young man from Middle America who was a marine in the Vietnam war, currently lives in a shabby New York apartment, and suffers from intense insomnia. So he becomes a cab driver, asks for night duty, and puts in ever longer hours. The film, which began with ghostly images of a yellow cab gliding through a hallucinated city, now turns into a bit of heightened quasi-cinéma-vérité about driving a cab through New York by night. It is a cinematic equivalent of the evocation of megalopolitan horror that poetry has done even better than fiction, starting with Baudelaire's *Tableaux parisiens* and Thomson's *City of Dreadful Night.* Scorsese, his prestigious young cinéaste-scenarist, Paul Schrader, and his less than distinguished cinematographer, Michael Chapman (remember the washed-out images of *The Last Detail?)*, accumulate such hellish visions as steam rising to engulf the cab for long seconds, or black hoodlums pelting away and breaking the rear window, and always, everywhere, night people: pimps, whores, pushers, weaving in and out of garish blotches of gaudy neon above them in the sky, around them in plate-glass reflections, below them in the mirror of wet pavements.

Yet even this imagery of the *ville tentaculaire* is overdone, and hammily shot by Chapman. Everything is ugliness: Travis seems hardly ever to drive through more prosperous neighborhoods or to get a decent fare. Orgies explode constantly just behind his back; every morning, as he tells us in voice-over narration, he has to "wipe the come off the backseat." *(Every* morning? Come, come!) At the Belmore Cafeteria, Travis exchanges stories with fellow cabbies; their unofficial chief, Wizard (a lovely acting job, as always, from Peter Boyle), tells no less weird ones than those that befall Travis. During his off-hours, our hero pops pills, swills brandy, fills his diary with pious platitudes, and hangs around porno movie houses. Why is the City so unremittingly cruel to him? Why doesn't he have an occasional pleasant adventure, even some friends? The cards are stacked, with no explanation given.

Even more problematic is the implicit connection: because the City is so wicked, so seductively diabolical, this poor bastard becomes unhinged. One day he sees a pimp roughly drag a barely teen-aged prostitute out of his cab; another day an obsessed man (played by Scorsese) makes him stop the cab and watch along with him, in a curtained but illuminated window, the passenger's wife make love in silhouette to a black man. The passenger describes in detail how he will blow her to smithereens with his Magnum. Nothing nice ever happens to Travis—except his glimpses of Betsy, a pretty campaign worker for Senator Palantine, a presidential candidate. From his dawdling cab, Bickle first watches her working behind the plate glass of the campaign headquarters; later, he begins coming in on various pretexts, and getting thrown out as a nuisance. Why does Betsy consent to go out for coffee with this obnoxious, importunate fellow? Why, since he is both boring and uncouth, does she go out on a date with him? And why would Travis, who sees her as some ideal, virginal creature, take her to a cheap porno theater, from which—and from him—she runs away disdainfully?

Motivation is extremely fuzzy here. Is Betsy a nice girl, genuinely interested in this odd fellow? Or is she a spoiled rich kid, merely playing with Travis? (I don't imagine one vote for Palantine can be worth that much trouble.) In either case, why would she give up that easily? The nature of the film is clear from the marquee, so why does Travis insist it is respectable, and Betsy believe him? The fact that she is played by the supremely untalented Cybill Shepherd, who here sinks to new depths of unblinking smugness coupled with prefabricated come-hither inflections, adds further layers of needless obscurity.

Equally mysterious and unexamined is Bickle's attitude toward Palantine, whom he once picks up in his cab, resulting in a mutually incomprehending but most polite conversation. Does he admire the candidate or envy and loathe him? And, in either case, why? He puts up Palantine posters on his walls, yet resolves to shoot him. All these things might be reconciled and resolved, if only the film probed deeper instead of trying merely to astonish and dazzle. Obviously, it is the offspring of an unholy union.

Paul Schrader is the product of a repressive Calvinist upbringing, aggravated by its midwestern locale; Martin Scorsese grew up hemmed in by Little Italy and orthodox Catholicism, complicated by his asthma and inability to make friends through participatory sports. Both kids looked to the movies as a panacea, both found dubious release in the fantasies Hollywood peddled and begat. But their fantasies do not necessarily mesh, any more than wounds inflicted by Calvin and Saint Augustine are cures for each other. Schrader is preoccupied with problems of psychometaphysical salvation and damnation, and knows little about New York. His interests are revealed in his book, *Transcendental Style in Film: Ozu, Bresson, Dreyer,* a pretentious and boring work, its foggy ideas and abstract language shuttling between the intellectual-mystical and the movie-buff-trashy. Scorsese, on the other hand, is possessed by the stifling city atmosphere, overripeness and repression, eruptions into violence: note the cameo roles he picks for himself—the hired gunman in *Mean Streets,* the brutal wife-killer-to-be in *Taxi Driver.* How shall we wed the children of Bresson and Dreyer to those of Sam Fuller and Raoul Walsh?

The movie now enters what might be its most fascinating phase, the lurid urban pastoral, as Travis meets Iris, the twelve-year-old whore, and Sport, her revolting yet not uncharming pimp. There could be a whole film in this unlikely triangle if only Schrader and Scorsese knew how to handle it. That they have desentimentalized the tale is correct; that, despite the impeccable acting of Robert De Niro, Harvey Keitel, and Jodie Foster, it neither moves nor sears us, is deplorable. A major problem may be what looks like excessive reliance on improvisation. All too often the dialogue proceeds by those fitful spurts and pauses that simply aren't the true rhythms of talk, however halting, uncertain, and inarticulate it may be. People need only think up what to say next, whereas improvising actors must worry about what to say next *in character,* which results in a stalling, stalking discourse unlike genuine conversations. Moreover, actors are not writers; their dialogue may be more natural, but is surely less artistic than that of a good writer, so improvisation doubles the loss.

The concluding violence (though Scorsese toned it down to avoid an X rating) is perhaps not so much excessively gruesome as lingered over with excessive enjoyment of the gruesomeness. Its almost slobberingly repetitive and protracted rehashing of images of blood and horror is ghoulish, made more absurd by being topped off with a twofold O. Henry ending: a cute reversal in the Travis-Betsy relationship and a paradoxical semihappy finale implying that in a mad society the murderous madman cannot be found guilty. What makes this offensive is not that it is necessarily untrue, but that it is presented much too glibly, with a patness that is almost cute.

Matching the cheesily posturing photography is an ungainly and bombastic score by Bernard Herrmann, who died the day after it was recorded. Herrmann had done yeoman's work in the movies, with effective scores for *Citizen Kane, Hangover Square, All That Money Can Buy,* and several Hitchcock films, among others, but here, perhaps fearing that this score would be his last, he tried to outdo himself. The resultant musical rant yields not complements to the images, but sputtering redundancies.

Taxi Driver is only very incompletely redeemed by exceptionally subtle performances, especially from De Niro and Miss Foster. And it is saddled with Miss Shepherd, whose presence is not even a tribute to Scorsese's healthy appetites: having gained weight, most noticeably in the face, she looks like Mussolini in drag.

Yet even the greatest sins of *Taxi Driver* are venial alongside *Gable and Lombard,* a supposed *hommage* to those charming cinematic personalities and off-screen lovers, which proves a dismal throwback and throwaway, making you either cackle unhealthily (because feeling superior to garbage does not make for healthy laughter) or just quietly throw up. Where am I to begin? There is Barry Sandler's attitudinizing, bottomlessly inane and illiterate screenplay, always unfunny except when it tries to be moving; and Sidney J. Furie's direction that does not miss a single cliché, and almost manages the unlikely feat of concocting a few new ones singlehandedly. There is the abysmal performance by James Brolin as Gable, who may not have been a great actor, but who was charming, sexy, and shrewd. Brolin comes out lumpish, loutish, and faintly imbecile, failing both as performer and as Gable impersonator. Staunchly assisted by Sandler and Furie, but mightily contributing himself, Brolin turns Gable into something midway between a stuffed shirt and an idiotic rube.

Jill Clayburgh does much better with Lombard. She has neither the looks nor the voice of the late star, but manages, except in a few totally reprehensible scenes, to remain a woman and an actress. There are even a few moments when she ennobles her material, an accomplishment that makes crossing the Alps with a Carthaginian army complete with elephants seem like child's play in comparison. But, in the end, she, too, is licked, rather less gloriously than Hannibal.

Imagine a movie that begins by trying to wrest suspense from suspenselessness with a scene in which Gable, in his officer's uniform, keeps nocturnal vigil at the foothills of the mountains where Lombard's plane crashed, in the hope that she may have survived, and proceeds to reminisce about their crazy, wonderful, topsy-turvy, heartbreaking, fun-filled (just add your own favorite cliché) romance. The film unfurls, figuratively, between a line like "I told her to take the train!" and another like "Don't go up there, Gable. It's not how she wants to be remembered." (Neither, I'm sure, is this movie.) In between, the filmmakers bog down in abject confusion: they want to make the story both into a screwball comedy of the kind Lombard often starred in, and into the sort of romantic drama we tend to associate with Gable. Even with talent, this would be an impossible blend to achieve; with Furie and Sandler, it is indigestible. Gable and Lombard, for instance, not only meet cute, they meet cute a dozen times over; and they suffer from Ria Gable's refusal to grant a divorce in a manner worthy of three handkerchiefs and ten Fannie Hursts. This, of course, leaves no room for the creation of real people, even if anyone here knew how to create them: as rich a character as Louis B. Mayer is turned into an exhausted commonplace.

Gable keeps saying he-manly things like, "Talk about no emotion, lady, you've got a wall up so thick you couldn't blast through it with a ton of dynamite"; Lombard is being ceaselessly madcap, as when the morning after their first sex Gable grouches over a perfectly good omelet, and she cracks jokes (not eggs) like "If you smile pretty, I'll throw in a couple of gizzards" (correction: egg, not joke). After the first big lovers' quarrel, we get parallel scenes, with her confidante asking, "He really meant something to you, didn't he?" and his sidekick inquiring, "First time a dame got to you, kid?" Add to this ugly, badly lighted photography by Jordan S. Cronenweth, and music by the insufferable Michel Legrand (endless, nauseating variations on a borrowed tune), and you have something that a billion gizzards thrown in could not save. Better throw it to the buzzards instead.

February 23, 1976

Technical Exercise, Exercise in Futility

THE FILMS OF John Cassavetes are, by and large, sterile actors' exercises. They are not even for all kinds of actors, but mostly for the friends of Cassavetes and amateurs like his family or his wife's family. They are doggedly pretentious and often of enormous duration; unless you are an actor, or a friend or relative of the director's, you should find them quintessentially trivial and boring. Cassavetes, who is quite a good actor but a bad director and worse writer, has insisted ever more emphatically over the years that his films are "scripted," though they seem to be taped and transcribed improvisations, possibly reenacted from such "scripts." At least I *hope* that this is how it is done; if Cassavetes is telling the truth, and he really writes this trash that postures as plot, characterization, and dialogue, he must be an even bigger simpleton than I take him to be.

It requires, either way, a rather arrogant folly to allow things like *Minnie and Moskowitz, Husbands,* and *A Woman Under the Influence* to buttonhole and protractedly assault our sensibilities as if they had anything to say. I gather that *Shadows,* which I missed, was a nice little try; *Faces,* thanks largely to the freshness of Lynn Carlin and Seymour Cassel, worked in part. But consider *A Woman Under the Influence.* It did not begin to enlighten us about whether the woman was demented or unjustly viewed as such, whether her husband loved her or not, whether her family and her doctor treated her rightly or wrongly. It did not remotely come to grips with whether she had extramarital relations, whether her love for her children was genuine or some form of infantilism and hysteria, and whether anything was changed after her return from the asylum. Many feminists hailed the picture as a major plea in behalf of oppressed womanhood; yet it was by no means clear whether and by what the heroine was oppressed, and whether her abject stupidity, indeed near-idiocy, made her a representative specimen.

But this near-idiocy is easily explicable. Cassavetes, Gena Rowlands (Mrs. C., who played the wife), Peter Falk (who played the husband), and the rest know precious little about blue-collar workers and their private lives. I have no doubt that in some bar or other they have stood a few construction workers a round of drinks in exchange for boozy self-revelations, or that they have, as struggling actors, occasionally driven taxis or waited on tables. But from there to a true insight into workers' minds and souls, and the ability to reproduce this on film, may be a longer way than they suspect. Writers, with the gift of imaginative projection that makes them writers, can do it; actors, with their gift for *mimesis* or imitation that makes them actors, generally speaking cannot. Moreover, because actors' improvisations are likely to be inconsistent—there being too many cooks for the broth to be homogeneous, and actors' moods varying from improvisation to improvisation—it is most probable that a film so arrived at will keep contradicting itself.

In any case, *A Woman Under the Influence* struck me as muddleheaded, pretentious, and interminable, fooling some people because of its factitious social significance. *The Killing of a Chinese Bookie,* cut from the same burlap, makes two strategic errors: its subject cannot even lay claim to significant social comment, and it tries for something like a thriller plot, for which Cassavetes and his pals have no real affinity. On top of kids playing with typical improvisations and cameras, we get kids playing with guns—disastrously.

The Killing of a Chinese Bookie concerns Cosmo Vitelli, who, after seven years, has just made the last payment to the mob on The Crazy Horse West, a strip joint on the L.A. Strip (which sounds like a redundancy, but isn't quite). Even this is much clearer from the printed synopsis than from the film itself, which is muzzy right from the start. We then follow Cosmo through a dull afternoon, during which he has an unlikely conversation with a cabbie who, for no discernible reason, follows Cosmo into an eatery where he deposited him half an hour earlier. The hackie offers to drive Cosmo home to his wife and children, which he hasn't got, and we are at liberty to guess whether the film changed tacks in midstream, or whether this was just a bit of irrelevant improvisation too cute to cut.

Next we see Cosmo at the Crazy Horse, where he "writes, directs, choreographs, and announces such acts as 'The Gunfight at O.K. Corral' and 'An Evening in Paris.' " These acts, consisting of a bedraggled homosexual comedian cracking humorless jokes or chanting pop songs totally off key, while several girls display their bodies and lack of talent, are not slick, sexy, or satirical, merely excruciating. They are, of course, meant to be untalented, but that's the problem: when not very bright or clever people try to convey to the movie audience that someone or something is supposed to be dumb, they sink to levels of stupidity and ineptitude that strike people of normal intelligence as positively feeble-minded.

So, for example, when Cosmo tells about two girls in Memphis who cut off a gopher's tail, ate it, and died of botulism, we wonder—there being no botulism outside of canned food—who is being inept: the character, the improvising actor, or the filmmaker. Later, when Cosmo phones his bartender and asks what act is on, and the bartender, even after painstaking explanations, cannot figure out whether he is looking at the Paris number, we cannot be sure whether he is meant to be a cretin, and, if so, why. And when a mobster claims that Marx was wrong, that opium is not the religion of the people, we cannot tell who is garbling Marx here, and to what purpose. And so on. Not only are ignorance and witlessness fulgurating in the movie, we do not even know whom to ascribe them to and how to evaluate them.

It seems most unlikely that Cosmo would gamble away twenty-three thousand dollars the day after he met his last painful payment on the club, and still less likely that he would agree without much demurral to kill a Chinese bookie for the mob in exchange for cancellation of his new debt. It is supremely unlikely that the mob, in turn, would pick the inexperienced, unskilled Cosmo to rub out what turns out to be a heavily protected bigwig, and monumentally preposterous that he would succeed at it in the simplistic manner we are shown. From here on in the movie becomes ever more clumsy and incredible: not only do things become totally divorced from sense, but also the filmmaking cannot or will not make clear just what happens during various key scenes. We do not find out just when Cosmo gets shot, what kind of wound he incurs, and why it seems insignificant and staunched when that suits the filmmakers, and profusely bleeding and presumably fatal when that makes for a splashier effect.

Not even Cosmo is decently examined and comprehended by the Cassavetes method; the other characters, except for an occasional touch of (usually spurious) colorfulness, remain total ciphers. So it would be interesting to learn more about Cosmo's affair with Rachel, a black stripper who works for him; why the girl still lives with her mother and Cosmo in their family house—a highly improbable arrangement; and why both Cosmo and Rachel are afraid of this mother, especially since she is played as a weak ninny by an amateur so rank she wouldn't last out one rehearsal of a high-school pageant.

Why go on? Ben Gazzara, an actor who can be forceful in the right part and ineffectual in the wrong one, can do next to nothing with the nonpart of Cosmo; we see much too much of him for what little we learn about him, and for what infinitesimal interest that little holds. But, under the circumstances, it is hard to assign and assess the blame. Azizi Johari, as Rachel, remains an attractive façade, and blank is not beautiful. Only the comedian, Mr. Sophistication, is given some identity, but as the playwright-scenarist Meade Roberts plays him, I can't imagine his being hired for the most down-at-heel drag show.

There is always the joker who says sneeringly, "Muddled, contradictory, stupidly bungling—that is just the way life is!" Maybe, but in that case give us *cinéma-vérité* rather than actors' improvisations posturing as life. If, on the other hand, you're trying to give us something more—art, perhaps—it is your obligation to probe a bit below the surface, to try at least to raise some questions worth the asking. Cassavetes offers up only a lot of extreme closeups and murky lighting—both literally and figuratively—and fails either to penetrate or to illuminate his subject.

I Will, I Will . . . For Now, if it weren't a movie but a person, would be a nonagenarian wheeled about a California old folks' home, and that institution's prime bore. It is one vast, nay, endless, unfunny clean dirty joke about risqué words that almost get uttered, sex that almost gets performed, nudity that never crosses the papal demarcation line, but waggles frenetically just this side of it. It carries on in 1976 as if the merest sexual innuendos were still going to send naughty shivers up and down one's spine, whereas what one feels is closer to progressive paralysis. It would be otiose to discuss the movie in detail, though this bit of senescent prurience deserves a historic footnote.

Once upon a time, in Hollywood's dreary forties, there was a pair of collaborators called Melvin Frank and Norman Panama. They reached their creative peak right away with *My Favorite Blonde* (1942), and were content thereafter to grind out mostly farces meant to titillate. It was a time, however, when the Production Code persecuted sex in much the same way that, a decade later, Joe McCarthy persecuted Reds; so one got Frank-Panama scandals such as *The Reformer and the Redhead, Li'l Abner,* and a couple of Hope-Crosby *Road* pictures, among others. In the mid-sixties, the team split up, and we are now treated to superannuated clean dirty jokes from both Frank and Panama separately. The former gave us, most recently, *A Touch of Class;* the latter, even more feebly, this. *I Will* can serve at best to remind us that the good old days of Hollywood could be just as rotten as the bad new ones, and that smuttiness winked and drooled at from a distance is no better than wallowed in at close quarters.

Something should be said also about the two leads. Even if Elliott Gould could act beyond the same old beady-eyed and slack-jawed expression and the same oily, petulant intonation that must convey everything from delicious roguishness to epochal self-pity, he would still be the possessor of one of the least palatable faces in Movieland—a face that vies with ontogeny in recapitulating phylogeny, but, unlike ontogeny, never quite makes it. Diane Keaton, who here looks better than I have ever seen her, and nimbly wears the exquisite outfits that Dorothy Jeakins, the highly gifted but underrated designer, has bestowed on her, is nevertheless a similar case. She can convey one thing on screen, a part in which Woody Allen, who has used her best, has consistently cast her. This is the lost urban neurotic, the young woman with vague, unfulfilled cultural and emotional appetites, who has a way of coming apart at the seams before your very eyes.

Miss Keaton does this very well—just as Gould can manage the Jewish schlemiel; try to get something else out of her, though, as Coppola did in *The Godfather,* and you get instant catastrophe. Then when you see her on talk shows and realize that that nervous, comic-pathetic flutter, those thrown-up hands or intonations, are of her very essence —just as Gould's recurrent screen persona is of his—you lose even what little respect you might have had for an authentic schtik. The only performer who emerges unscathed from this mess is Victoria Principal. It is high time that such a promising actress be rescued from the wretched movies she has been stuck in.

March 1, 1976

Through a Lens Falsely

THE MAYSLES BROTHERS, makers of *Grey Gardens,* have been busily producing cinéma-vérité films, for which they prefer the term "direct cinema," possibly because they are made uneasy by the word "truth," even when it is in French. Much has been made of the Maysleses' truthfulness, mostly by the brothers themselves. To James Blue, Albert Maysles has conveyed that "his cinema is one in which ethics and aesthetics are interdependent, where beauty starts with honesty, where a cut or a change in camera angle can become not only a possible aesthetic error but also a 'sin' against Truth. In things cinematic, Al Maysles is a religious zealot." Al Maysles has, moreover, been called by Jean-Luc Godard the "greatest cameraman in America," and the French critic Louis Marcorelles speaks of him as "a virtuoso who can do anything with a camera." His brother David carries the tape recorder and does much of the editing.

The first independent film by the Maysleses was *Showman,* about the producer Joseph Levine, which could never be shown publicly because Levine refused to grant permission, but was seen at various festivals. This may indeed be a truthful film—why else would Levine oppose it?—and I wish I had seen it: I have met Mr. Levine, and he strikes me as the last of the motion-picture-producer leviathans; short of having Nathanael West and George Grosz around to do him justice, I'd settle for the Maysleses' Auricon camera with Angenieux zoom lens, and their superlative Nagra tape recorder.

The next Maysles spectacular was *Salesman,* about a quartet of Bible salesmen selling an overpriced, tastelessly produced Bible door to door from New England to Florida. This was a fascinating film, raising many profound questions about religion, and one or two about the Maysleses' own religion of Truth. For, it seems, the Maysleses financed the salesmen's travel to Florida, where some of the most disturbing footage was obtained, as Walter Goodman recently reminded us in the *Times.* And *Gimme Shelter,* the Maysleses' next film, about the Rolling Stones' 1969 tour of America that climaxed bloodily at Altamont, was commissioned by the Stones themselves, and, as Pauline Kael was quick to point out, took some mighty fancy liberties with the sacrosanct Truth. But just as Catholic Bible salesmen were revealed to be less than holy, Truth salesmen, too, have their funny sidelights.

Now we get *Grey Gardens,* about two socially prominent recluses living in a sprawling East Hampton mansion where everything has gone to seed, and numerous cats, visiting raccoons, a widowed mother in her late seventies, and an unmarried daughter in her middle fifties are living amid monstrous untidiness and considerable filth. A flurry of scandal arose when the township tried to evict Mrs. Edith Bouvier Beale and her daughter, Edie, but failed to do so, possibly because they were relatives of Jackie Kennedy Onassis. Yet this issue is brought in by the Maysleses only liminally, as a bit of spice, without any further investigation of what may be a true social problem. Instead, our zealots of the Truth concentrate their attention on a mother who is, at the very least, eccentric, and a daughter who is, to put it mildly, spaced out, and who have made a *modus vivendi* out of confusing the past with the present, fantasy with reality, and communication with nonstop bickering. Direct cinema may always be an act of indiscretion; here, I think, it becomes also an act of indiscrimination and indecency.

The world is full of mentally disturbed people, and there is room for the "direct" filmmaker who wants to call attention to their plight—as, for example, Fred Wiseman did for the state-institutionalized patients of *Titicut Follies;* or to modes of treatment—as Allan King did for the troubled children in *Warrendale.* But what was the Maysleses' aim in recording the daily life of Edith and Edie, their interior and exterior messiness as it oozes out of and into them, even as day seeps into desolate day? Well, not entirely desolate, because old Edith, though mostly recumbent or semirecumbent, still has a good deal of fun; while middle-aged Edie skitters and fritters away an existence bitterly immured within a meaningless bustle. But, yes, totally disconsolate, when you consider that most of Edith's pleasure now stems from carping at, mocking, and lording it over Edie, to whose destruction she probably contributed very handsomely in concert with the departed and fondly remembered Mr. Beale.

How does scrutiny avoid becoming prying? Definitely not by getting its victims' wholehearted consent. For Edith is a born performer, always singing, reminiscing, philosophizing, bragging for an audience she needs more than anything else—the reason she retrieved Edie when she tried to make herself independent in New York City was, most likely, the need for a captive audience of at least 1 girl 1 over and above the hordes of cats and 'coons. And Edie also sings occasionally—not just tunelessly, but almost militantly antitunefully—and dances, horribly and ludicrously, sometimes trying to re-create her youthful drum-majorette routines. And when she does not dance, she wrangles with her mother, or flirts with the Maysleses, or yearns for the delivery boy whom she lures into tarrying in the house, or recites a litany of past and present grievances and absurd hopes for a better future. Now that the film is a mild *succès de scandale,* and Edie has been going around touting it, some of her dreams of glory may indeed seem to have been fulfilled, but at what price? The raucous, patronizing laughter of audiences at the Paris Theater, which gradually subsides, but not, I venture to say, from sympathy, only from bored indifference.

How, I repeat, does inquiry stop short of voyeurism? Not by disgracefully advertising this film as "a love story—sort of." There is only self-centeredness and resentment on display here, neither of which strikes me as compatible with the most approximative definition of love. And there is certainly no love of truth (with or without a capital letter) in filmmakers who, out of ostensible objectivity, do not ask any of the questions that need to be asked here, but assume that a truth will reveal itself. How? From the delusions, self-deceptions, nagging reproaches of these women? From the pandering to their need for an increased audience, which may lead them to distort their daily falsifications even further?

The only possible justification for "direct cinema" is that it can lead us closer to people worth getting to know better, or demonstrate a procedure, a *techne* (skill, craft, or art), or clarify a historical situation. But the hermits of *Grey Gardens* are not worth knowing—at least not in the very superficial way recorded in the film—nor do they shed light on social, political, or other important problems. Only the indirect cinema of a creative artist could have got at the inner truths of these women. The Maysles brothers, however, are merely pandering to morbid curiosity, sensationalism, and, worse yet, *schadenfreude:* look how low these once fine-looking, wealthy, upper-class women have fallen, and rejoice, dear friends, in how much better off you are in your mediocrity. Repugnant business!

March 22, 1976

Robin Hood and His Merry Menopause

"Perfection, everybody knows, is unattainble, but this film comes close." These being James Goldman's words about *Robin and Marian,* for which he wrote the screenplay, you might call them the perfection of impudence. Not quite, however, because Mr. Goldman chickens out and adds (in the introduction to the printed version), "That's not a judgment of my work, my writing is always full of flaws." Still, the finished film is "everything I ever dreamed. And more." Mr. G. can dream some rather trashy dreams: the play (later movie) *The Lion in Winter* was one of them; the musical *Follies,* another. Early in his rather less than literate introduction we are told about Goldman's youthful love for Giraudoux and Annouilh [*sic*]. Their style was not, it seems, a "solution" for him, so Mr. G. moved on. To what? Further poor imitation of Giraudoux and Anouilh, such as *The Lion in Winter* and *Robin and Marian.*

Intelligent reinterpretation is one thing; sensationalistic or smartass revisionism, quite another. Here we take Robin Hood, his merry men, and Maid Marian, but show them as middle-aged folk in an autumnal mood, at the end of their chivalric tether. We connect the story even more tightly than usual with Richard the Lionhearted by having Robin and Little John fight under him in the Third Crusade, and making the film begin at Châluz, where Richard meets his end. The historic Richard, whom various reversals seem to have wised up, and the legendary Richard, always righting his brother John Lackland's wrongs, is turned here into a war-maddened beast who spitefully commands Robin and John to slaughter Christian women and children. (What the historic Richard did at Acre was dreadful, but it must be remembered that to the medieval mind those heathens were not fully human.) He is made to die, ironically, of a hand-tossed arrow, pitched by an ancient, one-eyed, bowless man who cries out in language to make a Giraudoux or Anouilh shudder, "Lionheart, you are a pig." Only his derisory death prevents Richard from executing the faithful Robin and John.

That is revisionism for you! Knighthood, so far from being in flower, is mostly weeds and nettles, and even they are going to seed. Sir Walter Scott's hero-king has become a moody tyrant, and when legend is not countered with wanton deflation, facts are chosen for their somberness. Jailed by Richard, our boys sadly recall a Jerusalem seen only from a distance. True, however often he cruised about within sight of its walls, Richard never recaptured the city; still, the truce of 1192 wrested from Saladin free pilgrimage to the Holy Sepulcher, where the crusaders could worship before leaving the Holy Land. Mr. Goldman will have none of that. The brighter side is seen merely when a traditional villain is to be revisionistically whitewashed. The Sheriff of Nottingham becomes downright sympathetic; only his deputy is a treacherous, murderous bully—in fact, a pig. Even wicked King John is mostly ludicrous in his uxoriousness—toward a child-wife, at that!—and only perfunctorily despotic. When Robin, returning to a somewhat defoliated Sherwood Forest, is reminded of Maid Marian—now Mother Jennet, mother superior of a puny nunnery—he remarks laconically "Lovely girl; I haven't thought of her in years." And when Marian first hears Robin's call outside Kirkly Abbey, she exclaims, "Damn them all to hell," which is not your standard mother-superior jargon.

What's wrong with revisionism having a field day? A little of it, on acceptable historical premises, is perfectly welcome. Already in 1858, in *The Defense of Guenevere,* William Morris depicted a world where chivalry was, if not exactly dead, sorely beleaguered. Fair enough: the old romances, legends, folk tales, all have their darker sides; and history—well, we all know about history. But I find this systematic debunking quite cheap: what yields a shoddier, more facile effect than standing tradition on its head? It is not all that different from painting a mustache on the Mona Lisa.

What is it that Goldman and his director, Richard Lester, are after? In the already cited introduction, Goldman rambles on about providing an anti-heroic age with heroes suitably demythologized, yet also grand—which is how one arrives at Robin as "an aging hero with a swan song." The idea is to make us "laugh a little, cry a bit and have a thought or two about our heroes, where they've gone, and wouldn't it be wonderful to have them back again." Alas for that thought or two: where our heroes have gone is a thought never raised by the film; and wouldn't it be nice to have them back is a thought not worth raising. The little laughter and bit of crying we certainly do get (one for each eye) from a Robin and Marian who can blithely forget all about each other, then, after twenty years, come together—not to live happily ever after, which, heaven forfend, would be old-hat romance—but to die the most preposterous love death this side of grand opera.

Heroes haven't gone at all. It is only paltry sentimentalists like Goldman—and perhaps Lester, under his superficial toughness—that consider heroes a wonderful, lost breed; in fact, they exist as much, or as little, as they ever did, even if they no longer wield broadswords or longbows for the delectation of backward children in adults' clothing. Do not misunderstand me; the historical work—film, novel, whatever—that honestly tries to understand the age it deals with, and does not use it as a fancy-dress ball for jaded modern sensibilities or an easy way of capitalizing on anticlimaxes—and then, introducing a grand, old-fashioned climax after all, a lopsided *liebestod,* no less—is fine. But trying to have it every which way is, to me, contemptible.

And what kind of language does Goldman, the admirer of Giraudoux and Anouilh, who brackets himself with Coleridge, Wordsworth, and Haydn, write for his characters? A language, first, made up of titles of musical-comedy songs, as befits a man who collaborated on two failed Broadway musicals. In a single scene between Robin and Marian we get lines like "Where did the day go?" and "There's danger where you are" and "There'll be another morning"—every one of them waiting for Sheldon Harnick or Jerry Herman to continue them, and just itching for Jerry Bock or the other half of Jerry Herman to set them to music. There is, in the same scene, an entire speech that needs only the benefit of a short consultation with the rhyming dictionary, and right away Rodgers or Bernstein can set to work: "I'd go with you, go anywhere, live any way at all, do anything, be mother, sister, lover for you. I'll do anything but mourn. . . . I can't have found you just to lose you." It just takes a little rearranging: "Be mother, sister, lover for you,/Be glove and cloak and cover for you./I can't have found you just to lose you,/Is it for this love made me choose you?" and so forth. And, of course, one can always do a little discreet borrowing: "The wood, just now, was full of noises" is Caliban's island—"Be not afeard; the isle is full of noises"—turned into Robin's forest.

Next, we get that handy device inversion, archaic and poetic as all getout. "Round you were and hard and not a mark . . ." Or: "Some other girl it must have been . . ." Or yet: "A woman of your word, you are . . ." And, for the truly BIG MOMENTS, there is always the catalogue (another musical-comedy favorite): "Love you? More than all you know. I love you more than children, more than fields I've planted with my hands. I love you more than morning prayers or peace or food to eat. I love you more than sunlight, more than flesh or joy or one more day. I love you more than God." It is, of course, one thing to modernize the vocabulary, and quite another thing to travesty the spirit of an era. On the one hand, Goldman and Lester will introduce such authentic details as Robin using a twig to clean his teeth (a toothbranch?); on the other, we get such glaring anachronisms as Marian telling how, when Robin left their little cottage in the woods to fight in the Crusade, she tried to die by cutting her wrists. What medieval maiden ever heard of this routine? She'd have drowned or stabbed herself; but then she wouldn't have been one of us.

Lester's direction is equally divided. There is quite a bit of the Lester of *The Three Musketeers* and even the four Beatles here—debunking with wisecracks and sight gags; but there is also the Lester of *Petulia* and *Juggernaut* who, under a hard-boiled façade, slips in some hoary, sentimental heartbreak. I can see possible good in both approaches, but I object to their clumsy and meretricious miscegenation. There are, however, things of a more purely technical nature to be questioned. Why, for example, will Lester allow Robin and John to ride off in the opposite direction from Richard's funeral procession? Something more—or less—would have been demanded of former officers and prisoners. Or why, in another scene, does Lester permit Robin and John to ride away in the extremest of extreme long shots as tiniest dots in a verdant landscape? It is not at all a scene in which the surroundings are meant to overpower our heroes, nor is the point that they have found peace by blending into the world of nature. Such sequences are, I am afraid, all for effect, and to hell with everything else. Even John Barry's score is schizoid: inoffensive when just marking time, it becomes odiously sticky at the drop of a coif, maniacally bombastic at the toss of a javelin.

But *Robin and Marian* does have two assets so genuine as hardly to deserve them. One is David Watkin's cinematography, which will get a trifle syrupy in the sunlight-through-the-foliage shots, but which, the moment there are rising mists or overcast skies—when any kind of surrounding grayness or dimness lends a starkly perishable intensity to what it frames—is the equal of your purest ballad or epic. To Goldman's gestures and Lester's jests, Watkin adds the essence of the *chansons de geste.* And there is the acting. Let me take a leaf from Goldman's book and make a list. Can you ask for more than Audrey Hepburn and Sean Connery? More than Nicol Williamson, Richard Harris, and Robert Shaw? More than, even in the smallest parts, Ian Holm, Denholm Elliott, Esmond Knight? And each of them better than morning prayers or peace or food to eat? In fact, almost as good as food for thought.

March 29, 1976

From D.C. to W.C.

I HAVE NOT READ the book *All the President's Men,* but I have seen the movie. And I am delighted to report that the latter says it as well as any book could have said it, in sufficient but faster detail. It is a fairly long picture, but not once did I look at my watch; it is a screenplay by the usually gimcrack William Goldman, brother of James, but here nothing was offensive; it is an unending concatenation of performances by actors known and unknown, but without a single weak link. I was grateful for there being no romantic or heroic monkeyshines, and pleasantly aware of being instructed as well as entertained. I assume that everything I saw was true; but if there were little fictional additives to achieve an occasional extra fillip, I commend them for so handsomely enacting the truth.

No, I was not a Watergate buff. I was not glued to any television set, and did not even read the papers diligently. Having despised and loathed Nixon from the very beginning, having no faith whatever in associates chosen by him, and having, above all, very little hope for the integrity of politicians in general (at least those that manage to get themselves elected—I have known some perfectly beautiful losers), I all along expected the worst possible revelations, and was shocked and disgusted only once, at the very end, when Ford granted the prime culprit an unpardonable pardon. Recalling, however, a batch of movies of which Kurosawa's *The Bad Sleep Well* is perhaps the most distinguished, and Elio Petri's *Investigation of a Citizen Above Suspicion* the splashiest, I accepted the fact that, in films as in life, the bad need not end badly. I merely hope that someday we shall have a movie that tells, if only by implication, as much about Ford as this does about Nixon.

As a wag has suggested, the movie is admirable in never letting you forget who the real enemy was for Carl Bernstein and Bob Woodward: a composite of Walter Cronkite and the *New York Times.* Certainly our two journalist heroes never express the slightest concern for patriotism, justice, and similar niceties; getting the story and making it stick is all that matters—before, that is, the competition might get hold of it. These are not idealistic men, but they are bright, clever, and breathtakingly persistent. They are perfectly happy to lie in the good cause of getting their scoops, and there is always the consoling thought, for them as for us, that the trickster's art is an admirable one as long as it is directed against Them, who are far worse than tricksters.

Two things above all emerge about Them. Not very intelligent or in the least unflappable, they nevertheless inspire great fear. Time and again their clumsy method of squelching already leaked-out information proves a dead giveaway; yet their ability to keep subalterns scared and uncommunicative is worthy of any fascist or communist dictatorship. And then there is the magnificent hypocrisy of these subalterns when they do speak, and honesty is held in check by uncourageousness, so that the naming of mere initials, talking in riddles, and suggestive silences replace forthright utterance. This way, they feel, they have spoken without speaking, and their skins and consciences are unimperiled.

Alan J. Pakula, the director, must have given the picture the needed edge. A graduate of *Klute,* involving a big-businessman murderer, and *The Parallax View,* about an all-powerful U.S. corporation dealing in political assassination, he was just the man to sharpen the script's teeth: there is fine use made of videotapes of the actual people speechifying or testifying, as glimpsed on TV sets that punctuate the film's action and become part of its marvelously suggestive closing image. Altogether, the direction is taut, allowing for some sparse ironic touches but no needless embellishments, and is notably successful in capturing the atmosphere of the *Washington Post,* where, as at any similar publication, obscenity-studded horseplay and hard-edged horse sense mingle in a ruckus worthy of a downtown cafeteria during lunch hour.

Gordon Willis, the excellent cinematographer, has been made to curb his penchant for overgenerous lyricism, yet his sensitive camera does squeeze every legitimate drop of beauty out of Washington's not unphotogenic ambience, in particular some stunning shots from rooftops or, indoors, just under the Library of Congress dome, that nevertheless do not detract from the sober, quasi-documentary look of the film or detain its headlong pace. David Shire's background music is appropriately ominous, but both its menace and its quantity are kept within sensible bounds. High marks must go to the editing of Robert L. Wolfe, fast without being rushed, and the production design of George Jenkins, which makes reality and the sound stage merge seamlessly.

From Robert Redford and Dustin Hoffman down to the least bit player there is such perfection of acting as one scarcely associates with Hollywood filmmaking. And not only do the performers act and look convincing, they are even splendid likenesses, as far as I can judge: Hoffman, for instance, distinctly resembles Bernstein. (I can only hope for the sake of Woodward, whom I haven't met, that he looks as much like Redford.) There are, happily, no star turns, and even Jason Robards who, when he is not playing O'Neill, tends to get carried away by his enormous, free-flowing charm, holds back and gives what may be his finest film performance. It is well worth seeing *All the President's Men* twice; once for everything about it, and once more just for the acting.

The show-biz biography is standard movie fare of almost invariably substandard quality. The reasons are obvious enough: if the show-biz celebrity had, as often happens, a boring private life, you can't make much of a movie out of it; if the life, as happens equally often, was scandalous, and you have to make it conform with the demands of censors, rating boards, and worshipful fans, you end up with pap. And the production numbers based on old favorites, recast and re-created, are never a match for the old excitement.

The latest entry into this unpromising genre, *W. C. Fields and Me,* is no exception. Some of the infelicitous things that can happen to such films are (a) being based on a single source—in this case, the memoirs of Carlotta Monti—which means that the scope will be limited; (b) having for author a friend or, as here, a lover of the protagonist, which means a probably biased account; and (c) having an author who is still living and who can make sure that his or her limiting view is strictly adhered to. All of these contingencies seem to have nibbled away at what, in this case at least, might have been a moderately interesting story, because Fields was a man of impressive contradictions, and his work, catering to our more atavistic and antisocial instincts, made him into a bit of a maverick by Hollywood standards.

But for this to have happened, much more attention would have had to be given to psychological and social matters; as it is, the film does not even go into Fields's early years, and so does not begin to come to grips with the source of Fields's addiction to the bottle, well known as it is. Moreover, we get that not uncommon failing of such films, the attempt to make the protagonist's private life take on the style of his performing persona, so that, for instance, a failed affair with a fellow artiste is portrayed in slapstick terms, thus forfeiting a valuable additional dimension to the film. Yet the very attempts to deal with burlesque happenings in burlesque fashion miscarry; thus the pranks of Fields and his friends John Barrymore, Gene Fowler, and Dave Chasen lack outrageous hilarity as much as they do simple warmth.

I don't know whose fault this is, exactly: I have not read the book, and I mistrust equally the direction of Arthur Hiller and the screenplay of Bob

Merrill, a Broadway musical-comedy writer and presumable subject for a future screen biography, best remembered for his song "How Much Is That Doggie in the Window?"—a curious choice for writing a script about a man who hated doggies as much as babies and, no doubt, baby talk. There is also the additional problem raised by the casting of Rod Steiger as Fields. Actually, Steiger acts here with what, for him, is unusual restraint, and even manages to be moving from time to time. Still, I find it hard to forget that this face and this voice are Steiger's, which gives me a kind of audiovisual palimpsest. Furthermore, I wonder about the wisdom of Steiger's use of the Fieldian drawl—those sentences trailing off through the speaker's nose—in such a way as to force me to feel in the presence of an impersonation rather than a performance. Yet I am not sure whether an unknown face would have been necessarily better, and whether not duplicating such famous mannerisms would have been an improvement. It may simply be that screen biographies of people we remember intensely and, as it were, personally can never work, and should always skip a generation in order to play to audiences unburdened with memories. But with Fields's movies around, will this ever be possible?

W. C. Fields and Me, needless to say, re-creates some of the comedian's stage and screen routines, and here I must state that regardless of how well or ill they are rendered, they leave me rather cold, as does most of American film farce. What may need mentioning, though, is that I managed to miss Fields while I was growing up, and that seeing him later on may have been too late. On the other hand, I did see the Marx Brothers as a child, and even enjoyed them then, as I only very intermittently do now.

For whatever reason, then, *W. C. Fields and Me* does not stir up any nostalgia in me, although I cannot tell whether that works for or against it. I was, nevertheless, pleased as usual with the performances of Valerie Perrine and Billy Barty, and rather doubtful about Jack Cassidy as Jack Barrymore, given his propensity to substitute brazen slickness for genuine high polish. David M. Walsh's cinematography works very nicely. It has become almost *de rigueur* since *The Godfather* to give nostalgia vehicles a yellowish tinge, to evoke, I suppose, yellowing old photographs. Walsh, however, uses orange for his basic color, an orange that can slip into amber or tawny as need be. The effect suggests California oranges, which, at least in terms of cinematic achievement, are preferable to lemons.

April 5–12, 1976

Old Man Out

ALFRED HITCHCOCK, still chipper at seventy-six, is back with his fifty-somethingth picture—even the experts seem to have lost count, and disagree. The new one, *Family Plot,* is hardly worth counting, in any case. Though less pretentious and preposterous than *Torn Curtain* and *Topaz,* less ludicrous than *Marnie,* and less offensive than *Frenzy,* it is still late Hitchcock, and not very good. It is nearest in spirit to *The Trouble With Harry* in laughing at itself as it goes along: but laughter and suspense mix as badly as laughter and titillation.

The screenplay, by the glorified hack Ernest Lehman from a novel by Victor Canning, focuses on an unmarried couple: Blanche, a fake medium (I dare say all mediums are fake, but this one is the phoniest since the one in Menotti's opera), and Lumley, the stagestruck cabbie who chauffeurs her to the rich old women she is bilking. There is also another unmarried couple: Adamson, a wealthy and crooked jeweler, and Fran, occupation unspecified. Their avocation is abducting prominent people and keeping them hidden behind a fake wall in their garage until they are ransomed with the huge diamonds Adamson craves. Blanche extracts a secret from Mrs. Rainbird, one of her clients: the heir to the Rainbird fortune vanished long ago; for a healthy reward, Blanche and Lumley undertake to find him. The heir turns out to be Adamson, who mistakes Blanche and Lumley's nosing around his past for a threat, and vows to kill them. This much, I think, I can honorably tell you, though the rest will prove scarcely more suspenseful. Why?

I suspect that suspense, a genre in which speed, excitement, continuous surprise, are called for, is harder on an old man than something more introverted, contemplative, unfrantic. The thriller requires a mental and physical zest and celerity from its director that even a canny and still alert older man is unable to muster. Not only does a chase sequence take stamina to film, the direction also demands clever gimmicks more likely to pop out of a younger mind. Furthermore, working within the strict limitations of a genre uses you up more quickly; your inventiveness must function in a narrower range than if you turned out different types of films. The same hardening of the creative arteries overtook other genre directors such as Ford and Hawks.

In *Family Plot,* much goes very wrong, starting with the overlong initial expository scenes. Hitchcock, in a press conference, explained this as making the audience comfortable at the beginning, so that "you can then become purely cinematic and tell the story with pictures." Well, the audience seems to take longer than before, in Hitchcock's view, to become comfortable; though he denies it, he appears to have less faith than of yore in its perspicacity. For similar reasons, I suspect, his actors—Barbara Harris, William Devane, and especially Bruce Dern—are encouraged to italicize every expression and inflection to the point where the customarily unsubtle Karen Black seems to be positively underacting. Dern is particularly worrisome: an actor who can be extraordinary when a part fits or pleases him, as in *Smile,* he can become crudely excessive in meanness, as in *The Great Gatsby,* or in thickness, as here. His mugging now reaches a new low: even if Lumley is not meant to be brilliant, neither need he be a cretin whose facial muscles carry on like a Shriners' convention. At the end of the film, Barbara Harris winks at us broadly, and although Hitchcock has a tenuous explanation for this supererogatory gesture, nothing can explain or excuse the frenzied overacting throughout, except the mistaken notion that an electric blender can whip up comedy even when it has nothing inside it.

There are moments of inventiveness, here and there. When a woman tries to escape from a man in a cemetery whose paths are laid out like lines in a Mondrian painting (Hitchcock's own simile), there is something amusingly nutty about the pair's puny convergences and divergences, when mere cutting across a lawn could put an end to it all. In a high-angle shot, the thing looks as droll as a *pas de deux* for demented ants. How dreary, in contrast, is the big chase sequence with its strained humor consisting of Blanche's clutching, hysterically and ceaselessly, the wretched Lumley in ever more strangulating ways, making it ever harder for him to control their sabotaged car careering down a zigzagging mountain road. When they are miraculously saved, how does Blanche emerge from the overturned vehicle? By stepping squarely on the prostrate Lumley's face. Let no one tell me that Hitchcock is not expressing once again his deep-rooted dislike of women, which first struck me in his treatment of the Madeleine Carroll character in *The 39 Steps,* and which reached its unappetizing apogee in a couple of scenes in *Frenzy.* Yet I can forgive the antifeminism, but not the contrivance and overextension.

And speaking of miraculous rescue, do you know what breaks the impetus of that car hurtling toward disaster? A large wooden cross, of a kind unlikely in this landscape. And when are the miscreants apprehended? When their victim is a bishop, kidnapped from a cathedral during a religious service. And how is the heroine alerted to the danger that threatens her? By a telltale glimpse of the bishop's cope in a place where it shouldn't be. And what is the name of the chief malefactor? Adamson, the son of Adam and inheritor of his curse. And so on. French film critics and their disciples have long indulged in tracking down Catholic symbolism, hints of salvation through faith, in Hitchcock's work. What if the director denies such symbolism—might it not be unconscious, and all the more ingrained? In any case, *Family Plot,* with its deceptive cenotaph that may itself be religiously construed, should provide a happy symbol-hunting ground.

What it does not provide, along with suspense, is interesting clues. Thus when Blanche realizes that Adamson is the man she is looking for, it is no clue that guides her, only an unconvincing process of elimination and a vague hunch. Even such a very deliberate device as the assembling of an arbitrary topography by juxtaposing widely scattered parts of California does not yield the distinctive scenery Antonioni obtained by this method when he invented it for *L'Avventura.* Lastly, Hitchcock tends to pick obscure cinematographers, apparently to avoid being upstaged by his cameramen. Here he has come up with one Leonard J. South, whose name I have never encountered and whose work I have no desire to reencounter.

Michael Ritchie has struck me, ever since his first film, *Downhill Racer,* as a far more promising—indeed, delivering—director than such more highly touted young men with cameras as Paul Mazursky, Martin Scorsese, and Steven

Spielberg. It is not that Ritchie has already achieved the true film or films I believe he has inside him, but with the sole exception of *Prime Cut* (the one time the final cut was not his, and the producer's was anything but prime), his films have been consistently meritorious and challenging, full of good things even if not wholly successful. His latest, *The Bad News Bears,* is distinctly inferior to *Downhill Racer, The Candidate,* and *Smile,* but still charming and, in places, extremely clever. It should also prove his most popular film to date, for several bad reasons.

The Bad News Bears deals not only with baseball, America's favorite pastime, but also, being Little League baseball, with America's favorite people—kids. And not just any old kids, but a wonderful gallery of angelic kids, precocious kids, hilariously oddball kids, lovably ethnic kids, sweetly pathetic kids—in fact, everything but ordinary kids. Already you're ahead of the game, but it's only the beginning.

The kids are bunglers who turn into wizards: the Bears, duly beefed up with a tomboy pitcher and a dead-end-kid batter, evolve from dogs into lions. (Don't worry! Only a *near*-totally happy ending!) Moreover, the kids are foulmouthed, and when a blond WASP cherub lets loose with a four-letter word, it's the best of all possible worlds: the kid is no longer a sissy, and the word has sprouted angel's wings. For good measure, there is also Walter Matthau, as a once-promising minor-league player, now a swimming-pool cleaner addicted to boilermakers, who is hired to coach the runts of the league. In getting them out of the cellar, this cynical, amoral bum—needless to say—works out his own salvation and is headed for long-delayed romantic fulfillment with the star pitcher's mother, whom Ritchie and his scenarist, Bill Lancaster, wisely keep off the screen. Adult romance does not belong in a film like this, neither do adult marital problems, and a sparring married couple provides the movie's worst moment. The final bonus, though, is ethnic jokes; what the primitive in us craves as much as violence and sex has found a socially acceptable habitat in the mouths of babes. So one of them will exclaim in disgust: "Jews, spics, niggers—now *girls!*" and the audience roars with delight.

But the film has genuine virtues along with the spurious ones. Ritchie has directed the kids most persuasively, even when the script gives them deeds and dialogue that are not really credible. (At other times, though, they are.) From Matthau he gets one of his crustiest and unforcedly funniest performances, which does not let even such dazzling youngsters as Tatum O'Neal, Alfred W. Lutter, and Jackie Earle Haley steal the show. And Ritchie is marvelous at shooting action on the diamond, whether comic or tense. But he is most brilliant in moments of waiting, between plays or ploys, when people are nervously twitching or fidgeting, blinking or scratching themselves—when expectant emptiness begins to burst at the seams. Add to this fine cinematography by John A. Alonzo and jolly background-musical fiddling with the score of *Carmen* by Jerry Fielding, and you've got yourself a ball, if not a hit.

April 19, 1976

Bungle Gym

With the current *Stay Hungry,* Bob Rafelson demonstrates that a straining for eccentricity under the guise of originality, and basically trivial people and dialogue with a coating of the bizarre over them are his true hallmark. It is one thing to make a movie about body-builders, the ambiguous Mr. Americas or Mr. Worlds who muscle in on certain beaches where, like other beached whales, they become objects of mingled awe and ridicule; but it is quite another to make these fanatics of the superhealthy body with no room in it for a mind, healthy or otherwise, into a symbol of noble striving, a grand alternative to commercialism and greed.

Based on a novel by Charles Gaines, with a script by Gaines and Rafelson, the film concerns young Craig Blake, who, after the accidental death of his parents, becomes the heir to some steel money in Birmingham, Alabama, and to a southern mansion in a state of discreet decay. On his uncle's advice, he gives up a life of sport and idleness to become the silent partner to a remarkably crooked combine that seems to come straight out of a Charles Bronson movie; his assignment is to acquire inexpensively the solitary holdout on a block that is to be converted into a monstrous high-rise. This holdout is the Olympic Health Spa, where body-builders including Joe Santo, Mr. Austria and chief contender for the Mr. World title, are working out. (I may be wrong about the title; it may actually be Mr. Universe. Arnold Schwarzenegger, who plays the part, has been Mr. Olympic, Mr. World, and Mr. Universe so many times that even he probably no longer remembers which is which.) The Spa is run by Erickson, a gruff oddball of a giant who drinks, pops pills, has kinky sexual tastes, and probably a heart of gold. Certainly a head of mush.

As instructed, Blake infiltrates the rickety Spa—karate for ladies downstairs, serious body-building for gents upstairs—and befriends its colorful denizens like Joe Santo, who often wears a Batman outfit with mask, and Mary Tate Farnsworth, the cute little receptionist who used to be Joe's girl friend. You can guess that Blake gets more and more involved with the Spa, and with Mary Tate in particular, and concomitantly estranged from his snobbish class, "suitable" girls, and traditional way of life. In the end he defies the corporation and their gangster tactics; fights a terrific battle with Erickson, whom they have managed to corrupt; and chucks everything to marry Mary Tate (whom in a moment of recidivism he almost lost forever) and become the new manager of the Spa. The climax of the film is the brief takeover of Birmingham by the Mr. Universe contestants in their briefs—a veritable Invasion of the Body-Builders.

All this is clearly meant as a parable, the old American fiction of pastoral innocence against urban wickedness, but with a twist: goodness now lives in the heart of the city, a *rus in urbe* in the shape of the Olympic Health Spa, whereas the country is degenerating into greed, lust, and snobbish arrogance from which the façade of genteel tradition is rapidly peeling. Greater talents than the filmmakers' might just have carried off this urban pastoral (or, perhaps, urban postural?), but greater talents would have recognized the Spa people for the Snopeses they really are, and not tried to idealize them tritely and foolishly. They would have faced the disturbing implications of these exaggerated physiques—Concorde aircrafts made out of meat—and perceived the ominous parallels between a greedy urban development corporation and corporal developers who build hideous high-rises under their skins.

Rafelson tries for fewer fancy effects than is his wont, which would be fine if his unfancy effects were an improvement. After an ambitious beginning—a series of dissolves showing Blake and his horse idling through the countryside, while a practical-minded uncle speaks the contents of his admonitory letter in voice-over—the movie settles down to fairly straightforward action filmmaking and atmospherics. But that beginning gives away some of the basic weaknesses: the bucolic images lack genuine appeal, and the writing is platitudinous. The uncle, played by Woodrow Parfrey, has an attitudinizing voice, as of a young man straining to sound old; Victor Kemper, one of our least distinguished cinematographers, has a way of making nature look dull: his camera puts chlorine into the chlorophyll.

Still, a closer and more realistic look at the Spa people could have worked. But Joe Santo, for example, is shown as a simple, shy, unnarcissistic heterosexual who plays a mean country fiddle and advocates painstaking physical development with homespun philosophy about having to burn in order to grow. He also avoids prolonged relationships with women because one must "stay hungry"; I take this as an inversion of the Pauline teachings that it is better to marry than to burn. Why Blake, though, should be permitted the comforts of marriage to Mary Tate is unclear, unless it is an axiom that a Spa receptionist and champion water-skier will train your body rather than drain it.

It is yet more characteristic of Rafelson's ideological and technical confusion that he gives us simultaneously a melodramatic and a comic climax; the fight to the death between Erickson and Blake, and the body-builders turning all of Birmingham into an outdoor gym. Intercutting takes the sting out of the fight (itself preposterously exaggerated: blows and weapons that could stop a panzer column barely denting the human frame) and prevents us from savoring the comedy undisturbed. Even the casting and acting are not up to previous Rafelson standards; there are bad, or at least mannered, performances from R. G. Armstrong, Woodrow Parfrey, Helena Kallianiotes, Scatman Crothers, and a truly dull one from Sally Field, the former Flying Nun, as a definitely unsoaring Mary Tate. Arnold Schwarzenegger is a likable Santo, both when he fiddles and when he burns, but his muted delivery of every line becomes monotonous. Jeff Bridges (Blake) is good as always: natural and winning, and never resorting to the kinds of mannerisms that make, for instance, Miss Kallianiotes a continual pain to watch.

The Sailor Who Fell From Grace With the Sea, Lewis John Carlino's film based on Yukio Mishima's novella, is very pretty to look at and makes absolutely no sense. It concerns a small gang of boys in their early teens who kill a sailor about to marry the widowed mother of one of them—kill him because they feel he has betrayed the perfect order of things by abandoning the perilous, glorious sea for landlocked, bourgeois safety. They are, as you might guess, an unusual bunch of kids, who also dissect old household tabbies and dynamite seagulls in midair, and they do not in the least belong in the small seaside town of Dartmouth in Devonshire, where they could at best have been characters in some updated version of *Stalky & Co.* But even the kids that Mishima invented for the busy port city of Yokohama are only a shade more believable there.

In his Mishima biography, John Nathan, the English translator of *Sailor,* quotes from an autobiographical essay of Mishima's dating from the same period as the novella: "What remains then is the concept of death present, momentary, instant-to-instant death. It seems likely that to me this is the only truly enticing, truly vivid, truly erotic concept." In his important book, *The Nobility of Failure: Tragic Heroes in the History of Japan,* Ivan Morris instructs us that Mishima was an admirer of Wang Yang-ming, a sixteenth-century scholar-official and founder of a school of Confucianism whose followers "were men . . . forever mindful of their own deaths, knowing that their . . . refusal to compromise with the world's injustice would almost certainly lead them to a violent end. . . ." And we know how Mishima, impelled by his philosophical, political, and sexual propensities, did in fact end. The proper locale for the movie, then, would be neither Dartmouth nor Yokohama, but the theater of war inside Mishima's tormented psyche.

In the novel, though, the sailor is at least very nearly the central character, and his dual perception of life at sea as both fascinating and dreary contrasts interestingly with his complementary ambivalance about the young widow he gets involved with, who represents both *embourgeoisement* and death to him. Recollected images and adventures of the sea race through the hero's mind constantly, and form a compelling counterpoint to what happens on land; Carlino's screenplay and direction eliminate all of this except for one or two set pieces, and so the underlying doubleness of the book dwindles into simplistic singleness. But there is worse. The Devon land- and seascape, particularly as photographed by Douglas Slocombe with a kind of gorgeous Tchaikovskian schmaltz, are far more romantic than anything in the sailor's life as seen by the movie. So the yearning of our sailor, who now hails from Topeka, Kansas, for this demiparadise to settle into seems very much part of some perfect order of things.

And still worse: in a Japanese setting, the fanatical formalism of the boys becomes an almost credible motivating force; in a European milieu, what appears to motivate the widow's son is an erotic, Oedipal relationship to his mother, whom he watches through a peephole as she masturbates in the nude. In this Western context, we perceive a clearly Freudian situation, with the jealous son murdering the surrogate father. But this is not what Mishima has written and what Carlino has more or less followed, and the non- or anti-Freudian twists of the plot now seem perversely disorienting—or orientalizing. Moreover, the incidents that Carlino thinks up for the boys are either much too Nietzschean or quite self-contradictory. Particularly preposterous is the "Chief" of the group, probably the least convincing fictional child since

Hardy's Little Father Time. He is badly acted, besides, by Earl Rhodes; indeed, all the kids under Carlino's direction act and speak as if they had had starch poured over them.

There are some compensations. Besides the already mentioned scenic beauties, there is also the extraordinary sensual appeal and splendid performance of Sarah Miles, than whom no one has ever better conveyed naked sexual longing. Her masturbation scene, for example, is deeply erotic, without becoming in the least bit tasteless. For what makes Miss Miles such a genuinely sensual presence on screen is that she does not stop there—that she embodies a full-blooded human being in its manifold aspects, placing the sexuality in context, which is the only way to make us care for and share in it. Miss Miles is, moreover, stunning of face and body, and *mirabile visu,* incarnates perfectly one of Mishima's lines: "Her haughty breasts inclined sharply away from her body. . . ." Miss Miles's breasts are among the haughtiest and most inclining-away I have ever seen.

Kris Kristofferson, who has lost so much weight that he seems to be rattling around in his own clothes, plays the sailor without any expression, any suggestion of inner life. He has peculiar eyes, anyway; they look like two artificial craters cut into the massif of his face, with some insipid blue liquid filling them. Or perhaps they are conversation pits in which no one is conversing. However, Kristofferson has contributed a not unpleasing sea-motif to the otherwise undistinguished score by John Mandel.

Lipstick is a meretricious shocker based on a California case in which a woman shot the man who raped her. Any intelligent discussion of rape and its consequences would, of course, be very welcome, but this movie, aside from various other exploitative atrocities, has the victim's kid sister raped by the same man later on to justify big sister's shooting him dead. This cravenly evades the principal issue, besides being an excuse for further cheap thrills. Margaux Hemingway is good on the eye, terrible on the ear, and somewhere in between as a performer, but her real-life little sister, Mariel, is a genuine find. Lamont Johnson has directed flashily; Bill Butler has photographed sometimes brilliantly, sometimes only splashily; and there is a trashy score by Michael Poniareff that violates your sensibility. Among its lesser horrors, the film also features virulent anti-intellectualism.

April 26–May 3, 1976

Blue Bird of Sappiness

ALL TRULY GREAT CHILDREN'S BOOKS are aimed clandestinely at adults. Maurice Maeterlinck's graceful, and probably closet, drama, *The Blue Bird,* is no exception. By 1908, the Belgian writer had moved from symbolism (e.g., *Pelléas et Mélisande*), through neoromanticism (e.g., *Monna Vanna*), to an ultimate, allegorical mysticism. "Maeterlinck," wrote Max Beerbohm at the time of the London premiere of *The Blue Bird,* "is not less a sage than a poet." This "masterpiece of his later years" seems today ever so slightly dimmed, and when the great literary historian Albert Thibaudet refers to it as "a masterwork of the allegorical theater" and speaks of a switch from symbolism to allegorism, I detect a faintly elegiac note. Yet there is much to be said for the remark of another French critic, René Lalou: "Maeterlinck's art had never before deployed this easefulness that entertains children at the very moment it obliges adults to meditate on their destiny. Never has [this art] surpassed the profound beauty and pathos of the Cemetery and Gardens of Happinesses scenes."

Well, the current movie version omits precisely those two scenes (except for a fragment of the latter), but it is almost impossible to determine whether it is kinder to the scenes it omits or to the ones it includes. It turns a work for adults that children can enjoy into a charade for children that must sicken adults. And not even for all children—only very small or very tasteless ones. I saw the movie with a large group of underprivileged kids, infiltrated by a small group of manifestly privileged ones, and the only genuine laughter and cheers came at the very end, when the kids could finally go home.

Where to begin? To make a film as a politically prestigious U.S.-U.S.S.R. coproduction is an artistically risky undertaking, and the filming, we learn, has provided some of the most unsmooth sailing since that famous time the battleship *Potemkin* put to sea. But that is no artistic excuse, any more than the casting of Elizabeth Taylor in four parts is artistically excusable. It should have been obvious even to a producer that whoever plays the Mother and Maternal Love cannot, even if she had versatility, play also the Witch and Light, for it totally destroys the symbolism. And the lesson of previous productions or common sense (at least one of which should be available even to producers) could have demonstrated that Light must be played by (a) a golden blonde, and (b) an actress, since this is the pivotal role. Miss Taylor is about as much one as the other. Light represents that *amor intellectualis* that Maeterlinck perceived as, along with maternal love, a chief vital force, and to put an overcostumed, overbejeweled, overmade-up, and undertalented star with a voice barely more grown-up than that of little Mytyl into that role is something midway between the crassest exploitativeness and imbecility.

Consider, next, Ava Gardner. If someone must play Luxury, a part that does not exist in the original, why pick a performer who, histrionically as well as visually, at best suggests penury? And as a gross example of the film's corruptness, let me cite the end of the banquet episode. In the play, the carousing Fat Pleasures are swept away in a rout, and the scene changes to a garden where the Little Happinesses dance in a round. In the movie, a wind does arise, to be sure, but not so much to leave us with an image of vanity and desolation as to lift Miss Gardner's long skirt and provide us with a final vision of her last remaining asset: a pair of truly shapely legs. Very good for Miss Gardner's ego, but thoroughly destructive of the scene's point.

Take the very structure of the screen adaptation. The original begins with Tyltyl and his even smaller sister Mytyl waking up at night to look out of their humble cottage window and partake vicariously of the rich kids' Christmas feast across the way; we are not shown this, of course, and it is much more effectively conveyed through the eyes and words of the poor children. The film has them go out and trudge through the snow to an actual palace, which, among other bad things, militates against the dream journey to follow. The fairy Berylune (the movie's Witch) next appears in the play, anthropomorphizes domestic objects and animals, and the quest for the symbolic Blue Bird, longed for by the fairy's sick daughter, begins. The marvelous journey is only gradually revealed to be a dream rather than a miracle, just as the kids gradually discern that reality is no less beautiful than the dream: that their skimpy but not desperate circumstances are, in fact, the embodiment of all kinds of love and loveliness, if only you are en-Lightened enough to see through to the essence of creatures and things. And by way of confirmation, the neighbor woman turns out to be a replica of the old fairy Berylune, and her pretty little sick daughter the image of Light. Reality has come to meet the dream, and, in its modest but tangible way, to surpass it.

The movie, however, stupidly overexplains what is unmistakable by beginning with reality: the neighbor, the sick child, the rich kids' Christmas spelled out in garish literalness; later, their dream transformation is drummed in ad nauseam. The result is the diametrical opposite of the wanted effect: the dream becomes the beautiful but unattainable transubstantiation of oppressive reality. I know nothing of Hugh Whitemore, but from his coscenarist, Alfred Hayes, I would have expected more—except that he was probably working under duress. The scenes with the humanoid animals and objects are likewise cut or ruined. Throughout the play, they represent conflicting human tendencies in significant combat; the movie sees them mostly as curiosities, and severely curtails their roles. Often they are mere excuses for ballet sequences, poorly choreographed by Igor Belsky and Leonid Jakobson, and wretchedly, if at all, integrated into the action.

Here we come to the film's greatest failure, its lack of unified style. George Cukor, the director, cannot be blamed for everything—not, for example, for having shod Tyltyl and Mytyl. Neither the United States nor the Soviet Union would want to show such Maeterlinckian poverty as barefoot children; but what about the poverty of imagination? Granted, ballet is very hard to put on film, but must it be made to look so arbitrary, be shot so unlyrically, and vanish altogether from the expressive vocabulary once the characters stop dancing? Nowhere does the film manage to fuse its disparate elements: fantasy, naturalism, and a kind of cheap functionalism, as when dance floors are left looking exactly like well-waxed dance floors, rather than like ordinary spaces transmuted by the magic of dance. Worse yet is the way natural forest backgrounds, for instance, pop up in the middle of fantasy sequences—as if a Grimm fairy tale changed, in mid-paragraph, into Hemingway.

The production design by Brian Wildsmith is execrable: overblown without a trace of elegance or wit. Wildsmith is also guilty of the illustrations that turn into live sequences or vice versa; these illustrations are crude, and the transitions are anything but seamless. The costumes by Marina Azizian and, predictably, Edith Head for the principals—the Marxist egalitarianism of the

Soviet atmosphere cannot touch your Lizzes and Avas—are equal at least in their tastelessness. All concerned could have profited immeasurably by consulting, say, the Piazza edition of *L'Oiseau bleu* (Paris, 1945), illustrated by André E. Marty, for ideas about how things should look.

To come back to Cukor, however: why pick him for the project? There is nothing in his past to suggest that he can handle fantasy; what has distinguished him most is his ability to manipulate temperamental female stars, from Garbo and Hepburn on down. I do hope Hollywood votes him a special Oscar for a long career in lioness-taming, but as for his film-directing, consider only the rotten special effects he let pass here, such as a flock of bluebirds of sappiness to make Disney whirl around in his grave.

Scene after lovely scene, line after telling line, are omitted, toned down, misdirected, or misacted. Style means, among other things, unity of tone, and how do you get that by casting, for example, a very American Todd Lookinland as Tyltyl, and a pronouncedly British Patsy Kensit as his sister Mytyl? The same absurdity is repeated on the parental and grandparental levels, making the movie into a kind of parable of Anglo-American intermarriage. The Russian actors, carefully relegated to subsidiary roles, are dubbed into a lifelessly polite British, which clashes with the little bit of vitality they are allowed to show. None of the supporting players does well; shatteringly, even such excellent actresses as Jane Fonda and Cicely Tyson emerge inane, and that gifted and stunning little ballerina, Nadezhda Pavlova, makes less of a Blue Bird than an ass of herself.

And the children? Max Beerbohm sagely wrote: "It is essential that Tyltyl should be, or seem to be, a little boy . . . not a day more than eight years of age. To seem on the stage like a little boy of eight is beyond the powers of any actual little boy of eight; he appears as an awful little automaton of eighty. And five minutes of him appears as an eternity." Master Lookinland is not exactly an automaton; neither, though, is he a spontaneous innocent or genuine actor. Patsy Kensit is a cute Mytyl, but not much of an actress either, and further cursed with reminding one of Goldie Hawn—let us pray that she outgrows it. Even Robert Morley is miscast as Father Time, which brings me to one more horrible example I must cite. The scene with the two unborn children known as the Lovers lasts only a couple of minutes in the play, but is one of the most moving onstage love stories ever written; the movie trims it down to less than one minute, casts a couple of unisex kids who do not even suggest a man and a woman, omits a key line or two, and directs the remnant so undramatically that it might serve as an emblem for the imaginative failure of the entire film.

Let me add only that the music by Irwin Kostal and Andrei Petrov is unutterably banal, that Tony Harrison's lyrics are cutesy at best, and that even the cinematography by the usually magnificent Freddie Young, and Ionas Gritzus, who has at least sometimes done better, is disheartening. When Tyltyl opens the brass door behind which Night keeps the wars locked up, there pour out soldiers in various uniforms from medieval armor to that of (O the obviousness of it!) Nazi storm troopers. It would have been more appropriate to show the forces of Fox and Lenfilm at each other's throats while trampling on the prostrate form of Maurice Maeterlinck.

May 24, 1976

The Decline of the Western

THE WESTERN IS IN TROUBLE. Hailed by various Bicentennial hacks as the great American myth or great American art form, it may prove to be the great American embarrassment. For a long time it could thrive on shooting up Indians, until we recognized our national guilt, and shooting up Indians, at least as a heroic accomplishment, became taboo. Which left outlaws. You could still shoot *them* up and look good. But that began to give a funny image of the Old West: nothing but varmints shooting decent folk and lawmen shooting varmints, and in between a lot of frightened people gumming up the fireworks. Besides, after the millionth variation on the archetypal plot, it starts to pall on everyone except fanatics and simpletons—though these may never be in short supply, thus ensuring ever more farfetched, adulterated, and desperate westerns a ghoulish sort of immortality.

What hasn't been tried? Adult or psychological westerns, revisionist or pro-Indian westerns (e.g., *Little Big Man*), comic or parody westerns, musical and ethnic (i.e., black or Jewish) westerns, anarchic or pro-outlaw westerns (say, *The Wild Bunch*), antiwestern westerns (such as *Dirty Little Billy*), imported Italian or Japanese (spaghetti or sukiyaki) westerns—even children's westerns (e.g., *The Cowboys*), except that, in an important sense, all westerns are children's westerns. The salient fact about them is not that they preserve for us an idea of the hero, but that they preserve a particularly infantile idea of him. Even if he is not merely killing Indians or outlaws by the dozen, he is still a purely physical, anti-intellectual, American-imperialist hero—in short, an epic hero in an age that, everywhere except in the movies, has outgrown the epic. He stands for the most antiquated patriarchal values, and his attitude toward women in particular is equally unappetizing whether he lifts his ten-gallon hat off his ten-cubic-centimeter brain to them to salute his future cooks and breeders, or whether he whoops it up with them in the saloon-*cum*-cathouse, which is as far as he permits a few of them to range from the home on the range.

The most depressing part of a remarkably foolish and jingoistic piece on westerns by Grace Lichtenstein in the *Times* of May 16 was the news of a coming six-day conference in Sun Valley on "Western Movies: Myths and Images," whose participants will include: one western star, one western director, one western writer, one film historian, one Yale historian, one *American Heritage* magazine staffer, and two *Time* film reviewers. Whoever organized this convocation of giants was careful not to invite any Indian militants or film critics not known to salivate at the mention of the word *western.*

Let's face it: nothing so simple-minded as your basic western can be a work of art. Yet in his new book on John Ford, Andrew Sarris calls his subject "one of the cinema's greatest poets." More aptly, the late Charles Thomas Samuels, in *Mastering the Film,* a posthumous collection of his film writings, refers to Ford as a director having "a set of characteristic subjects frequently confused with a style." It is, of course, perfectly all right for the cinema to have its Robert Service or Joaquin Miller—both of whom, rolled into one, Ford may have been—but let us not confuse our little escapist pleasures with great poetry. Even so, Ford's "classic" westerns were at least honestly naïve artifacts like the paintings of Grandma Moses, far from the noxious new species of what might be called absurdist westerns, a genre pioneered by Robert Benton and David Newman and perfected by Thomas McGuane in the unbearably coy and phony *Rancho Deluxe,* and now in the still more coy and phony, as well as deeply distasteful, *The Missouri Breaks.*

McGuane (which must be an Anglicization of the ancient Irish name of McGuano) is also a repellent novelist, author of *The Sporting Club* and *Ninety-Two in the Shade,* both duly turned into repellent movies. With *The Missouri Breaks* he has surpassed himself as scenarist, exhibiting a charismatic gift for dragging down his betters with him—the worthy Arthur Penn, who directed, and Marlon Brando, who did something remotely resembling acting. McGuane, who lives on a Montana ranch, is quoted as saying he would have been a cowboy if writing had not kept getting in his way. By a curious coincidence, the same thing keeps getting in the way of his becoming a writer.

The Missouri Breaks starts out as a mere revisionist western. David Braxton is a powerful landowner who has taken justice into his own hands and casually hangs pleasant young cattle rustlers or horse thieves while discoursing to them about his extensive library—book-reading obviously makes a man mean as hell. Abandoned by his wife, he is hated by his daughter Jane, a spirited girl full of noble values until she starts crawling ludicrously to Tom Logan (Jack Nicholson), the leader of the gang of thieves, now posturing as a homesteader. Logan is compassionate, imaginative, brave, witty, and self-controlled, the very model of the varmint as the last Christian gentleman. True, his little band comprises hot young bloods and the occasional psychopath, but his second-in-command, the austere, elderly Calvin (well played by Harry Dean Stanton), had every right to go wrong as a youngster after his dad (or was it his stepdad?) shot the dog that was his only true friend. As further proof of how truthful, how honestly demythologizing, the film is, we are shown a brothel run, not by a grand, blowsy madam, but by a pitiful bunch of crones prostituting a bunch of bedraggled—scrawny or dumpy—young women.

Well, we have seen the hanging as a fiesta before, in *True Grit;* and the pathetic prostitutes in *McCabe and Mrs. Miller.* What we have not seen is the Shane-figure, here called a regulator, Lee Clayton, as a combination Dostoevskian Grand Inquisitor, Restoration-comedy fop, and Hibernian vaudeville comic. As conceived by McGuane and embodied—or should I say enlarded?—by Marlon Brando, he is as preposterous and odious a character as I have ever encountered in movies or fiction, and one in whom the moral sleaziness of the film comes into ghastly focus. For it is plain that we are supposed to love this fellow for his outrageousness while hating him for doing in the outlaws who are, after all, only trying to make a modest living at the expense of the likes of Braxton and the mighty Canadian mounties, good for many an anti-Canadian joke in the film. As it happens, our moral instincts would want to admire the man as a justicer and despise him for his inane antics, but this the thrust of the film forbids us to do. By the time Clayton at long last gets his comeuppance from Logan—in a scene whose controlled horror is the one truly effective moment in the entire movie—we are obliged, again against our better judgment, to cheer an outlaw's tracking down an adjunct of the law.

So, too, Jane Braxton is supposed to be an enlightened young woman, but must make herself into a servilely aggressive piece of jelly to the first man who comes along, Tom Logan, who does not even exhibit a sincere interest in her, to say nothing of visible accomplishments. Consistency of characterization is, of course, out of the question here: Why, for instance, should the ultrashrewd regulator not scan the remnants of a house he burned down for Logan's remains, rather than stupidly accept a gang member's word that Logan was trapped in there? Much greater than the offenses against logic, though, are the offenses against taste: men are killed in the middle of copulation or defecation; Lee Clayton and his horse eat the same carrot from opposite ends until their lips meet in a kiss barely dreamt of by *Equus;* there is a bathtub scene showing Brando in the nude, where it is hard to determine which, or who, is the tub.

What really hurts, though, is the dialogue. It is all studied quirkiness, self-congratulatory cuteness, and insipid pseudopregnancy. No one ever talked like this in the West, East, North, or South. Such diction might be appropriate to a film that sets out to be unrealistic, say, *Cat Ballou;* but a film that out of one corner of its mouth professes down-to-earth debunking cannot, out of the other, indulge in surreal fantasy, especially if the stylization is done with an unsure, wavering hand. For even stylization cannot explain why a regulator known to be such should pretend to be a crazy bird-watcher—unless he really is crazy, in which case how could he be so very nearly invincible? Too bad that I cannot quote you some of the horrendous dialogue, but I was either so dismayed or so disbelieving of what I heard that I did not know where to begin taking down things.

Utterly lamentable, too, is Brando's performance, even more slatternly and self-indulgent than his bloated physique. Starting with a correspondence-school brogue and bits of mannerism left over from his garish performance in *The Nightcomers,* he adds to them an effeteness and smarminess that would keep even the likes of Braxton from hiring him. He comes across as a mixture of Rod Steiger doing *Hennessy* and Tallulah Bankhead doing Tallulah. His cutesy *moues* in the notorious bathtub scene are matched only by the abject ineptitude of Kathleen Lloyd as Jane Braxton, who turns what needed to be only a badly written lost soul into a full-fledged driveling idiot. At UCLA, she won the 1969 Hugh O'Brian Acting Award, which, I assume, is given annually for the best impersonation of Hugh O'Brian trying to act.

Only Jack Nicholson comes out of this mess well-nigh unscathed, almost succeeding in turning the nullity handed him by the filmmakers into a living character—a not unremarkable feat. Michael Butler's photography is better than usual, but still has a long way to go; John Williams's score is brash and pointless. I do not understand Arthur Penn: What happens to all that charm, perspicacity, and worldliness he displays in conversation when he starts making pictures like *Night Moves,* and the still tawdrier and trashier *The Missouri Breaks?* He seems to be obsessed with trying to heighten genre films into art. Couldn't he pick something easier—say, making silk purses out of sows' ears?

May 31, 1976

Head Ache

READERS OF MY CRITICISM will know by now that its writer believes in film as art, and in art as a form of humanism. Consequently, the true enemy is not silly bits of exploitation like *Embryo,* bad as they may be; the enemy is pretentious nonart or anti-art posturing as art and subverting artistic integrity by turning inhuman pseudo-art into something the semiliterate, the inexperienced young, and the learned fools with anti-Establishment axes to grind can hail as daring, relevant, and artistically important.

I am sure that from idiot-savant movie buffs to sterile academics out to discover a new masterpiece, legions are standing by to proclaim the significance of Nicolas Roeg's *The Man Who Fell to Earth*—to write structuralist or semiological tracts about it, or simply to trumpet its profound meanings. In point of fact, it is, like all of Roeg's films, the blowing up of something simple or simple-minded to arrogantly bloated dimensions and purporting to be chock-full of hermetic truths merely awaiting their interpreters. But a plague of Roeg mystagogues is worse than a plague of locusts. When Roeg's first opus, *Performance,* a collaboration with an even more consummate poseur, Donald Cammell (who has since mercifully disappeared), came out, I denounced it in the Sunday *Times* as a prime example of the Loathsome Film, a genre that subsists purely on shock value, cheap thrills, decadent artiness, glorification of amorality, and sheer mystification. *Performance* duly became a cult film, and Roeg went on to such items as *Walkabout, Don't Look Now,* and now this—all "head" movies, turn-ons for addicts, which, however, is not the real problem. The real problem is that an illiterate or pseudoliterate age hails them as art. Indeed, when the Comparative Literature Association in a meeting at USC first deigned to address itself to a film, the picture chosen—with the approval of the chairman (John Russell Taylor) over the strenuous protest of the cochairman (me)—was *Don't Look Now.*

There is a sort of haiku by the German poet Arnfrid Astel that runs in its entirety: "I write. But he/against whom I write/cannot read." It exactly describes my feelings when, for the fourth time, I return to point out the ugliness of Roeg's filmmaking. Nick (as he was then known) Roeg was a very talented British cameraman, with films like *The Girl Getters, Nothing But the Best, Fahrenheit 451, Far From the Madding Crowd, Petulia* among his credits; unfortunately, he had to become Nicolas Roeg and set himself up as a director. A curse seems to hang over British cinematographers who follow this route. Jack Cardiff, who had shot such visually impressive films as *Black Narcissus, The Red Shoes,* and *War and Peace,* was, as director, to turn out stuff like *Scent of Mystery* and *The Mutation;* Freddie Francis, who had so sensitively photographed *Room at the Top* and Cardiff's own *Sons and Lovers,* is now churning out rot like *Tales From the Crypt, Tales That Witness Madness,* and other tales told by an idiot.

Roeg has fared no better; in fact, his pretentiousness makes it all considerably worse. *Performance* was a mindless tribute to drugs, androgyny, polymorphous perversity, and violence that invoked and vulgarized such prestigious names as Nietzsche and Jorge Luis Borges while stealing and debasing the cinematic inventions of Bergman and Antonioni. Mick Jagger's presence was one of the ugliest and sickest I have ever seen on film; James Fox, who costarred, reacted to the movie by giving up acting to become a religious proselytizer in the Midlands. Next, Roeg turned to a graceful, straightforward minor novel, *The Children,* by the Australian writer James Vance Marshall, and converted it, with the help of Edward Bond, into *Walkabout,* a hysterical indictment of civilization and science full of weird photographic effects, maniacal crosscutting and chronology-jumbling (his favorite devices), making sure that the story became all but impossible to follow.

With *Don't Look Now,* Roeg latched on to a tawdry horror story by Daphne Du Maurier, and proceeded to pump it full of grandly vacuous statements about life, death, love, art, religion, and whatnot (especially whatnot). There was, again, enough artsy crosscutting (particularly in the big sex scene) and flashing backward and forward to have Roeg arrested as a flasher. The shoddy underlying material, blown up, dragged out, worried to would-be metaphysical significance, became merely ludicrous, and, ipso facto, the delight of specialists in false profundity.

In *The Man Who Fell to Earth,* based on what I assume is an ordinary sci-fi novel by Walter Tevis, Roeg reuses all his old tricks, notably the oldest: casting a pop star with androgynous, unisex appeal in the lead—this time, David Bowie. But whereas Mick Jagger at least had some energy, however repugnant, Bowie comes across as an expressionless zombie. Correction: a zombie who, beyond a blank, has one expression that must do for both anxiety and bliss. It consists of suddenly baring the gums at the corners of the mouth—a horrible effect, like a nutcracker trying to smile. (I think I owe this trope to someone else; if so, would its owner please claim it?) It will, of course, be gleefully objected that since Bowie plays a being from outer space, his ephebic, expressionless quality is just right. But there must be a difference, at least histrionically, between the outer-space and the spaced-out, between the superhuman and the infrahuman, between enacting a certain impassivity and just being a blob.

I defy anyone to come up with a coherent synopsis of this film, let alone an explication of the individual scenes and resolution of the inconsistencies, contradictions, and preposterous non sequiturs that litter it from the very start. Thus the arrival of our space traveler on earth is already surveyed by a mysterious observer, presumably a member of the CIA (never named but clearly implied) who is to hound him and prove his undoing, even though as yet no such person could have been around. Why must our hero, who can have many plausible reasons for traveling decently, bum around the country suspiciously with a British passport? Or, later, be chauffeured in a superlimousine, but put up in cheap hotels? In other words, simultaneously try to avert and attract attention? What connection is there between his antagonist the chemistry professor's fatal attraction to very young girls, including (as far as I can unscramble it) cohabitation with his own daughter, and what follows? How, when, and why is the professor enlisted by the CIA? Why does our hero marry the well-meaning, silly elevator operator, Mary Lou, and then treat her as shabbily as he does? When he reverts to his outer-space identity and still wants to have sex (as near as I can make it out), what does Mary Lou see in his genital region that drives her berserk? (As usual in Roeg sex scenes, there had to be some cutting before the film could be released.) How does the CIA profit from meaningless defenestrations? Why is our hero's attempt to return to outer space foiled? What, if any, is the meaning of the closing scenes?

The point of all this is ambiguity, contradiction, or fuzziness for its own sake. If it is antinarrative and inscrutable, it is deep. And if it is deep, all you need is a fix while viewing it, and you can splash about in the private swimming pool of the Universal Mystery. Not only that; you are also partaking of a Great Artistic Experience. Small surprise that the main audiences for Roeg consist of "heads" without brains and academic "brains" without a head on their shoulders: Roeg has to be swallowed uncritically whole, or casuistically overexplicated; there is no other way.

Take the emblematic sequence when the hero is playing Ping-Pong with his earth-wife (this interstellar bigamist has a space-wife, too) in their eccentric desert domicile. Both are wearing expensive tennis (*not* table tennis) outfits. Smack on the Ping-Pong table, Mary Lou has to her right a full cocktail glass, to her left a fanciful container holding scores of balls, one of which she takes out for each new play. There is a low-hanging, elaborate chandelier just above the net. The walls, all around, are covered with a *trompe l'oeil* mural of autumnal woods, and the floor is strewn with actual sere leaves! A dart board hangs on one wall, presumably in case one wishes to complicate the game a little. Meanwhile the dialogue—as usual in this Paul Mayersberg script—is fraught with pregnant platitudes. Well, ladies and gentlemen, this is no way to make a significant movie; it is not even a way of playing Ping-Pong.

The cinematography, by Tony Richmond, is expert, and a few effects are quite exciting. The performances are mostly routine, with people like Rip

Torn and Buck Henry going through their standard motions. Even the make-up doesn't make sense: characters age at entirely different rates. The one serious performance comes from Candy Clark as Mary Lou, and though it is often affecting, it is, for that very reason, out of keeping with the rest of the film. As always in a Roeg film, there is a good deal of sexual intercourse, which gets intercut with something else. Here it is intercut with more intercourse—spatial intercourse, which differs from the terrestrial kind in that it is more boring to watch. There is also some interracial nudity, fantastic gadgetry, and opulent interior decoration. What is most on display, though, is Roeg's third-rate sensibility frantically aspiring to the second-rate.

June 14, 1976

Who Is Buffaloing Whom?

WE DESPERATELY NEED a major American film director: someone of our time, but not only for our time; someone with all the technical proficiency, but also the imagination that such proficiency must subserve. After the army of solid achievers that has distinguished American filmmaking, it is time for the unquestioned artist—the one Orson Welles began to be with *Citizen Kane,* the one we hoped Kubrick or X or Y or Z might turn into. Along came Robert Altman and our hopes perked up: *M*A*S*H* held out genuine promise, and even if his next few films ranged from the mildly to the wildly disappointing, there was a sense of an authentic technique and a willingness to take chances having joined forces and set out in search of a subject, a vision, a breakthrough into the core of humanity from some new angle.

Then *Nashville* came and was a qualified success—enough to make me wonder about the much longer version Altman wanted to release. There were good moments even in what we got, and quite a few of the risks taken paid off—less than lavishly, perhaps, but better than current interest rates. Above all, there was a laudable attempt to grasp a situation through a lot of representative characters and their interaction, which might have made for something new and valuable in movies, if only we could have had the four-, five-, or six-hour version that—in two parts, presumably—the film might have profitably justified.

But now we have *Buffalo Bill and the Indians or Sitting Bull's History Lesson,* and here, too, we have heard of problems with cutting and ending the film; yet seeing what is left inspires little confidence in any possible longer version. The two hours duration achieves nothing that could not have been done just as well in ninety minutes, and what sustains us much of the time is not absence of boredom but the assumption that so much artful quaintness must have something up its tasseled sleeve. In vain; this film makes me think that the center of Altman is made not of ideas, insights, visions, but of attitudes. And attitudes are not quite good enough.

The film is very, very remotely based on Arthur Kopit's play *Indians.* That was no great play, but it did latch on to and manipulate with some dexterity a good symbol: Buffalo Bill, the grand hero of the Old West, who was really William F. Cody, best at exterminating the buffalo, cheating the Indians, and befogging the public with self-serving spectacles presumed to be historical reenactments of American greatness. Out of this, and out of Chief Sitting Bull's having, in desperation, appeared for a while in Buffalo Bill's Wild West Show, Kopit was able to fashion a short play that had some suggestive images and resonant ironies. Also the good sense of not presenting a thoroughly rotten hero, fake all the way to his long locks (which the movie turns into a wig). For if he is to be the symbol of the deep ambiguities of our westward expansion, he must not be all bad. Yes, public and private injustices were committed left and right, but somewhere in the middle there was also a residue of heroism. Think of it: even the ancient Greeks, whom we revere above all peoples, took their peninsula by force from its previous inhabitants.

There are two sides to almost everything: William F. Cody was also a Pony Express rider, Indian scout, hunter, and entrepreneur of remarkable skill, however little you and I may value these talents. Neither is Sitting Bull an unequivocal figure. Was he Major James McLaughlin's, the Indian agent's, "mediocrity," inferior to many of his lieutenants; or, indeed, was he the arrogant coward described by E. A. Allison, the army scout who escorted him to Fort Buford, where he surrendered? Or was he the able, noble, and wise leader of Stanley Vestal and other revisionist historians? I don't know; what I do know is that Altman's sitting duck of a Buffalo Bill, this all black-and-white—or, rather, all red-and-black—history lesson with its consistently noble Indians and dependably ignoble whites will not wash. Not even if it is presented as madcap satire that is at times ingenious and amusing; there is, after all, more than one way of forking a tongue.

The screenplay Alan Rudolph and Altman have concocted is barely a screenplay at all; were someone to tell me that it was improvised *in situ* when shooting commenced in Alberta, Canada, I would readily believe it. For example, when Noelle Rogers, who plays the second of the opera singers Bill gets involved with, arrives on the scene, she sings a phrase from an obscure opera. "Handel's *Rinaldo,*" Bill announces with a knowing smirk. Now, the historic Cody had less than a year's schooling, and the film's protagonist is made into an even worse dunce; are we then to assume that bedding down with a few opera singers makes you into a tune detective? Actually, Miss Rogers was about to sing *Rinaldo* in real life, so the Handel got blithely thrown into the pot; and whereas a film can be as absurdist as it pleases, it cannot with impunity be inconsistent.

And it is not only the improvisational incoherences of the script that are problematical; there is also the notion that *texture* is all that matters, while *structure* can be allowed to shift for itself. It is not that I crave the overtailored plots of yesteryear; I do, however, want to see certain concepts worked out in dramatic terms. Let us call it a progression with intensification rather than mere brute accumulation of incidents. You could chop this movie up into tiny bits, splice them together in any order, and the result would not be appreciably less efficacious.

My point is that in order to deflate a balloon, you must first inflate it. Altman seems to assume that Buffalo Bill and the West are preinflated notions, ripe and ready for the pinprick. But are they? Cummings's famous "Buffalo Bill's Defunct" is a deflationary note that has resounded through numerous works of all kinds; for this film to be effective, some sort of pumping up was needed. Yet Altman begrudges his protagonist so much as his marksmanship; when a hated parakeet gets loose in his bedroom, Bill cannot hit it at almost point-blank range. And, in any case, two hours of unremitting deflation of one solitary subject makes *Buffalo Bill and the Indians* the longest pinprick on record.

It is not even as if Altman—or, at any rate, his film—weren't soft at the core. His Sitting Bull, too lofty to speak the palefaces' language, leaves all negotiations to his interpreter (well played by Will Sampson), and preserves throughout the movie a silence that becomes grander than golden—pure platinum. Annie Oakley, conceived and played by Geraldine Chaplin as a progressive finishing-school teacher, is magnanimous to the point of giving away most of her wardrobe to a needy squaw. And Ned Buntline (Burt Lancaster at his craggiest) cannot be a mere cynical potboiler-writer; he becomes a muckraker bordering on the philosopher-prophet, only part of which can be blamed on Lancaster's previous outing as Moses. Even Paul Lohmann's cinematography, espousing Remington's antiblue palette, achieves less irony than legend-bathed goldenness.

The problem, ultimately, extends beyond this picture to a certain monomania in Altman; it is all very well to want to knock off the American myths, one after another, but not to debunk the same one twice. The West already got kicked in the pants in *McCabe and Mrs. Miller;* show business got its comeuppance in *Nashville.* The present film, which is really a conflation of those two, thus ends up as a twofold tautology.

All this notwithstanding, there is, once again, substantial talent on display here. There is expert handling of the camera and actors (note especially the final barroom confrontation between Bill and Ned Buntline), some very able shooting of action and crowd scenes avoiding the usual clichés, apt use of the visual aside whereby the camera glancingly captures absurdities on the hoof, and intermittent but hearty comic sustenance for eye and ear. The editing is lively, the set and costume design consummate. Yet even some of this verges on cuteness, which seldom absents itself for very long, starting with the coy and confusing opening credits. The acting is a mixed bag: Paul Newman, just by being the fair-haired, blue-eyed boy in such a nasty context, cannot help scoring, and there is good work from many supporting players such as Joel Grey, Kevin McCarthy, and even Harvey Keitel, who seemed to me one-sided in the past but here neatly combines servile awe with asinine cockiness. But Bonnie Leaders strikes me as a poor singer, judging from her snatches of song, never mind actress; and Shelley Duvall, an Altman regular, is rapidly becoming one of the most predictably smarmy screen presences around.

I have no wish to talk anyone out of seeing this movie: Altman matters, and his very lapses are fringed with brightness. His quirks, though, have a way of getting the better of him—notably the mania for elaborately overlapping and studiedly blurred sound. I used to think that this was Altman's wrongheaded way of trying to approximate reality. It now looks more like a way of giving apparent significance to triviality—just as conceited people often talk extremely softly to make us strain for their every word. What good is Altman's celebrated eight-track sound if all it conveys is a one-track mind?

July 5, 1976

Hounds of Hell

THERE SEEMS TO EXIST a special kennel in Hollywood where pictures that were artistic dogs but popular successes are crossbred for the delectation of the great unwashed, and the even keener delight of the money men. Possibly the highest stud fees of the moment go to that champion hellhound, *The Exorcist,* and the prize bitch, *Rosemary's Baby,* whose latest whelp, *The Omen,* is certainly all dog from snout to tail. It was directed by Richard Donner, who comes from television serials, which may account for the film's being made up of isomorphic segments, each with its machine-tooled climax and archly suspenseful little hint about next week's installment, supposed to keep us on tenterhooks of delicious anticipation.

Actually, we cannot care less about what is going to happen to the manly American ambassador to the Court of St. James (Gregory Peck), his pretty but somewhat dense wife (Lee Remick), and their angelic five-year-old son—really a changeling spawned by the devil and about to grow into the Antichrist—and the mysterious hounds, peculiar nannies, and strange deaths that surround them. They range from the preposterous to the predictable, and nowhere can you glimpse a hint of subtlety or credibility. There is, however, quite a bit of amusement to be derived from a devil who allows photographs of his next victim to show seemingly inexplicable lines that point to the particular part of the anatomy where that unfortunate will be struck a mortal blow. I assume that this is done out of some spirit of sportsmanship, the Prince of Darkness being, after all, a gentleman. But theologians—who, no doubt, will ponder this movie as gravely as they did *The Exorcist*—may conclude that since early Christians believed that the arrival of the Antichrist would be followed closely by the Second Coming, it is precisely to the devil's interest to sabotage the coming of a harbinger of Christ's proximate victory, even if that harbinger is his own son.

The biggest laughs, though, come from a supposedly biblical prophecy translated into good American doggerel that serves as the movie's spiritual core; it predicts the coming of the Antichrist when, among other things, "the Holy Roman Empire rises," which the film's Bible exegetes interpret as the rise of the European Common Market! As for "the eternal sea" from which the Antichrist is to surface, it is interpreted as our turbulent politics, hence the smuggling of the imp into an ambassadorial family. Yet, surely, there must be a rival school of exegetes who read "the eternal sea" as the eternal C-pictures that Hollywood keeps churning out in A-picture trappings. The script is by David Seltzer, whose main previous credit is *The Hellstrom Chronicle*—clearly a man who believes that the world will perish not by fire or ice, but by insects or Antichrist.

The film has an elegant look, thanks largely to Carmen Dillon's art direction (though Pyrford Court, with its sixty-room mansion and thousand-acre estate, may be a bit too grand for an American ambassador, even if he is Gregory Peck), Gilbert Taylor's finely controlled color photography, and Lee Remick's stylish good looks. But this film is no place for some of the able supporting players to show off their talents; as for Peck, he worries and suffers as nobly as only a piece of granite can. Most annoying, however, is the music by that pretentious hack Jerry Goldsmith, who has cannibalized Stravinsky without crediting him.

Two footnotes. Gregory Peck must be bad at reading portents. As the star of a previous rotten film featuring impalement on a picket fence, you'd think he'd avoid another one with such an episode. And 666—the number of the beast in the Book of Revelation—figures so prominently in *The Omen* as to make me think it was intended as publicity for the Top of the Sixes.

Murder by Death can be described fairly accurately in terms of certain stock phrases, such as "a hilarious spoof of classic detective novels and movies," "vintage Neil Simon comedy," and "fun-filled ensemble acting by a distinguished cast." I say *fairly* accurately because the hilarity does take some serious dips here and there, because what Simon writes best (as he does here) is farce rather than comedy, and because the otherwise good to excellent cast has inflicted on it the worse than amateurish presence of Truman Capote. Hitherto I thought that Zsa Zsa Gabor was unique among performers in not even being able to play herself on screen; now Capote has snatched these sorry laurels from her. Though a good many of the film's jokes fall flat, Capote is the only one that is offensive. Enough said; *Murder by Death* is not a movie to write and read about, but to be seen and modestly enjoyed.

July 12, 1976

Unbabbling Brooks

IT IS A WELL-KNOWN FACT that, except once a year and then only for an hour, you cannot turn back the clock. Not in life, however much you might long to recapture lost youth; not in the economy, however much you may thirst for a good five-cent beer; not in art, however skillfully you might imitate Mozart or duplicate Vermeer. So, too, in movies there is something profoundly hopeless about trying to bring back the silents, as, for instance, Clarence Greene and Russell Rouse did with *The Thief* (1952). The thing smacked of gimmickry, was totally uncompelling, and happily started no trend.

It might, however, be supposed that Mel Brooks is on firmer ground with his new *Silent Movie,* a comedy about a once successful Hollywood director, ruined by alcohol, reformed and trying, with the help of two equally bungling sidekicks, to save a sinking studio by making a silent movie with some big stars. The rationale might be that silent comedy is believed by many to have been America's greatest contribution to the art of film, and that to emulate it even at this late date might prove beneficial—if only as a stimulant to that sense of visual comedy allegedly in abeyance since the heyday of Chaplin, Keaton, Lloyd, and the rest. Inspired slapstick, the argument might run, has no need of words, except perhaps for the occasional intertitle; and the nostalgia for "comedy's greatest era," as James Agee dubbed it, might provide a source of emotions ready to be tapped.

Against this, it can be claimed that nostalgia is one of the flimsier human sentiments, rather like crying over spilt milk; that Mel Brooks's comic gift, such as it is, is largely verbal and stands to lose too much in a silent movie; and that what was once done so well was done out of necessity, the need to overcome the limitations of a mute medium. Remove the necessity, which is the mother of invention, and you come up with test-tube babies of scant viability.

In the event, *Silent Movie* has some quite funny sight gags, though the invention wears progressively thinner; it also has exaggerated sound effects that have good and bad moments; it has, further, a puckish score by John Morris that sometimes merely puckers; and there are some amusing intertitles. The three musketeers, or *meeskites,* played by Mel Brooks (as the director, Mel Funn), the amiably bug-eyed Marty Feldman, and that overgrown flabby infant of a Dom DeLuise, are mostly struggling to enlist the elusive guest stars (Burt Reynolds, James Caan, Anne Bancroft, Liza Minnelli, and Paul Newman) or trying to outrun or outsmart the evil conglomerate tycoons, Engulf and Devour, and their minions. For Engulf & Devour will annex the studio—for whose chief, Sid Caesar, our boys are working—the moment it goes bankrupt; hence that silent movie must be thwarted, whether by skulduggery, violence, or a booze-inducing sex-bomb (Bernadette Peters).

The scenario is basically no sillier than those of the old silent comedies, but the innocence is gone. Some gags are too elucubrated and esoteric; others are take-offs on the old ones, and seem to kid something that depended on its deadpan dedication. Brooks is not an eloquent mime; Feldman is nearer the mark, but gets less good material; DeLuise, whose comic persona is that of a swish baby, is simply distasteful. Among the guest stars, the ones who kid themselves most wholeheartedly—Burt Reynolds and Anne Bancroft—come off well; the others are left stranded with nothing to play. Sid Caesar and Miss Peters work hard to little effect, and a growing desperation churns its way through the movie.

Yet it would be less than honest to say that there are no laughs; it must, however, be stressed that laughter, like other forms of sustenance, varies in taste. There are sweet or spicy laughs that leave a vivifying aftertaste in the mouth; there are sharp or sour ones that a good chef can likewise put to stimulating use. But there are also those laughs that are so stupidly bland, so bitter, or so distasteful as to leave behind an acrid taste or none at all. Such queasy laughs one is soon ashamed of having indulged in, and *Silent Movie* (sigh! sob!) has far too many of them.

July 19, 1976

Batting: Average

I AM GLAD that there are films like *The Bingo Long Traveling All-Stars and Motor Kings,* even if I don't particularly care for them. *Bingo* is fairly well made, fairly amusing, about a fairly interesting subject, and, though somewhat black-chauvinistic, fairly critical, too, of some blacks. Many people, of all colors and ages, will relish this movie, and far be it from me to begrudge them such innocent pleasures. It is just that I find all those *fairly's,* finally, a bit too bland for my taste.

Based on a novel by William Brashler, *Bingo* tells a tale that must be fairly close (that "fairly" again!) to actual events. In the late thirties, black baseball players were still not allowed onto white teams; in the Negro National League, however, many of them felt exploited by the club owners. So "Bingo" Long and Leon Carter, a star pitcher and catcher, decide to go it on their own, and form a barnstorming team that hustles engagements. Bingo and his All-Stars soon discover that, to cadge games, they must put on a bit of a minstrel show, and even perfect a few clowning Uncle Tom routines. Traveling in a couple of flashy touring cars, gaily bedizened, and singing and dancing their way to the shabby ball parks, they are beginning to do so well as to be soon plotted against by their former owners and roughed up by the latters' goons. Just when it seems that they must succumb to intensive harassment, they make a spectacular comeback by winning a game against the best of the Negro National League. The All-Stars become a team in the league, but their victory is Pyrrhic: already their most talented rookie is signed up by a white team. The days of black teams are numbered.

The film adheres closely to the old formula whereby, after so many comic and a few gloomy turns, there has to come a happy, although perhaps slightly wistful, ending. What makes it interesting is its atmosphere: the social undertones, the rollicking esprit de corps of the team, the laughter cunningly wrested from predicament. I have no idea how faithful this script by Hal Barwood and Matthew Robbins is either to the novel or, more important, to the way things were—and I thoroughly disliked *The Sugarland Express,* the previous Barwood-Robbins collaboration—but there is an engagingly bumptious vivacity here and that picaresque élan made more unusual by the supersession of the single *picaro* by two sardine-packed cars of pranksters.

The humor, however, is pretty elementary, and the laughs are not so much elicited as batted in. But John Badham, a director fresh out of television, has some dizzy old cinematic devices up his tricky mitt; it may well be that television is where traditional cinematic know-how has been nurtured by aspiring cinéastes. Badham gives us, for instance, that old-time fascination with the eccentric ingredients that make up a crowd, or the zany opticals, such as a pitched ball imploding into the image to start a new scene. It is not just baseball, it is even more cornball, but some of it works, especially as helped along by a perfervid, ebullient cast, comprising both authentic baseball players and actors who toiled to acquire the requisite athletic skills.

More than the writing and directing, more than Bill Butler's proficient but unspectacular cinematography, more than the comedy on the road or the comedy-drama on the diamond, what captivates us is the acting. As Bingo, Billy Dee Williams happily blends the virtues of the dedicated actor and the matinee idol. As Leon Carter, James Earl Jones demonstrates that he is at his best in down-to-earth comedy laced with a touch of seriousness; for farce, there are Richard Pryor and, some menace notwithstanding, Ted Ross. In fact, there's no loser in the entire large cast.

Yet there is no getting away from the fact that this is one of those films that have "human interest" scrawled large over every frame. That means that, while the filmmakers are not patronizing their characters, they commit the opposite error of drooling a little too lovingly over the characters' every foible, quirk, and wart. It also means that the film is more concerned with making you feel good about people than with having a good feel for individual reality. At any rate, the clichés of a certain type of comedy have a way here of obfuscating the small, hard-earned, underlying fund of truth.

July 26, 1976

Obsessions: On Land, Sea, and In Between

Paul Schrader is a curious specimen: a scenarist who combines highbrow and lowbrow tastes, theological and movie-buff concerns, he seems to be, according to anecdotes that drift eastward, at least as ghoul-haunted as Poe's woodland of Weir. There was obsessiveness at the core of *The Yakuza,* which he coscripted; his Travis Bickle, in *Taxi Driver,* was a man possessed; now we have the eponymous *Obsession,* which he wrote from a story by himself and his friend Brian De Palma, who directed. Or should I say ex-friend? Rumor has it that, owing to cuts and changes De Palma made in the screenplay, which are said to include the jettisoning of forty final pages, the friends have fallen out. As for the film, though I don't know who did what to which, one thing is certain: the result is an unholy mess. Intended as an *hommage* to Hitchcock—especially to his murky and pretentious *Vertigo* (itself a kind of unwitting tribute to Clouzot's *Diabolique*)—*Obsession* attitudinizes in three directions: toward the Hitchcockian thriller, toward the old-fashioned tearjerker, and toward the sophisticated European film, with cultural references strewn like bread crumbs along the way of Hansel and Gretel.

Such a mishmash could at least be endearing; as it happens, it is neither mish nor mash so much as mush. Briefly, it is the story of Michael Courtland, a rich New Orleans land developer who, partly through foul play and bad luck, but partly perhaps through his own improvidence, loses his adored wife Elizabeth and young daughter in a combination kidnapping and car accident. Unremittingly haunted by his unfulfilled love for Elizabeth, he returns, almost twenty years later, on a business trip to Florence, where she, fresh out of Bryn Mawr, first crossed his path. In the Church of San Miniato, where he and Elizabeth met, he espies atop a scaffolding a young woman, Sandra, who helps with the restoring of damaged artworks. She is a dead ringer for the dead wife; in fact, Michael takes her to be Elizabeth divinely restored to him as a second chance. He woos and wins her, and takes her back home to wed. On the eve of the wedding, after much preliminary anguish, the same disaster strikes again, leading to a bizarre climax one might call preposterous—except what, then, would one call the rest of the movie? A tissue of loopholes?

Now, I don't want to give away too much of the story, because all there is is the paltry but fiercely posturing plot. Still, I must say (close your eyes here if you wish to preserve your innocence vis-à-vis this rather corrupt film) that Sandra is really Elizabeth and Michael's daughter, a survivor despite appearances, now hell-bent on avenging her mother's death on the father, whom the real villain has smeared.

Schrader and De Palma have loaded their penny dreadful with allusions high and low. There are overtones of *The Winter's Tale,* the Bluebeard story, *Rebecca,* and, of course, *Vertigo.* There are quotations from Dante's *Vita nuova,* likewise a tale of loving obsession. And there is more: the fresco with whose restoration Sandra assists is by Bernardo Daddi; it is a Virgin and Child, whose damaging has revealed an earlier work underneath—which one of them is to be sacrificed for the other? Why such fuss over a lesser master such as Daddi, for whom Sandra and the restorers finally opt? Because Sandra's heart, however ironically and ferally, belongs to Daddy. And why the Virgin and Child? Because love between child and mother is what really motivates Sandra. And why is it the earlier work that is sacrificed? An anterior life must be abandoned both by Michael and Sandra for the sake of a *vita nuova.*

The movie is full of such otiose allusiveness and gamesmanship. Sandra's last name is Portinari—after Dante's Beatrice, of course. A minor character, said to be a bore, is called D'Annunzio after you know whom; another one is called Farber, although I can't say whether after Manny or Stephen. The place where Michael doesn't quite dare accost Sandra is the Ponte Vecchio, where Beatrice withheld her greeting from Dante. Since a staircase figures prominently in several Hitchcock films, photography, editing, and music combine to pump ominousness into the stairs of San Miniato, even though they have no dramatic function whatsoever. The first part of the film takes place in 1958—the date of *Vertigo.* The score was finished, just before he died, by Bernard Herrmann—the composer of *Vertigo.* And so on.

All this would be mere harmless minor nonsense if the plot as a whole weren't such a major piece of arrant absurdity. Sandra's behavior is *a priori* incredible, and it's only because we don't know till later who she is that we swallow the preposterousness that surrounds her. Thus, her supposed Italian mother sickens on cue, is tended by nuns at the hospital, exacts a deathbed promise of marriage from the already obsessed Michael and seemingly reluctant Sandra, then duly dies. Who is in on Sandra's scheme? The good sisters? A deadly virus? Or God? When Michael and Sandra share his New Orleans house, what's going on sexually? Are we to believe that these sophisticates shy away from premarital intercourse? Or that, incest being bad for desired PG ratings, they carry on blissfully off-camera? And why doesn't Michael age one bit over the quarter century covered by the film? Is it a clause in Cliff Robertson's contract? Plastic surgery? Or God?

Countless details are fudged in one way or another; if all else fails, there is always manic editing. Most incredible, though, is that the real villain should, with all his verve, choose so slow and risky a method of skullduggery as he does, and that the bright and decent Sandra should be so manipulable and obtuse. Toward the end, the behavior of all the characters becomes even less explicable, and the last slender links to sanity, indeed humanity, are frenetically severed.

De Palma's direction has its splashy slickness, but the people serve as mere props for the effects. The director was best at low-budget jobs like *Greetings* and *Hi, Mom;* considerably less good with medium-priced items such as *Sisters* and *Phantom of the Paradise;* and, if this is any indication, untrustworthy with bigger budgets. Vilmos Zsigmond, Hollywood's fanciest camera operator (I use the term advisedly), pulls all the stops out of his lenses and filters, and manages, for example, to make Florence look like something jointly concocted by Franco Zeffirelli, Max Ernst, and a light show commissioned by Perugina chocolates. New Orleans with overcast skies looks, by contrast, like something out of *Macbeth.* Worse yet is Herrmann's score, which can't consist of more than eight bars of music, as schmaltzy as the worst of Max Steiner or Victor Young, and becoming louder and nastier with every one of its thousand repetitions, until its obsessiveness surpasses the protagonist's. I don't know what Herrmann died of, but I wouldn't rule out shame as a possibility.

Nothing could have saved the film, but the acting might at least have humanized it. Geneviève Bujold may be almost the only leading lady in Hollywood today who combines looks, talent, and intelligence without having any of the prevalent freakishness; but as Elizabeth she has very little to do, and as Sandra very little that makes sense. At one point she is even misdirected into a kind of come-hither walk and expression that would have been excessive for Tondelayo. Maybe, however, overcompensation seemed called for opposite the near-perfect nullity of Cliff Robertson: the obsession he can muster is at best that of a stick in search of another to rub against in the hope of a spark. John Lithgow, who plays his partner, is just the stock exaggerated movie southerner. Can you rub together stick and stock?

Geneviève Bujold, for all her spunk, is wasted yet more mindlessly in *Swashbuckler,* a movie about evil governors and noble buccaneers in a bygone (or never-was) Jamaica that might better have been called *An Ill Wind in Jamaica.* Jeffrey Bloom's screenplay from Paul Wheeler's story is magisterially moronic, and cannot even make up its minuscule mind whether to play it straight or as a spoof of the pirate genre that might best be called *Captain Ketchup.* As a result, the incoherent whole is even worse than the scum of its parts. James Goldstone, the director, hasn't a clue about how to direct sword fights, derring-do, crowd scenes, romantic moments, orgiastic decadence, sight gags, or much of anything else; he is a little better with animals, but even there undependable: he gets a good performance from a monkey, but an undistinguished one from a rooster. What he really lacks is rhythm and timing; the opening sequence, an interrupted hanging, is a model of how not to achieve either comedy or excitement.

Several fine performers are perversely miscast in this movie, Goldstone having the inverse of the skill sought by the alchemists—the knack of turning gold into stones. Hence, no doubt, his name. Not only can he reduce good actors to indifferent ones, he can even make poor ones, such as Beau Bridges, look hopeless, and change a merely homely woman, such as Anjelica Huston, into a positive horror. Dependable craftsmen of the kind of the cinematographer Philip Lathrop and the composer John Addison, revert to tyros in *Swashbuckler.* To top it all, the film has a concept of homosexuality that is downright medieval. On the other hand, it may be the first movie to introduce the word *pederast* into the vocabulary of the hinterlanders, at whom it is clearly aimed. Still, there must be easier ways to build up word power.

Venturing a little less far into the briny deep, there is *Lifeguard,* which addresses itself with the most earnestly dogged idiocy to the profoundly existential question of whether its thirty-two-year-old—and consequently rather over-the-hill—hero should retain his integrity and freedom by continuing to ply the unfettered trade of lifeguard along the beaches of Santa Monica, bedding jolly stewardesses and an occasional underage groupie (the perils of jailbait!), or chuck it all, don his civvies, settle down to selling Porsches in "the Valley," and marry his high-school sweetheart, now an affluent divorcee with a cozy home, thriving art gallery, and lovable son (the perils of *embourgeoisement!*).

Ron Koslow, whose scriptwriting debut this is, spent his adolescent summers on the beaches of southern California, then five further, presumably adult, summers "hanging around with ocean lovers and [Los Angeles] lifeguards," and the results seem to be this movie and water on the brain. The humorless persistence with which he worries his hero's existential dilemma makes me wonder whether the movie isn't more Kierkegaard than *Lifeguard.* It is, at any rate, studded with inadvertently uproarious lines, like the one in which the hero confides that he prefers his job in winter, when the beach is deserted, because it allows him time to think.

Daniel Petrie has directed with veteran shlockiness, Ralph Woolsey's camera work is irritatingly picturesque or moodily washed-out, and the performances are unremarkable except for that of Sam Elliott as the protagonist. Elliott is so perfect as a befuddled beach Galahad, all mustache and suntan, as to make me worry about whether he could play any other part at all. Of the women who make his life sweeter but more difficult, the most fetching is

Sharon Weber, a former *Playboy* gatefold girl, as a fiery air hostess. Compared to such fire and air, the other elements, especially water, seem to be baser life indeed.

August 16, 1976

O.D.-ing on Billy Joe

ODE TO BILLY JOE was written by Herman Raucher (*Summer of '42, Sweet November,* and other trash) and produced and directed by Max Baer (*Macon County Line*), a former Beverly Hillbilly and son of the boxer of the same name. The movie is loosely based on Bobbie Gentry's song, and if you have been wondering for the last ten years what was thrown off the Tallahatchie Bridge, you can find out here. You can also find out that Billy Joe McAllister, the southern boy in love with Bobbie Lee Hartley, then jumped off the bridge himself, because he had had a single Homosexual Experience! Why he had that Homosexual Experience, or what it was all about, you do not find out, because this stupid little movie is totally incapable of making sense out of its more sensational twists—such as why Billy Joe should instantly have become a legend merely for drowning himself, or why Bobbie Lee at fifteen should then conceive an idea that only an over-the-hill hack of a screenwriter could come up with (going off to the City to have an imaginary baby), or how the girl's parents could let her get away with it, etc.

Only someone like Baer, who carries a two-million-dollar indemnity policy (as he told *People* magazine) so he can punch out "at least eight SOBs . . . who have it coming," and whose next movie will be a bawdy Women's Army Corps comedy entitled *WAC-Off,* could have made a film so redolent of imbecile sentimentality in which young lovers moon or fumble in picture-postcard shot after shot, and sometimes, thanks to slow dissolves, in what feels like two shots simultaneously. There is also lots of wonderful rustic atmosphere and rural humor thanks to assorted yahoos, Yazoo City whores, sweetly understanding parents, a dog named Dog, a comic minister, and quaint folkways such as people copulating with their clothes on, either because that's the way it is done in the Deep South or because that's the way one gets a PG rating.

The time is the Eisenhower era, and the McAllisters have neither electricity nor plumbing, which elicits a fierce indictment from Bobbie Lee. We unfortunately never see them get the electricity, but we do get to relish Dad's bringing home a toilet bowl with the bacon. The ecstatic scene between Bobbie Lee and the bowl is the one moment of genuine passion the film rises to. Glynnis O'Connor and Robby Benson, who were charming as the young lovers in *Jeremy,* are together again here; Miss O'Connor more or less keeps her head above the mush, but Benson plays the boy as if he were (a) demented, and (b) about to come apart at the seams from a lethal attack of the fidgets. Michel Hugo's cinematography should be sold at better card stores everywhere, and while your heart is being rent by the story, your stomach is being turned by Michel Legrand's score. The junior Baer has clearly directed with—for sentimental reasons—his father's gloves on. The film grossed fifteen million dollars in its first eight weeks in the backwoods, and if you want to help Baer keep up his premiums on the aforementioned policy, as well as make lots more enchanting movies, by all means throw in your ticket's worth.

There is so much *Ode to Billy Joe* these days in one form or another that one ends up distinctly O.D.-ing on Billy Joe. *Gator* is a kind of sequel to *White Lightning,* which I haven't seen, so there are, after all, some small mercies I can be thankful for. The current installment was written by William Norton and directed by Burt Reynolds, who also repeats his starring role as the lovable moonshiner Gator McKlusky. As in *Billy Joe,* we are in the Deep South, which is rapidly displacing the West and Southwest as the favored locale with which to rake it in in the hinterlands. One virtue of such movies is that they feature accents as impenetrable to the human ear as the Everglades are to the human foot, which permits frequent speculations about what might just have been said. In this way one keeps one's mind, not exactly usefully occupied, but at least partly distracted from the happenings on screen.

These involve, in the present case, the lovable moonshiner's moonlighting by doing a stint for the government, i.e., getting the goods on his former friend Bama McCall, the all-powerful crime boss of Dunston County, who, besides enjoying murder, arson, and graft, peoples his brothels with fifteen-year-old McCall girls. The movie tries to be both tough and witty, bloody and comic, which, given the quality of the writing (on the level of Jackie Susann trying to make like Raymond Chandler), makes you feel that you are watching an endless chain of people slipping on banana peels and breaking their necks. It is the kind of movie where a righteous but crazy bookkeeper insists that her pet pussycats be taken along on a perilous break-in to steal the secret ledgers of Bama McCall, and where Burt Reynolds and Lauren Hutton can, while all Dunston County is after them, spend an idyllic night of peaceful copulation on the beach.

There are two newish performers in the cast: Mike Douglas, the TV host, and Jerry Reed, the country-music star. Even a cameo role proves long enough for Douglas to forget his southern accent; Reed mostly flashes a powerful set of choppers that threaten to burst into song any moment. For supposed belly laughs there are Jack Weston and Alice Ghostley, but their frantic overacting is less humorous than Reynolds and Hutton's efforts at being Bogart and Bacall. Miss Hutton at least looks good when photographed from the right angle, though no such angle has as yet been discovered for Reynolds. You may, however, be taken with the undulant unisex haircut he manages to maintain even while plying his still at the heart of a swamp beyond the reach of man. Charles Bernstein's music is everything this film deserves, but William A. Fraker's cinematography is at times rather too good for it, even if it does pull out all the stops during the principals' ocean-side revels.

There exists a letter from Rilke to Friedrich Huch in which the poet chides the young novelist for betraying the truth about children, for depriving the little ones of their childhood by turning them into mini-adults. "You have done an injustice to childhood," this letter begins; what the writer-director Alan Parker has done to childhood in *Bugsy Malone* is no mere injustice, however. It is an indecency, an outrage. This man has taken children and adolescents and made them enact a gangster-*cum*-music-hall-*cum*-prizefight B-movie just as if they were jaded adult actors in a cynical thirties or forties picture. No reason is given (dream, fantasy, movie within a movie); the children are simply there in a studio-made New York of 1929, killing, brutalizing, swindling, and tarting it up. To be sure, the submachine guns spout marshmallows for bullets, yet their victims are "eliminated"; the dance-hall girls are not seen actually copulating, but the implications are there; the soft drinks are only suggestive of booze, but the glorification of violence and crime is real enough.

Wholesome youngsters have been duped into acting like adults—stupid, brutal, criminal adults, at that. And not even as such adults might really be, only as they were seen in the cheap movies of a bygone Hollywood. While the children are forced into specious adulthood, the movie returns to the infancy of the cinema, full of those romantically silly or repellently racist clichés that were considered harmless fun in those "innocent" days. Three minutes of *Bugsy Malone* might just pass for a bad cutesy joke; a whole film of it is as boring as it is offensive.

And don't tell me that children play at cops and robbers or cowboys and Indians, which are much the same games as this film. They are not. They are a child's vision and version of things; whereas the film's gimmick is to turn the kids into appallingly realistic scale models of full-grown brutes and trollops for the amusement of whom, I wonder? Pederasts and child molesters, certainly, who may find something deliciously provocative about tots got up as delinquent adults; some backward children, no doubt, who think this film exalts them; and adults benighted enough to perceive this offal as a lovable masquerade.

On top of its other troubles, *Bugsy* is a musical, with songs by Paul Williams, not one bar of which strikes me as music. Worse yet, the songs are dubbed in by adult voices, many if not all belonging to Williams himself. This makes the transitions from speech to song perfectly ludicrous, and has the further depressing effect of suggesting that the very mouths of these children have been violated. Even what I take to be Williams's natural voice, in the rendition of the title song, is somehow inhuman; the mere way in which he intones the name *Bohg-zee Mull-hone* is more cud-chewing than singing.

The sets, costumes, and cinematography are clever enough, and so, too, is the parodic quality of the choreography. But the kids aren't dancers; still less are they actors. Their attempts to sound tough are risible, which turns them into laughingstocks. The only professional performance comes from Jodie

Foster, the young actress who goes from strength to strength in bad movie after bad movie. Her deliberately stereotyped tough broad with a heart of gold is so good as to be alarming, which doesn't help much either.

Now, what could Alan Parker & Company do for an encore? The history of the Campfire Girls performed entirely by androgynous Oriental giants? A movie about horse racing with all the horses played by kangaroos? The life of Albert Einstein in which Einstein is portrayed by a dog postsynched by Paul Williams? An all-male, all-nude *Romeo and Juliet* with songs by David Bowie? In a world where *Bugsy Malone* can get a G rating, anything goes.

September 6–27, 1976

Affront

It would be nice to have a good movie about McCarthyism, and the blacklisting and other iniquities that went with it. This dark chapter of recent American history is, unlike some others, not so recent as to preclude some perspective on it. Yet it has hardly been touched by the movies, probably because Hollywood's role in it was among the ugliest, and because many of the victimizers (leaving aside the victims) are still alive and kicking people around. *The Way We Were* may be the only bigtime film in which the subject came up at all, and even there one or two proposed scenes were omitted. What remained could hardly have displaced an eyebrow.

One could have been hopeful about *The Front:* Walter Bernstein, the writer, Martin Ritt, the director, and several of the principal actors had all been blacklisted; here they could have discharged their accumulated experience and gall. But no such thing: *The Front* is all façade, posturing, clichés, and cutenesses; it might as well have been made by people whose information about McCarthyism came from a couple of magazine articles, and their knowledge of human beings from Earl Wilson's column. Even at that, the film may owe its existence to the fact that it deals with blacklisting on television only, and does not foul its own nest, however prefouled that may be.

The story concerns Howard Prince, an amiable goof-off who works as a cashier in a luncheonette when he is tapped by an old friend, Alfred Miller, a successful TV writer who has just been blacklisted. Prince is to become a "front": the man who will sign Miller's future teleplays in exchange for 10 percent of the fee. Before long, he is fronting also for two other blacklisted writers; living on the shirttails, if not in the lap, of luxury; and enjoying the favors of pretty Florence Barrett, a script editor in love with his "talent."

We observe right away that the film ignores the heart of the problem: if the network was dumb enough to believe that three quite different but gifted writers could be subsumed by Prince, a nonentity with no discoverable background or discernible foreground, it displayed an idiocy the film is duty-bound to explore. If, as is more likely, the network knew that Prince was a front, but cynically bought good scripts for modest newcomers' fees, this was corruption even more deserving of scrutiny. The film, however, is interested only in exploiting Prince's sometimes desperate stratagems for facile comic effects.

Which leads to the more serious shortcoming—that *The Front,* while ogling Significance, is content to cohabit with Farce. A serious problem can, of course, be treated as comedy, especially as black comedy, if it has been sufficiently dealt with as a serious problem in the past, if we have become tired of it when served up straight. But when its surface has barely been scratched, yokking up the subject seems at best evasive, at worst jejune. Nor are Woody Allen as Prince, and Zero Mostel as Hecky Brown, a comedian whom blacklisting drives to suicide, felicitous choices. Both are too glibly adept at churning out comic routines to get at the human beings behind those routines. Allen, moreover, is precarious casting for any kind of love object, and Mostel's part, as written, contains no hint of a tragic potential, so that, when tragedy pops up, it can only shock, not move us.

The very premise of the film is shaky. After plausibly showing us how even factitious success manages genuinely to corrupt Prince, it suddenly treats us to a heroic transfiguration, with Prince hurling a four-letter word at a congressional subcommittee, and smilingly marching off to prison, adored by his girl and exalted by all right-thinking persons. If heroism could come so cheap, and a facile obscenity could give McCarthy and his crew what-for, what was all the fuss about? The enemy in the film does not seem formidable enough to justify the death of a Hecky Brown even, and the serious points end up farcical without the comic ones becoming cutting.

There are, to be sure, some amusing bits here, though they tend to pertain to such marginal matters as Catskill resorts rather than to the central issues. Yet it is not comedy that the film exudes but a self-serving smugness: anyone who was blacklisted was ipso facto a hell of a guy, manifestly superior to anyone who did not make this honor roll. The clinching self-congratulatory note occurs in the final credits, where, after the names of writer, director, and several actors, parentheses proclaim the dates of their blacklisting. I am sorry to have to say the obvious, but however vicious blacklisting was, and however fell its consequences were, it did not, as the film implies, confer a badge of honor. To have been a Communist or Communist-sympathizer is not an automatic guarantee of moral and intellectual superiority, yet that is what the film would have us believe by making all characters at the center or right of center fools or scoundrels or both—enacted, like Remak Ramsay's consultant on loyalty, as monsters whose very silences are snarls. *The Front* is so simplistic that one learns with surprise that its creators were victims rather than persecutors, and one is forced to wonder how, had the political shoe been on the other foot, *they* would have behaved to anyone even slightly to the right of them.

Martin Ritt has directed with some skill in moving his actors about, and the film is not deficient in rhythm, to which Sidney Levin's editing must have made its handsome contribution. But Ritt's directorial vision is no more complex than Walter Bernstein's scenaristic one: the film is a congeries of skits rather than a credible organic development. Among the performers,

Michael Murphy as Alfred Miller and Charles Kimbrough as an odious congressional counsel come off best. As Florence, Andrea Marcovicci's voice is prettier than her face (even though much is made of her alleged gorgeousness), and her acting is only serviceable. In the relatively meaty role of a pusillanimous producer, Herschel Bernardi is pat and boring. Michael Chapman's cinematography and Dave Grusin's music are unobtrusive, which is fine; but they are virtually alone in this respect in an otherwise obstreperous and ultimately otiose film.

October 11, 1976

The Waxing of Wayne

The Shootist is one of those relatively few movies whose badness makes one feel genuinely sad. It is the sort of picture that, had it been made in almost any other country—i.e., any country that can see itself and its people straight rather than through a veil of myth and legend—could have emerged human and moving. Instead, it is superficial, cliché-riddled, and torn apart by conflicting aims of abiding by and debunking or transcending its genre.

On the right track are the direction and most of the casting; wrong are the screenplay and, to a lesser extent, the production values. Don Siegel is one of the very few remaining, tenaciously perdurable, intelligently workmanlike directors of genre pictures—pictures I shall define here, for the sake of brevity, as conforming to a firmly established type, such as the western, thriller, science-fiction film, etc.—and his technique, without being extraordinary, is in every way adequate to his modest yet not undemanding material. But that is where the problem lies: a novel by a run-of-the-mill author like Glendon Swarthout (*They Came to Cordura, Where the Boys Are, Bless the Beasts and Children*—all turned into paltry movies), adapted to the screen by his son Miles Hood Swarthout and the actor and dialogue coach Scott Hale, is hardly the material with which to transcend genre.

How have the formulaic, western-genre B-pictures (genre films are usually low-budget items) been transcended in the past? Either upward, into social documentaries like *High Noon,* cosmic statements with larger-than-life *mise en scènes* like *Shane,* or combinations of the two like *The Wild Bunch;* or else downward, into farce and travesty like *Destry Rides Again* and *Cat Ballou,* or into ultranaturalistic demythifying like *The Great Northfield, Minnesota Raid,* and *Dirty Little Billy. The Shootist* (a euphemism for gunman) is closest in spirit to *High Noon,* where the so-called solid citizens shamefully abandon the hero in his hour of need, and could have a slight edge on it, in that it realistically allows for a few more decent people in the world; but it loses that advantage by making the good ones too pure and the bad ones unrelievedly vile.

The plot concerns a celebrated gunman, John Bernard Books, who, it seems, was always on the side of the angels, which we had better believe since Books is played by John Wayne. Right away the film commits some crucial faux pas: it gives us a family album of shots from old John Wayne movies, provides the hero with an incurable rectal cancer (the real-life Wayne, we are forced to recall, won his bout with the Big C), and introduces Jimmy Stewart as kindly old Doc Hostetler who makes the fatal diagnosis. Nostalgia-mongering reliance on Wayne's past roles filing past us, the presence of Wayne's equally legendary costar, and a reference to Wayne's real-life drama are typically sentimental genre-film strategies that militate heavily against such a nongenre element as the hero's dying of an ugly, undignified disease. And the debunking elements of the story, characterized by such a casual remark of the hero's as "Bat Masterson always *was* full of sheepdip," are contravened by his demise being brought into an ostentatiously heroic-symbolic context: Carson City in 1901, where the action is set, is going urban and bourgeois—one of the villains drives an Oldsmobile, and the very first newspaper headline Books encounters proclaims the death of Queen Victoria. The Old West and the old leaders are fast dying out!

Against this weighty symbolism (is that Olds, by the way, derived from *Yojimbo,* where the archvillain sports a gun against the hero's samurai sword?), we get plenty of flimsy clichés. Doc Hostetler (Swarthout goes in for colorful monickers) sends Books to the boardinghouse of the widow Bond Rogers (Lauren Bacall, with her New York finishing-school accent, sadly miscast) and her sixteenish son Gillom (Ron Howard, so damned typical that it hurts). The mother naturally resents a boarder who is a gunfighter, but softens by predictable stages as she dips deeper into his four-square decency. Equally predictably, the boy, who at first foolishly venerates the killer of thirty men, is gradually more impressed by a courage based on prudence, and finally, with the tacit blessing of the expiring shootist, symbolically rejects life by the gun, as platitude is piled on platitude.

Things could be saved, perhaps, by a particularly novel treatment, but that is precisely what Siegel, despite his solid competence—or, more likely, because of it—does not come up with. Siegel may have been declared an *auteur* by *auteur* critics, but he is neither author nor co-author of his screenplays—not even, it would seem, a good judge of other people's screenwriting. The Swarthout-Hale scenario crawls with commonplaces: Books giving Gillom a shooting lesson; Serepta, Books's former sweetheart, turning out to be a calculating hypocrite who seeks to marry him now for pure gain; Dobkins, the prototypical yellow (in both senses) journalist who wants to write the hero's mendacious biography, etc., etc. Even worse is the dialogue: "You and Dobkins are two sides of a counterfeit coin"; "I must look a sight!"—"For sore eyes"; "Mrs. Rogers, you have a fine color when you're on the scrap. . . . I'm sure there is plenty of starch in your corset"; "I'm a dying man scared of the dark!"—"Damn you, damn you for the pain you brought into this house!" and so on.

The cinematography represents Bruce Surtees's marked advance over his previous camerawork—either the ultraromantic prettiness of *Play Misty for Me* or the undue harshness of *The Beguiled.* The score, by Elmer Bernstein, though by no means distinguished, is at least uninsistent and anodyne, which is saying a lot these days. Robert Boyle's production design is good, although perhaps too grand at times for this slender vehicle. Always, however, we come up short against the script: conventional at best, when not downright derivative and banal. Why could not the relationships between Books and Gillom, Books and Bond, and Books and Serepta (to say nothing of other, less important, ones) exhibit more juicy idiosyncrasy—why must it all be such out-and-out surrogate-father-and-son, good-man-and-pure-woman, good-man-and-impure-woman stuff? Even that bit of foreshadowing dialogue and corresponding dénouement about how the great westerners are brought low in the end by some no-account punk shooting from behind derives blatantly from *The Gunfighter.*

Something, however, is left. John Wayne gives a surprisingly effective performance as Books, a role somewhat more demanding than Rooster Cogburn in *True Grit,* his previous high. If at the age of sixty-nine, after forty-seven years in the movies, Wayne can truly have learned his trade, there is hope for every one of us, no matter how slow a study. James Stewart dithers delightfully; Bacall, if you can disregard the accent and a certain excess of sophistication, is all right; various guest stars and supporting actors perform smoothly. Ron Howard, I repeat, is disgustingly right as Gillom; the usually interesting Sheree North is defeated by the schematism of Serepta. Siegel's direction is well paced, actors and camera are moved about cogently, and there is sound albeit conventional wisdom about such things as low-angle and overhead shots. If only there were more originality about all this, other than that rectal cancer; how far can you travel on such rear propulsion?

August 23, 1976

Getting Winded

MARATHON MAN is yet another display of John Schlesinger's directorial smoothness. Smoothness is a shifty characteristic: at its upper edges, it becomes cleverness, which is a real but lowly virtue; at its lower end, it is mere slickness or flashiness, and no virtue at all. Whether it is a virtue or vice in its middle range is almost impossible to determine. It does very little for such good material as *Far From the Madding Crowd* or *The Day of the Locust,* but such dubious stuff as *Darling, Midnight Cowboy,* or *Sunday Bloody Sunday* has a way of glittering with an unhealthy sheen because of it. Schlesinger's best film, for me, is still his first, *A Kind of Loving,* though I am not sure how it would hold up today.

In *Marathon Man,* a tale of espionage and double agents, where the CIA is as villainous as the bigtime ex-Nazi now based in South America, the hero is a little Jewish schlemiel who, after he has been kicked and tormented too much, asserts himself and destroys all his torturers. It is a Steigian dream of glory in which Thomas Babington "Babe" Levy at last avenges his academic father, a victim of McCarthyism, and his elder brother Doc, a CIA (and double) agent whom the ex-Nazi kills, by becoming a better killer than any of them. It is the old story whose improbability borders on the sublime—that of the worm that turns and destroys the bigger, stronger, and far more numerous worms. Yet to make such a central figment palatable, everything surrounding it ought to reek of plausibility; only a scaffolding of eminent possibilities can prop up the lovely but frail edifice of the impossible.

To this end, Schlesinger has lavished realism on moments of terror and horror, as well as labored to extract a sinister beauty from them. Right away a contradiction crops up: Can or should the horrible look that pretty? There is, for example, the scene where a remarkably frightening Oriental attempts to garrote Doc on the balcony of his hotel room, perceived largely from the point of view of an invalid on a balcony across the way. As the life-and-death struggle staggers into the room, we see blood spurting on the billowing white curtains from within, to form a canvas rather better than any Jackson Pollock. When a woman is—apparently—killed under the arcades of a nocturnal Paris street, there rolls out of the pitch-black night around the anxious Doc a gleaming new soccer ball: it scurries toward and past him, and disappears. Aside from the fact that this is pure nonsense, there is the graver question of whether mayhem should be invested with such interior-decorator chic.

When the villain gets his final comeuppance among scattering diamonds rolling from his dying grasp into the Central Park reservoir, the image is redolent of keen, even if less than original, irony. By shooting from below through a grid, Schlesinger and his artful cameraman Conrad Hall make us feel as if we were standing at the center of a shower of deliquescent stars, and what should be primarily awesome emerges merely dazzling. Yet, sticking out of such glossiness, moments of true brutality appear either unbearably painful or, conversely, almost campy.

Underlying all this slickness is the even more unpleasant attitudinizing of William Goldman's novel and screenplay, the latter, we hear, touched up by Robert Towne. Even so, the screenplay does not bother to explain why certain people are killed, or why they are killed when they are, rather than at some other time. Gestures are repeatedly being made toward "the real thing," such as the sexual problems of the hero and heroine, interracial friction, or the relationship of history and current politics, but such matters remain mere psychological or intellectual cliff-hangers never decently explored. You may ask whether a thriller need bother its paltry head with matters of such pith and consequence, to which I answer, yes, if it lays claims to the prestige of extra dimensions, as this one steadily does. That such a synthesis is possible has been proved by films like *The Third Man,* owing, to be sure, to the considerably greater talents of Carol Reed and Graham Greene.

Incremental gloss derives also from fancy foreign locales, an international cast, and the presence of Laurence Olivier in a role for which any one of a number of Hollywood actors would have been sufficient. Certainly Olivier's Nazi, a combination of petty shrewdness, stolidity, and querulous self-pity, is refreshingly different from the usual arrogant demon; welcome, too, are the less-Prussian-than-usual accent and the wonderfully realized walk in which military bearing has begun to crumble into shards of senile stiffness. Likewise splendid is the Golders Green accent Olivier assumes when he pretends to be a London Jewish jeweler, though, of course, the Nazi whom he is playing could never manage that. For all this, one cannot help feeling that Olivier is slumming here.

Another very fine performance is Dustin Hoffman's Babe. Though the actor specializes somewhat limitingly in unadult bumblers whose humanity must crawl out from under a pile of inhibitions, he comes up here with more searing anxiety, more biting pain than usual; a scene (perhaps the best in the film) where he must find the right answer to an unfathomable question or be cruelly tortured, is played by Hoffman with the perfect blend of agony and comic absurdity that characterizes nightmares, and falls not a whit short of Olivier's marvelous mix of menace and preposterousness. The stock part of Doc is enlivened with extraordinary authenticity by Roy Scheider, an actor who unerringly hits the true note of humanity even among hoked-up circumstances.

The rest of the cast is defeated by the material, most sadly Marthe Keller, the Swiss actress who was so lovely and persuasive in the mediocre films of Lelouch and de Broca, but who here doesn't even look very good. Yet it is not as if Hollywood, as so frequently in the past, had transmogrified a simple, natural-looking European beauty into a Max Factor–Sidney Guilaroff–Edith Head zombie; Miss Keller was given what, by Hollywood standards, is the most natural, and ingenuous, of looks, and still appears woefully diminished. In Hollywood even the natural look is less natural than elsewhere.

October 18, 1976

Vicious Video

NETWORK inherits the Glib Piety Award direct from the hands of *The Front,* the previous winner. When it comes to sanctimonious smugness and holier-than-thou sententiousness, the new laureate is even more deserving of the unsavory prize. *Network,* moreover, is a further lap in Paddy Chayefsky's, the scenarist's, fascinating race against decrepitude and impotence, whose earlier laps we followed spellbound in *Middle of the Night* and *Hospital.* So we have two great contests to watch: Can the Universal Broadcasting System, a failing television network, make it out of the cellar of the broadcast league by out-intriguing its competitors; and can the advancedly middle-aged Max Schumacher, the UBS news president, make it with a ruthlessly ambitious and much younger woman? To add a third ring to the circus, there is also an overarching metaphysical question: Can the world survive the ravages of television? The on-screen result is worse than a three-ring circus, however: verbal and intellectual Grand Guignol.

The ostensible protagonist is Howard Beale, a UBS news anchorman who suffers a nervous breakdown on camera as he announces his last appearance, and proceeds to inveigh against capitalist America, materialism, television, etc., in perfectly sophomoric terms, though it is hard to tell whether

Chayefsky intends them as such or as the inspired fulminations of a new Old Testament prophet. Be that as it may, America is transfixed by the performance, and the UBS ratings mount markedly. Ruddy, the executive in charge, fires not only Beale (Peter Finch), but also his immediate superior, Schumacher (William Holden), the latter having permitted the disgraceful exhibition to pollute our pristine airwaves.

But there is an unscrupulous operator, Diana Christenson (Faye Dunaway), the newly transferred vice-president in charge of programming, who detects a chance for UBS to up itself. She persuades Frank Hackett (Robert Duvall), a brutally unprincipled senior corporate executive, not only to restore Beale and Schumacher to their jobs, but actually to build a big new show around the former. Ruddy is fired, and Schumacher's protests that Beale is a sick man in need of therapy are ignored; it is Diana who really pulls the strings, including those that yank Max Schumacher away from his wife and grown daughters and into her pad and bed.

Beale, the anti-Establishment spokesman for middle America, has been totally co-opted; soon Diana also purchases for UBS the Ecumenical Liberation Army (an amalgam of the Symbionese Liberation Army, the Black Panthers, and Angela Davis, and thus a veritable triumph of Chayefskian syncretism), which supplies the Beale Show with home movies of terrorist activities. The conglomerate that owns the network loves the show, but Arthur Jensen (Ned Beatty), the chairman of the board, must convert Beale to belief in the oligarchy of money, the true power that rules the world on both sides of the Iron Curtain. In the empty but still menacing boardroom, Jensen delivers to Beale a tirade worthy of the combined talents of Herb Gardner and Ayn Rand, and converts him to a Horror-Comix version of dollar diplomacy.

Plot summary being almost as odious as this plot, I shall stop here. It should be noted right away, however, that *Network* is not only uncertain of tone, floundering between the grim exposé and absurdist kitsch; it does not even play fair on the plot level. We are, for example, given specimens of Beale's radical populist oratory, but no sample of his postconversion right-wing populism, which must have taxed Chayefsky's ingenuity beyond endurance. The relationship between Max and Diana is psychologically preposterous, an uninterrupted series of reversals in a power play whose emotional basis is never believably conveyed. Even the question of whether their sex is good or bad, discussed repeatedly and at length, undergoes constant revisionist interpretations. Such things may exist in the world; where they do not have true existence is in Chayefsky's pedestrian plotting and shopworn prose.

Oh, the dreadful cuteness of it all! Max beds Diana on a romantic seaside weekend while she keeps talking shop until his mouth literally stoppers hers; unstoppered, she jabbers right on. Not only an old joke, this, but also heavy-handedly executed here; *Network* never attains the wicked charm it pants for. And when the fancy speechifying ends, and a man and a woman confront each other in a fundamental quandary, what do they utter? Utter banalities and platitudes; *this* week *East Lynne.*

Sidney Lumet, however, continues to improve as a director. His camera moves more and more easefully and fluidly—note, for instance, the slow tracking shot during a board meeting, and its echoing shot in the empty boardroom—and his grasp on pacing has become assured. Only one sequence is poorly directed, with Roy Poole as a Kunstlerish lawyer for the Ecumenical Liberation Army haranguing the UBS team. Though this may be largely the fault of Poole's customary rotten acting, it is Lumet, after all, who cast Poole. Owen Roizman supplies his dependably tangy cinematography, with things often assuming an off—but the right off—color. Thus in a panoramic shot of Manhattan, everything, even the sky, emerges sinisterly but beautifully viridescent, a cross between a patina and a wasting sickness.

The acting is impressive. William Holden, alas, has not aged well, but he does maintain his gracious, civilized presence; in the Jim Aubreyish role of the UBS strong man, Robert Duvall splendidly wipes away the bad taste left from his recent outing as Dr. Watson in *The Seven-Per-Cent Solution.* Peter Finch contributes that wonderful quality of his—troubled warmth—to the silly role of Howard Beale, and manages even to sound American except for a lapse or two; Faye Dunaway offers a persuasive blend of human and inhuman qualities. As a rejected wife, Beatrice Straight subtly treads the thin line between dignity and breakdown. Among many fine supporting performances, I single out Ned Beatty's bluffly threatening Arthur Jensen, and William Prince's gelidly self-possessed WASP of a Ruddy.

What makes *Network* such a repulsive movie, though, is its combination of nasty-mindedness and hypocrisy. The shallow jibes aimed at television, even if they contain a good measure of truth, are top-heavy with leaden sarcasm, and rather unseemly coming from the commercial product of a movie industry hardly in the position to cast stones at TV. There is no vileness attributed to television here of which the movies have not shown themselves capable, yet they never muckrake in their own house. Furthermore, almost everyone comes out base and buyable in this film; the meager supply of integrity is very nearly preempted by Max Schumacher, the author's alter ego.

Purporting to dispense wittily devastating inside information, this crude film really panders to whatever is smug and pseudosophisticated in an audience of self-appointed insiders; their smart-alecky laughter was not an inspiriting thing to hear.

November 22, 1976

Fairy-Tale Philadelphia, Demythified Hollywood

ROCKY is a pugnacious, charming, grimy, beautiful fairy tale. It is a small pearl of realism formed around a grain of storybook impossibility, which gets encased solidly in an accumulation of details that warm the heart without shaking the head. Still, basically, a fairy tale—not of glass slippers, to be sure, but of golden gloves. An obscure Philadelphia boxer gets a crack at the heavyweight championship, and comes very close to winning on points—would, in fact, have won except that champions are always favored; to unseat them, you have to lay them out flat. But Rocky, the likable nonentity whose tale this is, gains a moral victory (at some future time perhaps even the championship): the love of his girl and the respect of his fellow citizens.

Personally, I do not care for boxing. I am always amazed at attempts to suppress violence in the movies that serenely bypass what happens at prizefights on both sides of the ropes. Only the other day I was watching a fellow first-class airplane traveler responding to the filmed Ali-Norton fight by punching the hell out of the seat in front of him and yelling at Norton, "Hurt him! Hurt him! You never hurt him!"—quite as if the bout were taking place then and there, and these brutish exhortations might lead Norton to victory. Be that as it may, the boxing in *Rocky,* though extremely verisimilar and powerfully photographed, does not overshadow the humanistic values of the story, even if one approves of pugilism no more than of being an enforcer for a loan shark and punching out customers in arrears—which is Rocky's principal work as the movie begins. Rocky practices it with as much fraternal forbearance as the job permits.

What distinguishes *Rocky* from so many other boxing films is the precision with which the locales, the background activities, and the talk are evoked. There is none of the gutter exoticism of, say, *Fat City,* or of the moralistic attitudinizing of, say, *Golden Boy.* There are only ordinary people living in the seedier parts of Philadelphia, engaged in humdrum or mildly criminal activities, except when one or the other fellow starts slugging it out in the ring. For the ring, as we are shown, is an astonishing, schizophrenic place—as harsh, soiling, and mephitic as a coal mine, yet also the enchanted quadrangle where Kid Galahad may find the Grail of riches and glory.

John G. Avildsen, who was himself a cameraman as well as the director of semipornographic cheapies—along with two more serious ventures, the absorbing but deeply flawed *Joe* and the well-intentioned but vapidly pretentious *Save the Tiger*—exhibits an expert eye for seediness here. From James Crabe, the cinematographer, he gets an aura of dilapidation, a gray green shabbiness that coats everything, from human faces to the air itself. No less helpful atmospherically is the script that Sylvester Stallone, who plays Rocky, actually wrote for himself. It is a formidable accomplishment: dialogue that never sounds out of lowly character yet manages also to be artistic. The words encompass their objectives by their very inarticulateness, awkwardly clawing, biting into, bear-hugging their subjects, not letting go until their humble, clumsy, but true perceptions stand revealed. Even the pathetic thread of *you know's* with which Rocky embroiders his threadbare rhetoric is transformed into an urgent refrain, a hope for communication in the teeth of blighting indifference.

When people have nothing to say, the film allows them the dignity of silence. But the talk can be funny, mean-spirited, or suddenly generous. And as the talk is, so are the people. It may be a mite hard to believe in Adrian, the late-blooming virgin who overnight becomes Rocky's inspirational inamorata, but Talia Shire acts and looks the part so firmly and femininely that she compels our compliance. As Paulie, her coarse butcher brother, Burt Young convinces us, through appropriately slow unveilings, that a heart actually beats behind his gristle. Burgess Meredith, who has been known to overact lately, is restrainedly poignant as a hardy little trainer, an often thwarted man of integrity still wonderfully vulnerable to sparks of hope. Carl Weathers is splendidly haughty and sarcastic as a black champion who tempers his arrogance with wit. As a bigtime promoter, Thayer David persuasively radiates crookedness from behind perfectly fake bonhomie.

Even the smallest roles are well taken, and above all of them floats, securely and gracefully, Sylvester Stallone as Rocky. With the sharply etched yet always a bit sleepy face of a Roman patrician misplaced in a Philadelphia gutter, his eyelids almost always at halfmast, his voice seesawing between hopeful entreaty and ironic resignation, Stallone weaves through the film with a kind of indolent swagger. One restrains one's physical strength, he seems to be saying with gentle self-mockery; one comes to terms with life by keeping up a steady, bantering patter. But when the right woman or the goddess Fortune beckons, one deploys one's every decent resource to win. Rocky is the most likable and unaggressive of punks, and, certainly, an original. Stallone has imagined him with intense, bristling love, and plays him with relaxed affection.

Well, yes; a fairy tale. But can we be sure that miracles don't happen? Hasn't an obscure actor, after every kind of setback, delay, and disillusionment—his one real break came in *The Lords of Flatbush,* a movie awful enough to strangle talent in its cradle—come up with one of the best scripts and performances of the year to win a double crown no easier to come by than the heavyweight championship? Except for one very bad sequence—a prefight fantasy or dream of glory, conceived and directed as a television commercial—*Rocky* makes virtually no mistakes. It is an uppercut to the devil's jaw and an upper for the viewer's spirits.

The movie version of Fitzgerald's *The Last Tycoon* is an honorable failure. Honorable because it tries to serve its vision of the original faithfully; a failure because that vision falls considerably short of Fitzgerald's. Indeed, of the mating of Scott Fitzgerald's unfinished last novel and Harold Pinter's screenplay nothing totally good could come: the wedding of exuberance, even controlled exuberance, and minatory minimalism cannot bode well. Fitzgerald's striving is for capturing moments, feelings, people, with aching clarity; Pinter's game consists of making mundane words and trivial silences fill up with ominous nastiness. Can Fitzgerald's lucency thrive in Pinter's shadows?

I can see how Mike Nichols, the original director, would have been attracted to the trendy prestige of Pinter—and, for that matter, to the genuine international stardom of Jeanne Moreau—regardless of proper fit. But it is Elia Kazan who ended up directing, and his naturalism laced with expressionistic touches introduces further discord with both Pinter and Fitzgerald.

The omission of the so-called prologue, the airborne section of the novel, is probably all to the good; but the other major change, the foreshortened ending, strikes me as infelicitous. In this version, Monroe Stahr's downfall seems contrived; even the open ending—Stahr's eclipse may be only temporary—does not manage to disguise the fact that a conclusion has been hastily pressed into service where further development is indicated. Still, I can appreciate the filmmakers' unwillingness to make use of sketches and fragments of a story that Fitzgerald might have changed utterly had he lived to finish it. There may, then, be no way out of this hole; but a hole it is.

Next, it strikes me as unfortunate that the movie elects to underplay the period elements, to soft-pedal almost out of existence the lush fabric of topical references that holds the book together. One does not arrive at timelessness by discarding time and place, any more than one achieves universality by generalizing the individuality of characters. Fitzgerald's Hollywood is an atmosphere as thick as the Los Angeles smog; it is needed to set off the frail pathos of Stahr's emotional fiasco with Kathleen—a shining failure against a murky background of success.

But even granting that the film chooses to concentrate on the love story, it misses the point of that. Fitzgerald makes quite clear that, during a nocturnal drive with Kathleen, Stahr had his chance to get the girl to marry *him.* The novel shows that a tycoon who could be triumphant on the plane of empire-building could also be untrusting of his deeper feelings, snobbishly standoffish and irresolute before a lower-class young woman, and so let fulfillment elude him. The movie—or Pinter—chooses to make everything revolve around Kathleen's capriciousness, a force outside Stahr's character and thus not germane to the theme.

Pinter's additions are no more appropriate then his omissions. For example, there is a bit in which Stahr tells Kathleen that he can no longer remember what he and Minna, his dead wife, were like together. This is characteristic Pinterian nihilism; but Fitzgerald states plainly that Minna's terminal illness (in the film she is said to have died suddenly in her dressing room) brought the spouses closer together than ever; thus Kathleen, who outwardly so resembles Minna, turns into Stahr's all-important second and last chance—something the film fails to emphasize. Or Pinter invents a typically creepy incident: when the lights go on after a screening of rushes and everyone rises to leave, a cutter seems to have fallen asleep in his seat. It emerges that he is dead; rather than disturb the mighty Monroe Stahr, he chose to expire without so much as a sound. This is grandiloquent grotesquerie; absurdity in Fitzgerald is more mundane and evenly distributed—and thus more truly insidious.

Yet Kazan has directed with a technical solidity his recent undertakings, such as *The Arrangement* and *The Visitors,* made me think he had lost. The camera is always in a suitable place; the occasional bravura touch does not stridently call attention to itself; and even Pinter's obligatory long and sinister silences are dealt with intelligently. Sometimes they are supplemented with nice off-screen sounds such as the rolling of surf or the barking of a distant dog; sometimes facial play is built up to a pitch of dramatic eloquence. Even so, a pall of slowness enshrouds the movie.

Kazan also gets good work from a large cast. Among the roles that the scenario beefs up, that of an insecure leading man is acted with fine lunatic brio by Tony Curtis, and Jeanne Moreau almost manages to make the now cliché part of an anxiously aging actress seem fresh. Theresa Russell is a believable Cecilia as the film (wisely, for once) has simplified her; only Jack Nicholson has trouble toning down his innate dazzlingness to the unflashy part of a labor organizer.

One performance, however, nearly wrecks the film, while another makes it a virtual must. Ingrid Boulting is disastrous as Kathleen: prissy, with a ponderous deliberateness, a studied itch to be different. The very blankness of her voice is a way of jockeying for effect, and though her figure is exquisite, she has the face of a plastic woodchuck, with two stacked-up cubes surmounting a pointy, pyramidal chin. The total effect is insufficient, histrionically as well as visually. But Robert De Niro's Stahr is perfection itself. Here is that terrible soft-spoken irresistibility of the steamroller that can gracefully and speedily convince its victims that flat is not only beautiful but also necessary. De Niro does not so much obtrude his power as invite powerlessness in others. Yet he knows, too, how to be little-boyish and lost, how to beg with a silent cry.

There is also remarkable art direction from Gene Callahan, and a good though overabundant score from Maurice Jarre. But Victor Kemper's cinematography, though adequate indoors, turns washed-out outside.

November 29, 1976

Masterly Camera, Miscarried *Carrie*

BOUND FOR GLORY is the nearest thing on film to leafing through the album of a great photographer. It is nice to welcome Haskell Wexler, who may well be our finest cinematographer, back to unimpeded and undisguised work (impeded, for instance, in *One Flew Over the Cuckoo's Nest* and disguised in *American Graffiti*), after he had found little or no work because of his leftist sympathies. A film based on the autobiography of Woody Guthrie, and dealing mostly with the Depression, the Dust Bowl, the desperate people trying to get to California where new horrors awaited them, the difficulties of labor organizers confronted with worker apathy and management goons, would naturally have stimulated Wexler. It has done more than that, eliciting from him the most magnificent cinematography in an American movie in I don't know how many years. The phrase "Every frame is a work of art," so recklessly bandied about by film reviewers, may very nearly apply here. I have certainly never seen life in a windswept Texas town or the world of hoboes snitching rides from the railroads shot with such starkness and beauty without these contrary elements canceling each other out.

I wish this were the place for a close study of Wexler's camera work in the film—it is the one thing that sustains our continued attention to this serious and well-intentioned but rambling and superficial movie for which neither Robert Getchell's script nor Hal Ashby's direction—nor even Woody Guthrie's songs that David Carradine renders decently along with some of his own—can do much that is sufficiently antisoporific. In fact, this long and uninflected movie could easily be dismissed as a much lesser *Grapes of Wrath* with music if it weren't for the bitter lyricism of Wexler's camera. True, the many, often very brief, performances are mostly very good—as are Ronny Cox, Gail Strickland, and Randy Quaid in somewhat bigger parts. David Carradine gives a thoroughly sincere, quiet, and winning interpretation of Woody, exhibiting the low-keyed charm of the young Gary Cooper. Only Melinda Dillon is too manneristically Second City for a starving hick town.

But, oh, the photography, with its strictly subdued yet searing colors, its ability to suggest the monochrome skeleton under the world's many-hued flesh. *Bound for Glory* is almost the cinematic equivalent of the lavish Broadway musicals you leave humming the scenery; the difference is that you cannot really hum scenery, whereas nothing comes easier than singing the praises of Wexler's camera work.

It is hardly worth speculating about Brian De Palma's *Carrie,* a horror movie with grandiose aspirations to social satire. The horror is effective only once, at the end, and the attempts at humor are never very successful and come almost always when one is inclined to be moved by somebody's plight, so that the nonjokes yield authentic bad taste. The plot crawls with self-contradictions and improbabilities (even if one grants, as one willingly does, the central notion of telekinesis, the heroine's ability to move distant objects by thought control), and the bad characters are ludicrous while the good ones are saccharine.

Worst of all are the big effects, drawn out to impossible lengths and shot with trashy blatancy, as when a couple whirling about a dance floor are dwelt on with a monomaniacal insistence that gives the viewer an acute case of nausea. Or, again, when the pulling of a rope is made to last long enough to hoist all sails on a man-of-war. Such things do not exactly induce suspense; rather, they could replace narcosis in surgery. The performances are mostly humdrum or worse, except for that of Sissy Spacek in the lead: a touchingly unspoiled, intense, and various creation.

What could bear meditating on is the stack of good reviews from reputable critics. De Palma has been a critics' darling ever since his early irreverently anomic movies made on a shoestring and wildly diverting. But why should the critics persist in their fidelity to his early promise if De Palma himself has broken the faith.

December 6, 1976

Ape Rape and Other Indignities

The remake of *King Kong* rates very high on my list of unnecessary films. The new version tries hard to come up with things the original lacked: Freud, feminism, ecology, social satire, spoofing of astrology, and, above all, sympathy for the ape. In fact, the romance is now much more between beast and girl than between boy and girl, and the film can barely restrain itself from providing a *Liebestod* for the sweetly simian protagonist and the clearly zoophilic heroine. But for all this, nothing substantial has been added and something considerable has been forfeited.

The original version was genuine trash, like a novel by Jackie Susann or a painting by Norman Rockwell. Imagine, however, Nabokov trying to write a *Valley of the Dolls,* or Picasso trying to paint a *Saturday Evening Post* cover; the result would be much worse than Susann or Rockwell. Trash works up to a point because of its author's idiotic conviction that his product has genuine merit; there is no condescension and no fakery. The result is genuine, not fake, garbage. I am not saying that Lorenzo Semple, Jr., the scenarist of *KK* II, is a Nabokov, mind you; or that John Guillermin, the director, is a Picasso. Still, they are sophisticated well beyond the kind of innocence that yields authentic blooms of banality; they can produce only self-conscious kitsch.

The plot of *KK* II is close to that of *KK* I, but the dialogue is different and tries to be clever—as when the heroine reminds the beast on their second encounter of their initial "blind date"; or when, hoisted skyward in the beast's enormous paw, she tells him she is a Libra and asks what sign he is—Aries most likely. But this sort of thing is at best arch, at worst campy, whereas *KK* I had a primitive wholesomeness about it that *KK* II—even though the new Kong has expressions far more lovesick, eyes far more soulful or sorrowing than the old one—utterly lacks.

There are other disconcerting things about this twenty-four-million-dollar venture (thirty-nine million dollars if you count the promotion costs). The special effects are no better than in *KK* I—sometimes not even as good—and, with the passage of forty-three years, that is a serious lag. The cinematography of *KK* II, by Richard H. Kline, is just about the worst I have seen in so expensive a movie in years: Kline's lighting (which, as nearly everyone knows, is what cinematography is mostly about) is downright primitive, and makes large chunks of the movie look garish or washed-out. And Guillermin's direction is consistently uninteresting. But the director must have been laboring under an added handicap. With so major an investment, Dino De Laurentiis, the producer, clearly wanted to take no chances. Thus, advance rumors of nudity notwithstanding, the film has no sex other than the most implicit, and virtually no violence; we even got to see more of Fay Wray's bosom than of Jessica Lange's. Given all the things it doesn't have, a little sexual daring is about the only dubious asset *KK* II could have conjured up.

It would be quite pointless to try to discuss the acting in the human parts, although Charles Grodin manages to squeeze some juice out of the role of a comic villain. The beast, however—or the machine, or the man in the machine, whichever—achieves some touching moments, as when it showers its soiled baby doll in a waterfall, then dries her off by tenderly blowing on her. But the remake, alas, does not have anything like the grand philosophical closing line of the original—my God, is nostalgia creeping up even on me? And that is the worst thing about *KK* II: it is going to turn *KK* I, which it has contractually banned from showing, into a martyr—something great, sacred, and lost—when it too was, after all, only trash.

Voyage of the Damned is numbingly earnest in its intentions and crushingly dull in its execution. A pity, that, for several reasons. It is based on a shattering historical event with serious present-day implications; a good deal of effort by famous and capable people has gone into it; and the financing was lavish to the point of recklessness. There are fleeting instants when the power of the facts depicted, however inadequately, sears the screen; for the rest of its 158 minutes, Stanley Kramer might as well have been in charge, and the film be called *The Return Voyage of the Ship of Fools.*

In May 1939, the Nazis allowed the *St. Louis,* a ship of the Hamburg Amerika Line, to sail with 937 Jewish passengers; the destination was Havana, and all on board thought they had the necessary papers. Cuba, in the midst of its customary political unrest, refused, after great shilly-shallying, to let the passengers disembark, despite much passionate agitation, not least from the Jewish Agency. The ship, under the command of a sympathetic anti-Nazi captain, then sailed for Florida, from whose waters it was mercilessly chased away by Roosevelt's coast guard, a chilling development over which the film passes rather too rapidly. Meanwhile, of course, panic and disaster ran rampant among the passengers, climaxing with the realization that they were headed back for Hamburg and perdition. Goebbels and company, it seems, had planned the voyage partly as a smoke screen for espionage activities, partly foreseeing that no country would admit the voyagers, thereby tacitly corroborating the Nazis' treatment of the Jews. At the eleventh hour, Belgium, Holland, France, and Britain provided asylum for a quarter of the passengers each; but since three of those countries were overrun by the Nazis, some two thirds of the emigrants perished anyway.

The script by Steve Shagan and David Butler allegedly sticks close to a nonfiction account by Gordon Thomas and Max Morgan-Witts. Not having read the book, I cannot say; but the lush hokum of most of the screenwriting cannot help being indebted to the scenarists' incompetence. Shagan I know only too well from *Save the Tiger* and *Hustle;* about Butler I know nothing, unless he is that notorious butler who did it. Significantly, the production brochure, whose tonnage closely approximates that of the *St. Louis,* contains overgenerous information about everyone down to the composer and producer, but not a word about the writers. In any case, the dialogue they have concocted is so much flotsam and jetsam that gradually accumulates into a kind of Sargasso Sea through which the film can barely make headway.

The stories of these passengers and crew members—not to mention those of their supporters or impeders on land—would indeed require writers of exceptional talents to lift them out of the Grand Hotel triteness that almost always adheres to such cross-sectional ventures. Where there are so many characters, there is scant opportunity for developing any of them; so, if these slivers of humanity are to come alive, words, gestures, actions of uncommon authenticity must be found for them, well beyond the abilities of common hacks who could just barely pump some life into fewer characters with more time and space to disport themselves in. As it is, characterizations are reduced to formulas and platitudes, a shorthand that is the very antithesis of living art. Bad as it would be to inflict such treatment on fictional characters, it is worse yet to inflict it on real, tragic lives; thus watching this film makes one squirm and suffer, but only at the quality of the filmmaking.

The direction by Stuart Rosenberg (it is hard to believe that he once gave us the somewhat hokey but genuinely effective *Cool Hand Luke*) sails in a class lower than steerage—Stanley Kramer class: either grandly predictable, or so obvious as to seem predictable after the fact. Take the episode where a singer at a supposed predisembarkation masked ball brings tears of homesickness to the revelers' eyes. This could be moving. But the song is about Vienna and these are German Jews (as evidenced by the wildly incompatible accents Hollywood continues to be deaf to ethnic differences); the singer is Danish and could make only Germanic linguists cry at her pronunciation; and the schematic way in which the dancing couples stop at regular intervals, lift their masks by the numbers, and turn on the waterworks as if by faucets ruins everything. The model for this sort of thing is still the camp-show scene from Renoir's *Grand Illusion;* it eludes Rosenberg.

Or consider the characters of the two schoolteachers played by Paul Koslo and Jonathan Pryce; the latter, as his current stage performance in *Comedians* proves, a highly gifted actor, and Koslo, for all I know, no slouch either. But as Rosenberg directed them (and Shagan and Butler wrote them), rather than as teachers with sensitive minds wounded by having been in a concentration camp, they come across as stand-ins for King Kong. Or what about the double suicide of the young lovers, the least moving death scene I can recall in a long time? It is redeemed in part only by the superb acting of Max von Sydow as he discovers the bodies; but that extraordinary Swede rises from shambles after shambles, from *The Greatest Story Ever Told* to *The Exorcist,* unscathed, indeed triumphant.

Billy Williams's cinematography is, as usual, only workmanlike; Lalo Schifrin's scores have been steadily deteriorating, and this one is no exception; Phyllis Dalton's costume design is not even free of anachronisms; only Wilfred Shingleton's production design deserves commendation for, among other things, turning Barcelona successfully into Havana. Under the circumstances, the burden of carrying this albatross devolves on the actors, and given their roles, few of them can make it. Aside from Max von Sydow's captain, only Ben Gazzara as the Jewish Agency man, and Wendy Hiller, Luther Adler, Michael Constantine, Jose Ferrer, and Donald Houston in still lesser parts come off well. Oskar Werner, in an aggressive hairpiece that turns him into something midway between a gigolo from the Belle Epoque and a

Lhasa apso, underacts with a hammy vengeance; Lee Grant is unable to de-Americanize herself in the least; Victor Spinetti overdoes the humble bit while, as his estranged wife, Janet Suzman is far too grand; Malcolm McDowell looks too old for his part—in one night scene, downright wizened (why, when he is a young man?); and Orson Welles, as so often, cannot resist playing himself.

From some others we don't expect much. The wretched Helmut Griem, as the evil Nazi, is about as subtle as the script; Julie Harris does her standard schtik, although at least looking her age; Maria Schell, one of the world's most mannered actresses, drips tearful honey all over the place, and is as sticky as an unwashed breakfast plate; James Mason and Fernando Rey could not possibly score with their embryonic roles; and Sam Wanamaker, for all his years in England, where acting flowers, has learned nothing.

As for the leading ladies, Faye Dunaway does one of her routine jobs, though she can do appreciably better; Lynne Frederick is charming and spirited, and should travel far and undamned on future voyages; and Katharine Ross is so ludicrously miscast as a young German Jewess turned whore in Havana as to provide the film's only laughs. Mention must also be made of Laura Gemser, who does nothing except stand or sit leeward of Orson Welles and, with her beauty, steals every scene from him. *Voyage of the Damned* is a damned shame.

December 27, 1976

Varieties of Death Wish

REVIEWING THE BIG YEAR'S-END MOVIES is, I'm afraid, rather like compiling a list of the year's worst. Take, for starters, *Mikey and Nicky,* Elaine May's current debacle. This gifted comic artist has chosen to make something impossible: a film about two horrid fellows alternately abusing and greasily cajoling each other (and equally repulsive either way) when not getting into fights with other men or, for a little variety, maltreating the hapless women in their lives. Awful as this premise is, there is worse to come. One of these two old buddies may have a contract out on his life; the other is trying either to save or to finger him. Our sympathies are manipulated in such a way that we must keep switching allegiances: now we are dragged into feeling pity for an utter louse, now we are forced to recoil at the creepiness of a dedicated friend.

The idea seems to be to show us the relativity of emotional truths in a world where good and bad have become Gordianly entangled; where even the decent, long-suffering women are also frumps or doormats whom the swinish men exploit by means of a drop of charm or pathos mixed in with their meanness. It does not begin to work. Not just because you cannot be simultaneously Damon Runyon and Dostoevsky, but also because you can't make us care about people whose sweetness is virtually indistinguishable from their beastliness, so that the range of feelings with which we view their interminable, degrading squabbles extends only from distaste to boredom. Can you imagine two hours' worth of film about love, hate, and death among the cockroaches? And even that might be more interesting than this endless dawdling among people whose very souls are sweaty under their collars.

What truly sets one's teeth on edge, though, is that Miss May cannot forgo that cuteness which, when used aptly in zany, satirical comedy, adds an extra flavor to the zestful brew. Superimposed on this morose and morbid mess, however, it is unendurable—rather like a cloying perfume fighting a losing battle with an acrid body odor.

Now add to this technical analphabetism. Victor Kemper's always rather amateurish cinematography is further undercut by editing and continuity that are thoroughly shocking in a major film. Thus during one scene John Cassavetes is both shaven and glaringly unshaven; or fragments from the same bus ride will appear both before and after a long, maudlin cemetery sequence, with the fragments after it not even benefiting from an establishing shot of some sort. One becomes acutely aware of Miss May's endless, irresolute editing, of her unhealthy inability to be finished with something, to let go. On a more elementary level yet, the film never gives us the much needed exposition that would clue us in about who these characters really are, what their work is, and what Nicky has done or not done to incur his boss's lethal wrath.

As if that were not enough, there is also the acting. If you have felt that some of the Cassavetes films in which he, Peter Falk, and various others carried on ad infinitum improvising their modest brains out were the last gasp of drearily self-indulgent Method actors' exercises, you have another one coming. Here this non- or antitechnique is stretched out to even greater desolation, until you feel as though you had been locked into the Actors Studio for a week—a fate worse than any hell, Dante's, Sartre's, and Hieronymus Bosch's included. The only way to describe *Mikey and Nicky* is as a celluloid death wish, a desperate challenge to the audience to dare enjoy anything about the film. Like Miss May's writing and direction, the acting of Falk, Cassavetes, and the rest is not so much created as exuded or secreted, in the manner of some particularly nasty discharge. Two small but rotten performances, incidentally, are contributed by the well-known acting teachers Sanford Meisner and William Hickey. Altogether this is a film for audiences consisting solely of actors of the ingrown-toenail school of acting, and though they are numerous, there cannot be enough of them to keep this dismal film running.

There are also other ways, of course, for a film director to self-destruct, and Peter Bogdanovich's is to make the crudest, stupidest, unfunniest farce of this or any year, with two hours' worth of laughs guaranteed to stick in the craw if they do not sink to the pit of the stomach. *Nickelodeon* may well contain every gag—good, bad, or horrible—that ever crawled, crashed, or sashayed onto the stage or screen since Aristophanes or Méliès, and slapped together with minimal imagination or scruple. I can foresee only two possible uses for the film. One is as a catalogue of no longer usable gags, gimmicks, one-liners;

if they are in this movie, they are in so advanced a stage of decomposition that they can't even be buried without the gravediggers being issued gas masks. The other is as a sanity test: anyone who catches himself laughing at any of it at this late date should seriously consider commiting himself to the nearest mental hospital even though in his case a cure is hardly to be hoped for.

Ostensibly it all has to do with early filmmaking and the brutish warfare waged by the one big movie company against all the little ones; but it is only an excuse for Bogdanovich to tack every joke he has cribbed onto the one subject that means anything to him: moviemaking. *Nickelodeon* might more appropriately be called *The Night of the Walking Dead Gags,* except that they do not walk—they merely put one pratfall before the other. There must be some two hundred pratfalls, and there is nothing sadder than watching body after body falling through empty, laughterless space.

Amazingly, Bogdanovich is not even good with actors in this one; he can make the almost indestructible Brian Keith, playing one of those manic early producer-directors, come out not as an *hommage* but as a *dommage.* What he does to destructible actors shouldn't happen to a dog—one of which is actually in the movie and manages to be (a rare thing among film dogs) bad.

There are a couple of points of interest. The first is that Bogdanovich succeeds in making even one of the great scenes from *Birth of a Nation* interpolated into *Nickelodeon* look like mud; the second is that, told that he would not be bankrolled if he yet again starred his untalented girl friend Cybill Shepherd, Bogdanovich was able to unearth another model, Jane Hitchcock, even less tolerable than the previous one. Long ago I predicted that Bogdanovich's feeble, mostly imitative endowment would run dry as soon as he ran out of ideas to steal from the treasure trove of old movies he had sedulously memorized; even I did not suspect, though, that he would be so obtuse and brazen as to resteal the same ones.

And then there is the most expensive and arrogant of these aberrations, the re-remake of *A Star Is Born* with Barbra Streisand in what seems to be both the female and male leads. The first, 1937 version of the film was rather touching; the second, from 1954, though supererogatory and inferior, still had a nice scene or two. This third version is not only unneeded, it is emphatically uncalled-for. This time round it is the marriage of two rock stars—he declining, she rising—whose noisy disintegration is chronicled with condign oafishness. The oft rewritten script, attributed in its final version to John Gregory Dunne, Joan Didion, and Frank Pierson (the last of whom, nominally, also directed), cannot even begin to convey why the highly successful rock star John Norman Howard, played dimly by Kris Kristofferson, is going to pot—as well as to poppers, coke, and suicide—beyond ascribing it all to some undefinable death wish we are meant to take for granted in these post–Joplin-Hendrix-Morrison days.

This is a crazy quilt of the work of countless scenarists and directors, not least (except in quality) of Barbra Streisand and her mate, Jon Peters. Plot elements, like all the non-Barbra characters, including even Kristofferson, surface and vanish without making much of an impression. But, oh, is there ever Barbra! During the filming, she complained that there weren't enough closeups of her. Either she was mistaken then, or even more mistaken later, when she reedited the film to suit her immense ego; it is full of enormous closeups of a face that, even in medium-long shot, is an enormity.

Oh, for the gift of Rostand's Cyrano to evoke the vastness of that nose alone as it cleaves the giant screen from east to west, bisects it from north to south. It zigzags across our horizon like a bolt of fleshy lightning; it towers like a ziggurat made of meat. The hair is now something like the wig of the fop in a Restoration comedy; the speaking voice continues to sound like Rice Krispies if they could talk. And Streisand's notion of acting is to bulldoze her way from one end of a line to the other without regard for anyone or anything; you can literally feel her impatience for the other performer to stop talking so she can take over again. If dialogue there is, it is that between a steamroller and the asphalt beneath it.

Whenever possible, she gets herself shot with a halo of backlights from head to foot; yet she insists on wearing the most ridiculous glad rags, especially on horseback, where she looks like a takeoff on Brando in his *Missouri Breaks* granny outfit. Her clothes, a screen credit states, came out of her closet; if so, I am dead against *Schmatte* Liberation. Horrors of every kind abound, not least in the dialogue, which has her, in a climactic scene, yelling at Kristofferson, "I've had it with you! You can trash your life, but you're not going to trash mine!" Another line, which actually gets repeated, runs, "Are you a figment of my imagination, or am I of yours?" Asked reverentially about something she is tinkering with on the piano, she blurts out modestly, "Oh, it's just a little piece I wrote—it's going to be a sonata when it grows up." Kris tells Barbra, "When you hook into an incredible marlin, that's what it felt like hearing you sing." Funny; it feels like that to me when I see her face.

Barbra's singing? Amid the growing obstreperousness there are still a few pleasing bars when she doesn't push too hard. Even it can become quite unbearable, though, as in that closing scene whose unintentional humor is the one reward for those who can stick it out to the end. Here, giving her first concert after her spouse's demise, Barbra does a conscious or unconscious audiovisual impersonation of Mick Jagger by way of a tribute to her late husband, to whom, while the audience lights funerary matches and she herself is yet again haloed from top to toe by Robert Surtees's backlighting, she sings: "Your eyes are like fingers/Touching my body,/Arousing me so. . . ."

It is a moment of exquisite absurdity that makes me marvel at the megalomania of the whole undertaking. Could even people who accepted as valid the banal tribulations and factitious emotions of those overblown nonentities who seemed to make the screen even flatter than it is, fall for this piece of superbathos? Especially since the song, whether it is by Paul Williams, Kenny Ascher, Barbra herself, or one of several others who contributed to this seamlessly blending score, is as undistinguished as all the rest.

And then I realize with a gasp that this Barbra Streisand is in fact beloved above all other female stars by our moviegoing audiences; that this hypertrophic ego and bloated countenance are things people shell out money for as for no other actress; that this progressively more belligerent caterwauling can sell anything—concerts, records, movies. And I feel as if our entire society were ready to flush itself down in something even worse than a collective death wish—a collective will to live in ugliness and self-debasement.

January 10, 1977

Truth: No Stranger Than Fiction

THE NEW CINEMATIC YEAR begins with two documentaries that, though quite different, have this is common: they demonstrate that the nonfiction film can be quite as mediocre as the fiction film, even when addressing itself to subjects of profound or bizarre ready-made interest.

Harlan County U.S.A. is a well-intentioned piece of work about a coal miners' strike in Harlan County, Kentucky, that lasted thirteen months and led, after the brutal shooting of a miner, to the mine owners' acceding to the miners' demands, which were nothing more than the right to unionize. Along the way, this 103-minute film touches also on related matters: a major mine disaster, the Yablonski murders, other strikes and contract negotiations on the national level. The film is openly partisan: the miners are shown in a variety of places and situations; the mine owners and their scabs and goons are shown exclusively bossing around and gooning it up. My sympathies are with the underdog—just about any underdog—but I do not want to be manipulated. Yet that is precisely what the film does: it manipulates.

Let me start at the end, with one of the closing credits that reads: "Principle [*sic*] Cinematography: Hart Perry." Now, I am sorry, but I mistrust an illiterate filmmaker a priori; or, perhaps, since the credits come at the end, a posteriori. It is all right for these embattled coal miners to be illiterate: they can't help it, and it does not diminish their humanity, indeed nobility. But Barbara Kopple, the filmmaker, graduated from a university—even if it is only Northeastern. Still, she could have learned the difference between *principal* and *principle;* to allow the latter to impersonate the former in a card as big as life bodes ill for the culture of the filmmaker and the mentality of the film.

What a chasm there is between a great documentary by, say, Marcel Ophüls and Miss Kopple's *Harlan County U.S.A.* Yet the latter is not a total loss. After all, when people are trodden down to the point where their naked humanity is stepped on—when they at last take cognizance of the need to band together and fight against great and brutal odds—there are bound to be moments of courage and dignity, of warmth and suffering and even humor begotten by misery, that cannot help moving and sternly shaking us. All the filmmaker need do is be there. Let her push her way in with her cameras, and there is just about no way for her not to come back with some invaluable *objets trouvés* of grandeur under stress.

Such an enterprise should not be underrated, however. It takes vision and determination to conceive, shoot, and put together a *Harlan County U.S.A,* even if it is not done particularly well. There are sequences here as tragic or heart-warming as anything ever seen on film, despite the fact that they are usually, if not exactly botched, seriously impaired by being sprung on us out of adequate context, or by being held too long, or by remaining insufficiently analyzed to become illuminating. Thus the sequence of events stays unclear, and causality even more so.

But there are some wonderful details, as when old-timers who lived through the "Bloody Harlan" of the thirties draw stirring parallels between then and now while urging bloodless resistance, or when some remarkably staunch and levelheaded miners' wives assert themselves, or when a mother confronts the body of her murdered son (though this one is milked for too many audience tears—it would have been more effective shorter), or when a demonstrating Kentucky miner in New York City has a comic dialogue with a sympathetic but uninformed policeman.

Yet, I say, beware of people like Barbara Kopple, whose manifestly righteous indignation prevents them from seeing both sides of a question. People who are perfectly happy to do justice to one side only, granted that it is much the better one. Don't mine owners have problems too? And families? And responsibilities? Does being successful and rich automatically turn these people into slave-driving exploiters? Maybe so, but I would like to see the matter more thoughtfully examined. A doctor says that the health conditions for miners in other countries are much better than in the United States, but the film does not pursue and evaluate these differences lest some mine owners, somewhere, be proved humane. We learn that Boyle, the UMW president, was involved in the Yablonski murders, but we learn nothing about the motives: collusion with capital or simply personal rivalry?

There are other difficulties with the film. Miss Kopple and many of her coworkers being women, and probably feminists, the role of women in the strike seems to have been magnified. No doubt these wives and daughters were extremely brave, delightfully outspoken, and full of a saltiness that borders on sophisticated wit; still, we are given the impression at times that the pickets were almost all women, that among the leaders there were virtually no men. This may in fact have been the case, but I want some facts and figures. Facts and figures, however, are few and far between in this film—which is a pity, for when they are given, they are devastating, e.g.: management's profits up 170 percent; cost of living up 8 percent; miners' profits up 5 percent. So why not more of them?

There is, on top of all that, no rhythm to the film. No clear profile of the action, no real variety in the pace, no sense of the passage of time and growing hardships (if such they were) on the strikers. We do not get to know these people as we would in an Ophüls film, in large part because no one is asking them pertinent questions. Yet it must be pointed out in these filmmakers' defense that the Kentucky miners and mine owners lack the intellectual, educational, and verbal endowments of many of the people in an Ophüls documentary—even that glorious Irish gift of gab so evident in *A Sense of Loss.* And though the cinematography is adequate, the many songs on the soundtrack, generally written and performed by the miners themselves, are better as human documents than as words and music.

Still, you could do worse than see this film, and I personally was overcome by one aspect of it that surely never occurred to the filmmakers. As I watched some of these miners' wives already teasing their hair into preposterous beehives, I had to wonder what would happen to these good and gallant people if they were to get not only the modest increments they finally won for themselves, but also more: their full due in an affluent society. Gradually, I believe, these worthy folk would settle into their Pontiacs and color televisions, their decoy ducks on the mantelpiece and plaster dwarfs in the garden.

Before long, they would have their culture heroes, too, in Johnny Carson and Rex Reed, while the intrepid wives who nurtured guns for self-defense in their capacious bosoms would now clasp to them a Barbra Streisand and a Barbara Walters. And what—among the best furniture Grand Rapids can offer, the latest Literary Guild selections, and the children acting in school productions of *Our Town*—would become of all this noble, righteously embattled humanity? Who could still tell the miners from the mine owners? O Barbara Kopple, people are far more contradictory, questionable, weird, and fascinating than anything dreamt of in your philosophy!

Pumping Iron is a much smaller and specialized sort of documentary than *Harlan County U.S.A.* George Butler and Robert Fiore's film, based on a book by Butler and Charles Gaines (the latter responsible also for *Stay Hungry*), is about musclemen—body-builders, to give them their preferred, more architectural, title—and, to a much lesser extent, their families, trainers, fans. It is a film that cannot help having a certain freak-show appeal: monumental exaggeration—whether in architecture, conversation, musculature, or anything else—casts an unwholesome spell. These bodies, supposedly re-creating the marvels of Greek sculpture in living flesh, are actually rococo excrescences, grotesque hyperboles, delusions of fleshy grandeur. These mastodon muscles bursting from human frames are like a speedboat engine attached to a toy brigantine—worse yet, like an abattoir on Livestock Resurrection Day. Enormous hunks of dormant meat suddenly begin to ripple and bulge and swell into balloons. They exceed all shapes known to Myron and Phidias (or, for that matter, to normal man or beast), and turn whatever can be proportional and beautiful into frenzied hypertrophy, muscular megalomania, a deformity no better than abject scrawniness.

The most tyrannical and yet pathetic of fathers, who acts as both trainer and chief sycophant to his son—of all the body-builders in the movie, the least (or, depending on your definition, the most) anthropoid—informs his boy that he looks like something out of Michelangelo, though he looks much more like the Michelin Tire man—names similar enough, I suppose, to be confused by imprecise minds. Except for this doting father, however, there are almost no members of the musclemen's families to be seen, certainly not the wives and girl friends about whom we hear quite a bit. Nor is there evidence of homosexuality among the men and their fans; interesting, but is
 it a fact? We do not find out how these herculean beings get along with

people of ordinary dimensions; or even what the causes were that drove them to pushing themselves "through the pain barrier," as one of them says: grueling regimens to achieve gargantuan statures.

True, one man, we are told, was born with impaired hearing; another was teased by schoolmates for being Jewish and wearing glasses. But why did they choose to compensate in *this* way? No mention is made of narcissism, even when a body-builder called Mike has named his two children Michael and Michele, even when the most Cro-Magnon among these chaps is seen spending long, dedicated posing sessions before his mirror. Nor are we shown what becomes of these bodies after they are compelled to stop working out by advancing age or declining health—the pitiful dissolving into barrows of lard, something like a statue by Gaston Lachaise melting into a Medardo Rosso. We learn even less about the enthusiastic fans we keep glimpsing throughout, and what sort of power, sexual or other, the colossi have over them.

And yet the film has its riveting passages, as when we see the screen well-nigh explode with the superhuman, or superbovine, exertions of these body-builders, or when Arnold Schwarzenegger, the champion of champions, gives out with mischievous bits of witty cynicism. A thinking or, at any rate, wise-cracking giant—why, it's as good as a talking dog!

January 24, 1977

Star-Spangled Boner

WHAT IS ONE TO SAY about a film that, at this late date, acts as if *it* had discovered the Vietnam-Watergate two-act debacle on behalf of Hollywood filmmaking? That it is way too late? Sad to say, *Twilight's Last Gleaming* may well be the first main-line film that tries to take full account of our national shame even if it does not deal directly with any past events. For that is the extraordinary—or, knowing our movies, not so extraordinary—fact: except for passing references to them, an indefensible war and unconscionable administration have not yet been the subject of a fiction film, only of a documentary like *Hearts and Minds* or quasi-documentary like *All the President's Men.*

How eagerly, then, is one tempted to salute, how proudly would one like to hail, Robert Aldrich's *Twilight's Last Gleaming,* laid somewhere in the near future but trying to come to grips with our recent past and its possibly fearful consequences. Unfortunately, sincerity does not seem to exclude sensationalism. Aldrich is an ambiguous figure, a typical case of what can happen to quite a good man in Hollywood, where, to rephrase Oscar Wilde's famous epigram, some of us may look at the stars and still lie in the gutter. It is instructive to note the ambivalent view most film handbooks have of Aldrich. In his *Dictionary of Film Makers,* the Frenchman Georges Sadoul writes: "His style is powerful, persuasive, and a little hysterical." The Britisher Leslie Halliwell, in his *The Filmgoer's Companion,* says Aldrich has "declined from gritty realism to inflated melodrama." Another Britisher, Margaret Hinxman, in *The International Encyclopedia of Film,* notes: "Latterly his style has coarsened as his productions have grown in size and budget." And here is our own encyclopedic Pauline Kael about Aldrich's *The Big Knife:* "But with all these faults of taste, perhaps because of them, who could take his eyes off the screen?"

Go as far back as you wish—the coarseness is there in every Aldrich film, even in his best, *Kiss Me Deadly.* Yet the very beginning of that movie is the essence of what *film noir* is all about, and the tension barely lets up thereafter. Even as trashy a piece as Aldrich's recent *Hustle* has a certain class to it, not all of it Catherine Deneuve. Not for nothing has the man been assistant director (on the credit side) to Renoir, Chaplin, and Abraham Polonsky, as well as (on the debit side) to Milestone, Rossen, Losey, and Albert Lewin, among others. Something of the honest concern for people of the first group seems to have rubbed off on him along with much of the attitudinizing of the second.

There surely is no thematic consistency in his work, which includes such vastly different offerings as *Apache, Autumn Leaves, Whatever Happened to Baby Jane?,* and *The Dirty Dozen.* Andrew Sarris defines Aldrich as "a moralist in a man's world," which is pretty vague, but no worse than any other attempt at defining such elusiveness. Sarris is right to stress Aldrich's violence, but it must also be noted that the violence is almost always handled in an imaginative way, and was, in this respect, ahead of its time—though I am not sure whether that was a good thing. There is certainly a vision of evil in his films that tries to be apocalyptic, but usually ends up being ugly and faintly scabrous. Yet he does know how to generate genuine excitement rather than merely accumulate strident effects. In *The Flight of the Phoenix,* for instance, the thrills became more affecting because we got sincerely involved with the characters of the tale, something any old action director could not have given us.

Twilight's Last Gleaming, a good and histrionic Aldrich title, concerns Lawrence Dell, a provident maverick general who was busted and jailed on a trumped-up charge for wanting to stem the suicidal escalation of armament, as he sees it, and the dishonest maneuverings of the executive branch, which keep the people in the dark about cold- and not-so-cold-war machinations. He breaks out of military prison with three more or less unsavory fellow inmates, and they manage to infiltrate and take over a part of a Montana missile base. From this nearly impregnable position, they are able to launch nine Titan missiles aimed at Soviet targets. Dell is prepared to plunge the world into atomic destruction in order to prevent atomic destruction, a rather obvious self-contradiction that does not get pointed out to him until near the end of the movie, and then, of course, by his co-conspirator, ex-corporal Powell, who, like virtually all movie blacks, is staunch, streetwise, and cynical.

So there it is: ingenious, intrepid, indomitable, and foresighted Dell has the president, his cabinet, the military, the CIA by the proverbial short hairs, and duly comes within a short-hair's breadth of dispatching a Titan or two or nine. (I don't think I am giving away any plot here: even in these swinging days, Hollywood would balk at Armageddon.) But while successfully contending with a lot of double-dyed villainy—notably from the commanding general of SAC, who hatches truly diabolic schemes to get him—Dell manages to overlook the most obvious traps. O paradox!

Dell intends to get the president to fly off with him to some Third World stronghold, and thence broadcast the contents of a particularly nasty secret document to the people of the United States—a document so monstrous that the president, apparently totally unaware of it till now, reads it over twenty times and still, as he quaintly puts it, doesn't believe it. Even the most liberal members of the cabinet (which, naturally, includes one black) boggle at such a disclosure of double-dealing in high places; yet when its content is finally read out to us, it seems no different from that of a good many others that have long since found their way into the open. Maybe after careful preparation of the public, say these liberal statesmen, eventually, but not now! Well, all the brilliant Dell would have to do is to force the president's hand while Dell's finger is still on the red button. But no, he has to plump for that little airplane jaunt with the president as hostage. It is all right for the hero to have an Achilles' heel, but not in his head.

The film is based on a novel by Walter Wager, a former publicist whose most recent fiction is a King Kong spoof, and that may explain a good deal, if not everything. The rest is Aldrich, and the early action sequences have a commendable tautness and great, albeit controlled, brutality. Similarly, the early scenes showing President Stevens, a reasonably honest and sensible, but not extraordinarily bright or brave, fellow, trying to cope with the emergency—scenes that involve also a rather typical but not wholly uninteresting batch of cabinet members, and some even more typical but still not totally cliché military brass—are not without astute observation and a kind of propulsive raciness.

Even here, however, there is a good deal of posturing and some near-irrelevance, as in the scene involving an African head of state; but there is also a sufficiency of good acting—some of it from indifferent actors resourcefully type-cast—to cover up most of the weak spots. Later, however, the going and the dialogue both get thicker and heavier, more crudely conceived, and far less persuasive. Yet the Aldrich mark is still there: you giggle, get faintly repelled, feel infinitely superior to the obvious idiocy, but are not bored. Even the fact that you can guess the outcome, and think the entire thing ridiculous, does not propel you toward the exit.

Dell and his main sidekick, the often recalcitrant Powell, are played without much subtlety by Burt Lancaster and Paul Winfield, but the director manages to make their very crassness a part of their characterizations. Worse and very nearly unbearable is Burt Young, who carries the low-life mannerisms that served him in good stead in *Rocky* to revolting extremes. But everyone else is good to excellent; even the fact that Joseph Cotten, as the secretary of state, seems either ossified or mummified somehow works in context. Charles Durning, as a fat president (has adiposity ever proved eligible since the days of Taft?), is an amusing, idiosyncratic, and believable bundle of contradictions; Richard Widmark, as the SAC commandant, is quite marvelous: a handsome brute with just the right amount of surface suavity, sporting a sarcastic smirk that is almost engaging in its hearty enjoyment of the wickedness lurking behind it.

Several others make nice contributions, notably Gerald S. O'Loughlin as the president's adjutant, an irreverent, ribaldly outspoken, loyal friend who, when the president finally gets it, bursts into . . . I can't tell you what, because that would really be giving away things. Robert Hauser's cinematography is as routine as Jerry Goldsmith's score, but everything else about this American-German coproduction, especially the military hardware, looks convincing to these civilian eyes. If you have seen the two or three good movies playing around town, and can swallow the curious blend of over- and underwriting in this Ronald M. Cohen–Edward Huebsch screenplay, you may get some kicks out of this not good movie. Somewhere in middle America, heaven help us, *Twilight's Last Gleaming* may even make a dent where subtler and truer statements would not begin to register.

If you like latter-day variations on the private-eye movie—variations that consist chiefly of tongue-in-cheek deflations of the genre, of deglamorizing even its glamorous antiglamour—you may find *The Late Show* just your thing. It was written and directed by Robert Benton, one half of the *Bonnie and Clyde* writing team, and though its plotting is somewhat rudimentary and its illogic gigantic, it has oodles of atmosphere, oddball characters, snappy dialogue, affectionate allusions, and a likable way of not taking itself seriously.

Lily Tomlin, whom I have never previously liked, is totally winning as an absurd, aging hippie with solid instincts well hidden under layers of bizarre clothing, parlance, and behavior; there is also first-rate supporting work from Bill Macy, Eugene Roche, and Ruth Nelson. Only Joanna Cassidy continues to be a washout. And then there is Art Carney. This basic nonactor tries very hard, and manages to avoid obvious errors, but still fails to convince me. It may be that he is a little too successful at being as common as dirt even while he thinks he is charmingly matter-of-fact; whatever it is, Carney always makes me feel slightly unclean just watching him. Chuck Rosher's cinematography is unimpressive, but the art direction and set decoration make up for what it lacks. If only this entire genre, complete with its own brand of nostalgia, did not strike me as hopelessly juvenile!

February 14, 1977

See Jane Star

FUN WITH DICK AND JANE, which is basking in several choice locations, is rather like a crude American travesty of *The Wonderful Crook,* the brilliant Swiss film by Claude Goretta that is still waiting for a theater. If I am nevertheless recommending *Dick and Jane* to you, it is for one reason only: Jane Fonda. *Fun With Dick and Jane* is enormous fun with Jane; with everyone and everything else, including the insolent spaniel that plays Spot, the fun ranges from middling to muddied.

Let us now praise Miss Fonda who, I am convinced, is the only all-purpose actress we've got in Hollywood today. It may be that high tragedy is beyond her (though I doubt it), but everything else she handles with wit or poignancy, intensity or lightness, heart-warming or heartbreaking grace, whichever is called for. That she is probably sexier than anyone else around is only a bonus; the essential thing is that she is an actress through and through—yet she has been mostly misused or not used at all. No wonder she was driven into politics when there was so little of worth, and not much more of worthlessness, for her to do in her chosen profession that chose to treat her so shabbily.

When you come right down to it, there were only two occasions when Fonda was not handed fluff (e.g., *Sunday in New York, Cat Ballou*), muck (e.g., *Walk on the Wild Side, Hurry Sundown*), or earnest dead weight (e.g., *The Chase,* Losey's *A Doll's House*), not even to mention the sexual-exploitation trash to which her untalented ex-husband, Roger Vadim, subjected her. The two films that count are *They Shoot Horses, Don't They?* and *Klute;* in both she gave performances rich in technical virtuosity, psychological complexity, believability and charm. In the former, the charm was mostly tragic; in the latter, largely comic. Either way, it was supreme—this nearly undefinable quality which is the ability to persuade spectators that you are a person of value, that what happens to you really matters.

But only two such roles since 1960 (Fonda's film debut in the trivial *Tall Story*)? So she went into politics and, whatever one may think of her often excessive performances there, played parts that were more right than wrong, and played them gallantly—which, of course, was held against her in due time by the forces of reaction, and by those cowards who, without any affiliation, merely tremble at what boycotting by hawks *might* do to your box office. As a result, there was, for a long time, little or nothing of this greatly gifted actress to be had on our screens. So I say that even if *Fun With Dick and Jane* were a great deal worse (actually, it could only be a little worse), it would still deserve to be seen for Jane Fonda.

The picture seems to have had as many scenarists as those notorious Italian confections whose writers outnumber their casts. Only three are credited—David Giler, Jerry Belson, and Mordecai Richler—and at least from the last two I would have expected more. But there were others as well, one gathers, and the entire film looks like several months' worth of TV situation comedy by various hands, excerpted and slapped together. And not merely the highlights—quite a few lowlights, too.

Dick and Jane are an affluent young Los Angeles aerospace engineer and his wife who have been living normally beyond their means; when Dick is suddenly laid off, they find themselves in desperate straits. She has a go at working as a model, but makes a botch of it; he fails at a number of things, even at living off unemployment compensation and food stamps. The inevitable solution is a life of genteel crime: ripping off the rich and corrupt, and giving the loot to the deserving poor, namely Dick and Jane.

This is where the moral sleaziness comes in. Yes, the rich are shown as thoroughly immoral and unappetizing—small wonder that both the on-screen bystanders and the theater audience burst into applause when Dick and Jane hold up the Telephone Company, for instance. But then, just how deserving are Dick and Jane Harper? All they seem to be concerned about is that the swimming pool be as steamy, the wine as heady, and the grass even greener on their side of the fence. It is hard to invoke Robin Hood and Arsène Lupin on behalf of wallowing in the petty luxuries of consumerism, of O.D.-ing on creature comforts.

As for the thrown-together episodes, some are blatantly unfunny, some are funny but out of character (Jane would never be a klutz at modeling) or old hat (the take-off on gross opera divas and unruly supernumeraries has a beard longer than Barbarossa's), and some are funny but misdirected. I have no idea what kind of movies Ted Kotcheff might be good for, but comedies are definitely not his directorial meat. For example, the scene in which the Harpers' trees and plants are uprooted, their very lawn rolled up and carted off for nonpayment, is good comic material. But Kotcheff does not shoot and structure it right: neither the camera positions nor the rhythms are well calculated, and the laughs don't build so as to top one another.

The acting, too, is haphazard. Fonda is by far the most irresistibly smart-alecky wife since Myrna Loy's Nora in the *Thin Man* series, and more womanly to boot; as Dick, George Segal works hard and not ineffectually, but, as usual, without that apparent effortlessness that is the *sine qua non* of true comedy. Ed McMahon is good as an unscrupulous boss, as are John Dehner and Mary Jackson as smugly unhelpful parents, but these are easy parts. In crucial character bits there is much flubbing of opportunities, notably by Hank Garcia and Allan Miller, as a canny Chicano and a loan shark, respectively. There is, however, one small role played exemplarily: watch what Thalmus Rasulala does as a food-stamp inspector, down to the use of his eyes, as first one and then the other comes to quizzical life.

Most astonishing about the film is the amateurish cinematography by the usually accomplished Fred J. Koenekamp. He seems to have had special trouble with how to make the Harpers' front yard look sun-drenched in studio shots, and ended up with an effect that is like lemon juice in your eye. Nor must we overlook on the debit side Sean Frye, an all-too-typical child actor. But, I repeat, Fonda is back, casting so much incandescent humanity over the film that she almost redeems even such a bit of truly bad taste as a peeing sequence that can be described only as bathroom nonhumor. Please, you folks out there in Movieland, stop being mired in your myopia, and find roles for Fonda before it is too late—not for her, but for you.

Thieves may not be the worst movie I ever saw, but it may well be the most annoyingly cloying. Herb Gardner, who wrote it and ended up pseudonymously directing much of it, is one of those horrible examples of how an extremely limited, intensely self-satisfied, repetitious, and predictable cleverness can become—within minutes—more offensive than extended witlessness.

Ever since *A Thousand Clowns* (his one success, and that, to my mind, unmerited—when, in any case, will we learn that one hit does not entitle anybody to a lifetime of manufacturing well-financed turkeys?), Gardner has been turning out plays and movies of increasing self-indulgence, cutesiness, and indigestibility. In *The Goodbye People* on stage, and *Who Is Harry Kellerman . . . ?* on screen, his archness—really fallen archness—has reached the limits of human endurance. In *Thieves,* which he has now perpetrated on both stage and screen, it goes beyond them.

What we have here is another fun couple, Sally and Martin Cramer, whose marriage, along with her pregnancy, is in the balance. (For various cute reasons, she considers an abortion; in the end, for various equally cute reasons, she has her baby, and *we* get the abortion.) Martin, the principal of a fancy school for rich kids, has become stodgy over the years; Sally, who teaches in a ghetto school, has naturally preserved her swinging, committed purity—though which of the two is more insufferable remains a moot question. They live in a large Upper East Side apartment house, where they are beleaguered by the urban chicaneries students of Neil Simon's *The Prisoner of Second Avenue* and other such works will be familiar with, and then some. Simon's characters, at least, were never haunted by nameless street people who plague them, or by disembodied voices from other apartments muttering supposedly hilarious platitudes.

I shall spare you what passes for the plot, complete with daring little dabs at equally disembodied adultery, but must give you samples of the wit. "We do not love each other, so we have couples over, and they love us. We are held together by other couples." This epigram, by the way, is spun out, like most others, to much greater length than I was able to take down. "A stale corn muffin thrown away is still a corn muffin." This, of course, is metaphorical, though I no longer recall whether it functions as a right-to-life argument, or in the service of some other existential profundity. "I'm a goddamned dirty old man, but a dirty old man beats the hell out of a dead man." This is said—or bellowed—by the heroine's seventy-eight-year-old cabby father, who is the author's mouthpiece, the *raisonneur* of the film. But when a *raisonneur* spouts a ghastly mixture of smartass impertinence, crudely homespun philosophy, and cornball jokes that pile up into fuzzy monologues—which, moreover, are delivered by Irwin Corey—*dead* begins to look awfully good.

Charles Grodin plays Martin as if a sufficiency of slack in the mouth absolved one from all further comedic endeavor. As Sally, Marlo Thomas is the ideal Herb Gardner interpreter. Her face is always suffused with some sort of adorable, tough wistfulness, a wisecracking yearning; since it is a face that has clearly undergone intensive restructuring, it may be that the yearning is that of the remaining parts for those that are gone or have been shifted around. And she speaks exactly as she looks and as Gardner writes: with an embattled wryness, a sweet sophistication applied with a flat brush, and an impishness so pointed you could impale flies on it. I am forced to observe that after a certain overexposure a corn muffin becomes a liability, and had better be thrown out than thrown up over.

In nonspeaking parts, Mercedes McCambridge and Gary Merrill manage to over- and underact, respectively. But Ann Wedgworth, John McMartin, and Hector Elizondo are delightful in small roles, proving that flowers can bloom even on dung heaps.

February 28, 1977

Genuine Fake

NEXT TO THE RELATIONSHIP BETWEEN illusion and reality, I suppose, the one between the fake and the genuine has most exercised the human imagination. In a sense, of course, they are the same antinomy—if antinomy there is—which is what makes the question of whether a successful imitation is as good as what it imitates a matter of interest beyond the limits of art. If a fake Picasso, let us say, can be indistinguishable from a real one, this is of concern not only to those who buy Picassos, not even only to those who care about art; it is of importance to all who care about the meaning of life. In its broadest terms, this becomes the question of whether a convincingly faked experience can be as good as a real one: whether an imitation of love, friendship, contentment, say, can be as good as real contentment or friendship or love—whether, ultimately, there is any difference between the two.

Consequently, Orson Welles's new nonfiction film, *F for Fake,* could have been both fascinating and important. But it is, right off, rather like the Holy Roman Empire: it is not new, having kicked around for a couple of years already; it is not nonfiction, having a lot of mystification in it; and it is not quite a film, having been made for television. What makes it particularly fake, though, is that about forty minutes' worth of material has been stretched to almost three times that length, and that at least one of the purposes seems to have been the launching of an attractive but, on the available evidence, not especially talented young woman, Oja Kodar, the nature of whose usefulness to Welles may be worth some short speculation.

After Welles, the principal characters in the film are Elmyr de Hory (or Elemér Hoffmann), the late art forger; and Clifford Irving, the book forger, who figures here chiefly for having written *Fake!,* an account of Elmyr's forgeries. Conveniently, both of these men, the successful faker of Postimpressionist paintings and the somewhat less successful forger of a Howard Hughes biography, set up shop in Ibiza, or whatever it is that one sets up in that most exotic of Balearic Islands. The film purports to be an investigation of what is real and what is fake in art and perhaps life, and uses as its focal points the careers of Elmyr, some of whose fakes allegedly hang in leading museums and collections; of Irving, who became famous for a biography that proved to be even less than fiction; and of Welles himself, who, at age sixteen, began by fooling Ireland into believing that he was a Broadway star, and later made an ass of America with his radio program about a Martian invasion.

The purpose behind all this seems to be to suggest (1) that the so-called experts do not have any true expertise; (2) that art is whatever is good enough to pass for it; and (3) that the name of the painter matters no more than those of the builders of Chartres Cathedral, who remain anonymous. In another sense, the purpose may be to justify Orson Welles's later career—if that is the word for it—which has consisted largely of making movies that either never get made or never should have been made, and, of course, of raising money for these projects. I must say I've always been mildly puzzled by a man who comes to Los Angeles to plead for moviemaking money he is in desperate need of, and then lives in a bungalow of the Beverly Hills Hotel in a style befitting a pasha. No wonder the movies don't get made.

But let us get back to the three ostensible points of *F for Fake*. First, that the experts have no expertise. Much as Welles would like to believe this—needless to say, he equates film critics, whom he has compared to eunuchs, with the experts at the Museum of Modern Art, and possibly elsewhere, who have fallen for Elmyr's forgeries—it is not necessarily so. Though the eunuch analogy has gained popularity among film people (Mike Nichols and Peter Bogdanovich have quoted it with gusto), it is a curious one: Is art really comparable to a harem in which the point is to fornicate with the greatest possible number of concubines, and where the critic, poor castrato that he is, is excluded from the fun and consumed with corroding envy? With all due deference to poetic and other license, art is not—or should not be—screwing around, whatever Orson Welles's latest output might indicate. Some critics may be impotent, figuratively or literally, but to see films and evaluate them has nothing to do with making them, whereas to evaluate lovemaking does presuppose making love.

If a few, or even many, experts were taken in by Elmyr, this can mean only two things. Either they were poor experts (critics, scholars), or the stuff that was being faked so easily may not have been all that good in the first place. If it is so easy to paint Vlamincks, Van Dongens, Matisses, Modiglianis, Picassos, etc., maybe the originals were less than unique. Of course, what they have in any case (and the film does make this point, but immediately throws it away) is their original vision, which, too, can be copied, but cannot be created by a forger. Modigliani, for example, had a way of looking at a nude that is reproducible by skillful imitators; but first there had to be a Modigliani to look at the nude in that way.

Yes, you say, but afterward, is a convincing "Modigliani" worth any less than the real thing? That is a matter of opinion, and not a truly important issue except to the owner of a specific painting. To the person who doesn't know the difference, a fake is certainly as good as an original. The real problem, however, is how good Modigliani's vision is to begin with, and here anyone who can make out a well-argued, compelling case either way becomes worth listening to. There are no eunuchs or sultans in this game, only convincing or unconvincing persuaders, and the final test is that of time. In any case, for the film to have been of interest in this area, it would have had to go into a minute and extensive comparison of authentic works and fakes, delve into case histories of who was taken in and how, and what the consequences were. But *F for Fake* does not do this, partly for legal reasons, but largely because it is more interested in hocus-pocus, in dazzling us with fake cleverness, than in painstaking scrutiny.

Second problem: Is art ever merely what is good enough to pass for it? Yes, as I've already suggested, if it fools all (or nearly all) people for a very, very long time—decades, centuries, preferably aeons. Meanwhile, there is only informed guessing; the fact that some unnamed curators and art dealers may have been taken in by Elmyr, and some publishers by Irving, does not mean much. Ah, but you can't name names, for legal reasons. Well, in that case, forget about making this movie. Or just put some real paintings and fake ones on the screen, side by side, and have some intelligent experts (there are many unintelligent ones, too, as in other professions) discuss them. But that kind of movie would have no room in it for Orson Welles, let alone Oja Kodar.

Third, is the name of the creator unimportant? My guess—and all criticism is only a particular critic's guessing game—is: yes, if the work is as good as Chartres; no, if the work is as worthless as a dance by Merce Cunningham, a painting by Andy Warhol, a piece of music by John Cage, a stage production by Andrei Serban, a sculpture by Robert Morris, or a piece of criticism by a *Times* critic in which not even the name of the reviewer, only that of his publication, matters. Then all you have is the name, and that, I'm convinced, will be of little interest *sub specie aeternitatis.* For, in the long run, a Cézanne survives not because it is a Cézanne, but because it is good. Many of today's reputations are made by publicity, scandal, or cohabitation with the right persons; the rest is all the public's gullibility and greed. That a Jackson Pollock may go for two million dollars today does not mean you will be able to get two cents for it tomorrow. Of course, the real judgment is neither that of today nor that of tomorrow, but the judgment of eternity, or such part of it as mankind may enjoy before destroying itself.

But to get back to *F for Fake:* much of it was directed or executed by François Reichenbach, who figures in it in fifth place after Welles, Elmyr, Irving, and Oja. Now, Reichenbach strikes me as a perfect example of a fake: the handful of his films I have seen are all inept or unnecessary or both, yet the man enjoys a considerable reputation among supposed cognoscenti. He and Welles have put together a film that is now so fragmented, so rearranged out of all-important chronological sequence, so filled with sideshow trickery (rather than the imitation of life—to quote Aristotle, not Fannie Hurst), so patently catering to various kinds of self-promotion (Welles's ego; Kodar's body; the personalities of Elmyr, Irving, and Reichenbach), that it has virtually no light to shed on the subject at hand. Only Oja Kodar's looks are genuinely appetizing, but to swoon over them vicariously might truly expose one to the charge of being a eunuch.

March 7, 1977

California Splat

Ah, for the good old bad movies of yesteryear, as opposed to the bad movies of today, which are thoroughly rotten. In the old days, most movies were made by people who neither knew nor cared about art, and the result was presentable genre pictures: westerns, gangster movies, screwball comedies, etc., or, if you prefer, John Ford, Howard Hawks, and George Cukor (though you can't be quite sure about Hungarians—Cukor may have thought that he was making art). What they offered was, at best, honest craftsmanship; at worst, interesting trash. The stuff had no pretensions to ultimate truths or "literary" values, and therein lay its salvation.

Along came Vigo, Renoir, Buñuel, Bergman, Fellini, Antonioni, Bresson, and the rest, and the movies were dragged screaming into Film. Don't get me wrong: it was the right thing to do, and even such pioneers as Griffith and the early Russians were trying for it within their political and technological (and, in the case of Griffith, intellectual) limitations. But it was the highly personal styles of a Fellini or Bergman, the uncompromising elitism (a positive term) of an Antonioni or Bresson that created a more altitudinous atmosphere in films, even if the subject matter was ostensibly as mundane as the boredom of a bunch of jet setters or the emotional entanglements within a seedy traveling circus. To create such films and make them valid works of art, however, required something special: a culture, a civilization, and, above all, an intense and unique private vision backed up by intelligence and finesse.

When today's illiterates attempt to imitate these masters—sometimes without even realizing that they are imitating—the results are truly dreadful. There is no more genre framework, no more traditional trickery of the trade, no more cozy set of basic plots to provide guidelines, crutches, and, if worst comes to worst, a net underneath to fall into. The new illiterates are supremely pretension-prone: they think that the freedom that genius has come by at tremendous cost is theirs for the asking. What they should ask, of course, is: "Does my graduating from the UCLA, USC, NYU, or Columbia Film School—or my dropping out and bumming around—really entitle me to think that I am an artist?" But this sort of question is never asked by imbeciles, and therein, precisely, resides their imbecility.

These remarks are by way of an introduction to the latest horror, *Welcome to L.A.,* produced by Robert Altman and conceived jointly by Alan Rudolph (who previously worked for him as assistant director and screenwriter) and Richard Baskin (who previously worked for him as musical director, composer, and bit player). A fancy program note explains their intentions: to "stretch the edges of cinema" by a tale about Los Angeles where "Rudolph's impressions about collective privacy and the internal and external pressures of sexual behavior fused with Baskin's ideas about the difficulties of emotional contact." Both these young Los Angelenos "were certain that a designed use of music and film could deepen the emotional response of the story." Now, I ask, is there any use of music and film, however dismal, that is not designed? And what is "collective privacy"? What kind of pressures are there besides "internal and external"? And what, in any case, are the "pressures of sexual behavior"? And has there ever been a hoarier cliché with which to "stretch the edges of cinema" than "the difficulties of emotional contact"? And how about stretching the *center* of cinema a little for a change?

If this hollow, mindless jargon isn't enough for you, consider Rudolph's statement that "his painting source was Matisse." Baskin's "music source," I assume, was the junk heap of current pop music, and the result, in both cases, was pretentiousness, vulgarity, and stupidity. Yes, stupidity, which the old filmmakers, safeguarded by preestablished topics and structures, were protected from revealing in its nakedness. Nothing protects Rudolph and Baskin from revealing that they are artistic and intellectual basket cases.

Rudolph declares: "Each of us needs to be loved. And what to do with it once you've got it is the difficult part." The first statement is the quintessence of platitudinousness; the second, although it sounds good, has nothing to do with the cardboard cutouts that populate *Welcome to L.A.,* none of whom (I should say *which)* ever loves or is loved. Few, if any, of them can muster up even a bit of genuine lust. Of course, Rudolph may think that the sexual free-for-all he has slapped on screen actually represents various kinds of loving; if so, so much the worse for him. We get a bunch of Los Angeles characters, some show-biz and some not (though with no difference between the two), somewhere around Christmas (chronology and duration are as hazy as everything else), uttering relentless banalities while copulating, near-copulating, or refusing to copulate with one another.

This includes everyone of the least consequence in the movie, and is virtually the entire plot, with the exception of the burning problem of whether the great pop musician Eric Wood (insufferably mugged and squealed by Baskin) will turn the lyrics of Carroll Barber, a spoiled rich kid (who remains unenacted by Keith Carradine), into a bestselling album. That, clearly, was needed to allow Baskin and Carradine to play and pule ad infinitum the infantile, ungrammatical, cliché, and utterly unmusical songs that "deepen the emotional responses of the story." You might note, to begin with, that emotional responses are of an audience, never of a story.

But let me give you a typical bit of Baskin lyric-writing: "Your body held me for a while;/You could disguise with such beguile. . . ." First of all, *beguile* is a verb, not a noun, as Baskin's illiteracy would have it; but what of the meaning? "Your body held me for a while" is simply the ancient commonplace "Your arms held me for a while" made more needlessly explicit—and awkward—by substituting *body* for arms. "You could disguise"—what? This semiliterate phrase lacking an object presumably means "disguise yourself," in which case we are left with the thought "You could dissemble with such lovely dissembling"—something rather less than a penetrating insight. And so it goes throughout the lyrics, and the equally banal, tunelessly caterwauling score.

The idea, derived from *Nashville,* was to tell a story through more or less disjointed incidents, with a good many characters interacting almost at random within a very short period. But in *Nashville* there was some selectivity at work: the incidents chosen had some revelatory value; were small entities rather than tiny, disorienting fragments; and displayed at least a sense of rising action toward a climax, however unconvincing. In *Welcome to L.A.* there is no internal logic or order; incidents are often shown in incomplete, almost subliminal, form; and you seldom know where or when something is happening, to say nothing of why. For example, a husband and wife who have been copulating their separate ways are suddenly shown in bed together in the middle of the night in his furniture showroom, heaven knows how or why—though heaven, like us, surely couldn't care less.

People go around mouthing insipid or grandiose trivia. The most profound—or most obnoxious—character circulates quoting either the best-known phrase from Goya, which she takes to be by Ben Franklin, or bits and pieces from *Camille,* the movie version of Dumas' play. Significantly, you can never tell whether this character, moronically played by Geraldine Chaplin, is meant to be profound or obnoxious. She is the only character who exhibits something resembling development, and the only one who tries to understand what is happening. But the understanding is paltry, and the development histrionic, if not hysterical. Most likely, the filmmakers want to have it both ways. If you like the character, they will tell you, "Yes, isn't she splendid?" If you despise her, they'll say, "That was exactly our point—how silly, superficial, and pathetic all of these Los Angeles-dwellers are."

Well, you can't have it both ways, as this dumb and corrupt film would have it; what gets stretched here is our endurance—cinema merely gets shriveled. Special mention must be made of Dave Myers's grandiloquent cinematography, in which some of Sven Nykvist's most wonderful effects (e.g., dark silhouettes outlined by an edge of light) are reduced to visual vulgarisms. The direction is, at best, nonexistent, shrinking good actors into nonentities, and bad ones, like Chaplin and Viveca Lindfors, into thoroughgoing zombies. With typical uninventiveness trying to pass for cleverness, most of the characters have last names like Hood, Wood, or Goode. It would have made more sense to call them Sad, Mad, or just Bad. Only one actor survives the mess with a genuinely human performance: I doff my hat to Harvey Keitel. As for the rest of this indigestible Baskin-Rudolph confection, if Los Angeles is really as it is shown here, it does not deserve to be put on film. If, as is more likely, this is all our two jackanapeses can make of it, they should not be allowed to make movies.

March 21, 1977

Blight Entertainment

BLACK SUNDAY is one of those films that are perfectly enjoyable to watch but about which there is not all that much to say. One could call it (and many, undoubtedly, will) a somewhat less dazzling *Manchurian Candidate,* or one could fall back on that old reviewers' phrase, "good of its kind," and leave it at that, except that columns don't get filled that way.

In case you haven't heard it yet, *Black Sunday* concerns the joint effort of Dahlia Iyad, a beautiful young leader of the Black September terrorist movement, and her lover, Michael Lander, a former navy pilot brainwashed by the North Vietnamese, to detonate a special bomb in Miami during the Super Bowl game and kill the eighty thousand spectators, including the president. (Ford, indeed, might have been dumb enough to disregard all FBI warnings, but it is Carter who got elected, and it is his faked-in presence that detracts something from the overall credibility.) Racing against time and other dread obstacles to prevent disaster, are Corley of the FBI and Major Kabakov, an Israeli expert in counterterrorism, supported by a few assistants.

Immediately problems present themselves. Why should an Israeli major be virtually in charge of an American operation? How did this not-so-black Dahlia get to be Lander's mistress? How did Lander, dishonorably discharged, secure the six hundred thousand darts that go into his newfangled bomb? And how, for that matter, did Lander incur his sense of guilt that stems from the firebombing of a North Vietnam hospital, when he flew blimps and helicopters, neither of them any use in bombing missions? And if Lander was a pilot, how come he is such an expert engineer? And why would Dahlia, even after an invigorating night of lovemaking with her other lover, the Lebanese Nageeb, rush into recording a taped message to the American people, which could have waited quite a while longer, and thus not set off the boys from counterespionage?

Luckily, though, these unanswered and probably unanswerable questions are bunched up near the beginning of the movie, which, once properly under way, no longer strains our credulity. There is one structural error—the cutting out of a bit of throat-cutting by one of the terrorists needed to establish his fierceness and importance; but this was done to earn a PG rating, which, in the event, the MPAA foolishly withheld after all—so much for trying to play ball with that organization. Otherwise, John Frankenheimer's direction is consistently workmanlike, maintaining a sound pace, sufficient variety, and a decent measure of suspense.

If the movie is still less than totally involving, this may be the fault of the writing. In this screenplay by Ernest Lehman, Kenneth Ross, and Ivan Moffat from a novel by Thomas Harris, the dialogue, though never embarrassing, is generally flat, and the characterizations are routine and minimal. This may be inevitable in the suspense genre: either because art is something that compels us to slow down, to linger and reflect, which would be a roadblock in the breakneck progress of a thriller—to say nothing of allowing time for the detection of loopholes; or because the kind of writer who can do better things doesn't usually bother with thrillers. Anyway, because we do not much care for the characters, we cannot commit ourselves to the tale, especially since we can guess the outcome: no movie made in Hollywood will allow Arabs to outwit Americans and, what's more important yet, Jews, and permit eighty thousand sports fans, including one president, to be blown to kingdom come.

Under such circumstances, performances become all-important. It devolves on the actors to infuse human warmth and believability into the proceedings, and here Frankenheimer and his producer, Robert Evans, have chosen, for the most part, shrewdly. The minor roles, except where a football celebrity plays himself, are well acted, and all but one of the leads work swimmingly.

As Kabakov, the Israeli mastermind, the lately often irresponsible Robert Shaw gives a genuinely affecting performance. Without any fake frills, his oceanic gaze comes at us directly and majestically, wave upon blue wave, while his rich, slightly cracked voice, with a kind of mournful monotony, batters its way into our ears. The accent he uses is not exactly Jewish—it is vaguely Celtic mixed with working-class English, or, more precisely, all-purpose weird—but it works through its very mysterious vagueness: it might, for all we know, be an Esperanto accent, the dialect of Everyman, if only Everyman had a dialect. Above all, Shaw has power, the kind of power that always registers slow, considered, weighty, even when it is actually sudden, swift, even rash.

Power is the thing Marthe Keller lacks. When she was younger, slimmer, and cast in undemanding roles by Philippe de Broca and other Frenchmen, the German-Swiss actress was charming and crunchable *(zum Einbeissen,* as you might say in her native language, or *à croquer,* in her first adopted one), but in American movies and in English she is a dead weight. First, there is her thick German accent, which no jesuitical interpolations in the dialogue (a German mother, Swiss schooling) can make plausible in a Lebanese terrorist or bearable for a discriminating listener; then, there is the general thickness of face and body that, for whatever reason, was not evident in her French movies; lastly, there is the thick, clotted quality of her acting: no sinuous seductivity, no commanding persuasiveness—in short, no charisma.

With Bruce Dern's psychotically vindictive blimp pilot, things get better again. The part is simplistically written, and no actor on earth could make it entirely convincing, let alone sympathetic. Yet Dern does very nicely by the pathos, moodiness, sudden infantile rages, and despair of Lander, even if he stints a bit on the psychopath's notorious charm, an important characteristic, of which Richard Widmark is the past master. There is also a superb piece of acting by Steven Keats as Kabakov's aide; if ever a performance exuded authenticity in every visible and audible detail, this is it.

There is very solid work from others as well, notably from the craggily dependable Fritz Weaver, the pervasively slimy Michael V. Gazzo, and the ominously controlled Walter Gotell. And the filmmakers deserve a special citation for bringing back William Daniels after too long an absence; there is simply no one who can approach him in conveying officious clumsiness, pompous insecurity, and petty spite under a veneer of righteous concern. Here, in the tiny part of a Veterans Administration official, he conveys the noxiousness of bureaucracy in its full efflorescence.

Not to be dismissed either are John A. Alonzo's atmospheric cinematography, the not overhectic editing of Tom Rolf (closely supervised, I would imagine, by Evans himself), and the serviceable score by John Williams, even if it does rather repeat his shark theme from *Jaws.* All in all, a sound commercial film, the basic stuff of cinema, and an oasis in the current American movie output. And for those who like puzzles: Can you find the line of dialogue that is verbatim a line from a poem by T. S. Eliot?

April 4, 1977

Of Dimwits, Nitwits, and Halfwits

Even though I do not consider *3 Women* a good film, there are three good things about Robert Altman, who wrote and directed it. He is an accomplished technician; he can get remarkable performances from actors; he takes chances and keeps striking out in new directions. Sometimes, as in *3 Women,* he just strikes out. But his failures merit attention.

Actually, *3 Women* is not an entirely new tack; it is a film based on a dream of the director's, much as were *Images* and *Brewster McCloud.* It may just be that this is Altman's least rewarding vein, even if it is possibly his most audacious one. Dreams, a natural thing for the novelist and painter, have always been a hazard for the playwright and filmmaker, because there is serious difficulty in differentiating dream sequences from reality without becoming either too arty or confusing.

There is, however, the additional problem (which holds for writers as well) of how to justify the inclusion of dreams in one's work. For dreams are rather like children—infinitely fascinating when they're your own, but apt to be a bore and a nuisance when they're somebody else's. To be sure, the great romantic writers figured out how to make major use of dreams: as a way to tell parables or subvert the bourgeois stodginess of their time; as a mode of conveying the previously misunderstood or concealed irrational, neurotic side of human beings. In their works the dream became a symbol: it was shaped, controlled, and transformed until it achieved more than private significance.

It is the surrealists, alas, who ruined the dream for literature and possibly even for the cinema. By setting down what they dreamed in literal and solipsistic terms—and by gaining recognition for it—they turned out effusions in verse and prose of use to nobody but academicians, who can convert them into writing for profit without pleasure. Does anyone still read André Breton or René Char with the delight to be derived from Novalis or Nerval?

But back to *3 Women.* Briefly, it concerns the adoration lavished by Pinky Rose—an awkward newcomer to the ranks of the physiotherapists in a Palm Springs spa for the affluent, aged, and afflicted—on Millie Lammoreaux, a fellow Texan, who is really a silly and gauche girl full of *Cosmopolitan-Redbook* notions about life, but whom the cipherlike Pinky regards as the ultimate in sophistication and grace. They end up rooming together at the Purple Sage singles' apartment complex, where Pinky, except for secretly reading Millie's diary and putting on Millie's clothes, is a worshipful drudge sweetly overlooking the rebuffs Millie gets from practically everyone. Both girls frequently visit the Dodge City Ranch, a bar and amusement park of sorts where local policemen enjoy target practice and dirt biking. It is run by Edgar, a movie stunt man who mostly drinks and womanizes, and his pregnant wife, Willie, who gives off equally pregnant stares and never talks, only covers every conceivable surface, from walls to pool bottoms, with murals of half-human, half-animal creatures acting out a savage battle of the sexes.

When Pinky is relegated to the roll-away bed in the living room so Millie can booze and sex it up with Edgar in the bedroom, she attempts suicide by jumping into the pool. In the hospital, she remains comatose for a long time; Millie, bitterly repentant, tracks down Pinky's parents and summons them to the girl's bedside. The parents turn out to be benighted rubes—the father downright cretinous—and when Pinky comes to, she claims never to have seen them before. Out of the hospital, Pinky undertakes systematically what she played at earlier: she assumes Millie's identity. It is she who dominates now, drinks and has sex with Edgar, consigns Millie to the small bed, fraternizes (much more successfully) with all the Purple Sage's men, and becomes crueler than Millie ever was.

Willie is about to give birth but is abandoned by Edgar. The two girls rush to her cottage, and while Millie acts as midwife, Pinky is supposed to seek medical help, but instead stays to watch, mesmerized. When Millie discovers Pinky's presence, she strikes Pinky with hands still bloody from delivering a stillborn male baby. In the final scene, Millie has become a mother figure who quietly bosses around the other two women. Pinky has clearly turned into a daughter, though it is unclear whether Willie is another daughter or a grandmother. As the camera withdraws from the cottage, we see masses of abandoned motorcycle tires. Earlier, a piece of awkward exposition informed us that Edgar died of gun wounds (from one woman or all three?), and this final image may imply the death of all the men who swaggered around on dirt bikes, and the coming of matriarchy.

There are more improbabilities here than I can begin to list. No one can be as blank as Pinky and, on top of that, a physiotherapist; Millie is so perfectly average that there is no reason for either her idolization by Pinky or repudiation by everyone else; no Dodge City could be run by the ineffectual Edgar and Willie without outside help; there is no possible medical explanation for Pinky's coma: the leap from not very high might result in a freak death or fairly prompt resuscitation, nothing in between. Again, Pinky's parents are too old, their behavior subhuman, and they would have to be proved either real or impostors, not just fade out of the picture. When a woman left alone is about to have a baby, she calls an ambulance; at the very least that is what Millie would have done for Willie instead of dispatching Pinky for help. There is no credible reason for the first sudden reversal of roles between the girls, still less for the next one—a palinode's palinode. And so on and on.

But, Altman or somebody is bound to say, this is a dream—not meant to make logical sense. Very well, let's see what other kind of sense it makes. Even though much about the film leads us to believe that it is reality, let us assume it is all a dream and ask what it tells us. Can we derive a symbolic meaning of general applicability? That woman comes in three aspects: mother, daughter, and wife or whore? This could be conveyed better through a single woman than through a trio, and is, in any case, a hoary platitude. That women keep changing roles? Maybe, but so do men, and surely not so quickly, blatantly, extremely, and not *à trois.* That women will eventually join in systematically destroying a shared man, or indeed all men? Though a man who hates women or feels guilty toward them might come up with this notion, it is very hard to make art or even sense of it. Whichever way you twist Altman's dream (interestingly, in all three Altman dream films a woman or female fantasy creature causes a man's death), it yields unearnedly sordid or shallow meanings, or no meaning at all.

There is worse, however: derivativeness and pretentiousness in large doses. The spa sequences, with young people moving against a background of the decrepit and deformed, are out of *8½*; much of the suppressed violence, framed by bleached-out desert, stems from *Zabriskie Point;* making a whole film into a kind of dream containing more explicit dream sequences is dredged out of *Hour of the Wolf;* the transference of identities between women of unequal sophistication is lifted from *Persona.* In this film, you might say, Altman tries to elevate into art what is merely creative kleptomania.

The liftings are from the most prestigious sources: Fellini, Antonioni, Bergman. Here, among other places, is where pretensions bordering on megalomania come in. The transfer of identities in *Persona* comes about slowly and credibly between women who have genuine, conveyed identities; each has a past, a position in life, recognizable relationships with others. One woman, moreover, is a canny, even cunning, artist; the other is a naïve but decent bourgeoise; their fusion—enriching, demeaning, frightening—expands into the problem of the artist and the cultural consumer in their disturbing symbiosis, raising moral questions of some import.

But to whom does Altman transfer this transference of identities? To Millie, a dimwit; Pinky, a nitwit; and Willie—who paints dismal murals, says nothing, and cannot even call a hospital—a halfwit. A fine cast of characters through whom to make significant utterances. But they are figures in a dream, you protest. Sorry; utter nonentities are utter nonentities, even in a dream. Actions that are idiotic, hopelessly arcane, or self-consciously dipped in viscous ambiguity are unsatisfactory even in a dream context. To bestow the strategies of the subtle and profound *Persona* on these shallow or inchoate pygmies is a case of terminal pretentiousness.

There are extenuating circumstances. Altman does manage some funny lines or situations, and he knows how to convey the pettiness of certain strata and institutions as they flourish especially in the southern-California climate. Yet even here Altman's vision is unsteady and veers into excess or schematism. Tom, the neighbor who keeps dismissing Millie with a cough, coughs one time too often. If Pinky overhears Millie's diatribe against tomatoes, she later throws it back at her with a much too schematic exactness; if one character finds a California landscape very much like Texas, another is bound to find it totally unlike Texas. If a snotty set of twins is introduced as Pinky's nemesis once, this is soon reiterated x times, and further rubbed in when Millie alleges the twins' concern for Pinky's recovery. If Pinky is terrified of guns in the first half of the movie, she is sure to relish them in the second. Even the murals crop up with ponderous predictability, always heralded by the portentous music of Gerald Busby, meant, like Bodhi Wind's artwork, to be classy, but emerging as hollow posturing.

It would be easy to go on listing defects; I would rather point out a few genuine accomplishments. Thus Altman shows his usual technical command here, whether he uses protracted takes with a meditative fluency, or jolts us with rapid, dramatic cutting; he admirably suggests the atmosphere of a place by the choreography he devises for his camera and characters. From Chuck Rosher, his cameraman, Altman gets top-notch work, except in the clumsy dream-within-a-dream. And what impressive performances!

Sissy Spacek has already demonstrated her ability to shuttle between utter innocence and troubled quirkiness with the utmost ease, or to grow from ugly duckling into radiant maturity. As Pinky, she reconfirms it stunningly. Even more remarkable is Shelley Duvall, who improvised some 80 percent of Millie's dialogue, and deserves scriptwriter's credit. With gentle yet harrowing accuracy she embodies a submediocrity with delusions of mediocrity. And she creates an amiably aggressive gooniness that expertly allows charm and pathos to shine through—idiotic charm, but charm still.

Altman belabors his points hammer and tongs. Thus the girls whose nicknames are Pinky and Millie are, he tells us, both called Mildred; and Willie is only Millie with the initial upside down. But when Duvall learns that Spacek became Pinky in order to escape from a hateful name, she asks Spacek what she imagines Millie to stand for. As Spacek becomes aware of her gaffe, Duvall gives her a look—a short, quick look, yet brimful of amusement, exasperation, condescension, and complicity. *That* is art.

April 25, 1977

Belated Juvenilia

WITH *Annie Hall,* Woody Allen has truly underreached himself. Allen is easily our most literate comic, and may just be one of our most comic *littérateurs,* as readers of his humorous sketches know. But his new film is painful in three separate ways: as unfunny comedy, poor moviemaking, and embarrassing self-revelation. It is everything we never wanted to know about Woody's sex life and were afraid he'd tell us anyway. And now he does.

Here is the on-again, off-again love affair of a schlemiel and a meshuggeneh. (Much as I dislike Yiddishisms, there are times when one has no choice.) The obvious trouble with such an affair is that it is off even when it is on: we cannot feel real sympathy for the endless thrashings about of such nonentities. This is the almost brazenly biographical and autobiographical story of a comic called Alvy Singer and a would-be singer called Annie Hall (I almost wrote Annie Comic), who meet, love, live, and nag together; help, hinder, and berate each other; rub their respective analyses together to spark their dying relationship; have outbursts of frustration and jealousy, separate, come together again, part anew, and, if I remember correctly, stay parted. It is a film so shapeless, sprawling, repetitious, and aimless as to seem to beg for oblivion.

The jokes are tired and can often be seen dragging their feet toward us a mile off; when they finally arrive, we are more apt to commiserate than laugh. There are typical Upper West Side jokes and typical Upper East Side jokes, typical art-movie-house jokes and shrink jokes, meeting-his-or-her-family jokes and failed-lovemaking jokes. There is the hero's entire dreary past with his two previous unsatisfactory wives; and, though mercifully in less detail, the heroine's dreary past. Woody—I mean Alvy—will accuse one of his women in bed (I think they are watching TV): "You are using the Conspiracy Theory as an excuse for not having sex with me!" How much weaker this is than the scene from *Love and Death* where the bored young wife rejects her amorous husband in bed with "Please, not here!"

Such labored jokes! Alvy fumes while a pretentious idiot behind him in a movie line pontificates to his date about cinema, media, McLuhan; suddenly, Alvy produces from behind a billboard the real McLuhan to squelch the joker, then says to the camera something about if only it were like this in real life. (By the way, McLuhan delivers his two lines pitifully.) Or Alvy will say he read something in *Dissentary,* and explain that he understood *Dissent* and *Commentary* had merged. Now, if this cropped up spontaneously at a party, apropos of something in the conversation, it might be funny. But in the movie, where this gag about our interchangeably conservative Jewish-intellectual journals is dragged in out of New Left field, it sounds too deliberate to be funny.

Most of the gags, describable as nebbishy rubbish, have been done so many times before—by Neil Simon, for instance, or Woody Allen himself, especially in the likewise autobiographically slanted parts of *Bananas.* And then there is Diane Keaton's scandalous performance. Her work, if that is the word for it, always consists chiefly of a dithering, blithering, neurotic coming apart at the seams—an acting style that is really a nervous breakdown in slow motion—but it has never before been allowed such latitude to deliquesce in. Note especially the scene after a tennis game where Miss Keaton tries to latch on to Allen. She lurches into one of those routines where every uttered syllable is swathed in a nebula of half laughs and half sobs accompanied by a smile that keeps tripping all over itself. It is not so much an actress playing a role as a soul in torment crying out for urgent therapy—in bad taste to watch and an indecency to display.

Of course, it is not easy to turn one's own recent tragicomic past into material for comedy; clearly, both Allen and Keaton lack the necessary detachment. And to make matters more oppressive, Allen drags in a whole gallery of unappetizing show-biz personalities: Carol Kane, Paul Simon, and Christopher Walken, who has made himself into a complete zombie, along with others not even worth mentioning. Tony Roberts, in a part that has been cut to the bone, and Janet Margolin, in another one that seems also drastically pared down, come out ahead just by providing resting points for one's gaze. Roberts scores also by being the only major character who does not appear to be a candidate for a straitjacket.

Allen makes some attempts to turn *Annie Hall* into a fancier movie than his previous ones. There are such things in it as a split screen, Pirandellian devices, quotations from *The Sorrow and the Pity,* and cinematography by the distinguished Gordon Willis. None of these contributes much; it is arrogant to invoke Ophüls's great film about the real plight of the Jews as some sort of justification for these petty neuroses, and Willis's work here does not rise above the routine. Allen himself brings an unwelcome solemnity to playing himself, something he is happily free from when just playing; Miss Keaton is allowed to top her acting by singing two songs, which she does even less endurably: to compensate for her lack of vocal endowment, she goes in for even heavier mugging—it might as well be Central Park after dark.

Near the end of the movie, Alvy watches a couple of actors rehearse a play of his in which they enact Annie and him. The actress is played by Robin Mary Paris, who is new to me, but whose presence, brief as it is, lights up the film. It is she who should have played Annie, capable as she appears to be of keeping her head above a stagnant pond. The picture could at best be considered a love, or postlove, gift to Miss Keaton; it belongs in a gift-wrapped box, not on the public screen.

Joan Micklin Silver, whose *Hester Street* struck me as totally inept, has made her second feature film, *Between the Lines.* It is the story of the takeover of a Boston underground weekly, the Back Bay *Mainline,* by a newspaper tycoon who is the very embodiment of the Establishment. More important, it is meant to be a tale of deradicalization, of how a group of bright, undisciplined but idealistic kids who during the sixties put out a paper with some genuine bite to it ("We were dangerous then!") decline into slackness, indifference, jadedness, selling out. To make any sense, the action should be situated some eight years back, which is where, as I understand, the original scenario placed it. Updated to 1977, the movie taunts us with an unfillable lacuna: What kept these kids going till this day? Why is dissolution setting in now? Why haven't they already gotten over and safely beyond their disenchantment?

The film records, with however questionable accuracy, a particular period, and misplaces it; we feel that the kids might just as well be bemoaning the death of Pancho Villa. More troublesome yet is that we are not given a sense of anyone's former power. Harry, we are told, is a prize-winning investigative journalist; Michael, another reporter, has just written a book about the counterculture that has been sold so well as to permit his setting up shop as a writer in New York; Abbie, Harry's not-quite-ex-girl-friend, is said to be so good a photographer that she could easily exhibit her work if only she had the nerve to compete in an arena larger than the *Mainline.* None of this is conveyed, however: we do not experience these young people's talents; we do not believe that they were ever dangerous. Or are they phonies whom the picture is mocking?

Which brings us to the biggest difficulty with the film: the lack of a point of view. This was one of the troubles of *Hester Street,* too, where it was impossible to tell what value was to be placed on maintaining traditional Jewishness, and what value on Americanization. Are we to feel a sense of genuine loss in *Between the Lines,* or are we meant to laugh at these kids? Both, apparently, but, like double stops on the violin, *both* is too tall an order for a beginner—especially one who, like Mrs. Silver, exhibits no particular talent for her medium. The director makes the further mistake of not showing any ordinary things happening to her characters: everything is a bit too cute, clever, perilous, or bizarre. We begin to think that the glorious times are *now,* not then.

Even so, the film does mark some advances over *Hester Street:* its look is undistinguished rather than amateurish, partly because Kenneth Van Sickle's cinematography has improved, possibly aided by a bigger budget. There are even a few quite arresting scenes, including one with a conceptual artist on the rampage, but the approach, for the most part, is distinctly schematic. Note, for instance, how the big party scene is handled, with pedestrian cutting back and forth between the various principals and the orgiastic dancers and band. And the characters never diverge much from type: the scrounging, lecherous, con artist of a rock critic; the hard-hitting but self-protective editor; the pompous square of a business manager; the two-faced, feelingless tycoon; the gallant shrimp of a cub reporter; the dedicated secretary-receptionist, who is the unwobbling pivot of the whole operation; and so forth. It is not that such people do not exist, but that the film does not sufficiently individualize any one of them.

What does give *Between the Lines* some distinction is the excellent casting, under the supervision of Juliet Taylor. Some—one is tempted to say all—of the best rising young New York actors are in this film, many of them in tiny roles. There is virtually no unconvincing performance here, though I am slightly disappointed in the usually splendid Lindsay Crouse, whose Abbie is merely acceptable and not really able to arouse our concern. But there is ample compensation from the others, and it must not be forgotten that much of the dialogue was arrived at through their improvisations during rehearsal. I would like to praise dozens of performers individually, but must limit myself to the most outstanding pair.

John Heard, whom I have admired on stage, is impeccable as Harry. He brilliantly combines amiability with slovenliness, vestiges of involvement with near-pervasive disengagement, intelligence with intellectual laziness. His armor of charming cynicism shows the appropriate chinks that, rightly, are only chinks, not gashes. If Heard does not become a big star of stage and screen, either show business or I must be crazy. Equally fine in a less rewarding part is Jill Eikenberry as the receptionist. This extremely winning, technically accomplished, and subtly attractive young actress, who has never failed to impress me on stage, turns Lynn into an aggregate of virtues, without letting the goodness seem goody-goody—one of the harder tricks to pull off. Furthermore, she develops a character conceived as a generalization into a veritable individual.

Fred Barron, who wrote the screenplay with some help from David M. Helpern, Jr., worked on both of Boston's underground papers, the Boston *Phoenix* and the *Real Paper*. For all that, the script is as real as a real paper flower.

May 2, 1977

From War to Warhol

SAM PECKINPAH has examined many forms of brutality and warfare, but until *Cross of Iron* he and World War II had not met. As could have been expected, the encounter is an unusually violent one, probably one of the most harrowing accounts of that war ever filmed. But harrowing does not necessarily mean artistic, truthful, or even convincing. I would not be surprised if Peckinpah had succeeded in making war more violent than it actually is; but he has not made it truly shattering. Why?

The film tells of a German regiment withdrawing from Russia after the collapse of Hitler's eastern campaign. It begins in a forest, with the wiping out of a Russian bunker by a German platoon led by Corporal Steiner, who is a myth not only to his own men but to the entire regiment. This scene is extremely effective because it is a small skirmish in which Peckinpah cannot indulge himself in large-scale exaggeration and self-aggrandizement. And it is quite horrible enough. It makes entire pseudotough movies like John Sturges's *The Eagle Has Landed* look like hopscotch by comparison.

But things soon deteriorate: there is, unfortunately, a plot. It is mainly about the deadly conflict between Steiner and his nemesis, Captain Stransky, a cowardly, arrogant, cunning psychopath of a Prussian officer who lusts for the Iron Cross. Stransky feels that he must not only win that medal, without which he does not dare show his face back home, but also bring Steiner to heel or destroy him. It's a familiar motif—Stransky is a kind of Claggart figure and Steiner, though infinitely rougher and tougher, is his Billy Budd. They are surrounded not only by Steiner's adoring platoon, but also by Colonel Brandt, the commanding officer, a fine, old-fashioned, anti-Nazi military aristocrat (and a kind of Captain Vere, to continue the Melville parallel), and Captain Kiesel, the resident intellectual who makes most of the wry philosophical comments, whereas Brandt makes the wise, historical-political ones. For the sake of topicality, I suppose, there is even a pair of homosexual lovers—an officer and an enlisted man—whom Stransky is able to blackmail, and one of whom ends up wiping out, on Stransky's orders, most of Steiner's platoon. Yes, it's that kind of film.

I must confess I am curious about who wrote what here—although not curious enough to spend hours of research on it. At the basis of all this is a German novel by one Willi Heinrich, *The Patient Flesh,* which has been adapted by Julius J. Epstein (best remembered as one of the coscenarists of

Casablanca and *Four Daughters,* but also responsible for such marvels as *Pete 'n' Tillie);* Walter Kelley, the second-unit director; and James Hamilton, about whom we are told nothing. Yet, surely, Peckinpah's own ideas and tastes have also infiltrated this script, whose main themes are: admiration for the heroic Germans, hatred for the upper class, contempt for homosexuals, and a very equivocal view of women, who are there to be possessed and left, or killed and left (as the case may be)—some of them brave, but none of them to be trusted. Not the most attractive repertoire of themes, especially when you consider that war, which could do with some real hating, is viewed even more equivocally than women.

That very Peckinpah theme, mistrust and hatred for one's superiors, or for the aristocracy or ruling class, is carried here to an absurd extreme, to the point where Steiner hates even the good Brandt so much that he won't make common cause with him against the despicable Stransky. There is no comparable hatred of war, which is shown as, yes, terrible, but also magnificent—something that allows men to be really men, and some of them even invulnerable supermen, way above the common, pacific herd. Indeed, if there were no such thing as betrayal or, occasionally, bad luck, it would seem that none of the good guys would have to perish.

Still, one could forgive a lot if there were not such blatant improbabilities as, for example, a German platoon being able to shelter a very young Russian prisoner at a time when the official policy is to kill all captured Russians; a German nurse who has a clandestine affair with one of her patients (Steiner), exposing herself at dawn in a nightgown on his balcony; Steiner and his platoon trying to make their way back to headquarters through Russian-held territories, and sitting around a bright campfire as they burst into lusty song. Piffle!

Peckinpah shot the film in Yugoslavia and had the good sense to cast a lot of German and Slavic actors as the combatants. But then he also had the bad sense to cast in the leads one American, two Englishmen, and one somewhat Hollywoodized Austrian. Not only does that create a confusion of tongues—or, at any rate, accents—at the top, it also allows the principals to be shown up by the supporting actors. Well, James Mason almost gets away with it—not only because he has so expertly portrayed Rommel and other eminent or egregious Germans in various past movies but also because there is something truly international about his face and manner, even if not about his accent. And Maximilian Schell is a grand villain, though I would have preferred him a trifle less psychotic. But David Warner is indelibly British, and James Coburn unexportably American. Steiner is a particular problem: Coburn plays him as restrainedly as he can, but he is still full of Coburnisms that are as American and as histrionically eloquent as apple pie.

Nevertheless, Peckinpah is a notable director. He is positively Wagnerian in his ability to orchestrate violence. He does not use his favorite strategy of shooting in slow motion quite so promiscuously here, which is good; and the special effects are often breathtaking in their catastrophic verisimilitude. All the same, there are too many of them. There is also some commendable effort to do noncombatant scenes imaginatively—for example, a hospital party seen concurrently as it is and as Steiner's troubled mind imagines it; or memories of Steiner's men, alive or dead, haunting him at various crucial moments. John Coquillon's cinematography captures the terrible beauty of war, which poets like Apollinaire celebrated, with deadly precision, and there are unforgettable scenes, such as a Russian tank pursuing Steiner's platoon through the thickest obstacles—worthy of those two great previous tank pursuit scenes, in Andrzej Munk's *Eroica* and Grigori Chukhrai's *Ballad of a Soldier.*

Then, again, there are silly things, such as a group of Russian women fighters, almost all of them pretty enough to be Hollywood starlets; or a conventional score by Ernest Gold that is not fit to tie the shoelaces of, say, Pierre Bachelet's for *Black and White in Color.* The whole last section of the film goes from preposterous through incredible to utterly ludicrous. Even in it, though, there are redeeming features, such as the effective multiple freeze frames, each of them ending one character's story. However, Peckinpah cannot leave well enough alone; he has to follow this up with more of the stock footage with which the film began, quite derivatively enough. What is one to do about such talent, and such lack of discipline or even common sense? Worst of all, however, is the fact that the film emerges as a commercial for war, since the very best guys, I repeat, seem somehow to survive, and what viewer, however unheroic, does not identify himself with the very best guys? No, if you want to see what defeat at the hands of the Russians and their allies really looked and felt like, you have to go to films like *Italiani Brava Gente,* by Giuseppe De Santis, or *The Human Condition,* by Masaki Kobayashi. The last parts of both of these films make defeat as painful and tragic as Peckinpah's movie wouldn't know how to do even if it intended it.

From war to Warhol is not quite so big a leap as it might seem, for the kind of mentality that conceives, or at any rate produces, a film like *Andy Warhol's Bad* strikes me as a distinct social ill. Vincent Canby in his *New York Times* review sees *Bad* coming close to what the late Joe Orton achieved in plays like *Loot.* This strikes me as utterly wrong. *Bad* tells of an evil beautician, Mrs. Aiken (Carroll Baker), who, besides specializing in electrolysis, runs a little Murder, Inc., type of business on the side. For good money, her operatives, all women, kill adults, children, babies; they are also available for lesser jobs, such as wreaking havoc with property or murdering someone's pet dog. But the film is almost totally witless: where Orton is witty and manages to make his black humor comment on characteristic people and institutions, there is, except for one bent policeman, no one or no thing in *Bad* that isn't freaky or bred in a vacuum, cruel out of motives that have very little to do with recognizable human motivations. In other words, this screenplay, by Pat Hackett and George Abagnalo, directed by Jed Johnson—presumably all members of Warhol's "Factory"—has few valid points to make and very little wit with which to make those pointed. In the first scene, a sluttish blonde (Cyrinda Foxe—a name I don't believe) destroys somebody's store and bathroom, causing, among other things, the toilet to overflow with every kind of filth and junk. This scene, at least, I understand: it is Warhol's symbolic *hommage* to his mind.

From there on in, *Bad* becomes worse—but all the vicious people are women. The men in the movie, with one exception, are either patient, put-upon victims or, even if they are hired assassins, of the sort that take pity on an autistic child they are supposed to do in. The women, however, are beastly without exception: cold-blooded killers, lethal psychopaths, murderously vindictive neighbors, infanticidal mothers, or, at the very least, surly, crazed crones and near-cretinous slatterns. Joe Orton saw the whole world with his comically jaundiced eyes as wicked and ridiculous; though he was easily as homosexual as anyone in the "Factory," he was not of the woman-hating sort. *Andy Warhol's Bad* is revolting in its misogyny. But since no one in the movie can act, much of what in a better-performed film would be considered monstrous is viewed as cute. I wish that all the society hostesses who vie with one another to invite Warhol to their parties would take a close look at this film. But they are probably not bright enough to understand what it means.

May 23, 1977

Star Dust

STAR WARS is an impeccable technical achievement: a quantum—or maybe quasar—leap beyond *2001*. Yet Kubrick, the pioneer, had to be there to make it possible for young George Lucas to forge ahead in that direction, though we might well ask ourselves to what end. I don't read science fiction, of which this may, for all I know, be a prime example; some light years ago I did read *Flash Gordon*, of which *Star Wars* is in most respects the equal. But is equaling sci-fi and comic strips, or even outstripping them, worthy of the talented director of *American Graffiti*, and worth spending all that time and money on?

I sincerely hope that science and scientists differ from science fiction and its practitioners. Heaven help us if they don't: we may be headed for a very boring world indeed. Strip *Star Wars* of its often striking images and its highfalutin scientific jargon, and you get a story, characters, and dialogue of overwhelming banality, without even a "future" cast to them: human beings, anthropoids, or robots, you could probably find them all, more or less like that, in downtown Los Angeles today. Certainly the mentality and values of the movie can be duplicated in third-rate *non*-science fiction of any place or period.

O dull new world! We are treated to a galactic civil war, assorted heroes and villains, a princely maiden in distress, a splendid old man surviving from an extinct order of knights who possessed a mysterious power called "the Force," and it is all as exciting as last year's weather reports. Rather more can be said for the two robots that steal the show: one humanoid, British-accented, and with an Edward Everett Horton persona; the other, a kind of mobile electronic trash can, all nervous beeps and hearty bloops, waddling along in vintage Mickey Rooney style. There are glimpses, too, of interesting new animals and peculiar hybrids, but they don't do or say anything novel. For a while, this is funny, as it is doubtless meant to be; finally, though, we do yearn for something really new. Why, even the best fight is just an old-fashioned duel, for all that the swords have laser beams for blades.

The film doesn't even provide the good-looking hero and heroine of the old *Flash Gordon* strip; it has nowhere near the romantic invention of, say, Edgar Rice Burroughs's Martian novels, featuring that dashing Virginia gentleman, John Carter, and the lovely shocking-pink princess, Dejah Thoris. Here it is all trite characters and paltry verbiage, handled adequately by Harrison Ford as a blockade-running starship pilot, uninspiredly by Mark Hamill as Luke Skywalker (Luke for George Lucas, the author-director; Skywalker for his Icarus complex), and wretchedly by Carrie Fisher, who is not even appealing as Princess Leia Organa (an organic lay). The one exception is Alec Guinness as the grand old man Ben Kenobi (Ben for the Hebrew *ben,* to make him sound biblical and good; Kenobi probably from cannabis, i.e., hashish, for reasons you can guess). Sir Alec has a wistful yet weighty dignity of tone and aspect that is all his own; why he should waste it on the likes of Luke, whom he befriends, protects, and bequeathes the Force to, remains the film's one mystery.

John Barry's set design is compelling, as are John Mollo's costumes; John Williams's music is good when it does not heave too much; the cinematography is striking, as Gilbert Taylor's work always is. Kudos are due, no doubt, to each member of the production staff, which extends to an unprecedented four mimeographed pages. But what you ultimately have is a set of giant baubles manipulated by an infant mind.

And then there is that distressing thing called the Force, which is not a flat-footed allusion to New York's finest but Lucas's tribute to something beyond science: imagination, the soul, God in man. It is what Ben Kenobi passes on to Luke, making the receiver invulnerable, though it hardly protected the giver's skin. It appears in various contradictory and finally nonsensical guises, a facile and perfunctory bow to metaphysics. I wish that Lucas had had the courage of his materialistic convictions, instead of dragging in a sop to a spiritual force the main thrust of the movie so cheerfully ignores. Still, *Star Wars* will do very nicely for those lucky enough to be children or unlucky enough never to have grown up.

June 20, 1977

A Blunder Too Many

You could not ask for a more whopping mistranslation than the one William Goldman has perpetrated on the late Cornelius Ryan's *A Bridge Too Far* in fictionalizing it onto the screen. First, the precise military action of this attack on the Dutch Rhine bridges (supposed to shorten the war but turning into a major Allied setback despite extraordinary heroism) is never made fully clear. We don't truly get to fathom and follow who is doing what to whom, or exactly where and when. And as the British ground forces that are supposed to press to the rescue of the Allied paratroopers come to a halt a mile short of their objective for reasons less than perspicuous, it becomes clear that ours is not to reason why.

I suppose that some of the blunderers among the Allied leaders are still very much alive, while the heroic memory of some of the departed must not be more than slightly besmirched. So a cloud of unknowing may deliberately enshroud some of this screenplay. But much unfortunate, schematic invention has gone into it, too, such as the bespectacled fifteen-year-old Dutch underground agent, whose very glasses foretell early death. Much has also been changed (along with the names of many people) to make things more cinematic. For example, the German panzers razed Arnhem, and the few noble British paratroopers that hung on had to fight out of cellars, of course. But firing out of cellars is less photogenic than picking off tanks from high windows and rooftops—cellars, in fact, might look downright unheroic. So rooftops it is.

Most of all, some of the deeds and utterances of the people involved do not conform to current screenwriterish notions of foulmouthed, black-humorous, antiheroic heroes; so actions that were not picturesque enough were gussied up with bits of absurdist recklessness; sayings that had a sweet, almost Victorian, desuetude were recast in the tough-cute style of *Butch Cassidy, Waldo Pepper,* and other Goldman triumphs, where cowboys talk like drugstore cowboys, soldiers like bittersweet-chocolate soldiers, always with a 1960 or 1970 smartass New York–scenarist twang, even if the people of that remote time and place actually had all the unsmartness, uncuteness, and straightforwardness of real people, much more moving in their ordinary humanity.

For an obvious example, there is no strict analogue in Ryan's book for Colonel Bobby Stout, as portrayed in the movie by Elliott Gould. There couldn't have been a specimen like that in Operation Market Garden (as it was called) or in any other operation except the operating room in M*A*S*H, and he, too, was enacted by Elliott Gould. This combination of repellent aspect, insensitivity of delivery, arrogance pouring from every pore, and a voice brimming with infantilism can be matched on screen only by the ex–Mrs. Gould, the world speed record for on-screen odiousness being held jointly by the former spouses.

It is not that flamboyance and eccentricity do not exist on the battlefield, or cannot be adequately portrayed. Compare Gould's performance with the Lieutenant Colonel Vandeleur of Michael Caine, and you will see zaniness and cockiness humanized, made believable. Some of the difference is in the acting, some of it in charm, and some, surely, in intelligence. In fact, it would be highly educational to project Caine's and Gould's scenes simultaneously on a split screen. After which the same could be done with all the British and all the American actors' scenes to reveal to what remarkable extent the British come out ahead. Take, for instance, Ryan O'Neal, who is supposed to be the very capable James Gavin; in no way could O'Neal have made youngest general in the army—at best, he could have caused general consternation.

An equally unlikely performance is that of the usually able Gene Hackman as General Sosabowski, commander of the Free Polish forces assigned to the operation. Hackman's must be the worst attempt at a foreign accent I have ever heard—can you imagine a general serving in England pronouncing "general" with a hard *g?* That must be the ultimate Polish joke: Sosabowski is made out to be cranky, cantankerous, suspicious, morbidly brooding in corners, so that even an eventual bit of heroism tossed his way emerges as mere foolhardiness.

Here and there a few sequences work well enough, especially those with Anthony Hopkins as Lieutenant Colonel Frost, the hero of Arnhem, a potently understated and trenchant performance; Hopkins is so fine that, though I know him well from both stage and screen, it took me quite a while to recognize him, despite the fact that he wears no special make-up. And here we come to yet another profoundly disturbing thing about the film. However good it may be for your box office to stud your cast with 24-karat stars, it militates heavily against basic believability when even small supporting roles are played by an Ullmann or an Olivier. Even the Germans are played by such stars as Max Schell and Hardy Krüger, leaving only the scenes with seemingly anonymous Dutch men and women to ring true for us, whatever they may do for audiences in the Netherlands. If the stars happen to be also very good actors, and if the parts are big or good enough to allow for their acting ability to display itself, things might be different, but such is not the case in *A Bridge Too Far.*

It is too bad also that producers do not see other people's movies, or have no memories, or, perhaps, just no taste and judgment—otherwise Joe Levine would not have chosen Richard Attenborough, the director of *Oh! What a Lovely War,* to stage so similar an all-star martial disaster. Not that Attenborough hasn't done a professional enough job, but three hours of scripting by William Goldman require more than professionalism as an antidote. The director lacks even such small but essential gifts for a war film as being able to make clear where the shooting comes from; instead, people in an attic, say, suddenly keel over without our comprehending whence and how the bullets came.

John Addison, who used to compose such handsome scores, with genuine concert-hall values, now merely accumulates sonorously aggressive platitudes. But Geoffrey Unsworth's cinematography maintains its luster without any sacrifice of starkness, and the production design seems authoritative throughout. There are moments when all hands combine to give us a genuine sense of awe, but they don't last. At altogether too many other times the film is almost an insult to the dead, the survivors, and the truth.

No less a producer's film is *The Other Side of Midnight,* only Frank Yablans prefers to put the money not into stars in bit parts but into sets and costumes, or at least landscapes, for what the film is selling is luxury and voluptuousness, fancy sex in sumptuous settings—in short, the kind of opulence and ostentation that only a housewife in a steamy kitchen or a shopgirl whose feet are killing her can dream up so gorgeously, passionately, and tastelessly. And the movie is selling something else as well, very important to the underprivileged (and who among us is not a have-not compared to Greek shipping magnates and their movie-star mistresses?), to wit, suffering. For after one has indulged oneself in unlikely identification with guilty squanderings, orgies, and even worse excesses, there must also be a vicarious comeuppance. Unless those glamorous grasshoppers pay through their noses (or antennae) for their indecently good times, how can we ants accept going back to our everyday drudgery?

So, in the manner perfectly understood by the late Jackie Susann, Sidney Sheldon, who wrote the underlying bestseller, and the brace of archetypal hacks, Daniel Taradash and Herman Raucher, who adapted it to the screen, see to it that there is hell to pay. But somebody dared to go a step further and let one of the superrich get off scot-free despite much ruthless deviltry. But that man, in a yet more unconvincing trick ending, turns Prince Charming for the Cinderella figure. Is the rewarding of sweet innocence justification enough for letting a rich rotter off the hook? For the answer to this momentous question we must wait until the box office has its last, solemnly juridical, word.

By way of plot summary, suffice it to say that this is the story of unleashed passions, of the uncontrollable love of lovely Noelle Page, a sweet little French beauty turned fashion model and movie star with a little whoring in between, for Larry Douglas, the dashing and debonair American flying ace and schmuck, who knocks her up and leaves her. Against a turbulent background of the German occupation, high fashion, low morals, and postwar prosperity, this tale of two great cities, Paris and (ugh!) Washington, and one small country, Greece, unfolds the profound and profane love-hate of Noelle for Larry; also the sacred love of pure and gentle and dipsomaniacal Catherine for the same Larry in sweet and innocent America; and Noelle's fury that pursues Larry across the world, until vengeance turns to lust again, and lust to attempted murder, and so, gloriously, forth.

Marie-France Pisier, a pert, winning, and bright actress, is not at all the irresistibly gorgeous idiot the part of Noelle calls for; she plays it with intelligent underacting that would be as commendable elsewhere as it is misplaced here. As the good and spunky American alcoholic, Susan Sarandon is winsome and, amazingly, almost believable; which is more than one can say for Clu Gulager as the high-powered but gentle ad-agency head who suppresses his honorable love for her for reasons known only to high-powered but gentle ad-agency heads. As the Hellenic tycoon who buys Noelle with the money that launched a thousand ships, Raf Vallone repeats his performance from Jules Dassin's *Phaedra*, even though it hasn't aged particularly well—but then excessively old vintages aren't very good either. Worst of all is John Beck as the man all women crave, for reasons that the Delphic priestess might have had difficulties elucidating—a huge but shapeless hunk of man, equipped with the jawbone of an ass that keeps ascending until it turns into a semblance of a brow after having in the process buried two small and inexpressive eyes. Beck's cinematic raison d'être is inscrutable—it certainly has nothing whatsoever to do with talent.

Michel Legrand has ground out his usual molasses-and-noise score; Fred J. Koenekamp's once artful cinematography has become fearfully literal-minded. John De Cuir's production design is unabashedly, indeed ferociously, costly-looking, and Irene Sharaff's costumes do not trail far behind. You can see exactly where every last dollar went, and tracing its itinerary is, alas, the movie's only interesting trip. The producer, Frank Yablans, is said to be the smartest salesman in the business, and he may have set up the whole thing as a challenge to himself: if you can sell *The Other Side of Midnight,* the Brooklyn Bridge should be child's play.

Please, Frank Yablans, if you are the honest and intelligent man you strike me as being, get rich in some other way—not by feeding this stale garbage to the public, however much they may want to lap it up.

June 27, 1977

Flaws

THE FIRST THING we see on the screen, after some amusing fish swimming around the credits, is Jacqueline Bisset's breasts encased in a white bathing suit that, underwater, becomes translucent, and affords us a fair idea of this magnificent matched pair of collector's items. The camera dives along with them (not being human enough to dive into them), in a glorious exordium, after which *The Deep* is downhill all the way.

Jaws was, in its trashy way, a clever and spirited film that, though stagnant on land, always came to life in the water. In the movie of *The Deep,* based on Peter Benchley's follow-up to *Jaws,* the excitement is supposed to be equally intense on land and in, or under, water; alas, in neither element is Peter Yates's film in its element. Perhaps, like the dying Cleopatra, Yates considers himself fire and air; to the other elements, he has certainly given lesser life. From the screenplay by Benchley himself and Tracy Keenan Wynn, the director has fashioned a movie that advances the cause of underwater cinematography almost as prodigiously as it retards the cause of filmmaking.

A rather silly "fun couple," David Sanders and Gail Berke, dive for treasure in Bermuda, and, with beginner's luck, hit upon a kind of wreckage palimpsest: a World War II wreck containing a treasure in morphine ampoules underneath which is an eighteenth-century wreck loaded with rare jewels with which a king of Spain wooed a stand-offish noblewoman. (The morphine looks convincing enough, but the rare gems have a curiously curio-shoppe look about them.) They hook up with a rough but honest local diver and adventurer, Romer Treece, who will help them with the treasure for half the profits, and fall afoul of Cloche, a sinister Haitian dealer in narcotics, whose gang first tries to scare them into leaving Bermuda immediately and, later, to assist them in leaving this earthly life equally precipitately.

Suffice it to say that none of the plot holds water half as well as the brains of the scenarists. Cloche and his gang, early on, abduct David and Gail; by applying intimidation and torture a little more skillfully (or even by a little bird-dogging), they could easily have wrested the location of the treasure from the dopey couple and recuperated it themselves. True, there would have been no movie then; but this would have benefited an overwhelming majority of the population—everyone, in fact, except the tiny minority that stands to make a profit from having concocted *The Deep.*

And speaking of minorities, the film has been accused of racism because all the heavies are, supposedly, black, and all the good guys white. Actually, however, there is also Eli Wallach in the rather unsympathetic role of a treacherous rummy, and he, to all appearances, is white. Moreover, the good guys are not all that good, and, some of them—like Gail and David—not even very smart, so I think the charge of racism might as well be dropped (or, in this context, scuttled); unless, of course, one takes the position that *The Deep* is unfair to the human race, which it may well be, and which is the worst kind of racism. Certainly the fish that float around most of the sequences behave with much greater dignity and innocence.

To be sure, even among the fish there are villains—moray eels and gray sharks—but, since the heroes elude them while the evildoers do not, they cannot be excessively faulted. There is indeed an eerie beauty about the world of the deep, which the underwater cinematography of Al Giddings and Stan Waterman, presumably overseen by the overwater cinematographer, Christopher Challis, admirably exploits. But for this sort of thing one still prefers Captain Cousteau at the helm; Captain Yates's hokum, even abetted by a highly efficient five-man team of special-effects people, founders on the reefs of incredibility.

Among the performers, the lovely Miss Bisset looks better than ever in Ron Talsky's clever costumes that have not so much elegance perhaps as an understated ostentatiousness; and Robert Shaw is immensely likable as Treece, though his ever-more-bizarre accent and voice production—every syllable erupts like the bark of a splenetic old seadog—make him only marginally comprehensible. Still, I did make out his telling Miss Bisset that Nick Nolte (who plays David) is not the king of Spain. This is debatable: with his attenuated forehead and befogged eyes, his prognathous and semicretinous aspect, he looks very much like one of those late and degenerate Hapsburg monarchs of Spain whom not even the brush of Velázquez could, or would, whitewash. Not only can he not act, he cannot even look and sound halfway intelligent during the rare moments when the screenplay calls for it.

The others, including Lou Gossett as a smoothly menacing Cloche, do the best they can with a foolish and sometimes inscrutable script. *The Deep,* however, has a fascinating history of production, and is a prime representative of a newish cinematic genre that is gaining in popularity. It is a type of film whose making is fraught with so much complication, so much deployment of technical resourcefulness, so many brilliant coups of logistics and publicity, that what really matters is not the film but the filming. What the public rushes to see, in other words, is not so much a moving picture as a set of illustrations and footnotes to all those fascinating accounts of bizarre incidents and triumphs of technological ingenuity one read about for months before the film's release. One does not go to *see The Deep,* only to *verify* it.

There can be no doubt, however, that *Exorcist II: The Heretic,* without the benefit of special diving equipment, sinks infinitely deeper yet. Whereas it is impossible to designate even approximately the worst film one has ever seen, there is a very strong probability that *Exorcist II* is the stupidest major movie ever made. I hate to sound that categorical, because it may send collectors of imbecilities scurrying off in droves to see this execrable product; but, then, I suppose, collectors of imbecilities *are* the fitting audience for this film, and they deserve each other.

The original *Exorcist* was garbage enough, but at least it was garbage with a point of view, however confused, and a plot, however crude. In this quasi-sequel, taking up the story of Regan four years later, there is no plot, but all kinds of disparate plot fragments churning around chaotically; and there is decidedly no point of view (Richard Burton as a crazed, fanatical priest yells at the top of his voice, "I am *not* a fanatic!") except the determination to exploit everything that is exploitable, from zoom lenses to religion, from boutique décor carried to absurd heights to aerial photography sinking to new depths of eye-blasting pretentiousness.

I shall not insult you and myself by trying to summarize this plot, which is incomprehensible anyway, though not nearly so incomprehensible as what motives besides greed could have led a director like John Boorman, who in some of his earlier films showed a certain intelligence as well as some craftsmanship, to concoct this foul-smelling witch's brew of meaningless turbulence, this storm not exactly in a teapot, but in a vessel of a somewhat similar sort. The script is by one William Goodhart, described by the program as a "hit Broadway playwright," but for all that I put on my other, drama critic's, hat I cannot recall a single work by this renowned Broadway hit man. "The inspiration for the story," we are further told, came from Father Teilhard de Chardin, and though I am not exactly an admirer of that worthy but fuzzy pietistic protoscientist, I must say that the script has less bearing on Teilhard than on the latest lunatic cult that may have sprung up in one of the obscurer crannies of Los Angeles.

In any case, would you believe a film in which an actress mother, away on location, never even telephones her deeply troubled daughter? Or a film in which a skyscraper's penthouse terrace has a parapet with enormous, deliberate gaps in it, so that a sleepwalking Linda Blair could more easily hurtle off it? (This may become the first film ever to be condemned by the Building Code Enforcement Bureau.) And in which that same Linda Blair, teetering somnambulistically on the edge, does not fall off—surely a scene that surpasses in ridiculousness even the notorious final scene of *The Fountainhead,* the previous champion in the bottom-scraping skyscraper division.

Linda Blair, not a very talented or prepossessing youngster then, is even less interesting now, though considerably more bovine; I doubt whether a postpubertal acting style can be made out of mere chubbiness. Poor Richard

Burton, as Father Lamont, although the script buffets him about as the infernal gust does the souls in the second circle of Dante's hell, does not manage to look much more tormented than the average sufferer from colic. Louise Fletcher looks uncannily like Ellen Burstyn here, but doesn't contribute much else, while Max von Sydow, Kitty Winn, and a number of others, deserve some sort of recognition for being able to play parts of surpassing absurdity without bursting into mad laughter. The audience sometimes does, but not often enough to justify going to the movie as a comedy, either. Richard MacDonald's art direction is even more baroque here than it was in some of Joseph Losey's films. William A. Fraker's cinematography would be impressive if the context permitted it, but the gifted Ennio Morricone's music sounds rather like the outtakes from the sound effects for the plague of locusts that frequently descends in the film, whereas it should descend *on* it.

But the greatest plague in the movies these days is the plague of sequels. If there is one relatively easy thing the public can do now to help improve the state of American movies, it is to stay away resolutely from sequels and remakes. If cinematic follies have to be committed, let them at least not be committed in duplicate.

July 4, 1977

Empty Generalities

WHAT IS ONE TO SAY about a film like *MacArthur?* That it is bigger than a bread box and shorter than *A Bridge Too Far?* That Gregory Peck's long career as our most ligneous actor reaches its apotheosis here—for whatever the real MacArthur may have been like, the piece of wood that the screenwriters, Hal Barwood and Matthew Robbins, and the director Joseph Sargent, offer us could not have garnered a more suitable interpreter than Peck, unflinchingly handsome as ever, even in his convincing MacArthur make-up, and perfectly ageless? To tell his years, in fact, you would have to saw him in two and count the rings. He certainly won't allow the movie to age him very much either, and plays the eighty-two-year-old retired general looking not a day over seventy. You might say that not since Hardy's poem about the slow but ineluctable coming together of the *Titanic* and the iceberg fate nurtured for its undoing, was there so fatal a convergence of the twain as that of Peck and his current role.

The actor tries hard to be granite but never gets much beyond walnut. What is more, he means occasionally to be sensitively brooding, but it comes out as a solemn sullenness; his few ostensibly funny lines he delivers in so hieratic a monotone that it takes us several seconds of reflection to determine whether they were meant to be jokes. Maybe MacArthur really was like this; if so, he, too, could have been converted very nicely into a coffee table. On the other hand, Peck is not much helped by a script that is consistently, determinedly ambivalent, following a formula perfected by *Patton,* its immediate ancestor.

The trick is to show a famous commander as both a hero and a bit of a menace, so that both the pacifists and warmongers in the audience have something to latch on to while conveniently shutting their eyes to the rest. There is, in other words, no point of view, and the general is exalted in some scenes and ridiculed in others. But, you might ask, isn't this fairer than oversimplifying, and didn't Shakespeare himself in his histories wisely mix black and white into gray? Well, yes; but he mixed them rather than merely alternating them.

What in a true artist emerges as complexity and scrupulous fairness is in lesser men merely mealymouthedness and schematism. An artist humanizes all contradictions, embeds them deeply in flesh and blood, discovers the troubled and turbulent center from which such antithetical impulses spring; a hack simply daubs schematic antitheses on his lay figures—beneath the contraries there are more contraries, and no living, idiosyncratic core. Men like Barwood and Robbins do not even instill in us the urge to puzzle out the enigma of character; instead, they slickly manipulate us toward whatever oversimplification suits our prejudices or, if we haven't any, toward shrugging the whole thing off with a formula like "a living paradox."

So we get the usual superficial history or near-history lesson; moving pictures from the life and times of Douglas MacArthur. It is a primer with a few facile ironies and wisecracks added in the hope of elevating it from the freshman to the sophomore level. The method is to surround the hero, lushly ambiguous, with an array of stick figures ranging from adoring friends and associates to cynical underlings and rivals, and allow every shade of extreme or intermediate attitude perfunctory hearing. In between, there is action footage that, as Joseph Sargent directs it, looks curiously like stuff from the routine war movies of the forties and fifties. Still, inasmuch as the scenes of personal confrontation, loyalty, and intrigue, of strategy and politicking are handled no more resourcefully, the result is at least very much of a piece, though I shall tactfully refrain from telling you of what.

The supporting performances range widely in quality, from the fussily unconvincing FDR of Dan O'Herlihy, to the quite ingenious and arresting Harry Truman of Ed Flanders—if only he didn't rattle off his lines quite so hectically. On the whole, though, the casting and make-up people have performed wonders in getting the portrayers of the famous people to look and sound remarkably right; but the fun in that is an idiot's delight at best.

A much bigger disaster, however, is *New York, New York,* all 2 hours and 33 minutes of it. It is devilishly hard even to figure out what Martin Scorsese, the director, and Earl Mac Rauch and Mardik Martin, the scenarists, had in mind here (if anything), for the film, aside from being terrible in every way, makes no basic sense. It is a movie musical about the supposedly torrid romance of a saxophone player, Jimmy Doyle, and a band singer, Francine Evans, who after an unorthodox courtship enter upon a tempestuous marriage that soon breaks up. They become famous and rich—she as a movie-musical comedienne, he as a jazzman who has his own popular club—and almost get together again, but finally don't. It may not sound like much of a story, but it is even less, dragged out as it is to unconscionable length.

It may be about the passing of the big bands; but if so, the reason for it, or for anything else, is never made clear. The filmmakers obviously couldn't decide what to do with their material. Sometimes it looks as if they were trying to revive the grand old movie musical; at other times, they seem to be spoofing it. Actually, they have come closest in plot to *Alexander's Ragtime Band*, but that was genuinely unpretentious and guilelessly believed its own sillinesses; besides, it had Irving Berlin.

The greatness of the confusion is carried over even into the production design. Some sets simply cannot decide whether to be realistic or stylized, straightforward or caricatural. The Moonlit Terrace, for instance, is both a tribute to and a distortion of the Rainbow Room; a railway station looks moderately real, but the train in it is a cutout; a forest scene has very real-looking trees up front and gross travesties farther back. The production numbers in the movie-within-a-movie similarly cannot quite opt either for tacky Busby Berkeley take-offs or for cleverness and spectacle in their own right.

The aura of uncertainty engulfs everything. The rather too flamboyant costumes at least stick to their period, but the dialogue is full of anachronistic slang. Though the characters are conceived along the cliché lines of the old big-band and backstage musicals, the actors are allowed to overemote and overact (notably Robert De Niro as Jimmy) as if they were in a Soviet film about victims of czarist oppression. Indeed, if there is any idea in this pitiful, hyperthyroid film, it is to take the old clichés and blow them up bigger and bigger—to bursting and beyond.

As a symptom of this disease, consider the night-club signs. The movies of the age of relative innocence developed the convention of conveying the wild and wondrous life of Nighttown by a montage of neon signs heralding the names of nightclubs. These signs were to dazzle us with the quirks of their names and lettering, with the ingenious ways in which they were splattered across the screen (vertically, horizontally, diagonally; in high- or low-angle shots; in superimposition or quick dissolves; in color, whenever possible), and with their flashing on and off to the beat of the background score. You would think that if he used it at all, Scorsese would exaggerate or travesty or otherwise improve on the device; instead, all he gives us is more and longer montages. Vapid quantity is all.

This, regrettably, is the formula for the screenplay, too. No one has bothered to make the characters the least bit believable and sympathetic. They love, quarrel, separate, and yearn for no compelling reasons (sometimes not even for uncompelling ones), but they do it in bulk. So we try to decide just what to do with the two and a half hours plus at our disposal: laugh, feel nostalgic, admire the filmmakers' encyclopedic knowledge of clichés, or what? In the end, the easiest solution is to lean back in indifference and try to endure the excruciating boredom with the greatest possible dignity.

Quantity as the basic ingredient is apparent also in the way the dialogue is spun out. A fundamental concept—say, that the touring Francine, now singing for her husband Jimmy's band, wants to go back to New York to have her baby—is stated by her in a declarative sentence. Then Jimmy inverts it into a question, roughly, "You wanna go to New York to have the baby?" She then repeats her affirmation more emphatically. Whereupon he questions her more sarcastically. This may be good for one or two more exchanges, after which a small additional detail is appended, and we're off again on the shuttle. It is with such proto-Wittgensteinian linguistic analysis that the movie inches, or tautologizes, its way ahead. Were those depressing reiterations of banalities pruned from the movie, we could all have gone home an hour earlier; but *New York, New York* is made as if the filmmakers' chief aim were to demonstrate that they could get their matériel wholesale.

The only other idea—if you can call it that—was to encourage Liza Minnelli as Francine to act and sing as much as possible like her mother, which she usually does anyway. The result is rather like urging someone who has been spontaneously walking to walk consciously, which leads him, of course, to paralysis or to falling on his face. In any case, the big difference between Garland and Minnelli is that Garland, though less than comely, was not (until near the end) grotesque and goony; that Garland, even if overacting, did so in her own style at least; and that, though one sometimes refused to cry with Garland, one can never help giggling at Minnelli.

The songs that John Kander and Fred Ebb wrote for the film (some golden oldies also stud the soundtrack but tend to get short shrift—in fact, only a record of the Hot Club of France playing "Billets Doux" that the distraught Francine listens to manages to sound like real music-making) are appropriately flavorless. The lyrics are downright embarrassing, even when they are not stealing the title of the well-known Comden-Green-Bernstein show song that also becomes the title of this eclectic movie. Ron Field's choreography is minimal in invention, and, like the other minimums here, gets stretched beyond its elasticity.

The minor roles are conceived so stereotypically that even such an oddball actor as Lionel Stander emerges as a platitude; in what looks like a severely cut role, Mary Kay Place alone maintains a modicum of individuality. Everything finally devolves on De Niro and Minnelli. De Niro apparently decided that maniacal drivenness was the only thing that could be played in his part; he may have been right, but should nonetheless have tried for a little less of it, eking out the rest with some charming nonchalance. As it is, he quickly becomes grating, and it is Minnelli, as ever a desperate display of synthetics forlornly straining for the real thing, that comes out ahead. Pathos, even in its most extreme and unsavory form, is less unappetizing than the combination of arrogance and monomania.

But the person who comes off least well here is Martin Scorsese, whose directorial vision seems to be no greater than that of a man driving through a downpour without turning on his windshield wipers.

July 11, 1977

Rough Riding

IT REQUIRES ENORMOUS ARROGANCE to remake a classic film like Henri-Georges Clouzot's *The Wages of Fear* (1953), which in its own melodramatic way was quite brilliant, as a specimen of gross and unintelligent commercialism, and then dedicate it to the memory of Clouzot. But that is precisely what William Friedkin has done, and, by way of further dishonesty, he entitled the mess *Sorcerer,* after the name painted on a truck, so that the gullible folk who fell for *The Exorcist* should fall farther yet into believing this to be a sequel to that egregious piece of goods.

A genuine tribute to Clouzot would be the re-release of his film in the uncut version, never shown commercially in this country. Based on a novel by Georges Arnaud, this was, first of all, an impassioned indictment of strangulating poverty in a Latin American country fostered by the collusion of United States business interests and domestic dictatorship. Out of this arose the story of four desperate men who undertake to convey a hypersensitive shipment of nitroglycerin in two battered trucks across impossible terrain in return for enough money to get them out of that country. The film was a banner achievement in atmosphere and suspense, and, in the light of subsequent history—in Chile, for instance—would have added meaning for the present time.

Friedkin, however, spent twenty-one million dollars to perpetrate a film that could be usefully studied in courses on how not to make movies. First (with his screenwriter, Walon Green) he gives us four vacuous episodes about the backgrounds of the quartet of future explosive-conveyers. The episodes are paragons of pointlessly spent money and film time, dragging in expensive foreign locales and irrelevant violence, and look rather like Friedkin's attempt to prove his ability to make capsule versions of *Black Sunday, The Godfather, The Other Side of Midnight,* and even, heaven help us, *The Next Man.* They are boring and confusing in themselves, and merely subtract from the whole. By establishing all four principals as swindlers or murderers, they effectively kill off sympathy for them, so that when the great ordeal comes, we do not care whether anyone lives or dies.

The banana-republic atmosphere in Friedkin's film is conventionalized and depoliticized to the utmost. Though a despotic *presidente* and some discreetly ruthless American businessmen are still there, the emphasis is on general squalor (sets that seem to be made of papaya-mâché), melodramatic confrontations between police and populace, and our four principals weaving in and out of hovels and flophouses, brushing against sinister fellow outcasts, and exchanging snippets of murky dialogue or long, supposedly significant, glances across seedy distances.

When the main plot finally does get under way, the emphasis is still not on the effect of stress upon character, but on stress upon stress upon stress. Unlike in Clouzot's film, the men remain ciphers, and have hardships piled on them so thick and fast that the result borders on the ludicrous. Thus a suspension bridge is crumbling away under a truck, the rope that helps pull the vehicle across is rapidly fraying, the trestle to which the rope is tied is getting uprooted, and torrents of rain and great gusts of wind are further sabotaging human endeavor. There are no moments of relaxation, let alone of feeling. Even the acting is rendered uninteresting by the dimensionless roles. The cinematography by John M. Stephens and Dick Bush looks retrograde, with blues and greens running amuck. The music by Tangerine Dream is undistinguished except in the Paris sequence, when it switches, without credit, to Ravel's String Quartet. This could be the doing of Mrs. Friedkin, in public life Jeanne Moreau, who may be trying to civilize her husband's soundtracks. Still, piracy is a rather odd species of civilization.

In *The Story Behind the Exorcist,* Travers and Reiff quote Friedkin: "I have a theory of criticism: If a film is liked by the critics and the audience, it's probably a great film. If a film is liked by the audience, but not by the critics, it's still probably a great film. If a film is liked only by the critics, it is a piece of shit!" I regret not being able to give you an exact evaluation of *Sorcerer* because Friedkin's otherwise comprehensive schema fails to provide the *mot juste* for a film disliked equally by audience and critics.

I Never Promised You a Rose Garden is a sincere and, at times, affecting movie version of the popular novel about sixteen-year-old Deborah Blake, schizoid and suicidal, who spends three anguished years in a psychiatric hospital and is in the end apparently cured through the ministrations of Dr. Fried, a wise and humane woman psychiatrist. I haven't read the book; the movie strikes me as decently struggling to be honest, but remaining less than compelling artistically and much less than convincing clinically. The problem with movies about psychotherapy (as I have often said and am, alas, obliged to repeat once or twice yearly) is that they are doomed to foreshorten and overdramatize a process that is slow, tedious, and wholly unspectacular, thus giving an impression as delightfully misleading as those nature documentaries in which the life cycle of a plant or insect is reproduced in seconds. A psychiatric cure in a movie always looks like black magic or outright mendacity. Deborah's trouble, moreover, seems to be so deep-seated, possibly more psychotic than neurotic, that the simplistic and accelerated solution looks even less persuasive. This is particularly regrettable because Anthony Page has directed individual scenes scrupulously and forcefully.

Furthermore, like other such films, *Rose Garden,* its generally intelligent screenplay by Gavin Lambert and Lewis John Carlino notwithstanding, fails to make Deborah's fantasy world seductive enough for us to sympathize with her delusions. These hippiefied cavemen are sentimental clichés, not even up to the romance of prehistory as purveyed, for example, by the novels of J.-H. Rosny. Moreover, there seems to be no way of preventing the antics of the insane from striking a fatuous audience as riotously funny, which makes one feel embarrassment on top of depression.

Still, even if we do not get a sense of three endless years in an asylum, we experience clearly enough patches of exasperation and terror. There are moments of self-destruction with burning cigarettes and jagged bits of tin, of brutalization by fellow inmates or sadistic guards, of spiritual humiliation by uncomprehending parents or therapists that are portrayed with aching accuracy not devoid of artistry. The camera captures certain spasms and outcries with a matter-of-factness that is more effective than any attempt to emotionalize or editorialize. Basically, though, one feels in the presence of dedicated artisans rather than of inspired artists. If a single sequence from, say, Bergman's *Persona* or *The Passion of Anna* were edited into this film, the entire venture would be shown up for the brave journeyman work it is.

Yet, I suppose, we must be grateful even for this much from an American movie, even one with a British director and one British scenarist. And there is the flawless performance of Kathleen Quinlan as Deborah. Miss Quinlan has been good as a precocious tomboy in *American Graffiti* and overeager jailbait in *Lifeguard,* but I was unprepared for the staggering, unaffected integrity of this performance. There must be two tremendous temptations, especially for a young actress, in a role such as this: to act the sweet, lovable, lost soul, or, simply, to overact. Miss Quinlan will have none of this: she is pitiful, ugly, even horrible, by turns, as called for, always in a manner that I must describe, for lack of better words, as crisp and efficient, and never suggests (as so many actresses would) an uncontrollable personal dementia of her own, only the sensitive and sensible enactment of it.

A very solid performance comes from Bibi Andersson too, as expected, though she is hardly the visual and vocal type for Dr. Fried, a kindly Jewish psychiatrist. In fact, Miss Andersson has yet to feel more at ease with acting in English; otherwise, however, she performs with admirable honesty—almost nobility—in her avoidance of both mannerism and any strategy of ingratiation. It is not her fault if the role is, in the last analysis (so to speak), a trifle unrealized and tepid.

The numerous supporting roles are imaginatively cast and soundly performed (although Ben Piazza and Lorraine Gary, as Deborah's parents, form a rather unlikely couple), and there is honorably professional camerawork from Bruce Logan and music by Paul Chihara, names new to me. If you can see this film for its incidental virtues and ignore its overarching inadequacy, it will prove modestly rewarding.

August 1, 1977

Legionnaire's and Other Diseases

THE LAST REMAKE OF BEAU GESTE contains a few, a very few, genuinely comic moments, but otherwise Marty Feldman's parody is very much a graduation piece from the Mel Brooks school of farce. It is no better than the similar graduation piece by a fellow student, Gene Wilder, in which Sherlock Holmes rather than Beau Geste was given the treatment, and is not appreciably worse than most of the works by the beloved master himself.

There is something mildly repulsive to me about the very idea of parodying *Beau Geste,* either the novel by Percival C. Wren, or the antepenultimate movie version by William A. Wellman. Both works strike me as decent and unpretentious, rather like a harmless, not very sophisticated, but ever so obliging maiden aunt, whom it really does not do to kick in the backside. There is not even a Beau Geste cult or mystique to lampoon—not so much as a T-shirt.

Feldman and Michael York are identical twins (!), orphans whom Trevor Howard, the half-crazy lord of Geste Manor, adopts and names Digby and Beau. The one grows up splendidly, the other shabbily, until a wicked young stepmother arrives in the person of Ann-Margret, after which the family heirloom disappears, and it's the Foreign Legion—well, you know the story, more or less, and Feldman knows it about that much too, and is only too eager to maul it beyond recognition.

The scene at the orphanage is mildly amusing because Trevor Howard is a splendid actor and has, in Irene Handl, a comedienne to act against. There is also some quite pleasant kidding of cinematic clichés, where Feldman has something worth kidding. When the film, however, switches to black-and-white to parody a silent comedy and record Digby-Feldman's inept jailbreak, in which everyone from the prison governor down tries to assist and only Feldman keeps flubbing, there is again no idiocy worth satirizing.

Nor are things funny in the Foreign Legion, partly because there was never much of a legionnaire genre *(Beau Geste* and *Between Two Flags* are all most people remember) and what there was of it was far too long ago. And here the material becomes unspeakably clumsy: the running—or, rather, hobbling—gag being Sergeant Markov's peg leg. Neither Peter Ustinov as Markov nor Roy Kinnear as his sidekick can lend these leg jokes much of a helping hand, though neither of them sinks as low as Henry Gibson as a French general (and possibly a take-off on Mel Brooks—though who knows or cares?). Ann-Margret adds to her other no-talents a no-talent for farce; and the worthy Michael York, who rose undented from the debacle of *Dr. Moreau,* is well-nigh destroyed by this one. Marty Feldman shows some restraint: he sometimes actually retracts those endlessly extrudable eyes. The film suffers not so much from ocular jocularity as from a hypertrophy of Feldman himself, a little of whom pops a long way.

Do not allow the first few minutes of *Outrageous!* (or, indeed, the title) to turn you against this winning little Canadian film written and directed by Richard Benner. You see a scene in a "gay" bar, moments from the home life of a homosexual hairdresser, and a young girl escaping in hospital attire from a mental institution through matutinal Toronto. There is some rather schematic crosscutting between the homosexual in his apartment and the running girl; when she tells him she wants to stay with him and he reluctantly agrees, and their life together begins, the framing of shots is routine for a while, and the camera movements seem paltry. Beware of concluding that you are in for yet another conventional story about the heartbreaking, not-to-be-consummated affection between a homosexual and a promiscuous but tenderhearted girl—the sort of thing that was treated, openly or disguisedly, in films such as *I Am a Camera, Darling, A Taste of Honey,* and *Cabaret.* Above all, do not walk out. Because soon you will be sitting up and attending: this dialogue is fresh and spirited, witty and lifelike; these characters behave like people, disturbed or disgruntled, but swimming in their miseries rather than sinking in them, and not viewing themselves—or being viewed by the filmmakers—with unseemly sentimentality.

Other characters come into the picture: hairdressers and their clients in a jesting but acrid symbiosis; an overanxious mother and a seemingly callous, but possibly wise, psychiatric nurse; various homosexuals and mental patients—and casual pickups of Liza, the girl, or friends of Robin, the hairdresser. These people, with the exception of Liza's excessively standard mother, are pertinently observed, in no way oversimplified, and allowed to interact in the odd but finally compelling ways in which their natures prod them. Why, there is even a psychiatrist who rings true—one of the rarest things in movies.

By now we have forgotten that we are watching a film shot in 16 mm and less than satisfactorily blown up; the camera placements and movements have become more persuasive; the editing is secure, including some nicely timed lateral wipes, allowing the story to unfurl in varying but credible tempos. The characters continue to grow on us. Robin is not an idealized portrait of a homosexual; Liza is not a particularly lovable schizophrenic. But both are believable human beings, inflicting and sustaining pain, helping and hurting each other and themselves, prone to precariously improvised happinesses, and trying to meet with dignity the indignities life metes out to them.

Liza attempts to publish some of the writing she does "for all the crazies of the world," and also, against strictest medical orders, to have a baby; Robin sets out to make a professional success out of his talent for impersonating female movie stars and singers. How they thrive or fail in Toronto and New York City, in various homosexual or heterosexual night spots, in maternity hospitals or with magazine editors, and in a number of apartments—how they diverge and converge again—you will have to find out for yourselves. I can only assure you that you will be often amused and repeatedly touched, and never uninvolved.

My guess is that the understanding of mental illness comes from Margaret Gibson, on whose story the film is based, and that the sympathetic insight into the homosexual world stems from the screenwriter-director. Neither ambience is belittled or embellished; and though it may be that the anguish of inversion and insanity is a bit too glibly equated in the end with the universal condition—that craziness is placed a trifle too cavalierly above dull sanity—this is done with tactful ambiguity. A beleaguered person is speaking to his even more severely endangered friend, so the statements have to be taken with a grain of salt—whether the salt of irony or that of tears will depend on the individual viewer.

Outrageous! is much more moving and amusing than it is outrageous, though it does provide what I assume to be honest views of homosexual life at its not exactly raunchiest, but far from most attractive: there is, for example, real sadness in a scene in which the pretty but perturbed Liza looks in vain for sexual recognition among the habitués of a black-leather bar; and there is some genuine insight into how camp or homosexual wit is generated out of the bitterness and frustrations—but also the devil-may-care relaxedness—of homosexual hangouts. The drag queens who parade about riotously in front of their audiences, only to wrangle rancorously behind the scenes, are split between contrary urges of masculinity and feminity, but fight their dichotomy gallantly with the only weapons available: blade upon blade of flashing, lacerating wit.

There are some very apt supporting performances, among which I must single out Richert Easley's Perry, a clumsy, obstreperous, but finally extremely appealing homosexual sidekick of Robin's, especially funny when he is impersonating Karen Black in *Airport '75.* Yet the film lives particularly off its two acute principals. Hollis McLaren, as Liza, has the gift of humanizing craziness without falsifying it, and of managing to convey that something is faintly askew even during moments of remission. Craig Russell, as Robin, is not only a highly accomplished female impersonator (as in real life), but also an authoritative on-screen presence, often not so much playing as playing with his role, as befits the character.

A final proof of Richard Benner's directorial shrewdness is that, unlike Anthony Page in *I Never Promised You a Rose Garden,* Benner never shows us the fantasy creatures that persecute his heroine. Whereas Page and his scenarists made their film ludicrous each time those preposterous figures invaded the screen, Benner genuinely moves us when Robin joins Liza's efforts to ward off her nemesis, the Bonecrusher, even though he can see him no more than we can; and he manages to frighten us no less truly when, while we hear Liza's frenzied pleading, the camera focuses on the empty, harmless, sundrenched corner of the room where the terror is supposed to dwell. This was Bergman's technique in *Through a Glass Darkly,* and T. S. Eliot's in verses like "There, the eyes are/Sunlight on a broken column." Benner could not be in better company.

August 8–15, 1977

Of Superhuman Bondage

THERE IS A KIND OF MOVIE that can get away with everything, and deserves to. The latest James Bond, *The Spy Who Loved Me,* belongs in that class. Like other 007 epics, only perhaps even a little more so, this picture comes at you winking with both eyes and saying something like: "For heaven's sake, don't take any of this seriously. This violence isn't real violence, this sex isn't anything like real sex; all this is fantasy, escapism, slick entertainment. If you believe any of this, you are a bigger fool than if you think you are married to Sophia Loren, will become president of the United States, and live forever.

You might just as well believe that this is art!" And so you wink back, don't believe any of it, and have a damned good time, smiling from ear to ear when not actually letting out a hoot and a holler.

This is the first 007 film that is not based on an Ian Fleming novel, only a Fleming title, according to the late novelist's own instructions, we are told. And, to be sure, when you have a good title like *The Spy Who Loved Me;* the veteran Bond producer Albert Broccoli (who used to team up on these ventures with Harry Saltzman, but who has done quite well on his own, broccoli being tasty even unsalted); the tried Bond scriptwriter Richard Maibaum together with a new hand, Christopher Wood; Lewis Gilbert, the director of another Bond film, *You Only Live Twice,* and of some rather more respectable other movies, including the severely undervalued *Alfie*—why, then, shouldn't everything go swimmingly?

Actually, things start out skiingly in the pretitle sequences—and a jolly set of deviltries they are!—and end swimmingly. In between, of course, there is every other kind of sport, from sex with a gorgeous Soviet spy to blowing up a couple of atomic submarines programmed to send New York and Moscow into that great détente in the sky. And there is, first of all, yet another of those tricky title sequences, during which a stunning, seemingly nude, female silhouette (or rather a whole set of such silhouettes) carries on rapturously and moderately kinkily behind the credits with the barrel of Bond's gun. It is the sort of thing that might make fanatical feminists go berserk, but even they, surely, have better things to become enraged by.

After that, we are off on a plot about which I couldn't do anything more idiotic than try to tell you the first thing. In geographical terms, however, I can promise you marvelous sights from Egypt to Sardinia; in terms of colorful villains, you can look forward to everything from suave, Continental, ultracerebral evil in the person of Curt Jurgens to a more mechanical menace in the person of Jaws, a seven-foot-three-inch golem, equipped with steel teeth that can bite through and kill an attacking shark in the water, not to mention a massive frame, which can survive everything from the collapse of an Egyptian temple on top of it to a direct hit by a torpedo on the floating marine laboratory housing it. Best of all, in gadgets, I can guarantee you more fantastic ones than you have seen heretofore—but to give away even a single Bond gadget would be infinitely greater malpractice than rattling off the entire plot.

So what *can* I report on? The performances? But are there ever performances in a Bond movie? Well, there used to be Sean Connery, whom I may not have sufficiently appreciated. He had a sort of double-bottomed look on his face—an ironic expression that meant that he could be either superman or an ass, that what he was saying could be taken at face value or as an outrageous pun—and, lo, what happened next, in its predictable unpredictableness, matched his expression and sweetly slippery, brogue-suffused tone. Or, to put it simply, you could believe that Connery was cunning and apt enough to think up the clever things he said, and execute the mighty maneuvers he undertook. Not so Roger Moore, who looks handsome enough to be the mold from which the world's most expensive clothing dummies are cast, but who has absolutely no way with an expression, let alone with a line. You might say that, as 007, he does justice only to the first two thirds of his role.

As the spy who loves him and collaborates with him when she is not trying to kill him, there is Barbara Bach, who does not exactly act up a storm either—still less a Russian storm—but who may just be the most beautiful woman ever to enter the Bondian universe. Let us say for Miss Bach that her personality is utterly pleasant (which is more than one can claim for many previous Bondstresses), and that her looks are the absolute best that America can produce, which, for me as for Henry James, is very probably the loveliest loveliness there is. It is, in effect, the triumph of symmetry over asymmetry, or European beauty, which usually has it all over symmetry, except when symmetry happens to be perfect, fearful symmetry. In which case there is nothing insipid about it any more, only the peace that passeth understanding—and let us not be so churlish as to fiddle with the spelling of that "peace."

If I have any quarrel with *The Spy Who Loved Me*—blissfully photographed by yet another veteran, Claude Renoir, and grandiosely designed by the usual Bond production designer, Ken Adam—it is with its PG rating. When the smoothly vicious Curt Jurgens has Miss Bach tied to his couch and prepared for a fate that, for a sophisticated superspy, is considerably less bad than death, how dare that officious PG come between every man and his vicarious desire? Oh, sure, some youngsters might then be denied the film, and the box office their contributions; but for every debarred adolescent I would be willing to guarantee Mr. Broccoli two or three lecherous adults that would take his place and come back more than once. If I am wrong, call me Asparagus.

Jodie Foster deserves better than she gets in *The Little Girl Who Lives Down the Lane.* This is a totally improbable and ham-fisted movie about a thirteen-year-old who moves into a rented house in a small New England town and fools all of its residents into believing that her celebrated poet father is alive and living with her, only working or sleeping or lunching in New York with his publisher whenever people try to see him. She keeps this pretense up indefinitely. What is there about the population of a small New England town that makes it so much dumber than a New York movie audience that sees through little Rynn Jacobs's stratagem in a matter of minutes? But I am not the one to tell you what or whom supersmart, ultrasophisticated, and tougher-than-tough-talking Rynn keeps in the cellar. If you are a New York moviegoer, or anyone else of average intelligence, you'll know soon enough. But, of course, if you are a small-town New Englander, you may not know even after seeing the movie, which keeps everything that might be a problem—whether inadequate logistics or excessive horror—safely out of sight.

Rynn also has a love affair, duly consummated, with the slightly older Mario (nicely played by Scott Jacoby), and things fluctuate between adorable precocity and still more adorable lapses into childishness. Since Miss Foster seems destined to play prematurely adult and cynical moppets (except when she is a child genius gallantly dying of an incurable disease), she has become a past master at this sort of fakery. She puts on a dazzling display of speaking in a moody monotone, staying nearly poker-faced throughout, being a monster of precocity if not of monstrosity, and still remaining likable and almost believable. But the way this delightful youngster is being nudged into being Carole Lombard one year, Gloria Grahame the next, and God knows who thereafter (Mae West? Gloria Swanson? Thelma Ritter?), it will be a miracle if she survives her juvenilia.

With that heavy-lidded hard-bittenness, that curling-lipped condescension, that weary or jaded impassivity of tone, this adolescent seems as old as Walter Pater's Mona Lisa! And that, unlike anything else in this poor movie, is scary. It is a measure of the obviousness of the script Laird Koenig has fashioned from his novel that if a character is a nasty anti-Semite, this has to be rubbed in in a dozen leaden little ways, and if another is a villainous child molester, it is prefigured by everything from his walking muddy-booted across other people's clean floors to torturing a hamster with a burning cigarette before throwing the luckless beastie into the flaming fireplace. Nicolas Gessner's direction does little to palliate the obviousness, and cannot begin to tackle the implausibility. Alexis Smith and Martin Sheen play the heavies heavily, but at least they are not Piper Laurie and John Beck.

When Mort Shuman appears as a kindly Italian policeman, the last smidgen of credibility is forfeit. I suspect that Shuman, who looks about as much like a kindly Italian policeman as he does like Golda Meir (considerably less, in fact)—or like an actor—is engaged to perform in movies only because he can do double duty as composer or, as here, music supervisor. And his composing or supervising is every bit on a par with his acting. Here he supervised a score by Christian Gaubert and Frédéric Chopin, a team mismatched for all his surveillance.

Judging from names involved on both sides of the camera, the film seems to have been made in a French-speaking region. Let me hope that it is Walloon, Swiss, or Canadian: I'd like to keep some illusions about France.

August 22–29, 1977

Basketball, Baseball, and a Sheriff Who Wouldn't Play Ball

ONE ON ONE is being hailed in some quarters as another *Rocky,* which, believe me, it isn't, except perhaps in its head; one reviewer has proclaimed it the best movie ever made about basketball, which may be true—for all I know, it may be the best movie about jai alai, too, though that game is never played in it. Written by its star, Robby Benson, and his father, Jerry Segal, who probably have different names to avoid being confused like Dumas *père* and *fils,* it concerns a Colorado high-school athlete—part bright, part naïve—who finds, upon accepting a cushy athletic scholarship to "Western University" in Los Angeles, that college athletics are both tougher and meaner than he ever dreamed they could be. And better organized, for both good and ill, though not so well as to preclude the determined and gifted individual's triumphing over the deadly system.

If that sounds obvious and yawn-begetting in briefest précis, try the movie itself for predictability, clumsiness, and almost total boredom. There is a limpness, a caducity about this whole film, which comes across like the last thin-blooded scion of a long line of intermarrying distant relatives, quite incapable of staying alive. Motivation here is as compelling as the case for car-battery additives: relationships are formed and dissolved, an athlete is favored or rejected, a game is won or lost for reasons no more persuasive than that a certain father-and-son writing team would have it so. The family that writes scripts together may stay together; it is the scripts that fall apart.

Lamont Johnson is supposed to have made one decent film, *The Last American Hero,* before the studio recut and then scuttled it. I cannot say, not having seen either version. But I have seen other Johnson pictures with minimal enthusiasm, and *Lipstick* with considerable revulsion. Here, in any case, Johnson avoids the cliché shot very rarely, and then only at the price of a certain amateurishness that lacks even the charm of innocence. Consider only the unbearably stereotypical scene in which Henry, our young hero, first sneaks onto Western's empty basketball court at night: the timid turning on of one light, then the reckless switching on of all, accompanied with the obligatory circular panning shots and the voices of an imaginary crowd cheering, cheering in ghostly choirs.

Perhaps it could all have been, not saved, just alleviated by a strong central performance. But Robby Benson, who was quite nice in *Jeremy* and has steadily waned since, offers an anemic piece of nonacting and big blue eyes intruding on the world as shyly as bicycle lamps on a Los Angeles freeway. His voice is not just soft, it has all the eloquence of goose down; when he asserts himself in justified indignation against an arrogant heckler or a corrupt and unscrupulous coach, his anger could move molehills. His acting has a liquid quality—or, rather, the quality of a liquid in search of a container.

The supporting cast, with one exception, is no better. Annette O'Toole, who was good in *Smile,* cannot overcome the witless writing, particularly damaging to a character who is supposed to be dartingly witty; G. D. Spradlin, as the coach, enunciates so badly (as does also Benson) that one begins to wonder whether it is done out of misplaced compassion for the audience. Melanie Griffith is miscast in a PG picture, where she is obliged to hide her one talent (or two, depending on how you count it . . . them). But Gail Strickland infuses her breezy elegance into the crude role of the coach's administrative and nymphomaniacal assistant. Let me hope that Hollywood recognizes her value sooner than it did that of the splendid Alexis Smith, whom she so resembles both in looks and talent, without, however, being in the least epigonic.

After such pretentious garbage, it feels almost good to turn to plain, old-fashioned, unassuming garbage like *Final Chapter: Walking Tall.* This purports to be the last segment of the more or less biographical trilogy about the life and death of Sheriff Buford Pusser, the embattled Tennessee lawman who cleaned up McNairy County with—of all things—a large wooden club, losing in the process his wife, part of his jaw, and, if we are to trust the implication of this *Final Chapter,* his life. Actually, I am not much concerned with how truthful the film is to chapter and verse, as long as we can trust the message of hope contained in the word *final.*

The movie was directed by Jack Starrett, an expert cheapie-maker, who, it would seem, directs with a club, and has a plot that neatly alternates clichés and holes. But there is one thing here that makes the proceedings watchable: Bo Svenson's performance as Pusser. The actor still has a bit of a Swedish accent, incongruous here, but in every other way gives a performance of such controlled intensity, intelligence, and sensitivity that one can imagine oneself watching a far classier operation than one of those sure-fire hinterland crowd pleasers of the Billy Jack or Billy Joe variety. That he is consistently cast in rubbish makes him as much in need of preservation as the bald eagle, the coyote, and the timber wolf. Well, as Catullus said in a somewhat different context, *Passer* (or Pusser) *mortuus est;* so on to other things.

One *Bad News Bears,* directed by Michael Ritchie, was relatively good news; two *Bad News Bears*—actually *The Bad News Bears in Breaking Training,* directed by Michael Pressman—is bad news indeed. Sometimes you don't even have to go up to three for it to be a crowd. The film itself is overwhelmingly uninteresting, but the audience I watched it with in Yorkville was fascinating. Though they were predominantly black and Puerto Rican, they roared for every one of these rotten white kids at bat as though it were Hank Aaron, Geraldo Rivera, or the Second Coming. Enough lousy films like this, and we could unite all warring factions. Shucks.

September 12, 1977

Berlin on $50,000 a Day

In Fred Zinnemann's film from Lillian Hellman's story "Julia," there is a moment when Lillian (Jane Fonda) tells her lover Dashiell Hammett (Jason Robards) that she enjoys fame—being recognized when she goes to buy a jar of mayonnaise. I doubt whether the filmmakers are aware of their gaffe: the best known mayonnaise in America is Hellmann's, though it has no connection with the author of "Julia" and *Pentimento,* the book of memoirs of which that story is a part. What viewers ought to recognize in seeing the movie is some sort of truth about people and life; instead, they get a famous brand name. The interest up there is theoretically sustained by the names of Lillian Hellman, and "Dash" Hammett, along with the names of the stars, who include Vanessa Redgrave portraying the heroic Julia, written, directed, and acted with such nobility and goodness that butter, let alone mayonnaise, would not melt in her mouth.

Very little of what happens in the film is intrinsically interesting, so that for the nonmegalopolitan public essentially ignorant of who Hellman, Hammett, Dorothy Parker, and Alan Campbell were, the film loses its main selling point. For the more cultivated moviegoer, however, the film can function only as a comic-strip version of what it is like to be a famous writer, or a dedicated anti-Nazi fighter such as Julia; indeed, considering how the film handles them, Dorothy Parker and her husband could easily go unrecognized by the most sophisticated viewer. Here I think a statement by the director, Fred Zinnemann, is highly significant: to have shown Parker, the cynical wit, in the solemn context of anti-Nazi struggle and death, he said, would have been an obscenity.

Nonsense. The truth, as represented by an artist, is never obscene; and humor, cynical or even frivolous, is never out of place, as Shakespeare, among others, has proved. I doubt whether there is anything as valuable to someone on the threshold of death as a good laugh—hard as it may be to come by. It is only a paltry mind that has to be utterly solemn in the face of a Major Theme. Still, the simplistic mentality of Zinnemann and Alvin Sargent, the screenwriter, is matched by Lillian Hellman's apparent unawareness of what she was doing in her story. She was trying (ostensibly) to extol the heroism of her friend Julia, about whose underground activities, however, she knew and knows precious little. So we have to admire a shadowy figure about whom we are continually told that she lived and died nobly in a noble cause; but whom we can see and feel for far too little for identification. Hence it is Lillian's smuggling fifty thousand dollars into Germany for the anti-Nazi underground that becomes the film's big event, even though Hellman is careful to present herself as somewhat of a bumbler, and even though various members of the underground watch over her and guide her steps all along the way.

Still, it is Hellman who emerges as the not exactly unsung heroine of a work that might more honestly have been called *Lillian.* Aware of the dearth of material about Julia, Zinnemann and Sargent have eked it out with other bits of *Pentimento* and anecdotal matter about Hellman, who apparently kept a wary eye on the filming. As usual, film has been unsuccessful in conveying a writer's struggles to write, not very dramatic stuff intrinsically, even if it has been souped up here to such moments of close combat as an angry Lillian throwing her typewriter out of the window. Further mileage was squeezed out of the somewhat hectic relationship between Dash and Lillian (toned down and purified as it is in the movie), all of which merely unbalances the proceedings, with Julia fading farther and farther into the nebulous background.

Zinnemann, who many years ago was able to make decent pictures, now chokes on his own portentousness. Fonda is handed some relatively undistinguished bits of Hellman's prose to deliver in voice-over narration whose tone, for naked awe, matches that of a television commercial plugging an expensive funeral parlor. The gambols of young Julia and Lillian (invented for the film) are shot in a setting in which *Vogue* might pose the latest high fashions. The last meeting between the friends in a Berlin restaurant is filmed as if a trip to the lady's room were fraught with immense personal danger, and as if a man watching the women from a table near the door were plotting their doom rather than merely savoring their faces and figures.

Douglas Slocombe is the cinematographer *par excellence* to make everything glitter *(The Great Gatsby, The Sailor Who Fell From Grace With the Sea),* and so even a vicious Nazi-staged riot at the University of Vienna looks like an elegant farandole that unaccountably got out of hand. The acting, too, seems reverential to a fault, with Fonda (a far too unplain Jane to portray Lillian) always suggesting weights suspended from her limbs and voice, and Redgrave relentlessly posing for a portrait of Joan of Arc. The supporting cast has little chance to do anything but assume stances, although Maximilian Schell and Lisa Pelikan, who plays the young Julia, manage to sneak bits of the third dimension into the general flatness.

The film never even comes to grips with what this great bond between Julia and Lillian is truly based on, since they certainly don't see each other much, and do not really share activities and interests. This is the sort of shallowness exhibited by another current "feminist" film, Agnès Varda's *One Sings, the Other Doesn't,* in which we are asked to believe in an intense relationship between two women who do not see each other for periods of ten years. But, in general, films today do not seem to ask any of the key questions about personality and relationships, about the very significance of human behavior.

And, while we are on the subject of questions, did this supposedly historic Julia actually exist? Clearly not, otherwise she would by now be a famous heroine, complete with full-length biographies and public monuments—maybe even a street or two named after her—to her credit. As it is, she was invented only to provide Miss Hellman with a little chance for self-glorification.

In a piece of vulgar and inept—but mostly well-reviewed—filmmaking such as James Ivory's *Roseland,* for example, we are supposed to sympathize with a very rich middle-aged matron who spends most of her time at the dance hall where her live-in lover is a sort of resident gigolo. That the man (played by Christopher Walken in his customarily surly manner) is vaguely reprehensible, Ruth Prawer Jhabvala's trashy script makes reasonably clear; but what about the matron who keeps him, cossets him, indulges him, and sits or dances around Roseland endlessly, mindlessly, contentedly? That something must be gravely wrong with this woman (unsubtly played by Joan Copeland), the film does not begin to suggest.

Yet we are supposed to feel for her, and for the other superficially observed and sentimentally inflated puppets in this movie. There are performances here—such as the appalling hamming of Lilia Skala as a former cook who pretends to have been an opera singer and comes to Roseland to relive the glory of a concocted past—that ought not to pass muster in a dinner theater where the management would give away the food.

Now, what we really need is a movie about Hellmann's mayonnaise. How did it become rich and famous? Who put its owners and their wives into Cadillacs and sables, or their equivalents? How did it beat out other brands of mayonnaise? As for the pious platitudes about writing and man-woman relations exchanged between this other Hellman and her equally cardboard lover, dashed if I can care about them.

November 25, 1977

Double Whammy

LOOKING FOR MR. GOODBAR is the sort of clever trashy novel out of which a talented director could have made a better than average movie. Needless to say, a good script would also have been required. Unfortunately, Judith Rossner's book got a poor scriptwriter as well as a crass director—both in the person of Richard Brooks—a double whammy no work could survive. What the film could have taken over from the novel and developed further is the quiet sordidness of a gray, petit-bourgeois, sin- and sickness-haunted childhood falling prey, as it grows into womanhood, to megalopolitan amorality. Everything would have had to be kept low-keyed: Theresa, the limping, unbeautiful, freckle-faced redhead, moving from an oppressive home life into an unliberating liberation; the singles bars that had not yet gone disco and offered only booze and the promise of one-night stands; and, somewhere in the background, Theresa's daytime existence as a dutiful schoolmarm.

Brooks was not content to mine this minor vein. Instead of an acridly detailed New York, he creates, by conflating various towns, an Unreal City under the brown fog of William Fraker's moody cinematography. Instead of a run-of-the-mill Catholic upbringing and parents who just did not pay much heed to Theresa, he comes up with a fanatic father and a dithering mother; above all, the girl herself has to be made much less damaged in body and considerably prettier, thus removing the principal sources of her insecurity.

Whereas the novel begins honestly at the end, and then proceeds to examine what led up to its heroine's slaying, Brooks, with extraordinary shallowness, wants a thriller: since even people who haven't read the book know that this girl gets killed, let us at least make a guessing game out of which one of her outlandish men will do her in. Let, therefore, even a perfectly nice lawyer be turned into a voyeuristic, presumably impotent, social worker. Then, too, Brooks dawdles over Theresa's teaching deaf children and turns her into some kind of saintly miracle worker. The split between decent teacher and sexual drifter is not enough for him; for the sake of a sermon on the evil effects of liberation, we must get Miss Jekyll and Ms. Hyde.

Yet even that apparent intention remains unclear in this thoroughly muddled and lurid movie, concluding with a gimmicked-up murder that is obviously meant to out-*Psycho Psycho,* to which end the weapon is changed from a skull-crashing lamp to a repeatedly stabbing knife. What is certain is that the movie lacks even the superficial social curiosity of the novel, and that casting the achingly adorable or psychically slatternly (depending on your evaluation of the Woody Allen Woman) Diane Keaton as Terry is an instant edulcoration of the character. Though Keaton gives her best performance to date (which is not saying all that much), she does revert to Woody's neurotically giggly virgin-whore during the film's rather embarrassing sex scenes. And we never sense Theresa's dismal compulsion, and must assume that this basically winsome girl is merely on a somewhat overextended lark.

The film is manipulative and, finally, exploitative; in short, ugly. Richard Gere contributes a convincing bit as Terry's most showily unbalanced swain; the other actors don't get enough of a chance, or are handed parts that beg to be oversimplified. Brooks proves inept even on the basic technical level: wishing, for example, to ape better filmmakers, who are able to slip fantasy sequences into the proceedings so subtly that we realize only gradually what they are, he manages to drop in such sequences so clumsily that we remain confused all the way. He is so careless, moreover, as not even to include in the film the dive named Mr. Goodbar, which gives the work its facilely ambiguous, heavily symbolic title.

His greatest omission, however, is life—the little incidents and details that make a film, aside from whatever else it is, real. Take the moment in the novel when Terry, wanting and fearing to be deflowered, watches her beloved professor and "the water that he was pouring into the top of the glass thing . . . dripping down to the bottom as coffee." Such grains of actuality are missing from the movie. In an interview, Brooks said that "the point of the story . . . is that it could have happened on any day . . . and to any of a number of other people." Maybe so, but you do not start from a generalization; you start with specifics, with the personal and intimate. If this is well enough imagined and felt, you can trust it to become universal by itself.

Even more portentous a piece of speciousness is *Equus,* Peter Shaffer's adaptation of his highly though undeservedly successful play. This is the story of a disturbed stableboy prey to a masochistic cult of a self-created horse-god, Equus, and how the boy gets sexual satisfaction from rubbing naked against horses (always stallions!) until, failing in an attempt at intercourse with a girl in the stable, he stabs out the eyes of six surrounding horses in a rage of shame. Placed in the care of Dr. Dysart, a provincial psychiatrist married to a frigid Scottish woman dentist—a man, by the way, whose unfulfilled sexual yearnings are fixated on statues of Greek gods (not, it seems, goddesses)—the boy is cured with ridiculous ease, while Dysart mourns having had to change such a wonderfully passionate youth into an ordinary, "normal" human being for whom horses are merely something to bet on.

This well of Democritus of a play, which had Broadway audiences giving nightly ovations—sometimes even standing ones—to Dysart's speech in defense of the boy's impassioned aberration, can be read in two ways: either as a thinly veiled paean to pederasty (for a detailed analysis, see my article in *The Hudson Review,* Spring 1975), or as a warning against marrying female Scottish dentists. On stage, at least, in John Dexter's dazzlingly stylized production, the play had the superficies of theater; in Sidney Lumet's mostly but inconsistently naturalistic movie version, literal-mindedness lends added repugnancy and preposterousness. Still, movie audiences likewise cheer Dysart's grand sophistic tirade extolling the boy's right to stand "in the dark for an hour, sucking the sweat off his god's hairy cheek."

The worst thing about *Equus* is that viewers, softened up by Richard Burton's ultratheatrical monologues, for which Lumet has been unable to find a cinematic format (probably no one could), may think that such solemnity is a powerful argument for individualism and nonconformity, what with the boy's proper father being shown up as a fraud, and his mother as a self-righteously speechifying schoolmarm. Sanity, clearly, is nothing but an ignoble compromise with the mundane. Even the score by the distinguished English composer Richard Rodney Bennett is a sellout—typical movie mush by a man who can write solid concert music.

Burton acts his part with the called-for metapsychiatric *Weltschmerz,* and Peter Firth re-creates his role as the boy with the kind of loutishness considered nowadays an earnest of youthful purity and authenticity. Some excellent actors are wasted on stilted supporting parts, and Oswald Morris, the fine veteran British cameraman, supplies enough chiaroscuro for an entire exhibition of Mannerist painting. He usually allows only one eye of Burton's to be out of the shadows, making it look as if one of *his* eyes had been gouged out too.

December 9, 1977

Whistling in the Dark

BY FAR THE MOST ATTENTION-GETTING FILM at the moment is Steven Spielberg's *Close Encounters of the Third Kind,* the latest example of a possible trend toward science-fiction superproductions. This seventeen- to nineteen-million-dollar item (or, counting the advertising budget, twenty-two to twenty-five-million-dollar) must be the most expensive piece of sci-fi to date, appropriate for an age that finds cost at least as impressive as quality. The thirty-year-old director-screenwriter set out to make something even more astounding than his last one, *Jaws;* if the watery epic left viewers with their mouths more agape than a shark's, this skyey paean to the UFOs was to leave them saucer-eyed. And, sure enough, at the populous preview I attended, the special effects got lusty applause; the plot, characters, and dialogue got nothing.

The one salient feature of Spielberg's script is that it makes no sense whatever. This may have something to do with its having been shot over a period of three years and with five different cinematographers (sometimes the same car has different license plates). But it must have more to do with a basic contempt for consistency—not just the petty kind ridiculed by Emerson, but the very basic sort that turns acts into behavior and brain waves into thought. Thus Spielberg's UFOs, though meant to be manned by benevolent, superior creatures, play nasty practical jokes on mankind, and are criminally careless of human safety.

If there is little justification for such cat-and-mouse games, there is still less for these supermen, or, as they are finally represented, super-hermaphrodites, encoding their proposed trysting place with the earthlings in a conundrum: it seems that these giant intellects that have mastered Zoltán Kodály's sign language for teaching deaf children music are unable to decode and learn ordinary human speech. Worse inconsistency: only a handful of people deign to look up into the skies and take note of the UFOs carrying on there like a planetarium gone haywire.

Human behavior and relationships run counter to minimal common sense throughout. When the hero—Roy Neary, a power-company lineman—is haunted by the vision of a cone-shaped object, there is no reason for him to plunder his neighbors' chicken wire and half the objects in his own house and garden to build a cone up to his living-room ceiling. And nothing could be more arbitrary than the way Roy's wife packs up her children and leaves home instead of getting her husband an appointment with a psychiatrist. When Roy falls in love with Jillian, a fellow UFO-watcher whose four-year-old son Barry has been abducted by a saucer, he promptly abandons her to go off with the spacemen or space-epicenes on a ride that may last days, years, forever, as she dopily snaps pictures of his departure. Roy's car is, at one point, practically demolished by unmotivated UFO interference; next minute, we see it drive off in one piece.

Major and minor contradictions ooze out of this movie. A French scientist, Lacombe (an excuse for casting François Truffaut), seems at times to run the entire U.S. Army and Air Force UFO project; at others, he is in complete ignorance of strategy—as when the area around Devil's Tower, the cone-shaped Wyoming mountain where the UFOs will land, is to be evacuated by a sinister military stratagem. Sometimes Lacombe speaks decent English; sometimes he is lost without an interpreter. Eluding pursuit on foot and by helicopter, Roy and Jillian make it up the near-perpendicular slope of Devil's Tower—a marvel of mountaineering as well as of stupidity, seeing that the installation for the UFO landing is clearly at the base of the mountain.

And the sheer contrivance of it all! The French interpreter, who used to be a cartographer and happens to be there only because of Lacombe, is the sole person who can figure out that the UFO signals refer to the longitude and latitude of the proposed trysting place. Little Barry, an ordinary small-town tot, has more electrical toys than you could find in the toy department of the biggest metropolitan store. Jillian, his mother, has a splendid house without any visible means of support—she doesn't have to go to work at any time.

The film's myriad self-contradictions allow for three possibilities: (1) Spielberg has the memory span of a four-year-old—a possibility reinforced by little Barry's being the closest thing to an auctorial alter ego among the dramatis personae; (2) Spielberg, like a true child of his era, considers any kind of logic an outdated hangup; (3) Spielberg is incapable of elementary ratiocination.

Indeed, under the many layers of contradiction, we come at last to the bedrock of solid nonsense. In the film's grand finale, the visitors' glittering mother ship, looking like an enormous flying carrousel in full Christmas regalia, lands at the army station for a musical parley with the earthlings' building-sized audiovisual electronic organ. Finally, some U.S. airmen who disappeared with their planes in World War II (an actual occurrence) are disbursed by their supersaucer—earlier in the film, their aircraft were discovered miraculously intact in the Arizona desert—and are, thirty years later, not a day older or a jot wiser; the one, presumably, through a time warp; the other, no doubt, through a brain warp. A bunch of U.S. galactonauts, in firehouse-red space suits, are duly blessed by a padre and embark in the visitors' craft. Why, when the World War II crews clearly have returned to earth in a state of utter hebetude? True, they didn't have fire-red suits or a chaplain's blessing.

Meanwhile, dimly perceived, the space creatures dance before their ship. One of them accosts Lacombe; as devised by Carlo Rambaldi (the creator also of King Kong II), it is spindly, moon-faced, androgynous, and seemingly made of plasticene. It grins like an anonymous Halloween pumpkin, though Pauline Kael has identified its rictus as "Jean Renoir's lopsided grin," beneficently bestowed on Renoir's admirer François Truffaut. Meanwhile Roy has donned a crimson space suit—the army must always have a few spares around—and has blithely joined the delegation to the great beyond. Lacombe gazes after him enviously, and bemoans his ungratifiable yearning to join him, although nothing about the Frenchman makes him appear anything but expendable.

Why, you might wonder, do these supersane extraterrestrial minds inhabit such sickly bodies? To make them, I suppose, closer to objects, which Spielberg always prefers to people. The movements of machines and gizmos of every kind are made volatile and manic: they zoom at us with exaggerated suddenness and fury. In his *Duel,* the true protagonist is a mean-looking, homicidal truck, whose driver is never seen. In *The Sugarland Express,* cars and helicopters act up a storm, while the people remain ciphers. In *Jaws,* an electronically operated shark is by far the most real character. Now, in *Close Encounters,* the hypertrophic gadget is literally exalted, enskied, while people become mere counters.

But, then, reification of persons and deification of machines has been par for the sci-fi-film course. These filmmakers—whether they be Kubrick with *2001,* George Lucas with *Star Wars,* or Spielberg—seem afraid, perhaps even incapable, of genuine feelings. Kubrick may pretend that his point is precisely the affectlessness of the space age—but why, then, are his other films, about the past and present, similarly affectless? Lucas may evade the issue by telling a children's adventure story in which sexuality and love do not belong by definition. Spielberg elides the whole thing with a few moist glances and one perfunctory clinch, ostensibly to keep the action racing ahead—indeed, he shoots nearly every sequence as if it were a noisy, frantic, breathless climax: a car door cannot open or close without implications of Armageddon, what with fast cutting, tricky camera angles, and a soundtrack turned on high enough for the most belligerent discothèque. Only with extreme reluctance does the director-screenwriter accord us a few scenes of relative quietude; before we know it, all zap and zowie breaks loose again. Anything to avoid addressing oneself to the relations of grown men and women.

This is not to say that Spielberg isn't capable of shooting certain climactic scenes with genuine ability; but after all those bogus climaxes, all that fake excitement, the real thing begins to look specious and, worse yet, anticlimactic. So it is when the visitors finally become visible—all female, it would seem, and looking from a distance like body-stockinged toadstools in a chorus line. When one creature comes closer, she (he? it?) looks like a cross between Lillian Gish and an embryo. As it did in *Jaws,* John Williams's score heaves heroically to convey momentousness, and sometimes actually succeeds at the price of redundancy—repeating what is already visually explicit for the benefit, one presumes, of blind children, to whom neither the film's images nor the Kodály hand signals would be of any use.

To evaluate performances in a movie like this is like trying to determine which of the soccer-playing dogs in the Soviet Circus is the best player. There is nothing much for actors to do here; only Richard Dreyfuss, as Roy, gets to scurry, rant, and sizzle quite a bit; but his character, too, remains underdeveloped. His very name is so infrequently mentioned that one tends to think of him only as "the Dreyfuss character"—or, perhaps, the Dreyfuss case. Still, Melinda Dillon and Teri Garr manage to look convincingly midwestern; Truffaut, a director who has been photographed almost as much as his actors, looks only like himself and so out of place.

A further token of the film's extravagance is that, though Vilmos Zsigmond gets "director of photography" credit, four other major cinematographers are also listed, along with seven special-effects or second-unit photographers. Some of this has to do with the long and sporadic shooting schedule of the film, but some of it, surely, is the kind of conspicuous waste that characterizes Spielberg's approach.

To clarify everything and make things cohere would have required, as Spielberg remarked in a press conference, a four-hour movie instead of the present one, slightly over half that length. Yet four hours of sense would go by faster and more pleasantly than two of nonsense. Moreover, I doubt whether anyone who could make a shorter period this nonsensical could have made much more sense at any length. Spielberg—which in German means toy mountain—may indeed have made the most monumental molehill in movie history, conveniently cone-shaped to serve as a dunce's cap for an extremely swelled head.

When American movies are not diving into the future, they tend, with equal determination, to totter backward into a synthetic past. Take *The Turning Point,* that supposedly trail-blazing look both at the ballet and at what lurks behind its scenes. Now, ballet has become enormously popular with American audiences during the last few years, but not since *The Specter of the Rose,* a baroque extravaganza of 1946, has an American movie tried to come to grips with it. It might be supposed that the present scenarist, Arthur Laurents (who wrote the books of such dance-oriented Broadway musicals as *Gypsy* and *West Side Story*), the director, Herbert Ross (a former dancer and choreographer), and the assistant director, Nora Kaye (Ross's wife and a distinguished ex-ballerina of the American Ballet Theater), would be just the people to give us both the visible and hidden truths about the ballet.

Not so. They have concocted instead the balletic version of all those countless sentimental backstage musicals and comedy-dramas of yesteryear. In essence, it is the story of two former aspiring ballerinas, now middle-aged. At the turning point, Deedee gave up her career to marry the fellow dancer who had made her pregnant and settled down in Oklahoma to raising a family and teaching ballet; Emma, however, after counseling Deedee not to have an abortion, snatched the lead in a new ballet and went on to become the prima ballerina of the American Ballet Company (not so much a disguise as a fig leaf for the American Ballet Theater) at the cost of remaining single, having unsatisfactory affairs, and now facing supersession by younger talents, to be followed by sterile retirement. The two women meet again and battle it out over Emilia, Deedee's daughter and Emma's godchild, who has joined the company to become its improbably swiftly rising prima-designate. Envious of each other's lives, Deedee and Emma also fight it out between themselves with accusations old and new in a knock-down drag-out fracas that starts in acrimony, continues with blows, and ends in sisterly laughter—and exists only in movies of a markedly factitious kind.

But everything here is spurious. Emilia's meteoric rise to the top; the simplistic love affairs in which the women get involved, and promptly disinvolved, entirely by rote; the schematic backstage camaraderie and rivalries; the homespun aperçus and the burlap epigrams. The fact that this is a *pièce à clef,* with mildly acidulous sketches of recognizable ABT personalities, only worsens things: stingless satire on such colorful people is less than no satire at all. Thus, in an age that could face the prevalence of homosexuality among male ballet dancers and the curious situations into which this forces the female dancers, the film offers exactly two brief references to inversion, one of them hypocritically mentioning the "old days" when most male dancers were "presumed to be fairies." Actually, no such presumptions ever existed: the old days were too naïve; our times are not naïve enough.

Most of the acting is as unconvincing as the script. Shirley MacLaine's Deedee looks like a smug, middle-aged kitten who has swallowed enough canaries to bloat her middle. When contented, her smirks are holier than thou and cuter than all getout; when provoked, she can work herself up to a positively majestic simper. Anne Bancroft's Emma is a trifle more convincingly dancerish, if only because she looks thin and drawn; yet she has a way of wearing her haggardness as if it were a layer of stubborn dirt that has defied all cleansers.

There is agreeable work, though, from Leslie Browne, who makes a credible Emilia, even if she is, in the dance scenes, naturally outclassed by Mikhail Baryshnikov as Yuri, the company's *danseur noble* and somewhat less noble philanderer. When he dances on screen, Baryshnikov is almost more spellbinding than on stage, but he is no actor—not even a comprehensible speaker of English. Among the supporting cast, Alexandra Danilova manages with infectious bounce an ex-prima turned into a benevolent dragon of a teacher—

which, unfortunately, belies one of the premises of the movie: that a gaping nothingness awaits the woman who chooses career over marriage. Not bad either, in his poker-faced, effete nastiness, is Daniel Levans as an Eliot Feldish whiz-kid choreographer of the new school; but here the script oversimplifies the meanness, just as it oversimplifies the goodness of Deedee's patient husband, however roundedly Tom Skerritt tries to play him. In a character apparently compounded out of Oliver Smith and Jerome Robbins, James Mitchell is doubly dull.

Still, dragged down by clichés as it is, *The Turning Point* does take a hefty step ahead in filmed ballet. Herbert Ross may be an indifferent director, but he was a choreographer and knows where the camera should be for maximum efficacy during every moment of the dance sequences. And Robert Surtees has so lighted and shot them that the dancers never get lost in the backgrounds. When Baryshnikov does one of his variations, the audience gasps and cheers—and applauds something worthier than special effects.

December 23, 1977

Too Small for Their Britches

A TRIO OF NEW American films is conspicuous without being noteworthy. The three all have energy, drollness, and flashiness; what they lack is an original—or, at least believable—vision, textural and moral consistency, and that almost perennial American desideratum, adulthood. Even in such a basically frothy genre as farce, the Europeans can (or could) give us grownups behaving childishly. In American farce, we get children pretending to be adults.

Take Neil Simon's latest contribution to the screen, *The Goodbye Girl.* Marsha Mason plays a not-so-young Broadway musical-comedy dancer who has lost out both with her ex-husband, the father of ten-year-old Lucy, and with the actor-lover who just walked out on her. We are to believe that in this day and age one marriage and one prolonged affair constitute a checkered sexual history—for a Broadway dancer, of all people!—and that these two failed relationships prove our heroine to be a "goodbye girl" who brings some kind of undermining pessimism to her involvements with men.

Here is a subject rich with possibilities, but Simon makes almost nothing of them. His protagonist is simply a hard-bitten woman (though not sexually so: like the good Jewish puritan he is, Simon insists on quasi-virginal heroines) who has had bad luck with men and jobs. When Richard Dreyfuss, as a young Chicago actor getting his first crack at off-Broadway as Shakespeare's Richard III, arrives on a rainy night to claim Mason's apartment (the rat who ran out on her sublet it to him), immediate hatred springs up between the predestined lovers. Eventually, they uneasily compromise by sharing the apartment, each grudgingly adapting to the other's quirks. Hers—quite improbably—include balking at Dreyfuss's female visitors; his include Zen chants and nocturnal guitar strumming which helps him sleep and keeps others awake. Finally, it is his tantras against her tantrums; all of which amounts to meeting cute, co-existing cute, and, eventually, getting involved cute, in which the daughter is, naturally, a cute catalyst.

Virtually none of the film's comedy stems from what the characters are supposed to be about. The ambitious young actor falls in love like a lamb, which makes the goodbye girl, who does worry a mite overmuch (but only a mite), no longer a scold, or ungiving, or a saboteur of relationships. Everything glibly ends well, and the jokes are mostly set pieces. Our hero, to satisfy a crazy, avant-garde director, must play Richard as a flaming queen; our heroine, obliged to sell cars at an auto show, forgets her spiel, and is saved from the sack only by Dreyfuss's wily impersonation of an enthusiastic customer. The fun—good or bad—is extraneous, adventitious; some of it, moreover, is as hoary as passers-by getting into the act when lovers squabble in the street.

Still, good performances, especially from Dreyfuss and little Quinn Cummings; serviceable, unpretentious direction from Herbert Ross; and, of course, some undeniably droll gags from Neil Simon do add up to a tolerable movie. But it could have been so much more.

Next, consider Mel Brooks's latest, *High Anxiety,* a much more febrile farce, purporting to be a take-off on the films of Alfred Hitchcock. Already the premise is questionable: How can you satirize something that is as neat, taut, efficacious—even witty—as the best of Hitchcock? Significantly, the only fully successful bits of parody concern scenes from *Psycho* and *The Birds,* two of Hitch's more outrageous items. For the rest, the main merriment is irrelevant to Hitchcock, and often talks down to the audience, as when a speaker at a psychiatric congress feels obliged to use baby-talk terms for certain bodily functions because a couple of kids have strayed into the audience. On the other hand, a sight gag like the photomurals behind the rostrum representing psychiatry's giants—Freud, Jung, Adler, Rank, and Joyce Brothers—is funny because it dares to be mystifying to the ten-year-olds.

Brooks plays a Harvard psychiatrist entrusted with running a weird California mental institution where the sadistic head nurse and her masochistic lover (one of the staff psychiatrists) murdered the previous director, and are now devising Brooks's demise. Brooks has acrophobia, and the sanatorium is atop a beetling oceanside cliff—hence the film's title, and some dizzy allusions to Hitchcock's *Vertigo.* There is a romance between Brooks and Madeline Kahn, as the plucky daughter of an unjustly institutionalized millionaire, himself earmarked for murder. Little of this is adult comedy, though some of it does elicit our childish laughter.

Occasionally, though, we get a glimpse of mature funniness, as in a song Brooks performs with the band in a cocktail lounge to impress his ladylove. Written (both words and music) by Brooks, and called "High Anxiety," it is the ultimate send-up of those irrelevant and nonsensical title songs that nowadays clutter up movies, and Brooks renders it with the appropriate dastardly aplomb that requires a microphone to make obscene love to, a trailing cord to be swished about behind one like a train of royal ermine, members of the audience to be inanely flirted with, and a dance floor across which one sashays like a randy gazelle.

In a different vein, *Saturday Night Fever* is supposed to be an exposé of how working-class kids in a poorer Brooklyn neighborhood find outlets in things like disco dancing, intermittently leavened with a little gang warfare, back-seat copulation, and the performing of *rites de passage* on the parapet of the Verrazano Bridge. The hero, Tony, played by the latest heart-throb, John Travolta, comes from an oppressive, mutually face-slapping, Catholic blue-collar family, whose dreariness is made neither believable nor sufficiently quaint to be successful caricature. It is only at the 2001 Odyssey discotheque that Tony, a splendidly feline dancer, feels fully in his element, particulaly if he can get for his partner and girl friend a snooty young woman (Karen Lynn Gorney), who, because she has a questionable job in Manhattan and some garbled rudiments of cocktail-party erudition, acts vastly superior to him.

The film chronicles the events through which boy finally not only gets girl, but also gets escape from family and Brooklyn into fabled Manhattan, which has not been so glorified as the Promised Land since Whitman stopped rhapsodizing about it. It is all, I am afraid, poppycock; the move to Manhattan for today's Brooklyn kids would hardly be a medieval quest through the Forest Perilous, only a chthonian subway ride. What is truly dismaying, though, is the script by Norman Wexler (*Joe, Mandingo*), which patronizes young and old alike, although the dialogue does have its scattered pungencies. Not even the disco scenes are done with sufficient choreographic abandon—the director, John Badham, opts for mushy sentimentality on the dance floor. But Travolta does give an exceptionally convincing performance, a seamless blend of cockiness and vulnerability. What remains to be seen is whether it is really acting, or merely type-casting.

February 17, 1978

Truth—for Beginners

SOMEWHAT LATE IN THE GAME, Hollywood is beginning to try to come to grips with the effects of Vietnam. *Coming Home* is meant to illustrate the impact of that war on three groups of people: paraplegic or otherwise scarred veterans; average, gung-ho Americans, who faced disappointments over there and back home; and wives who were left behind. Roughly, it is the story of the emancipation of a typical, sheltered officer's wife, who, while her husband is having a hard time of it in Vietnam, starts doing volunteer work in a Los Angeles veterans' hospital, gets involved with a wonderfully virile paraplegic pacifist, and begins to see, in bed, both colored lights and *the* light. When her husband returns, disillusioned but still hawkish (also male chauvinist pig), she reluctantly but hopefully chooses him over her lover; but the by now highly neuroticized husband, after threatening murder, commits self-sacrifice.

There could have been a fine film in this—Nancy Dowd, the author of the original screenplay, claims there was, before it got rewritten by Waldo Salt and Robert C. Jones—but *Coming Home* is, for most practical purposes, yet another musical remake of *A Star Is Born.* As period songs blare away ceaselessly and maddeningly on the soundtrack, the wife (Jane Fonda) slowly emerges from her cocoon; the cocky husband (Bruce Dern), his smug antebellum values shattered, ends by neatly folding his uniform on a beach, then swimming off naked to a briny self-immolation.

The paraplegic lover (Jon Voight), to be sure, is a new kink in the old *topos;* and the fact that Fonda gets her first orgasm from him in a torrid scene that contrasts heuristically with an early one in which hubby's avid lovemaking leaves her as unengaged as she hadn't been since her stint with a client in *Klute,* is even newer stuff. With a paraplegic, that is; otherwise, first *real* orgasms, lovingly recorded by the camera, are getting to be, as it were, an anticlimax.

There are perfectly splendid performances by Jane Fonda and Jon Voight, but they cannot make up for a script in which preposterousness vies with tendentious banality. For example, we are asked to believe that a supposedly brilliant young veteran who is clearly mentally deranged (but not so clearly brilliant) is not confined to the hospital's psychiatric ward. When the spirit moves him, he locks himself into the open and abandoned dispensary, uses a hypodermic with lethal efficiency while his buddies watch helplessly without breaking down the door, and, by the time the orderly returns (apparently from Timbuktu), is, naturally, dead.

Again, Hal Ashby, an undistinguished director at best, has left it up to the actors to improvise a number of scenes—a device that unfailingly fails. If it looks only like awkward dawdling here rather than an abject fiasco, it is because the written parts of the dialogue are not that much better. Above all, though, the film depends on facile sensationalism: the inept pleasuring by the husband; the fabulous loving of the paraplegic, who, with the mere help of a few pillows to prop him up, makes it good business to hire the handicapped; the gross paranoia of the husband, especially as portrayed by Dern, who has made creepiness bordering on craziness his stock in trade. Why couldn't the contest have been between personalities and ideologies rather than between glossy or grotesque oversimplifications?

Haskell Wexler, that master cinematographer, has shot the film handsomely, though probably deliberately less dazzlingly than he did his last one for Ashby, *Bound for Glory.* There are some good supporting performances, but also carelessnesses: after much has been made of a ramp built to Fonda's back door to make her place accessible to wheelchairs, Voight, in the climactic showdown, rolls right up to the inaccessible front door. And if you are going to get a body model for some nude shots of Fonda (curious, considering that others are unmistakably of her), try not to get one with stubby, plebeian fingers, when Fonda's are long and aristocratic.

An Unmarried Woman is Paul Mazursky's best film to date. True, Mazursky has always aimed for an adult, European style of filmmaking, with modest production values but a more searching investigation of personal problems and conflicts, usually centering on the arduous process of self-discovery. But the Scylla of triviality and the Charybdis of coarseness lay steadily in wait for the writer-director, and in every previous film, he ran up against one or the other, or, frequently, both.

Mazursky now seems to have observed and listened to married and unmarried women of his acquaintance with ripe sympathy but without the excessive self-involvement and sentimentality that previously led him astray. So he gives us the story of Erica, a well-to-do wife and mother in her late thirties, living on Manhattan's posh Upper East Side, who, when her stockbroker husband leaves her for a younger woman, finds herself unmoored and adrift. This, despite a genteel job in a SoHo art gallery, a nice and intelligent teenaged daughter, three warm female friends to exchange tales of woe with, a goodly number of peripheral men still avidly ogling her by no means tarnished charms, and, of course, one obligatory psychotherapist who feeds her some bolstering platitudes.

Most traumatic for Erica is the need to start "dating" again, in spite of her mature age, her present edginess about men, and the exaggerated sexual expectations of casual companions, based, presumably, on previous experience with easy divorcées. It is this area of sociosexual awkwardness that the film handles most effectively and, for American movies, originally. It should have stuck to this, rather than waste footage on chronicling the typical breakup of a schematic New York marriage, or on the resolution, when Erica meets a dreamboat of a divorced painter whose virtues are as overwhelmingly concrete as his work is wishy-washily abstract (courtesy Paul Jenkins). This part of the film is too precipitately idyllic by half, and, to obviate a conventional happy ending, Mazursky paints himself into a conclusion that is arbitrarily ambiguous and equally unconvincing.

There are many keenly and generously perceived incidents and details, as Erica, for instance, elicits outbursts of self-pity from the friends she needs compassion from; as her daughter (well played by Lisa Lucas) innocently enhances her nervousness; as seemingly innocuous oafs are turned, by taxicabs bound for home, into noxious would-be wolves; and as casually satisfactory sex proves no more filling than Chinese food. Mazursky, a former and still intermittent actor, has a sharp sense of casting, and wonderful performances pop up all over the movie. The only bad work, in fact, comes from the director's real-life analyst, who plays Erica's shrink: it is hard to say whether she emerges worse as a thespian or as a therapist.

Most impressive of all is, appropriately, Jill Clayburgh's Erica, a woman rendered in all the complex interplay of antithetical impulses, ranging from subservience and vulnerability to angry or hopeful resilience. The actress exudes a wealth of inner activity and an ample repertoire of fascinatingly changing expressions, better than any kind of static, conventional prettiness. Thus, in a skating scene in Rockefeller Center, the camera comes in tight on her for what seems like an unconscionably long time as Erica has her first sense of being blessed by freedom. A lesser actress would have portrayed the sort of outburst of eudemonia that is occasioned by a superior detergent in a

TV commercial; Miss Clayburgh gives us something as gradual and miraculous as the opening of a flower followed through all its stages by a nature documentary. She goes from smiling disbelief to ever more confident laughter with an authority that the film, good as it often is, ultimately lacks.

April 14, 1978

Creeping Shabbiness

THE MOST INTERESTING THING about *Fingers*—correction, the only interesting thing—is Pauline Kael's review of it. So let's save that for the end.

Fingers is a cross between a small boy's dream of glory and a bigger boy's masturbation fantasy. James Toback, the writer-director, is the author of the dreadful screenplay for Karel Reisz's *The Gambler;* of a book called *Jim,* about James Brown, the football player turned movie actor, with whom Toback lived and orgied while he wrote this piece of mixed hero-worship and self-love in which the two Jims become fused like the nurse and the actress in *Persona;* and of a number of magazine articles, including a tribute to that supreme macho megalomaniac, Norman Mailer.

For anyone who knows Toback even slightly, *Fingers* is full of autobiography—or, rather, psychobiography; and what a congeries of bravado, self-pity, arrogance, and sheer mean-spiritedness it is! All of which matters less, though, than the fact that it is a totally amateurish job of writing and filmmaking; only Toback's fast-talking slickness and the gullibility of the producer, George Barrie, can explain how the thing ever got made.

It is the story of Jimmy Angelelli, the son of a Mafia loan shark and a now-institutionalized Jewish concert pianist; he is a young man torn by contrary heritages. Note the name: Jimmy, as in Toback; Angelelli, as in "angel" and "(h)ell." There is already enough autobiographico-metaphysical symbol-mongering in this to make one queasy.

We encounter Jimmy seated one day at his piano (though the way he carries on, he might as well be seated at his organ, even if not in Sir Arthur Sullivan's sense), while the camera takes an unconscionable time to move in on him. Harvey Keitel, who plays Jimmy, is going through the contortions of the damned, along with agonized croonings that would be the envy of Glenn Gould and the nausea of anybody else. But—and here is part of the way he's split—in the street and even in restaurants, he carries with him a blaring tape deck, usually of the Jamies (another variation on Toback's name) giving out with "Summertime, Summertime," a noxious piece of junk Jimmy adores as much as Bach.

The film tells us nothing about how Jimmy comes by his fancy pad in New York's most expensive section, not to mention the concert grand or the professional recording-studio equipment. We follow him now on a wenching expedition, then humoring his aging father as, dutiful son of a *mafioso,* he roughs up a debtor by way of collecting papa's dough. In this same tough-guy capacity, he enters another debtor's swanky club, follows that big *mafioso*'s girl friend into the ladies' room, and there, half by obscenity-studded compliments, half by force, possesses the girl perpendicularly against the bathroom wall. The *dernier cri* in orgasms he promises her looks a bit wham-bam-thank-you-ma'amish to this viewer; but, then, I hear that the MPAA people snipped a lot of sex and violence out of the film, for which—this once—we have reason to be thankful.

On the finer, maternal side of things, we find Jimmy practicing and practicing the Bach Toccata in E-minor, going to see his mother at the sanatorium, with disastrous results, and auditioning for a concert manager unsuccessfully—but only, I daresay, because of the insecurity his warring parents bequeathed to him. Under slightly more auspicious family circumstances no one could have tickled those ivories like Jimmy except perhaps the trunk of a mother when they were still tusks on her beloved offspring's face.

Meanwhile, Jimmy has also been pursuing Carol (Tisa Farrow), an eccentric sculptress with a SoHo loft, whom he also bulldozes into bed and a leporine orgasm, and whom he follows into a shady bar whose black owner is named, with yet another splendid burst of schoolboy symbolism, Dreems. He is played, of course, by Toback's wish-fulfillment alter ego, Jim Brown. As several reviewers have remarked, Brown is the true love-object here, scrutinized and swooned over by the camera as no woman in the film is.

Dreems takes Carol and Jimmy for some sex *à quatre,* of the kind Toback describes in his book about Brown. They go to the posh pad of lovely Christa (Carole Francis) in the Hotel Plaza. Dreems encourages the two girls, who have been bussing, nuzzling, and licking him, to kiss each other, while Jimmy looks on in a mixture of agony and ecstasy. When they prove reluctant, a ghastly incident occurs. Here is Toback himself recounting it in a short but unreadable article inappropriately entitled "Notes on Acting" in *Film Comment* (January-February 1978): "Shortly after I had lived in his house in L.A. and written a book about our adventures together, [Brown] was arrested (though the charges were later dropped) for whacking together the heads of two girls. I knew as soon as I heard about the incident not only that I could 'transform' it but that it had *happened* so that I could transform it."

I don't know whether Brown's whacking or Toback's whacking-off over it is more deplorable—or, for that matter, the fact that Brown, a celebrity, got off scot free; what is most pitiful, though, is Toback's arrogance, which views this act as occurring for his art to transform it. Toback, alas, could transform water into wine as easily as a coarse event into art. Needless to say, as he boasts in the article, Toback had Brown perform another real head-whacking for the camera, which only goes to show how desperate some actresses are for employment, and at best transforms a performer into a patsy.

But why go on? Toback often doesn't even manage to frame a shot properly, has no feeling for rhythm, cannot make a scene look lifelike (consider, for instance, the one where a little girl in a park is playing in the margin of the main action, and her playing is made to look arbitrarily erotic and stilted), gets poor, washed-out cinematography from Michael Chapman (an inferior cameraman, but never before this bad), and has no skill for making anything credible. Thus, for the final showdown, Jimmy saunters into the big *mafioso*'s club as easily as into a ladies' room, finds the gangster alone, promptly gets him onto a deserted back stairway, reduces him first to defenselessness by squeezing his testicles, then to jelly by repeatedly shooting him in the eyes, so that a mixture of blood and eye squirts onto our hero's face. He then goes home, strips naked, and stares forlornly out of the window, his bite no better than his Bach.

Now, as promised, Pauline Kael's review. It is a masterpiece of equivocation that nevertheless manages to bring in, however ambiguously, Orson Welles, Sir Carol Reed, Dostoyevsky, Conrad, Kafka, Mailer, and Tennessee Williams to gild Toback by association. The review has to be read *in toto* to reveal America's most loved and feared film critic tergiversating in the most pathetic and ludicrous way, e.g., "Yet the film never seems ridiculous, because [Toback has] got true moviemaking fever." What that means in plain English is that if you are this desperate to make a movie, you deserve high marks even if you lack the requisite talents. It is as if a doctor said: "The patient died, true enough, but look at the beautiful parabola of his fever chart."

Be it noted that for a couple of years now James Toback has been one of Miss Kael's steadier escorts around town. Like an unfunny Falstaff, Toback is not only shabby in himself, but the cause that shabbiness is in others.

May 12, 1978

Coming of Age in Sodom

LOUIS MALLE has made two impressive films, *The Fire Within* and *Lacombe, Lucien,* and some valuable documentaries about India. But his problem seems to be a certain affectlessness: his films are less about feelings than about the need to have them. However charming, the joys of incest, as portrayed in *Murmur of the Heart,* are merely excogitated—Malle does not seem to be alive to their real implications; Lucien Lacombe's moral *anomie* and lack of feeling are accepted a bit too casually; Alain, the hero of *The Fire Within,* kills himself a trifle too promptly when his youthful good times appear to be over.

Pretty Baby, Malle's latest, is about Violet, a child prostitute in a brothel of Storyville, just before that famous New Orleans red-light district was closed down in 1917. Violet's mother is Hattie, a girl in Nell's bordello, who—when one of those accidents occurred, as they often did—allowed a child to be born to her. At first, Violet merely watches the life of the brothel with a mixture of curiosity and cold-bloodedness. Then she gets interested in Ernest Bellocq, a dedicated photographer who specializes in whorehouse scenes and particularly enjoys photographing Hattie. At twelve, Violet is deemed to be of age, and is auctioned off in a kind of sex-show-*cum*-slave-sale to the highest bidder, a man who (as we hear but are not shown) roughly sodomizes her.

But Violet enjoys the luxuries of whorehouse living—unlike Hattie, who is yearning to get away from it all and finally gets a man to marry her and take her off to respectability, even though it means leaving Violet behind for an indefinite period. Meanwhile, Bellocq has become quite enamored of the trick baby (as child whores were called), and she eventually seeks him out, moves in with him, and gets him to marry her. Though the union of the obsessed photographer and the doubly spoiled brat is a messy one, Bellocq is shattered when Hattie and her husband come to reclaim Violet, who does not seriously resist being carried off to school and the bourgeois life.

This could have made an interesting movie if only it had had a clear point of view: some penetrating psychological insight combined with a social content, not necessarily redeeming. The trouble is that Malle, apparently, does not know what he is doing, beyond wishing to express his fascination with a child born into, and coming of age in, a whorehouse; and with New Orleans jazz, born, or at any rate fostered, in brothels, where the black pianists were treated with considerable respect. On two such pianists, Tony Jackson and Jelly Roll Morton, the character of the Professor in *Pretty Baby* is based—a remote and imperturbable dandy, who keeps whatever feelings he may have well hidden.

The heroine derives from a real-life model, "Violet," the pseudonymous trick baby interviewed in old age by Al Rose for his well-researched book, *Storyville, New Orleans,* the chief source of the film. As for Bellocq, he is, of course, the photographer whose pictures of Storyville prostitutes brought him (alas, only posthumous) fame. But Malle misses his chance to delve into the reality—and therewith the possible meanings—of his characters, even though he is quoted in an interview in *Film Comment* (May/June 1978) as admiring "Violet" for her "straight attitude," her acceptance of the brothel and the world as they really are. Rose's book, in fact, reveals a girl who at ten was already casually wiping off her mother's clients; soon thereafter selling oral sex; and, at twelve, auctioned off, together with another little virgin, for a double defloration.

Malle shows the amorality of the child only outwardly; for MPAA ratings' sake, or other reasons, he goes neither into the sexual experiences of the girl nor into a full exploration of their psychic resonance. His Violet thus emerges less hardened than her prototype must have been; and the life she leads, thanks to the luxuriousness of the *mise en scène* and camerawork, more romantic than even a child's view of it. In the same interview in which Malle praised the real "Violet" for her no-nonsense approach to her past, he describes his heroine's vision as that of a child and "very distorted." But the twelve-year-old "Violet" was clearly not very different from the old woman she turned into, even if she did give up prostitution for marriage along the way. She could not have been a youngster living in a "dream world," as Malle would have it; she had to be prematurely jaded about our quotidian sources of wonder.

Malle evades this issue, just as he shirks the true nature of Bellocq. Keith Carradine's photographer is modeled outwardly on Degas (who actually spent time in New Orleans living with relatives): a pale, languidly handsome, bearded young man, strangely impervious to easily available flesh, although, unlike Degas, he has no sexual problems. The real-life Bellocq, in contrast, made sense as Toulouse-Lautrec did: a dwarf (in Bellocq's case also near-hydrocephalic) living among the despised, who could not look down on him. His misshapenness prevented Bellocq, like Lautrec, from becoming seriously involved with the whores; his talent enabled him to portray their sensual essence, thus also granting him vicarious possession. A seemingly normal and attractive but sexless Bellocq is an uncompelling enigma, more prurient than sympathetic.

Even less real than the main characters are the peripheral ones: mere unhaunting ghosts. We never get to know, for instance, whether Hattie truly cares about her daughter; whether the Professor has any feelings and, if so, of what kind; why Violet suddenly moves in with a Bellocq who, however enamored, has little to offer her; and why, having married him, she is so easily severed from him by a mother who had abandoned her for so long. Nell, the madam, is all platitudes (badly played and postsynched by Frances Faye); the whores are interchangeable, and their customers even more so. The jazz, though present on the soundtrack, comes no more significantly alive than the people in the film who create, consume, or ignore it.

There is, however, much lush production design, although there are few outdoor shots of New Orleans despite location filming. Malle's coscenarist was Polly Platt, the ex-wife of Peter Bogdanovich, whose earlier films she ably designed. Her only previous writing credit was her collaboration on the rather primitive script for *Targets;* small wonder that *Pretty Baby* looks more designed than written, even though Platt herself is not credited with its production design. And the opulent décor is photographed with such seductive brilliance—by Sven Nykvist, Bergman's cinematographer—that competition from action and dialogue is desperately needed if we are not to be turned from moviegoers into museum visitors.

The acting is not much help. Susan Sarandon, through her charm, and Antonio Fargas, thanks to his suggestively simian face, make something of Hattie and the Professor, respectively. But young Brooke Shields is merely very beautiful as Violet—neither actress nor even nymphet enough to carry the film. As for Carradine, he continues to be the sullen, slightly oily-looking, pinched-voiced lout he has been all along. But the problem does not really rest there, or even with the self-censorship that may have created the psychological lacunae and lapses in continuity. The problem is that Malle, with all his elegance and technical command, has made a film that, for lack of import, has little or no impact.

June 9, 1978

Dishonest Denim

WHY HAS THE BLUE-COLLAR WORKER been so neglected by American movies? Because his life does not usually lend itself to that combination of melodramatic sensationalism and escapist fantasy on which Hollywood thrives. There are no opulent furnishings, exotic journeys, or even, presumably, clever repartee in such a life. Its violence and crimes are considered merely sordid, except when they become so spectacular as to turn the movie into a genre film, a gangster or caper picture, a *policier* or *film noir.* In short, a film that no longer concerns itself with the everyday realities of working-class life.

Rightly or wrongly, working-class reality is assumed to be something that the blue-collar moviegoer wants to transcend as soon as possible; or, having risen above it, never look back upon. Yet one aspect of workers' lives is dynamic and dramatic by any standard: the labor union movement and the struggle upward on the economic ladder. But that is explosive material, not calculated to please the capitalists who finance movies, and apt to displease, no matter how it is handled, one or another class of viewers. Manual labor itself is not considered photogenic, except perhaps in a short documentary about toy makers, glass blowers, or steeplejacks. As for full-length documentaries—or any narrative films that might resemble them excessively—they are as welcome at the box office as the Black Death.

It is, therefore, a characteristic of American films that dare begin in a blue-collar milieu to veer away from it as fast as possible: thus *Five Easy Pieces* abandons the oil rigs and the lives around them very quickly. Films that deal with workers' lives in some detail either concentrate on picturesque toil on the earth with lots of tragic acts of God (e.g., *The Southerner),* or follow workers through some exceptional crisis (e.g., *The Grapes of Wrath),* or concentrate on a psychiatric case (e.g., *A Woman Under the Influence),* or have to be made abroad and are barely seen in the country they deal with (e.g., *Give Us This Day,* an adaptation of *Christ in Concrete).*

So it is still a bit of rarity for two working-class films like *Blue Collar* and *F.I.S.T.* to come along almost simultaneously. But Paul Schrader's initially realistic *Blue Collar* very rapidly turns into a highly improbable, funny caper movie, then hurtles into farfetched melodrama. Moreover, it fails even in its early sequences to convince us that the workers' lot is bad enough to require their desperate stratagem—otherwise how could they afford the expensive drug-and-sex orgies they are seen indulging in. For Schrader, Zolaesque naturalism is just an excuse for kinkiness and bizarrely savage effects.

F.I.S.T., on the other hand, is a thinly disguised fictionalization of the rise and fall of Jimmy Hoffa, and purports to tell an atypical but not incredible working-class life story as it really happened, or really might have happened. Typically, this film, directed by Norman Jewison from a screenplay by Sylvester Stallone and Joe Eszterhas, can hardly wait to introduce us to corrupt or exploitative management figures in the Cleveland of the 1930s, where it begins, so that evil is to be perceived less as poverty, overwork, and boredom than as sadistic meanness from those on top toward those below, and so the stage is set for rebellious heroics.

Jewison has directed the scenes of labor violence well enough, though without particular distinction. But the brief scenes in which we observe Johnny Kovak (Stallone) and his best friend in their family circles or courting their women (played as well as circumstances permit by Melinda Dillon and Cassie Yates) are conventional in the extreme. Not much better are the scenes in which Johnny, now a growing force in the labor movement, gets involved with a former friend turned petty gangster (nicely acted by Kevin Conway), and eventually with a bigger racketeer, Babe Milano (Tony Lo Bianco, good although somewhat schematic). All this would be derivative and second-rate in any case; based on pungent reality, it is depressingly insipid.

We are to be impressed by Kovak-Hoffa's charisma, but here, too, things are made unduly hard for us. Both Johnny's rabble-rousing oratory and his tough speeches during negotiations are essentially uninspired, and Stallone, repeating his Rocky performance minus some of its charm, fails to move us. Sometimes the thickness of his speech renders him incomprehensible; sometimes his jauntiness coarsens into mere arrogance. Still, he does have good moments when his hangdog features clamber into cockiness, and he gets fine support from such able actors as Peter Boyle, Peter Donat, and Ken Kercheval, among others.

The film was originally planned as much longer than its present 145 minutes, and was then shortened simplistically by having its middle cut out. So we have a rather lame before-and-after construction, further marred by dishonesty in crucial matters. Thus Kovak never commits a single truly bad deed: he does acquire the help of underworld goons, but this is represented as the only way of overcoming management goons backed by the police; he does once, during a riot, batter an unconscious man to death, but this is shown as hardly more than self-defense tinged with righteous anger; and he does make deals with Babe Milano, but only for the good of his Federation of Inter State Truckers (hence the acronym F.I.S.T., even if "Interstate" is really one word and, from what one reads of Stallone's tantrums during production, F.I.T. might have been more appropriate). Never, though, does he take anything for himself and his family, and his rise to the presidency of the union is so clean, his downfall so undeserved, that we cannot even weep for him: our tears would be too saline for such sweetness.

It is equally improbable that his idealistic buddy, however estranged, would rat on Johnny in this particularly holier-than-thou and inept, yet still damaging, way to a congressional investigation committee. And the ending (one of three that were tried) is just too obvious and flat-footedly executed. But the film does have one imaginatively directed and strikingly photographed (by Laszlo Kovacs) sequence in which bargaining for an 8.5 percent wage increase is made visually exciting. Furthermore, Rod Steiger turns a Kefauver-like investigating senator into someone interestingly ambiguous: his muckraking is so smug and self-righteous as to cast doubt on his high-mindedness. This touch of complexity is achieved, perhaps only inadvertently, through Steiger's basic unlikableness, but it does give the movie a bit of much-needed shading.

June 23, 1978

Unfocused Comedy

As OTHERS, too, have remarked, this spring and summer (so far) have been the Sahara and Gobi of the movies. Foreign imports have proved no less barren than the domestic product; under these circumstances, an insignificant item such as *Heaven Can Wait* looms on the horizon like a lush oasis, even though it is only a middling mirage. For all its opulently colorful outdoor look, this remake of *Here Comes Mr. Jordan* (1941), a romantic comedy-fantasy with metaphysical overtones, already exercises a weaker hold on my memory than the grubby black-and-white, relentlessly studio-made original version.

The expensive remake, written by Elaine May and Warren Beatty (and owing more to the original screenplay than the credits care to admit) and directed by Beatty and Buck Henry, changes its hero, Joe Pendleton, from a boxer to a quarterback for the Los Angeles Rams. Joe is snatched up to Heaven prematurely by an overeager neophyte escort (Buck Henry); the error is caught by the mysterious Mr. Jordan, who may be God, and is certainly, and infelicitously, James Mason. Since Pendleton's body has already been cremated, a new fleshly envelope must be found for Joe; this is to be the body of Leo Farnsworth, an unscrupulous and eccentric billionaire whom his wife and private secretary (her lover) have just poisoned.

Joe agrees to become Farnsworth only because he falls for a pretty English girl (Julie Christie) who is in Los Angeles to protest an ecological crime one of the nabob's enterprises is about to commit. The Joe-ified Farnsworth is a quixotic do-gooder who also buys the Rams so he can still play quarterback in the upcoming Super Bowl. But the scheming wife (Dyan Cannon) and secretary (Charles Grodin) get him anyway, and Joe has to be moved again, which makes Heaven rather busier than the Seven Santini Brothers. He ends up inside a fellow quarterback killed in the game, and wins for the Rams. He must now forget his former identity, but love triumphs even over the transmigration of souls and attendant amnesia.

It was a silly plot even in 1941, but we and the movies were both much younger, and fantasy in those unrealistic days did not look that much different from other, supposedly more truthful, Hollywood genres. Vincent Canby, of the *New York Times,* has speculated that in time of war this concern with death and survival, either in Heaven or by reincarnation, seemed more urgent and acceptable. I think, rather, that World War II, genocide, and all the subsequent historical catastrophes have made this type of fantasy inadequate to our needs, unless it is as witty and irreverent as *Blithe Spirit* or as philosophically charged as Sartre's *Les Jeux sont faits.* The prevailing mood among today's moviegoers seems to be an agnostic materialism, but even twice-born Christians are unlikely to fall for the woolly eschatology of *Heaven Can Wait.*

So the emphasis is now on comedy (the comic villains have become much more important) and on whatever electricity the on-screen teaming of the once celebrated off-screen lovers Beatty and Christie can generate. For me, Elaine May's wit has long since faded, and though she still manages a few genuine laughs here—many of them due to the superb expressions and comic timing of Charles Grodin—much of the humor misfires, often because (as Canby has rightly observed) the movie lacks a sense of period. Some of the ecological and racial gags are fairly up-to-date; but a weird billionaire with bedeviled servants and heavenly personages either bungling or resolving things are strictly forties-or-earlier vintage. Somehow jokes such as a ship of souls built like a white marble Concorde and the previously always hatted Farnsworth suddenly going forth bare-headed, to the butler's astonishment, don't belong in the same picture.

Neither does the romantic element jell for me. Julie Christie has lost much of her former appeal, and her taste in hairdos has been steadily worsening. Here she looks like someone whose youth has been painted onto her face, and whose hair has been frizzed to a frazzle. As for Beatty, who also produced the film, he is just not believable as a nice, average Joe Pendleton; I kept expecting him to turn Machiavellian or at least neurotic on us: innocence sits on him like an overtight suit whose seams will burst any moment. As I recall it, Robert Montgomery and Evelyn Keyes were much more credible and winning as the avatar-crossed lovers.

Several supporting players are fine, though: notably Grodin, Joseph Maher as the very model of a manservant, and Jack Warden as a decent, befuddled Ram coach. Other parts are overdone, e.g., by Dyan Cannon and Vincent Gardenia (as a police inspector); or underdone, e.g., by James Mason, a complex, ironic actor who cannot act and sound unambivalently benign; or not done at all, e.g., by Buck Henry, who has almost always struck me as an essentially unfunny funnyman. The production is handsomely designed by Paul Sylbert and photographed by William A. Fraker, but trappings do not a movie make.

A different backward glance is taken by *The Cheap Detective,* Neil Simon's new film, directed, like his *Murder by Death,* by Robert Moore. This is a parody of Humphrey Bogart movies—chiefly *Casablanca* and *The Maltese Falcon,* spiced with added allusions to *The Big Sleep* and *To Have and Have Not.* The problem is evident: the political pieties and bittersweet romanticism of *Casablanca* are a far cry from the private-eye toughnesses of *The Maltese Falcon.* Parody, a small, precise genre, demands perfect accuracy and self-control: to swat with different implements at diverse projectiles is, like trying to play tennis and hockey simultaneously, a mess.

The execution, moreover, is a tangle of self-indulgence. One corpse discovered in the exact position it assumed while alive is funny; a whole series of such corpses is not. Naming all three policemen after Italian-American baseball players is too much or, depending on how you look at it, too little. Having a character's name turn out to be something else every few seconds is a running gag that soon runs out of steam. Everything here is milked to the point where, if it were a cow, it would trample the dairymaid to death.

This is not to say that there are not, as always with Simon, a few funny sight gags and one-liners. Yet even they are rare here, and suffer from the weight of the all-encompassing heavy-handedness. James Coco and John

Houseman in particular are victimized by a lack of funny material; Dom DeLuise, despite a pretty good take-off on Peter Lorre, has for his comic mainstay the fact that he exudes an unbearable stench. A character in a Feydeau farce can turn bad breath to good comic account; stinking all over is considerably less funny. The parodist, mocking vulgarity, must not himself fall into worse vulgarity.

Among the generally undistinguished performances, Louise Fletcher's Ingrid Bergman take-off is particularly disconcerting: a character meant to be boring is played quite literally boringly. The very Hispanic Fernando Lamas is unintentionally ludicrous as a Frenchman; his prototype in *Casablanca,* Paul Henreid, was not very French either, but Lamas's un-Frenchness is not an ironic jab, only Hollywood's perennial insensitivity to telling details. Peter Falk is insufficiently inventive as a comedian to carry the main role, and I wish that his baby-talk version of Bogey's speech would stick in his craw instead of mine.

August 4, 1978

Bergmania

WOODY ALLEN has made his first serious film, *Interiors,* and its condition is worse than serious, it's grave to the point of disaster. Whether it makes you bite your lips in rage or roll over with helpless laughter, you will concede that there is not one real, original character in it; that almost every line of dialogue is, at best, hackneyed, at worst, ludicrously stilted; and that virtually every shot is derived from some other filmmaker, usually Bergman or Antonioni. In fact, most of the film is taken over from Bergman in a misunderstood and mismanaged way, particularly from *Cries and Whispers*—one of Bergman's poorest films, but we can hardly expect anyone tasteless and foolish enough to make *Interiors* to know what to copy.

When Allen made his last drearily inept film, *Annie Hall,* not only was he hailed with unprecedented critical hosannas, but Vincent Canby of the *New York Times* even went so far as to declare him our Ingmar Bergman. And Allen, who, as we know from *Love and Death,* has a Bergman complex, was fool enough to believe Canby. Right from the titles of *Interiors*—simple white on black, and, as in the rest of the film, no music—we know we are in Bergman country.

The first few shots are empty interiors of a tastefully antiseptic beach house, all muted colors: gray, beige, fawn, taupe. Later in the movie, black, white, and steel blue will occasionally be added. And so it remains, with one hammy exception, throughout. After these dead interiors (out of *Persona* and *Face to Face,* as well as Antonioni's *Eclipse),* we see a character, Joey (Marybeth Hurt), appear first as a reflection in mirrors or the glass over a picture. Presently, she stares out of the window at a bleak seascape. Next, we see her sister, Renata, pressing anguished fingers against another windowpane giving on autumnal trees. Her face (Diane Keaton's living cliché of a countenance) agonizes, and the fingers are in near-paroxysm; right off unearned effects usurp the place of character in action. Forthwith, it is the turn of the women's father, Arthur (E. G. Marshall), to stare out at a New York cityscape through the plate glass of his skyscraper office and rehearse banalities about their family past. Even if the words were not dismal ("Looking back, of course, it was rigid . . ."), the schematic cutting among these three anxious window-dwellers is the height of obviousness.

The film purports to record a brief but agitated period in the lives of a WASP family, who, even with no last names, are supposed to exude gentileness. Arthur, a successful and rich lawyer, is insensitive (possible) and totally obtuse (unlikely); he was put through law school by his whiny and fluttery wife, Eve, an interior decorator who is in and out of suicide attempts and sanatoriums; she speaks and behaves in an *outré* way throughout, but this is probably only Geraldine Page's old and by now threadbare Method acting.

The eldest daughter, Renata, is a successful poetess published in *The New Yorker,* but is now, as she reveals in a monologue to an invisible analyst (monologues to unseen interlocutors are another Bergman device), unable to write: "My impotence set in a year ago, my paralysis." Later she adds, "What am I striving to create anyway? To what purpose, to what end, to what goal?" Is this a poetess or a master tautologist? Why would *The New Yorker* print anything by someone who says: "I can't shake the real implication of dying—the intimacy of it embarrasses me"? In a small college magazine, in a bad month, perhaps . . .

The second daughter is Flyn (Kristin Griffith), a movie and TV actress who is passed by when "classy roles" are given out, and who sniffs cocaine. She does not look or sound at all like either of her sisters and clearly doesn't interest Allen much. The youngest is Joey (a name that comes, after Renata and Flyn, as a bit of an anticlimax), who is very bright but ungifted: "Poor Joey, she has all the anguish and anxiety of the artistic personality but none of the talent . . ." (From that redundancy, you know who is speaking.) Joey, who has been an editor and is now a copywriter, is no mean hand at pleonasm herself. "At the center of a sick psyche," she tells her mother, "there is a sick spirit," which helps drive Eve to her ultimate suicide. Joey is terribly earnest and says things like: "I feel a real need to express something, but I don't know what to express and how to express it." Why this should stop her—given the precedent of Woody Allen—I cannot say.

Renata is married to Frederick (Richard Jordan), a novelist who exclaims, "I don't know whether I lost it or never had it," and consoles himself by drinking and writing exceedingly nasty book reviews, often of novels by his friends: "I was extremely cruel about it, and I took great pleasure in my cruelty." When not writing, he teaches at Barnard—Phys. Ed., one hopes.

Joey lives with Mike (Sam Waterston), a political activist of some kind, though nothing is shown us of his activities. This is not surprising, because throughout the film Allen is incapable of showing anything. Everything is *told,* by one character about another, or by a character about him or herself, in endless, utterly inept palaver: "One day an enormous abyss opened up beneath our feet," or "[I don't want to] be swallowed up in some anonymous life-style." Or, from the poetess *in extremis:* "It was as if I had a clear vision where everything seems awful and kind of predatory . . . I felt precarious. It was like I was a machine, but I could conk out at any minute." On and on, they verbalize in language that one would think was persiflage if Allen himself had not announced repeatedly that he was dead serious in the film.

The camerawork is just as derivative. There are the large surfaces of white walls in front of which characters suffer and recriminate—out of Antonioni. There is a staircase whose banister seems to imprison Frederick—an angle shot through the railing, shamelessly out of Bergman's *Shame.* There are three fighting and reconciling sisters right out of *Cries and Whispers.* A family narrative with flashbacks of the sisters when they were children is even more flagrantly out of that film, as is Joey writing in her diary with inserts of the past (close enough to be labeled plagiarism). A cutting-away from Eve's drowning (a scene rather out of Altman's *The Long Goodbye)* to the other people in the cottage sleeping in their respective beds strongly suggests Fellini's *I Vitelloni.* The funeral, at which all the principals pop before the stationary camera with the identical single white rose in their hands but carefully differentiated facial expressions, is a cinematic cliché seen most recently in Truffaut's *The Man Who Loved Women.* There are all those shots in front of mirrors or windows that are acutely Bergmanian, as are the lacerating quarrels between lovers or spouses. Except that these, in Bergman, are passionate and insidiously subtle, and inflict palpable psychic wounds. In Allen they are all posturing: shoddy verbiage and no real passion.

And the vulgarity of it! When the father introduces Pearl (Maureen Stapleton), his new wife-to-be, to the family, there she is in sudden bright red in the midst of all those earth tones, and henceforth she will always wear red or loud prints. She is, by various obvious implications, Jewish; but is she meant to be an infusion of real life into this bloodless WASP milieu, or is she to be viewed as a ridiculous vulgarian? During a dinner-table discussion of a Broadway play about the Algerian war that is meant to bring out how the characters' minds work, everyone spouts clichés or banalities. Thus our poetess observes, "If you've read Schopenhauer, Socrates, Buddha, even Ecclesiastes, they all say it very convincingly," on which Pearl comments, impressed, "They should know!" What is one to make of this scene (and indeed the movie)? Are we to laugh at WASP pretentiousness—Socrates and Buddha, after all, wrote nothing—or are we to chuckle at Pearl's Miami Beach ignorance? Or are both equally ridiculous? But Allen insists there is no joke in the movie; are we, then, to take both positions seriously? Joey says about the play: "The writer argued both sides so brilliantly you didn't know whose side he was on." I submit that it is equally possible to argue both sides so ineptly that the only side the writer can be assigned to is that of his own megalomania and incompetence.

While the film purports to sound the deeper aspects of human misery, it is quite unable to handle narrative and psychology on their simplest levels. Thus Joey announces her pregnancy to her lover, Mike, and, over his weak protestations, seems to decide on an abortion. That is the last we hear of it, one way or the other. When Joey bemoans her lack of creativity, Mike suggests that she take up photography again, a suggestion she categorically rejects. Yet in a later scene we see Renata and her husband looking at photographs Joey has submitted for their opinion. When Arthur arrives to introduce Pearl to the family, Renata sends her small daughter upstairs to play by herself. Ludicrous: any grandfather after a long absence would want to see his grandchild; but Allen clearly doesn't know how to deal with children in a movie.

He is not much better with adults. Under no circumstances would Arthur get remarried at the beach house to which his suicidal ex-wife, Eve, has free access, and where she does show up with fatal consequences. Joey, however outspoken, would not say those crushing things to her mother on Arthur's wedding day. And what kind of a political activist would live in the lap of bourgeois luxury at the expense of his girl friend's father? Yet that is what Mike does without a twinge of conscience, and without so much as a little reproach from Joey during their frequent fights. *Interiors,* which in one speech actually feels obliged to explain its own title, never quite discovers on which side of the epidermis to search for the soul.

Gordon Willis is an expert cinematographer, and he has clearly obliged Allen in every detail. But, however subtly lighted and shot, all those supposedly WASP, muted tones are finally as much of a strain on the eye as constant eruptions of primary colors would be. Indeed, Allen forces Willis into all kinds of photographic hamminess. Thus when Joey and Mike are driving home after the initial family meeting with Pearl, we first see the couple riding in almost complete darkness; in the next shot, some street lights they drive past illumine their somber faces; in the third shot, darkness swallows them again. It is highly charged visual maneuvering, but what does it say that couldn't be conveyed without that expense of chiaroscuro? Effect without meaning is mere affectation.

The acting is painfully uneven. Maureen Stapleton, because she has the one part endowed with quasi-comic relief, and because she has played the simple-minded earth mother long enough to be an earth grandmother, comes off rather well. By entirely avoiding any sort of acting—something that comes all too naturally to him—Sam Waterston, as Mike, manages to be inoffensive. Marybeth Hurt, a multifariously gifted young actress, almost succeeds in giving life to Joey, by dint of hard and intelligent work. The others are catastrophic. Marshall and Page I have already discussed; Kristin Griffith, as Flyn, has no part to play, and finds no way of transcending the banalities.

The nadir, however, is Diane Keaton (Renata). She is yet another of those nonactresses this country produces in such abundance—women who trade on the raw materials of their neuroses, which has nothing to do with acting. What we get is an untransmuted dithering-and-blithering session of the kind that goes on across the continent, from est to West; but when, in every Keaton performance, we get the same decomposition of voice, disintegration of features, and dissolution of mind, we begin to wonder whether the performer needs a critic or a clinic. To the above repertoire, Miss Keaton now adds repeated loud intakes of breath, another device out of Bergman, but exaggerated to sound like a vacuum cleaner in heat. Alas, she has become the darling of reviewers and audiences, and the recipient of an Academy Award. From me, she gets the Sandy Dennis Prize for Instant Deliquescence. As for her sometime lover and permanent employer, Woody Allen, I urge him to ponder the remark Pliny attributes to Apelles: *Ne sutor supra crepidam!* which can be Englished as, "Comic, stick to your one-liners!"

September 29–October 13, 1978

Heavenly Daze!

To NO MOVIE have I been more favorably predisposed than to *Days of Heaven.* I rate Terrence Malick's first film, *Badlands,* above all other American pictures of the last few years, and so I awaited the philosophy-instructor-turned-film-maker's second work—which met with various delays and had a hard, slow coming—with uncommon eagerness. The first few minutes of *Days of Heaven,* sure enough, promised to fulfill all expectations. The titles, against a background of period stills (1916 or thereabouts), provided a highly evocative sequence, even if the device is becoming overused; by the time we leave the Chicago steel mill where the hero, Bill, has killed a tyrannical foreman in a fight, we have witnessed images of explosive beauty and a dramatic event staged with stark economy.

When Bill, his teen-aged sister, Linda, and his girl, Abby, set off by train for the Texas Panhandle, we get a shot of such overwhelming magnificence as one rarely encounters on screen. It is a long shot in silhouette of a train crossing a bridge, but the way the entire span of the train precisely fills up the wide-screen frame, the manner in which these archaic-looking railroad cars and engine blackly detach themselves from the cerulean background, the cunning interplay of intricate train and bridge shapes, and something else that I cannot explain—perhaps the presence of some *deus ignotus*—add up to a breathtaking vision of technology in the ascendant.

But already there is trouble, too. Linda's voice-over narration, which will be with us through most of this otherwise austerely taciturn film, is delivered in a present-day New York street-kid voice and vocabulary. The performer—Linda Manz, a tough, scarred, street-wise urchin who was discovered in Central Park rather than at Central Casting, and seems to have made up much of her narration by herself—simply doesn't sound right for the period and place. She tells us that Bill and Abby will pass themselves off as brother and sister so that the migrant farmhands whom they are about to join won't molest Abby. Here begins a strained parallel to the Book of Genesis, where Abraham and Sarah in Egypt, expecting the beautiful Sarah to catch Pharaoh's eye, pass themselves off as brother and sister on the assumption that a brother will be spared where a husband might not be. And Sarah does becomes Pharaoh's concubine, just as Abby ends up marrying the rich, supposedly dying young farmer on whose land she, Bill, and Linda are working. Bill himself urges her to wed (the man will soon die, after all), so that our trio's toil may turn to dalliance in the wealthy man's eerie Victorian house that juts out of the wheatlands as if Edward Hopper had tossed it there.

Yet what makes sense in the penumbra of legend does not hold up in 1916, even if you refer to those last agrarian times as days of heaven. The field workers would quickly notice what goes on between Bill and Abby (in the film, only one of them does, and is promptly silenced by Bill's fists), and would take as unkindly to being lied to as they would to incest. What, in any case, is the point of the scriptural parallels? Malick's film never makes it clear, thus leaving an unpleasant aftertaste in the mind. And how could such vast domains and so large a house be run solely by the solitary Farmer (no name given, presumably for allegorical purposes) and his foreman, without help from kinfolk, servants, or anyone else except the migrant field hands? Given such arbitrariness, one need hardly quibble with a love scene in a patch of June snow such as you might get in Canada, where the film was shot, but not in the Panhandle, where it is set.

Strange things keep happening. At the Farmer and Abby's wedding, we see an inscription in an outlandish alphabet, left totally unexplained. Later, a tiny, fly-by-night flying circus drops out of the sky, its three scruffy performers possessed of two fancy aircraft, one of them a Fokker triplane. Though the Farmer has been given only a year to live, next year's harvest finds him seemingly in the pink. Such things could, of course, be made a bit more credible with some effort, but Malick, in both his script and his direction, exults in leaving them as enigmatic as possible.

Linda Manz, though suitably hard-boiled, does not, as I mentioned, sound right. As Bill, Richard Gere is out of place in his fancy 1970s haircut, trim clothes, actorish speech, and less than earthy performance. The sultrily nonchalant Brooke Adams (Abby), with her oblong, downward-curving mouth and pointy chin, who sometimes verges on plainness only to bounce back into fierce beauty, is very much more believable; the playwright Sam Shepard is perfect as the Farmer, all dolefully suspicious eyes, properly slicked-down hair, and bumblingly irregular teeth. Robert Wilke (the foreman), his implacably azure-eyed face craggier and more crevassed than the aging W. H. Auden's, is the very image of avenging angelhood. When Bill commits his second homicide and the chase is on, the film finally becomes more involving, but also, regrettably, too close for comfort to *Badlands.* And the closing sequences lapse into contrivance and utter inscrutability.

Nevertheless, the visual splendor remains throughout, as does Malick's gift for eliciting poetic as well as Gothic *frissons.* A plague of locusts and, on its heels, an all-destroying fire (biblical echoes again!) are staged and shot with a marvelously consubstantial sense of aesthetics and drama. Here Malick's downright notorious perfectionism reaps (to use an appropriately agrarian, perhaps even prebiblical, metaphor) a harvest of stunned admiration. Yet at times aestheticism preponderates: Are there not too many shots of prelapsarianly innocent herds of buffaloes and antelopes, and even time-exposures of seeds sprouting into plants, more suited to nature documentaries? And what about a quite gratuitous shot of a dropped champagne goblet coming to rest gracefully on a river bottom?

Still, Malick had the excellent sense to hire Nestor Almendros, the remarkable Cuban-born cinematographer (from whom Malick exacted work even more gorgeous than he supplies his European directors); and, when prior commitments forced Almendros to leave, to bring in one of America's greatest cameramen, Haskell Wexler, to provide seamlessly matched additional camera work. Furthermore, Malick obtained the services of Ennio Morricone for a score that, though perhaps not among the celebrated Italian's very best, still soars above the Hollywood norm. One looks and listens with rapt wonderment; every prospect, every permutation of the simple, basic melody, pleases, and only man is vile.

Yes, the people and their story remain inchoate and sordid, as the depressing tale and characters of *Badlands* never were. That film was about alienation, too, but alienation situated in a culture whose aridity was strikingly suggested, and relieved by a grim but undeniable sense of humor. Here the humor appears only once or twice, and many of the bizarre goings-on seem as gratuitous as the pretty but empty scene in which the main characters watch President Wilson's private train rattle past them: a haunting nocturnal vision but totally uncontributive to any larger structure. After two such films, I begin to worry that alienation is, for this highly talented filmmaker, not so much subject as symptom.

December 22, 1978

For Consenting Adolescents

ONE OF THE MAJOR GENRES of American filmmaking has commonly been labeled "adult love story." There is something odd about the term: Is there such a thing as a children's love story? Well, I suppose there is: child meets dog (horse, hamster, parakeet . . .), child loses dog, child wins back dog. The more pertinent question, then, is why are there so few truly adult love stories in the American cinema? In the past, whether things ended happily or tearfully, the goo, the schmaltz, the treacle were seldom out of camera range. And these days, a supposedly enlightened movie such as *An Unmarried Woman* goes all mushy and muddle-headed—albeit in a "contemporary" way—the moment the heroine meets her ideal mate.

Recently, we have been getting a whole batch of doomed attempts at the genre. *Comes a Horseman* is ostensibly a latter-day western and love story; but the hero (James Caan) is a fellow who inexplicably got out of the Vietnam war early on, and the mere presence of Vietnam in the background vitiates the conventional western maneuverings in the foreground. These concern a ruthless cattle baron (Jason Robards) who wants to own the entire Colorado valley of which he already has the lion's share; the son of a former associate (George Grizzard), who wants to dig up the whole valley in search of oil; and the tough and stubbornly independent daughter of a double-crossed friend of Robards's (Jane Fonda), whom Robards seduced in her salad days, but who now holds out tenaciously against his designs on her body, her hand in marriage, and the little bit of valley property she owns. Part of this ranch, which Miss Fonda runs with one faithful old cowpoke (Richard Farnsworth), she has sold to Caan, whose buddy has been killed by one of Robards's men. Reluctantly, like the tough, stubbornly independent creatures they are, Caan and Fonda make common cause against Robards; slowly, taciturnly, and almost unwillingly (as befits the genre), they end up as lovers.

The clichés continue to proliferate. Farnsworth, like all such faithful retainers, heads for the inevitable, heart-rending last roundup, even as the battle between the forces of good and the forces of evil builds toward a predictably preposterous climax, in which good triumphs not so much by its wisdom as by evil's stupidity. Alas, the film's love story is just as hackneyed as its heroics, which is surprising from a director such as Alan J. Pakula, who, in a previous film with Fonda, *Klute,* managed to save the man-woman relationship from the foolishness of the rest of the script. Here the scenario by Dennis Lynton Clark clearly defeats him.

Gordon Willis's cinematography, although sometimes verging on the arty, is often breathtaking; I, for one, am glad that it concerns itself so much with the weather and the light, which are manifestly the only gold in them thar hills. Noteworthy, too, is the incisive performance by Jane Fonda, who has finally shaken the last vestiges of her Vassar accent, the one small blemish on some of her previous outstanding work. Farnsworth, too, is good in a stock way; the others rely on their respective histrionic shortcuts, of which Caan's is the shortest. Caan allows his glistening teeth to wag his entire performance, and there are a few nocturnal exterior long shots in which the whole valley seems to be illuminated solely by the light of those silvery teeth.

A still more obvious love story—more obvious in every way—is John G. Avildsen's *Slow Dancing in the Big City,* which has to do with the smiling-through-tears and weeping-through-gags romance of a hefty New York columnist of the Jimmy Breslin school and the icy, remote, fanatically dedicated ballerina who wants none of him. Each has a secret. His, unbeknown to him, is that under his tough hide and lingo beats a heart of molasses, so that he will actually risk his safety for the little people he writes about. Hers, which she discovers midway through the movie, is that under her impeccable physical discipline lurks a dread muscular disease: if she does not stop dancing, she will lose even the ability to walk.

In the best cinematic tradition, she keeps her secret from everyone (just as the singlehanded hero clandestinely seeks out the lair of some Hispanic hoodlums in an attempt to save a bright little Puerto Rican boy from the heroin addiction into which his criminal elder brother is pushing him), and she has her one great triumph in Lincoln Center, at the end of which the hero (whom by now she loves) has to carry her onstage for the curtain calls. The hero himself almost doesn't make it to the theater on time: he has been searching for the Puerto Rican boy, whom he was going to redeem by taking him to the ballet, but who has died pitifully from an overdose given him by his brother. Still, against a background of lost lives and careers, hero and heroine face a future of radiant happiness.

If this summary of Barra Grant's nauseating screenplay is not enough for you, let me assure you that the details of the dialogue and direction are sufficient to suffocate all but the gushiest sentimentalists. Miss Grant's verbal invention is an awesome amalgam of Ben Hecht (remember *his* ballet film, *Specter of the Rose?)*, Jean Kerr, and Richard Brautigan; Avildsen's direction, on the heels of the same director's *Rocky,* gives us a *Rocky* on points. Paul Sorvino, who is a very able actor, plays the columnist as the world's biggest, cuddliest teddy bear; Anne Ditchburn, a Canadian ballerina and choreographer, acts the doomed dancer as someone who will never act again. Miss Ditchburn has an inexpressive face and a gray, monotonous voice; even the ballet she has choreographed to Bill Conti's vulgar music is a gross travesty of *The Rite of Spring,* so earnest as to constitute the film's only true humor.

But surely the most misbegotten of today's stories is *Once in Paris* . . . , written and directed by Frank D. Gilroy. Gilroy once wrote a good, honest play, *Who'll Save the Plowboy?* (1962), which remained unappreciated; then went on to win every possible prize with a highly commercial play, *The Subject Was Roses;* and has proceeded to turn out stage and screen pap ever since. The hero of *Once in Paris* . . . is a happily married screenwriter (Wayne Rogers, an awful actor) who, commissioned to rewrite somebody's screenplay now being shot in Paris, comes to that city for the first time, relatively late in his life. (And very late in ours, as viewers of movies about the overphotographed *ville* Lumière et Méliès.) Rogers, who divides his and our time between faltering bouts with his French phrase book and wide-eyed wonder at the sights and folkways of Paris, exhibits a lack of tourist savvy that would do discredit to a John Wayne.

He promptly gets involved with a hipsterish chauffeur (Jack Lenoir), who introduces him to the joys of Gallic living, and a glamorous neighbor at the Hotel Régina (Gayle Hunnicutt, whom it is nice to see again, though the Régina, after similar use in *The Other Side of Midnight,* begins to pall), who initiates him into the pleasures of cosmopolitan adultery. Watching this movie is comparable to reading an article in *Seventeen* about the glories of Paris, while sipping a *vin ordinaire* gone slightly sour. After a parade of visual and aural clichés—shot, directed, and acted true to stereotype—we are finally treated to a slightly ambiguous ending, but this presumably adult element is scarcely more thought-provoking than the standard shot of the Eiffel Tower.

The film is made even more embarrassing by its obvious air of autobiography: the shy-making expiatory confession of what I take to be an early peccadillo of Gilroy's. One is confirmed in this belief by the fact that the dreadful revised scenario of the film-within-the-film ends with a freeze frame, just as the film does; and by the fact that the sincere, naïve, thoroughly decent bore of a hero corresponds to the auctorial persona Gilroy has been painstakingly evolving. Unless he gets rid of the sentimental blarney, Gilroy risks remaining a *homo unius libri.*

January 5, 1979

Lame Deer

ALREADY ON ITS WAY to becoming the most controversial movie of both 1978 (when it was shown for a week to qualify for the Oscars) and 1979 (when it is going to play the major cities across the country as a road-show attraction) is *The Deer Hunter,* a three-hour film that Universal considered a white elephant and almost didn't release. The movie has garnered many glowing write-ups, as well as the New York Film Critics' prize and other awards, and will doubtless gain further official accolades; it is also incurring the wrath of journalists and other people with Vietnam experience—mostly "doves" who feel that it falsifies the Vietnam war and our involvement in it.

Why shouldn't the director, Michael Cimino—possessor of a Yale M.F.A., protégé of Clint Eastwood, and writer-director of the latter's *Thunderbolt and Lightfoot* by way of main previous experience—falsify the war, considering that he falsifies just about everything he touches? This is the story of three Russian-American steelworkers from Clairton, Pa., a real town that Cimino turns into a fantasticated one. Though quite small, it boasts a gigantic Russian Orthodox church; though conventional in every way, it permits Michael and Nick, two of the three principals, to share a mobile home rather than live with their families until they themselves take wives, as Steven, the third musketeer, appropriately does. The heroine, Linda, when her drunken father slaps her around once too often, moves into that mobile home, one or both of whose owners she is apparently in love with.

All highly unlikely in a tight, provincial ethnic milieu. Moreover, there are hardly any families in evidence. Steven has a shrewish mother who figures noticeably enough (too noticeably, in fact, considering how badly Shirley Stoler plays her); but Linda's alcoholic father quickly vanishes, and the principals are left with no appendages other than a gaggle of giggly blondes, meant mostly to fill the wide screen with their bodies and guffaws. Steven is about to marry an older woman who is pregnant by another man—again an unusual circumstance that the filmmakers don't ever bother to explain. The screenplay is by Deric Washburn (a failed playwright), from a story by Cimino, Washburn, Louis Garfinkle, and Quinn K. Redeker—quite a few cooks for one broth.

The Deer Hunter begins with a farewell drinking session following our threesome's last day at the steel mill: they have enlisted and are off to join the 101st Airborne Division. (Why so late in the game? Why weren't they drafted?) The next major scene is Steven's Russian Orthodox wedding; the third is an interminable wedding-plus-sendoff party at the Legion Hall. This derives clearly from the ball in Visconti's *The Leopard,* but does not justify its inordinate length by the schematic representation of our heroes and their gang as stereotypical boozers, brawlers, and pranksters. (One Green Beret who inexplicably wanders into the proceedings and answers our boys' questions with concise obscenities is a steal from *Baby Blue Marine;* he is just about the only sign of war in the film's early sequences, even though the year must be 1972.) And despite Meryl Streep's strong presence in the role of Linda, women hardly exist in this movie, and matter even less; the concern is with men: their friendship, ritual camaraderie, love, and perhaps something more—although Cimino has vehemently denied any homosexual implications.

Next morning, the gang goes hunting in the mountains; whereas the others exhibit various degrees of indifference or incompetence, Michael hunts with ritual dedication and brings down an abundantly antlered stag cleanly, with a single bullet. Meanwhile, an invisible choir sings Russian hymns and the snow-capped peaks glisten in crystalline approbation. Later, the guys wax sentimental when one of them, fat Welsh, the bar owner, plays Chopin on the piano—fat chance! Thereupon, with a quick cut, we are in the Vietnam inferno.

Here everything proceeds with ruthless speed and disorienting confusion. But this is not the confusion of an individual caught up in the war; rather, it is a confusion the filmmakers wish to implant in the viewers' minds, probably because it is also in their own. It is not clear who is killing whom and why, though it does appear that the Americans are less vicious than the Vietcong or North Vietnamese, or whoever they are. Forthwith, our three friends are reunited as captives of a bunch of monstrous yellow enemies. The next sequences are staged, acted, shot, and edited with the utmost forcefulness; the only trouble is that they make no sense whatsoever.

We are asked to believe that the VC or North Vietnamese would set up their torture camp in a fully exposed site on a riverbank policed by American helicopters; that they would torture the prisoners by, among other things, forcing them to play Russian roulette while heavy bets are placed on which player will survive. We are to swallow the assumptions that the captors are stupid enough to have no guards surrounding the shack where the game is played; that they would idiotically fall for Michael's scheme and allow a pistol to be loaded with three bullets instead of one; and that, even so, this would prove enough for the tortured and weakened Michael and Nick to kill off all their tormentors, despite the submachine guns trained on them. I am afraid that the preposterousness of all this outweighs its technical brilliance.

From here on, this supposedly realistic film goes completely berserk: not a shred of historical, logical, chronological, or psychological credibility remains. I can concentrate only on the major absurdities. After they escape—mainly through Michael's resourcefulness, courage, and strength—our buddies are separated. Nick becomes psychically unbalanced and goes AWOL. He soon turns performer in a Russian-roulette casino; we are to understand that the game has become a sport in Saigon, involving large sums for participants and bettors, and that the bodies of losers pile up outside the casinos like torn-up betting tickets at our racetracks. It is in such a casino that Michael and Nick meet up again (after what they've been through, they are as likely to hang out there as to let a favorite sister marry a North Vietnamese), but Nick, unaccountably, runs away from Michael.

Later, Michael goes home, reluctantly becomes Linda's lover, and restores Steven to his unhappy wife and child. Steven, an unreconstructed double amputee, has been lingering in a VA hospital where Nick sends him lavish checks from Saigon. (How does the by-now-amnesiac Nick manage to do that? How does Steven cash these checks without anyone's noticing?) Only now does Michael realize that Nick is alive (why not before?); he rushes back to Vietnam just as Saigon is falling (how does he wangle his way back in?). After ludicrous coincidences and incredible maneuvers, he tracks down Nick at a Russian-roulette casino that has moved somewhere upstream, in which South Vietnamese war profiteers, who in reality would now be running for their lives, calmly continue their gambling.

The amnesiac Nick has now become the champion Russian-roulette player; he has broken the bank in Saigon—not to mention the law of probability—and after months of playing he is still around to cash in. Michael, whom he does not recognize, in desperation challenges him to a game; only after he has started the cylinder rolling does Nick find his brain clearing—merely to have it promptly blown out by a bullet. As so many times before, we watch blood and brains explode from a temple; remarkably unsplattered, a weeping Michael rocks his true love in his arms, even though only a moron would so shake a dying man.

But never mind the preposterousness of this scene; consider rather the ridiculousness of Russian roulette as the master image for war. There is, of course, no evidence of the game's thriving either as a form of torture or as a spectator sport in Vietnam. It is something that could have been invented only by a jaded Western civilization; it is antithetical to Oriental history, culture, and *Weltanschauung.* Worse yet, it does not function artistically as a metaphor for war: soldiers may survive through sheer luck, but they do not keep gambling voluntarily with their lives. Worst of all, it contradicts Cimino's governing concept of the survival of the fittest: for it is the staunch, self-sacrificing, self-disciplined Michael (his very name, as Pauline Kael notes, makes him the director's alter ego) who emerges unscathed—indeed ennobled, for he no longer kills defenseless deer. His less brave buddies pay with their limbs or lives.

For all its pretensions to something newer and better, this film is only an extension of the old Hollywood war-movie lie. The enemy is still bestial and stupid, and no match for our purity and heroism; only we no longer wipe up the floor with him—rather, we litter it with his guts. The average moviegoer gets no antiwar message from *The Deer Hunter;* he simply identifies himself with Michael—the best—and envisions himself as survivor and hero of the next war to come along. By way of crowning lie, the film ends with the survivors, after Nick's nice, homey funeral, singing "God Bless America"—not exultantly, to be sure, but without a trace of doubt or irony.

It is no wonder that Michael Cimino has made so mendacious a film, since he himself is a liar. As Letitia Kent, who interviewed him for the *Times,* discovered (but, alas, only after the interview), he is not thirty-five but thirty-nine; his M.F.A. from Yale is not in architecture but in the less prestigious field of graphics (hence, no doubt, all those graphically shown horrors); he did not enlist in 1968 in patriotic fervor elicited by the Tet offensive but joined the reserve in 1962 and continued his studies; during his brief service, he was not, as he claims, a medic attached to a Green Beret unit, but had an office job; and all of this took place well before the war really got under way.

All right: Cimino can direct action sequences; and his cast, led by Robert De Niro, Christopher Walken, Meryl Streep, John Savage, and John Cazale, performs expertly before Vilmos Zsigmond's sensitive camera. But is this reason enough for the film to rake in raves, amass awards, and ask the public, when they send in for their expensive, reserved seats, to "specify three alternative dates"? A more reasonable alternative would be to stay away altogether from this dear *Deer Hunter,* the kind of movie dreamed up by kids in a college snack bar over beer and hamburgers.

February 16, 1979

Of Pods and Porn

It is idle to remake a piece of cinematic trash; idler yet if it was a well-made and, on its own terms, highly successful piece of trash; and idlest of all if the remake is far surpassed by the original. That, however, is the case with Phil Kaufman's remake of *Invasion of the Body Snatchers,* Don Siegel's fetching sci-fi thriller of 1956. The story of a small town taken over by "pods" that appropriate the bodies of human beings and destroy their souls—and that become feelingless, conformist nonentities hell-bent on eliminating any remnants of genuine humanity—was particularly timely then. Although it was apparently Siegel's comment on Hollywood, liberals of every stripe were able to interpret it as an attack on McCarthyism, which, indeed, the film may also have been intended to be.

What made Siegel's movie interesting to me was that it did not waste footage on elaborate pseudoscientific explanations and special effects, but concentrated instead on showing what happens to a decent young man in a provincial town who finds that his fellow citizens are, one by one, becoming pods out to get his soul; who never knows which of them is still human and which isn't; and whose girl friend, to his horror, is eventually turned into a pod that lures him into abjuring his soul. There was a routine cop-out forced on the director, to the effect that the FBI was going to stop this plague (how?), but otherwise the film was honest, unassuming, and scary in the profoundest sense: morally.

The new version, from a screenplay by W. D. Richter, goes in for all sorts of bogus metaphysics and biology, wallows in special effects (excellently done, but sidetracking the horror into mere nausea), introduces cutesy *hom-*

mages and in-jokes (it is also a very parochial San Francisco film in various ways), and finally bogs down in second-rate chase sequences. These lead up to an ending that lacks the original's stark simplicity, and becomes rather more tricky than—if I dare use a big word in a humble context—tragic. The hero is now a government food inspector; the heroine is his assistant, who becomes his lover after her boy friend, a kind of TV-sports-besotted pod *avant la lettre,* turns into a bona fide pod and tries to get her, with the help of a psychiatrist (played by Leonard Nimoy with ploddingly unctuous sinisterness) who is a pod master strategist. The podification of a sod is of small concern to us, and the psychiatrist is so obviously evil that he couldn't fool anyone but the most shrink-hating analysand.

The anti-pod faction is similarly trivialized. The hero is far too smart-alecky and is played by Donald Sutherland, who, even when he is good (as here), is pretty bad. As his girl, Brooke Adams is attractive, with her husky-voiced languor—one can never be sure whether it betokens sensuality or somnolence—but the menaced purity of Dana Wynter in the 1956 version made her ultimate co-optation more poignant than Miss Adams's, which also gives rise to a totally unwarranted nude scene. The other virtuous pair is a young married couple, owners of a steam bath; he is a griping, anti-Establishment poet; she, a devoted wife who looks after him and does all the work. Veronica Cartwright is very affecting; Jeff Goldblum merely trots out his by now standard countercultural maunderings.

Particularly annoying are Denny Zeitlin's blatantly electronic score—which carries on as if the movie were only the visual adjunct to its musical dramatics—and all the in-jokes, such as Robert Duvall making a gratuitous appearance as an ominously idling priest on a playground swing (a shaggy dog-collar story?), or the director and the star of the original *Invasion* (Don Siegel and Kevin McCarthy) popping up in cameo roles. The cinematographer, Michael Chapman, continues to unimpress me. One of the more pedestrian toilers in a field that now has many true creators, Chapman is a favorite with certain trendy directors and reviewers for reasons I find unfathomable.

Equally unrelated to any existential truth, though in a different way, is Paul Schrader's *Hardcore.* This is the story of a Grand Rapids furniture manufacturer (George C. Scott), a staunch Calvinist, whose daughter winds up, through a series of nebulous circumstances, making hardcore pornographic movies in southern California. When a sleazy private detective (Peter Boyle) proves no better than the police at tracking her down, Scott himself goes out to Los Angeles and searches for his daughter high and low—or, rather, low and lower—through the world of porn filmmaking, massage parlors, prostitution, etc. By pretending to produce a homosexual porn film, he tracks down one of the actors in a movie the girl is in; then, with the help of a young prostitute (Season Hubley), he finally finds his daughter in San Francisco, now the mistress of an utterly vile producer of snuff films (in which sadistic murders are actually perpetrated). Boyle kills the escaping villain—highly unlikely for a mere private eye to do, for both legal and psychological reasons—and Scott is at last alone with his wayward daughter. She calls him a disgusting creep (in language much worse than this), proclaims her love for her producer-pimp, and refuses to go back to her allegedly loveless home. A minute later, however, she is lovingly reconciled with her daddy and obediently follows him. And Scott, who promised Miss Hubley that he would help get her out of her unsavory life, fumbles a feeble attempt at help, then leaves her in the lurch.

Clearly, the two key relationships in *Hardcore* are Scott's with his daughter and Scott's with the young hooker who becomes a kind of surrogate daughter to him while they search together—she doing it for the money at first, then out of a certain respect for Scott.

Take the first relationship. In the early sequences of the film, life in a midwestern Calvinist family is presented as warm, congenial, full of heartening solidarity. There is no indication whatsoever that the teen-aged daughter could have any reason for resenting her father. The vital scenes of how she is recruited for hardcore work, and how and why she takes to it, are simply omitted. So her final rejection of a seemingly splendid father makes—in the film's terms, at least—no sense at all. And, given that rejection, her prompt reversal makes even less sense: it is having both a tough, realistic ending and a cozy, upbeat ending at one foul swoop.

Now take the Scott-Hubley nexus. She belongs to the Venusian Cult, he is a pillar of the Dutch Reformed Church. They talk about their religious beliefs without affecting each other. She tries to have sex with him, which he easily refuses. It emerges in a conversation that his wife left him, presumably because of his lack of concern for her sexual well-being, but very little is made of this. Finally, when Miss Hubley has become more of a daughter to him than his real daughter, Scott nevertheless ditches her. Throughout the movie, he is preposterously invulnerable, resourceful, efficient, indomitable. Yet, somehow, even he is made out to be an emotional failure. Nobody learns anything from anyone.

Schrader has stated that the film is a tribute to his Calvinist father, but it is an equivocal tribute at best. Despite some possibly authentic glimpses into California's sexual underworld, it does not go deeply enough into character; it cannot show people in the process of changing—it can only show them having undergone sensational turnabouts, or rubbing shoulders without rubbing off on each other. The notion that Scott could impersonate a swinging middle-aged producer of homosexual hardcore is totally unbelievable. A man with the requisite flexibility and wit could never be such a rigid Calvinist at his hard, inflexible core. Except for illustrating Schrader's love-hate for his origins and, I suspect, an unhealthy curiosity about a morbid world (there is no real understanding for its victims save for a superficial pat on Miss Hubley's back), the film has no human, truth-telling value. In a supposedly earnest, artistic film, can the lack of sympathetic insight and the mechanistic manipulation of character be so readily forgiven as the mostly respectful reviews imply? Perhaps our critics could themselves use a dose of Calvinism.

March 16–April 13, 1979

Timely and Untimely

WHATEVER ELSE IT ISN'T, *The China Syndrome* must be the luckiest film ever made. This story of near-disaster in an atomic power plant was heralded by circulars from various scientific bodies assuring us that it was a disaster movie of the worst kind because its scare tactics had a more realistic look and played on more fundamental fears than all those supercolossal potboilers about blazing skyscrapers and killer bees. Yet hardly had the film opened across the nation when a strikingly similar incident occurred at the Three Mile Island nuclear facility located at a town named, with the perfection of a press agent's dream come true, Middletown. A line in the film says that such an accident could wipe out an area the size of Pennsylvania—which is where Middletown is. What has Columbia Pictures done to deserve this much from fate?

In *The China Syndrome* (a metaphoric term for a catastrophic meltdown in a nuclear reactor), Jane Fonda plays a rapidly rising Los Angeles TV reporter who is straining for more serious assignments; she and her cameraman, Michael Douglas, an unreconstructed sixties student radical, find themselves on a routine tour of a nuclear power plant. A near-catastrophe (later pooh-poohed by the management) occurs, and Douglas surreptitiously films it. The footage, almost as explosive as the atom bomb, is shelved by the pusillanimous TV station manager (Peter Donat), under pressure from the powerful chairman of the board of the power plant—to Douglas's utter and Miss Fonda's considerable rage. Douglas steals back his film while Miss Fonda gets in touch with Jack Lemmon, the plant supervisor, in whom she stirs up doubts about whether the event was really so trivial as they had been told, and even about the desirability of nuclear power plants.

Lemmon does a bit of research and finds out that some of the equipment was inadequately tested, but that the management refuses to incur the loss of revenue proper corrective testing would entail. He proposes to reveal these facts to an outside investigation that is under way, but the strong criminal arm of management is by now out to get him and anyone else who could hurt the corporate interest. One of Douglas's assistants, carrying Lemmon's evidence, is nearly killed, and the evidence is absconded with; Lemmon has no choice but to lock himself into the bulletproof-glass control room of the plant and threaten to blow it up unless Miss Fonda and Douglas are permitted to interview him *in situ* for television, thus alerting the public to the danger from the flawed plant.

I should not reveal any more of the plot, but I must say that this taut, intelligent, and chillingly gripping thriller turns in the end unduly melodramatic—a bit too improbable even for a genre that thrives on exaggeration. The conclusion is both false and bathetic. Getting the story on television by making a hitherto frightened assistant of Lemmon's talk into a microphone is giving that questionable medium an undeserved halo; and an explosion in the plant, which surely would have permitted perilous radiation to escape, is glossed over as harmless. The idea was to have shots of terrifyingly collapsing structures without making the film too scary: having your catastrophe without losing your box office. Worst of all, Lemmon, so resourceful and strong till the end, must suddenly and improbably turn to jelly.

Still, even aside from its extraordinary timeliness (life, which has been known to imitate art, has now included cinematic melodrama in its repertoire), *The China Syndrome* has other robust virtues. Recent movies have laid the blame for the world's ills on everyone from the Mafia to Mom, but have tended to spare big business, which here at last gets its well-deserved lumps. Its kid-gloved sinisterness is shown as hiding some mighty knuckle-dusters, and not till the end does the script itself turn heavy-handed with overstatement. The efforts of a sexy but also talented TV newswoman to upgrade herself from soft to hard news are chronicled with a fine irony that speaks louder than feminist frenzy. There is a whole slew of convincingly delineated minor characters, and the plant supervisor in his agonizing dilemma very nearly becomes a genuine tragic hero. Jack Lemmon trenchantly portrays this unspectacular man's rise to great moral heights as well as his ultimate collapse: no one can convey specious cheerfulness better than Lemmon or make you feel more clammily sweaty under the collar.

The only trouble is that, however good he is, Lemmon somehow remains himself; Jane Fonda, conversely, seems born anew with every dead-on-target performance. Here, it is exciting to watch the character's awakening social consciousness overpower but never quite dislodge a fund of show-biz egomania. Michael Douglas is boringly himself as the cameraman, and the fact that he often mispronounces "nuclear" as "nucular" does not further endear him. In general, though, the film's strongest suit is the casting: excellent but little-known supporting actors (among whom Wilford Brimley as the intimidated assistant is outstanding) give the film a documentary quality, assisted also by the no-nonsense direction of James Bridges, even if it may lean a trifle too heavily on the old device of crosscutting. The screenplay by Mike Gray, T. S. Cook, and Bridges pays laudable attention to details, including much near-subliminal dialogue that nevertheless has cumulative impact in, say, evoking the chaotic shenanigans of TV broadcasting. James Crabe's cinematography, incisive without artiness, hits the spot, as does George Jenkins's production design. Even without Three Mile Island, *The China Syndrome* would be worth seeing; with it, it may well be a must.

There was no good reason for making a movie out of the musical *Hair* at a time too early for nostalgia and too late for anything else. Miloš Forman, the director, got the interesting young playwright Michael Weller *(Moonchildren,* etc.) to supply a story line for what was essentially a plotless stage show. This proves a double deprivation: for the sake of plodding padding, several good songs had to be cut. Still others, like the title song, no longer fit into the scheme of things: what have prisoners jumping all over their jail to do with "Hair"? Forman, in fact, has made some extraordinary mistakes, such as engaging a major choreographer, Twyla Tharp, and then allowing the camera to perform a rival choreography of its own, undercutting and, finally, almost obliterating the world according to Tharp.

Even more serious a problem is that of sympathy, which Forman clearly—and rightly, in this context—wants to go to the flower children (whatever they may have been like in reality); yet the actors portraying them—and particularly Treat Williams, as their leader—are so thoroughly unappetizing that one finds oneself rooting for the wealthy stuffed shirts, the police, the army, and all the other adversary powers the film would have us reprehend. Moreover, Forman has cast as Sheila, the upper-class heroine whose conversion to hippiedom is the crux of the tale, Beverly D'Angelo, whose lack of talent, charm, looks, and hauteur is such that she could no more pass for upper-crust than a camel for the thread in a needle's eye.

With the exception of Miles Chapin, who plays a typical preppy to frightening perfection, and Cheryl Barnes, who brings a grave poise to the cliché part of an unwed and abandoned black mother, there are only undistinguished or bad performers at work. John Savage, so fine in *The Deer Hunter,* plays the naïve farm boy who turns hippie and then near-cannon-fodder stolidly, like someone to the manure born and not to be weaned from it. There are two good things about *Hair,* however, but only two. One is the "Black Boys, White Boys" number, in which a homosexual draft board comically lusts for the inductees; the other is a sequence in which the brilliant camera of Miroslav Ondriček captures in terms of chiaroscuro the fate awaiting a long line of soldiers marching into, and being engulfed by, a transport plane for Vietnam. For this, Forman's eye also deserves praise, as it does for the sudden cut to a field of military graves. But even two swallows do not make a summer.

May 11, 1979

Hokum of Yore

In their current desperation, movies will stop at nothing—not even at turning back the clock to a time remote enough for the clock not yet to have been invented. As a nostrum against feminism, for example, we have now a spate of pictures about variously invalided young women, rendered weak enough to be sorely in need of old-fashioned male protection. And then there are all-around tearjerkers whose suffering heroes and heroines live in times that have not the slightest lived-in look.

Consider Franco Zeffirelli's *The Champ,* a remake of the 1931 King Vidor movie (rancid even in its own day) in which everything is brought up to date except the film's mentality. We are to believe, in this Walter Newman script, that Jon Voight, a former world-champion boxer, is reduced to being a stableboy at the Hialeah race track in A.D. 1979, and also an incorrigible boozer and gambler. But ever since his wife, Faye Dunaway, walked out on him to marry a millionaire gerontologist and set herself up as a leading fashion designer (from rags to riches in a few years, perhaps; but from rags to haute couture?), Voight has been bringing up their son, little Ricky Schroder, with the kind of paternal solicitude we have come to expect from a morally untarnished crap-shooting alcoholic.

To complete the film's unreality, Voight has no sex life, keeps the boy spotless inwardly and outwardly, and never speaks ill of the boy's supposedly dead mother, even while he walks horses rather than making a boodle out of TV commercials and, say, a string of restaurants. Needless to say, remarried mother and seven-year-old cherub meet cute at the race track, and Faye almost makes a mint by betting on the filly that the boy won cute. But, while in the lead, the horse takes a tumble and throws its jockey. The horse recovers: they don't shoot horses that are injured cute, do they? On the other hand, or hoof, the miraculously restored horse is not permitted to win another race and make its precocious owner rich: a victory at Aqueduct would mean a defeat at the tear ducts.

I will spare you the rest of the story, but must tell you a bit more about Zeffirelli, who, not content with having reduced *Romeo and Juliet* to a kind of musicless *West Side Story,* has gone on to film nauseating biographies of Saint Francis and Jesus Christ. If this great Christian is not stopped in time (as his colleague Pier Paolo Pasolini, whom he resembles in every way except talent, was—albeit in a gruesome way one would not wish on anybody), he will manage to turn every saint in the calendar into a feebly animated waxwork lacking even the simple, primitive piety of an ex-voto. In an early film of Lina Wertmüller's, a bankrupt husband says to his spoiled wife who is nobly simpering about shared poverty, "Your idea of poverty is a garret in *La Bohème* designed by Franco Zeffirelli."

In Zeffirelli's world, a loving father can safely abandon his adorable son on a street corner in the shadiest section of town; a mother's love expresses itself through Faye Dunaway's lunging at Ricky Schroder across a bed as if to drag him instantly between the sheets (Miss Dunaway's playing late-blooming mother love as a rampant form of libido doesn't help); and transitions between scenes are effectuated by cutting to a shot of shocking-pink flamingos or a skyful of pelicans (unless they, too, were flamingos—my eyes were too tear-clouded to tell the difference) flying in formation. Miss Dunaway is allowed to give a performance unworthy even of *The Eyes of Laura Mars;* Voight, his talent not entirely dimmed even by *The Champ,* is nevertheless made to speak and behave in dem-dere-dat terms; and precious Master Schroder could lose even his cooking-oil commercials—who wants to cook with syrup? Fred Konekamp, a good cinematographer, is obliged to shoot rigorously color-coordinated backgrounds, even when the locale is a stable or police station, as if he were a fashion photographer gone slumming.

May 25, 1979

Nattahnam

AT THE ROUND EARTH'S IMAGIN'D CORNERS—or, at any rate, in four theaters throughout this eponymous borough—we can now see Woody Allen's *Manhattan*. This is a bittersweet comedy about Isaac Davis (Woody Allen, in more ways than one), who gives up a lucrative job as a TV comedy writer to undertake a serious novel about life in Manhattan. His best friends are Yale, a Hunter College English prof grinding out a book on Eugene O'Neill, and Yale's wife, Emily. Isaac has been twice divorced, latterly from Jill, who left him for her lesbian girl friend, Connie. Jill got custody of their son (unlikely!) and, to make matters worse, is bringing out a book with intimate details about their marriage and divorce. Isaac's girl friend is Tracy, a forthright, unspoiled seventeen-year-old who, when others boast about their literary lives, answers the question, "And what do you do?" with a disarming "I go to high school."

Isaac is a bit bothered by Tracy's youth, even though she is loving, kind, and (literally) incredibly wise. So when the married Yale pushes Mary Wilke, a suddenly bothersome extracurricular flame, at him, Isaac, though initially repelled by the militantly cerebral ways of this snotty young woman of letters, ends up getting involved with her.

He leaves the heartbroken Tracy for bright and brittle Mary, sophisticated but intensely neurotic and still hankering for Yale. When the latter's virtuous resolve runs out, Mary rushes back to him; Isaac, deeply hurt and furious, races back to Tracy, now eighteen and "legal." She is on her way to London to study drama—just what Isaac used to urge her to do. Now he tries everything to stop her, and if she weren't on the way to the airport and didn't have her parents waiting in London, she might indeed desist. The wise, newly legalized young girl tells the anxious forty-two-year-old child whom she still loves: "Six months isn't so long. Not everybody gets corrupted. You must have a little faith in people."

Manhattan is a profoundly and multifariously dishonest picture. It can be read in both directions, as if it were written simultaneously in English and Hebrew. As *Manhattan*, it is the story of a decent little fellow who shakes off TV commercialism, moves into a more modest apartment, and tries to authenticate his life as an artist. His conscience protests against his affair with a minor, his basic honor resents his ex-wife's shenanigans. He disapproves of Mary's pretensions and condescension, her narcissism, her adulterous affair, and her excessive dependence on her shrink: "You don't see anything suspicious when your analyst calls you up at three in the morning and weeps on the telephone?" Nevertheless, he loves and does right by her, only to be double-crossed by both her and his best friend, Yale. Finally, he recognizes—better late than never—what true love is, and the film ends on a sadly sweet note of hope.

Read backward, however—and the continuous flip humor demands that it be read thus—*Nattahnam* is all tongue-in-cheek cynicism. Isaac is a bit of a schnook, redeemed only partially by his wisecracks; Mary, though dazzling, is also a fool and a sickie; Tracy has previously had three affairs with boys and is, for all her extolled precocious perspicacity, also childishly uncomprehending—as when she comments about aging TV performers with face-lifts, "Why can't they just age naturally?" Jill and Connie are clever, cold women, obviously created during a milk-of-human-kindness strike; Emily is a cipher—of the kind, incidentally, that no true artist would allow in his film.

What remains is a set of sometimes funny one-liners parading in front of a background of Manhattan's most spectacular vistas, most with-it hangouts, and most romantic nooks, to the accompaniment of a score of Gershwin favorites played by two separate but equally symphonic orchestras. Yet even Manhattan is undercut: when Isaac and Mary row around Central Park Lake, his hand trailing in the water gets caught in a piece of oversized offal.

Look at that closing speech of Tracy's, in response to Isaac's fear that she will lose her innocence and her love for him: "Six months isn't so long." Very sensible. "Not everybody gets corrupted." Why is the dear little cherub even talking about corruption? Surely what Isaac is afraid of is the long separation and other men or boys. So could that irrelevant "corruption" express a secret wish of the angel to tangle with the world, the flesh, and the devil? In which case, her "You must have a little faith in people" (this to Isaac, who has always had too much faith in people) is the final sardonic twist. Or is it?

Or take that Gershwin score in monstrous overorchestrations by the New York and Buffalo Philharmonics. Is it as grand and romantic as New York, or are we being buffaloed into swallowing overblown pretensions—nice little tunes Mantovanied up into a huge crock of mammoth soup? I submit that art does not work like this.

If I invoke art as a criterion, it is because the shy and shrinking Allen insists, in his numerous recent interviews, that his film is serious art and presents a view of Manhattan and its denizens ready for encapsulation in artistic eternity. It is also because the majority of reviewers and audiences have hailed *Manhattan,* even more than *Annie Hall,* as a masterwork, thus allowing Allen to see himself more and more as what some have called him: the American Ingmar Bergman. (Several tributes to Bergman in the film corroborate this.)

Art, to be sure, does not have to provide answers; indeed, the greatest art is probably always ultimately ambiguous, leaving us finally with a question mark. But it also leaves us with insights, epiphanies, a climate of elation in which it is easier to breathe in the perennial problems, more possible to live with them according to our individual lights. *Manhattan,* however, is two-faced rather than ambiguous: both a self-serving exaltation of Allen and his values, and, if one were to challenge them, a perfect setup for Allen and his collaborator, Marshall Brickman, to snap back: "You simpleton! Don't you see that it's all satire, all a put-on?"

But is it? When Yale and Mary play a cocktail-party intellectuals' game of smirkingly nominating members for "the Academy of the Overrated"—Mahler, Mailer, Lenny Bruce, Jung, Böll, Fitzgerald, van Gogh, and Bergman are swiftly disposed of—we are clearly to side with Isaac, who makes fun of this nonsense. But later, when Isaac himself dictates to his tape recorder the things that make life worth living—Groucho Marx, Willie Mays, the second movement of the *Jupiter* Symphony, Louis Armstrong's "Potatohead Blues," Swedish movies, Frank Sinatra, Marlon Brando, apples and pears by Cézanne, the crabs at Sam Wo, and Tracy's face—we are patently invited to take this absurd hodgepodge seriously. (And what, by the way, is wrong with the other movements of the *Jupiter?)*

Or is Isaac-Allen also a figure of fun? We are, for instance, constantly told about his successes with women, his good looks, his great amatory technique. This is meant partly in jest, but partly also, I am sure, as truth. After all, a sexy lesbian was moved to marry him, little Tracy adores him (for reasons that are never made remotely clear), and even brainy, beautiful Mary, who "could have had the entire MIT faculty," chooses Isaac over MIT as a cure for Yale.

But if the film and its hero are a joke, why all this self-adulation and Manhattan-boosting? And if the film is a "serious" comedy, why must Isaac, even at the height of his jealous grief and rage, wisecrack with Yale ("You think you're God!" "I've got to model myself after someone!")? Why must even semivirginal Tracy consider corruption? Why must there be ludicrous dung in the enchanted lagoon? Because Allen is insecure, as no true artist is, but as a fellow who wants to be both Groucho Marx (or Woody Allen) and Bergman (or Mozart, or Cézanne) will be. Having it both ways is not having it at all.

On the credit side, we get fine performances by both Mariel Hemingway (Tracy) and Meryl Streep (Jill), and spectacular black-and-white cinematography from Gordon Willis. On the debit side, there are also the other performances, especially those of Diane Keaton, who, as Mary, is yet again not acting but mugging and blithering; and Michael Murphy, who, as Yale, is even more nondescript than his part. But don't get me wrong: *I* am not ambivalent. *Manhattan* and *Nattahnam* are bad movies both.

The film—or films—should also be recognized as a moral, human failure—its ethics as deficient as its aesthetics. To start with a couple of specific examples. One of the high points of hilarity occurs when Mary, during an already comic sequence, gets a phone call from which it emerges that her analyst—whom she calls Donnie, and who is given to phoning her at 3 A.M. and crying on her shoulder—is in a coma from having taken an overdose of drugs. This is presented as a laugh line and has the audience duly in stitches. There may, of course, be the odd psychiatrist who does go to pieces, but the implication here is that—like most artists and almost all intellectuals in the film—psychiatrists are frauds as a group. In any case, nobody's coma is a laughing matter, except in an absurdist context; that, however, is not the framework in which this film operates. And the joke is particularly offensive coming from Allen, who has been in psychotherapy for years.

Worse yet is a wisecrack during a storm scene in Central Park. Isaac grouses about the danger of being struck by lightning: "I don't want to turn into one of those guys who sell comic books outside Bloomingdale's." The jocular reference here is quite specific: to one particular wretched man, a victim of cerebral palsy or something like it, who sells old comic books outside Bloomingdale's. This seems to be triply reprehensible. First, because the poor fellow, who has indeed been knocked over by an occasional gust of wind, is hardly a fit subject for mirth, least of all from someone as successful and rich as Allen, who, instead of ridiculing him, could afford to help out financially. Second, this awkward and unsightly creature does not look so very different from Allen himself, who owes his self-deluding success with women to the sexual appeal of power, which alone permits him to condescend to his *semblable* and *frère* outside Bloomingdale's. Third, Allen lacks even the courage of his inhuman convictions: he changes the *single* man outside the department store into "those guys"—either to dilute, however piddlingly, the sting of the remark, or to avoid legal complications should a champion of the unfortunate fellow present himself.

Yet the bad moral climate of *Manhattan* is not confined to such isolated moments. As in *Annie Hall,* there is again, and still more strongly, the implication that women are wicked or boring and can be redeemed solely through loving Woody Allen, the only decent male on the scene. Thus Isaac's two former wives have not only left him, but also gone on to lives that are perceived as absurd, if not contemptible. The second wife, the lesbian Jill, even publishes a tasteless book about the failed marriage, gratuitously or meretriciously exposing Isaac's foibles to the world of prurient gossip. Emily, the wife of Isaac's two-timing friend Yale, is a dull and pathetic creature, clumsily trying to hold on to her husband by wanting a baby, which would only make for yet another miserable life. Mary, of course, is a total mess, morally, mentally, and emotionally. Only the teen-aged Tracy, who adores Isaac even after he throws her over, may have true moral stature.

And the men? Yale is a liar, cheat, weakling, and exploiter of his best friend; Jeremiah, the ex-husband whom Mary keeps talking of as an intellectual giant and sexual demigod, is revealed to be a puny and unappetizing nonentity (played by Wallace Shawn—perhaps the only actor in New York who looks worse than Woody Allen), or, as Isaac puts it pleonastically, a "little homunculus." Even marginal male figures turn out to be such unsavory things as directors of pretentiously pseudo-intellectual pornographic movies.

Oh, but Isaac is good and pure and lovable for all his filigree peccadillos—indeed, because of them. He is a loving father to his son and even maintains good feelings for the boy's faithless, lesbian mother; he does not make a play for Mary until Yale hands her over on a platter of silver-tongued lying oratory; he lets down Tracy in the most forthright, sympathetic, and paternally concerned way, and then becomes a patient and supportive lover to the infuriating Mary; finally, when he returns repentantly to Tracy, although he does try to prevent her sensible and justified departure for London, his behavior is not inconsistent with genuine albeit belated passion, and he does give in gracefully and touchingly as the film ends. And even in his righteous anger and hurt, Isaac confronts Yale without falling into undignified pathos or violence; quite improbably, he keeps cracking jokes and winning at wit while losing in love.

Yet even this unappetizingly smug self-exaltation is not the ultimate moral (and intellectual) failure of the film. Most irresponsible is the implication that a thoroughly decent man of forty-two can find fulfillment in love and sex only with a seventeen-year-old girl. Mind you, it is neither Tracy's age nor the difference in ages between Tracy and Isaac—not even the underlying real-life nexus between Allen and Hemingway—that bothers me: if Humbert Humbert and Lolita could have found happiness together, I would have been all for it. What I deplore is the notion that maturing corrupts people, and that only beings as privilegedly childlike as Isaac and Tracy (though even *she* may be corrupted by six months in swinging London) can truly love. If there is anything our era does not need—on screen or elsewhere—it is a paean to immaturity, an attempt to pass off infantilism as the sole protector of our amatory relationships.

Alien is an expensively produced space-horror picture in which interstellar voyagers find their spacecraft invaded by a virtually indestructible monster that devours them one by one. The movie, directed by Ridley Scott (who seems to have a Conrad fixation: his first feature, *The Duellists,* was a misguided adaptation of a Conrad story; here, the space ship is called the *Nostromo),* has the usual number of inconsistencies, improbabilities, and outright absurdities characteristic of the sci-fi and horror genres. What is interesting, though, is its hostile critical reception, despite the excellent visual values, direction that is no more hokey than usual in such films, dialogue that (when it is decipherable) is par for the course, and acting that is generally superior.

What earmarks *Alien* as a probable audience hit and certifiable critical flop is merely that the horror is more horrible than usual, and the loathsomeness—for loathsomeness there certainly is—basically unfudged. In other words, cinematic horror is running into the same problem that sex and violence ran into earlier. The appetite for sex and violence seems inexhaustible and, by and large, unimpeded as long as these are rendered grotesquely, unbelievably, or just plain ineptly. Thus sex and violence—and now horror—are convicted only for their convincingness—conviction for conviction, as it were. For fanciers of horror, among whose numbers I do not count myself, *Alien* is recommendable, provided that they are free from hypocrisy and finicky stomachs; the leading performance by the appealing and gifted Sigourney Weaver can be recommended to others as well.

This summer may go down in cinema history as the summer of the horror movies, but none of these can match Barbra Streisand and her latest offering, *The Main Event.* The screenplay, mothered by Gail Parent and forged by Andrew Smith, is a set of absurd contradictions meant to make Streisand appear simultaneously tough, vulnerable, witty, deliciously screwy, brilliant, lovably dumb, skillful, fumbling, feminine, butch, and everything else plus its opposite. It attempts to make both a shark and a goldfish out of a nasty little piranha. Miss Streisand has never looked uglier or acted worse than in this movie coproduced by herself and her husband, which, even in its attitude toward cinematic man-woman relations, cannot make up its nonmind whether the time is 1940 or 1979.

The story concerns a cosmetics millionairess who, suddenly penniless, finds her only asset to be the contract of a worthless boxer (Ryan O'Neal, intended as a tax loss for the heroine, and a dead loss as an actor), a chap who prefers running a driving school built in the shape of a giant boxing glove to getting his pretty face mauled in the ring. By a mixture of shrewdness and happy ineptitude, impudence and alleged charm, Streisand gets O'Neal to become (a) a terrific fighter, (b) her lover, and (c) a quitter who gives up boxing on the verge of triumph to turn into Barbra's undented love object—though I should think that dodging that formidable nose in a clinch might be harder than evading the mightiest uppercut. I leave it to you to determine which of those three plot developments is most preposterous. There is decent supporting work from Paul Sand, Whitman Mayo, and Patti D'Arbanville; Howard Zieff, who nominally directed, cannot be held responsible: directing Streisand must be like trying to get a rogue elephant to cross a street on the green light.

June 22–August 3, 1979

$30 Million in Search of an Author

APOCALYPSE NOW is finally here, so belatedly that even its marketing technique has been anticipated by *The Deer Hunter.* There is a sense in which three years of supercolossal gossip and a cost of at least thirty million dollars cannot be topped by any actual performance, and it is to the film's credit that at least sizable chunks of it are not anticlimactic. Even so, it is a deeply depressing film, because it exhibits to an almost unprecedented degree what T. S. Eliot (who is quoted in it to bad effect) called dissociation of sensibility.

To Eliot this meant that, starting with later seventeenth-century poetry, "the language became more refined, the feeling more crude." So it is in *Apocalypse Now,* where the cinematic language can do just about anything, but the ideas and feelings of the director, Francis Ford Coppola, and his coscenarist, John Milius, are not only crude but also immature and pretentious. Even the notion that Conrad's *Heart of Darkness* could provide the basis for a large-scale attack on the Vietnam war, and modern warfare in general, is puerile and self-serving. Conrad's darkness is a metaphysical darkness that merely manifests itself in existential events; his heart is the everyday, noncombatant heart that we like to imagine as a valentine, but that Yeats taught us is a foul rag-and-bone shop.

The Vietnam war, as Coppola is often able to convey in his film, was a completely un-Kurtzian horror of politics and technology running amuck hand in hand; the last thing it teaches (and, if at all, only incidentally) is the corruptibility of the individual—that a little extra power and relaxation of moral discipline can turn any auricle or ventricle into a chamber of horrors. Captain Willard (Conrad's Marlow), an intelligence officer and proven assassin, is entrusted with the secret mission of killing the charismatic Green Beret Colonel Kurtz who, having become the idol of a rabble composed of Montagnard tribesmen and sundry defectors, crossed over into Cambodia, apparently went berserk, and is engaged in some unspeakable war of his own.

A patrol boat takes Willard upriver. Along the way, every kind of spectacular, grotesque, and horrifying adventure befalls him and the crew. At last, he and the two surviving crewmen make it to Kurtz's Angkor Wat–like headquarters, where bodies hanging from above and heads protruding from below ground greet them everywhere, along with a sinisterly scowling soldiery or mob. After a ridiculous game of cat-and-mouse between Kurtz and Willard (and an obvious uncertainty on Coppola's part about how to end the movie), the captain quite easily kills the colonel, walks through hostile ranks back to his boat, and takes off.

The Conradian plot elements are forcibly and fuzzily superimposed on unrelated matter. Most obvious is the upriver trip by boat, when a helicopter would have been faster and safer. As a crowning absurdity, there is mail for Willard that arrives handily by helicopter to meet him near his destination, which he reached only by the skin of his teeth. The Willard-Kurtz relationship, for all that Willard dutifully studies Kurtz's dossier on the way upriver, never amounts to anything like a Conradian secret sharing of two lives. The Kurtzian horrors depicted here are banal and hardly worse than what Willard and we have been seeing all along, and there is no clear sense of their stemming from a potentially basic human loss of control, from fallibility of moral choice. Certain incidents, such as an attack with poison darts, make sense in Conrad's Africa only, and are, in any case, small beer compared to the wholesale slaughter that surrounds them. Every allusion to Conrad strikes me as gratuitous—as a desperate attempt to confer shape on the shapeless, prestige on the epigone.

The opening shots of the film are among the best: lush tropical trees shuddering as helicopters whiz by so close that the eye can barely fathom what it sees; next, the trees go up in flames. The image subsumes and virtually makes expendable all that follows. We are immediately put off by Willard's a little too arbitrary-looking suicidal tantrums: a strategic error, for we need an initially sane Willard if his gradual deterioration is to have deeper meaning. But Coppola feels he must start with a bang if he will end with a whimper. (Kurtz, by the way, recites "The Hollow Men" to his followers, a notion whose ludicrousness is surpassed only by the way Marlon Brando reads the famous verses.)

Things improve, however, in the scene in which a general and his henchmen test and brief Willard for the mission of having Kurtz "terminated with extreme prejudice." G. D. Spradlin is marvelous as the general of whom it is hard to say whether he is more or less derailed than his designated victim. The entire scene, culminating in a hearty last supper, has a subdued, unreal, unstated ghastliness about it that is more dreadful than anything to come.

Still, Coppola is very good at capturing the grandiose dementia of war, the murderous efficiency that has a certain gorgeousness to it as long as one is not on the receiving end. Whether the merrily unhinged Lieutenant Colonel Kilgore (perfectly played by Robert Duvall) is conducting a cavalry-charge-like helicopter raid on a village or, as a surfing freak, is ordering his men to perform aquatic stunts before the smoke has settled and blood has dried; whether this officer comments on a blazing jungle, "I love the smell of napalm. . . . It smells like victory," or whether American patrol boats are playing live-ammunition-shooting bumper cars with one another, there is believable horror galore. But then we veer into unbelievable horror.

When an outpost company that is fighting insanely responds to Willard's inquiry about who their commanding officer is with a serious "Ain't you?"; when, deep in VC territory, a huge nocturnal fest is arranged, with *al giorno* illumination, for *Playboy* bunnies to entertain troops who start rioting and constitute a prime aerial target; when, again by night, a strategic bridge is festooned with more lights than an amusement park's roller coaster and is duly bombed to smithereens by the enemy—well, you begin to wonder whether this is still a legitimate vision of war, even making allowances for surrealism and absurdism, or whether it is a Coney Island of the minds of Coppola and Milius.

Then, when Willard, a burnt-out case to begin with (played stolidly by Martin Sheen), reaches Kurtz—a Brando who has become an obscene, secular Buddha with shaven head and ballooning midriff, whose voice emerges like the squeal of a mouse from a ridiculous mountain (actually, they had to use a less fat body model for the few shots in which it isn't only Brando's head that we divine as it drowns in chiaroscuro)—two dullards confront each other over a thin gruel of pretentious platitudes or portentous understatement, and the film becomes worse than bad—abject.

There are two large problems that envelop even the positive aspects. Vittorio Storaro's cinematography is remarkable, catching, as it were, the half tones and quarter tones of the color scale, and Coppola knows how to hurl the camera into the action so as to stop just short of self-annihilation—the way an acrobat dives from a tower into a shallow trough of water. But all this exhilaration and lyricism of war (I am reminded of Apollinaire's even more wonderful, but equally suspect, war poems, such as *"Merveilles de la guerre,"* or the one beginning, *"Ah Dieu! que la guerre est jolie")* is not really licit, is not decent stuff to put into a movie that purports to excoriate war. Battles may seduce the desperate or crazed combatant, but what is an allegedly antiwar filmmaker doing mucking around in this tainted ecstasy?

Finally, I feel uneasy letting this footage (only an infinitesimal fraction of what was wastefully shot) suck me into the screen: these multicolored flares, incandescent floodlights, infernal conflagrations; or conversely this opulent vegetation, fulgurating foliage interrupted now and then by the carcass of a helicopter impaled on the branches it ravaged; or just these squadrons of superbly drilled whirlybirds photographed inside and out from every enticing angle. It makes me wonder: Did a mind make this movie, or did thirty million dollars do the trick? Can you toss out a net of so much money, so much brute busyness, and not capture something, though possibly something not worth the price? Was this movie thought out and directed, or was it merely bought with an arriviste's wealth?

September 28, 1979

A Crime Film That Pays

The Onion Field is an utterly honorable movie; therein lie both its strength and its weakness. Joseph Wambaugh, the policeman-turned-novelist, found the film versions of two of his previous novels so offensive that he resorted to litigation to regain control of this one, then went into hock to finance it and have it produced as he wanted it. He wrote the script and closely supervised all stages of the filmmaking. The result is a movie that is faithful to the book—a long book, however, that forced the filmmakers to use a telegraphic style where more leisurely development was needed.

Indeed, *The Onion Field* is a picture with far too many transitions left out, so that the plot twists and climaxes come at us thick and fast, often puzzling and sometimes even seemingly arbitrary, despite the fact that this is a true story. It is all rather like a controversial lecture full of provocative and haunting pronouncements, but with the dialectical underpinnings elided. One is often left in the awkward situation of having to take the truth on faith.

The story concerns two policemen, officers Hettinger and Campbell (John Savage and Ted Dannon), who, on a typically restless night in downtown Los Angeles, stumble on two petty criminals—a white man, Greg Powell (James Woods), and a black, Jimmy Smith (Franklyn Seales)—driving forth on one of their routine liquor-store holdups. Powell, a dangerous psychotic, and Smith, a smalltime loser in and out of jail, manage to disarm the officers and force them to drive to a lonely onion field near Bakersfield, ostensibly to be abandoned while the punks make their getaway. But Powell evokes the Little Lindbergh law that, he mistakenly believes, carries mandatory death sentences for the kidnappers of policemen, and shoots Campbell while Hettinger somehow escapes. The last thing Hettinger sees is that someone pumps four more shots into his prostrate colleague.

The two culprits are eventually caught and brought to trial, with Hettinger obliged to testify again and again at hearing after hearing. The official position of the police is that he is responsible for his buddy's death, which, along with reiterated enforced relivings of the horror, drives Hettinger into severe mental disturbances. He turns kleptomaniac out of the unconscious need to be caught and punished, and is made to resign from the force; he has recurrent nightmares, becomes impotent with his devoted and understanding wife and harsh with his children; finally, he is flirting with suicide.

Meanwhile Powell and Smith are condemned to death, but during the protracted legal maneuverings Powell becomes a self-taught lawyer of exceptional shrewdness; when the verdict is appealed, the new trial becomes the longest in Los Angeles history, and Powell and his team manage to obtain life sentences for both Powell and Smith, chiefly because, though the pair confess everything else, neither admits to that final vicious fusillade. In 1983, Smith, still a shiftless jailbird, and Powell, now a legal as well as an evil genius, will be released from jail, with who knows what consequences. True, Hettinger is ultimately saved by his good wife and a Voltairean cultivation of his own garden that eventually leads to a nice horticultural job; but the brutally murdered Campbell remains dead, and the world seems more unsafe than ever.

The film has sundry virtues. The unsavory, messy, yet ludicrous private lives of the criminals are tersely and tellingly conveyed; the precarious existences of policemen, caught between the devilish murderers and the deep blue sea of police bureaucracy, are no less well evoked, though here the shortening of the novel into movie format is somewhat damaging. It is even more so when the psychopathic punk suddenly emerges as a dazzling lawyer, and when Hettinger's decline has to be traced with insufficient gradualness, and when the endless, unconscionable juridical jockeyings and legal equivocations cannot be conveyed in all their Dickensian convolutions. Thus the volcanic outburst of an incensed young district attorney (David Huffman) rendered impotent by the cool casuistry of the defense loses authenticity because of the suddenness with which both the character and his exasperation are thrust upon us.

The film has other flaws, too. There is some unhelpful sentimental dawdling over the staunchness of the dead policeman's mother and the surviving one's wife, both of whom emerge with more ichor than blood in their veins, and there are certain plot developments—especially the acrobatics of jurisprudence—that become obscure even beyond the limitations of foreshortening. That we never learn who did that heinous extra shooting no doubt follows the facts of the actual case, but it is artistically disruptive; it urges the mind into bootless puzzle-solving and so distracts it from the film's larger issues of law and morality, of how much we have the right to demand from a policeman, of whether a mandatory death sentence would not be best in some cases, of just how many murderers can dance through the loopholes of the law. And though the acting ranges from good to excellent (Seales is splendid, and Woods, without a trace of exaggeration, stunningly terrifying), I have trouble with John Savage. Although he plays Hettinger with the stolid near-impassivity with which a simple, decent man would teeter on the brink, there is something a bit too boyishly cute about his looks and too innocuous about his aura to make his downfall and agony as moving as that of a visibly larger and stronger man.

Nevertheless, under Harold Becker's efficient, no-nonsense direction, and with Charles Rosher's customary unsensuous cinematography contributing a documentary quality, *The Onion Field* gives us several scenes of unusual maturity and philosophical impact seldom found in American movies. I admire particularly the various scenes in which the expert homicide detective, Pierce Brooks (compellingly played by Ronny Cox), tirelessly probes the criminals' psyches with a gently Dostoyevskian doggedness, and the sequence in which Hettinger, his anguish exacerbated by the unstoppable howling of his baby, is driven to striking the infant and very nearly going further, only to crumple into abject remorse a moment later. The baby-hitting scene is so powerful that even the callous theater audience with which I saw the film, and which took to violence like a fish to fish food, let out a gasp of human horror.

Not much need be said about *Yanks,* John Schlesinger's elaborate imitation of a 1940s war-on-the-home-front movie (take anything from *Since You Went Away* to *Mrs. Miniver),* except that it is carefully made, doughy, and absolutely pointless. Dealing with the nervous romances of Yanks stationed in England on the eve of D-day, it differs from forties flickers only in one gratuitous scene of racial violence in our armed forces (the lack of integration here is more artistic than social), and in a couple of bedroom scenes that show a little nudity but, alas, no passion.

The screenplay by Colin Welland and Walter Bernstein is hackneyed, full of characters who are supposed to be saved from becoming stereotypes by having an occasional arbitrary idiosyncrasy slapped on them; as for the fresh, country dialogue, it all comes out of a can. The movie drags on for over two hours and features performances ranging from the skilled (Rachel Roberts and Tony Melody as the kind of shopkeepers that made Britain a nation of heroes) to dull (Richard Gere as a respectfully amorous army cook) and slightly offensive (William Devane as an unconvincingly upper-class American captain). In the part of the sweetly provincial English heroine, Lisa Eichhorn, an American, is charming and wholly believable. Vanessa Redgrave, as a discreetly straying upper-crust officer's wife, is competent but prematurely dowdy. Schlesinger's direction consistently confuses polish with excitement. Why was this film made?

November 9, 1979

Mature Movies, Hollywood Style

THE MOST POPULAR FILM currently on our screens is Blake Edwards's *10,* about an aging bachelor, George (Dudley Moore), a pop-song composer living in reasonable, if not close, harmony with Sam (Julie Andrews), his girl friend of similarly mature years but also, unlike him, mature attitudes, and his lyric writer, a likewise aging fellow who, however, is a homosexual and has troubles with his young lover. Then George spots Jenny (Bo Derek), the perfect 11 on a scale of one to ten, and becomes intransigently infatuated with her on what turns out to be her wedding day. Through a series of intricate farcical maneuvers he manages to move into the same Mexican hotel where Jenny is honeymooning, and then, even closer, into her bed—only to discover that a featherweight brain and fly-by-night sex are a turnoff. Predictably, he ends up with Sam, who simmers down and forgives.

The plot is simple and old, which would not matter if Edwards, who wrote as well as directed it, were not simplistic and old-hat. On the one hand, *10* attempts to be a seriocomic examination of midlife crisis, of our sexual mores, and of what constitutes, in the parlous new parlance, a meaningful relationship; on the other, both Moore and Edwards are farceurs for whom the basic unit is not the scenario but the skit, the blackout sketch, the gimmick. Hence there is not so much a plot based on the interaction and development of characters as a concatenation of funny and not so funny bits, often unrelated to the profile of the action and strung together with a looseness that courts promiscuity.

Let me explain. There is no reason for a film having a perfectly good fundamental problem and seriocomic situation to base most of its humor on such irrelevancies as George's being stung by a face-disfiguring bee during Jenny's wedding ceremony, or finding the sand at the Mexican beach too hot to walk on, or having to get four cavities filled at one excruciating swoop merely to extract one piece of information about Jenny from her dentist father. An entire scene is wasted on a meeting between George and Jenny's minister (Max Showalter, and very obvious) in order to allow the minister, a frustrated songwriter, to inflict a lengthy and heavy-handed travesty of a song of his own devising on defenseless George and us. And, irrelevancy within irrelevancy, the minister's old and purblind housekeeper serves tea by bumping into the furniture and all but spilling everything. Even if such things can be funny, they are out of place here, and are invariably milked a little longer than the humor can sustain. Comedy *can* undercut comedy: a comic's patter is not helped by his dropping his pants.

There is worse. George has a neighbor who keeps throwing orgies that George watches through a telescope, only to be occasionally spied on in turn by the orgiasts. Much low-comedy footage is wasted on this subplot that is not even a subplot, only an aside; when George finally makes it over to one of these orgies, he is too self-conscious to score. But the film does not make any significant connection between this and his subsequent fiasco with Jenny, any more than it makes anything incisive out of the episode with Mary (Dee Wallace, and excellent), a tragic divorcée who adoringly goes to bed with George. When he proves impotent with her, she breaks down, blubbering about her unhappy marriage and how she jinxes all her men. It could be a touching sequence were it integrated into the story, though perhaps slightly out of keeping even then. As things stand, it is merely maudlin and gratuitous.

Equally mystifying are the semidrunken conversations George has with the sympathetic bartender at the Mexican hotel who admires his songs. These sequences are as prolonged as they are pointless. For a while it looks as if some sort of implicit homosexuality were aimed at to balance the story of George's lyricist, but this proves not to be the case. The film is merely maundering—perhaps for some arcane autobiographic reason known only to its makers, or else to fill in gaps between the supposed comic highlights. Finally, the grand rejection of Jenny occurs for no better reason than that she has an open marriage and a rather empty head, and that the record of Ravel's

"Bolero" that she uses as an aphrodisiac has come to an end and requires someone to get out of bed to restart it.

These might constitute sufficient reasons for spiritual detumescence if George were shown as having anything resembling a soul. As it is, his failure to enjoy what he wanted on terms not so different from those he had hoped for suggests either some kind of industry censorship or that Sam must win out because she is played by the director's wife. Still, if *10* were treated from beginning to end as farce, without interludes of wistfulness, mawkishness, and preachment, the anticlimax (in both senses) might work, although even then it would have to be staged with more brio than Edwards musters.

As things are, there are a few performances worth watching (albeit not that of Bo Derek—who, incidentally, though white, cornrows her hair in a most unbecoming fashion), and a few good comic sequences without true comic logic. How, for example, can the inept and cowardly George manipulate a catamaran by himself and rescue Jenny's husband who is about to drown in treacherous currents? And why? Surely he would like nothing better than to console the bereaved widow in her honeymourner's bed. A self-indulgent film, this, and one that sacrifices comedic structure to cheap laughs and easy pathos. Yet it contains one astounding innovation: *our* Julie Andrews goes, for the first time, not exactly topless, but see-through-braless! Why, it's as if Mary Poppins burst into four-letter words!

Starting Over, which Alan J. Pakula directed from Dan Wakefield's novel, is a nice idea that does not really make sense in James L. Brooks's screen adaptation with Pakula's inappropriate casting. This heavily autobiographical tale obviously concerns three homely and slatternly people, desperately undistinguished, even if they may not view themselves as such. To cast the devilishly virile Burt Reynolds as the magazine-writer and junior-college-teacher husband ditched by a glossy Candice Bergen for his boss (this part is rather fudged by the final cut, which renders it almost incomprehensible) and for a show-biz career is all wrong; even Jill Clayburgh, though essentially a *jolie laide,* is probably too *jolie* for the jolly and tomboyish schoolteacher with whom, after many misunderstandings and missteps, he finally finds happiness.

Yet Clayburgh can convey a certain averageness; Reynolds and Bergen, however, are far too glamorous for the parts they are playing, and their Fifth Avenue apartment is a veritable showplace. Hence the romantic flounderings and sexual ineptitudes of the characters are quite out of sync with the performers; it is all rather like watching a film about the problems of immensely obese people enacted by a lithe, athletic cast. You end up feeling as if you had a detached retina—whatever that may be like.

Pakula's direction is adequate, but catches fire only in the two best scenes: one on a staircase to a church basement where a departing divorced-male consciousness-raising group crosses an arriving feminist consciousness-raising group, and the other an incident in a department store's furniture section where Reynolds starts hyperventilating while testing a connubial bed. But Brooks's screenplay is basically TV sitcom stuff, and, like *10,* falls short of even the mild seriousness about man-woman relations that the film aspires to along with the laughter.

Nevertheless, Reynolds handles himself very well in an unsuitable role. Clayburgh has some juicy moments, and even Bergen is beginning to look ever so slightly less cellophane-wrapped. The minor characters, however, are pure clichés, and Sven Nykvist, Bergman's great cinematographer, here unappetizingly revels in a palette that seems to be all mauve and maroon. *Starting Over* never takes one step into realism without taking two into cuteness: a purposeful lunge yields to much too fancy footwork.

January 4, 1980

Benton Versus the Truth

AWARDS AND ACCOLADES have begun to pour on Robert Benton's *Kramer vs. Kramer,* which, with *Breaking Away* and *The Onion Field,* is one of the best American movies of the past year, though that is only knee-high praise. It is a film in which noteworthy acting, direction, and cinematography collude to make us—some of us—overlook the flimsiness of the writing. Based on a novel of some years ago by Avery Corman, Benton's screenplay is a superior tear-jerker about the fight of divorced parents over their golden little boy. The theme is legitimate and adult—with minor differences, it served well in *Medea* and *A Midsummer Night's Dream;* what makes it soap, or chopped-onion, opera here is the distance from Euripides and Shakespeare to Corman and Benton.

Though I haven't read Corman's novel, I gather that it is more satirical and wry than the largely sentimental film. It may be from the novel, however, that the movie inadvertently takes over its most glaring factual error: Ted Kramer, the rising Mad-Av account executive who won't let his wife, Joanna, work, makes thirty-two or thirty-three thousand dollars (I forget which) a year, on which his family, including six-year-old Billy, lives in high style high up on the Upper East Side. When Ted, in desperate straits, must take a lower-paying job at twenty-eight thousand dollars or so, he can still pay his lawyer fifteen thousand dollars in a custody suit. Corman's antiquated figures are ridiculous in Benton's inflationary world.

This may seem unimportant, yet it is just such inattention to detail that can hurt a film that revels in the authenticity of observed minutiae. (Indeed, the film is behind the times in more important matters as well, such as the handling of child-custody cases. The bias in favor of the mother is no longer automatic, as the film assumes, and no present-day court, at least in New York, would fail to talk to the child and try to discover his wishes in the matter.) Benton may have retained the faulty figures for sentimental, popularity-getting reasons: to retain the unenvious good will of lower-income-bracket audiences. But a lie is a lie and makes us lose confidence—add also the fact that Billy goes to PS 6, whereas everything else about the Kramer style of living points to a private school. Benton recently told Andrew Sarris that he did shoot the scenes in which Ted interviews a spectrum of candidates for the job of housekeeper, but that the ethnic humor came out nasty and patronizing *on screen,* and had to be cut. Well, that is how soap operas are made: by omitting any details that might give offense to anybody. So you end up with the absurdity of a mother who has flown the coop, a father who puts in extra-long hours at the ad agency, and a six-year-old who presumably walks himself home from school and takes care of himself for several hours thereafter.

Ah, yes, the story. Ted Kramer comes home exulting over "one of the five best days" of his life: his boss has put him in charge of a major new account with a vice-presidency attached to it; at that very moment Joanna declares that she is leaving him. Eight years of marriage to an overbearing egocentric are enough; because he has even squelched her professional development, she feels obliged to abandon their son to him, as better able to provide for the child. Ted is faced with explaining her departure to Billy, and the almost superhuman task of Stakhanovite work on the new account along with the endless, often infuriating, demands of child care. Obviously Benton avoided filming the earlier parts of the novel because showing Ted's evolution from driven egocentric to paragon of combined parenthood would have placed a similarly huge burden on the writer-director.

Remarkable as Ted is, he makes his heartless boss, O'Connor, feel that he is placing paternity above publicity. Billy, at first highly critical of his father's (often genuinely amusing) attempts at being an all-around parent, gradually educates Ted into model parenthood. Now father and son enjoy home life even more, until, eighteen months having passed, Joanna reappears, and O'Connor fires Ted. Joanna now has improbably gainful employment and a dazzlingly restored self-confidence, both acquired in California, where such things are indigenous. She wants her son back, and the eponymous lawsuit, Kramer vs. Kramer, begins. The movie charges ahead, open throttle and tear ducts, into fierce courtroom drama, with warring but fundamentally decent parents and a suffering but brave kid. Everybody makes sacrifices, flowers of nobility sprout from harsh urban asphalt—and I haven't even told you yet how noble Margaret Phelps, the Kramers' neighbor and friend, is. Abandoned by her own husband, the faithful Margaret becomes Joanna's best pal and defender; still, after watching Billy thrive under Ted's growing solicitousness and wisdom, she becomes Ted's champion and witness in court. And although she and Ted could eminently comfort each other sexually, too, they do no such thing, noble souls that they are.

Speaking of sex, how does Ted fill that vacuum in his life? Once, only once, he brings home a woman, Phyllis, a fetching colleague from the agency. When the naked young woman gets up in the middle of the night to go to the toilet, sure enough she collides with Billy, on the same errand. Sophisticated Phyllis gets all flustered, improvising a bra and fig leaf with her arms, and making awkward small-tot-talk. Although the contretemps ends happily, Ted, it seems, never brings a woman home with him again.

It is painfully evident that Benton is hell-bent on not offending anyone. I get the distinct impression that Joanna's mean lawyer, playing dirty courtroom pool, is carefully counterweighted with Ted's tough but essentially honest one; that the heartless O'Connor is counterbalanced by the brass at the other agency, who, in the midst of a hectic Christmas party and the rush to catch vacation-bound planes, still manage to give Ted a much-needed job. Above all, Joanna's character and Ted's treatment of his wife are minutely calculated not to offend either feminists or patriarchalists in any more than momentary ways. Art must take the measure of man and woman—but with artistic vision, not with calipers.

What, then, makes *Kramer vs. Kramer* still eminently worth seeing? First, Benton's direction, which is as solid as his writing and thinking are unreliable. Well beyond his work on *Bad Company* and *The Late Show,* Benton displays a true sense of pacing and framing, of camera placement and movement, as well as of working with actors and allowing them (especially young Justin Henry) to feel their way into a scene. An occasional fault in continuity—a meeting agreed upon at the Central Park Boat Pond that actually takes place on the Mall—hardly matters. The performances of Dustin Hoffman, Meryl Streep, and that extraordinary youngster, Justin Henry, are flawless; in supporting roles, there is exceptional work from, among others, Jane Alexander, who, as always, radiates an understated or even wordless eloquence of the heart; and George Coe, who infuses just enough humanity into O'Connor to make him a believable, almost pitiable, monster—which cannot be said for Bill Moor as Joanna's attorney.

Finally, there is Nestor Almendros's cinematographic palette, supremely sensitive to nuances of light and color, yet remaining unpretentious—note especially the goodnight scene in Billy's semidarkened room. Thanks are due also to intelligently used music both old and new, well-scouted locations, and a canny eye for details of production design and set decoration. Go, enjoy, and weep—both for the true pathos and for the missed truth.

Mark Rydell's *The Rose,* a fiction closely resembling a biography of Janis Joplin, is worth attending. Though laden with clichés of the backstage-romance genre, it is also an entertaining and sometimes illusion-piercing account of the life, tribulations, and death of an idol whose vitality, indomitableness, and humor triumph over a mediocre talent and worse countenance. With disarming pungency and flamboyant frumpishness, Bette Midler manages to make the messy career and drug-induced death of Rose the rock star into something funny and touching as well as absurd and appalling; she gets first-rate support from Frederic Forrest as her supremely devoted but finally defeated swain. Though the film falls short of the shrewdest observations on success without foundation, on celebrity without sobriety, it does make us partake of the coruscation and doom of a human meteor.

February 8, 1980

Stodgy Satire, Dodgy Satyr

JERZY KOSINSKI, the Polish-born American novelist, is a curious phenomenon. After two very interesting and in many ways impressive early novels, *The Painted Bird* and *Steps,* Kosinski has become more successful and famous, has had more and more professorships, awards, TV appearances, and other honors and emoluments heaped on him, even as his later novels (mostly mere novellas) have become weaker and more strained. Thus, I imagine, Kosinski has a special affection for Chance, the hero of his novella *Being There,* which he has adapted faithfully, except for some expurgations, to the screen. For Chance is a naïf who keeps repeating the same inanities to a society that insists on reading profundities into them until he becomes rich and powerful and very probably the next president of the U.S.A. Kosinski himself has only made it as far as president of the PEN American Center up to now—but, then, *he* is anything but a naïf.

Chance is an orphan who served as a gardener to a rich Washingtonian; he never left his employer's house and high-walled garden, and spent his leisure time watching television. When the old man dies, Chance puts on one of the boss's expensive suits and goes forth into the world. A very rich woman's car slightly injures him, and the millionairess, Eve Rand, brings him to the palatial mansion she shares with her much older husband, Benjamin, a slowly dying reactionary tycoon, friend and adviser to the president, but a pretty decent fellow withal. Soon our almost completely feelingless simpleton—whose name and occupation, misheard, turn him into Chauncy Gardiner—becomes the confidant and guru of Benjamin, the counselor of the president, the semiplatonic lover of Eve (television having taught him only the earlier phases of lovemaking), the darling of TV talk shows, and the lion of Washington society. He ends up as heir to the dead Benjamin's wealth and widow, and the likeliest candidate for the presidency.

Everything works for him. His dead boss's expensive old custom-tailored suit has just come back into high style; his vacant stares and inability to converse are mistaken for circumspectness and inscrutability; his intensely enunciated banalities based on gardening or TV-watching are perceived as metaphoric and philosophical utterances of the highest order. That no government agency or reporter can dig up any background information on Gardiner means that he is the safest political bet, free from any past that could be used against him, and so on, and, alas, on—for what could make a good short-short story or long anecdote, but was too much even for a slim book, and is way too much for a two-hour movie.

The novella, of course, is written in the absurdist mode, which never quite works on film, where too much reality rushes into the camera's purview. Absurdism is rather like a demented algebra, and though it can work on stage where unrealistic words can hold their own among stylized sets, it fails on screen, where images of the things of this world crowd in, and there is no way for a real sky, landscape, street, crowd of passers-by to pretend that they are x, y^2, and z^3. Hal Ashby, the director, has tried to increase the unreality by proceeding at a slow, stately pace amid settings of ponderous pomp (Biltmore House, the sumptuous Vanderbilt mansion in North Carolina, serves as the Rands's Xanadu), photographed by the talented Caleb Deschanel in tones varying from burnished to brooding. But the effect is only one of carefully nurtured stasis rather than of psychological dislocation, and the work's single joke—Chance's imbecilities taking on ever greater luster—becomes more stifling with every new solemn camera setup.

Peter Sellers's performance has garnered critical kudos, but his Chance seems to me more sinister than innocent: there is no spontaneity in his platitudes, no bewilderment in his too knowingly emptied-out gaze. His pompousness is comic all right, but it has a way of suggesting a pompous ass rather than a mere simpleton. The others are all good, often ingeniously cast, and Melvyn Douglas's Rand is the warmest yet unsappiest crotchety Croesus you will ever see. Toward the end, Kosinski and Ashby blow their cool and have Rand buried in a mausoleum shaped like the pyramid on the dollar bill, while Chance blithely walks on water. But even that cannot further hurt an already seriously damaged movie.

When the book *Being There* appeared, several reviewers recognized the title's allusion to Heidegger's *Dasein,* with which, however, the story has nothing to do. Rather, it is *Candide* in reverse, with the naïveté, instead of wreaking disaster, reaping vast benefits. The Pangloss is television, whose facile optimism is never belied by catastrophe. Eve, the Cunégonde, stays adoring and faithful throughout, and the hero's ultimate bliss stems from remaining in—not leaving—Eldorado. All this could be more amusing—especially the satire on television—if, as Robert Asahina has justly noted, there were not two serious inconsistencies in it. One is that Chance watching TV sometimes arbitrarily imitates what he sees on it; and sometimes, equally arbitrarily, does not. The other is that he, who has manifestly learned everything from TV, often reveals himself ignorant of precisely the things TV bombards us with. In the crazy but algebraically exact equations of absurdism there is room only for the most ruthless logic. Otherwise, the absurd becomes silly.

All That Jazz is Bob Fosse's unauthorized autobiography. Like Fosse, the protagonist, Joe Gideon, is a combination Broadway choreographer-director and filmmaker at work simultaneously on a Broadway musical like *Chicago* and on a movie, not just like but actually *Lenny,* about Lenny Bruce. He is driven, mildly drug-addicted (uppers and downers), and devoted with equal fanaticism to his work and his womanizing. Among the women who surround Joe are his ex-wife and leading lady (Leland Palmer, whom Fosse has turned into an alter ego of Gwen Verdon, his actual ex-wife and leading lady); his principal dancer and *maîtresse en titre* (Ann Reinking, who has functioned in both capacities in real life), a new dancer-mistress, Victoria (Deborah Geffner, with doubtless an analogue in reality, though whether it is Miss

Geffner herself or someone else, I don't know); Angélique, a kind of Angel of Death with whom Joe has portentously vacuous existential colloquies (Jessica Lange, another real-life Fosse girl friend); and Michelle, Joe's teen-aged daughter, with whom a tough-tender father-daughter and choreographer-dancer relationship flourishes (beautifully played and danced by young Erzsebet Foldi, although Fosse's real-life daughter, Nicole, is also in the film playing a subordinate dancer).

The others in Joe Gideon's life include producers, composers, directors, and sundry theater folk—many of them recognizable caricatures—as well as the doctors and hospital staff with whom he gets involved after his near-fatal heart attack and open-heart surgery; the attack, to give the movie a convenient but facile ending, is converted into a fatal one. The film is part movie musical with very good (though no longer very original) Fosse dance sequences, part hospital tragifarce (complete with bypass surgery), part backstage satire. The latter layers are much less compelling; worse yet are two quasi-refrains that run through this jagged montage of levels of reality and superreality. One has Cliff Gorman (who played Lenny on stage) spouting from a Movieola Brucisms that apply to Fosse-Gideon's frenzy; the other has Ben Vereen (a former Fosse star) offering from a TV screen an introduction to Joe's appearance on a variety program—an introduction that becomes more sardonic each time it is repeated. Through all this weaves the metaphysical colloquy with the insipid angel (the screenplay is by Fosse and the late Robert Alan Arthur, and disastrous) that spans everything from satyriasis to eschatology in a series of verbal *grands jetés*.

A vapid, vertiginous farrago, this, clearly derived from Fellini—call it Fosse's *Beat Me, Daddy, 8½ to the Bar.* The film is both too close and not close enough to a rather sleazy reality that this kind of self-serving apotheosis makes grimier yet. But all the dancing and much of the acting (notably Roy Scheider's callow yet likable Joe), beautifully shot by Fellini's cameraman Giuseppe Rotunno and trickily edited by Alan Heim, exude a blend of titillation and hypnosis that is not without interest.

February 22, 1980

Love and Money

PAUL SCHRADER'S LATEST, *American Gigolo,* is a recasting of that hoariest of clichés, the whore with a heart of gold, into the male hustler with a heart of gold. We need not dwell on the simplistic pseudo-intricacies of the plot, which record the activities of Julian (Richard Gere), a highly paid but still rising Los Angeles gigolo, among whose valuable services are proficiency in several languages, access to the L.A. Country Club, intimacy with the maître d' of the Polo Lounge, a wardrobe designed by the celebrated Giorgio Armani, and unequaled gifts for soft talk and hard loving.

Julian is conned into a kinky S & M job of a sort he otherwise does not stoop to and is promptly framed for the murder of a masochistic wife by her sadistic bisexual husband. The latter is in cahoots with a black pimp who has it in for Julian, and with Senator Stratton, whose beautiful but neglected wife, Michelle (Lauren Hutton), has fallen helplessly in love with our hero. Michelle's love, whose very existence, let alone magnitude, the film is unable to make credible, pursues Julian like a combination Hound of Heaven and Daddy Warbucks. When Julian is finally apprehended for the supposed S & M murder as well as the defenestration of the pimp, of which he is the accidental cause, Michelle fights everyone and everything for him: her jealous and powerful husband, the law, and Julian's own deep-seated resistance to any love that is not bought. At last—need I tell you?—love triumphs as Julian sobs into the little window through which, an imprisoned Pyramus, he must communicate with his Thisbe: sobs about why it took him so long to accept the gift of love. I wish I had his exact words, but I was too convulsed with laughter to get them down.

Schrader is that sinister figure Hollywood turns out intermittently: the hack with a dangerous bit of learning. Equipped with a smattering of literature, philosophy, art history, and theology, he clearly thinks that he has created in Julian (whose full name is Julian Kay, a probable allusion to Kafka's Joseph K.) an existential hero for our times out of Camus, Céline, and Dostoyevsky. Actually, he has written and directed something out of Kerouac with a touch of watered-down Colette. Julian emerges, first of all, as stupid. When, during body-building exercises, he is learning Swedish from phonograph records, he repeats not only the Swedish phrases but also the English ones! (He may, of course, need to build up his English, too.) When he first meets Michelle in the Polo Lounge, each pretends to be French and fools the other, despite a command of Racine's tongue that would hardly pass muster in Racine, Wisconsin.

Now for a sample of Julian's sexual spiel: "I can make you relax, relax like you've never relaxed before. Make you aroused like you've never been aroused before. Excited. I know how to touch you. Where to touch you . . ." And so on. If this is high-class gigolo talk, what could the diction of medium-priced lovers be like? Grunts, I daresay. But the Armani *couture* is *haute* enough, and Schrader's camera lovingly pans across well-stocked closets and drawers filled to bursting. Julian's other worldly goods are likewise scrutinized (expensive car, various electronic gadgets, etc.), but the seamier side of his trade is cravenly elided. We never see him escorting a truly old or ugly woman, and we see him in bed only with Lauren Hutton, which would present no problems even for the rankest amateur.

As *American Gigolo* would have it, Julian's troubles stem only from that one kinky trick he was tricked into turning—the kind of trivial misstep a reputable writer might make by publishing once in the wrong magazine. The moral questions of Julian's existence are never even remotely confronted, and his defense of his calling (bringing joy to the needy) is written, staged, and photographed for maximum persuasiveness. Toward Michelle, he comports himself like a perfect, albeit loveless, gentleman, preferring to sacrifice his freedom and very life perhaps rather than involve her in any way, a veritable Sir Kay of Arthur's court. No wonder, then, that his redemption is brought about as gratuitously and unconvincingly as his previous gallantry was sentimentally contrived. If you take also Gere's superficial performance and Hutton's better but still insubstantial one, what have you got? A terrific commercial for Giorgio Armani.

April 4, 1980

Christ Without Christ; Nijinsky Without Nijinsky

JOHN HUSTON'S *Wise Blood* very nearly does justice to Flannery O'Connor's first novel, on which it is based. Though the novel may be Miss O'Connor's least successful fiction, for a movie to have captured its spirit is enough to place it quite high on the film scale, and in a category of its own. In November 1963, after Albee's adaptation of *The Ballad of the Sad Cafe* reached Broadway, Miss O'Connor wrote to a friend: "Did you ever consider *Wise Blood* as a possibility for dramatizing? If the times were different I would suggest that, but I think it would just be taken for the super-grotesque sub–Carson McCullers sort of thing I could not stand the sight or sound of." There is something unfortunately McCullersish about the novel itself (the real, great O'Connor was to come later) and so about the movie.

Yet this tale of Hazel Motes, the preacher's son who tries every way to escape Jesus and cannot, has much of the funny awfulness of Flannery O'Connor's best works, dealing with the phenomena that once almost blanketed the South and still thrive in many a not so isolated pocket. In a somewhat different, less extreme form, they may indeed lurk in human nature everywhere. *Wise Blood* is the *credo quia absurdum* justified by all those absurd poor-white southern lives: if being is so absurd, why shouldn't belief, and the truth itself, be likewise? This is also, as it were, a prose version of "The Hound of Heaven," with Christ relentlessly tracking down the would-be sinner protagonist until he dies as a martyred quasi-saint. It is all horrible and funny, with the horror and funniness in a stranglehold so tight that they take even the audience's breath away. And it is so outrageous you have to believe it; something so crazy, tormented, pitiful has to be beyond anyone's ability to invent.

The screenplay is an extremely faithful adaptation by Michael and Benedict Fitzgerald (whose parents, Robert and Sally, were among Miss O'Connor's closest friends), and Huston has not indulged himself in directorial liberties. True, the flashbacks to Hazel's childhood are shot in a kind of fuchsia monochrome, but what haunts someone has the right to be garish; and, to save money, present-day Macon, its one high-rise brazening it out in the background, is allowed to stand in for an unidentified city of the late forties—yet who is to say that this story is not entitled to timelessness?

Otherwise, I repeat, there is no great directorial inventiveness, but no directorial flaw, either. When a Huston film works, it is either because the script (often an adaptation) was well chosen and just rolls along—as in *The Maltese Falcon, The Treasure of the Sierra Madre,* and *The Asphalt Jungle;* or because the material is slapdash or *outré* enough to lend itself to a certain directorial flashiness and condescension—as in *Beat the Devil, The Roots of Heaven,* and *The Man Who Would Be King.* But when Huston picks the wrong material, the result, as we know from so many bitter experiences, can be catastrophic. Still, Huston is more justly served by the unpretentious Leslie Halliwell's description, "unpredictable but occasionally splendid," than by the more fanciful Robin Wood's assessment, "a somewhat coarsened sensibility."

The briskness with which Huston approaches his queasy subject here pays off. The simple way in which Hazel beds down with an obscenely obese whore or the matter-of-fact manner in which he runs over a false prophet with his car has the proper low-key dreariness from which the horror and humor shine forth all the more glaringly. But there is also artistry of a less obvious kind. Take the scene in which Motes preaches from the hood of his godforsaken jalopy and proclaims: "I preach the Church Without Christ . . . where the blind don't see and the lame don't walk and what's dead stays that way." It is a fine touch to show Motes and the small band of bemused idlers who listen to him only in tight and medium shots until "and what's dead stays that way"—on which line we get a zoom-out. What better words to accompany the distant, cold eye of the camera as it miniaturizes the weirdly pathetic preacher, the humdrum bunch propelled by boredom into listening, and the honky-tonk city sprawling under a gray sky in lackluster light, denied even the doubtful purification of rain?

As so often, Huston has cast the film with great canniness and obtained flawless performances. Brad Dourif's lack of any kind of quality except humorless conviction is just right for the protagonist. Even when he is saying something polite or conciliatory, Dourif has the gaze of a hunted rat about to bite back, a jaw cantilevered into defiance, and a colorless voice that can gain volume but never inflection. Dourif provokes our awe while rightly leaving our empathy alone. Similarly, Mary Nell Santacroce, a local amateur playing the elderly landlady who mysteriously falls in love with Hazel, is so invincibly ordinary, so lacking in physical and spiritual identifying marks on top of her puny common sense, that we are made to understand how such personified anonymity would be drawn to a maniacal paradox. She is as pathetic without pathos as Hazel is Christian without Christ.

There is very good work also from Dan Shor as a genuinely simple-minded and not oversweet Enoch; Harry Dean Stanton as a scary as well as scarred Hawks, the fake preacher and false blind man (the scene wherein Hazel discovers that the man can see is a brilliant stroke: very short, compressed between two symbolic blackouts, and shot in extreme closeup, alternating between Hawks's self-betraying and Motes's disabused eyes looming huge, while the ominous flame of the match flickers like a feeler of hell-fire at the bottom of the frame); Amy Wright, perhaps a bit actressy as Sabbath Lily, but steeped in the innocent nastiness of that dunghill flower; and Ned Beatty as the troublingly smiling pitchman Onnie Jay Holy, the maker and breaker of prophets.

Yet even the smallest roles, filled by sundry townsfolk, come off superlatively; only Bill Hickey, as the nonentity whom Holy promotes into Hazel's rival, is too obvious a halfwit. Buttressed by Gerry Fisher's nicely noncommittal cinematography and Alex North's jauntily rustic score, *Wise Blood* hops and lurches to its trivial, tremendous climax in a manner Miss O'Connor would have approved—which is praise enough.

Nijinsky is the exact opposite of *Wise Blood:* a gaudily splendiferous surface and hollowness inside. Years ago, Rudolf Nureyev was set to play the title part, and might have carried it off with bravura, even though Albee was to write the script and Ken Russell was supposed to direct. The chap who did direct, Herb Ross, was defeated from the outset by picking for Nijinsky George de la Peña, an undistinguished dancer with a bland face and no acting ability. He neither looks like Nijinsky nor conveys that human battlefield of genius and madness. Unlike in *The Turning Point,* where Ross could train his camera on Baryshnikov and let the dancing do the rest, here every subterfuge must be enlisted: slow motion, jump cuts, superimposition, framing that cuts off the legs—to deflect attention from de la Peña's dancing.

Then there is Hugh Wheeler's simplistic script that takes silly liberties with truth. Accordingly, everything is turbulently wonderful while Diaghilev and Vaslav bask in mutually devoted homosexual love. But when various intriguers take over (Baron de Gunzburg, whom the script unwarrantedly turns homosexual and Machiavellian; Romola de Pulszky—misspelled as "Pulsky"—who, as played by Leslie Browne, is a crashingly dull gatecrasher), a heterosexual marriage destroys the idyl, and the walls of sanity come tumbling down. Wheeler also concocts a plethora of mediocre epigrams, e.g., Diaghilev's "My taste is impeccable, even when it is bad" or "Nobody loves a fat faun." The errors of omission are graver yet: the most interesting events, characters, complexities have a way of being minimized or totally absent.

Still, there are the convincing backgrounds; accurately evoked faces, sets, costumes, bits of choreography; and a few exquisite performances: from Alan Bates, Alan Badel, Anton Dolin, and Carla Fracci in particular. Perhaps Rex Reed's statement—used, incredibly, in the ads—sums it up best: "Towers above nine out of ten other mindless entertainments on the screen today."

May 2, 1980

Mythopoeic Madness

IF *Star Wars* struck me as no worse than harmless junk, the reason may have been the novelty of combining the hardware of *2001* with the software of Tolkien. But the sequel, *The Empire Strikes Back,* subtitled *Star Wars: Episode V,* is malodorous offal, and not only because it promises three prequels to its predecessor and four sequels to itself. Yet that, too, is repulsively commercial: George Lucas—whether directly, as in *Star Wars,* or indirectly, as here, through his new scenarists (the late Leigh Brackett and Lawrence Kasdan) and new director (Irvin Kershner)—had just enough vision for one intermittently diverting piece of nonsense. In the sequel, everything is stale, limp, desperately stretched out, and pretentious. And without innocence.

What innocence there may have been in the original *Star Wars* was surely forfeited by the exploitative industries that sprang up around it: unprecedented devices for blood sports such as parent-bleeding and piggy-bank-sticking. You might say that the Disney people were not exactly guiltless of megalo- or meta-marketing, from Mickey Mouse watches to Disneylands and Disney Worlds, those Forest Lawns of the mind. But those were secular realms, whereas *Star Wars* is a religion, as the sequel makes even clearer, and religious cults are better than lay ones at mulcting their adherents.

In *The Empire Strikes Back,* the evil Empire, under the demonic leadership of Darth Vader, has regained stability after having been shaken by the powers of good under that platonic *ménage à trois,* Princess Leia, Luke Skywalker, and Han Solo. These redeemers have now gone into hiding deep under the snows of the ice planet Hoth, where they are being tracked by octopus-shaped mechanical probes of the Empire. Luke goes investigating on his stylized kangaroo steed (the Lucas imagination recapitulates a primitive bestiary) and is attacked by a powerful snow creature he finally manages to kill. But he would freeze to death (after dark one must be sheltered in a Hoth house) if Han Solo did not ride out to find him in that endless wilderness of ice, which he promptly does. Swiftly, singlehandedly, he builds an igloo, without sacrificing so much as a finger to frostbite or verisimilitude.

Later, when the Empire attacks with several snow-walkers (slow, long-leggedly swaying, turtlelike tanks) that are impervious to Princess Leia's most elaborate weaponry, Luke destroys one by winding a steel wire around its legs, another by giving it a dynamite hotfoot. Still later, when Leia and Han in their Millennium Falcon are pursued by the imperial flotilla, they give Darth Vader the slip—first by steering into a field of asteroids, then by landing atop his Death Star and riding it piggyback, unnoticed by anyone. As you can see, the plot devices are superannuated, preposterous, or imbecile, or a combination of the above. Even science fiction can use a little credibility and originality.

But there is worse. There is a romantic subplot in which Han and Leia play the love-hate game of 1930s screwball comedies, where, at least, the hero and heroine ended up in a conjugal bed. Here a chaste kiss or two is the ultimate consummation, as tepid and infantile as the repartee that preceded it. *Infantile* is the operative word, for nothing in *Empire* must interfere with the blessed infantilism of children and the blissful regression of adults. Nevertheless, at film's end, when Han Solo is carbon-frozen into an oversized paperweight and carried off by a bounty hunter for undisclosed purposes, Leia seems to veer back to Luke, and simple-minded triangularity is restored.

This witless banality is made even less bearable by the nonacting of the principals. Harrison Ford (Han) offers loutishness for charm and becomes the epitome of the interstellar drugstore cowboy. Mark Hamill (Luke) is still the talentless Tom Sawyer of outer space—wide-eyed, narrow-minded, strait-laced. Worst of all is Carrie Fisher, whose Leia is a cosmic Shirley Temple but without the slightest acting ability or vestige of prettiness. Though still very young, she looks, without recourse to special effects, at least fifty—the film's only true, albeit depressing, miracle. It turns out, as part of the movie's barbershop Freudianizing, that Darth Vader is really Luke's father; by the time we get to the next episode, Leia may easily be his mother.

Most painful, however, is the dime-store mysticism that runs through the picture. Obi-Wan Kenobi, who periodically reappears from the other dimension into which he has been translated, informs Luke that the Force he has inherited must be perfected by studying with the supreme master Yoda, Kenobi's own guru, on the swamp planet Dagobah. Off zooms Luke to Dagobah, accompanied by R2D2, who, of course, gets into all sorts of robot mischief. The great and wise Yoda (yoga with soda?) is a cute cross between a gnome and a lizard, and gives Luke a brand of Zen training that consists mostly of learning to spout platitudes while standing on one's head. (Does an upside-down cliché equal a mystic insight?) Ultimately, Luke is to perform wonders like the one pulled off by Yoda when, by sheer concentration and will power, he raises Luke's aircraft from the ooze that engulfed it. Yet before Luke has mastered half the curriculum, he rashly rushes off to save Leia, Han, and C3PO from terrible dangers. They are being betrayed by Lando Calrissian (Billy Dee Williams), lord of the cloud city of Bespin, into the hands of Darth Vader.

Lando is really the intergalactic black hipster, who soon proves to be a decent rascal by reverting to his old camaraderie with Han Solo, and siding with Han, Leia, and the by now dismantled C3PO, whom Chewbakka the Wookie is gradually reassembling. Lando serves the dual purpose of giving blacks someone to identify with in the great beyond and teaching white kids to love their street-wise black brethren. But I worry about the way Lando ogles Leia; there is no telling what might happen by episode VII or VIII.

I really can't go on feeding you more of the plot (which also includes plentiful references to the ancient Knights of Jedi, whose return will be chronicled in the next installment) without making morons of all of us. Suffice it to say that the ending is a double or triple cliffhanger, and to assure you that, even though Darth Vader in a duel unto deathly boredom chops off Luke's hand, the bionic replacement will undoubtedly prove as good as the old limb—after all, the bionic hands that wrote and directed this sequel seem to have incurred no falling off at the box office.

The danger is only that as we get, spread out over two decades or more, the remaining episodes, a whole generation of kids may grow up with the Force as their faith, the Jedi knights as their apostles, Luke (i.e., Lucas) Skywalker as their Savior, and Obi-Wan Kenobi as their Paraclete. I am not sure whether Darth Vader is to be reclaimed—a prodigal dad reverting to benevolent paternal godhead—or whether Han and Leia will turn into a ruling divine couple with Luke as their Oedipal son; but I suggest that, unless it is already too late, an energetic campaign be mounted against this nascent theogony and theocracy.

Meanwhile, the special effects, which alone can make this sort of *olla podrida* even vaguely palatable, are conspicuously inferior to those in *Star Wars*—perhaps because the ingenious John Dykstra did not ply his recondite craft on this one. For whatever reason, *The Empire Strikes Back* strikes out in most of its special effects, which look like a second-rate comic strip. The program lists five and a half pages of credits; it would take at least twice that space to list the debits.

If you have any lingering doubts about the mentality of George Lucas, which informs this epic ennead in the making, consider the northern-Californian cinéaste's remark to the *New York Times's* Aljean Harmetz: "Hollywood is not where my home is, my wife is, my dog is. I like to be in my own bed watching television." Lucas should make love, not star wars, to his wife, his dog, his very own television set, and stop contributing to the sappiness of nations. Parents beware! Lucas and your kids may land you in bankruptcy court.

June 13, 1980

Horribile Visu

EXCEPT FOR THE MYSTERY FILM, no genre requires more rigorous logic than the horror movie. The supernatural forces may be as weird as they like, but they must play by some set of rules. If ghosts, for example, cannot cross water in the first reel of the movie, they must not trip it merrily across a lake by the second reel. Rigorous consistency provides that modicum of credibility that allows for suspension of disbelief; without belief in it, the horror merely strikes the mind as horribly silly. It may be that in any case, but the point is to let the spine enjoy its brief *frisson* while it may.

Stanley Kubrick's *The Shining* is bad in many different ways, the worst of which is surely that it does not scare us in the least, because its horror abides by no rules. I do not know the underlying novel by Stephen King, but I am told that Kubrick and his coscenarist, Diane Johnson (in other genres, a gifted writer), have played fast and loose with it. Illogic is piled up so high that the most supine mind should feel superior to it, if I may coin a paradox. Even the basic premise, that the enormous and luxurious Overlook Hotel in the mountains of Colorado would close down for five winter months rather than function as a ski resort, is as preposterous as anything that follows; inaccessibility and snowdrifts are no explanations in 1980.

Next, we are to swallow that this vast hotel will hire for a given winter one measly, totally inexperienced outsider to see to its upkeep. Jack Torrance, an ex-schoolteacher struggling with a novel, accepts this job even though his wife, Wendy, will have nothing to do for five months and their six- or seven-year-old son, Danny, will obviously be missing school. The Overlook, it seems, has a doubly guilty past: it was sacrilegiously built on the site of an old Indian burial ground (though when the ghosts start materializing, there is nary a red one among them—all whited by the sepulcher, no doubt); and the previous caretaker went stir-crazy and butchered his wife and two daughters with an ax before killing himself (the daughters' ghosts, however, are the wrong ages and have British accents—for no better reason than that Kubrick now lives and works in England). Credibility be damned—along with the dead.

When the Torrances settle in for the winter, they must use the hotel's huge kitchen (no smaller facility anywhere?) and, though their isolation is an obvious economy measure, they keep all the lights burning to produce an electric bill bigger than in midseason. They are a supposedly happy family, even if Jack had a drinking problem that once drove him to dislocate his son's shoulder; in penance, Jack gave up alcohol. Now all seems to be right again, but the film never establishes anything tangible about the family and their relations. Is Jack Torrance a genuine writer? Do Jack and Wendy love each other? Does the Overlook drive them crazy because they are already flawed? Is Danny's gift of "shining"—some form of ESP that operates on so many contradictory levels as to present a hopeless tangle in itself—connected with his imaginary friend, Tony, a boy who lives in and talks through Danny's mouth while also activating his index finger? Or is Tony with his *basso profundo* a mere bow to *The Exorcist?* Is or isn't Danny compensating for parental neglect?

As usual, Kubrick exhibits his basic inability to deal with people—the single, and not entirely successful, exception being *Paths of Glory.* Except in *Dr. Strangelove,* where the characters were meant to be cartoons, Kubrick's comic-strip approach to mankind has proved steadily detrimental. *2001* became amateurish the moment it forsook apes, hardware, and special effects for people. *A Clockwork Orange* reveled in the iconography of the future as *Barry Lyndon* did in that of the past, always to the detriment of the characters. In two and a half wearying hours, *The Shining* fails to make credible a single man, woman, or child.

What about the ghosts when, at long last, they do appear? Every Torrance sees them sooner or later, but it remains unclear why at one time and not at another, and whether different Torrances see the same ghosts, and if not, why not. Sometimes the implication is that it is all in people's minds, sometimes that it is all palpably real, and the two dispensations alternate with dizzying inconsistency. Key plot developments are left unexplained. Thus after Wendy manages to lock the murderously mad Jack into the larder, we are not shown how he gets out. Clearly the ghostly butler did it; but, if so, why doesn't he help Jack with other locked doors?

There are dozens of such glaring contradictions lying in ambush for the most willingly suspended disbelief. Why, for example, does the hotel's cook, also gifted with shining, come all the way from Miami to help Danny at great expense and risk (and without taking minimal safety measures), though he offered little or no warning when there was still time? And, having come, why does he fail to make use of the shining to protect him against an obvious pitfall? Yet the ghosts are even more inconsistent than the people; some can see and talk to Jack; others can't, though they rub shoulders with him. Some ghosts are young and strapping, some turn hideously old when clasped, some are already moldering skeletons. Danny is haunted by two recurrent visions: the little girls inviting him to play, which makes ghostly sense; and torrents of blood pouring from an elevator shaft until an entire corridor is awash in gore, which does not. Who would have thought two little girls and their parents to have had so much blood in them?

There are other problems related to Kubrick's megalomania. The film must be big at all cost, thus everything is dragged out beyond its usefulness. Danny, pedaling along in his little car through the Overlook's corridors, covers more ground than the contestants in an international racing event—merely to provide our technology-struck director with a crack at the longest low-angle rear-tracking shots in movie history. The final chase in the snowy topiary maze outside the hotel takes long enough for a Theseus to have slain a dozen Minotaurs, and for us to succumb to the most drawn-out anticlimax in the annals of cinema. And wouldn't Danny have been just as safe in his initial, indoor hiding place? What drives him out where he would logically freeze to death even before he could be chopped up by the paternal ax?

And still more forms of absurdity. Throughout the film, we get title cards, e.g., "3 O'CLOCK," "TUESDAY," or "SATURDAY"—as if what was being recorded were D-day or the bombing of Hiroshima rather than merely Kubrick's delusions of grandeur. And for weeks on end Jack types away fanatically at his novel; when Wendy finally looks at the manuscript, it is several hundred pages' worth of one sentence: "All work and no play make Jack a dull boy," albeit in the most diverse and complex typographical arrangements. With such talents as a typographer, who needs to turn out novels? And if a man is that far gone even before his crackup, wouldn't his wife have had sufficient cause for action earlier?

Finally, *The Shining* was shown at first with an epilogue that put a very different light on the proceedings; when audience responses proved unfavorable Kubrick simply took his ax to it and lopped it off, putting a quite changed interpretation on plot and characters. Can anyone with so little loyalty to his vision be seriously considered an artist?

Jack Nicholson hams atrociously from the outset; Shelley Duvall is better, but unable to fashion a whole character out of disparate fragments; little Danny Lloyd is as obdurately dour as other child actors are relentlessly cute. One thing the film does teach us; stymied creators are a bad lot: if they don't murder their families, which is bad enough, they come up with things like *The Shining,* which is worse.

June 27, 1980

Protean Bull

HOLLYWOOD MUST CONSIDER it axiomatic that summer makes people completely besotted. There exists, accordingly, a canicular film-releasing pattern that manages to depress the lowest common denominator—as well as the civilized moviegoer—a little further yet.

Take a film like *Urban Cowboy,* with which John Travolta hoped to efface the memory of *Moment by Moment* (or *Aeon by Aeon,* as it struck those of us who had to sit through it). This one is based on an *Esquire* cover story by Aaron Latham, a Texas-born journalist and Princeton Ph.D., whose doctoral thesis about Fitzgerald in Hollywood was published in book form. The screenplay, by Latham and James Bridges, the film's director, ostensibly explores the lives of Texas blue-collar workers who, off the oil rigs, like nothing better than to mount the mechanical bull at Gilley's, near Houston, the world's biggest bar, which can hold eight thousand Texans (God only knows how many Rhode Islanders!), and caters to all the recreational needs of these eponymous urban cowboys. Donning cowboy gear, they drink, dance, brawl, and wench at Gilley's (for which the movie is an excellent though overlong commercial), and, of course, ride the mechanical bull. Gilley's is the self-styled "biggest honky-tonk in America," and *Urban Cowboy* may just be the biggest rinky-dink among the summer's movies.

Bud, a young toiler in the oil refineries, is torn between his estranged tomboyish bride, Sissy, whom he resents because she can outlast him on the mechanical bull, and Pam, a spoiled rich girl who, out of her craving for Bud, destroys a conciliatory note Sissy left in the mobile home she used to share with him. Sissy, as a love offering, has cleaned the place in Bud's absence, but Pam stoops so low as to pretend that *she* did the cleaning. Sissy, however, sinks even lower by becoming the mistress of Wes, an ex-con who knocks her about and tries to hold up Gilley's. But Bud, who has just beaten Wes at mechanical bronco busting, foils the latter's robbery attempt, beats Wes at savage fisticuffs as well, and, having obviously come to his senses, blissfully resumes his marriage with Sissy. *Urban Cowboy,* as you may gather, is pure mechanical bull.

What makes the film truly reprehensible, though, is the filmmakers' stance. On the one hand, the principal characters are made into utter clods, lacking any individuality, imagination, or intelligence; on the other hand, they are accorded every kind of mythic resonance. Latham calls this a love story, even though the groupings and regroupings of the characters resemble those of atomic particles. Only one older couple (Bud's uncle and aunt) can be said to exhibit anything like real love, but they are presented in such cliché terms—their every gesture and utterance a sentimental stereotype—that they make love as absorbing as a TV commercial seen for the hundredth time.

As for Bridges, he perceives these characters as "honest, open and direct, possessing simple values." But "simple" need not mean simple-minded, any more than "open" need suggest a door banging about in a gale. So unable are he and Latham to invest these people with interesting mentalities and turns of phrase, even individual quirks, that their "directness" leads directly to dullness. I suspect that Latham and Bridges want to have it both ways: let these creatures be exemplars of "the cowboy, the most enduring symbol of our country [who] must be reinvented by each generation of the West," (Latham) for naïve viewers, while allowing more sophisticated audiences to feel pleasurably and smugly superior to them. I find that intellectually dishonest and morally distasteful.

Travolta sounds Texan enough part of the time (though there is the other part) and looks handsome from some angles (though there are the others, from which he looks inane). His acting, however, is all beatific grins or outbursts of petulance. Scott Glenn, as Wes (a character made to appear unearnedly sympathetic at first, then, suddenly and contrivedly, unduly antipathetic), does reasonably well under the circumstances. Madolyn Smith, as the rich Pam, whose entire character is hypostatized rather than motivated, can merely look sleek and gleam at the camera. However, Debra Winger, as Sissy, conveys an arresting combination of waif, brat, and incipient woman, and may develop into an actress to reckon with. The soundtrack relentlessly grinds out the kind of music appropriate to Gilley's, which isn't calculated to endear it to me; Roy Villalobos's cinematography is routine stuff. Yet all those shots of petrochemical refineries, sleazy housing developments, and all-night diners have their horrible fascination. If only something besides the oil were refined!

Samuel Fuller is the writer-director of some twenty B- (that's putting it kindly) features that have a fanatical following among movie buffs and auteur critics. Andrew Sarris, for instance, considers Fuller's *Shock Corridor* "a distinguished addition to that art form [*sic*] in which Hollywood has always excelled—the baroque B-picture." Fuller's films, whether gangster melodramas, war epics, westerns, or quasi-political thrillers, do not so much display "a primitive artist at work" (Sarris) as they proclaim a poster artist at his glaring worst. The dialogue is as simplistic as the ideology; the characterization as primitive as the sexuality, which is also infantile and puritanical; ferocity and jingoism are everywhere. "The strong, violent, and idiosyncratic handwriting" that Gavin Millar (in *Cinema: A Critical Dictionary*) detects in this oeuvre looks more like chicken tracks to me. Nicholas Garnham, in his book on Fuller, proclaims him "one of the major creative talents in the contemporary cinema"; for some readers it may suffice to know that Fuller was one of the principal influences on Jean-Luc Godard, who pays him a fulsome tribute in *Pierrot le Fou.*

The Big Red One is a film that comes close to being imbecile. Lee Marvin plays the tough Sergeant (he has no name—to make him more epic) who guides four teen-aged wetnoses through World War II. As members of the U.S. Army's First Division, the five men see action in North Africa, Sicily, Normandy, Belgium, Germany, and Czechoslovakia, and provide us with a travelogue across the major battlefields of the European theater. The four boys, like the Sergeant, are perfect stereotypes: Griff, a sensitive sharpshooter who has difficulties with killing (Mark Hamill, even more wonderful than as

Luke Skywalker); Johnson, a blond pig farmer who becomes worldly-wise through World War II (Kelly Ward, a nonentity); Zab, a pulp novelist who walks through the entire war with a cigar in his face—if the cigar isn't always the same, the face certainly is (Robert Carradine, the last chip off the old block, let's hope, and surely the least); and Vinci—why not Buonarotti or Alighieri?—an Italian street-kid and former saxophonist (Bobby Di Cicco, and typical).

Thanks partly to the Sergeant's shrewdness, partly to the "four horsemen's" quick learning and prowess, and partly to the absurdity of the script, our boys come through the war with nary a scratch while around them everywhere men are dying like flies. Replacements pour into the platoon to be mowed down within the range of flicked cigar ash from our heroes, who just wisecrack away as their buddies bite the dust. The obvious message to the pig farmers, sharpshooters, pulp novelists, and saxophone players in the audience is that war, though hell, is, if you have the right Sergeant, also a hell of a lot of fun.

There is a weasel prologue set in World War I, where the Sergeant, unaware that armistice has been declared, kills a German soldier. In the weasel epilogue, the Sergeant, again unaware that the war is over, stabs his opposite number, a ubiquitous German noncom. This time he will do everything to revive the not-quite-dead German; as the film tells us over and over again, what is killing in wartime is murder in peace. We are to know that we are watching privileged brutalities and may enjoy them accordingly.

Yes, there are some clever shots throughout *The Big Red One,* although Adam Greenberg's cinematography is mediocre, and Dana Kaproff's music further vulgarizes whatever it underpaints. If you cannot, like Godard, say about a Fuller film (*Forty Guns*) that it "is so rich in invention—despite an incomprehensible plot," you may find this offensive propaganda—not so much for a vulgar brand of America *über alles* as for a kind of hack Hollywood filmmaking apparently unaware that an armistice has been declared.

August 8, 1980

Ars Longa, Vita Brevis

FAME, directed by Alan Parker, who gave us those two abominations, *Bugsy Malone* and *Midnight Express,* marks a step up for the director. It concerns, first, the way boys and girls audition to get into New York's High School of Performing Arts; then how the work and lives of some of them interlock; how, in some cases, the teachers affect them; and how, after adventures and misadventures, they all graduate with a glorious splash. The stories of the youngsters make absolutely no sense—one smart, tough girl gets suckered into making porn movies against her will, and one homosexual feels like a lonely pariah, whereas the school must teem with his likes—but the early sequences of more or less desperate, wryly comic auditions carry some conviction (though they are unduly gimmicked up) and a good deal of energy, which is the film's chief virtue.

The trouble even here is that the audition as an *objet trouvé* of storytelling has lately been overexploited: we've had *A Chorus Line* on stage and its cinematic derivative, *All That Jazz.* Yet *Fame* owes even more to Miloš Forman's treatments of the theme: first in his Czech student film, *Competition,* then in his American reworking and expansion of it, *Taking Off.* There exist, it appears, subjects that film cannot use more than sparingly without making them look repetitious, derivative, all but plagiarized. Still, the comic vitality of its initial sequences makes *Fame* viewable in a season of famine.

A somewhat more interesting, though still faulty, film is *The Great Santini,* which had a troubled prehistory. A failure in several cities where it was sneak-previewed, it was sold by Orion, the production company, to Home Box Office and to the airlines for in-flight showing under its previous, equally infelicitous title, *The Ace.* On the strength of good reviews, however, it is making a bit of a theatrical comeback, and it surely deserves more than a half-life on and in the air. Written and directed by a former, not untalented, playwright, Lewis John Carlino, from an autobiographical novel by Pat Conroy, this is an uneven achievement that nevertheless contains enough of value to justify catching it.

The Great Santini concerns Colonel Bull Meechum, a marine flying ace chomping at the bit of peace, who, though a brilliant flier and a crack officer, has been trouble for the Marine Corps, what with his daredeviltry and practical jokes. He is now transferred to Beaufort, S.C., where a squadron of sadsacks needs his genius to make men and pilots out of them. Unfortunately, the entire military side of the film is reduced to a few vignettes, mostly farcical without being very funny. What we get more of is Bull's family life with Lillian, the loving, understanding, but often sorely tried wife, and their two sons and two daughters, whom Bull is rearing in the toughest marine tradition, as if they, too, were a recalcitrant squadron. Yet, of course, along with the sternness there is also the love and horseplay postulated by this cinematic genre. The film focuses mainly on the Oedipal triangle involving Ben, the eighteen-year-old eldest, Bull, and Lillian; but even here, despite some vibrant incidents, much is amiss.

Stanley Kauffmann has suggested that Robert Duvall, a powerful portrayer of lower-class fanatics, does not convey a man who belongs to the military elite: instead of a member of an aristocratic warrior caste, we get a scrappy plebeian in aspect, accent, and demeanor. But, I dare say, officers can be of all types; the trouble is that we do not see what drew the obviously refined Lillian to him; even his occasional sophisticated banter with his children issues contradictorily from his tough, often foul, mouth. The rivalry between the aging champion and the sensitive son who is beginning to overtake him is compelling, both funny and moving, but the side of Bull's character that elicits transcendent loyalty from wife and son even in the midst of justified exasperation is fatally shortchanged. Still, Duvall is commanding enough in his lowbrow way, and Blythe Danner and Michael O'Keefe are splendid as Lillian and Ben.

More than splendid: they are able to take stock parts and make them resonate in our sensibility as if we had never encountered them before. Such acting cannot be described: it has to do with personality, charm, sincerity, and great self-control. It is enough of an art to be enjoyable even independently from the context, although, of course, it fits perfectly into it. The three younger children have less rewarding roles and are not persuasively matched. But Stan Shaw, as a young black who befriends Ben and later comes to a horrible albeit too obviously tear-jerking end, is also very fine in a fairly standard part. Yet Meechum's death—because he will not parachute from his burning plane while it flies over Beaufort and might kill the townfolk—is arrant nonsense: it must take all of two seconds for the fast-flying plane to clear the tiny speck that is the town. Still, the father-son clashes are often gripping and keep a decent enough progression going. The cinematography, unfortunately, is plodding; but Carlino's theatrical background helps with the personal confrontations, and there are moments of savory family banter, as well as a couple of dramatic scenes between father and son that are turbulent, disturbing, and finally touching.

September 5, 1980

Murder Most Fulsome

SUDDENLY, THE SUMMER HAS one mighty critical success that is also proving a sweeping audience favorite (though some boos are also heard): Brian De Palma's *Dressed to Kill.* David Denby has hailed this as the first great film of the eighties; Pauline Kael has splattered panegyrics across four pages of *The New Yorker.* Two-page ads in the *New York Times* are studded with hearty albeit shopworn superlatives, and the lines outside theaters where the film is playing look as if a bank were giving away—in the current, detestable pleonasm—free gifts. What *Dressed to Kill* dispenses liberally, however, is sophomoric soft-core pornography, vulgar manipulation of the emotions for mere sensation, salacious but inept dialogue that is a cross between comic-strip Freudianism and sniggering double entendres, and a plot line so full of holes as to be at best a dotted line.

We begin with music by Pino Donaggio that, even if it is (but is it?) meant to be trashy, has no business being tailored for a future album of Music to Grit Your Teeth To. Angie Dickinson (or, mostly, a body model) is in the shower while her husband is shaving with a straight razor—the ubiquitous razors are perhaps the only straight thing about this film, but even they are put to crooked uses. Angie is loving herself up—not masturbating, mind you, which might make sense, but doing all those crotch caressings and nipple squeezings that soft-core porn wallows in, and doing them endlessly—establishing right away that this is a movie without psychological integrity. A stranger suddenly overpowers her from behind and makes violent love to her, while the husband just keeps shaving. Thus we catch on that this is all the fantasy of an unfulfilled wife.

In the next scene—essentially redundant after the foregoing—the husband is pumping away at Angie in bed while the weather report drones from the bedside radio. Angie pretends to be enormously aroused and having a mile-high orgasm, though even a crazed and subnormal bull could tell that she is faking. The husband, of course, promptly rolls off his wife in that textbook way of inadequate lovers, while Angie lingers glumly supine. There is multiple derivativeness here. The sexual-fantasy beginning presented as if it were reality stems from Buñuel's *Belle de Jour,* where, however, it serves to establish the heroine's crucial masochism. Here, Angie's excessive lasciviousness widely overshoots the mark of rendering her pathetic sexual frustrations. The rape in the shower comes, of course, from Janet Leigh's murder in *Psycho,* but that scene, because of its relative sobriety (leaving much to the imagination) and dazzling editing, managed to be both sexier and scarier than De Palma's epigonous piddling. The unsatisfactory intercourse scene owes something to Jane Fonda in bed with a john in *Klute,* where, however, the woman's uninvolvement is conveyed much more economically and forcefully by a surreptitious look at a wristwatch than by this insistent and overexplicit weather report.

The sequence between Angie Dickinson and Michael Caine, her matinee-idol psychiatrist, is, again, unconvincing. Earlier, a scene with her scientific genius of a son (Keith Gordon) at work constructing a computer was more credible; here, you feel that everything is planted to further the preposterous plot rather than to give dimension and plausibility to the characters. Even though Caine is dapperly British and his furniture impeccably Scandinavian, his professionalism is not much greater than that of the thirties and forties shrinks usually played by Sig Rumann with a Teutonic accent as thick as their sconces.

The heart-warming headshrinker is administering to his long-time patient a simplistic brand of therapy that suggests that neither of them has been involved with this sort of thing before. Such lack of credibility—and psychiatric explanations escalate into ludicrous absurdity as the film proceeds—matters only because De Palma is being hailed as a serious artist. If he were that, even his light entertainments or Gothic thrillers would have some bearing on at least a stylized reality, which is what distinguishes the fluff of an artist from the machinations of a manipulator.

Angie goes off to what is supposed to be the Metropolitan Museum but is actually its Philadelphia cousin, where she sits before a huge, junky portrait by Alex Katz and jots down shopping reminders into her agenda. The contrast between the museum setting and the scribbled trivia would be enough for a director with taste, but De Palma must drag in the photorealist portrait of a gorilla *(pintor*—to me—*ignotus)* from the opposite wall for what seems to be a further ironic comment. But what does it mean? (I wonder, incidentally, whether this atrocity actually hangs in the Philadelphia Museum of Art.)

The fact that Angie's eager head—she appears to be using the museum as a pickup place—is often shot against the crotch of a Philip Pearlstein nude *is* an unmistakable comment, though not one a director with finesse would find it necessary to make.

There ensues an elaborate pickup ritual with a handsome stud—whose behavior is, by the way, completely self-contradictory—involving a deliberately dropped glove that may or may not be picked up, may or may not be returned, and may or may not be accepted if returned. There is also a profusion of tracking shots through the museum's galleries, ending with Angie's jumping into the taxi from which the stud ungallantly waves the missing glove. To the horrified delight of the cabbie watching in the rear-view mirror, the stud promptly administers his brand of oral resuscitation, of which, as a detective later remarks in a typical sample of De Palma's verbal wit, the driver gave "a blow-by-blow description."

Angie goes to the man's nifty apartment and is rendered ecstatic by having, apparently, all her connubial lacunas filled. Yet since the man is sleeping like a log all the time she is getting dressed, and since what we saw of his performance was not markedly different from the husband's, we feel as manipulated as Angie does when, in the process of writing a gracious thank-you note to her snoozing lover, she discovers in his desk drawer an urgent summons to report for treatment of his venereal disease. One of our film critics actually perceived this as evidence of De Palma's high moral purpose: punishment for Angie's infidelity. Yet the swain's cloddish sleeping-it-off is ironic comeuppance enough; only De Palma's infantile sense of humor requires that the poor woman, about to be sliced to ribbons by a mad killer, agonize first about impending gonorrhea.

As a distraught Angie gets into the descending elevator, we catch a glimpse of the killer lying in wait for her on the fire stairs. But he doesn't follow her into the conveniently empty elevator. On the way down, Angie discovers that she forgot her diamond solitaire by the bed where she committed her well-nigh solitary vice. So she must ride back up again to meet her doom; how did the waiting killer know that she would return? And what does the ominous stare of a little girl who, led by her mother, rides part-way up with Angie, mean? Pure effect without cause. Then the killer, a tall, dark-spectacled blond floozie—or perhaps a transvestite—gets into the elevator and starts cutting up Angie with a straight razor.

Meanwhile, waiting downstairs for the elevator, is the real heroine of the film, Nancy Allen, a.k.a. Mrs. Brian De Palma, whom, until death or divorce do them part, De Palma will undoubtedly inflict on us in film after film. She portrays (badly) a witty, intelligent, stylish, and basically pure hooker, who carefully invests her earnings in stocks and bonds, and may be the cinema's first whore with a heart of gilt-edged securities. The character, as written by De Palma, is yet another sophomoric sex fantasy, just as Angie Dickinson is the schoolboy's lubricious dream of the beautiful older woman in a state of continuous arousal and availability.

Nancy is with a john, gleaning tips on investing before divesting for him, as the elevator doors open, revealing Angie streaming blood and extending a slashed, imploring hand for help. De Palma squeezes every bit of horror and fun, not to mention improbability, out of crosscutting between the gory murder and the comic Wall Street chatter and the john's craven flight. Unable to leave unwell enough alone, he must show us—as Nancy runs from the scene of the crime for which both police and perpetrator will be after her—a last grisly shot of a bloodied limb protruding from the elevator door and twitching in the paroxysm of death. In view of the encomiums De Palma has been getting, Oscar Wilde must have been right: nothing succeeds like excess.

The murder scene is profoundly distasteful. Not because of the gratuitous brutality, and not because of the comic crosscutting, though both are bad enough. But because of the choreographic, interior-decoratorish way in which it is staged and shot. Angie's smart attire and the glistening high-tech elevator contrast cutely with the killer's campy getup and the generous helping of blood. Angie's vain gestures of self-defense or imprecation and her subsequent slow crumpling into a corner of the elevator are studiedly counterposed to the killer's showily swordsmanlike brandishing of the razor (which displays at various times in the film meticulously photographed reflections of the victim) and erect clinging to the wall of another corner in an attempt to avoid detection as the doors open. This is to treat murder (quite unlike Hitchcock, for all his serving as model to De Palma) as fashion-magazine chic *à la* Helmut Newton—perhaps the unholiest form of titillation. Claims by De Palmists notwithstanding, this is neither unblinking stoicism nor, more preposterous yet, the meting out of poetic justice. It is moral aphasia, and something uglier still: the drawing out of murder into languorous, lascivious excitation.

I have no room—and feel no obligation—to analyze any more of *Dressed to Kill,* with its repeated formula of mixing jokiness, sexuality, and deadly violence. But I must comment on a set of final sequences, which includes a shower scene for Nancy to complement Angie's and involve the young woman's dreams or fantasies. Framed as the film is by this matching prologue and epilogue, it confronts us forcibly with the notion that the chief functions of women are (a) to indulge in elaborate dreams or fantasies of a largely masochistic sort, and (b) to provide men—both as filmmakers and as filmgoers—with objects for *their* sexually aggressive and murderous fantasizing.

Much has been made of De Palma's alleged brilliance in handling the camera. He is certainly not inept with it, but here, too, he cheats. Thus in Nancy's dream, he fools around with a threefold point of view—the girl's, the killer's, and the director's—that has nothing to do with the way dreams work. But, of course, he doesn't want us to know that dreams are dreams: we are supposed to get all excited about watching something that, though bizarre, is apparently real, then let him off the hook because it was, after all, only a dream. But dreams, too, have their logic; only De Palma is completely devoid of it, as he is also of any moral sense.

Ralph Bode's cinematography is routine, but there is one charming and persuasive performance: by Keith Gordon, as the young scientific genius who seems to find true happiness with our whorish heroine. Yet even this character is unconvincing: a wiz in everything electronic and an illiterate in biology—again merely to suit De Palma's whims. There is one clever and scary madhouse sequence, not quite enough to merit Pauline Kael's paean: "It is hardly possible to find a point at which you could tear yourself away from this picture." As I remarked earlier, the story line is so full of holes as to be, at best, a dotted line. You can easily tear yourself away along it.

September 5–19, 1980

Sandy Stardust

WHEN WOODY ALLEN DISCOVERED Underlying Seriousness in *Annie Hall,* he may have gained the world, but he lost those of us who prefer, even on screen, an honest stand-up comic to a dishonest social commentator, metaphysical seeker, and existential sniveler. *Stardust Memories* merely reaffirms his strategy of having it both ways: self-aggrandizement that tries to pass for self-irony, virulent misanthropy that masquerades as amusement at the human show, artistic pretentiousness that copies major filmmakers while pretending to be good-natured pastiche.

Stardust Memories is an almost plotless movie that tells about Sandy Bates, a comedian turned successful filmmaker, who, harassed though he is by the contingencies of his trade and success, agrees to a weekend at the Stardust Hotel (presumably somewhere on Long Island, but the topography is rearranged and fictionalized as in *L'Avventura*). There is to be a screening of his new film along with seminars for buffs and fans conducted by Bates and a female movie critic (modeled on Judith Crist and her Tarrytown movie weekends). What we see on screen is a mixture of what happens at the Stardust with scenes from the film and occasional dreams and fantasies of Sandy's, the three elements not clearly identified and made deliberately confusing. There may be some little life yet in this hanky-panky with Illusion and Reality, but not when we don't care about the protagonist and his problems. As it is, the technique palls almost before it registers.

To be sure, it is a device perfectly suited to the dishonest evasions of the overarching strategy. If something is too preposterous or repellent for the viewer to accept as Sandy's life (i.e., the Truth), it can always be assumed to constitute part of Sandy's satirical film. If it is too absurd or ugly even for that, consider it one of Sandy's daydreams or nightmares. But there is also a higher, all-embracing dishonesty at work here. Almost everything we are told or shown about Sandy Bates is true of Woody Allen, yet with just enough deviations from strict autobiography to allow Allen to declare it presumptuous to equate him with his protagonist.

What, then, are Bates's problems? They pertain, first, to his work: like Woody, he used to make pure comedies, but awareness of, ugh, Reality has made him seek deeper and darker subjects. "Human suffering does not sell tickets in Kansas City," he is told by the production people who keep bugging him throughout, and his quest in the movie (insofar as kvetching is a quest; perhaps kvesting would be better) is derived from Preston Sturges's *Sullivan's Travels.* But here lies the big lie in all its naked ugliness: when Sandy says, "I look around the world and all I see is human suffering," what does this Sandy-Woody really mean? From his chauffeur-driven Rolls-Royce (in the film as in life), from his fancy apartment protected by a battery of agents, secretaries, cooks, and other amanuenses, how much reality can he perceive? The apartment is decorated with wall-sized photomurals of himself, Groucho Marx, and the Saigon police chief executing a prisoner point-blank; since when is narcissistic Groucho-Marxist radical chic a panorama of human suffering? Well, pigeons do flutter around his plate-glass windows, and an enraged Sandy chases them: he calls them "rats with wings." Is that cliché used deliberately? You never know with Woody.

Allen's strategy is one of instant self-deflation. He promptly tells his fans at the Stardust that, though he has been accused of narcissism, the mythological character he identifies himself with is not Narcissus but Zeus. Loud laughter. By this making fun of yourself you achieve triple *captatio benevolentiae:* you are funny, you are big enough for self-mockery, and—who knows?—maybe, just maybe, you really are the Zeus of current American filmmakers and lechers. Throughout the film—as a running, crowding, suffocating gag—we get ever more ludicrous and creepy fans (interspersed, however, with the odd pretty girl asking for an autograph on her left breast) saying and requesting ever more ludicrous and creepy things. It begins with someone saying she loved all of Sandy's films, "especially the early, funny ones." Later, aliens from outer space repeat this statement. We are to understand that the new, unfunny ones are even better, merely beyond the comprehension of fools.

Pretty soon, in between preposterous requests to read a comedy script about mass suicide and contribute a used truss to a collection of memorabilia, Bates is told, "You are a master of despair," and, again, with utmost reverence, "You have such a degenerate mind!" Clearly, since they are all such super-Fellinian grotesques and behave like stampeding pigs, the fans (for which read: the public) are the kinds of loathsome pests that do not leave you a private minute, and demand not mere autographs but dedications such as: "To Phyllis Weinstein, you unfaithful, lying bitch!" Gradually, however, it is insinuated that perhaps even such phony swine recognize genuine pearls when they are cast before them. And when one of them asks for an autograph on a copy of *Tom Sawyer,* Sandy, unflinchingly, signs it. Bates-Allen is Mark Twain *redivivus.*

Yet there is some authentic self-incrimination—perhaps even self-loathing—here; a trait that, however genuine, is less than endearing, let alone exonerating. Thus when one of Sandy's women accuses him of flirting with a girl of fourteen and he vehemently denies it, we glimpse yet another photomural—an incriminating blowup of a newspaper article whose truncated headline reads: INCEST BETWEEN FATHER AND . . . Another time, a seemingly teen-aged girl has bribed her way into Sandy's bed; she has been driven from Bridgeport by her husband, a Bates fan who considers it a privilege to sleep outside in the car while Sandy is cuckolding him. When Sandy demurs, the girl upbraids him: "Empty sex is better than no sex!" And she switches off the light; the ensuing blackout may or may not mean consummation. In a sense, Bates the adolescent-lover is like those murderers who leave behind notes begging the police to catch them.

But when it comes to playing the great lover with more or less adult women, Sandy-Woody knows no self-irony. Small, Jewish, and ugly, Sandy (like Woody) has an insatiable yen for big beautiful shiksas, to be conquered as plentifully and publicly as possible. Michael's Pub, where he plays the clarinet, is Woody's real-life Deer Park; in the film, Sandy uses both the set on which he directs and the Stardust Hotel as hunting grounds. He dallies with Charlotte Rampling, who stands for crazy, aristocratic English beauty; Marie-Christine Barrault, who represents voluptuous French earth-motherhood; and Jessica Harper, who embodies bright, very young, crunchy American neurosis with artistic leanings. (Allen and Miss Harper have been "romantically linked" in the gossip columns.) All three are shown either panting after or profoundly satisfied by the runty Sandy: "You are the best kisser," burbles one of them; to which Sandy replies: "It was my major in college." It's a joke, but with serious, self-serving overtones.

Stardust Memories cribs from everywhere. There are Antonioni's white-walled cages in which the high-rise-dweller molders and maunders; there are Buster-Keatonesque views of the empty screen inviting speculations on Film and Reality; there is the Bergmanesque mute prologue (with only a clock ticking) where Sandy is imprisoned in a hideous train with dismal fellow passengers while on a parallel track beautiful people are living it up on a scrumptious train; there is the sequence in which the hospitalized, deeply disturbed Miss Rampling monologizes heart-rendingly while a tight camera makes quick cuts from one take to another—out of *The Four Hundred Blows* via *Winter Light;* there is the flashback, out of the end of *Wild Strawberries,* to a happy past, where everything is white, luminous, peaceful—in this case, Miss Rampling prone on Sandy's carpet, the Sunday paper before her and her legs waggling behind, while Satchmo on the hi-fi sings "Stardust." And, above all, there is Fellini, in all those quick, bittersweet cuts back into childhood, and those visions of people in mysterious long shots that make bizarre behavior look supernatural. The film has been called Woody Allen's *8½*, but it is too dumb for that; it is really his *Juliet of the Spirits.*

Bates-Allen tries to be disarming, like that unsightly woman who, hoping to be contradicted, asked Oscar Wilde: "Am I not the ugliest woman in France?" Bowing deeply, Wilde answered with exquisite courtesy: "In the world, madame, in the world." Thus Sandy worries: "I am not talking about my stupid little film here; eventually there's not going to be any Shakespeare or Beethoven!" Clearly, we are to exclaim in dread, "And no Woody Allen!" So when Bates-Allen mentions "Art and masturbation—two areas in which I am an expert," I say there is no doubt about it—he just has difficulty figuring out which is which.

November 28, 1980

Men or Beasts?

THE ELEPHANT MAN is a thoroughly bad movie, but its badness is nothing compared to its dishonesty. A title card announces that this film is based not on the Broadway play but on the true life story of John Merrick, the Elephant Man. This is a double lie: the film deliberately falsifies and sensationalizes the story by means of various shabby, unimaginative fabrications, and it does crib a number of not particularly distinguished conceits from Bernard Pomerance's play, *The Elephant Man.*

By now, most people will have heard about the case of John Merrick, a late-nineteenth-century English victim of neurofibromatosis, a congenital disorder, which hideously deformed most of his head, body, and limbs (his left arm and genitals were spared). He was cruelly exhibited in sideshows as far afield as Belgium, and was rescued only when Frederick Treves, a brilliant and humane young surgeon, put him in London Hospital, Whitechapel, where his four last years were made tolerable. With the approval of Treves's superior, Carr Gomm, and thanks to the public's generous response to a plea for funds, Merrick could enjoy books and learn to speak despite dreadful impediments (Treves, in his 1923 memoir, called Merrick the most disgusting specimen of humanity he had ever seen). He became a sort of mascot of high society, whose members visited him and showered him with presents, and was even sneaked into his beloved theater—under heavy veils and through secret passages into a curtained box—thanks to the kindness of Madge Kendal, a leading actress of the day.

The monstrous, incurable, yet sweet-natured Merrick scored a noble victory for the human spirit; by the time he died, aged twenty-seven, in 1890, he had even built, with his good left hand, a fine model of Saint Philip's, the church he could see from his window. Frequently Treves heard him say, "I am happy every hour of the day." And yet Merrick committed a kind of suicide. Because of the weight of his enormous head, he could not sleep in the normal way, but had to be propped up with pillows, his head resting on his knees. One night he chose to lie down to sleep; rupture or compression of his spinal cord made the sleep terminal.

The story, which needs tact and taste in the telling, was, unfortunately, produced by Mel Brooks, not known for either. Brooks entrusted its direction to young David Lynch, whose only previous credit is *Eraserhead*, a low-budget horror film. From Eraserhead to Elephant Man was obviously the shortest distance (even if not exactly a straight line) for Lynch and his coscenarists, Christopher DeVore and Eric Bergren. As a result, we get a film shot in black-and-white, exploiting the seaminess of industrially blighted Victorian London, with a screenplay that is all melodrama and horror show.

To begin with, we are teased in every way with expectations of the monster until we are finally accorded a view of the wretch in his full ghastliness. (Good as the make-up is, incidentally, it still looks like make-up.) Then follows a concocted story fraught with fake reversals. Not only is Bytes, Merrick's initial keeper, a disgusting bully (derived, clearly, from the corresponding character in the play), but there is also another bestial fellow, a hospital orderly who sells nocturnal admissions allowing gawkers to inspect Merrick in his hospital room (lurid scenes of jeering and sexual arousal among the gapers) even though one word from Merrick to Treves would have put an end to such a practice.

The evil orderly is instrumental in Bytes's kidnapping of Merrick for further sideshow exhibition abroad; this gives Lynch a chance to play at being Tod Browning, with all the freaks pitching in to help Merrick narrowly escape from his tormentor. Then there is a ludicrous scene in which the orderly, unmasked by Treves, threatens physical violence, only to be comically knocked out by the crusty head nurse brandishing a well-stuffed laundry bag. Or take another hammy scene, in which the hospital board considers evicting Merrick from his shelter at the instigation of a nasty board member; at the last moment, in sweeps kindly Princess Alexandra and makes the vile fellow eat crow. Or there is the scene wherein Mrs. Kendal and Merrick read from *Romeo and Juliet* in his room (again derived from the Broadway play), with the English actress portrayed by Anne Bancroft, a.k.a. Mrs. Mel Brooks, as a smug, smarmy American without a trace of Englishness.

But the nadir is reached when, shortly before his death, Merrick is shown relishing a Christmas pantomime in an open loge. This unfortunate, whose aspect, the film keeps telling us, made strong men blanch and trained nurses run in panic, mingles happily with fellow box-occupants, then receives a curtain salute from Mrs. Kendal—platitudes delivered by Miss Bancroft with a sickening smirk, vocal as well as facial—and gets a standing ovation from an audience that beams at him rapturously. Based upon the true life story of Hollywood hackery, this vulgar and mendacious film gained enthusiastic reviews from Pauline Kael and Vincent Canby, among others. Yet the very opening shot is a giveaway. Merrick used to remark that his mother must have been frightened by a circus elephant when she was carrying him. So Lynch begins his film with a sequence in which a pretty, well-dressed young woman—supposedly Merrick's mother—is weltering on the ground and silently screaming while a herd of wild African elephants tramples all around her, in slow motion, no less. Too good to waste on a mere prologue, this sequence returns at film's end.

John Hurt gives a sensitive and touching performance from behind his impenetrable Elephant Man mask, and Anthony Hopkins (Treves), John Gielgud (Carr Gomm), Wendy Hiller (head nurse), Freddie Jones (Bytes), and some others do the best they can with unrewarding material, while Freddie Francis's camera spews up moody chiaroscuro as if the film had been shot by flashlight. Wild elephants shouldn't drag you to this one.

What is Martin Scorsese's *Raging Bull* really about? Adapted from the ghosted autobiography of Jake La Motta, the ex-middleweight champion, by Paul Schrader and Mardik Martin (and revised by the director and his star, Robert De Niro), this is the story of a *bête humaine* who lives to pummel his opponents, in and out of the ring, to a pulp and to possess his fine-looking blond wife, Vickie, body and soul. But even these two driving motivations are not truly examined. It is possible to interpret them in reverse—to view Jake's boxing as a kind of kinky sexual fulfillment, and his mad jealousy and brutalizing of his wife as the assertion of an ego and virility corroded by self-doubt.

There is no continuous story, only an accumulation of "big" scenes: brute meets girl, possesses and knocks around girl, loses girl. Brute wins fights, throws fight for the Mafia, is rewarded with crack at championship, wins title, loses title. Then, suddenly, a much fatter and jollier La Motta runs a night club in Florida, which he loses after he is jailed on a morals charge. Having been a comedian at his own club, he is shown now backstage at New York's Barbizon-Plaza as he rehearses a speech from *On the Waterfront,* which, along with selections from Shakespeare, Tennessee Williams, and others, as well as some comic doggerel, he is about to perform for an audience. Where did this new La Motta come from?

The film, though it revels in accurate reconstructions of the Bronx in the forties, the ring, Mafia lairs, yesteryear's night clubs, and the like, does not have any social statement to make. Thus Jake and his brother Joey—his manager, sparring partner, and mentor—are not shown in a full Italian family context: they seem to have no parents or in-laws, only wives and children; and even Jake's first wife disappears tracelessly when Jake gets involved with Vickie, and Jake and Vickie's children are conveniently out of the picture except for two token appearances.

Similarly, the Mafia (which is never named) seems to enforce an ironclad rule on the ring it controls: unless Jake will throw a fight for the Brotherhood, he gets no shot at the title. Then how does an honest black—as Sugar Ray Robinson, who wrests the championship from Jake, is portrayed—get the title without the Mafia's support? The way that particular bout is staged, it looks as if Jake were doing penance for something—but for what? And what about the economics in the film? La Motta owns his Florida night club and a fancy house, but cannot raise ten thousand dollars for his bail when he is caught serving liquor to two teen-agers—and (though this, like much else, is fudged) presumably indulging in sex with them. Don't ex-champions have that much credit in a sports-happy society?

The film is technically Martin Scorsese's most accomplished work to date, and the black-and-white photography is Michael Chapman's best yet. But even the cinematography is trendy in its currently favored "honest" monochrome, as well as in its brief espousal of grainy color for interpolated home-movie sequences of the La Mottas' early, fleeting conjugal bliss. (I am sorry to say that even Bergman has succumbed to this sort of thing in his latest, *From the Life of the Marionettes.*)

I am thoroughly convinced by Scorsese when he conveys to me—through tight shots, hand-held camera, fast editing, visual blurs, heightened or vanishing sound, and the obtuse spondees of blows—what it feels like to be battered senseless; I am even more impressed when he gleans a novel insight: how frayed the ropes of the ring have become from bodies that have scraped against them—with the implication of what the ropes, which surely fought back, must have done to those bodies. But when Scorsese tries to tell me something about people—assuming he has any ideas on that subject—even the most polished technique amounts to no more than a stammer.

Raging Bull does not even communicate what the rage of this bull is about: why he is so preternaturally jealous (even for a street-bred Italian) of his faithful wife, why he will turn even on his loyal and helpful brother, how he works out his eventual salvation—if that is what it is. Putting a prestigious but irrelevant biblical quotation on a final title card is merely a hollow gesture, an intellectual rabbit punch. And for all the good acting from the entire cast (especially Joe Pesci as the devoted but uncloying brother) the film finally misses out because of blindness and deafness to human meaning.

One final example: throughout, we get obsessive reiteration of one gross participle, which here emerges as midway between "foaking" and "focking." This Homeric epithet—which, alas, is not allowed to nod for a moment—is meant, I suppose, as a secular litany, a ritual assertion of toughness and savvy. But its thump, more persistent than that of leather on bone, soon becomes an indictment of minds incapable even of invention in obscenity. An ironic comment by the filmmakers? Certainly not, in a film whose entire comment is "No comment."

January 23–March 20, 1981

Second-City Blues

SOME CONSPICUOUS MOVIES of the past year unaccountably eluded my coverage, most notably *Ordinary People,* Robert Redford's directorial debut, now up for six Academy Awards—if that sort of thing still means anything to you, which I sincerely hope it doesn't. *Ordinary People* is an earnest, well-meaning film, determined to be forthright and searing, to reveal the lives of quiet desperation under the well-waxed façade of Lake Forest, Illinois, affluence. Yet everything remains a bit propaedeutic, a mite primitive, as if someone, instead of creating a work of the imagination, had dramatized a self-help book.

The Jarretts are a family carrying on gallantly after tragedy has struck. Calvin continues to be a prosperous, cheerful, considerate tax attorney, husband, and father, and Beth is still a fine, elegant, crisply efficient wife who, without full-time help, keeps a sizable house shipshape enough for a round-the-world cruise should it be cut from its Chicago moorings. And cut it was, by a sailing accident in which Buck, the popular elder son, was drowned, and which Conrad, his more introverted younger brother, blamed himself for surviving. Conrad then attempted suicide, spent months in a hospital receiving shock treatment, and is back now uneasily repeating junior year in high school. Beth, it turns out, adored Buck, but has no real love for Con, whom she perhaps blames for Buck's death, though this is not made clear. Cal, full of good intentions, tries feebly to mediate between mother and son, who keep talking past each other.

Conrad broods and sulks until Dr. Berger, a Jewish psychiatrist, helps him let out his repressed WASP emotions (a rather Jewish notion of gentile life, not unlike the one in Woody Allen's *Interiors,* prevails here). Even Calvin is aided by the tough yet kind, messy yet wise Berger, and finally father and son see behind Beth's mask. Revealed in her ungivingness, she leaves, and Cal and Con are united in a bursting nova of affection, with Con apparently beginning a wholesome relationship with Jeannine, a delightful schoolmate.

I have oversimplified a little, but the film's message, drilled in with tactful but unremitting understatement—like major surgery under local anesthesia—keeps iterating its twin ideas: let it all hang out lest you hang yourself; and love, love, love one another or perish. A brace of plausible enough points, these, and probably worth their billionth restatement, human imperfectibility being what it is. Nevertheless, to survive all that competition from ceaseless repetition, they have to be handled with pristine sharpness of observation, strategically sound deployment throughout a plot, characterizations that have both solidity and complexity, and, finally, a certain breathing space for the characters—room for some ambiguity, idiosyncrasy, nonpurposiveness, so that quirky life does not get chopped down to fit the Procrustean bed of pseudo-art.

On most, if not all, of these counts *Ordinary People* fails. Judith Guest's bestseller, on which Alvin Sargent's screenplay is based, is not really a better work, but it does have two good instincts the movie lacks: it tries to fill in the characters' backgrounds and environments (admittedly easier in a novel), and it strives to inject some humor, however second-rate, into the gloomy proceedings. The movie may have foreshortened too much; it has certainly become more long-faced and antiseptic, more relentlessly purposeful. We get a sense of every scene, however short, having been carefully programmed to make its single point before proceeding to the next scene, with its equally neat, cleanly made point, and so on throughout this entire lecture, sermon, or mathematical demonstration that is *Ordinary People.*

At the very beginning, when Beth, Cal, and another couple emerge from what seems to have been some dismal little-theater production, Cal asks with an unnerved laugh, "Well, did we like it?" Aha, we say, here is a man unsure of himself and trying to find a socially ingratiating way out of his insecurity. A little later, during the film's only classroom scene, a particularly odious English teacher (probably not meant that way, but who knows?) asks Conrad about Hardy's Jude: "Do you think he was powerless in the grip of circumstances, or could he have helped himself?" Con hesitates: "I don't know. Powerless? I guess he thought he was." Ah, yes! The problem in a nutshell, along with the solution squeezed right in with it: as long as you think you are powerless, you are. So change your way of thinking.

But problems, in life or art, are not readily fittable into nutshells, and there are capricious winds that dislodge and efface the existential signposts. Beth's cold efficiency is steadily, stridently underlined. If her son won't immediately eat the French toast set before him, into the shredder it goes; if Cal, in bed, wants to make love, she will let him do so, but with what seems feigned responsiveness. But, then, why did this woman love Buck so much and Conrad so little? And now that Con is all that is left to her, wouldn't she, so well trained in deception and self-deception, transfer at least a semblance of affection to him?

The film suffers from ideological schematism that often does not seem psychologically thought through. And Redford's generally competent direction nevertheless reinforces the didacticism. Thus Beth and Cal come home from that theater in a sequence in which the camera shoots through the balustrade their legs winding their way up an inner staircase toward their sleeping quarters. Yes, yes: life as the placing of one foot ahead of the other along a closed-in path—an orderly routine mechanically pursued. Our feet can do our living for us. There is no room for the unpredictable in this kind of filmmaking—for the lint of irony, the fluff of ambivalence that in an art conversant with truth adheres to the steeliest certainties. When, for example, in Rilke's great *The Notebooks of Malte Laurids Brigge,* the lovely, somewhat lost mother sighs to her son, "There are no classes for beginners in life, Malte," there is just a chance that this may be only her despairing view. When Dr. Berger tells Con, "Feelings are scary: sometimes they're painful, and if you're not going to feel pain, you are not going to feel anything else either," we must allow as how this is a powerfully unambiguous verity. And also dangerously close to a platitude.

Still, there are some decent things in this film, even if its general intellectual level and its view of psychotherapy are not quite of their number. There is, for instance, no last-minute effort to whitewash Beth and no attempt to tell us whether her departure is temporary or conclusive. Yet that final shot of Con and Cal in a tearful albeit manly embrace—echoing a somewhat earlier and less likely parting hug between Berger and Con—is a bit too pat in its paternal-filial bliss. And Redford the director is still opting for fairly obvious camera placements and movements, though he does manage to set and maintain a brisk narrative pace.

Best of all are three pieces of acting. Elizabeth McGovern breezes into believability as Jeannine, all uncluttered, outgoing warmth and yet beset by little slips of youthful ineptitude, which the actress conveys with a marvelous coltishness that seems to grow into a rich femininity before our very eyes. Donald Sutherland gives his best performance in years as Calvin; all too often miscast in roles too extreme for him to handle without blatancy, here, as a middling man of good will, he stumbles toward ripeness with a good deal of winning, unexaggerated pathos. The most remarkable work, however, is in the Conrad of Timothy Hutton, a precociously pared-down actor already free of any form of special pleading such as cuteness, unearned intensity, pseudohonest befuddlement translated into excessive pauses and hesitancies, and all the rest. Instead, Hutton confronts Conrad's uncertainties and reversals head on, allowing us to see the forming of thoughts, the genesis and repression and outbursts of feeling with a vocabulary of expressions that is articulate but never prolix.

Alas, *Ordinary People* also has two flaws that consign it below the respectable mediocrity to which it otherwise manages to cling. One is Mary Tyler Moore's Beth, whose initially convincing frigidity (it has the look of typecasting rather than acting, but, so long as it works, who cares?) soon spills over into a slackness in and around the eyes, and shades, in scenes of climactic intensity, into something that looks like sheer bloated stupidity, quite ungermane to the role. The other is Marvin Hamlisch's truly loathsome score that begins with Pachelbel's already overexploited Canon and proceeds to ring a series of ever more unwelcome changes on it—including bizarre pop arrangements and finally even human voices—implicating us in its musical cud-chewing. How one longs to give this soundtrack a sound trashing!

April 3, 1981

Rainbows in Your Eyes

JONATHAN DEMME is probably the most gifted young filmmaker to come out of Roger Corman's stable; his very first "serious" feature, *Citizen's Band*, was a lovely, hilarious, semisatirical folk comedy, needing only a better ending: neither of the two that Demme tried was quite satisfactory. This scintillating little fable promptly died at the box office, was given a new title, *Handle with Care,* and re-released only to die equally promptly, despite valiant efforts by individuals and institutions to keep it going. After this twice-born *succès d'estime* came *Last Embrace,* a stillborn disaster. Demme's third, *Melvin and Howard,* treated by Universal as a stepchild despite fine reviews and various awards, may have received a new lease on life thanks to Oscars for Bo Goldman's screenplay and Mary Steenburgen's supporting performance.

Melvin and Howard has what *Citizen's Band* had, but in simpler, sweeter, purer, and slightly less brilliant form. Without the absurdist, satirical overtones, it is a goofy comedy about lovably zany, gently outrageous people that rings true even at its most preposterous and makes you care for characters whom it would be easy to condescend to and dismiss. It is the basically true story of Melvin Dummar, a near-ne'er-do-well, who once saved an injured bum from dying of exposure in the nocturnal Nevada desert. That bum claims to be (and is) Howard Hughes, a crotchety, surly fellow, whom Melvin, without believing him, humanizes as he drives him back to Vegas. He makes the old-timer sing, first, a silly song written by Melvin, whose tune cost our eccentric hero $70 shelled out to a mail-order composer ("And well worth it!" Melvin declares), and then "Bye, Bye, Blackbird," which Hughes dredges up from his childhood along with other tender memories.

The film's ostensible story concerns a historic trial: how a will of Hughes's turned up mysteriously, leaving $156 million to Dummar—a will that was contested and eventually thrown out of court. But the real story is about the lives of Melvin, his two wives, Lynda and Bonnie, and their children; about Melvin's friends and employers and lawyers; about the game shows on which Melvin hopes to get rich; about the white-elephant consumer goods he acquires on down payments, only to have them quickly repossessed; about marriage, family, divorce, sex, and other curious involvements in the westernmost reaches of these United and disunited States. It is about quick-marriage chapels, motels, strip joints; about work as a milkman or in a magnesium factory; about office Christmas parties; about preposterous giveaway shows on TV, and winning money easily and losing it no less easily.

Yet though these people are simple-minded, childishly impetuous, and even screwy, they do not lack for a crazy sort of imagination, an originality in shuffling and brandishing platitudes. They have comic-strip values and mess up large chunks of their lives, but they pursue their touchingly foolish dreams with a vivacity and dedication bordering on the heroic. Their energy is inspiring, their directness disarming, and their follies not all that different from those of sophisticated people. In the end, they are a strangely moving lot, whose very ludicrousness wrings your heart. You laugh and cry simultaneously, which makes rainbows in your eyes. The most terrible thing Lynda can say to Melvin, whom she has remarried but is leaving for a second time (now with two kids instead of one), is "You're a loser, Melvin," which he achingly, ardently denies. Fundamentally, all these characters are losers, but they do not admit it, and therein lies their glory: they are the gallantly walking, waltzing wounded, too dizzyingly busy to lie down in defeat.

Demme and Goldman see this lower-middle America plain, but they see it with affection. They observe its follies without minimizing them, but also without patronizing, sentimentalizing, or judging them. In a Reno strip joint, one of the girls dances naked but for a cast on her forearm; in a drive-in marriage chapel, an aged professional witness gets a minor heart attack from the effort—or joy?—of kissing the bride; Lynda, in curlers and just getting out of bed at her mother's place, consumes a quickie breakfast from orange juice to coffee while Melvin woos her over the long-distance phone into another go at marriage; Melvin and his daughter Darcy watch *Easy Street,* their favorite giveaway show, through fancy, dimestore sunglasses; a pretty married woman seduces her milkman (Melvin, now Milkman of the Year) in the most guileless, almost virginal, fashion; a counterman in a drugstore (played by the real-life Melvin Dummar) watches approvingly as Lynda uses the store's mustard, ketchup, salt, pepper, and whatnot to spruce up a homemade farewell sandwich for her daughter, whom she is sending back by Greyhound to her father.

The film teems with such spunkily observed visual details, but the spoken ones are just as pungently original. Leaving him for the second time, Lynda tries to explain to Melvin how absurd it was to acquire on down payment a huge Cadillac with a still bigger motorboat in tow (he sits in it on dry land, having switched from cowboy hat to captain's cap, and radios the Santa Monica Coast Guard for a weather report), given how poor they are. Melvin protests: "Not poor. Broke maybe; not poor!" But she is leaving, adamant: "*C'est la vie,* Melvin." "What's that?" "French, Melvin. I used to dream of becoming a French interpreter." "You don't speak French!" "I *told* you it was a dream." Could any parting dialogue sound weirder, sadder, truer? And what of the fat, saucy marriage-parlor proprietress who, asked what kind of wedding music she can supply at $5 extra, announces, "I've got inspirational: 'Because'; Hawaiian: 'The War Chant' . . ." And when Melvin sheepishly observes that he had not counted on the decrepit witnesses' fee, the marriage vendor tartly replies, "Well, they've got to eat, too."

Equally juicy is Demme's handling of the camera. When Melvin rejoices in the prospect of his inheritance, he is a tiny figure in extreme long shot in the lower left corner of the frame as he dances before the Great Salt Lake, and we sense that he is up against something too big: the force that won't let small-time losers turn big-time winners. When Melvin and his second wife, the practical Bonnie who nevertheless was the one who proposed to the impractical Melvin, are in a heated conversation, how casually the camera picks up, between and slightly behind them, the television set on which a newscast shows highlights from the just-ended life of Howard Hughes. When Melvin takes the witness stand in the courtroom, how effectively, with one 360-degree pan, the camera captures all the different presences, swiftly epitomizing diverse personalities and attitudes.

The performances are all flawless, the very looks of the actors revealing more than reams of dialogue. As Lynda, Mary Steenburgen is both pretty and extremely ordinary, with a life-battered face full of virgin hope; wonderfully, she can become submerged up to her chin in whatever feelings assail her or can hurl herself into ludicrous activities with a natural grace as good as the greatest dignity. As Bonnie, Pamela Reed combines ingenuous optimism with levelheadedness, her cunning child's face absolutely ageless. As Darcy, Elizabeth Cheshire is an earnest yet unprecocious youngster; her countenance, though gravely confronting adversity, has not given up on childhood. Paul Le Mat is an infectiously engaging Melvin, puffed up with hope and aglow with obsessions, yet capable of becoming discouraged with a wistfulness that is even more endearing. And how patiently logical he can seem while chasing the wildest of geese! As Hughes, Jason Robards is both canny and otherworldly, an emaciated anchorite with desert winds nestling in his mane and beard, but under whose crustiness and suspicions a little amusement and wonder are still shyly aglimmer.

The best, the most enchanting, thing about *Melvin and Howard* is that it merrily explains the mystery of Hughes in terms of the marginal chimeras of penny-ante eccentrics. In a world where everything is irrational, unpredictable, askew, each person finds the bizarreness that fits him. And yet, the bizarre, the absurd, can be humanized: by singing in the night, like Melvin and Howard, or by loving each other, like Melvin and Lynda, after each is married to another.

June 12, 1981

CRITICAL MATTERS: REVERSING THE ANGLE

The Bloody Sport of Film Criticism

OF ALL AREAS OF CRITICISM TODAY, the most bloodily contested is that of film criticism. There are several reasons for this. Film is now the most popular art form, outdistanced only by rock music and television, which, however, are not arts. So film has both the popularity that comes from easiness—just consider how much harder it is to absorb a concert, an art show, or a book than to let a movie wash over you—and the cachet of being a legitimate art form. It is now one of the most sought-after college subjects, and English, theater, art, and communications departments fight among themselves for the right to teach it. And since not all students of film can make films, the next best thing, presumably, is to write about them.

Moreover, everybody who goes to the movies fancies himself a film critic, opinions about movies being easier to entertain than those about any other art; not even theater is quite so available, in both senses of that word. With the whole world talking about film and half the world wanting to write about it, the professional critic becomes the loved and envied cynosure—if not exactly a superstar, certainly a media personality, given the least bit of innate panache. So, like the competitive athlete, the film critic is cheered or cursed and egged on against his fellow critic.

Ever since Pauline Kael (well before that ultrarespectable publication *The New Yorker* curbed her tongue) started calling her colleagues to account for having views different from hers, the arena of film criticism has become progressively more sanguinary. The more so since film is such a new form, film as consciously artistic expression newer yet, and film criticism the newest of all. There are relatively few established values thus far, not many reputable books of theory and criticism, and a mere handful of practicing critics of more than local fame. Consequently, anything goes, and X believes that if he can only outsmart Y and outwrite Z, he can corner the critical market. And the blood sport is on.

But it is not so much the sanguinariness of film critics as the nature of their backgrounds that is the problem. Most of them started either as fans or as buffs. Now, movie fans are perfectly harmless creatures to everyone but stars, whose clothing they try to tear off. Luckily, few fans become reviewers, and if they do, they become something like Rona Barrett or Rex Reed and need not be taken seriously by anyone. Film buffs, however, are universally dangerous, particularly when they become critics, which they very often do: unlike fans, they elevate the useless accumulation of movie data from a passion to a pseudophilosophy and pseudoscience.

The temptation of a blinkered, monomaniacal cinematic omniscience is great indeed. Film, after all, is a small territory compared to the other arts with their long histories. No critic of literature, music, or the fine arts would presume to know everything about the entire field: that is where specialization comes in. With film, however—thanks to revival houses, cinemathèques, reruns on television, festivals, as well as subtitles that minimize language barriers—it is possible to aspire to absolute knowledge, which is the buff critic's ambition.

Yet film, even more than opera, is a true *Gesamtkunstwerk,* the total work of art subsuming all others. Hence the ideal film critic would need to be fully conversant with all the arts and (while we are dreaming) all languages, because subtitles are never quite adequate and usually wretched. There is an enormous need for the film critic to cultivate his mind and taste in every way—not least by living, for which film buffs watching their nonstop movies have hardly any time at all. The axiom, then, is simple: The better the buff, the worse he is as critic. Dwight Macdonald clearly understood this rule: when he was writing his distinguished film criticism for *Esquire,* he had his sons and trusted friends sift movies for him; he himself saw no more than five or six a month.

By and large, though, the serious film critic finds himself in a uniquely unhealthy situation. A book reviewer is not expected to read all the bestsellers and ephemera that come out, yet even the most fastidious film critic, unless he wants to sit around idly for weeks on end, is compelled to review schlock. Can you imagine Lionel Trilling reviewing Rod McKuen, or Edmund Wilson having to write a critique of Jacqueline Susann? Yet that is what a film critic must do—such is the pressure from below. And there is also a pressure from above—from the academics who are invading the field and foisting on it their fancy theories, such as structuralism or semiology, with which no respectable working critic can do anything.

Look at the most illustrious American film critics of the past: James Agee, Otis Ferguson, Robert Warshow. They had no theories, no academic games to play—only their intelligence and good taste. They loved film, but not blindly. Yet they too must have been beleaguered by fans and buffs with questions like, "What's the matter with you? Don't you like film?" Can you imagine a serious literary critic being asked by lovers of literature whether he *really* likes books?

Of course, in film as in the other arts there are critics as well as reviewers, and there are a good many definitions of the difference between them. Most simply put, a reviewer has opinions; a critic can back them up with reasons. I would add that a critic is someone I want to read even when I disagree with him. A reviewer is someone who, if he tells me that he reads me regularly and with steady agreement, makes me seriously apprehensive.

To be a film critic, you need, besides the obvious requirements for any kind of criticism—intelligence, taste, the ability to write well—three special prerequisites. First, courage. Because films cost millions of dollars, there is immense pressure on critics and their publishers not to rock so expensive a boat. Second, integrity. Again because of the hugeness of the stakes, not only producers and film companies but also directors, screenwriters, and actors are apt to court the more powerful film critics with insidious flattery. Third, space. Because film is such a complex art form, the true critic can't do justice to all its aspects without enough room to stretch his mind in. At fewer than fifteen hundred words a critic is condemned to being a reviewer.

July 1978

The Great Pop Critic

No one sufficiently interested in film to read on beyond this point needs to be told what a new collection of Pauline Kael's reviews from *The New Yorker* is all about or reassured that it is worth reading. At the risk of redundancy, I will nevertheless say that *Deeper into Movies* is worth rereading even if one enjoyed the pieces as they came out; Miss Kael's zest, wit, sharpness, knowledgeableness, and fierce idiosyncrasies shine on unabated. Miss Kael has become so much of a mythic phenomenon and household commodity, a still voice lurking at the back of many an unconscious and a thundering critical avalanche gathering adherents as it rampages on, that it is time to assess the manifestation itself. Who is Pauline Kael really, and what can be done with, or about, her?

It is possible to get the essence of this collection, and therewith the essence of Pauline Kael, by reading the last two pieces in it: "Alchemy," which is a panegyric to *The Godfather,* and "Collaboration and Resistance," which begins with a list of films that opened between March 1971 and March 1972 and made this, for her, "a legendary period of movies." We must ask ourselves then why so astute a critic would proffer as summit achievements *The Conformist, McCabe and Mrs. Miller, Sunday Bloody Sunday, The Last Picture Show, Fiddler on the Roof, Murmur of the Heart, The Garden of the Finzi-Continis, Cabaret,* and *The Godfather?* To be sure, *Murmur of the Heart* is a delightful little music-box of a film, and *Cabaret* a big, flawed but still quite effective contraption; the rest, however, range from slick commercialism, through pretentious posturing, to downright junk. And, on a slightly lower level, Miss Kael enshrines even *Made for Each Other* and *Billy Jack!*

I would say that Miss Kael suffers from two rather touching (because profoundly human) but deleterious (because profoundly uncritical) fallacies: one social and one existential. The existential fallacy consists in confusing movies with life or, more precisely, using film as a surrogate for life—being so involved in living the movies that one cannot properly evaluate them. Repeatedly Miss Kael comes out, in this as in her previous collections, in defense of certain kinds of trash. Thus *Bob & Carol & Ted & Alice* earns high marks even if it is "slick" and "whorey" and "unabashedly commercial"—after all, "it's so damned easy to be cultured." "Sometimes when things go terribly wrong in a movie," we are told elsewhere, "it's more fun than if they'd gone right." A piece of moral and aesthetic garbage such as *The Honeymoon Killers* comes in for some left-handed compliments because it resembles the old Republic cheapies. A contemporary comedian's rage "could become a lasting part of our culture, like Edgar Kennedy's slow burn." Well, if that's what culture consists of, it is indeed damned easily come by.

The bad old formulaic movies are faintly praised for having at least tried to give the audience *something;* it is acknowledged that "some fine American movies were made as plain, honest jobs of hack work." (Significantly, no names mentioned.) Defensively, Miss Kael declares: "I don't trust critics who care only for the highest and the best; it's an inhuman position, and I don't believe them. I think it's simply their method of exalting themselves." In other words, highbrows are ipso facto phonies. Protesting against the genteel qualities of *Long Ago, Tomorrow,* she affirms, "I can enjoy a sleazy, silly old movie," and proceeds to equate, more or less, vulgarity with vitality. Refinement and tidiness are qualities she profoundly mistrusts. Characteristically, the term "classic" becomes a mild pejorative: one film has a "classical, middlebrow banality," another "feels like a 'classic,' and that's not how a film that really speaks to us feels," and in still another "tired expertise" is equated with a "classical" quality. Conversely, *Is There Sex after Death?* is, at least in part, "*Mad* Magazine sophomoric in the best sense . . ."

"There is a sweet, naive feeling in *Billy Jack,"* we learn, "even when it's atrocious"; apropos *Fiddler on the Roof,* we are told that in "movies vulgar strength has been a great redemptive force, canceling out niggling questions of taste." Elsewhere, Miss Kael announces that "your whole primitive moviegoer's soul cries out" for the beleaguered heroine to pull the trigger; she admits that "movies more than satisfy my appetite for trash." What made *Bringing Up Baby* great was "that it was a *romance"*—an italicized romance, no less.

What emerges from collating these bits of ludicrous overpraise or pathetic true confessions is that the shoddy films Miss Kael extols all possess one or more of the following characteristics: they are reminiscent of the kind, of movies she uncritically devoured in her early years; they exalt so-called healthy vulgarity as a way of life or filmmaking; they undermine the middle-class values from which Miss Kael sometimes (though not consistently) wishes to feel liberated; and they feature a homely or butch heroine who nevertheless achieves romantic fulfillment.

It is almost dotting the i's to point out that these are the hallmarks of filmgoing for purposes of wish fulfillment, escape, rebellion against parental authority, and nostalgia. They are all to a greater or lesser degree immature and neurotic, and though they perfectly validate movie-buff sentiments, they are not quite so satisfactory as critical apparatus. Perhaps the clearest proof of this existential fallacy—in this case of the use of film as a sex surrogate—lies in the very titles of Miss Kael's four books: *I Lost It at the Movies, Kiss Kiss Bang Bang, Going Steady,* and now *Deeper into Movies.* Of course, a critic is human and must be expected to have his little human peculiarities and weaknesses that will color his criticism. But if he is a responsible critic as well as a slaphappy consumer, he will try to detach and distance himself a little and, not repress his idiosyncrasies, but recognize and label them as such.

Even more pronounced, however, is Miss Kael's social fallacy, her need to use film as a way to become part of a great, powerful, cozy, convivially laughing, crying, and booing mass, The Audience, for whom she is filled with childish affection, maternal recriminations, and the shrill love-hate of a hysterical inamorata. There is hardly a page in this collection on which Miss Kael does not dispense accolades or spankings to her fellow moviegoers, does not agonize about why they loved some violent, brutal scenes, or rejoice at their lapping up something she herself relished.

Movies (the demotic term she prefers to the more formal "film") should be, she keeps insisting, "a great popular, democratic art form," and she delights in those "best popular movies [that] come out of a merger of commerce and art," that succeed in "blurring the distinction" between "high" and "popular." Accordingly, "you get a good feeling when you're in an audience that spontaneously breaks into applause for outrageously silly jokes," and you have a soft spot even for those old-time "generally tawdry films [that] contributed to our national identity—such as it was." It is so that a paean to the gross and inept Liz Taylor ends with "She's Beverly Hills Chaucerian, and that's as high and low as you can get."

These, clearly, are the views of a loner yearning to become part of the community, of a person endowed with superior intelligence but gladly willing to sacrifice some (though not all) of it for the sake of warming herself at the bosom of the crowd. In this way Pauline Kael strives to become, despite certain misgivings, the Great Pop Critic, and succeeds, not completely but alarmingly enough.

If, however, you feel that art is not in the smelting of high and low, not in the kicking over of the priorities of searching penetrancy and uncompromising effort to express the ineffable; if, in short, you believe that art, though it keeps its doors open to all who care to enter, is not a democratic fun house but a place of comic or tragic insight available fully only to an enlightened perception—a spiritual aristocracy—Pauline Kael is not your critic, even if she may at times concur with you in spite of herself. She is a lively writer with a lot of common sense, but also one who, in a very disturbing sense, is common.

March 30, 1973

Genteel Razzle-Dazzle

Penelope Gilliatt has brought out a collection of her film and drama reviews chiefly from *The New Yorker* and some of the more high-toned British weeklies under the curious title *Unholy Fools,* and the explanatory subtitle *Wits, Comics, Disturbers of the Peace.* She is, clearly, more at ease with comedy, and the book contains at least a half dozen disquisitions on the nature of farce, each more or less contradicting the others. But serious stuff can be brought in under the catchy catchall, "Disturbers of the Peace," which Miss Gilliatt herself prefers not to be: one is almost halfway into her book before the first really damning review appears. Except in the occasional profiles and recollections of beloved children's books, which are open love letters, Miss Gilliatt generally espouses the tone of our glossiest magazines: the *via media* between hyperexquisite sensibility and unabashed pizazz. As a contriver of genteel razzle-dazzle, she is just about tops.

Of course, she is a fiction writer first of all, not the least when she is writing criticism. At its best, this yields a lively, imaged style and a bustling rhythm; at its worst, it means that she is rewriting, reinventing a play or movie in her mind—certainly the things she says about *Desperate Characters* or *Petulia,* for instance, though pretty enough in themselves, have precious little to do with what happens on screen. To the characters in such films she will ascribe motives, experiences, behavior—even articles of clothing or jewelry—that are of her very own coining. Yet it is her style that is often most distressingly fictional, because it is the style of bad fiction. Miss Gilliatt will rely heavily on extended metaphors and similes, sometimes even tropes within tropes, that are farfetched, overelaborated, and exceedingly hard to follow.

Thus "the Woody Allen comic character . . . left to himself . . . would lie on his back and play with a yo-yo, which is a very difficult thing to master, or look at a nude magazine in the spirit of besotted awe about the professionalism of the beloved, like a dumb sweetheart mooning over a book of her fiancé's calculus." The imagery here, like that original Penelope's web, is constantly unraveled and rewoven, leaving the readers in the roles of the bewildered, frustrated suitors. Of the characters in a Gogol play we learn that "their anxiety is totally inert, a sensibility that is almost submerged in an unstirring pool of Slav warm temperament, like the one emergent eye of a hippopotamus cooling off underwater." How a Nilotic hippo could cool itself off in a pool of Slavonic warm temperament, and how such a warm temperament can be totally inert, and how indeed an anxiety comes to be a sensibility, are conundrums beyond my ability to unriddle.

Miss Gilliatt's metaphors are the main carriers of her humor, but carriers that often miscarry—as when Feydeau's farce, *A Flea in Her Ear,* "is like a deckle-edged Greek tragedy with an RSVP at the end of it," which may once have meant something to God, but can now have meaning only for its author. Such witty images are rather like the humor of a poet in one of Miss Gilliatt's own short stories, which "seemed entirely immobile," expressing "no energy in any direction." The author will, moreover, fall in love with her own clevernesses and repeat them: on page 54, two friends "chat by laminating two monologues"; on page 203, we read about "dialogue more like two monologues laminated." She seems, in fact, enamored of the word "laminating" to the point of aberrancy: *No More Excuses* is said to be edited "with a slapping rhythm to it like the timing of a skilled sandwich-maker laminating bread and innards and mayonnaise in a drugstore at lunchtime." I will take one of those with mayo, but hold the metaphor.

Even without metaphors, in mere exposition, Miss Gilliatt can be impenetrable. "The prisoners . . . spend a lot of time emptying the cesspool, and the impulse that makes one of them disappear to add to it in the interest of making the job more his own is . . . very funny" is a statement guaranteed to make no sense to anyone who has not seen *The Elusive Corporal,* to which it refers. But when we are told that Fellini in *The Clowns* "catches the look of loss on a million faces, and, beyond that, a kind of felicity," even those of us who know the film may read this with a look of loss.

Often Miss Gilliatt means the opposite of what she seems to be saying: when she writes that "many precedents . . . are to be laid at Mr. Simpson's door," this ominous-sounding phrase turns out to be a compliment; when we are told that the butts of music-hall jokes are male, this does not mean that men are being ridiculed but that what is laughed at is what men find ridiculous—most often women. It may, of course, be useless to expect clarity from a writer who will have a woman "begetting" a child, will use "who" for which, "wrack" for rack, "self-deprecation" for self-depreciation, "imbecilic" for imbecile, "anxious" for eager, "aggravate" for irritate, "inchoate" for chaotic, and will fall into the pleonasm of "false disguises," the jargon of "identify with" and "intrigued by," the vulgarism of "incredibly bad," and the sheer ungrammaticalness of "prevent him staying" and "stop him enjoying."

But what of Miss Gilliatt's critical acumen? She has a penchant for the solemnly proclaimed platitude: "Like all Shakespeare's greatest plays, *Henry IV* is immensely complex and also very simple"; or "nearly every . . . Russian play . . . includes one character that is unmentioned in the cast list, and that is Russia herself"—a discovery that would be more impressive if it applied to nearly every Flemish or Bolivian play. There is also the fake aphorism: "A lot of good work is cheek"; and the fake discovery: "Concealment of one kind or another characterizes a lot of American humor—W. C. Fields concealing his booze and his bank accounts, and Groucho Marx his terror of Margaret Dumont, and Laurel and Hardy their fear of being only two, and Lenny Bruce his panic at the way [of] the world . . ." where some of the propositions are the openest of secrets, and some of them so well concealed that only Miss Gilliatt's eye—or imagination—could ferret them out.

Mention must be made also of Miss Gilliatt's cuteness, as when she tells us that "*Thark* . . . is a title of genius: better than *Henry IV, Part I,* when it comes down to brass tacks"; of her inappropriate short-story writer's trick of ending a review with an insignificant detail, a dying fall; of her unfortunate ordering of the pieces in this book not chronologically or geographically or generically, but by some artificial scheme so befuddled as to make the discussions of later works by Kubrick and W. C. Fields, for instance, precede those of the earlier ones. There is also the gushy tendency to hero worship, as when all things become different in Jean Renoir's presence, or Max Ophüls is equated with Beckett, and his gimcrack *Lola Montès* described as "immortally pacifying"—whatever that means. Then, too, there is the need to show off, as when the title *Putney Swope* reminds Miss Gilliatt of the Middle English words *mukel swink,* which is stretching parallelism to the vanishing point. Such ostentation is not even backed up by genuine erudition: we read about "the Gorgon," when, in fact, there were three, one of whom was *the* Medusa, whom our author means; and though Miss Gilliatt prides herself on her French, she writes *"folie de grandeur"* for *folie des grandeurs.*

But at least her criticism has, in one case, inspired her fiction. The statement in a 1965 review that Brecht "had the courage to find nothing better than anything" becomes in her screenplay for *Sunday Bloody Sunday:* "There are times when nothing *has* to be better than anything." So for those of you who liked that movie, Miss Gilliatt's criticism may, after all, not have been a total waste.

August 3, 1973

Mudpack-Raking, Sinking Hindenburgs

How did Rex Reed come to pass? Did Andy Warhol's Frankenstein concoct him to spread the camp sensibility into the bloodstream of silent America via the Hearst Syndicate? Or did the media fabricate him to add a touch of Bill Blass class to the low couture of Johnny Carson's "Tonight Show"? Actually, Reed was wafted north by a breeze from the Gulf to make a writing career in New York, and I have heard both Gloria Steinem and Liz Smith take rueful credit for helping him get published in their mass magazines. Soon he was film critic for Igor Cassini's malodorous and ephemeral *Status;* when that mule was shot out from under him, he began appearing as an interviewer in the Sunday *New York Times* and *Esquire,* and as a columnist in *Women's Wear Daily* and *Holiday.* He acquired a reputation for clever bitchiness and supposedly revelatory interviews with aging prima donnas, an activity best described as mudpack-raking.

What was Reed's open sesame with the celebrities? First, that he wasn't really that bitchy, or that clever; a few feuds with declining divas were soon patched up, and now, with the possible exception of Richard Harris, he has no conspicuous enemies. Second, his current outlet, the Chicago Tribune–New York News Syndicate, gives the interviewee maximum exposure, and few performing-art luminaries have the sense to realize that all they need to hang themselves is enough tape. The occasional smartass comment by Reed hurts no one, and to be interviewed by him carries almost as much prestige as having one's hair done by Mr. Kenneth himself or being recognized by the headwaiter at Lutèce. About the bitchiest line in Reed's fourth and latest collection of interviews, *People Are Crazy Here,* is the remark about Cybill Shepherd's acting career, "It beats jerking sodas back home in Memphis." Even if Miss Shepherd recognized this as less than laudatory, it hardly makes a very formidable enemy for our intrepid epigrammatist.

Reed fails to meet my basic requirements for an interviewer. Except when he is forced to concentrate on atmosphere, as when Joe Namath apparently would not talk to him and all that was left was Namath's restaurant and its clientele, or when, in the profile of Grace Slick, he had extra space to kill, he does not give you much sense of the ambience in the forty pieces included in *People Are Crazy Here.* In the item about Adolph Zukor's one-hundredth-birthday party, not even the city where the eerily nostalgic goings-on took place is named. Yet the *genius loci* is not the only genius missing here.

As a portraitist, Reed is just as deficient. Rightly, he tries to concentrate on his subjects' eyes. So George C. Scott has "small cumulus clouds that make tiny swirls of hypnotic vertigo if you look in their direct focus"; rather than visualize eyes, we wonder why a small cumulus cloud isn't simply a cirrocumulus, why clouds should cause vertigo, why vertigo should be hypnotic, and how one can look into the direct focus of eyes—or what, for that matter, would be indirect focus? Bette Midler's eyes are "glittering green venetian blinds from which stars are shooting like emeralds," and one is forced to wonder whether green venetian blinds are in fact shutters, and whether one has ever seen an emerald shoot—and shoot in a cowardly fashion, from behind venetian blinds, painted green, no doubt, as camouflage for an emerald. Tennessee Williams is "shy, pursued by visions of hell, and blind in one eye." Curious collocation: Is it the hellish visions or the shyness that blinds you in one eye? And does one get the visions of hell in the blind or in the seeing eye?

Reed's hearing is no sharper than his vision. Sylvia Miles has a voice "so low it would make a dulcimer jealous," where Reed clearly cannot tell his dulcimer from his double bass. Joan Hackett has a "crisp, cool voice that sounds like a poet reading Little Orphan Annie," where one speculates whether the poet might be Edith Sitwell, Carl Sandburg, or Frank O'Hara, each of whose reading of Little Orphan Annie would differ considerably from the others'. George C. Scott has a "rasping Rasputin of a voice," from which we get only a Rasp put in for frivolously verbal reasons. Tuesday Weld gives out with a "freckled whisper of a gurgle, lonely and little girlish and faraway," which carries synesthesia to new depths, and makes for a fallacy pathetic enough to squeeze tears out of stones.

Can Reed at least conjure up a human presence as a whole? Well, George C. Scott is "a sour green apple with a soft core, hounded by the furies all his life," leaving open the question whether the Eumenides were after that pomiform Orestes for his sourness or his soft core (the hard-core version, by the way, was censored by Hollywood). Tuesday Weld has a "rosebud mouth on her gentle, uncharted face" that "should be erupting into a graceful discourse," with Reed clearly mistaking "uncharted" for unlined, and illiterately assuming that a graceful discourse can erupt like Krakatoa. Here is Bette Midler at the Continental Baths: "Up from the stygian depths of New York's steamy, seamy night-spas Bette is emerging like a nymphet Lorelei, singing and tempting her eclectic audiences right onto the comfortable-rare rocks of laughter and sentimentality." Quite aside from the fact that Miss Midler is rather overaged for a nymphet and facially underendowed for a Lorelei, the rocks onto which a siren tempts one are hardly a laughing matter, and sentimentality does not have a rocklike consistency. And how is an audience eclectic?

What Reed means is heterogeneous (though, to be sure, there is little that is hetero about Miss Midler's audiences), but he doesn't know words any better than he knows history (the stage version of *Gone With the Wind* "sank . . . like the *Hindenburg*"), zoology (he absurdly uses the giraffe's movements as an example of clumsiness), physics ("the vibes in the room are kinetic"—what else can they be?), fine arts (Portsmouth, England, looks "like an Utrillo watercolor"), opera (he wrote in a column that the Cockettes, a transvestite act, "came down the aisle like the Anvil Chorus from *Aïda,*" and when I pointed out to him that "The Anvil Chorus" is a piece of music sung in a stationary position and located in *Il Trovatore,* he merely changed this in reprinting it here to "like the chorus from *Aïda,*" which is meaningless), ballet ("she takes a ballet pose like a white swan turning discreetly away from her odious black sister"—a totally garbled reference to something that does *not* occur in *Swan Lake*) or drama (he refers to "Doreen [*sic*] in *Tartuffe*"—maybe in *Tartuffe Goes to Hollywood*). Still, his insensitivity to words remains his most disastrous feature: he writes that Bette Davis moves "like a ravishing barracuda," though the only creature that could be ravished by a barracuda is another barracuda.

Why, then, is Reed such a popular success? Because besides slaking the public's thirst for gossip, he mirrors the public's vulgarity and sentimentality. Here is his list of the finer things in life: "koala bears [they are not bears], Harold Arlen songs, country tomatoes served with fresh dill, St.-Jean-Cap-Ferrat at four in the afternoon, . . . any house Gloria Vanderbilt lives in, Concord Bridge . . . in . . . mid-October, the smell of gingerbread baking, and, of course, Kay Thompson." Something for everyone, jet setter or rube, old-timer or child, reader of Suzy Knickerbocker or the Eloise chronicles. And Reed reflects and serves the basic public dichotomy by simultaneously crawling in both directions: though Los Angeles is a place that "guarantees a loss of a few IQ points each year" to its inhabitants, "MGM was . . . the symbol of perfection and glamour" to "a lot of critics . . . like myself." And this is the reason I have gone on so long about Reed: the fact that he has conned a lot of Americans into endowing their image of the critic with his own mental and physical lineaments. Pascal defined man as a thinking reed; Rex, alas, is a Reed of another sort.

July 5, 1974

Wayne Damage

Praise for old John Wayne, I should have realized as I wrote last week's review of *The Shootist,* is almost always a bit premature. No sooner was my piece about *The Shootist* locked into type than along came Molly Haskell's tribute in the August 16 issue of the *Village Voice,* "What Makes John Wayne Larger Than Life?," making clear that the Duke had goofed again. It is one thing if an attack casts an unfavorable light on its subject; the attacker may be biased. It is quite another when an homage makes it subject look bad; that, I fear, has to be believed. We read:

> John Wayne keeps working. He turns down scripts that are too dirty (like *Dirty Harry),* or cleans them up. For instance, *The Shootist* was, he felt, too graphic in its description of the cancer, too heavy, too downbeat in its ending. In the original, before Wayne had it altered, the Ron Howard character is a thoroughgoing punk, who not only is unredeemed at the end, but performs the final ripoff of the dead gunfighter. Wayne had it cleaned up morally and made funnier.

So even if his performance was decent, Wayne managed to muck up the movie in other ways.

I have since consulted the Glendon Swarthout novel, which, such as it is, stacks up considerably better than the film script. Particularly in the end—the death of the hero and what the juvenile does after that—the novel has it all over the movie. But, of course, Wayne had to have things "cleaned up morally" and turn Gillom into a Norman Rockwell all-American boy, and have the dying Books, unable to talk, signify his blessing on the youth for discarding his gun. Don't misunderstand: I don't consider an upbeat ending automatically inferior. But it has to be earned by what goes before, and the tone of the movie does not prepare us for it. So it ends up looking goody-goody, contrived, and dishonest.

What I found most interesting about Miss Haskell's article, however, is that, confronted with Wayne, it abandoned every vestige of critical responsibility. It is an extraordinary piece of special pleading, worth scrutinizing because it is so typical of the kind of fan clubbery that, in film criticism more than anywhere else, passes for judiciousness. Haskell numbers herself among "those . . . who have always known [Wayne] was one of the greats." One of the great whats, we might ask; surely not *actors*—not for managing to be competent in undemanding and repetitious roles, and sometimes not even competent? Do you remember him as Genghis Khan, for instance, or Commodore Perry? Do you recall his ludicrous delivery of the one line he had in *The Greatest Story Ever Told?* Shall we say: one of the great lummoxes and great stars? For one can be both; what one cannot be is both starstruck and a critic.

After minimizing the importance of Wayne's rotten politics—with which assessment, from the critical point of view, I agree, for politics has nothing to do with acting (but neither, alas, has most of everything else Wayne does)—Haskell goes on to declare that "it would be a mistake to take as the sum of the man" the stereotype compounded from his politics and his lesser roles. Instead:

> Consider the xenophobic, violently anti-Indian Ethan Edwards of *The Searchers,* the arrogant and obtuse cattle driver of *Red River,* the prudish male chauvinist of *The Quiet Man,* the fanatic Spig Wead, Naval commander in *The Wings of Eagles.* These subtle and complex Wayne performances in no way correspond to the image of the neanderthal he-man . . . etc.

Well, blow me down! The xenophobic, Indian-hating, arrogant, obtuse, prudish, chauvinistic fanatic is *not* a Neanderthal he-man? Strange; but there is stranger stuff to come. Haskell now launches into several paragraphs bulging with things like

> Wayne was not a lusty sort in the oh-ho-ho fanny-pinching tradition. . . . Wayne had his own mission, his own promises to keep—to a woman, to a batallion, to a dead friend. . . . Wayne didn't wear his heart on his sleeve. . . . His relationships with women were shy, but giving. . . . He hadn't yet come to understand what he generally *would* come to understand: that men and women could be not only lovers but friends.

And so on and on. This is ridiculous in two, if not three, ways.

First, can you imagine anyone in his right mind writing: "Olivier was a man haunted by the evil wife whom he had to kill to be rid of, which may explain in part why he later strangled a sweet and innocent wife of whom he was insanely jealous. To be sure, his quasi-incestuous feelings for an adulterous mother who married his father's fraternal murderer may well have unhinged him where women are concerned, a condition exacerbated by his sometimes being a clubfooted hunchback among handsome courtiers and, at other times, an unwelcome Moor among haughty Venetians." Yet this is exactly what Haskell is doing: an astonishing thing from a critic, though quite common among fans. TV soap-opera actors have told me about the desperately concerned letters they keep getting from viewers, warning them not to marry the too-too-sweet girl next door, to stop trusting their business partners, to try to give up the bottle, and so forth. For these unfortunate addicts, the soap opera and its characters have become real life, actual people—worse yet, part of their own lives.

Of course, Miss Haskell, Wayne isn't an oh-ho-ho fanny-pincher any more than he is an arrogant and obtuse cattle driver; he is (to give him the benefit of the doubt) the *actor* John Wayne enacting those parts more or less imaginatively and persuasively—which would need to be argued, demonstrated rather than asserted with a couple of casual epithets. And here comes the second absurdity: our critic implies that because Wayne had his own mission, which he didn't sidestep to pinch a few fannies, because he was shy but giving with women, and kept his sleeve unencumbered with organs that do not belong on it, and because by his, roughly, 150th movie he learned that women can be friends as well as lovers, he was somehow a better actor—if not indeed, third absurdity, a better man.

Oh, how Haskell praises Wayne for acting opposite older actresses, for becoming "quite frankly a father figure," and other such achievements of the calendar or the casting director. These and similar things, without any histrionic illustrations tendered, must be understood to make Wayne a great actor. And a great man, too, for didn't Haskell begin by saying "it is a mistake to take as the sum of the *man*" (italics mine) his politics and lesser roles; clearly, then, we should take as the sum of the man his better roles and the fact that "women unblinded by the prejudices of fashion have always responded to the authentic, nontough-guy Wayne—witness Joan Didion's lovely tribute to him. . . ."

That lovely tribute by Miss Didion, though fairly ludicrous, at least had the honesty to call itself "a love song," and to describe Wayne's face as one more familiar than one's own husband's—which, were I John Gregory Dunne, her husband, would give me pause. Didion, quite openly, was writing from the crotch—as, less consciously, is Haskell. Witness her defense of Wayne's attitude toward women by a parenthetic "and frankly, does any woman really want a crybaby for her john?," where that *john* is very curious: a pun on Wayne's (assumed) Christian name and—what? A *john* is not an ordinary swain, but a prostitute's *trick,* to be mulcted and despised.

However, it is not my purpose to analyze what lies behind the sexual imagery of Miss Haskell's piece—imagery that would be all right from any *other* critic, whose mainstay is not her feminism—but only to show how deluded, confused, and, above all, star-struck this criticism is. Thus Haskell refers to "the brawling, Oscar-winning Marshal Cogburn of *True Grit,*" bringing to mind such other Oscar winners as Sir Thomas More, Professor Higgins, and Eleanor of Aquitaine. I am, simply, against the blurring of the role, the actor, and the man—blurring that crops up even in such revealing lapses as Haskell's reference to Carson City, the locale of *The Shootist,* as Culver City, the once hallowed home of Leo the MGM Lion.

That Miss Haskell's performance is representative of much that today passes for film criticism (which alone justifies such a lengthy scrutiny) was confirmed by the chorus of critical hosannas that greeted Wayne's work in *The Shootist.* Perfectly good it was, as I, too, was more than willing to affirm, but hardly anything to require the combined forces of the Trapp Family Singers and the Mormon Tabernacle Choir to do it justice. "The legend must be preserved," Haskell writes about Wayne, who, she assures us, has become "the preeminent figure in American folk mythology." I ask merely what is the function of criticism: to help create myths and legends, or to try to assess what is good acting and when, where, and by whom it is practiced?

August 30, 1976

Elegy for a Critic

DEATH BY HIS OWN HAND at the age of thirty-eight was, I am sure, the only thing that prevented Charles Thomas Samuels from becoming the most important film critic of our time.* For it must be remembered that a critic is a writer who ages differently from, say, a poet or a novelist, from whom he differs hardly if at all in literary prowess. A lyric poet is apt to be at his height at a very early age, a novelist usually in his early-middle or middle years, whereas a critic is just beginning to get into his own at thirty-eight. For criticism is not primarily a matter of invention or of response to things as they come along, and formulation of the response with brilliant artistry; it is a matter, above all, of prolonged, profound involvement with the art criticized—a continuous savoring, weighing, reflecting upon, comparing and contrasting, and living with, let us say, films; then placing them in the context of other arts and art in general; finally, situating them in life—as a critic must also have found time to live it.

The apprenticeship of a critic, then, is much longer than that of other literary artists, which is not to be construed as a value judgment—an elephant is not superior to man because its gestation is almost thrice as long as a human being's—it is merely a statement of fact. My point is that Samuels's film criticism, like his literary criticism, had every chance of becoming even better than it already was at the time of his death, and that the loss to us is qualitative as well as quantitative. That only four sections of his book on the

* Charles Thomas Samuels died in 1974. John Simon's essay appears as the foreword to a collection of Samuels's film criticism, *Mastering the Film and Other Essays,* edited by Lawrence Graver and published by the University of Tennessee Press.

major directors survive—and those not necessarily in their final form—is for us a deprivation of inestimable magnitude.

Still, like everyone else, a critic must be judged on what he achieved, not on what he might have done. And we are lucky indeed that Samuels left us as much as he did, and that a posthumous collection now brings together what was previously scattered or unpublished. There would have been much more of it had Samuels elected to become a full-time film critic, had he not felt that there were too few good movies around, week by week, to keep a fastidious mind regularly occupied. But even if he could have been a full-time film *and* literary critic, he would not have been happy because of his horror of the Big City where such critics must ply their trade, and because he loved teaching too much to give it up for anything.

At Williams College he had an almost ideal setup. He could teach both English and film, he lived with his wife and two daughters amid delightful surroundings, and he was not so far from New York City but that a mildly enervating drive could provide him with material for one of his quarterly columns for *The American Scholar.* It was on these lightning visits that I most often saw him, our talk sandwiched in, along with a couple of actual sandwiches, between two of his movies, or a movie and a ballet or play. For all his espousal of the careful and deliberate, Samuels was also extremely quick, quick-witted, almost driven. One of the topics that hardly ever failed to come up was his loathing for megalopolitan life—its unconduciveness to relaxed ratiocination and inducements to literary dog-eat-doggishness. Samuels preferred to write about a film after viewing it several times in succession with his students in a film course, then, upon brisk discussion with them and his wife, Nada, writing out of slowly ripening reflection.

He wrote carefully, perhaps even painfully, but the result justified the pains taken. There is a solidity and finality about Samuels's best criticism, a pregnancy and lucidity that many an easier, more fluent writer never arrives at. If his style lacks anything, it is sensuousness and, to a lesser extent, that wittiness Samuels the man possessed in abundance. Whether his writing, becoming more relaxed, would have acquired these features as well, I do not know, but by comparing the earlier and later pieces, the reader may make his own inferences. What is notable in all the writing, besides the good sense and keen insight, is a marvelous absence of fudging, an absolute concision. By this I mean the special grace that knows exactly where lies the line between cryptic overconcentration and flabby overelaboration. And then there was his judicious, idealistic sternness.

Film criticism, being such a new discipline, is still very undisciplined, especially when one considers that film and writing about it have, until very recently, been mainly acts of rebellion or escape: rebellion against the supposedly narrow confines of the so-called higher arts, and escape from harsher realities against which film was presumed to provide a shelter made of glittering fantasies and womblike darkness. Hence much that passes for cinematic criticism to this day is—unless it is mere reviewing—the spinning out of preposterously cloying tributes and the fabrication of outlandishly abstruse theories by people who are really movie fans or buffs—enthusiasts or fantasts who either worship all films or conceive of film criticism as a means of justifying irrelevant cravings. Movies are adored just because they are there, or because they allow free association in the guise of scholarship. Samuels, however, was of a different cast. For him films had to be as good as the very best work in the other arts, and as the best films he had seen in the course of his devoted, intense but critical moviegoing. I suppose I am merely saying that he had standards acquired through learning, teaching, cultivated diversification, and, of course, that mysterious thing we call discrimination or perception or simply taste.

Samuels the man was, with the one exception noted above, as nearly as possible identical with Samuels the critic. This was greatly to the benefit of the latter. Whatever the man experienced, felt, thought, believed was faithfully and unaffectedly placed at the service of the critic. And Samuels the critic felt as much accountable for Samuels the man as he did for any of his lectures or publications. This, alas, may not have been to the ultimate benefit of the man. Charles (forgive me if I drop the pretense of impersonality and call him as I would have called him when alive) suffered some critical setbacks with his books *Encountering Directors,* savaged by a number of journalistic reviewers, and *The Ambiguity of Henry James,* which endured the fate common to many university press books of passing by almost unnoticed. As a result of this, and certain disappointments with his own behavior that only an ultrasevere critic would have found disconcerting—and in spite of some academic honors that simultaneously came to him—Charles condemned himself to nonexistence.

Let me make it clear: I do not subscribe to the romantic notion that unjust reviews can kill a sensitive literary plant; psychiatry could doubtless find some highly plausible explanations for Charles's suicide. But I do believe that over and above everything he thought he had "killed" others in his reviews and that, not having lived up to his gallantly extravagant and intransigently perfectionist expectations of himself, he had to draw what must have looked like a logical conclusion to his depressed mind. His friend Leonard Michaels, the short-story writer, put it succinctly and well when he said of Charles's suicide, "It was a mistake." No more, and no less.

His students loved him—this I know at firsthand from a good many of them who have written or talked to me about him. They loved him despite his being perhaps the toughest grader on campus, because they knew he cared about them as much as he did about literature and film, to the point of strictness. But Charles had a remarkably gentle severity, one that patiently explained its reasons, could laugh at itself, and never denied a student, filmmaker, or writer another chance. He was eminently capable of spotting something good in the midst of insufficiencies, as witness his treatment of Hitchcock; or of rescuing an unjustly slighted reputation, as witness his treatment of Carol Reed. And he could be fiercely demanding of those he loved best, like Bergman and Bresson. And so it was not only the young, but also distinguished elder colleagues, such as Stanley Kauffmann, who respected his gifts.

What cannot be overstressed is his love for teaching, of which criticism was for him a natural extension. How often he urged me to return to the classroom, and how—affectionately yet forcefully—he would lecture me on what he perceived as the pedagogical errors of my criticism. He certainly had what all good teachers possess: the ability to reprove without condescension, to correct errors without making such corrections emerge as a mode of self-promotion, let alone a source of glee. His criticism is, even at its most negative, unfailingly dignified.

But what, one might ask, was the final critical contribution of Charles Thomas Samuels? Did he leave some useful critical tools—a methodology perhaps, or a theory? No, thank goodness. When he was offered Christian Metz's *Film Language* for review by *The New Republic,* he turned it down after scrupulously struggling through it; a "semiotics of the cinema" (as the book is subtitled) was for him not even worth refuting.

What does come out of Samuels's work is what we receive also from our other best critics—James Agee, Otis Ferguson, Robert Warshow (why do they all have to die prematurely?)—the example of a limpid mind working from the best available aesthetic, psychological, philosophical, and social—which is to say humane—criteria. And working in so aboveboard a manner, with every move open for inspection, that even if you disagree with some of the premises or conclusions, you cannot help learning from the clarity and persuasiveness with which they are set forth. I want to believe that we can learn by watching a master-critic—a teacher—at work, which is the way other skills and disciplines are taught or transmitted to us: by example. But even supposing that we cannot learn from it, there is pure delight in observing a masterly performance.

November 1977

Bits of Fluff

Though I tend to disagree with Andrew Sarris's taste in movies and to despair of his stylistic insufficiencies as a writer, I have always relished Sarris on two subjects: politics and sports. Hence I was predisposed to enjoy *Politics and Cinema,* a collection of those of his reviews from the seventies that deal with films having political or social relevance. Unfortunately, these thirty pieces, all but three reprinted from Sarris's *Village Voice* column, manage to have enough cinema in them to smother the sensible observations on politics under Sarris's critical woolgathering.

One of the problems is that "politics" here is interpreted too broadly—as befits, I suppose, a practitioner of *politique des auteurs*—so that many of the pieces have little or nothing to do with it. Still, when the subject is unmistakably political, as in the discussion of Costa-Gavras's *State of Siege* or Susan Sontag's attack on Leni Riefenstahl, Sarris can make wonderful sense. He can see equally clearly the absurdities of the left and the right, not because he is a centrist, but because he is that unusual centrist who is what he is by conviction rather than by indifference, and not too lazy to do his homework.

But even though Sarris often declares that he places his aesthetics above his politics (or, more pretentiously, his poetics above his politics—as if every Greek-born critic were an Aristotle), the fact is that these reviews are aesthetically undernourished. Sarris is entitled to admire films I consider appalling (*The Night Porter, The Assassination of Trotsky, Mon Oncle Antoine)* and to disparage others that I value *(The Candidate, Slaughterhouse Five, Hearts and Minds);* what he may not do is discuss them as if they were mere ideological constructs, a set of social or political attitudes. It is surprising to what extent this champion of aesthetics does *not* discuss such matters as acting, dialogue, editing, set design, and other aspects of film as art and craft.

Downright astounding, however, is the scant attention paid to the feature of filmmaking that Sarris the auteur critic considers of paramount importance, "the director's attitude toward the spectacle." In these reviews, there is hardly any mention of camera placement and movement, of the dialectic of montage and deep focus, to which Sarris's occasional theoretical statements pay assiduous lip service. So much for Sarris the critic; as for Sarris the film historian, he is mostly a listmaker. Let there be a striptease in a movie, and he will rattle off all the stripteases in previous films; let him review Mailer's *Marilyn,* and he will give you a long list of other blond stars—but, with scrupulous historical accuracy, only those who worked for Miss Monroe's studio, Fox—"from torchy Alice Faye to tip-tappy Betty Grable," and so on.

Sarris's style is mostly punch-drunk Mad Av, with alliteration and assonance running amuck (often governing and deflecting the meaning), and dreadful wordplay like "less chilly Chile" or "ants in his angst." There is no foreign language Sarris doesn't mangle: Italian ("O Solo Mio"); French ("nouvelle libertinage"); German ("Weltschmertz"); Greek ("the other hoi polloi"); even, alas, the language of the cinema. Thus the Brazilian Cinema Novo becomes "Nuevo"; the famous director Gillo Pontecorvo, "Gilles"; and the distinguished film theorist Béla Balázs, "Balasz." But the worst indignities are reserved for English, where, for example, we get a sentence like "But such was not to be"—and even worse mistakes in paragraph after paragraph.

Auteurism, to Sarris, is also "describing the cinema personally rather than nonpersonally" (he means, of course, impersonally), and this gives him license, paralleled only by Pauline Kael's in her pre-*New Yorker* days, to litter reviews with autobiographical detritus. We follow Sarris as he plays hooky from a conference at CUNY, spends a year in Paris after his first Cannes festival, or, repeatedly, listens to the news as he drives to or from Long Island.

Is there anything of merit, then, in *Politics and Cinema?* Yes, partly because most current writing about cinema makes even less sense, and partly because Sarris does make shrewd observations about politics and society, some of which are even felicitously expressed, e.g., "Confession may be as good for sales as for the soul," or "When the Arabs claim that they don't hate Jews, but only Zionists, they are merely expressing a preference for the Jew as victim to the Jew as victor." But fuzzy-mindedness is never far away: in a discussion of Susan Sontag's literary style we read that it is "spare, severe," yet a few lines later her prose is said to be "intellectually sensuous." Even assuming that that phrase could be made sense of, would it not contradict the spareness and severity?

Still, Sarris is one of our leading film critics and an associate professor of film at Columbia University, whose press published *Politics and Cinema.* Things being what they are, none of this is surprising. What does shock me, however, is that a leading university press should have such deplorable copy editing as is exhibited throughout this book, so that even the numerous French names and words, left accentless by the *Village Voice*'s poor typography, have not regained their lost accent marks. Truly, this is film criticism with a different accent.

February 19, 1979

Index